Mastering the

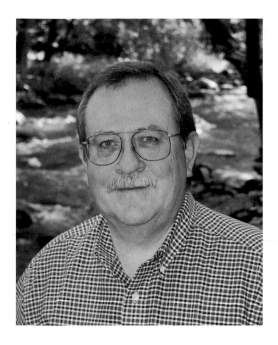

Darrell Young (*DigitalDarrell*) is a full-time author and professional photographer with a background in information technology engineering. He has been an avid photographer since 1968 when his mother gave him a Brownie Hawkeye camera.

Darrell has used Nikon cameras and Nikkor lenses since 1980. He has an incurable case of Nikon Acquisition Syndrome (NAS) and delights in working with Nikon's newest digital cameras.

Living near Great Smoky Mountains National Park and the Blue Ridge Parkway has given him a real concern for the natural environment and a deep interest in nature photography. You'll often find Darrell standing behind a tripod in the beautiful mountains of Tennessee and North Carolina.

He loves to write, as you can see in the Resources area of the Nikonians Online community (**www.Nikonians.org**) and at his Master Your Nikon blog (**MasterYourNikon.com**). He joined the Nikonians community in the year 2000, and his literary contributions led to his invitation to become the founding member of the Nikonians Writers Guild.

Mastering the Nikon D810

Darrell Young

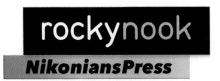

Darrell Young (aka Digital Darrell)

Editor (Rocky Nook): Jocelyn Howell
Editor (Nikonians): Tom Boné
Layout and Type: Almute Kraus, www.exclam.de
Cover Design: Helmut Kraus, www.exclam.de
Printer: Sheridan Books, Inc.
Printed in USA

Cover photo: Nikon USA
Back cover photo: Don Ridgway

1st Edition
© Darrell Young 2015
Rocky Nook Inc.
802 E. Cota Street, 3rd Floor
Santa Barbara, CA 93103
www.rockynook.com

Library of Congress Control Number: 2014954977

Distributed by O'Reilly Media
1005 Gravenstein Highway North
Sebastopol, CA 95472

This book is dedicated to:

My wife of many years, Brenda; the love of my life and best friend…

*My children, Autumn, David, Emily, Hannah, and Ethan,
five priceless gifts …*

*My mother and father, Barbara and Vaughn, who brought me into this world and
guided my early life, teaching me sound principles to live by …*

*My Nikonians editor, Tom Boné,
without whose assistance I could not possibly write books …*

*My friends J. Ramon Palacios and Bo Stahlbrandt, who make it possible to belong to
Nikonians.org, the world's best Nikon Users' Community …*

*The wonderful staff of Rocky Nook, including Gerhard Rossbach, Scott Cowlin,
Joan Dixon, Jocelyn Howell, Maggie Yates, and Matthias Rossmanith …*

And, finally, to Nikon, who makes the world's best cameras and lenses.

Special Thanks to:

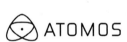

Tony Trent of **www.atomos.com** (503-388-3236) for allowing me to use a powerful Atomos *Ninja Blade* external HDMI video recorder. The revolutionary Ninja Blade is the go-to "Smart Production Weapon" for Nikon HD-SLR camera owners who want to record the highest quality, uncompressed video their camera can output.

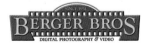

Brad Berger of **www.Berger-Bros.com** (800-542-8811) for helping me obtain a Nikon D810 early in its production cycle so that I could write this book. I personally buy from and recommend Berger-Bros.com for Nikon cameras, lenses, and accessories. They offer old-time service and classes for your photographic educational needs!

Table of Contents

Nikonians Gold Membership

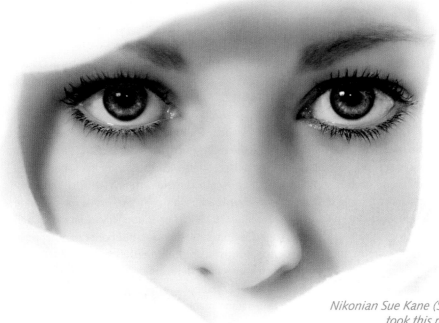

Nikonian Sue Kane (Sue A)
took this picture
suek.redbubble.com

Enter the following voucher code to obtain a *50%* discount for a Nikonians Gold Membership: Ni3Rn4AuD81Z

gold

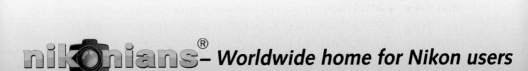
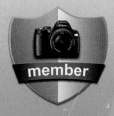

Foreword

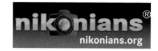

Through the past 12 *Mastering the Nikon DSLR* books authored by Nikonian Darrell Young (known to us as Digital Darrell), we have been delighted to witness an amazing evolution in the author's steadfast devotion to perfecting his craft, ever since becoming Founding Member of the Nikonians Writers Guild almost 15 years ago.

The new Nikon D810 is a world-standard-setting camera, like its predecessors the D800 and D800E. In addition to the many published official changes, the D810 has more upgrades internally than most readers will expect, with many new menu items and various improvements to previous camera systems. The D810 is one of the most flexible digital cameras ever made, with plenty of pixels for cropping capability in the medium-format range (36 MP), a fast enough frame rate for action photography (5–7 fps), and a deep feature set that makes it superior to other cameras for almost any type of personal, artistic, and commercial photography.

As engineers add and perfect features, each new camera introduced in the Nikon digital single-lens reflex inventory has exponentially become harder to describe in an easy-going and simple-to-understand manner. Yet Darrell has proven equal to the task by spending significant time with each camera in real-life photographic situations, discovering the unique personality of each new Nikon, and by adjusting his descriptive writing style to fit the needs of the reader. Camera complexity vanishes as the reader begins to understand each feature well and is able use his or her new Nikon to make superior images.

Before writing each book, Darrell's first step is to read the user's manual. Once he grasps the concepts and basic directions available through the manual, he takes those same concepts and directions into the field. He makes sure he understands how each feature works for basic photography and how it can be applied to specialty applications such as landscapes, weddings, events, and portraits. Once satisfied that he has mastered each new feature, he then translates his experience into a simple-to-understand sequence of profusely illustrated steps, and then goes on to recommend the best initial settings and shooting techniques to match. As you read the chapters that follow, you will be the beneficiary of his diligence and painstaking attention to detail.

This joint venture between nikonians.org and Rocky Nook has developed a strong following in the "camera instruction" genre, and Darrell's fastidious attention to detail has been the key ingredient in that trend.

We are proud to include his impressive credentials and body of work in the ever-growing and never-ending resources for our community, such as the forums,

The Nikonian eZine, Nikonians Academy Workshops, Nikonians News Blog, Nikonians podcasts, and our Wiki. Our community continues to grow as we now surpass 500,000 members on record.

Nikonians, now in its 14th year, has earned a worldwide reputation as a friendly, reliable, informative, and passionate Nikon® user's community, thanks in great measure to members like our own Digital Darrell, who have taken time to share the results of their experiences with Nikon imaging equipment. Nikonians, where photographers of all skill levels share, learn, and inspire.

Enjoy this book, the Nikonians community, and your Nikon.

J. Ramón Palacios (*jrp*) and Bo Stahlbrandt (*bgs*)
Nikonians Founders
www.nikonians.org

P.S. At the end of the Table of Contents you will find a 50% discount voucher for a one-year nikonians.org Gold membership. Use it. You will discover why members say, "A Nikonians membership, the best investment ever made after my camera." Enjoy this book, the Nikonians community, and your Nikons.

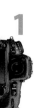

Camera Setup and Control Reference

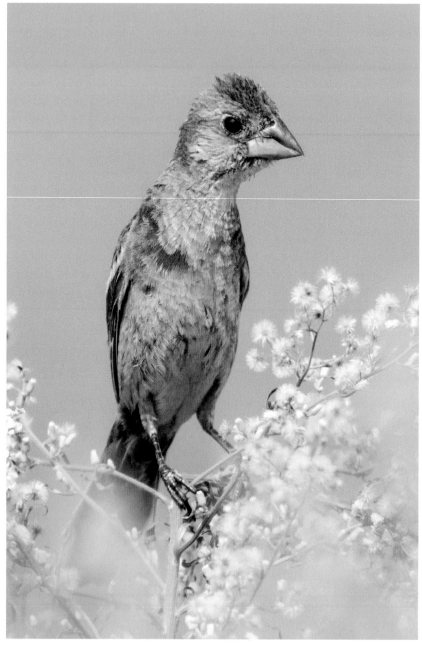

Elmer the Juvenile Blue Grosbeak © Jackie Donaldson (*bhpr*)

Congratulations! You've purchased, or are about to purchase, Nikon's professional-level, smaller-bodied, full-frame (FX) format camera: the Nikon D810.

While no digital camera is inexpensive, the D810 provides passionate photographers with a professional-level camera with medium-format resolution at an attractive price. It is weather and dust sealed with a magnesium-alloy body and frame and a rubberized coating that makes it strong and reliable for years of faithful service.

The 36.3-megapixel imaging sensor and supporting Nikon Scene Recognition System (SRS) allow you to take complete creative control of the scene in front of your lens.

The camera has advanced firmware that does things like automatic chromatic aberration reduction and full color optimization via selectable Picture Controls, which allow you to create the best pictures you've ever made.

This book will explore your incredibly feature-rich camera in great detail, using everyday language. We'll cover virtually every button, dial, switch, and setting, giving you how, when, and why information so that you can become a master of your new, powerful imaging instrument. Your passion for excellent photography can be fully expressed with your Nikon D810. Let's take control of it!

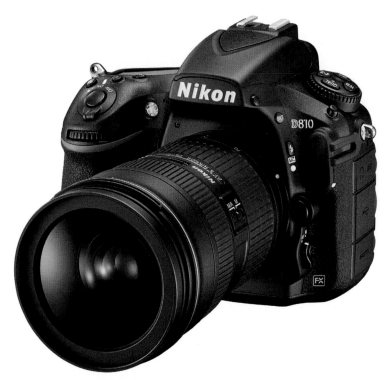

Figure 1.0 – Nikon D810 with AF-S Nikkor 24-70mm F2.8G ED VR lens

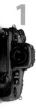

Medium-Format Resolution Sensor

In the olden days, pre-2002, I loved medium-format cameras. You would often find me in Great Smoky Mountains National Park lugging around a heavy Mamiya RB-67 Pro SD medium-format camera, which gave me a large 6×7 cm Provia F transparency. As film started fading away and digital photography rose supreme in most people's eyes, true medium format went away for the everyday photographer. Sure, one could buy a nice Hasselblad digital medium format for $20,000, but few could afford that level of camera.

Now, with the exciting Nikon D810 camera, Nikon has returned medium-format resolution to the everyday photographer who wants it. No longer will we have to find a lab to process our 120 film, be forced to lug around huge medium-format film bodies, and have to settle for standard-size digital images.

At 36.3-megapixel resolution, the D810 moves soundly into medium-format territory. What's the difference between the D810 and a much more expensive true medium-format camera back? Although the D810 provides similar resolution, the imaging sensor on some medium-format cameras can be twice the size of the D810's, at 36.7×46.1 mm compared to the D810's 35.9×24.0 mm CMOS (FX) sensor (figure 1.1).

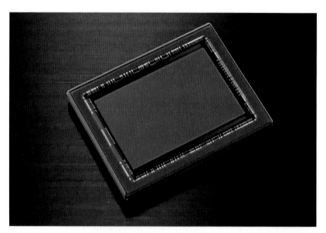

Figure 1.1 – Nikon D810's 36.3-Megapixel Imaging Sensor (FX) 35.9×24.0 mm

Obviously, the larger medium-format camera backs will have larger pixels, providing better light-gathering capability and less noise. However, the cost entry point for most medium-format digital camera backs is around $10,000 and goes up very quickly with the number of megapixels. For about one-third of the lowest medium-format back price for a new D810, I'm inclined to tolerate a little more noise in

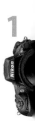

higher ISO shots. However, the Nikon D810 has excellent noise control, even better than its predecessor, the Nikon D700, and that camera is well known for its excellent, low-noise images.

With the new D810, you can make an image with 36 megapixels (7360×4912 pixels). Do you realize the camera creates a 16×24-inch (40×60 cm) native print at 300 dpi (using FX format)? With careful post-processing and enlargement, the images can be made, as National Geographic photographer Jim Brandenburg says, "as large as a house!"

Imagine the expansive landscape shots with the massive detail that comes with the resolution of the D810. Imagine being able to make large portraits to hang on your wall. Think of how your clients will enjoy the various crops you'll be able to make from the huge image file. Consider the extra income from stock photography you'll gain from the larger pictures.

Medium-format resolution has distinct advantages, with only the disadvantage of having to store the much larger images. Of course, you could use the DX mode in the D810 for smaller image size and still have images of comparable size to the 16 megapixel Nikon D7000. Such flexibility!

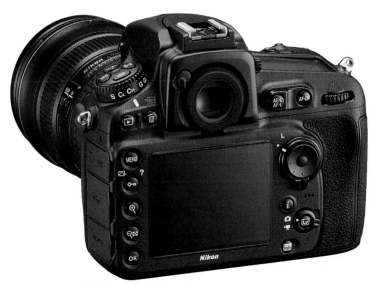

Figure 1.2 – Back of Nikon D810

The Nikon D810 is indeed a camera that sets new standards other manufacturers will have to scramble to approach. Nikon can at times seem slow about bringing out new technology, but when it does, nothing else on the market even comes close.

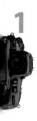

This camera is a very mature high-definition (HD) imaging device designed to provide years of usage; you can put your money into better lenses instead of a new camera. Few photographers will need more power than the Nikon D810 can deliver. With this camera, you are well equipped for years to come.

Now, let's start learning about this powerful, medium-format, high-definition, single-lens reflex (HD-SLR) camera!

How to Use This Book

The upcoming sections and chapters are best read with your camera in hand, ready for configuration. There are literally hundreds of things to configure on this advanced HD-SLR. In this chapter, I'll give new D810 users a place to start. Later, as you progress through this book, we'll look at all the buttons, switches, dials, and menu settings in detail. That will allow you to fully master the operation of your Nikon D810.

There is a chapter or section for each menu in the camera. Plus, there is additional information on how to put it all together in chapters like **Metering, Exposure Modes, and Histogram**; **White Balance**; **Autofocus, AF-Area, and Release Modes**; and **Movie Live View**. Because the Nikon D810 is a camera for advanced users, this book assumes you have knowledge of basic things like depth of field, lens focal length, and angle of view and how the aperture, shutter speed, and ISO sensitivity control exposure. If you need brushing up on those subjects, may I please refer you to one of my other books, *Beyond Point-and-Shoot*. It assumes absolutely no previous knowledge of photography and covers the basics for new users of DSLR cameras. You can find out more about *Beyond Point-and-Shoot* at my website:

http://www.PictureAndPen.com/BeyondPS

If you would like to contact me directly to comment on the book, ask questions, or report errata, please use the contact link at my website, **www.PictureAndPen.com**.

You can also join my Facebook group, **Master Your Nikon**, and my Google+ group, **Nikon Digital Camera & Photo Enthusiasts (NDCPE)**, at the following web addresses:

https://www.facebook.com/groups/MasterYourNikon/
https://plus.google.com/communities/110426867121786060811

You will find a series of downloadable resources for this book, along with any errata, at the two following websites:

http://www.Nikonians.org/NikonD810
http://rockynook.com/NikonD810

For excellent support of your new Nikon D810 and other Nikon equipment, be sure to stop by and visit with the fine members of **www.Nikonians.org**, the best Nikon users' community on the web, full of friendly and knowledgeable world class photographers. There is a voucher with a 50% discount on a Nikonians Gold Membership in the front of this book. Use the code to start or renew your Nikonians membership.

Nikon User's Manual Page References

Since many people appreciate additional reference points for research, I've included appropriate Nikon User's Manual page references under the subheadings through-out the book. Using these references is entirely optional and not necessary for complete understanding of your camera. However, many people, myself included, enjoy having a different perspective on things they are studying, especially when the subject is as complex as an HD-SLR.

Colors and Wording Legend

Throughout the book, you'll notice that in the numbered, step-by-step instruc-tions there are colored terms as well as terms that are displayed in italic font.

1. Blue is used to refer to the camera's physical features.
2. Green is for functions and settings displayed on the camera's LCD screens.
3. *Italic* is for textual prompts seen on the camera's LCD screens.
4. *Italic* or ***bold italic*** is also used on select occasions for special emphasis.

Here is a sample paragraph with the colors and italic font in use:

Press the MENU button to reach the Setup Menu and then scroll to the Format memory card option by pressing the down arrow on the Multi selector. You will see the following message: *All images on Memory card will be deleted. OK?* Select Yes and then press the OK button. Please make sure you've transferred all your images first!

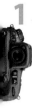

What's in the Box?

The golden box containing the highly desirable Nikon D810 and accessories contains a total of 14 items in the American version. There may be slight differences in versions from other countries, but this will give you a good idea of what should be in your camera box.

Following is a list of each item shown in figure 1.3:

1. English User's Manual and Quick Guide
2. Spanish User's Manual and Quick Guide
3. The Golden Box from Nikon
4. Nikon D810 camera body
5. View NX 2 installer CD
6. BF-1B body cap
7. EN-EL15 Li-ion battery with terminal cover
8. UC-E22 USB cable (USB 3.0)
9. AN-DC12 neck strap labeled Nikon D810
10. BM-12 monitor cover
11. USB cable clip for tethering
12. HDMI cable clip for tethering

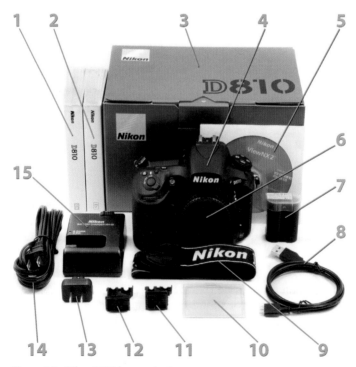

Figure 1.3 – Nikon D810 box contents

13. AC wall adapter (for battery charger) *
14. AC wire (for battery charger) *
15. MH-25a battery charger
16. Warranty registration card (not shown)

* Your camera will include either the AC wall adapter (13) or the AC wire (14) for your region's power outlet type, but probably not both. This varies with the country and region.

Initial Hardware Considerations for New Users

Although the D810 is a camera for enthusiasts and professionals, some new DSLR users have purchased a D810 as their first digital single lens reflex (DSLR) or HD-SLR camera. New users may not know how to attach and remove a lens, insert or charge the battery, and format and insert memory cards. The majority of this book's readers, however, already know how to perform these tasks. I do not want to ask a more experienced DSLR user to read over the basics of DSLR use in this advanced book, so I've created a PDF document called **Initial Hardware Considerations for New Users**, which you can download from either of these websites:

http://www.Nikonians.org/NikonD810
http://rockynook.com/NikonD810

The document explains the basic information you will need to get started using your new camera. There are also other articles of interest to new Nikon D810 users on these web pages. To use these documents, you'll need Adobe Reader, which you can download for free at **www.adobe.com**.

Initial Camera Setup

This section is devoted to the first-time use and configuration of the camera. There are five specific settings you should configure when you first turn on the camera, before you shoot any pictures. I'll walk you through the settings. Later chapters will cover virtually all camera settings in detail.

When you first insert the battery into a factory-fresh Nikon D810, you may notice the word CLOCK flashing on the camera's upper Control panel and rear Monitor, if you press the info button. If you don't see CLOCK flashing, then your camera may have already been set up for initial use.

You may want to go through these steps even if the camera has been in use previously. That way you can make sure the initial settings are best for you.

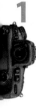

Setting the Camera's Language – Step 1

The D810 is multilingual, or multinational. As partially shown in figure 1.4, the menus can be displayed in 36 languages. Most likely the camera will already be configured to the language spoken in your area because various world distributors ship their cameras somewhat preconfigured. However, you may want to check and make sure.

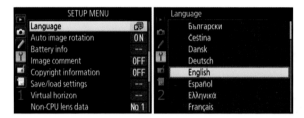

Figure 1.4 – Selecting a Language setting

Here are the steps to select your language:

1. Select Language from the Setup Menu and scroll to the right (figure 1.4, screen 1).
2. Use the Multi selector to scroll up or down until your language is highlighted (figure 1.4, screen 2). It may already be selected if your camera was set up by your distributor.
3. Press the OK button to select your language.

Next, let's move to the second screen in the setup series, the **Setup Menu > Time zone and date** screen.

Setting the Camera's Time Zone – Step 2

This is an easy screen to use as long as you can recognize the area of the world in which you live. Use the map shown in figure 1.5 to find your area, then select it.

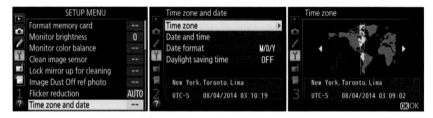

Figure 1.5 – Selecting a Time zone setting

Here are the steps to select the correct Time zone setting for your location:

1. Select Time zone and date from the Setup Menu and scroll to the right (figure 1.5, screen 1).
2. Select Time zone from the Time zone and date screen and scroll to the right (figure 1.5, screen 2).
3. You'll now see the Time zone screen with yellow arrows pointing to the left and right on either side of the small black and gray world map. With the Multi selector, scroll to the left or right until your world location is highlighted in yellow. You will see either a vertical yellow strip with red dots or a tiny yellow outline with a red dot. At the bottom of the screen, you will see the currently selected time zone. Mine is set to New York, Toronto, Lima (UTC-5), as shown in figure 1.5, screen 3.
4. Press the OK button, and your Time zone setting will be locked in place.

Ok, let's examine the third screen in the series, the Date and time screen.

Setting the Camera's Date and Time – Step 3

This screen allows you to put in the current date and time. It is in year, month, day (Y, M, D) and hour, minute, second (H, M, S) format. Once you've configured this function, check to see if the blinking CLOCK notice has gone away from the top Control panel and Info screen.

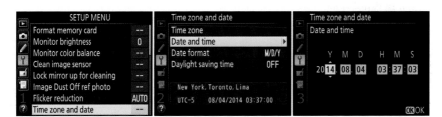

Figure 1.6 – Selecting a Date and time setting

Here are the steps to configure the Date and time setting:

1. Select Time zone and date from the Setup Menu and scroll to the right (figure 1.6, screen 1).
2. Select Date and time from the Time zone and date screen and scroll to the right (figure 1.6, screen 2).
3. Using the Multi selector, scroll to the left or right to select the date and time sections. Scroll up or down to set the values for each one (figure 1.6, screen 3). A 24-hour clock is used for the time values (see page 325 for a 12- to 24-hour conversion chart).
4. Press the OK button when you've finished inputting the Date and time.

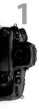

Next, we'll consider the fourth step in the series, setting the camera's date format.

Setting the Camera's Date Format – Step 4

The English-speaking world uses various date formats. The Nikon D810 allows you to choose from the most common ones. There are three date formats you can select:

- Y/M/D – Year/Month/Day (2015/12/31)
- M/D/Y – Month/Day/Year (12/31/2015)
- D/M/Y – Day/Month/Year (31/12/2015)

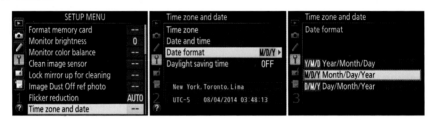

Figure 1.7 – Selecting a Date format setting

American residents usually select the M/D/Y (Month/Day/Year) format. However, you may prefer a different format. Here are the steps to select the date format you like best:

1. Select Time zone and date from the Setup Menu and scroll to the right (figure 1.7, screen 1).
2. Select Date format from the Time zone and date screen and scroll to the right (figure 1.7, screen 2).
3. Using the Multi selector, scroll up or down to the position of the date format you prefer (figure 1.7, screen 3). I chose M/D/Y.
4. Press the OK button to select the format.

Now, let's configure the last screen in our series, and your camera will be ready to use.

Setting the Camera's Daylight Saving Time – Step 5

Many areas of the United States observe daylight saving time. In the springtime, many American residents set their clocks forward by one hour on a specified day each year. Then in the fall they set it back, leading to the clever saying, "spring forward and fall back."

You can use the Daylight saving time setting to adjust the time on your D810's clock forward or back by one hour, according to whether daylight saving time is currently in effect in your area.

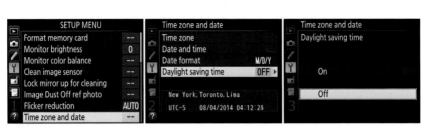

Figure 1.8 – Selecting a Daylight saving time setting

To enable or disable Daylight saving time, follow these steps:

1. Select Time zone and date from the Setup Menu and scroll to the right (figure 1.8, image 1).
2. Select Daylight saving time from the Time zone and date screen and scroll to the right (figure 1.8, image 2).
3. There are only two selections: On or Off (figure 1.8, image 3). If daylight saving time is in effect in your area (spring and summer in most areas of the United States), select On. When daylight saving time ends, you will need to manually change this setting to Off (via the Setup Menu) to adjust the clock back by one hour.
4. Press the OK button to select your choice.

This is not an automatic function in the Nikon D810 camera; it simply allows you to adjust the camera's clock quickly by selecting On or Off. Therefore, you must remember to return to this setting whenever daylight saving time begins and ends. When you change the clocks in your home, it's a great time to change the clock in your camera as well. If you don't, your images will have metadata reflecting a time that is off by one hour for half the year!

In the next section, **Control Location Reference**, we will take a look at each of the buttons, dials, and switches on the camera to see what each control is named and where it is located.

Control Location Reference

Following are the locations and names of all the controls mentioned in this book. You may want to place a bookmark here so you can refer back to this control location reference list when an unfamiliar control name is mentioned in the book. This list covers 70 separate external camera controls, showing their locations and Nikon-supplied names.

I have also created a document titled **Control Function Reference** that you can download from either of the following websites:

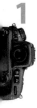

http://www.Nikonians.org/NikonD810
http://rockynook.com/NikonD810

The Control Function Reference provides a deeper discussion of each button, dial, and switch on the camera.

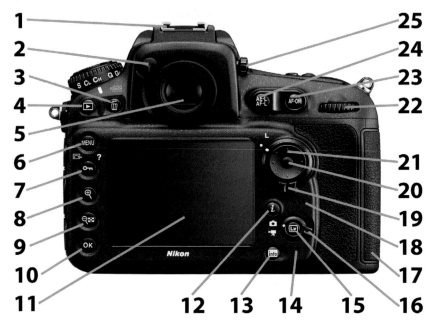

Figure 1.9 – Back of camera

Back of Camera (figure 1.9)

1. Accessory shoe (hot shoe)
2. Eyepiece shutter lever
3. Delete/Format button
4. Playback button
5. Viewfinder
6. MENU button
7. Protect/Picture Control/ Help button
8. Playback zoom in button
9. Thumbnail/Playback zoom out button
10. OK button
11. Monitor
12. *i* button

13. info button
14. Memory card access lamp
15. Live view button
16. Live view selector
17. Memory card slot cover
18. Speaker
19. Focus selector lock
20. Multi selector center button
21. Multi selector
22. Main command dial
23. AF-ON button
24. AE-L/AF-L button
25. Diopter adjustment control

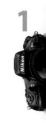

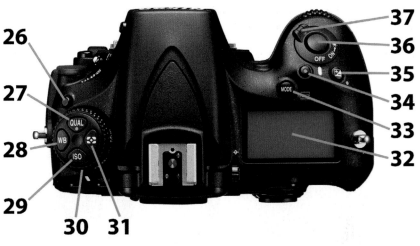

Figure 1.10 – Top of camera

Top of Camera (figure 1.10)

26. Release mode dial lock release button
27. QUAL button (image quality and size)
28. WB button (white balance)
29. ISO button (ISO sensitivity)
30. Release mode dial
31. Metering button
32. Control panel
33. MODE/Format button (exposure modes)
34. Movie-record button
35. Exposure compensation button
36. Shutter-release button
37. Power and backlight switch

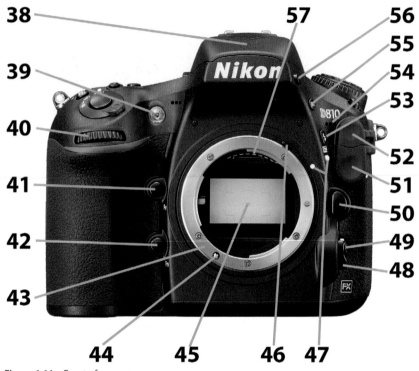

Figure 1.11 – Front of camera

Front of Camera (figure 1.11)

38. Built-in flash (closed)
39. AF-assist illuminator
40. Sub-command dial
41. Depth-of-field preview button
42. Fn (function) button
43. Lens mount (F-mount)
44. Screwdriver AF lens focus driver
45. Reflex mirror (shutter, sensor is behind)
46. Meter coupling lever
47. Mounting index (lens)

48. Focus-mode selector switch
49. AF-mode button
50. Lens release button
51. 10-pin remote terminal cover
52. Flash sync terminal cover
53. Flash mode/compensation button
54. Stereo microphone
55. BKT button (bracketing)
56. Flash pop-up button
57. CPU contacts (body to lens)

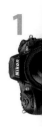

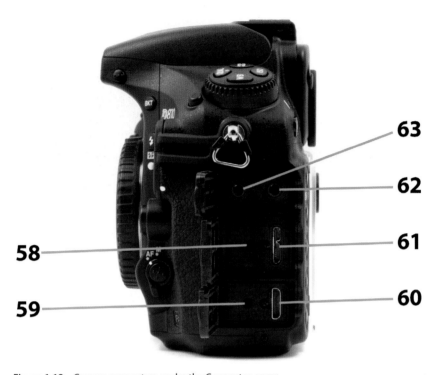

Figure 1.12 – Camera connectors under the Connector cover

External Connectors (figure 1.12)

58. USB cable clamp mount hole
59. HDMI cable clamp mount hole
60. HDMI mini-pin connector (Type C)
61. USB connector (USB 3.0)
62. Connector for external microphone
63. Headphone connector

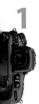

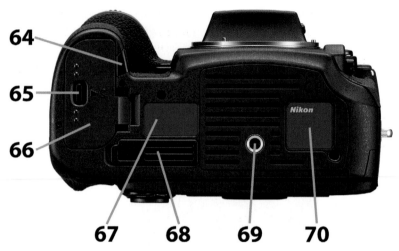

Figure 1.13 – Bottom of camera

Bottom of Camera (figure 1.13)

64. Power connector cover
65. Battery-chamber cover latch
66. Battery-chamber cover
67. Compliance and information plate
68. Contact cover for optional MB-D12 battery pack
69. Tripod socket
70. Camera ID, battery info, and serial number plate

For a deeper discussion of each button, dial, and switch on the camera, download the bonus **Control Function Reference** document from either of the following websites:

http://www.Nikonians.org/NikonD810
http://rockynook.com/NikonD810

The **Control Function Reference** follows the same numbering pattern as the **Control Location Reference** (this section).

Using the Nikon D810 Menu System

The next several chapters will consider the camera menu subsystems. The D810's menu system consists of six menus, as shown in figure 1.14.

There are literally hundreds of configuration options in these six menus. Additionally, there is a seventh menu (not shown in figure 1.14) called Recent Settings.

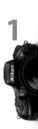

My Menu is the default final menu in the camera, and you can toggle between My Menu and the Recent Settings menu by selecting it under *My Menu > Choose tab* or *Recent Settings > Choose tab*. We'll discuss these two final menus and why they work this way in the chapter titled **My Menu and Recent Settings**. The Recent Settings menu always contains the last 20 functions you've adjusted on your camera, while My Menu lets you place your favorite, most-configured menu selections under your own custom menu.

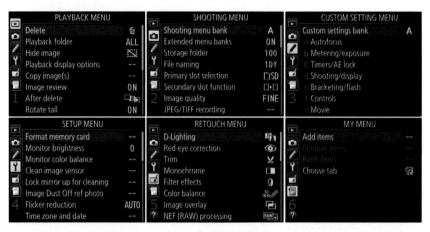

Figure 1.14 – Six primary menu systems in the Nikon D810

In case you've never used a Nikon DSLR before, you enter the menu system by pressing the MENU button next to the top left of the camera's Monitor. As you scroll up and down on the toolbar at the left of each menu you will scroll through the six available menus.

Author's Conclusions

This first chapter helped you get your camera ready for initial use. It also provided camera control descriptions, locations, and references like few other books on the market. With this book you have a complete reference for your Nikon D810 camera.

We'll examine each setting on each menu, starting now. Do you have your camera near you? You'll need it to test the numerous ways each function can be configured. You'll learn and remember the functions much better if you take the time to adjust your camera while you are reading.

Congratulations on purchasing one of the most powerful Nikons this author has ever seen. Let's get down to examining its details!

Playback Menu

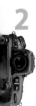

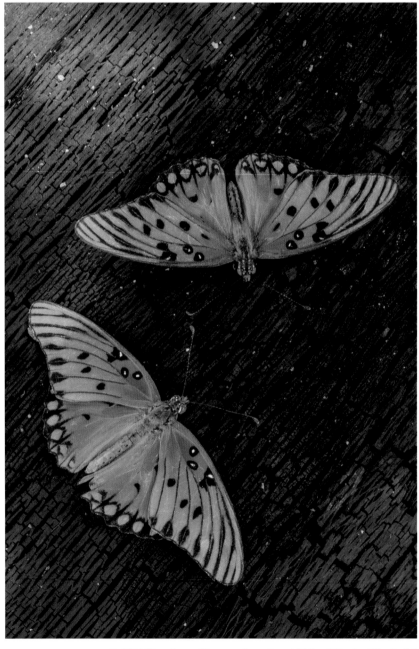

Gulf Fritillary Butterflies on a Burnt Log © Richard Higgins (*HigginsR1*)

The Nikon D810 has a big 3.2-inch high-resolution OLED Monitor, which you can use to examine in great detail the images you have taken. You can zoom in past the 100 percent pixel-peeping level to make sure an image is sharp enough. You can view, copy, delete, and hide images and examine detailed shooting information on each picture. You can even use the Monitor to view a slide show or output the show to a much larger HDMI device, such as a television (HDTV).

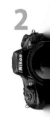

The Playback Menu has everything you need to control your camera's image playback and copying and printing functions. You'll be taking thousands of pictures and will view most of them on the Monitor; therefore, it is a good idea to learn to use the Playback Menu well.

By now you may have quite a few pictures on your camera's memory card. Let's consider how you can best view, move, and print those images using the Playback Menu. The Playback functions are as follows:

- **Delete** – Allows you to delete all or selected images from your camera's memory card(s).
- **Playback folder** – Allows you to set which image folders your camera will display if you have multiple folders on the camera's memory card(s).
- **Hide image** – Lets you conceal images so they won't be displayed on the camera's Monitor.
- **Playback display options** – Controls how many informational screens the camera will display for each image.
- **Copy image(s)** – Gives you functions to copy images between the two memory cards.
- **Image review** – Turns the camera's post-shot automatic image review on or off.
- **After delete** – Determines which image is displayed next when you delete an image from a memory card.
- **Rotate tall** – Allows you to choose whether portrait-orientation images (vertical) are displayed in an upright position or lying on their side on the horizontal Monitor.
- **Slide show** – Allows you to display all the images on your camera's memory card(s) in a sequential display, like the slide shows of olden days (pre-2002). No projector required.
- **DPOF print order** – Lets you print your images directly from a PictBridge-compatible printer without using a computer—either by using digital print order format (DPOF) directly from a memory card or by connecting a USB cable to the camera.

Now, let's examine each of these settings in detail, with full explanations on how, why, and when to configure each item.

2

> ### Technical OLED Monitor Information
>
> As mentioned previously, the D810 has a 3.2-inch Monitor with enough resolution, size, and viewing angle to allow you to really enjoy using it for previewing images. It has VGA resolution (640×480), based on a 1,229,000-dot, or 1.2M-dot, organic light-emitting diode (OLED) panel. The bottom line is that this 3.2-inch screen has amazing clarity for your image previewing needs. You can zoom in for review up to 46x for Large (L) images, 34x for Medium (M) images, and 22x for Small (S) images. That's zooming in to pixel-peeping levels.
>
> Now, if you want to get technical, here's the extra geek stuff:
>
> If anything you read says the OLED Monitor has 1,229,000 pixels of resolution the writer is uninformed. Nikon lists the resolution as 1.2M dots, not pixels. Technically, an individual pixel on your D810's Monitor is a combination of four color dots—red, green, blue, and white (RGBW). The four dots are blended together to provide shades of color and are equal to one pixel. This means the Monitor is limited to one-fourth of 1,229,000 dots, or 307,250 pixels of real image resolution. The VGA standard has 307,200 pixels (640×480), so the D810's Monitor has VGA resolution.
>
> The white dot color used on the D810 Monitor is an added feature that many camera monitors do not have. This extra white dot color allows the Monitor to have better contrast and more accurate color. The D810 Monitor isn't any higher in resolution than that of its predecessors, the Nikon D800 and D800E, which also have VGA resolution but are limited to RGB colors, with no extra white dots. The D800 and D800E cameras have 921,000 red, green, and blue dots, which when divided by three (one-third) equals 307,000 pixels, or basically the same resolution as the D810.

Which Memory Card and Folder?

Before we get into the individual functions on the Playback Menu, there is something you need to understand that will help you avoid confusion as you use your camera's menu functions. Because the D810 has multiple memory cards (playback slots) and image folders (playback folders), you will need a good way to know which memory card and folder contain a particular image. The information in this section explains how the camera informs you of where a highlighted image is stored.

The D810 has multiple card slots, so many functions can affect multiple memory cards when *Playback Menu > Playback folder > All* is selected (see the upcoming section, **Playback Folder**).

How can you tell which memory card and folder is being affected by the current function? As an example, I am using the first setting on the Playback Menu, the Delete image function. However, this concept of card slots (i.e., CF and SD) and folders (e.g., 100ND810 and 101ND810) applies to many functions in this camera. You can use this knowledge as you work your way through the entire book.

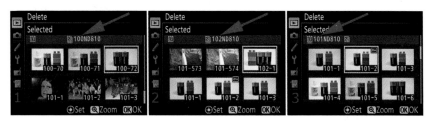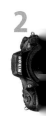

Figure 2.0A – Active memory card slot

Notice in figure 2.0A that there are two tiny memory card symbols above the image thumbnails (see arrows). Each card slot is labeled. One is CF and the other is SD. If your camera has only one card inserted, the other card will be grayed out.

As you use various functions that affect displayed images, the memory card symbol will be underlined for the card containing the image you are modifying, and the playback folder name will be displayed to the right of the card slot name (red arrows in figure 2.0A). In figure 2.0A, it is apparent that there are two memory cards in use because neither card is grayed out. The selected card is highlighted in yellow and the other card is white.

The three screens in figure 2.0A represent what appears on the Monitor while scrolling through images. Moving from left to right in the three screens, you will notice the playback folder number is different in screens 1 and 2 (red arrows). Screen 1 shows that the SD card has a folder named 100ND810, while screen 2 shows that the SD card has a second folder, named 102ND810. If you look at the highlighted pictures in screens 1 and 2, you will see that folder 100ND810 has 72 pictures and picture 100-72 is selected (figure 2.0A, screen 1). The number 100 represents the folder in use and the number 72 represents the image number in that folder. In the folder named 102ND810 picture 102-1 is selected (figure 2.0A, screen 2). It is apparent there are no more pictures after 102-1 because you don't see a continuance of the 102 picture count in the next picture; it stops with 102-1 and continues on the next row with 101-1, a different folder. Now, in figure 2.0A, screen 3, you can see that I have switched to the CF card. There is only one playback folder showing and it is named 101ND810.

The camera automatically switches between these cards and folders as you scroll through images if *Playback Menu > Playback folder > All* is selected. However, if *Playback Menu > Playback folder > ND810* or *Current* is selected, the choice of folders and images may be more limited. See the section called **Playback Folder** later in this chapter for information on the Playback folder option.

Had there been only one card in the camera, the other card would have been grayed out and not selectable. The memory card containing the currently selected image will always be underlined and highlighted in yellow. As you scroll through the images, notice that the yellow underline and highlighting will jump to whatever card and folder contain the image that is highlighted at that moment.

What if you don't want to take the time to scroll through hundreds of images trying to determine which playback folder they are in? Fortunately, there is a shortcut for selecting images on only one card or in one playback folder. Again, I am using the Delete function as an example, but this method applies to multiple functions in this book (figure 2.0B).

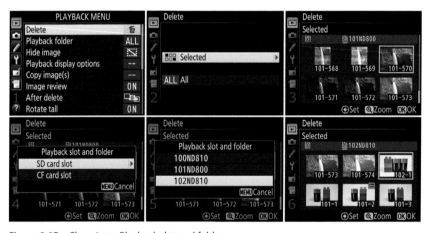

Figure 2.0B – Choosing a Playback slot and folder

Figure 2.0B shows the method used to choose a playback slot (memory card) and folder. Many functions in the book affect one of the two memory card slots. You can choose which slot is affected by a current function by using the method discussed here. (Be careful! I am using the Delete function as a sample only. We are not currently deleting images, so don't actually execute this sample Delete function to completion. I will discuss how to delete images in the next section):

1. Select the Delete function (sample) from the Playback Menu and scroll to the right (figure 2.0B, screen 1).
2. Choose Selected and scroll to the right (figure 2.0B, screen 2).
3. While the screen shown in figure 2.0B, screen 3, is on the Monitor, press the Thumbnail/Playback zoom out button.
4. The menu shown in figure 2.0B, screen 4, will now appear. This Playback slot and folder menu gives you a choice of the active playback slots (memory cards) the

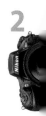

camera is currently using. Choose one of the two (SD card slot or CF card slot) and scroll to the right.

5. Now choose which playback folder you want to use and press the OK button (figure 2.0B, screen 5). Playback folder 102ND810 is selected in figure 2.0B.

6. You will now note in figure 2.0B, screen 6, that the yellow rectangle is surrounding the first picture in the folder 102ND810 on the CD card. There is only one picture in this folder currently (102-1).

You can use this method anytime you want to drill down into a specific card and folder to use or modify a certain image or images. This method of moving between cards and folders will apply to many functions throughout this book, so always be on the lookout for which memory card and playback folder contain the picture you are working with.

Why am I talking about these two functions at the beginning of the chapter instead of adding them to each individual section? Simply because many functions use this same methodology and there is no point in wasting book space to repeat the same instructions over and over. Just remember, please, that anytime you see a Monitor screen full of images, you can likely press the Thumbnail/Playback zoom out button and open the Playback slot and folder menu to select a particular memory card and folder.

Also, I am putting this information at the beginning of the Playback Menu chapter because it is so closely controlled by the settings of the *Playback Menu > Playback folder* function. You need to learn this well so that you can use this information as you study this book and when you are using your camera in the field.

Now, let's examine each of the settings on the Playback Menu in detail.

Delete

(User's Manual – Page 252)

The Delete function allows you to selectively delete individual images from a group of images in a single folder or multiple folders on your camera's memory card(s). It also allows you to clear all images in the folders without deleting the folders. This is sort of like a card format that affects only images. However, if you have protected or hidden images, this function will not delete them.

Note: I wish Nikon had chosen to put Playback folder first on the Playback Menu instead of the Delete function. Delete, which is first, does different things according to how you have Playback folder configured. It is really best to understand and configure Playback folder before using the Delete function.

There are two selections on the **Delete** screen: Selected and All. Let's consider each of them.

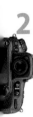

Selected

You can use the Selected method to delete individual images on the camera's memory card. This function does not delete all images at once, unless you want to take the time to mark each image for deletion individually. Deleting all images at once is done with the All method (next subsection). Figure 2.1A shows the menu screens you'll use to control the Delete function for selected images.

Notice in screen 3 of figure 2.1A that there is a list of images (and possibly videos), each with a number in its lower-right corner. These numbers run in sequence from 1 to however many images you have in your current image folder, or on the entire memory card. The number of images shown on the Monitor will vary according to how you have the Playback folder settings configured. (See the next section of this chapter, **Playback Folder.**)

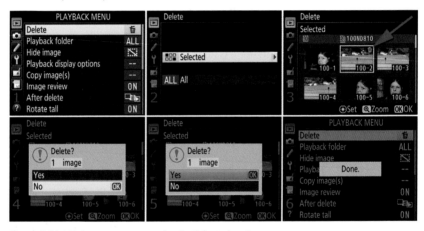

Figure 2.1A – Delete menu screens for the Selected option

If you have Playback folder set to Current, the camera will show you only the images found in your current playback folder. If you have Playback folder set to ND810, the camera will display all the images created by the D810 in any folder on your camera's memory cards. If Playback folder is set to All, the camera will display all images on both cards, whether they were created by the D810 or another Nikon camera. The safest setting when deleting images is to use *Playback Menu > Playback folder > All.*

Here are the steps to delete one or more images with the Selected method. These steps will work however you have *Playback Menu > Playback folder* configured; however, you will be limited in the number of images you can see to delete when you are using the *Playback Menu > Playback folder > Current* setting.

1. Select the Delete function from the Playback Menu and scroll to the right (figure 2.1A, screen 1).
2. Choose Selected and scroll to the right (figure 2.1A, screen 2).

3. Locate the images for deletion with the Multi selector and then press the Multi selector center button. This button will mark or unmark images for deletion. It toggles a small trash can symbol on and off on the top right of the selected image (red arrow in figure 2.1A, screen 3). Only one image is selected, number 100-1. However, you can select as many images as you want by highlighting them with the yellow box and pressing the Multi selector center button.
4. Select the images you want to throw away and then press the OK button. A screen will appear asking you to confirm the deletion of the images you have selected (figure 2.1A, screen 4).
5. To finish deleting the images, select Yes and press the OK button. To cancel, select No and press the OK button (figure 2.1A, screen 5).
6. A final screen will appear briefly with the word *Done* over a grayed-out Playback Menu and then the camera will return to the normal Playback Menu.

While you are selecting or deselecting images to delete, you can press the Playback zoom in button to see a larger version of the currently selected image. This lets you examine the image in more detail to see if you really want to delete it. You can also use the Thumbnail/Playback zoom out button to open the Playback slot and folder menu, allowing you to select a particular memory card and folder (as discussed at the beginning of this chapter).

Now let's discuss how you can delete all images from a memory card without removing the folders on it.

All

This option is like a formatting a card, except that it will not delete folders, only images (figure 2.1B). As mentioned previously, it will not delete protected or hidden images, either. Using this option is a quick way to format your card while maintaining your favorite folder structure.

Here are the steps to delete all images on the card (or in the current folder):

1. Select the Delete function from the Playback Menu and scroll to the right (figure 2.1B, screen 1).
2. Choose All and scroll to the right (figure 2.1B, screen 2).
3. Select the slot from which to delete images. You can select either SD card slot or CF card slot (figure 2.1B, screen 3). If there is a memory card missing from one of the slots, it will be grayed out and unavailable. Press the OK button to choose the slot.
4. A screen will appear asking you to confirm the deletion of all images. All means what it says, as step 5 more deeply discusses. Read it carefully! You must understand that how you have the Playback folder option (the next function in the Playback Menu) configured affects how many images will be deleted. See the next section of this chapter, **Playback Folder**, for information on the Playback folder option.

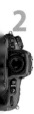

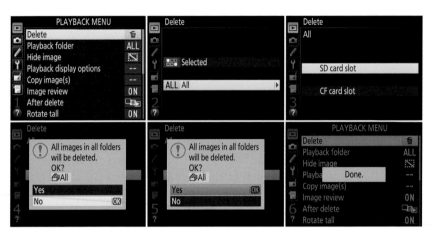

Figure 2.1B – Delete menu screens for the All option

5. Choose Yes from the next screen with the big red exclamation point and dire warning of imminent deletion (figure 2.1B, image 5). **Be very careful from this point forward!** If you have Playback folder set to ND810, the camera will delete all images in *every* folder that was created by the D810, and the warning will say, *All images will be deleted. OK?*, followed by ND810. If you have Playback folder set to Current, the camera will delete only the images in the folder that is currently in use, and the warning will say, *All images will be deleted. OK?*, followed by Current. If you have Playback folder set to All, the camera will delete all images in all folders, and the warning will say, *All images in all folders will be deleted. OK?* The camera is prepared to delete every image in every folder (created by any camera) on the selected memory card if *Playback Menu > Playback folder > All* is selected.

6. When you select Yes and press the OK button, a final screen with the word *Done* will pop up briefly, informing you that the deed has been accomplished (figure 2.1B, screen 6).

Being the paranoid type, I tested this thoroughly and found that the D810 really will not delete protected and hidden images. Plus, it will keep any folders you have created. However, if you are a worrier, maybe you should transfer the images off the card before deleting any of them.

Settings Recommendation: I don't use the *Delete > All* function often because I usually don't create special folders for each type of image. If you maintain a series of folders on your memory card(s), you may enjoy using the All function. Most of the time, I just use the Selected option and remove particular images. Any other time I want to clear the card, I use the Format memory card function in the Setup Menu or hold down the two buttons with the red Format label next to them. We'll

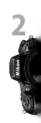

Recovering Deleted Images

If you accidentally delete an image or a group of images, or even if you format the entire memory card and then realize with great pain that you didn't really mean to, all is not lost. Simply remove the card from your camera immediately and do not use it until you can run image recovery software on the card. Deleting or formatting doesn't permanently remove the images from the card. It merely marks them as deleted and removes the references to the images from the memory card's file allocation table (FAT). The images are still there and can usually be recovered as long as you don't write any new data to the card before trying to recover them.

It's wise to have a good image recovery program on your computer at all times. Sooner or later you'll have a problem with a card and will need to recover images. Many of the better brands of memory cards include recovery software either on the card itself or on a separate CD that comes with the card. Make sure you install the software on your computer before formatting the brand-new memory card!

---

discuss formatting the memory card in the chapter titled **Setup Menu**, under the heading **Format Memory Card**.

Another way I rid myself of images I don't want is to view them on the Monitor by pressing the Playback button, and then press the Delete button on the top left of the camera back (labeled with a trash can symbol). You have several convenient ways to rid yourself of unwanted images with the D810; choose your favorite.

Playback Folder

(User's Manual – Page 281)

The Playback folder setting allows your camera to display images during preview and slide shows. You can have the D810 show you images created by the D810 *only*, in all folders; images that were created by the D810 and any other Nikon cameras, in all folders; or only the images in the current folder.

If you regularly use your memory card in multiple cameras, as I do, and sometimes forget to transfer images, adjusting the Playback folder setting is a good idea. I use a D810, D300S, and D7000 on a fairly regular basis. Often, I'll grab an 8 GB card out of one of the cameras and stick it in another one for a few shots. If I'm not careful, I'll later transfer the images from one camera and forget that I have folders created by the other camera on the memory card. It's usually only after I have pressed the format buttons that I remember the other camera's images on my memory card. The D810 comes to my rescue with its *Playback folder > All* function.

With All set, I can see all the images in all folders on both memory cards from all Nikon cameras.

Let's look at how the Playback folder function works by first looking at what each selection does and the steps needed to select the best function for you (figure 2.2). The three selections (ND810, All, and Current) are described as follows:

- **ND810** – The camera will display images created by the D810 from all folders on both the SD and CF memory cards. This is good to use if you are interested in seeing only D810-created images, wherever they may reside.
- **All** – The D810 will obligingly show you every image—created by any Nikon camera—it can find in all the folders on both memory cards. During playback, or before deletion, the D810 will display images from other Nikon cameras you've used with the current memory card. Each camera usually creates its own unique folders, and normally the other folders are not visible. When you select All, the D810 intelligently displays its own images and any other Nikon-created images in any folder on the two cards.
- **Current** – This is the most limited playback mode. Images in the image folder the camera is currently using will be displayed during playback, whether the images were created by the D810 or another Nikon camera. No other images or folders will be displayed.

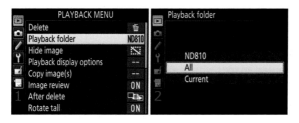

Figure 2.2 – Selecting a Playback folder source

Use the following steps to select the folder(s) from which your camera will display images:

1. Select Playback folder from the Playback Menu and scroll to the right (figure 2.2, screen 1).
2. Choose ND810, All, or Current and press the OK button (figure 2.2, screen 2).

Settings Recommendation: Using anything except All makes it possible for you to accidentally lose images. If you don't have any other Nikon cameras, this may not be a critical issue. However, if you have a series of older Nikon cameras around, you may switch memory cards between them. If there's an image on any of my memory cards, I want to see it and know it's there. Until I started using the All setting, I was sometimes formatting cards with forgotten images on them. From my pain comes a strong recommendation: Use All!

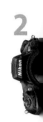

Playback Folder and Hidden Images

The display of images to select for hiding (see the next section) obeys the *Playback Menu > Playback folder* selection that we considered in this section. You can hide only the images you can see in the Hide image selection screen. If you don't have All selected for *Playback Menu > Playback folder*, you may not see all of the images on the card. If you regularly hide images, you may want to leave your Playback folder set to All. That way, all the images on the card will appear on the Hide image screen and you can select any of them to hide.

Hide Image

(User's Manual – Page 281)

The Hide image function lets you mark images so they won't show up on the camera's Monitor. If you sometimes take images that would not be appropriate for others to view until you have a chance to transfer them to your computer, this setting is for you. You can hide one or many images, and when they are hidden, they cannot be viewed on the camera's Monitor in the normal way. After they are hidden, the only way the images can be viewed again in-camera is by opening the *Playback Menu > Hide image > Select/set* function again, which displays the hidden images (figure 2.3A, screen 2).

There are two selections in this menu: Select/set and Deselect all. Let's consider both of them.

Select/set

This selection allows you to hide one or several images (figure 2.3A, screen 3), or you can use this function to unhide images that have already been hidden. Here's how to hide or unhide an image:

1. Select Hide image from the Playback Menu and scroll to the right (figure 2.3A, screen 1).
2. Choose Select/set from the list and scroll to the right (figure 2.3A, screen 2).
3. Scroll to the image you want to hide and press the Multi selector center button to select the image. You'll see a little dotted rectangle with a slash symbol appear in the top-right corner of the image you've selected (red arrow in figure 2.3A, screen 3). You can do this multiple times to select several images. Both picture numbers, 100-11 and 100-12, are set for hiding in screen 3. (**Note:** To unhide a single image or several images, simply press the Multi selector center button while highlighting an image with the hide mark showing.)
4. Press the OK button to hide or unhide the image(s). *Done* will appear on the Monitor when the process is complete (figure 2.3A, screen 4).

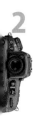

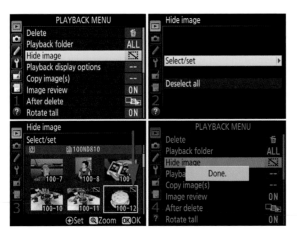

Figure 2.3A – Hide images with Select/set

The number of images reported does not change when you hide images. If you have 50 images on the card and you hide 10, the camera still displays 50 as the number of images on the card. A clever person could figure out that there are hidden images by watching the number of images as they scroll through the viewable ones. If you hide all the images on the card and then try to view images, the D810 will tersely inform you, *All images are hidden*.

You can also use these steps to unhide one or many images by reversing the process described earlier. As you scroll through the images, as shown in figure 2.3A, screen 3, you can deselect them with the Multi selector center button and then press the OK button to unhide them.

While you are selecting or deselecting images to hide, you can use the Playback zoom in button to see a larger version of the image you currently have selected. You can also use the Thumbnail/Playback zoom out button to open the Playback slot and folder menu, allowing you to select a particular memory card and folder (as discussed at the beginning of this chapter). This lets you examine the image in more detail to see if you really want to hide it.

Deselect all

This is a much simpler way to unhide the previously hidden images on the card all at once. Here are the steps to unhide (deselect) all images marked as hidden:

1. Select Hide image from the Playback Menu and scroll to the right (figure 2.3B, screen 1).
2. Choose Deselect all from the list and scroll to the right (figure 2.3B, screen 2).
3. When prompted with *Reveal all hidden images?*, select Yes and press the OK button. All hidden images on the card will then be viewable (figure 2.3B, screen 3).
4. After the images are unhidden, the Monitor will display the message, *Marking removed from all images* (figure 2.3B, screen 4).

Losing Protection When You Deselect All Images (Unhide)
If you have images that are both hidden and protected from deletion and you unhide them, the deletion protection is removed at the same time.

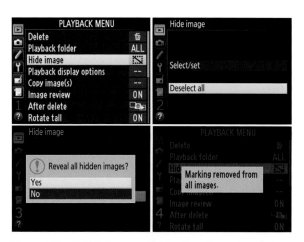

Figure 2.3B – Unhide images with Deselect all

Note: As mentioned previously, you can also use the steps connected to figure 2.3A to unhide a single image or a few images instead of unhiding all hidden images at once with the steps shown for figure 2.3B.

Playback Display Options

(User's Manual – Pages 282, 238)

The *Playback display options* selection allows you to customize how the D810 displays several histogram and data screens for each image. You get to those screens by displaying an image on the camera's Monitor and scrolling up or down with the Multi selector.

When you want to see a lot of detailed information about each image, you can select it here. Or, if you would rather take a minimalist approach to image information, simply turn off some of the screens.

If you turn off certain screens, the camera still records the information—such as lens used, shutter speed, and aperture—for each image. However, with no data screens selected, you'll see only two screens when you scroll up or down. One is the main image view, and the other is a summary screen with a luminance histogram and basic shooting information. I have not found a way to turn this summary screen off. You get to the screens by using the Multi selector to scroll vertically. I leave my camera set so I can scroll through my images by pressing left or right on the Multi selector. Then I can scroll through the data screens by pressing up or down on the Multi selector.

Here are the selections in this menu:

Basic photo info
- Focus point

Additional photo info
- None (image only)
- Highlights
- RGB histogram
- Shooting data
- Overview

When you modify these selections, be sure to scroll up to Done and press the OK button to save your setting (figure 2.4A, screen 3).

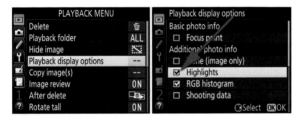

Figure 2.4A – Playback display options menu screens

Use the following steps to enable or disable any of the six playback display screens:

1. Select Playback display options from the Playback Menu and scroll to the right (figure 2.4A, screen 1).
2. Choose any of the six available screens by highlighting a line in yellow with the Multi selector and scrolling to the right to put a check mark in the box for that item (red arrow in figure 2.4A, screen 2). You must scroll down to see the final selection, Overview, which does not show on the main screen. In figure 2.4A, only Highlights and RGB histogram are selected.
3. After you have put check marks in the boxes for all the screens you want to use, press the OK button.

Now, let's look at what each of these selections accomplishes (figures 2.4B to 2.4K).

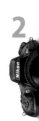

Focus point

If you are curious about which autofocus (AF) sensor was focused on your subject during an exposure, use this mode to easily find out. If you are using Single-point AF or Dynamic-area AF, you'll see a single red AF indicator where the camera was focused when you took the picture (figure 2.4B, screen 2). If you are using Auto-area AF, you'll see all the AF points that were providing autofocus in your image. This is a useful function for reviewing how the camera's AF system performs in different imaging situations. In figure 2.4B, screen 2, you can see the red AF indicator on the cheek of the young man holding the smartphone, which is the focus point of this image.

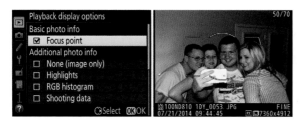

Figure 2.4B – Enabling the Focus point display

None (image only)

This setting is designed to give you a somewhat larger view of the current image, using all of the available screen space to show the image (figure 2.4C, screen 2). There are no text overlays, just the image by itself. This is a good selection for when you want to zoom in to the image to look at details. Since only the image itself is displayed, it is easier to scroll around within it for deep looks when using the camera's two zoom buttons (zoom in and out). You can zoom all the way in to 46x the normal image view. There is a tremendous level of detail buried inside each 36.3-megapixel image. You have an easy way to view it with None (image only).

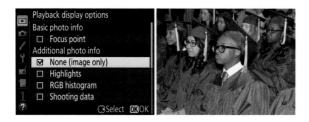

Figure 2.4C – Enabling the None (image only) display

Highlights

If you decide to use the Highlights selection, as shown in figure 2.4D, you will turn on what I call the "blink mode" of the camera. You'll see the words RGB Highlights at the bottom left of the image. When any area of the image is overexposed, that area will blink white and black. A rectangle surrounding the word RGB will blink from black to yellow at the same time.

This is a warning that the areas of the image that blink black and white are overexposed and have lost detail. You will need to use exposure compensation or manually control the camera to contain the exposure within the dynamic range of the camera's sensor.

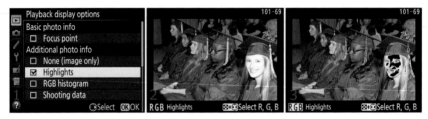

Figure 2.4D – Enabling the Highlights display

Look at the young woman who is closest to the camera in figure 2.4D, screens 2 and 3. In screen 2, you can see that her face is overexposed. She was too close to the flash unit, which caused her face to be burned out in the image. If you were looking at this image on your camera's Monitor, you would see the girl's face repeatedly blinking white to black.

When you have Highlights enabled and you see an area blinking white and black in an image on the Monitor, it means that area of the image has turned completely white and lost all detail, or has blown out.

If you examine the histogram for an overexposed (blown-out) image, you'll see that it's cut off, or clipped, on the right side. Current software cannot usually recover any image data from the blown-out sections. The exposure has exceeded the range of the sensor and the image has become completely overexposed in the blinking area. We'll discuss how to deal with images that have light ranges exceeding the sensor's recording capacity in the chapter called **Metering, Exposure Modes, and Histogram**.

Highlights mode conveniently warns you when you have surpassed what the sensor can capture and lets you know that portions of the image will be overexposed.

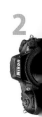

RGB histogram

A histogram is a digital readout that shows the range of light and color in an image. If there is too much contrast, the histogram display will be cut off. We'll examine the histogram in more detail later. For now, let's see how to turn the display on and off.

I like this feature since it allows me to view not just a basic luminance (brightness) histogram as some cameras do, but all three color (chrominance) histograms—red, green, and blue—and a luminance histogram on one screen (figure 2.4E, screen 2). The D810 stacks the four histograms on the right side of the screen, with luminance on top (white histogram) and the RGB color histograms underneath.

It is quite useful to see each color channel in its own histogram because it is possible to overexpose, or blow out, only one color channel. The luminance (white) histogram usually looks similar to the green channel histogram because green is the most common color and the luminance histogram is weighted toward green. We'll discuss more about the luminance histogram, and the three RGB channel histograms, in the chapter called **Metering, Exposure Modes, and Histogram**.

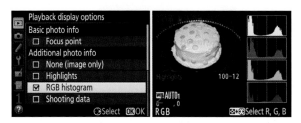

Figure 2.4E – Enabling the RGB histogram display

Shooting data

This setting gives you four additional image shooting data screens to scroll through (figure 2.4F). Normally these shooting data screens overlay a pale version of the image they represent, so you will see a faint image beneath the screens. However, to make the information on the screens more legible, I took pictures of a gray background. The data on these screens includes the following information.

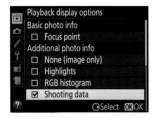

Figure 2.4F – Enabling the Shooting data display

Shooting data, screen 1 (figure 2.4G)

- Light meter in use (Matrix, Spot, or Averaging), Shutter speed, and Aperture
- Exposure mode (P, S, A, M) and ISO sensitivity
- Exposure compensation value and optimal exposure tuning
- Lens focal length
- Lens overview data (e.g., 24–85mm /3.5–4.5)
- Focus mode and VR (vibration reduction)
- Flash type and commander mode (CMD)
- Flash sync mode
- Flash control and compensation
- Commander mode info (if used)

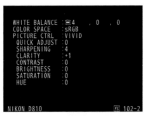

Figure 2.4G – Shooting data, screen 1   **Figure 2.4H** – Shooting data, screen 2

Shooting data, screen 2 (figure 2.4H)

- White balance (WB), color temperature, WB fine tuning, and Preset manual
- Color space (sRGB, AdobeRGB)
- Picture control detail (i.e., Standard, Neutral, Vivid, Monochrome, Portrait, Land-scape) and adjustments: Quick adjust and Original Picture Control, Sharpening, Clarity, Contrast, Brightness, Saturation and filter effects, and Hue and toning.

Shooting data, screen 3 (figure 2.4I)

- High ISO noise reduction, Long exposure noise reduction
- Active D-Lighting (Off, Low, Normal, High)
- HDR exposure differential and smoothing
- Vignette control
- Retouch history
- Image comment

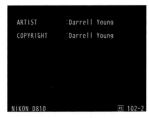

Figure 2.4I – Shooting data, screen 3   **Figure 2.4J** – Shooting data, screen 4

Shooting data, screen 4 (figure 2.4J)

- Artist
- Copyright

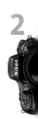

Overview

This screen provides an overview of the image detail for each picture (figure 2.4K). It is packed with 28 items of information on each image, all in one convenient place. With this screen and the always-available File information screen (figure 2.4L), you will have enough information to determine the most important details about a particular image. Whether you select any other screens is entirely up to you and is determined by how much information you want for each image you have taken.

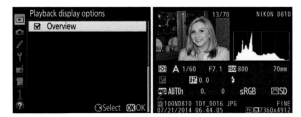

Figure 2.4K – Enabling the Overview screen

File information

This screen is not selectable under the Playback display options for the simple reason that it is always turned on and available for each image (figure 2.4L). You cannot turn it off; although, if you have *Playback display options > Focus point* enabled, the Focus point and File information screens will combine into just one screen. File information includes a large, clear view of the picture with only basic image details.

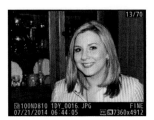

Figure 2.4L – File information screen

GPS screen

If you take a picture with a GPS unit attached and active on your D810, you'll have an additional screen available (figure 2.4M)—even if you don't have Shooting data selected. It will not show up unless a GPS unit is attached to the camera when the picture is taken. We will consider the details of the GPS function and screen in the chapter named **Shooting Menu** under the **GPS** heading.

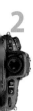

That's a lot of screens to scroll through, but they provide a great deal of information about the image. Look how far we've come from the days when cameras wrote date information on the lower-right portion of an image (permanently marking it) or between the frames on pro-level cameras.

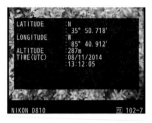

Figure 2.4M – GPS screen

Settings Recommendation: The screens I use all the time on my D810 are as follows: None (image only) as seen in figure 2.4C, Highlights (figure 2.4D), RGB histogram (figure 2.4E), and Overview (figure 2.4K).

I like None (image only) because I love to drill down deep into these enormous 36-megapixel images to see what detail I've been able to capture. The D810 gives me such deep, overwhelmingly detailed images. I enjoy this setting because it lets me examine the image with no text overlay distractions.

The Highlights screen is very useful because at a glance I can see where I have overexposed an image and can take immediate corrective action. The black and white blinking action grabs my attention and I can change my settings for the better immediately.

The RGB histogram is also important to me because it allows me to see all the color channels, just in case one of them is being clipped off on the light or dark sides (no detail). It also allows me to see how well I am keeping my exposure balanced for light and dark.

The Overview screen gives me, at a glance, most of the important information I need to know about the image, along with a larger luminance histogram. If I only had one screen, I'd want it to be the Overview screen.

The Shooting data and Focus point screens are not very important to me personally. Also, if I have the Shooting data screens enabled, I'll have to scroll through four more screens to get to the screens I like to use.

However, those are my preferences. If you want to examine a large amount of extra image data, then you should enable the other screens, too. Nikon gives us very thorough picture detail screens. Use what you like best.

Copy Image(s)

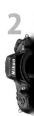

(User's Manual – Page 283)

The D810 provides a means to copy images between the camera's two card slots. If you've been shooting and decide you want a backup on the card in the other slot or want to give images on one of your cards to someone else, you can use this function to copy images between the two cards. You must have memory cards in both slots to use Copy image(s), otherwise the menu selection will be grayed out.

This convenient function has several steps to copy images. First, select a source card—if both cards have images—and the source folder, then select the images to copy, and then select the folder on the destination card in which you want to place the images. Figure 2.5A shows the screens used to copy images.

If Select source is grayed out, there are two potential reasons; see them following the step-by-step instructions shown next.

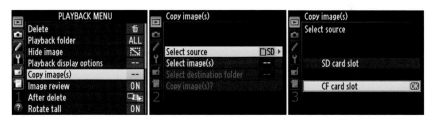

Figure 2.5A – Selecting a source for images to copy

Refer to figure 2.5A and follow these steps to select a source card:

1. Select Copy image(s) from the Playback Menu and scroll to the right (figure 2.5A, screen 1).
2. Choose Select source from the list and scroll to the right (figure 2.5A, screen 2).
3. Choose one of the card slots. I use CF card slot as my primary card slot, so figure 2.5A, screen 3, shows that I selected it as the source. **Note:** You can use *Shooting Menu > Primary slot selection* to choose which card slot is primary for your camera.
4. Press the OK button to lock in your choice.

Why is Select source grayed out? – When I first opened the menu shown in figure 2.5A, screen 2, I found only one item available: the Select image(s) choice. The rest of the choices were grayed out. I was quite puzzled at first, but then I figured out that there are two reasons Select image(s) may be the only option available.

First, there might be images on only one of the cards. Think about this for a moment. If only one card has images on it, it has to be the source. This is the most likely scenario.

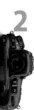

Accidentally Inserting a Write-Locked Card

The camera cannot write to an SD card with the write lock set to On. If the locked SD card is the only one inserted into the camera, you will see the word *CArd* blinking on the top Control panel (yes, for some reason it has an uppercase *A*). Also, if you press the Shutter-release button, a message will appear on the Monitor, saying, *Memory card is locked. Slide lock to "write" position.*

If there are two memory cards in the camera and one of them is locked, a blinking card slot icon will appear on the Control panel and Information display screen (press the info button once for the Information display screen). The blinking card symbol on the Information display screen will have a key icon in the middle, symbolizing that the card needs to be unlocked (it is protected). If you don't notice the blinking card icons, it may take a while to realize that you've accidentally moved the write-lock switch to the locked position on one of the cards.

The camera is smart enough to write to the other available card slot when it can't access one of the two memory cards, so you may be happily snapping images thinking they are being saved to the primary card when they are actually being sent to the secondary card, or vice versa.

The camera will continue displaying images found on the locked card if it contains images and Playback folder is set to All in the Playback Menu. The D810 can still read the card and display images from a write-locked card.

There are only a few CF cards on the market with a write-lock switch available. On the other hand, virtually all SD cards have a write-lock switch. In most cases, problems with a locked card are caused by an SD card, which is relatively easy to write-lock accidentally upon insertion.

Second, an SD card's (or in rare cases a CF card's) write-lock switch might be in the On position. This usually happens when the SD card is inserted into a card reader or a camera at a slight angle. The switch is on the side, and sometimes it accidentally gets moved from the Off to the On position. See the sidebar **Accidentally Inserting a Write-Locked Card** for more information about what happens when a write-locked card is inserted into one of the camera's memory card slots.

The following instructions assume that you have a card in each slot and there are images on both cards. If you have images on only one card, you can skip this process. Refer to figure 2.5A and follow the steps to select a source card.

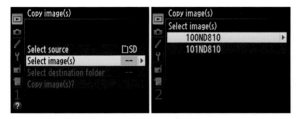

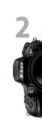

Figure 2.5B – Selecting a source folder for images to copy

When you have chosen a source, it's time to select images to copy. First, follow these steps to choose a folder:

1. Choose Select image(s) from the list and scroll to the right (figure 2.5B, screen 1).
2. Choose the folder that contains the images you want to copy (figure 2.5B, screen 2). My cards currently have two folders available and I chose the folder named 100ND810. Your cards may have several existing folders or only one. After you have chosen a folder, scroll to the right.

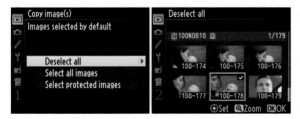

Figure 2.5C – Deselecting all images to copy

3. There are three options for copying images: Deselect all, Select all images, and Select protected images (figure 2.5C). Each option has a slightly different way of doing things (the description for each option is listed between steps 3 and 4). Choose one option for your copy operation, follow the directions for your chosen option, and continue with step 4.

- **Deselect all** (figure 2.5C) – Choose Deselect all from the Images selected by default menu and scroll to the right. Deselect all opens a list of images, none of which have been selected. It sounds a little weird to select images for copying while using a function named Deselect all, but this means that the camera automatically deselects all the images so you can choose which images to copy. You'll need to scroll around with the yellow rectangle and select images one at a time. Mark an image for copying by pressing the Multi selector center button, and you'll see a small white check mark appear in the top-right corner of the image thumbnail. Figure 2.5C, screen 2, shows only one picture selected, number 100-178. It is the only one with a check mark. Now move on to step 4.

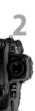

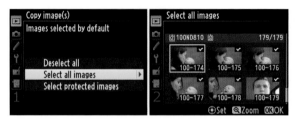

Figure 2.5D – Selecting all images to copy

- **Select all images** (figure 2.5D) – Choose Select all images from the Images selected by default menu and scroll to the right. The Select all images screen will appear, with all images selected. If you want to copy all of the images, move on to step 4 now. If you want to deselect a few of them before copying, scroll to an image and press the Multi selector center button. This action will remove the check mark from the image thumbnail. After you've unchecked the images you don't want to copy, move on to step 4.

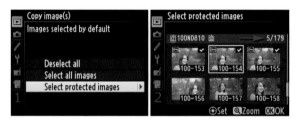

Figure 2.5E – Selecting protected images to copy

- **Select protected images** (figure 2.5E) – Choose Select protected images from the Images selected by default menu and scroll to the right. If you have used the Help/protect button to mark images as protected, they will appear with a little key symbol and a check mark in the list of images, indicating that they are already checked for copying (figure 2.5E, screen 2, pictures 100-153 to 100-155). If you have a lot of images on the card and only a few are protected, it may be hard to find the protected images. Rest assured that the camera knows which ones to copy. It will display all the images but only copy the protected ones. You can see the number of protected images that will be copied in the upper-right corner of the display (red arrow in figure 2.5E, screen 2). This figure shows that I will copy 5 protected images out of 179 images on the CF card from folder 100ND810. Now move on to step 4.

4. After you have selected all the images you want to copy, press the OK button and the Monitor will display the Copy Images(s) menu. Now it's time to select a destination folder into which you'll copy the images (figure 2.5F).

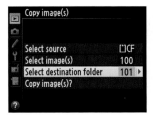

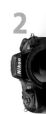

Figure 2.5F – Selecting a destination folder

5. Choose Select destination folder from the Copy image(s) menu and scroll to the right (figure 2.5F). You will have two options: Select folder by number or Select folder from list (figures 2.5G and 2.5H). Before we move on to step 6, let's investigate these options. Pick an option, follow the instructions for your option, and then move on to step 6.

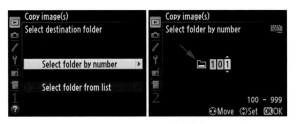

Figure 2.5G – Selecting a destination folder by number

• **Select folder by number** (figure 2.5G) – Choose Select folder by number from the Select destination folder menu and scroll to the right. The next screen will display a folder number that can be changed to any number between 100 and 999 (figure 2.5G, screen 2). If you select a number for a folder that already exists on the destination card, the images will be copied into that folder. If you select a folder number for which a corresponding folder does not exist on the destination card, the folder will be created and the source images will be copied into the new folder on the destination card. Notice the little folder symbol the red arrow points to in screen 2. The folder symbol appears only when you are copying into an existing folder. My cards already contained existing folders 100ND810 and 101ND810, as seen in figures 2.5B and 2.5H. In figure 2.5G, screen 2, if I had scrolled up where the yellow highlighted 1 is, changing it to a 2 instead, the camera would have created a folder on the destination card named 102ND810 in preparation for copying the files. Now move on to step 6.

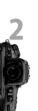

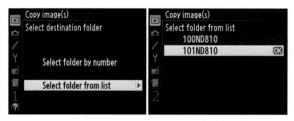

Figure 2.5H – Selecting a destination folder from a list of folders

- **Select folder from list** (figure 2.5H) – If there are no existing folders on the destination card, this option will be grayed out. Obviously, you can't copy images to a folder that doesn't exist, so use the Select folder by number option to create a new folder. If this option is not grayed out, choose Select folder from list and scroll to the right. The next screen will show you a list of folders. My list in figure 2.5H, screen 2, has two folders in it. I chose to use the folder named 101ND810. After you have selected the destination folder, move on to step 6.

6. Now it's finally time to copy some images. We've selected a source card and folder, some images, and a destination folder. Notice that you don't have to select a destination memory card. Since we've already selected a source card, the other card automatically becomes the destination. The D810 does not support copying images to the same memory card; you can copy only to the other card. All that's left is to select Copy image(s)? and press the OK button.

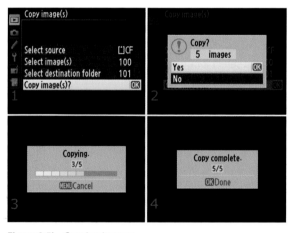

Figure 2.5I – Copying images

7. Figure 2.5I shows the screens for this step and step 8. After you have selected Copy image(s)?, you'll see a screen asking for verification. Mine says, *Copy? 5 images* (figure 2.5I, screen 2). Select Yes and press the OK button. Figure 2.5I, screen 3, shows that the camera is copying 5 pictures from the source card to the destination card. Notice how the *Copying* screen shows the progress of the copy action with a green progress bar. This will take several minutes to complete if you are copying a large number of images.

8. When the copying is finished, you will see a small white box that says, *Copy complete* and the number of images successfully copied, in this case five of five (5/5). You must press the OK button to return to the Copy image(s) screen. That completes the copying process.

There's one more screen to be aware of, in case you try to copy images into a folder where they already exist. If an identical file name already exists in the destination folder, you may or may not want to overwrite it.

The camera will warn you with the screen shown in figure 2.5J, helpfully showing you thumbnails of both images. You can view the two thumbnails and choose Replace existing image, Replace all, Skip, or Cancel.

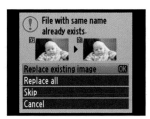

Figure 2.5J – Image overwrite warning

Image Review

(User's Manual – Page 287)

Image review does exactly what it says; it displays an image you've just taken on your camera's Monitor. With this function set to On, you'll see each picture you take just after you take it. You can review the image for quality and usefulness.

With Image review set to Off, you won't see each picture unless you press the Playback button afterward. This saves battery life. However, the camera's battery is long lived because the D810 does not use a lot of power. If you prefer to review each image after you take it, then you'll need to set this feature to On.

You can control how long each image is displayed on the Monitor before it shuts off by adjusting *Custom Setting Menu > c Timers/AElock > c4 Monitor off delay > Image review*. This custom image review time can be adjusted to display pictures

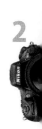

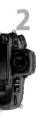

from 2 seconds to 10 minutes. We'll discuss this in more detail in the chapter titled **Custom Setting Menu**.

There are two Image review settings, as shown in figure 2.6:

- **On** – Shows a picture on the Monitor after each shutter release.
- **Off** – Causes the Monitor to stay off when you take pictures.

Here are the steps to choose an Image review setting:

1. Choose Image review from the Playback Menu and scroll to the right.
2. Select On or Off from the Image review screen.
3. Press the OK button.

Most of us will turn this feature on right away. Otherwise, the only way to view an image after taking it is to press the Playback button.

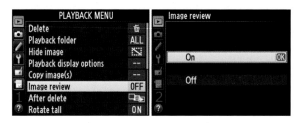

Figure 2.6 – Enabling Image review

Settings Recommendation: Because the camera's battery lasts a long time, I leave Image review set to On. I am an unashamed image chimper (see sidebar **Are You a Chimper Too?**) and always examine each image, if there's time. Photography is enjoyable, and one of the good things is the satisfaction you feel when you capture a really nice image. However, if you are shooting a sports event and blasting through hundreds of shots per hour, there's not much time to view each image. It all boils down to how you shoot. If you aren't inclined to view your images as you take them, then it may be a good idea to set Image review to Off—merely to save battery life.

After Delete

(User's Manual – Page 287)
If you delete an image during playback, one of your other images will be displayed on the camera's Monitor. The After delete function lets you select which image is displayed after you delete an image. The camera can display the next image or the previous image, or it can detect which direction you were scrolling—forward or backward—and let that determine which image appears after you delete another.

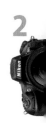

> ### Are You a Chimper Too?
>
> *Chimping* means reviewing images on the Monitor after each shot. I guess peo-
> ple think you look like a monkey if you review each image. Well, I do it anyway!
> Sometimes I even make monkey noises when I'm chimping my images. Try say-
> ing, "Oo, Oo, Oo, Ah, Ah, Ah" really fast when you're looking at an image and are
> happy with it. That's chimping with style, and it's why the word was invented.

The three selections on the After delete menu are Show next, Show previous, and
Continue as before (figure 2.7).

- **Show next** – If you delete an image and it wasn't the last image on the memory
  card, the camera will display the next image on the Monitor. If you delete the
  last image on the card, the previous image will be displayed. Show next is the
  factory default behavior of the D810.
- **Show previous** – If you delete the first image on the memory card, the camera
  will display the next image. If you delete an image somewhere in the middle or
  at the end of the memory card, the previous image will be displayed.
- **Continue as before** – This weird little setting shows the flexibility of computerized camera technology in all its glory. If you are scrolling to the right (the order
  in which the images were taken) and decide to delete an image, the camera uses
  the Show next method to display the next image. If you happen to be scrolling to the left (opposite from the order in which the images were taken) when
  you decide to delete a picture, the camera will use the Show previous method
  instead.

Use the following steps to choose an After delete setting (figure 2.7):

1. Choose After delete from the Playback Menu and scroll to the right (figure 2.7,
   screen 1).
2. Select one of the settings from the After delete screen (figure 2.7, screen 2).
3. Press the OK button to lock in the setting.

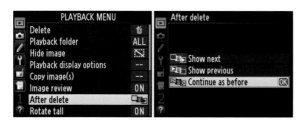

Figure 2.7 – Playback Menu – After delete

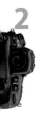

Settings Recommendation: When I delete an image, I'm not overly concerned about which image shows next—most of the time. However, this functionality is handy in certain styles of shooting and when I am deleting rejects.

For instance, some sports or wildlife shooters might like to move backward through a long sequence of images, starting with the last image taken. They can then delete the images that are not usable in the sequence, and the camera will immediately show the previous image for review. When they reach the first image in the sequence, the entire series is clean and ready to use.

I leave my camera set to Continue as before, as shown in figure 2.7, because it will use the direction I was scrolling to decide which image to display after deleting one.

Rotate Tall

(User's Manual – Page 288)

When you shoot a portrait-oriented (vertical) image with the camera turned sideways, the image can later be viewed as a horizontal image lying on its side or as a smaller, upright (tall) image on the camera's horizontal (wide) Monitor.

If you view the image immediately after taking it, the camera's software assumes that you are still holding the camera in the rotated position and the image will be displayed correctly for that angle. Later, if you are reviewing the image with the camera's playback functionality and have Rotate tall set to On, the image will be displayed as an upright, vertical image that is smaller so it will fit on the horizontal Monitor. You can zoom in to see sharpness detail, if needed.

If you would rather have the camera leave the image lying on its side in a horizontal view, forcing you to turn the camera 90 degrees to view it, you'll need to choose Off.

The following two settings are available on the Rotate tall menu (figure 2.8):

- **On** – When you take a vertical image, the camera will rotate it so you don't have to turn your camera to view it naturally during playback. This resizes the view of the image so that a vertical image fits in the horizontal frame of the Monitor. The image will be a bit smaller than normal. When you first view the image after taking it, the camera does not rotate it because it assumes you are still holding the camera in a vertical orientation. It also senses which end of the camera is up—if the Shutter-release button is up or down—and displays the image accordingly.
- **Off** – Vertical images are left in a horizontal direction, lying on their side; you'll need to turn the camera to view the images in the same orientation as when they were taken. This provides a slightly larger view of a portrait-oriented image.

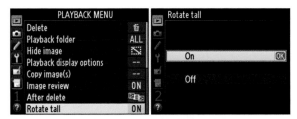
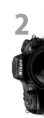

Figure 2.8 – Playback Menu – Rotate tall

Here are the three steps to choose a Rotate tall setting:

1. Choose Rotate tall from the Playback Menu and scroll to the right (figure 2.8, screen 1).
2. Select On or Off from the Rotate tall screen (figure 2.8, screen 2).
3. Press the OK button to finish.

There is another camera function that affects how this works. It's called Auto image rotation, under the Setup Menu. We'll discuss this function more deeply in the chapter titled **Setup Menu**. Auto image rotation causes the camera to record the angle at which you are holding it as part of the image's metadata. Auto image rotation should be set to On so that an image will report how it should be displayed on the camera's Monitor and on your computer.

In other words, Rotate tall and Auto image rotation work together to display your image in the correct orientation. Rotate tall gives you the choice of how the image is viewed based on the orientation information it finds in the image's metadata. *Setup Menu > Auto image rotation* causes the camera to store how the image was taken so it will know whether the image has a vertical or horizontal composition. It can then report this information to the Rotate tall function.

Settings Recommendation: I leave Rotate tall set to On. That way I can view a portrait-oriented image in its natural, vertical orientation without turning my camera. Be sure you understand the relationship between this function and Auto image rotation, which stores orientation data with the picture. I always set *Rotate tall* and *Setup Menu > Auto image rotation* to On.

Slide Show

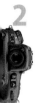

(User's Manual – Page 288)

A slide show is a convenient way to view a large number of images instead of having to scroll through them one by one. The camera can also be connected to an HDMI display device to show a slide show on a larger device. With the size of some of today's flat-screen televisions, we've come full circle to the old days of family slide shows. With the D810's big 3.2-inch Monitor for viewing immediately or its HDMI output for viewing later, slide shows are back! But instead of a portable screen and slide projector, we have the D810 and an HDTV.

Note: Connecting to an HDTV requires the separate purchase of an HDMI (Type A) to mini-HDMI (Type C) cable (not included with camera). The D810 uses the Type C, mini-HDMI connector, while the HDTV uses the larger Type A connector.

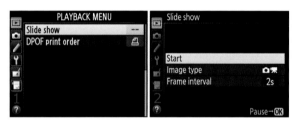

Figure 2.9A – Playback Menu – Slide show

As shown in figure 2.9A, the easy way to start a slide show is to simply select the *Playback Menu > Slide show* setting, scroll right, select Start, and press the OK button. The slide show will commence immediately with a default display time of 2 seconds (2s) per image.

   You can control how long each image is displayed with the Frame interval setting. If you want to allow a little more time for each image to show, you'll need to change the Frame interval (display time).

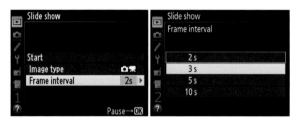

Figure 2.9B – Playback Menu – Slide show Frame interval

Figure 2.9B shows the menus where you can make the Frame interval changes. Your choices are as follows:

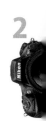

- 2s – 2 seconds
- 3s – 3 seconds
- 5s – 5 seconds
- 10s – 10 seconds

To start the slide show after you change the Frame interval setting, repeat the steps shown in figure 2.9A. The slide show will now run at the speed you chose.

Settings Recommendation: I usually set the Frame interval to 3s. If the images are especially beautiful, I might set it to 5s. I've found that 2s is not quite enough, and 5s or 10s may be too long. I wish there were a 4s setting, but 3s seems to work well most of the time.

Changing the Slide Show Image Flow

There are several options that affect how the images are displayed during the slide show. None of these options are in the camera menus; they are available through the camera's controls only. Your options are as follows:

- *Skip back/Skip ahead* – During the slide show, you can go back to the previous image for another viewing by simply pressing left on the Multi selector. You can also see the next image with no delay by pressing right on the Multi selector. This is a quick way to skip images or review previous images without stopping the slide show.
- *View additional photo information* – While the slide show is running, you can press up or down on the Multi selector to view the additional data screens. The screens you will see depends on how you have configured your camera's *Playback Menu > Playback display options* settings, such as Focus point, None (image only), Highlights, RGB Histogram, and so on. See the section called **Playback Display Options** earlier in this chapter. If any of these screens are enabled, they can be used during the slide show.
- *Pause slide show* – During the slide show you may want to pause, change the frame interval, or even exit the show. If you press the OK button, the slide show will be suspended and you will see the Pause screen (figure 2.9C).

Using the screens shown in figure 2.9C, you can select any of the following:

- *Restart* – Selecting OK or scrolling to the right with the Multi selector continues the slide show, starting with the image following the last one that was viewed.
- *Frame interval* – Scrolling to the right with the Multi selector takes you to the screen that allows you to change the display time to one of four values. You can choose 2s, 3s, 5s, or 10s. After choosing the new Frame interval, you'll have to select Restart to continue the slide show where you left off.
- *Exit* – Selecting this option exits the slide show.

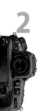

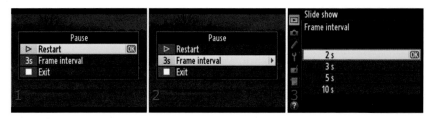

Figure 2.9C – Playback Menu – Slide show Pause and Restart

Exiting the Slide Show

There are several ways you can exit a slide show while it is running:

- *Press OK to pause* – Then select Exit from the Pause menu (figure 2.9C). The camera jumps back to the Playback Menu with Slide show highlighted so you can start again quickly.
- *Exit to the Playback Menu* – If you want to quickly exit the slide show, simply press the MENU button and the camera will jump directly back to the Playback Menu, with no items selected.
- *Exit to playback mode* – You can press the Playback button to stop the slide show and switch to a normal full-frame or thumbnail view of the last image seen in the slide show. This exits the show on the last image viewed.
- *Exit to shooting mode* – If you press the Shutter-release button halfway down, the slide show will stop. The camera is now in shooting mode, meaning that it is ready to take some pictures.

These days, instead of hauling out a slide projector and boxes of slides, you can simply plug your D810 into the closest high-definition (HD) device, such as an HDTV, because the camera has a high-definition multimedia interface (HDMI) port. We'll talk more about HDMI in a later chapter.

DPOF Print Order

(User's Manual – Page 267)

At first I thought it was odd that Nikon chose to put image printing functions in the Playback Menu. Then I realized that printing is a permanent form of image playback. You play (print) the images to your printer and then view them without a camera or a computer. What a concept!

There are two ways to print images from your camera without using a computer. One way is to use DPOF to create a print order on a memory card. This function is called Print set (DPOF). The second way is to plug in a USB cable and print directly to a PictBridge-compatible printer. Both of these methods are generally used by nonprofessional camera users to print pictures from Joint Photographic Experts Group (JPEG) files at home or at the local lab, with no post-processing.

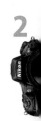

Most advanced amateur and professional users of the D810 will want to post-process their images in computer software such as Nikon Capture NX 2, Lightroom, Photoshop, or Aperture before printing, so this functionality is not used as often as other functions. However, it can be useful for someone who would rather simply take pictures and print them at home or at a store than manipulate images on their computer.

Since these seldom-used functions require multiple pages to describe and many people do not use them, I have relegated this information to a detailed document called **DPOF Print Order** and included it in the downloadable resources at **http://rockynook.com/NikonD810**.

Note: DPOF print order can be used only with JPEG images. It does not apply to NEF (RAW) files.

Author's Conclusions

Wow! The D810 sure does have a lot of playback screens and menus. I remember the old days when if you wanted to see your images, you'd have to find the old shoebox full of pictures or open an album and flip pages. Sometimes I miss photo albums. I have a bookcase full of old prints from the film days, but no digital prints. Hmmm.

You know what? I'm going down to the superstore right now to buy several albums. Then I'll have some images printed and put them into the albums. Better yet, I think I'll go buy a PictBridge-compatible printer so I can print my own images for the albums. Do you have new albums full of digital prints? If not, why not? They're awfully convenient and fun to view.

Anyway, let's move on to the next menu system in the camera, the Shooting Menu. This is one of the most important menus because it affects how the camera is configured to shoot pictures. Learn these upcoming settings well!

Shooting Menu

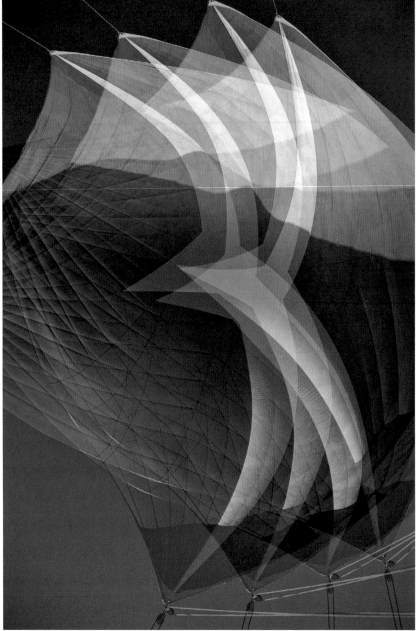

Spinnaker Sail Multi-Exposure Resembles a Flying Tern © Jim Austin (*Jimages*)

The Shooting Menu settings are some of the most-used functions in the camera. Spend time carefully learning about each of these selections because you will use them often. They affect how your camera takes pictures in all sorts of ways.

Here is a list and overview of the 25 items found on the D810 Shooting Menu. Each of these items can be configured in different ways by using the four available Shooting menu banks.

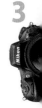

- **Shooting menu bank** – Allows configuration of the camera in four separate ways so that it can act like four different cameras as you change banks (A, B, C, and D).
- **Extended menu banks** – You can save not only the internal camera Shooting Menu function configurations but also the exposure mode and shutter speed (when you use S and M exposure modes) and the exposure mode and aperture (when you use A and M exposure modes). Later, when you select a Shooting menu bank, the exposure mode and the aperture or shutter speed setting will be recalled along with that bank's previous configuration.
- **Storage folder** – Selects the folder into which subsequent images will be stored on the camera's memory card(s).
- **File naming** – Lets you change three characters of the image's file name so that it is personalized.
- **Primary slot selection** – You can select either the SD or CF memory card slot to be the primary slot that receives images.
- **Secondary slot function** – Allows you to select either the SD or CF memory card slot to be the secondary slot that receives image overflow or copies.
- **Image quality** – You can select from eight image quality types, such as JPEG fine, NEF (RAW), or TIFF.
- **JPEG/TIFF recording** – Allows you to choose the Image size for JPEG and TIFF files, as well as the type of compression you want to use for your JPEG images (JPEG compression). For Image size you can choose to shoot Large (7360×4912, 36.2 MP), Medium (5520×3680, 20.3 MP), or Small (3680×2456, 9.0 MP) images when using FX mode. This image size will vary according to whether you have FX, 1.2x, DX, or 5:4 Image area modes selected. For JPEG compression you can select Size priority or Optimal quality for your best JPEG images.
- **NEF (RAW) recording** – Allows you to choose the Image size for NEF (RAW) files, including: RAW L, or Large, and RAW S, or Small. You can also set the compression type and bit depth for NEF (RAW) files.
- **Image area** – You have the choice of letting the camera automatically select DX mode when a DX lens is mounted, or you can select that it stay in FX mode (On or Off). You have four different image areas available for your pictures. They are FX (36×24), 1.2x (30×20), DX (24×16), and 5:4 (30×24).
- **White balance** – You can choose from nine different White balance types, including the ability to measure the ambient light's color balance (PRE).

- **Set Picture Control** – You can choose from several Picture Controls that modify how the pictures look.
- **Manage Picture Control** – Lets you save, load, rename, or delete custom Picture Controls from your camera's internal memory or card slots.
- **Color space** - You can choose either the industry printing standard Adobe RGB or the Internet and home use standard sRGB color space for your camera.
- **Active D-Lighting** – Allows you to select from several levels of automatic contrast correction for your images. The camera itself will protect your images from a degree of under- or overexposure.
- **HDR (high dynamic range)** – You can create a two-exposure HDR image. The camera will automatically combine them. Use for JPEG or TIFF images only.
- **Vignette control** – This function allows you to automatically remove various amounts of the corner darkness resulting from using certain lenses at maximum aperture with a full-frame sensor. Provides for three levels of vignette control when using an FX lens of the G or D type. Excludes DX and PC lenses.
- **Auto distortion control** – With a G or D type lens (PC, fisheye, and certain other lenses excluded), the camera can automatically reduce barrel distortion when using a wide-angle lens and pincushion distortion when using a telephoto lens. May cause image edge cropping as the distortion is automatically removed. Can reduce distortion in DX lenses when the camera is in DX mode.
- **Long exposure NR** – Uses the "dark-frame subtraction" method to significantly reduce noise in long exposures. A very powerful and useful function if you make long exposures because it is not as damaging to the image as blurring noise reduction. Slows camera frame rate and reduces memory buffer size when turned on.
- **High ISO NR** – Uses a blurring and resharpening method to remove noise from images shot with high ISO sensitivity values.
- **ISO sensitivity settings** – Allows you to manually set the ISO sensitivity between ISO 32 (Lo 1) and 51,200 (Hi 2), or let the camera decide for you automatically with Auto ISO sensitivity control.
- **Multiple exposure** – Allows you to take more than one exposure in a single frame and then combine the exposures in interesting ways.
- **Interval timer shooting** – You can put your camera on a tripod and set it to make one to several exposures at customizable time intervals.
- **Time-lapse photography** – Similar to Interval timer shooting, except more movie oriented. You can make a time-lapse movie with this function, obeying the options selected in *Shooting Menu > Movie settings*. Shooting things like a time exposure of a flower opening becomes easy with the D810.
- **Movie settings** – You can use this to set the movie quality, frame size, and frame rate of the video stream in Movie mode. You may also select how the Microphone works, choose the Destination card slot for the movies, and select how the ISO sensitivity level is configured when shooting a movie.

Now, let's consider each of these 25 Shooting Menu functions in more detail.

Shooting Menu Bank

(User's Manual – Pages 291)

The *Shooting menu banks* are unique to professional-level cameras. Most Nikons have a Shooting Menu, but only the best have multiple Shooting menu banks. Using the four banks, your D810 can change from a pro camera to a point-and shoot, and anything in between, with just a few button presses. Let me give you a couple of examples of what I mean.

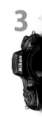

It can shoot RAW files using ISO 100 in Adobe RGB Color space with the Fn button assigned to Spot metering for serious professional shooting, and very quickly change to Normal quality JPEGs at ISO 400 in sRGB Color space with high image sharpening for that party where you don't want to think about anything but having a good time. These are only two variations of the many available combinations of bank settings you can design.

The D810 has not only four Shooting menu banks, but also four Custom settings banks (covered in the next chapter). There are no direct relationships between the Shooting menu banks and the Custom settings banks, although you could create one by naming them in a similar way and configuring them for similar purposes.

You can easily configure the functionality of each bank with different settings, name them accordingly, and use them to quickly change the way your camera behaves. Multiple cameras in one!

There are four default bank names: A, B, C, and D. You can add your own labels to any of these. In this chapter, we'll assume that your camera banks have not yet been adjusted and that you are not entirely familiar with the process. Let's learn how to label bank A with a more useful name and set its individual features. When you've done this once, you'll be ready to set up your camera for special uses and switch between banks quickly.

We will fully configure only a single bank in this chapter (bank A). Just repeat the same process for each bank, with different settings.

Following are the steps to create a label for Shooting menu bank A. Repeat the steps to label the other three banks (B–D):

1. Notice in figure 3.1A, screen 1, there's a selection called Shooting menu bank with an A after it. This means the camera is using Shooting menu bank A. If any letter other than A is showing, you are using a different Shooting menu bank. Let's give Shooting menu bank A a new label so you'll be able to see at a glance what this particular bank is set up to accomplish. Select Shooting menu bank from the Shooting Menu and scroll to the right.

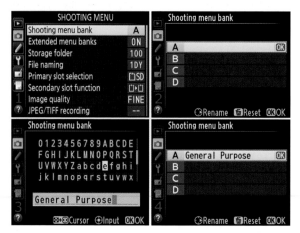

Figure 3.1A – Selecting and changing a Shooting menu bank

2. Assuming you haven't yet renamed any of your Shooting menu banks, you'll see the four banks called A, B, C, D, with a blank line following each letter (figure 3.1A, screen 2). The factory default for an unnamed bank is simply a blank field following the letter. Using the Multi selector, scroll to the right on the bank you want to rename (figure 3.1A, screen 2). If you press the OK button instead of scrolling to the right, you will simply select the bank. You must scroll right when the bank is highlighted in order to modify its name.

3. As shown in figure 3.1A, screen 3, you'll see a series of numbers and letters at the top of the screen. There is a space character at the end of the lowercase letters, after the small z. You can find various symbols by scrolling down below the numbers and letters. Notice the line of dashes in the gray text field at the bottom of the screen. This field is where you will enter the text that renames the bank. I added the words *General Purpose* there (figure 3.1A, screen 3). To add the new name for your camera's bank A, scroll around with the Multi selector and use the Multi selector center button to select letters, numbers, and symbols with the yellow cursor. You should see each character appear in the gray text field when you select it with the Multi selector center button. You can hold down the checkered Thumbnail/playback zoom out button and use the Multi selector to move back and forth in the gray text field. If you want to delete a character from the gray text field, move the darker gray cursor over the top of the letter and press the Delete button (garbage can). You are limited to 20 characters in the new bank name.

4. Press the OK button to save the new name. When you check the bank's name under the Shooting menu bank A setting, you'll see the bank's new label (figure 3.1A, screen 4). If you were renaming bank A, it is now selected also.

Settings Recommendation: I generally name my banks as shown in the following list. Each of the label names describes at a glance how I intend to use a bank when shooting. You may want to use different names and settings for each bank, but this list may give you some ideas:

- *Bank A – General Purpose*: Bank A is my general purpose bank. I use it when I'm just walking around with my camera doing general photography. I will often modify the camera's settings when using bank A. I know to check before shooting when using this bank. I generally shoot in RAW mode but might switch to JPEG as needed. This is a completely variable bank and the only one I modify regularly.
- *Bank B – Best Quality RAW*: Bank B is for when I am shooting commercially, with the best quality my camera can muster. I use this on any type of shoot that requires me to post-process the images in-computer. My critical settings for bank B are Image quality at NEF (RAW), with *NEF (RAW) recording > Type* set to Lossless compressed and NEF (RAW) bit depth at 14-bit, Image size set to Large, Image area set to FX, White balance to AUTO, Neutral (NL) Picture Control, Color space to Adobe RGB, Active D-Lighting to Off (or Low), ISO sensitivity to ISO 100, and Aperture-priority mode with the aperture set to f/8. (If *Shooting Menu > Extended menu banks* is set to On, the camera will remember the last exposure mode and aperture or shutter speed, saving it under the current bank with the rest of your settings for that bank. See the section **Extended Menu Banks** for more information.) Once it's set, I rarely modify this bank. If I'm shooting landscapes from a tripod, I may lower the ISO sensitivity to ISO 64 by holding down the ISO button and turning the rear Main command dial.
- *Bank C – Best Quality JPEG*: Bank C is for when I have no time to post-process the images. I need them as soon as I shoot them but must have maximum quality. My critical settings for bank C are Image quality set to JPEG fine, Image size set to Large, Image area set to FX, JPEG compression to Optimal quality, White balance to AUTO, Standard (SD) Picture Control, Color space to Adobe RGB, Active D-Lighting to Low, and ISO sensitivity to ISO 100. Once it's set, I rarely change this bank. I also use Extended menu banks set to On with Aperture priority mode selected and aperture set to f/8.
- *Bank D – Party JPEG*: When I am going to a party with friends, I'll simply switch to this bank and fire away. I could use bank A, but then I'd have to reset it to higher quality later. Instead, I use this bank to have some fun with my camera and friends. The images must be high enough quality to get good prints, at least 11×14 inches (27×35 cm) in size. The critical settings for bank D are Image quality set to JPEG fine, Image size set to Medium (20.3 MP), JPEG compression set to Size priority, White balance to AUTO, Standard (SD) Picture Control, Color space to sRGB, Active D-Lighting to Normal, and Auto ISO sensitivity control set

3

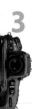

to On, with a Maximum sensitivity of ISO 1600 and Minimum shutter speed of 1/60s. Even though I turned on Auto ISO, I also set ISO sensitivity to ISO 400. I'll explain why in the upcoming note. Finally, I set Extended menu banks to On with Programmed auto exposure mode selected for thought-free shooting. My camera is like a heavy Coolpix point-and-shoot for party time while still giving me 20-megapixel JPEG images.

Note: Why did I set a manual ISO sensitivity in Shooting menu bank D – Party JPEG? I also turned on the Auto ISO sensitivity control. Shouldn't that automatically handle all my ISO sensitivity needs? Good questions! I set a manual ISO sensitivity because of an undocumented feature in most Nikons. If you set ISO sensitivity to a certain number when you have the Auto ISO sensitivity control enabled, the ISO you set manually becomes a minimum ISO, while the Auto ISO sensitivity control sets the maximum ISO. So, in my case, by setting an ISO of 400, I set a minimum ISO that my camera will not go below. The Auto ISO sensitivity control is set to never exceed ISO 1600 in my bank D setting. I have now created a range of ISO 400 to 1600 that my camera can shoot within, adjusting ISO sensitivity automatically, as needed, in my set range.

Alternate Shooting Menu Bank Access

If you would prefer, you can access the Shooting menu banks without pressing the MENU button. Instead, you can access the Shooting menu banks from the Quick Menu screen (figure 3.1B).

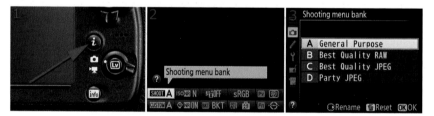

Figure 3.1B – Accessing the Shooting menu banks with the *i* button and Quick Menu screen

Use these steps to change Shooting menu banks quickly:

1. Press the *i* button once (figure 3.1B, screen 1). This will cause the Quick Menu screen to appear.
2. Scroll to the Shooting menu bank position and press the OK button (figure 3.1B, screen 2).
3. The Shooting menu bank screen will now appear, allowing you to change quickly to a different bank (figure 3.1B, screen 3). Notice the names of my fully configured Shooting menu banks.

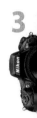

> ### Combining Shooting Menu Banks and Custom Settings Banks
>
> Can you see how flexible having these four Shooting menu banks will make your D810? You can create your own bank names and apply the underlying settings however you wish. If you want, you can match these Shooting menu banks to similarly named Custom settings banks, which allow you to set things like the Autofocus and Metering/exposure types. When the Shooting menu banks and Custom settings banks are combined in this manner, the D810 becomes a very powerful camera with strong flexibility to match different photographic needs and styles. There are **no** direct connections between the Shooting menu banks and Custom settings banks. I make my own mental connection by giving both similar names and then changing to them at the same time.

Working with Shooting Menu Settings

Each of the settings mentioned in my list of banks are Shooting Menu settings. We will discuss each of them in this chapter. If you don't know where to find them, do not attempt to set up your own banks until you have read over this chapter. You may have a completely different idea on how to configure your banks. Think about the way you shoot, and then name and configure the banks accordingly.

To select a particular bank, simply go to *Shooting Menu > Shooting menu bank*, highlight a particular bank, and press the OK button. The letter for the bank should appear to the right of the Shooting menu bank, as seen in figure 3.1A, screen 1.

We are using Shooting menu bank A as our example and must now set up the camera functionality for this bank; there are 25 functions left to set. Let's scroll down in the Shooting Menu and configure each individual line item available there. They will each be saved as part of bank A, which we renamed and selected. Changes in one bank do not affect changes in another bank. Each bank is a standalone bank with separately stored function settings, with a few exceptions that affect all four Shooting menu banks at once, as follows:

- Multiple exposure settings
- Interval timer shooting settings
- Time-lapse photography settings
- Changes to White balance preset settings

If you change any of these settings, they will affect all four banks (A–D) simultaneously. Changing other settings affects only the bank your camera is currently using. Since each bank can be configured with most items having different settings, your D810 can act like four different cameras.

Extended Menu Banks

(User's Manual - Page 292)

Extended menu banks is a simple function that sounds complex. All it does is ask your camera to remember the last exposure and flash modes you used in a particular bank (P, S, A, or M) and the aperture if you are using A or M or the shutter speed if you are using S or M. Here is how it works:

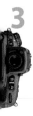

- *Scenario 1* – Let's say you are using bank A with fill flash and the exposure mode is set to Aperture-priority (A) mode with an aperture setting of f/8. You now switch to bank B where you use Shutter-priority (S) mode for awhile. Even if your camera is set to Shutter-priority in bank B, when you switch back to bank A, the camera remembers that you were previously using fill flash in Aperture-priority mode and an aperture setting of f/8 and sets the camera back to those settings automatically.

- *Scenario 2* – You are using bank C and the exposure mode is set to Manual (M) with an aperture of f/11 and a shutter speed of 1/125s. Now you switch to bank D, which is using Programmed auto (P) mode. You shoot with bank D for awhile, then switch back to bank C. The camera, upon entering bank C, remembers that you were using Manual mode with an aperture of f/11 and shutter speed of 1/125s previously and sets the camera back to those settings.

- *Scenario 3* – You are using bank B with the exposure mode set to Shutter-priority (S) and a shutter speed of 1/2000s because you are shooting an air show with flying airplanes. You decide to take a picture showing the crowd, so you switch quickly to bank A, which is using Aperture-priority mode. When you are done shooting the crowd, you switch back to bank B and the camera remembers that you were using Shutter-priority and a shutter speed of 1/2000s previously and sets the camera back to those settings. You continue shooting the air show.

With Extended menu banks enabled, your camera will remember the last exposure mode and related settings used for each bank. The following list shows which settings it remembers for each exposure mode selected:

- *Programmed auto (P) mode* – The camera will remember that you were using P or P* (flexible program) modes. Since P mode asks the camera to automatically adjust the aperture and shutter speed, it will *not* remember your previous aperture and shutter speed settings when you switch banks. However, if you have overridden P mode by placing the camera into flexible-program P* mode, the camera will remember that you were in P* mode and the aperture you were using when you switched away from the bank. It also remembers which flash mode you were using.

- *Shutter-priority (S) mode* – The camera will remember that you were using Shutter-priority mode and the shutter speed you last used before switching away from the bank. It also remembers which flash mode you were using.
- *Aperture-priority (A) mode* – The camera will remember that you were using Aperture-priority mode and the aperture you last used before switching away from the bank. It also remembers which flash mode you were using.
- *Manual (M) mode* – The camera will remember that you were using Manual mode and the shutter speed and aperture you last used before switching away from the bank. It also remembers which flash mode you were using.

The camera remembers the information about the mode and settings without you manually saving anything. When you switch away from a bank and then return to the bank, it will remember your previous settings without you doing anything more than having Extended menu banks set to On. If you set Extended menu banks to Off, the camera will not remember any of your flash, exposure mode, shutter speed, and aperture settings for each bank.

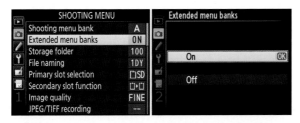

Figure 3.2 – Enabling or disabling Extended menu banks

Use these steps to configure the Extended menu banks setting:

1. Select Extended menu banks from the Shooting Menu and scroll to the right (figure 3.2, screen 1).
2. Choose either On or Off from the menu (figure 3.2, screen 2).
3. Press the OK button to save the setting.

Settings Recommendation: I leave this turned on because I find it to be quite convenient. Having the camera remember my last exposure mode setting lets me enter a familiar shooting environment when I return to a particular bank. If I used a certain exposure mode previously with that bank, the odds are very high that I will want to use similar settings in the future. If you do not want the camera to remember your previous exposure mode settings, leave this set to Off. It will not affect how the camera remembers any of the other Shooting Menu settings.

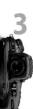

Storage Folder

(User's Manual – Page 293)

The D810 automatically creates a folder on its primary memory card called 100ND810. This folder can contain up to 999 images. If you want to store images in separate folders on the memory card, you might want to create a new folder, such as 101ND810 or 200ND810. Each folder you create can hold 999 images, and using *Storage folder*, you can select any folder as the default folder.

This is a good way to isolate certain types of images on a photographic outing. Maybe you'll put landscapes in folder 100ND810, and people shots in 101ND810. Whenever the camera senses that the current folder contains 999 images or when an image reaches a file number of 9999, a new folder is created, with the value of the first three digits of the folder name increased by one. If you are using a folder named 100ND810, the camera will automatically create a new folder called 101ND810 when you exceed 999 images or reach image number 9999 in folder 100ND810.

When manually creating folder names, you may want to leave room for the camera's automatic folder creation and naming. If you try to create a folder name that already exists, the camera doesn't give you a warning; it simply switches to the already existing folder. Let's look at how to create a new folder with a number of your choice, from 101 to 999 (101ND810 to 999ND810).

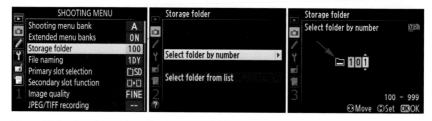

Figure 3.3A – Creating and numbering a new folder

Use these steps to create or select a folder with a number of your choice:

1. Select Storage folder from the Shooting Menu and scroll to the right (figure 3.3A, screen 1).
2. Choose Select folder by number and scroll to the right (figure 3.3A, screen 2).
3. You will now see a screen that allows you to enter a folder number between 100 and 999 (figure 3.3A, screen 3). Create your new number by scrolling up or down in any of the three available number positions. This number will have ND810 appended to it when you are done, and a new folder by that name will appear on the camera's current primary memory card. Notice the little folder at the point of the red arrow in screen 3. This little folder appears only when you

have an existing folder with the number shown on the screen. Were I to change the number to 105, the little folder would disappear because my camera does not have a folder named 105ND810. If I actually tried to save the settings from screen 3, the camera would not create a new folder named 101ND810 because it clearly already exists. Instead the camera would simply switch to that folder.

4. Press the OK button to create the new folder or switch to an existing folder.

When you see a folder next to a folder number, as shown in figure 3.3A, screen 3, you should take note of how full the folder is. In screen 3, the camera indicates that there are existing files in the folder by showing it with a white filler. There are only three settings: empty (no white fill), partially full (partial white fill as in screen 3), and full (all white fill). If the folder contains fewer than 999 images, it is considered partially full. If it has 999 files, or a file numbered 9999, the folder will show as full.

You cannot create a folder with any number less than 100. Remember that the three-digit number you select will have ND810 appended to it, and the actual folder name will look something like 101ND810 when you have finished.

Once you have created a new folder, the camera will automatically switch to it. What if you want to simply start using an existing folder, choosing it from a list of folders instead of making a new one? The D810 makes that easy with the following screens and steps (figure 3.3B).

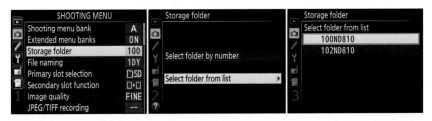

Figure 3.3B – Selecting an existing folder from the list of available folders

Use the following steps to choose an existing folder from a list of folders:

1. Select Storage folder from the Shooting Menu and scroll to the right (figure 3.3B, screen 1).
2. Choose Select folder from list and scroll to the right (figure 3.3B, screen 2).
3. Choose a folder from the list of current folders (figure 3.3B, screen 3). My camera happens to have two folders on it. If yours only has one, that is all you will see in screen 3 (most likely 100ND810).
4. Press the OK button and the camera will switch back to the Shooting Menu main screen, with the first three numbers of the selected folder showing next to Storage folder.

All images will now be saved to this folder until you exceed 999 images in the folder or manually change to another.

One note of caution: If you are using a folder named 999ND810 and the camera records the 999th image or if it records image number 9999, the Shutter-release button will be disabled until you change to a different folder. Normally, when those conditions occur, the camera increments the folder number by one and creates a new folder with the incremented number, and the next image simply goes into the new folder. However, if you are using folder number 999 (999ND810), the camera cannot create a new folder because it cannot increment larger than 999 on a folder number. Therefore, it locks the Shutter-release button until you remove the memory card containing folder 999ND810 or create a new folder manually. In my opinion, it is not wise to create a folder numbered 999, especially if you shoot a lot of images and may exceed 999 pictures in the folder.

Settings Recommendation: As memory cards get bigger and bigger, I can see a time when this functionality will become very important. Last year I shot around 125 GB of image files. With the newest memory cards now hitting 256 GB, I can foresee a time when the card(s) in my camera will become a year-long backup source. Of course, the image files are so much larger on this D810, with its medium-format resolution, that large-capacity memory cards are very welcome. At the present time, I do not use the Storage folder functionality all that much, but I guarantee you I will in the near future. This is a good function to learn how to use!

File Naming

(User's Manual – Page 295)
File naming allows you to control the first three letters of the file name for each of your images. The default is DSC, but you can change it to any three alphanumeric characters provided by the camera. The D810 defaults to using the following file naming convention for your images:

- sRGB color space: **DSC_1234**
- Adobe RGB color space: **_DSC1234**

According to the color space you are using, the camera adds an underscore character to the end of the three DSC characters in sRGB or to the beginning in Adobe RGB. I use this feature on my camera in a special way. Because the camera can count images in a sequence (see Custom setting d5) from 0001 to 9999, I use File naming to help me personalize my images. The camera cannot count images higher than 9999. Instead, it rolls back over to 0001 for the 10,000th image.

When I first got my D810, I changed the three default characters from DSC to 1DY. The 1 tells me how many times my camera has passed 9999 images, and DY are my initials, thereby helping me protect the copyright of my images in case they are ever stolen and misused.

Because the camera's image File number sequence counter rolls back over to 0001 when you exceed 9999 images, you need a way to keep from accidentally overwriting images from the first set of 9999 images you took. I use this method:

- First 9999 images: 1DY_0001 through 1DY_9999
- Second 9999 images: 2DY_0001 through 2DY_9999
- Third 9999 images: 3DY_0001 through 3DY_9999
- Fourth 9999 images: 4DY_0001 through 4DY_9999

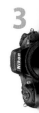

See how simple that is? The listed numbers show a range of just under 40,000 images. Since the D810 is tested to the pro level of 200,000 images, you will surely need to use a counting system like this one.

My system works up to only 89991 images (9999 × 9). If you wanted to start your camera at 0 instead (0DY9999), you could count up to 99990 images.

If Nikon would ever give us just one extra digit in our image counter, we could count in sequences of just under 100,000 images instead of 10,000 images. I suppose that many of us will have traded on up to the next Nikon DSLR before we reach enough images that this really becomes a constraint.

This is merely the way I'm using this useful feature in my D810. If my method doesn't work for you, you could use the three characters to classify your image names in all sorts of creative ways.

To rename your three custom characters, please refer to figure 3.4. This works similarly to the method for naming the Shooting menu banks discussed in the section **Shooting Menu Bank** at the beginning of this chapter (figure 3.1A), except that you have only uppercase characters and numbers from which to select.

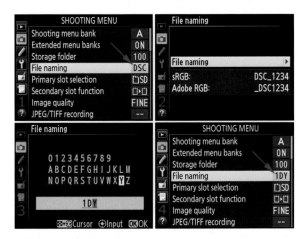

Figure 3.4 – File naming

Here are the steps to set up your custom file naming characters:

1. Select File naming from the Shooting Menu and scroll to the right (figure 3.4, screen 1).
2. Figure 3.4, screen 2 shows the sample screen that lets you view the current formatting for file names. If you have changed the characters to something other than DSC, those characters will be shown in the sample file names below the File naming selection in screen 2.
3. Use the Multi selector to scroll through the numbers and letters to find the characters you want to use (figure 3.4, screen 3). Press the Multi selector center button to select and insert a character. You can move around within the three characters by holding down the checkered Thumbnail/Playback zoom out button and moving left or right with the Multi selector. Highlight a character to delete and the press the Delete button (garbage can) to remove it, or simply overwrite it with a new character.
4. Press the OK button to save your three new custom characters. They will now appear at the beginning of each new image file name as shown at the red arrow in figure 3.4, screen 4.

Settings Recommendation: We discussed how I use these three custom characters in the beginning of this section. You may want to use all three of your initials or some other numbers or letters. Some will even leave these three letters at their default of DSC. I recommend at least using your initials so that you can easily identify the images as yours. With my family of four Nikon shooters, it sure makes it easier for me! If you use my method, just be sure to watch for the images to roll over to 9999 so that you can rename the first character for the next sequence of 9999 images. With the longevity of a Nikon and your prolific shooting habits, I am sure the numbers will be rolling over often!

Primary Slot Selection

(User's Manual – Page 86)
Primary slot selection allows you to select which memory card (SD or CF) you want to use as the primary card for writing images and recording movies.

This function and the next, Secondary slot function, are concerned with where your camera stores its image files. If you're using two memory cards, an SD and CF, you will need to set these two functions to control where files go and what happens when a card fills up.

You'll need to decide which card type you want to shoot with most often. If you have more of one type than the other, or simply like one card style better, this function will let you choose your favorite.

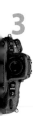

File Number Sequence

Custom Setting Menu > d Shooting/display > d6 File number sequence controls the File number sequence. That function works along with File naming to let you control how your image files are named. If File number sequence is set to Off, the D810 will reset the four-digit number—after the first three custom characters in File naming—to 0001 each time you format your camera's memory card. I made sure File number sequence was set to On as soon as I got my camera so it would remember the sequence all the way up to 9999 images. The factory default is On for File number sequence, but I would check it just in case. I want to know exactly how many pictures I've taken over time. We'll talk more about File number sequence in the chapter titled **Custom Setting Menu**.

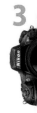

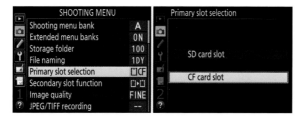

Figure 3.5 – Choosing the primary card slot

Here are the steps to select the primary card slot:

1. Select Primary slot selection from the Shooting Menu and scroll to the right (figure 3.5, screen 1).
2. Choose your favorite card slot from the Primary slot selection screen. Your choices are SD card slot and CF card slot (figure 3.5, screen 2).
3. Press the OK button to lock in your choice.

Settings Recommendation: I happen to prefer the CF cards for my D810, merely because they seem more robust. Therefore, I set my primary slot to CF card slot. If you upgraded from a less costly DX Nikon DSLR, you may want to use the SD card slot as the primary slot because you'll probably have several SD cards from previous cameras. However, you may prefer the CF card type, especially if you previously used a D700/D800/D800E or will use the D810 as a companion to a D3s or D4s professional camera. You don't have to use both cards slots if you don't have one of the two types; the camera will work fine with just one card. If you have Primary slot selection set to the SD slot—with a CF card in the CF card slot—and then accidentally leave the SD card out of the camera, the camera is smart enough to use whatever card type it can find—in this case the CF card.

Secondary Slot Function

(User's Manual – Page 86)

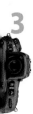

The Secondary slot function is designed to let you do image flow control. You decide where and when images get written to the memory card combo. You can make the camera fill up one card and overflow onto the other when the first is full, write to both cards at the same time, or write a separate NEF (RAW) and JPEG image to each card.

Here is a deeper description of the three different ways you can set the Secondary slot function (figure 3.6):

- **Overflow** – Have you ever gotten the dreaded "Card full" message? Well, if you select Overflow, it will take a lot longer to get this message. Overflow writes all images to the card you have selected under Primary slot selection. Then when the primary card is full, the rest of the images are sent to the secondary card. The image number shown on the Control panel will go down as you take pictures and they are written to the primary card. When the image count hits zero, the camera will switch to the secondary card and the available image count number on the Control panel will increase to however many images will fit on the secondary card. It is a good idea, although not absolutely necessary, to use cards with a similar capacity when using this function. The camera will gradually fill up all available space on both cards as you take pictures.
- **Backup** – This function is a backup method for those shooting critical images. Every image you take is written to both the primary and secondary memory cards at the same time. You have an automatic backup system when you use the Backup function. If you are a computer geek (like me), you'll recognize this as RAID 1, or card mirroring. Because your camera is very much a computer, a function like this is great to have. Be sure that both cards are of equal capacity or that the secondary card is larger than the primary card when you use this function. Otherwise, you'll have reduced capacity shown for the primary card. The camera is required to write a duplicate image to each card, so the smallest card in the two slots sets the maximum capacity of the camera's storage.
- **RAW primary, JPEG secondary** – For those who like to shoot NEF (RAW) files, this function can save some time. You'll have a JPEG for immediate use and a RAW file for later post-processing. When you take a picture, the camera will write the RAW file to the primary card and a JPEG file to the secondary card. There is no choice in this arrangement—RAW always goes to primary and JPEG to secondary. Also, this function works as described only when you have *Shooting Menu > Image quality* set to some form of NEF (RAW) + JPEG. If you set Image quality to just NEF (RAW) or JPEG fine alone—instead of NEF (RAW) + JPEG fine—the camera will

simply write a duplicate file to both cards instead of a RAW on one and a JPEG on the other. In other words, if Image quality is set to NEF (RAW), the camera will write two NEF files; if set to JPEG, two JPG files; and if set to TIFF (RGB), two TIFF files—one on each card. Basically, unless you set *Shooting Menu > Image quality* to some form of NEF (RAW) + JPEG, this function acts like the Backup function mentioned previously.

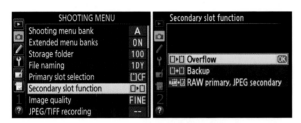
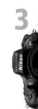

Figure 3.6 – Choosing the Secondary slot function

Here are the steps to select a Secondary slot function:

1. Select Secondary slot function from the Shooting Menu and scroll to the right (figure 3.6, image 1).
2. Choose one of the three selections from the Secondary slot function screen (figure 3.6, image 2).
3. Press the OK button to lock it in for use.

Settings Recommendation: When I'm out shooting commercially or for any type of photography where maximum image capacity is of primary importance, I select Overflow. This causes the camera to fill up the primary card and then automatically switch to the secondary card for increased image storage. If I'm shooting images that I cannot afford to lose, such as at a unique event like a wedding or graduation, I'll often use the Backup function for automatic backup of every image.

If I want both a RAW and JPEG file, I'll use the RAW primary, JPEG secondary function. This lets me have the best of both worlds when card capacity is not worrisome. This too allows a measure of redundancy, like the Backup method. In a sense, you are still backing up the same image, they are just in different formats—one RAW and one JPEG. RAW primary, JPEG secondary also benefits you by providing a JPEG for immediate use and a RAW file for later post-processing. I use each of these three selections from time to time, but my favorite is Overflow.

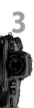

Image Quality

(User's Manual – Pages 79, 489)

Image quality is simply the type of image your camera can create. You can shoot several distinct image formats with your D810 (NEF/RAW, JPEG, and TIFF). We'll examine each format in detail and discuss the pros and cons of each. When we are done, you will have a better understanding of the formats and can choose an appropriate one for each of your styles of shooting. Following are the screens and steps to select an Image quality setting.

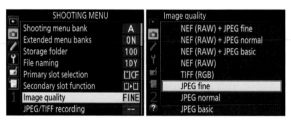

Figure 3.7A – Choosing an Image quality setting

Use these steps to select an image quality via the Shooting Menu:

1. Select Image quality from the Shooting Menu and scroll to the right (figure 3.7A, screen 1).
2. Choose one of the eight Image quality types listed. Figure 3.7A, screen 2 shows JPEG fine as the selected format.
3. Press the OK button to select the format.

You can also use the QUAL button above the Release mode dial to set the image quality. This can be much faster than using the menus.

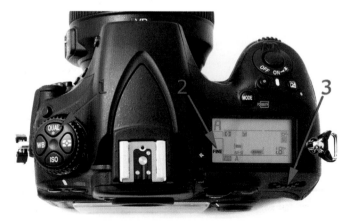

Figure 3.7B – Setting the Image quality with external controls

Use these steps to select an image quality with external camera controls (figure 3.7B):

1. Hold down the QUAL button (figure 3.7B, number 1).
2. Look at the Control panel to see the Image quality values (figure 3.7B, number 2).
3. Rotate the rear Main command dial (figure 3.7B, number 3) to change the Image quality setting (i.e., RAW, TIFF, FINE, NORM, or BASIC). The FINE, NORM, and BASIC settings all refer to JPEG formats, with each having a stronger compression ratio. Again, I had FINE selected, as shown at the red number 2 on the Control panel.
4. Release the QUAL button to lock in the modified Image quality settings.

The camera supports the following eight Image quality types (figure 3.7A, screen 2):

- NEF (RAW) + JPEG fine
- NEF (RAW) + JPEG normal
- NEF (RAW) + JPEG basic
- NEF (RAW)
- TIFF (RGB)
- JPEG fine
- JPEG normal
- JPEG basic

New DSLR users may feel unsure about which format is best to use. In fact, it is a good idea to use all three formats at different times. We will briefly discuss the basics of the formats, as a nice review for all shooters:

- **NEF (RAW)** – The 12- or 14-bit NEF (RAW) format is designed for those photographers who have the time and inclination to work on, or post-process, each image. The camera merely captures light information when shooting in RAW but does not process the data into a usable image. It is up to you to develop a workflow that allows finalizing the image within the computer. The reward for this extra work is the highest possible image quality that can be achieved with the camera. Note: The D810 also has a NEF (RAW) processing function on the Retouch Menu that allows you to convert to JPEG from a RAW file on the memory card. A D810 NEF (RAW) is in the 40 to 50 MB range when Lossless compressed NEF files are used. Uncompressed, a NEF file is around 70 MB in size.
- **JPEG** – The 8-bit JPEG format is for those times when you must have a finished image right now! The image comes out of the camera in ready-to-use form. JPEG is a lossy format, however, and it throws away a considerable amount of image data when the camera converts the 12- or 14-bit RAW file down to 8 bits. The image data that is left is of the highest quality and is ready to use. However, a JPEG cannot be modified and resaved more than a time or two without JPEG compression losses damaging the image. Use JPEG when you have to use the

image right away or when you do not have the time or inclination to work with RAW images. JPEG files are smaller than NEF files by far, with an average size for a JPEG file being from 4 to 25 MB, according to the complexity of the scene and compression ratio used. The camera uses the following compression ratios for a JPEG file: JPEG fine = 1:4, JPEG normal = 1:8, and JPEG basic = 1:16. The smallest Large (L) JPEG file I've seen out of my own D810 is about 4 MB (bland subject) and the largest is about 24 MB (very complex subject).

- **TIFF (RGB)** – The 8-bit TIFF file type, as created by the camera, is basically like a JPEG with no compression routines applied. The image file can be used immediately without conversion. The 12- to 14-bit RAW file is converted into an 8-bit file, throwing away considerable data, so TIFF is initially a lossy format, losing from 4 to 6 bits of image data. However, once the file is created, you can modify and resave it without compressing the data or losing any more image detail. If you are in a situation that requires an immediate-use file and a JPEG won't do because image modification is required, and you have no interest in or experience with NEF (RAW) files, the TIFF format is a good candidate. The biggest drawback to a TIFF file is its large file size. An average TIFF file is a little over 100 MB in size. It won't take many of those to fill up a memory card or two.

Combined NEF and JPEG Shooting (Two Images at Once)

Some shooters use the three storage modes at the top of the list in figure 3.7A, screen 2, whereby the D810 takes two images at the same time—NEF (RAW) + JPEG fine, normal, or basic. This gives you the best of both worlds in that the camera captures a NEF file and creates an additional JPEG file each time you press the Shutter-release button. Here are the first three modes found at the top of the *Shooting Menu > Image quality* setting list:

- NEF (RAW) + JPEG fine
- NEF (RAW) + JPEG normal
- NEF (RAW) + JPEG basic

You can set the *Shooting Menu > Secondary slot function* to write the NEF (RAW) file to one card and the JPEG to the other.

You can use the NEF (RAW) file to store all the image data and later process it into a masterpiece, or you can use the JPEG file immediately with no adjustment.

There is no need to go into any amount of detail about these modes since the NEF (RAW) + JPEG modes have the same features as each individual mode. In other words, the RAW file in NEF (RAW) + JPEG mode is just like a normal RAW file if you were using the standalone NEF (RAW) mode. The JPEG in the NEF (RAW) + JPEG mode is just like a standalone JPEG fine, normal, or basic image without the NEF (RAW) file.

Settings Recommendation: Which format do I prefer? Why, NEF (RAW), of course! However, it does require a bit of a commitment to shoot in this format. The camera is simply an image-capturing device, and you are the image manipulator. You decide the final format, compression ratios, sizes, color balances, and so on instead of letting Nikon's software engineers decide. You create the final image when you post-process it with your computer and save it in a final format, such as JPEG. Your RAW file stays untouched and ready for reuse.

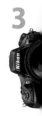

By shooting in NEF (RAW) mode, you have the absolute best image your camera can produce. It is not modified by the camera's software and is ready for your personal touch. No camera processing allowed!

If you get nothing else from this section of the chapter, remember this: When your camera is processing the images in *any* way, it is modifying or throwing away image data. There is only a finite amount of data for each image that can be stored on your camera, and later on the computer. With JPEG or TIFF mode, your camera optimizes the image according to the assumptions recorded in its memory. Data is being thrown away permanently, in varying amounts.

If you want to keep *all* of the image data that was recorded with your images, you must store your originals in RAW format. Otherwise, you'll never again be able to access that original data to change how the image looks. A RAW file is the closest thing to a film negative or a transparency that your digital camera can make. That's important if you would like to modify the image later. If you are concerned with maximum quality, you should shoot and store your images in RAW format.

Later, when you have the urge to make another masterpiece out of the original RAW image file, you'll have all of the original picture data intact for the highest quality image.

I shoot in NEF (RAW) format for my most important work and JPEG fine for the rest. Some people find that JPEG fine is sufficient for everything they shoot. Those individuals generally do not like working with files in-computer or do not have time. NEF (RAW) files are not yet usable images and must be converted to another format. You'll use both RAW and JPEG, I'm sure. The format you use most often will be controlled by your time constraints and digital workflow. Most of us use TIFF only when we convert a RAW file in-computer into that format. I rarely, if ever, shoot images in TIFF. There are just not enough benefits in TIFF files to deal with the larger files and slower transfer speeds, in my opinion. Shoot RAW for the best and JPEG for the rest!

JPEG/TIFF Recording

(User's Manual – 81, 83)

JPEG/TIFF recording allows you to choose the Image size for JPEG and TIFF files, as well as the type of compression you want to use for your JPEG images (JPEG compression).

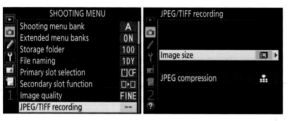

Figure 3.8A – JPEG/TIFF recording subfunctions

Figure 3.8A, image 2, shows the two subfunctions in the JPEG/TIFF recording function: Image size and JPEG compression. Let's consider each of the two functions.

Image Size

(User's Manual – Page 83)

Image size lets you shoot with your camera set to various megapixel (M) ratings.

The default Image size setting for the D810 is Large FX, or 36.2 M (36.2 megapixels). You can change this rating in quite a few ways, based on the Image area settings discussed later in the chapter.

Image size applies only to images captured in TIFF (RGB) or JPEG fine/normal/basic modes. If you're shooting with your camera in any of the NEF (RAW) + JPEG modes, it applies only to the JPEG image in the pair. Image size does not apply to a NEF (RAW) image.

This setting is relatively simple because it just affects the megapixel size of the image. Following are the screens and steps to select the Image size.

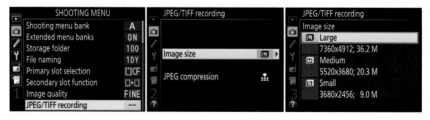

Figure 3.8B – Choosing an Image size setting

1. Choose JPEG/TIFF recording from the Shooting Menu and scroll to the right (figure 3.8B, screen 1).
2. Select Image size from the JPEG/TIFF recording menu and scroll to the right (figure 3.8B, screen 2).
3. Choose one of the three Image size settings listed. Large is selected in figure 3.8B, screen 3.
4. Press the OK button to choose the size.

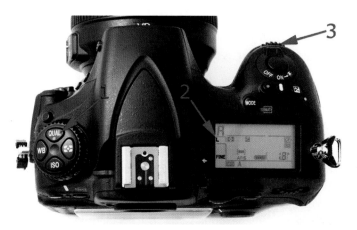

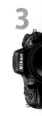

Figure 3.8C – Setting Image size with external controls

You can also choose the Image size by using external camera controls, as shown in figure 3.8C. Use the following steps:

1. Hold down the QUAL button (figure 3.8C, number 1).
2. Look at the Control panel to see the Image size values (figure 3.8C, number 2).
3. Rotate the front Sub-command dial (figure 3.8C, number 3) to change the Image size setting (L, M, or S). Large (L) is selected at number 2.
4. Release the QUAL button to lock in the modified Image size settings.

I normally shoot at the largest possible size and crop the image if needed. However, there are reasons to shoot at the lower megapixel levels, such as when a smaller resolution image is all that will ever be needed or if card space is at an absolute premium. Even medium and small size D810 images are plenty big!

Setting Image quality to JPEG basic, Image size to Small, and JPEG compression to Size priority allows the camera to capture 19,000 images on a 32-gigabyte card. The pictures are 9.0 MP in resolution and are compressed to the maximum, but there are a large number of them. If I were to set off today to walk completely around the earth and I had only one 32-gigabyte memory card to take with me, well, my camera would give me 19K images on one card—so I could at least document my trip well.

Taking Still Images in Movie Live View

If you want to take still images that closely match the format of an HDTV or modern flat-screen computer monitor, you can do it by taking still images in Movie live view mode's 16:9 aspect ratio. FX and DX mode still images created in Movie live view have the following Image sizes:

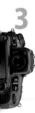

FX format in Movie live view mode (16:9)
- Large – 6270×3776 – 23.7 M
- Medium – 5040×2832 – 14.3 M
- Small – 3360×1888 – 6.3 M

DX format in Movie live view mode (16:9)
- Large – 4800×2704 – 12.9 M
- Medium – 3600×2024 – 7.3 M
- Small – 2400×1352 – 3.2 M

Settings Recommendation: You'll get the best images at 36.2 M (FX), of course. Using the smaller sizes won't affect the quality of a smaller print, but it will limit your ability to enlarge your images. I recommend leaving your camera set to Large unless you have a specific reason to shoot smaller images or you have low-capacity memory cards, which is anything under 16 GB with the D810.

The D810 gives you several image formats that match various industry standards. I recommend trying the different formats by adjusting the Image area (next section). The maximum image size is provided by the FX Image area setting. However, the FX image size from the D810 is so large (Native FX = 16x24 inches, or 40x60 centimeters, at 300 dpi) that you will have room to use various image crops. If you don't like any of the provided Image area formats, you can crop to your own specifications in your computer. Having such a large image size gives us maximum flexibility. Cropping is back!

JPEG Compression

(User's Manual – Page 81)

JPEG compression allows you to fine-tune the level of compression in your JPEG images. The JPEG format is always a compressed format. The Image quality settings for JPEG images include fine, normal, and basic. Each of these settings provides a certain level of compression of the picture's file size, as we've discussed briefly in a previous section. In review, here are the compression specifications:

- **JPEG fine** – 1:4 compression ratio (25 percent of original size)
- **JPEG normal** – 1:8 compression ratio (12.5 percent of original size)
- **JPEG basic** – 1:16 compression ratio (6.25 percent of original size)

The compression ratios listed are best-case scenarios. JPEG files will normally vary in size when the subject of one image is more complex than that of another. For instance, if you take a picture of a tree with lots of leaves and bark against a cloudy blue sky, JPEG's compression formatting has a lot more work to do than if you take a picture of a red balloon on a plain white background. All those little details in the leaves of the tree cause lots of color contrast changes, so the JPEG file size will naturally be bigger for the complex image. In the balloon image, there is little detail in the balloon or the background, so the JPEG file size will normally be much smaller. The less detail in an image, the more efficient JPEG compression is.

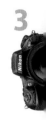

What if you want all of your JPEG images to be the same relative size? Or, what if file size doesn't matter as much to you, while quality is very important? That's what the JPEG compression menu allows you to control, the final quality of your JPEG images, by varying the amount of compression. Let's examine the two settings:

- **Size priority** – This compression setting is designed to keep all your JPEG files at a certain uniform size. The size will vary according to whether you selected JPEG fine, normal, or basic in the Image quality menu. Image quality controls the regular, everyday compression level of the JPEG file, while Size priority tweaks it even more. How does it work? With Size priority enabled, the camera's software tries to minimize file sizes, keeping them as uniform as possible while still maintaining good quality. If a JPEG file has lots of fine detail, it will require more compression than a file with less detail in order to maintain the same file size. By enabling this function, you are telling the camera that it has permission to throw away however much image data it must to get each file to a somewhat uniform size. How uniform? I did a test where I shot a relatively bland subject and the file size was 8.5 MB. Then I shot a medium-complexity subject and got a file size of 10.0 MB. Finally, I shot a very complex subject and the file size was 13.0 MB. So, the camera maintained a range from 8.5 to 13.0 MB on subjects with varying complexity. This type of compression could lower the quality of a complex landscape shot much more than a shot of a person standing by a blank wall. Size priority instructs the camera to sacrifice image quality—if necessary—to keep the file size fairly consistent. Use this function only for images that will not be used for fine art purposes. Otherwise, your image may not look as good as it could.
- **Optimal quality** – This setting really doesn't do much extra to your images; the camera simply uses less compression on complex subjects. In effect, you are telling the camera to go ahead and vary the file size so that image quality will be good for any subject, complex or plain. Instead of increasing compression to make an image of a complex nature scene fit a certain file size—as Size priority does—the camera compresses the image only to the standard compression level based on the Image quality setting you selected (JPEG fine, normal, or basic). Less image data is thrown away, so the image quality is higher. However, file size will vary significantly, depending on the complexity of the subject. How

much variation? I shot the same subjects as before with Optimal quality enabled this time. On the plain subject, the file size was 9.7 MB. On the medium-complexity subject, the file size was 11.4 MB. Finally, on the complex subject, the file size jumped up to 24.2 MB. Whoa! As you know, 9.7 MB to 24.2 MB is quite a variation in file size. Clearly, the camera is not compressing the images with complex subjects nearly as much as when Size priority is enabled. Image quality will be higher on complex subjects, and on low-detail subjects the quality will be similar to what it would be with Size priority enabled. Nikon states that the camera's internal memory buffer capacity is reduced when you use Optimal quality, as would be expected with the larger file sizes.

Why not test this for yourself and see what file sizes you get between the two modes? Now, let's examine how to select one of the JPEG compression types.

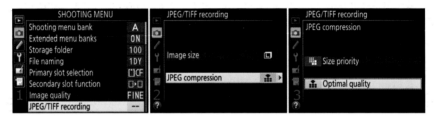

Figure 3.8D – Choosing a JPEG compression type

Here are the steps to choose a JPEG compression type:

1. Choose JPEG/TIFF recording from the Shooting Menu and scroll to the right (figure 3.8D, screen 1).
2. Select JPEG compression from the Shooting Menu and scroll to the right (figure 3.8D, screen 2).
3. Choose Size priority or Optimal quality (figure 3.8D, screen 3).
4. Press the OK button to choose the compression type.

Settings Recommendation: I normally use Optimal quality when I shoot JPEGs since the whole JPEG concept is one of lossy image compression and I don't want the potentially heavier compression of Size priority to lower the image quality.

Size priority just adds more potential image quality loss, so I tend to avoid it. The only time I use Size priority is when I'm shooting snapshots. When I'm at a party taking pictures of friends having a good time, I'm not creating fine art and won't make an enlargement greater than an 8×10-inch (20×25 cm) size. In that case, I don't worry about extra compression. In fact, I might just welcome it to avoid storing larger-than-needed images on my computer's hard drive. Using Size priority lets the camera use fairly consistent files sizes. When consistent file size is not critical but maximum JPEG quality is, I use Optimal quality.

NEF (RAW) Recording

(User's Manual – Page 81, 85)

NEF (RAW) recording is composed of three menu choices—Image size, NEF (RAW) compression, and NEF (RAW) bit depth, which deals with color quality. We will look into all three of these choices and see how our photography can benefit from them.

Image Size

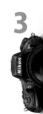

The Nikon D810 provides a 9.0-megapixel RAW Image size, called RAW S (Small) within the Nikon manual and menus. This new format, not found in the Nikon D800 or D800E, was inherited from the Nikon D4s professional camera. The standard 36.2-megapixel RAW file is now called RAW L (Large) in the camera menus and manual.

The RAW L image is a true RAW file, containing image brightness data along with color markers and other settings. However, the color markers and other settings are stored in the image's metadata and are not applied to the RAW file permanently. Therefore, you can easily modify a RAW L file after the fact, completely changing how it looks, without damaging the image.

The RAW S file is not a true RAW file because image setting data and color information is baked into the file permanently. The RAW S setting uses a 12-bit uncompressed format, which, in my opinion, makes it like a small TIFF file in many ways. It provides the quality of a file that is not compressed and can contain plenty of color and brightness data for later post-processing. The file size of a RAW S file is about half of a RAW L file, making it a legitimate format for those who want to work with a file that is better than a compressed JPEG, but don't want to store the very large RAW L files. Let's examine how to choose one of the two RAW formats.

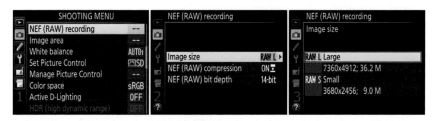

Figure 3.9 – Selecting a large or small RAW format

Here are the steps to choose an Image size for shooting in RAW format:

1. Choose NEF (RAW) recording from the Shooting Menu and scroll to the right (figure 3.9, screen 1).
2. Select Image size from the NEF (RAW) recording menu and scroll to the right (figure 3.9, screen 2).

3. Choose RAW L Large or RAW S Small (figure 3.9, screen 3).
4. Press the OK button to lock in the NEF (RAW) recording Image size.

Now let's examine how to select one of the available compression levels for a RAW L file.

NEF (RAW) Compression

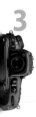

In previous sections, we discussed how JPEG files have different levels of compression that vary the size of a finished image file. NEF (RAW) also has compression choices, though not as many. The nice thing about the RAW compression methods is that they don't throw away massive amounts of image data like JPEG compression does. NEF (RAW) is not considered a lossy format because the file stays complete, with virtually all the image data your camera captured.

One of the compression methods, called Compressed, is very slightly lossy. The other, Lossless compressed, keeps all the image data intact. Let's discuss how each of the available compression methods works. There are three NEF (RAW) formats available, as follows:

- NEF (RAW) Lossless compressed (20–40% size reduction)
- NEF (RAW) Compressed (40–55% size reduction)
- NEF (RAW) Uncompressed (No compression – full file size)

Note: NEF (RAW) compression applies to RAW L (Large) files *only*. The RAW S (Small) format always uses an uncompressed 12-bit format, regardless of the settings in this function.

Here are some details on each of the choices for RAW L files:

- ***NEF (RAW) Lossless compressed*** – The factory default for the NEF (RAW) format is NEF (RAW) Lossless compressed. According to Nikon, this compression will not affect image quality because it is a reversible compression algorithm. Because Lossless compressed shrinks the stored file size by 20 to 40 percent—with no image data loss—it's my favorite compression method to use. It works somewhat like a ZIP file on your computer—it compresses the file but allows you to use it later with all the data still available.
- ***NEF (RAW) Compressed*** – Before the newest generation of cameras, including the D810, this mode was known as "visually lossless." The image is compressed and the size is reduced by 35 to 55 percent, depending on the amount of detail in the image. There is a small amount of data loss involved in this compression method. Most people won't be able to see the loss because it doesn't affect the image visually. I've never really seen any loss in my images using this method. However, I've read that some have noticed slightly less highlight detail. Nikon says that this is a nonreversible compression, so once you've taken an image using this mode, any small amount of data loss is permanent. If this concerns

Card Capacity Reporting

Why does your memory card's remaining image capacity seem to stay the same in NEF Lossless compressed and Compressed modes as in Uncompressed mode? Shouldn't it show lots more capacity in the compressed modes since they make the image smaller by 20 to 55 percent? The reason your camera does not show any increased image capacity on the Control panel in the compressed modes is because the D810 has no idea how well it will be able to compress a particular image.

An image with a large amount of blank space, such as an expanse of sky, will compress a lot more efficiently than an image of a forest with lots of detail. The camera shows a certain amount of image storage capacity in NEF (RAW) modes—a little over 400 images with a 32-gigabyte card. You'll find that in the compressed modes, the D810 does not decrease the image capacity by one for each picture taken, as it does in Uncompressed mode.

This means that the camera will decrease the number of available images only every two or three shots, according to how well it was able to compress each image. When the card is full, it might have more than twice as many images stored as it initially reported it could hold. Basically, your D810 deliberately underreports storage capacity when you are shooting in either of the NEF (RAW) compressed modes.

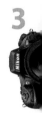

you, then use the Lossless compressed method discussed previously. It won't compress the image quite as much (20–40 percent) but is guaranteed by Nikon to be a reversible compression that in no way affects the image.

- **NEF (RAW) Uncompressed** – No compression is applied to the image. The main drawback to this mode is that your images will be quite large. Each will be in the 70-megabyte range, so it will take larger storage media to contain your images. With Lossless compressed available, I feel that this method is semi-obsolete.

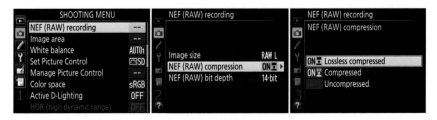

Figure 3.10A – RAW (NEF) compression

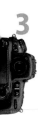

Here are the steps to select one of the NEF (RAW) compression types:

1. Select NEF (RAW) recording from the Shooting Menu and scroll to the right (figure 3.10A, screen 1).
2. Select NEF (RAW) compression from the NEF (RAW) recording menu and scroll to the right (figure 3.10A, screen 2).
3. Select one of the three compression methods. I chose Lossless compressed (figure 3.10A, screen 3).
4. Press the OK button to save your selection.

Settings Recommendation: I shoot in Lossless compressed RAW most of the time because I'm concerned with maximum quality along with good storage capacity. The Lossless compressed method makes the most sense to me. It gives me a file size significantly smaller (45–50 MB) than the Uncompressed setting's results (70+ MB). I do not use Compressed simply because Lossless compressed is available. Even though I might not be able to see any image quality loss, it bothers me that it is there, if only slightly. The 10 or 15 percent extra compression is not worth the potential small data loss to me. If I were running out of card space but wanted to keep shooting RAW, I might consider changing to Compressed temporarily. Otherwise, it's Lossless compressed for me!

NEF (RAW) Bit Depth

NEF (RAW) bit depth is a special feature for those of us concerned with capturing the best color in our images. The D810 has three color channels: one for red, another for green, and the final one for blue. It combines those color channels to form all the colors you see in your images. You may have seen the acronym RGB in your camera study. RGB stands for red, green, blue—the three color channels. Let's talk about how bit depth, or the number of colors per channel, can make your pictures even better.

With the D810, you can select the bit depth stored in an image. More bit depth equals potentially better color gradations. The default for the D810 is 14-bit (16,384 colors for each RGB channel), or you can switch it to 12-bit (4,096 colors per RGB channel). The more color bit depth in your images, the better they can look, if there is a lot of color in your subject in the first place.

Why would anyone set their camera to a lower bit depth and reduce its color capacity and smoothness? Older DSLRs used to suffer from a slower frame rate when shooting bursts of images in continuous high-speed (CH) shooting mode. The D810 does not have significantly slower frame rates from 14-bit shooting.

However, a 14-bit image file is bigger and will make the internal buffer space in the camera hold less. Also, the additional file size from the greater color capacity in a 14-bit image can lead to a little slower image writing to the memory cards and transfer to the computer later.

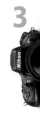

Therefore, people who are concerned about maximum camera speed will often shoot in 12-bit mode. A photographer shooting a football game will not have as great a concern for maximum color depth; he wants shooting speed to capture the shot. On the other hand, a landscape artist wants as much color depth as her pictures can contain. She wants beautiful color gradations and maximum color fidelity.

Most serious sports shooters will opt for a camera like the Nikon D4s with an extremely high frame rate of up to 11 fps, instead of the D810's 5 fps in FX mode or up to 7 fps in DX mode. I would think that the majority of D810 owners are more concerned with the biggest and best image they can make, or they would have purchased a different camera.

At the time this book was being written, DxO Labs rated the sensor in the D810 with a new highest score ever of 97. This score exceeded digital medium-format cameras costing many thousands of dollars more than the D810. That's pretty impressive! Who wants to waste a sensor with that much quality by lowering its color capacity? Not me! If you do not fully understand the reasoning behind NEF (RAW) bit depth, please take a look at the next section, **Channel and Bit Depth Discussion**.

As mentioned earlier, the D810 has the following two bit depths available for RAW L images (**Note**: NEF (RAW) bit depth applies to RAW L (Large) files only):

- *12-bit* – 4,096 colors per channel
- *14-bit* – 16,384 colors per channel

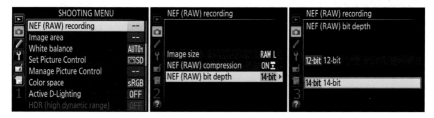

Figure 3.10B – NEF (RAW) bit depth

Here are the steps to choose a bit depth:

1. Select NEF (RAW) recording from the Shooting Menu and scroll to the right (figure 3.10B, screen 1).
2. Select NEF (RAW) bit depth and scroll to the right (figure 3.10B, screen 2).
3. Select 12-bit or 14-bit from the NEF (RAW) bit depth menu. I left my D810 at the 14-bit factory default (figure 3.10B, screen 3).
4. Press the OK button to save your selection.

Settings Recommendation: Which bit depth setting is best? Well, I always use 14-bit because I want all the color my camera can capture for the best pictures later.

If you read my tutorial on bit depth in the next section, you'll understand why I feel that way. However, my style of shooting is nature oriented, so I am concerned with capturing every last drop of color I can.

There are some disadvantages to using the 14-bit mode. If you choose 14-bit, be aware that your file sizes will be 10 to 20 percent larger than they would be in 12-bit. There is a lot more color information being stored, after all. There's another drawback to the 14-bit mode that some may find objectionable. The internal camera buffer that stores images taken and being written to the memory card is about 47 frames with 12-bit Lossless compressed NEF (RAW) files. However, that drops to 28 frames if you shoot in 14-bit mode (see User's Manual page 489). Therefore, if you're a sports or action shooter, you might not want to use the 14-bit mode. If you're a nature shooter and don't need the highest frame rates and biggest internal buffer storage, 14-bit is best for the image.

Channel and Bit Depth Discussion

Many experienced D810 users may already have a handle on this bit-depth information. However, I decided to include this short tutorial in the book because it is very important information to a digital photographer. This information is a good review for most of us.

An image from your camera is an RGB image. As mentioned previously, RGB stands for red, green, blue. Each of the colors has its own "channel." If you are shooting in 12-bit mode, your camera will record up to 4,096 colors for each channel. Therefore, there will be up to 4,096 different reds, 4,096 different greens, and 4,096 different blues. Lots of color! In fact, almost 69,000,000,000 (69 billion) colors (4,096 × 4,096 × 4,096).

However, if you set your camera to 14-bit mode, instead of just 4,096 different colors per channel, the camera can now store 16,384 different colors in each channel. Wow! That's quite a lot more color—almost 4,400,000,000,000 (4.4 trillion) shades (16,384 × 16,384 × 16,384).

Is that important? Well, it can be, because the more color information you have available, the better the image. I always use the 14-bit mode now that it's available. That allows for smoother color changes when a large range of color is actually in the image. I like that!

Of course, once you save your image as a JPEG or TIFF, most of those colors are compressed, or thrown away. Shooting a TIFF or JPEG image in-camera (as opposed to a RAW L (Large) image) means that the D810 converts from a 12- or 14-bit RGB file down to an 8-bit file. An 8-bit file can hold only 256 different colors per RGB channel, or a little over 16,700,000 colors (256 x 256 x 256). That sounds like quite a lot of color, and it is. However, when you compare the 16.7 million colors in a camera-created 8-bit JPEG or TIFF image to the potential 4.4 trillion colors in a 14-bit NEF (RAW) file, the 8-bit color potential is relatively small in comparison.

That's why I always shoot in the 36 MP RAW L (Large) format, so that later I can make full use of all those potential extra colors to create a different look for the same image if I'd like. Even the RAW S (Small) file, with its 12-bit format, can contain about 69 billion colors, which is way more than the D810's 8-bit JPEG and TIFF formats can handle. Therefore, the RAW S format does have some benefits for those who want to use the small (9 MP) images for great quality and maximum storage.

If you shoot RAW L and in 14-bit, you can later save the file as a 16-bit TIFF and not lose any color information. The D810 will not create a 16-bit TIFF; it is limited to an 8-bit TIFF. Remember, 16-bit files can contain 65,536 different colors in each of the RGB channels. Some photographers save their files as 16-bit TIFFs when post-processing RAW files. TIFF is a known and safe industry-standard format that will fully contain all image color information from a RAW file. However, a 16-bit TIFF file from a D810 image is well over 200 MB in size. That's about four or five images per gigabyte of storage space. I will often post-process my images and save the intermediate results as a 16-bit TIFF file. However, once I have saved the post-processed TIFF file as the final JPEG file for image use, I delete the TIFF. The RAW file remains untouched and ready for reuse.

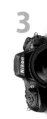

Lossless compressed NEF (RAW L) is the best way to store your D810 images long term, at only about 45 to 50 MB each, with all potential color information included in the file.

Image Area

(User's Manual – Page 74)

Image area is a convenient built-in crop of the FX image to a smaller size. Where the FX (3:2) "area" is 36×24 mm, the camera can provide three additional image areas: 1.2x–30×20 mm, DX (1.5x)–24×16 mm, and 5:4–30×24 mm. If you need these particular image areas, you will be familiar with the industry-standard formats they provide.

There are two parts to the Image area function: Choose image area and Auto DX crop. Let's consider both of them.

Choose Image Area

The camera offers four Image area formats. Let's examine a series of pictures I took using all four formats (figure 3.11A). These pictures are of a Kodak Brownie Hawkeye like the one my mother gave me in 1968, getting me started on a lifetime of photography. I did not vary the camera position at any point when taking these images, so you can see how the change in Image area affects the size (crop) of the subject.

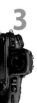

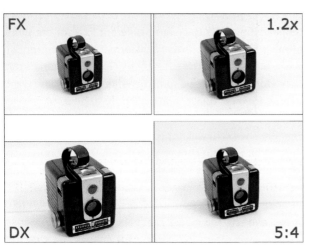

Figure 3.11A – The four Image area formats

Following is a detailed list of specifications for the four available image areas, including sensor format crop (mm), Image size, pixel count, and megapixel (M) rating:

FX (1.0x at 3:2) Image area (36×24 mm):
- Large – 7360×4912 – 36.2 M
- Medium – 5520×3680 – 20.3 M
- Small – 3680×2456 – 9.0 M

1.2x Image area (30×20 mm):
- Large – 6144×4080 – 25.1 M
- Medium – 4608×3056 – 14.1 M
- Small – 3072×2040 – 6.3 M

DX (1.5x at 3:2) Image area (24×16 mm):
- Large – 4800×3200 – 15.4 M
- Medium – 3600×2400 – 8.6 M
- Small – 2400×1600 – 3.8 M

5:4 Image area (30×24 mm):
- Large – 6144×4912 – 30.2 M
- Medium – 4608×3680 – 17.0 M
- Small – 3072×2456 – 7.5 M

Now let's see how to select one of the Image area formats for those times you need to vary the Image area crop.

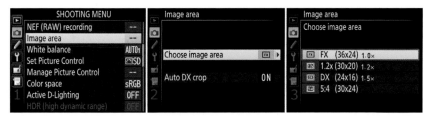

Figure 3.11B – Choosing an Image area format

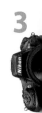

Use the following steps to select one of the Image area formats:

1. Choose Image area from the Shooting Menu and scroll to the right (figure 3.11B, screen 1).
2. Select Choose image area and scroll to the right (figure 3.11B, screen 2).
3. Select one of the four Image area crops. FX is selected in figure 3.11B, screen 3.
4. Press the OK button to save the Image area setting.

Note: You can also assign Image area to a camera button, such as the Fn, Preview, or AE-L/AF-L button. Then you can adjust the area on the fly without using the Shooting Menu. We will consider how to make the assignment in the next chapter, **Custom Setting Menu**, in the sections for Custom settings f4, f5, and f6.

Auto DX Crop

The camera can automatically switch to DX mode when it detects that you have mounted a DX lens. Or, you can set it so that it stays in the FX format (or the other three formats) unless you select DX. You will use Auto DX crop to make that decision.

If Auto DX crop is set to On, the camera will automatically switch formats when you mount a DX lens, using only the part of the sensor covered by the image circle of the DX lens.

Setting Auto DX crop to Off means the camera will ignore the lesser sensor coverage of the DX lens you have mounted and stay in its current FX format, using all of the sensor. With many DX lenses you will detect a strong vignetting in the viewfinder and in any images taken if Auto DX crop is set to Off.

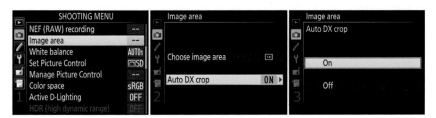

Figure 3.11C – Choosing Auto DX crop

Use the following steps to enable or disable Auto DX crop:

1. Select Image area from the Shooting Menu and scroll to the right (figure 3.11C, screen 1).
2. Choose Auto DX crop and scroll to the right (figure 3.11C, screen 2).
3. Select On or Off from the Auto DX crop menu (figure 3.11C, screen 3). Factory default is On.
4. Press the OK button to save the setting.

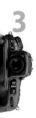

Settings Recommendation: Being a nature shooter, I normally leave my camera set to FX, its largest image area. If I need a little extra reach, I may switch the camera to DX mode for convenience, although I could also simply crop the image later in the computer. These Image area formats are merely for convenience, to prevent you from having to manually crop the image later. Each Image area format is designed to match a standard someone needs to use. If you need any of these standards, you have them available. I choose the largest (FX). I can always crop later if I need something special.

White Balance

(User's Manual – Page 148)

White balance is designed to let you capture accurate colors in each of your camera's RGB color channels. Your images can reflect realistic colors if you understand how to use the White balance settings.

This may be one of the most important things to learn about digital photography. If you don't understand how white balance works, you'll have a hard time when you want consistent color across a number of images.

In this chapter we will look at white balance briefly and learn only how to select the various White balance settings. This is such an important concept to understand that an entire chapter—titled **White Balance**—is devoted to this subject.

Please read that chapter very carefully. It is important that you thoroughly learn to control the White balance settings. A lot of what you'll do in computer post-processing requires a good understanding of white balance control.

Many people leave their cameras set to Auto White balance (figure 3.12A). This works fine most of the time because the camera is quite capable of rendering accurate color. However, it's hard to get exactly the same white balance in each consecutive picture when you are using Auto mode. The camera has to make a new white balance decision for each picture in Auto. This can cause the white balance to vary from picture to picture.

For many of us this isn't a problem. However, if you are shooting in a studio for a product shot, I'm sure your client will want the pictures to be the same color as the product. White balance lets you control that carefully when needed.

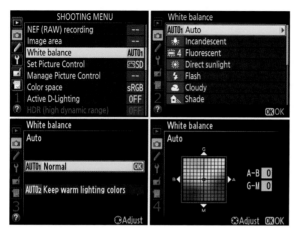
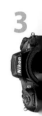

Figure 3.12A – Choosing a White balance setting

The steps to select a White balance setting are as follows:

1. Select White balance from the Shooting Menu and scroll to the right (figure 3.12A, screen 1).
2. Choose a White balance type, such as Auto or Flash, from the menu and scroll to the right (figure 3.12A, screen 2).
3. If you choose Auto, Fluorescent, Choose color temp., or Preset manual you will need to select from an intermediate screen, shown in figure 3.12A, screen 3. The other settings will skip screen 3 and go directly to screen 4. Auto presents two settings: Auto1 – Normal and Auto2 – Keep warm lighting colors. Fluorescent presents seven different types of fluorescent lighting. Choose color temp. lets you select a color temperature manually from a range of 2500 K (cool) to 10000 K (warm). Preset manual (PRE) shows the stored white balance memory locations d-0 through d-4 and allows you to use one of them. If you are unsure which is best, choose Auto1 – Normal for now. The chapter titled **White Balance** will explain how to use all these settings; therefore, consider this section an introduction to how to choose a white balance.
4. If you scroll to the right instead of pressing the OK button, as shown in figure 3.12A, screen 4, you'll arrive at the White balance fine-tuning screen. With this screen you can adjust how this particular White balance setting records color by introducing a color bias toward green, yellow, blue, or magenta. You do this by moving the little black square in the middle of the color box toward the edges

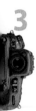

of the box in any direction. If you make a mistake, simply move the black square to the middle of the color box. Most people do not change this setting.

5. After you have finished adjusting (or not) the colors, press the OK button to save your setting. Most people press the OK button as soon as they see the fine-tuning screen so they do not change the default settings for this particular White balance setting.

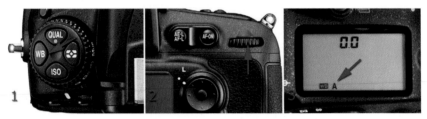

Figure 3.12B – Setting White balance with external camera controls

You'll also find it convenient and even faster to change the White balance settings by using external camera controls. Here are the steps to do so (figure 3.12B):

1. Hold down the WB button above the Release mode dial (figure 3.12B, number 1).
2. Turn the rear Main command dial (figure 3.12B, number 2) as you watch the WB icons change on the Control panel (figure 3.12B, number 3).
3. Release the WB button to lock in your choice.

Settings Recommendation: Until you've read the chapter on white balance, I suggest that you leave the camera set to Auto White balance. However, please do take the time to understand this setting by reading the dedicated chapter carefully. Understanding white balance is especially important if you plan on shooting JPEGs regularly.

Set Picture Control

(User's Manual – Page 170)
Set Picture Control allows you to choose a Picture Control for a shooting session. Nikon's Picture Control system lets you control how your image appears in several ways. Each control has a specific effect on the image's appearance. If you shot film a few years ago, you will remember that each film type has a distinct look. No two films produce color that looks the same.

In today's digital photography world, Picture Controls give you the ability to impart a specific look to your images. You can use Picture Controls as they are provided from the factory, or you can fine-tune Sharpening, Contrast, Brightness, Saturation, and Hue.

We'll discuss how to fine-tune a Nikon Picture Control later in this section. In the next section, Manage Picture Control, we'll discuss how to save a modified Picture Control under your own Custom Picture Control name. You can create up to nine Custom Picture Controls.

I'll refer to Picture Controls included in the camera as Nikon Picture Controls because that's how Nikon refers to them. You may also hear them called Original Picture Controls in some Nikon literature. If you modify and save a Nikon Picture Control under a new name, it becomes a Custom Picture Control. I'll also use the generic name of Picture Control when referring to any of them.

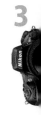

The cool thing about Picture Controls is that they are shareable. If you tweak a Nikon Picture Control and save it under a name of your choice, you can then share your control with others. Compatible cameras, software, and other devices can use these controls to maintain the look you want from the time you press the Shutter release button until you print the picture.

Now, let's look closer at the Picture Control system. As shown in figure 3.13A, screen 2, there is a series of Picture Control selections that modify how your D810 captures an image. They are as follows:

- SD – Standard
- NL – Neutral
- VI – Vivid
- MC – Monochrome
- PT – Portrait
- LS – Landscape
- FL - Flat

Each of these settings has a different and variable combination of the following settings:

- Sharpening
- Clarity
- Contrast
- Brightness
- Saturation
- Hue
- Filter Effects (applies only to MC – Monochrome)
- Toning (applies only to MC – Monochrome)

You can select one of the controls (SD, NL, VI, MC, PT, LS, or FL) and leave the settings at the factory default, or you can modify the settings (figure 3.13A, screen 3) and completely change how the D810 captures the image.

Note: If you are shooting in NEF (RAW) mode, the D810 does not apply these settings directly to the image as it does with a JPEG or TIFF, but it stores the settings with the image, allowing you to change to a different Picture Control later, in-computer using Nikon Capture NX-D or Nikon View NX 2, if you so desire.

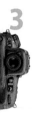

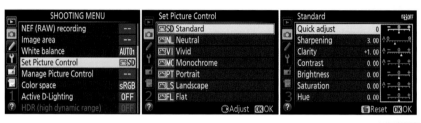

Figure 3.13A – Choosing a Nikon Picture Control from the menus

Here are the steps to choose a Picture Control from the Shooting Menu:

1. Select Set Picture Control from the Shooting Menu and scroll to the right (figure 3.13A, screen 1).
2. Choose one of the Nikon Picture Controls from the Set Picture Control screen (figure 3.13A, screen 2). At this point, you can simply press the OK button and the control you've chosen will be available for immediate use. It will show up as a two-letter name in the Shooting Menu next to Set Picture Control. You can see this in figure 3.13A, screen 1, where SD is shown next to Set Picture Control. You can also modify the currently highlighted control by scrolling to the right instead of pressing the OK button.
3. Scroll to the right when using the Set Picture Control menu shown in figure 3.13A, screen 2, and your camera will present the Picture Control fine-tuning screen, as shown in figure 3.13A, screen 3. You can adjust the Sharpening, Clarity, Contrast, Brightness, Saturation, or Hue by scrolling up or down to select a line and then right or left (+/-) to fine tune the value of that line item. Please notice the Quick adjust selection at the top of figure 3.13A, screen 3. By highlighting Quick adjust and scrolling left or right, you can change Sharpening, Contrast, and Saturation all at once in +2/-2 steps. Clarity, Brightness, and Hue remain individual adjustments only. By using Quick adjust instead of adjusting the individual settings, such as Sharpening or Saturation, you may tend to keep the control more in balance while making the effect of the control stronger or weaker. If the Quick Adjust setting is sufficient for your needs, make the adjustment, press the OK button to set the values for that Picture Control, and skip the rest of these steps. However, if you want to fine-tune each setting individually, continue with step 4.

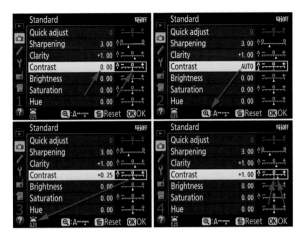

Figure 3.13B – Leaving Picture Control individual setting Auto (A) mode

4. Figure 3.13B starts where figure 3.13A leaves off. Please notice that Contrast is selected in figure 3.13B, screen 1. We will use Contrast as our sample; however, you can use the information in this step for any of the individual settings (e.g., Clarity). As you can see, Contrast is currently set at 0.00 (screen 1, red arrows). You can adjust Contrast in 0.25 increments up to +/- 2.0 steps. You can also select AUTO mode for an individual setting by pressing the Playback zoom in button. AUTO will appear after Contrast, and the tiny yellow pointer on the adjustment scale will point to A instead of 0, as shown in screen 2. AUTO means the camera will decide how much contrast to add to the image. In screen 3, you can see that the pointer on the adjustment scale has been moved toward the + side (higher contrast). Fine adjustments can be made in 0.25 step increments by turning the front Sub-command dial (screen 3, red arrow). Or you can adjust the contrast in larger, 1.0 step increments by pressing left or right on the Multi selector (screen 4). Notice that there are two tiny indicators showing at the point of the two red arrows in screen 4. The one that is bright yellow (right arrow) is the new adjustment position you have selected. The one that is a pale dim yellow (left arrow) is the current (old) setting for Contrast. Until you have made a new selection permanent, you will always be able to see where the current setting is in relation to the new setting based on the position of the dim pointer.

5. Repeat step 4 for any of the individual settings you want to adjust for this Picture Control. Once you are finished, press the OK button to lock in the setting.

Now that you have adjusted a Picture Control away from its factory default settings, it would be good to know how to return the control its default settings. Let's consider how to do so (figure 3.13C).

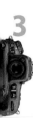

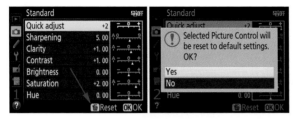

Figure 3.13C – Resetting a Nikon Picture Control

Use the following steps to reset a Picture Control:

1. Open the adjustment screen for the Picture Control you want to reset, and then press the Delete button (garbage can; figure 3.13C, screen 1).
2. A box will appear that says, *Selected Picture Control will be reset to default settings OK?* (figure 3.13C, screen 2). Select Yes and press the OK button to return the Picture Control to its factory default settings.

Note: If you choose to modify a Picture Control using Quick adjust or with the individual line item settings (Sharpness, etc.), it is not yet a Custom Picture Control because you have not saved it under a new name. Instead, it is merely a modified Nikon Picture Control. We'll discuss how to name and save your own Custom Picture Controls in the upcoming section, **Manage Picture Control**.

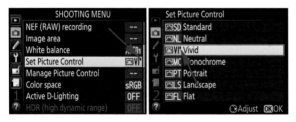

Figure 3.13D – An adjusted Nikon Picture Control (see asterisks)

Figure 3.13D shows an asterisk after the Vivid control (VI* - Vivid) in both Shooting Menu screens (see red arrows). This asterisk appears after you have made a modification to any of the Picture Control's inner settings (Contrast, etc.). The asterisk will go away if you reset the Picture Control to its factory settings.

Because many of us change Picture Controls often, Nikon has given us a handy external button to quickly open the Picture Control menu (figure 3.13E).

Use the following steps to set a Picture Control by using an external camera control button:

1. As shown in figure 3.13E, you can press the Picture Control button, which is a combo button that has the rather long full name of Protect/Picture Control/

Help button (as evidenced by the other symbols above it). If there is nothing showing on the camera's Monitor and you press the Picture Control button, the menu shown in figure 3.13E, screen 2, will open, giving you immediate access to the Picture Controls.

2. Choose one of the Picture Controls and press the OK button.

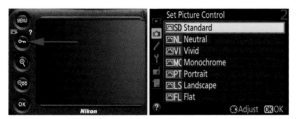
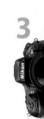

Figure 3.13E – Using the Picture Control button to open Set Picture Control

Protect/Picture Control/ Help button details: If you press the button shown in figure 3.13E, screen 1, when a picture is showing on the Monitor, the camera will protect that picture from deletion (Protect button). When you press the button with nothing on the Monitor, as mentioned in step 1 of the preceding steps, the Set Picture Control screen opens (Picture Control button). Finally, if you press the button when a menu item is showing, it will open a Help screen describing the functionality of that setting (Help button).

Let's examine the basic functionality of each of the Picture Controls.

Examining Picture Controls

Now it's time to break out my red, green, and blue (RGB) Lego blocks as sample subjects for Picture Control Sharpening, Clarity, Contrast, Brightness, Saturation, and Hue variation comparisons.

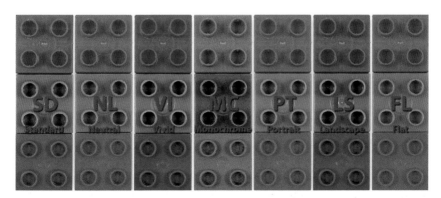

Figure 3.13F – Sample color variations among Nikon Picture Controls

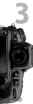

Figure 3.13F provides a look at the differences in color saturation and shadow with the various controls. Due to limitations in printing, it may be hard to see the variations, but they are clearly visible in a picture. Saturation and Contrast depth increase within these Picture Control choices, in this order: FL (very low) > NL (low) > SD (medium) > VI (high). PT appears to be a modified form of the NL control, and LS seems to be a modified form of the VI control.

The following is an overview of what Nikon says about Picture Controls and what I see in my sample images taken with the various controls (figure 3.13F).

- **SD**, or **Standard**, is Nikon's recommendation for getting "balanced" results. Nikon recommends SD for most general situations. Use this if you want a balanced image and do not want to post-process it. It has what Nikon calls "standard image processing." The SD control provides what I would call medium saturation, with darker shadows to add contrast. If I were shooting JPEG images in a studio or during an event, I would seriously consider using the SD control. I would compare this setting to Fuji Provia or Kodak Kodachrome 64 slide films.
- **NL**, or **Neutral**, is best for an image that will be extensively post-processed in a computer. It has the widest available dynamic range of any of the Picture Controls. It too is a balanced image setting, but it applies minimal camera processing, so you'll have room to do more with the image during post-processing. NL has less saturation and weaker shadows, so the image will be less contrasty (wider dynamic range). The effects of the NL and SD controls are harder to see in figure 3.13F because there's not a marked difference. However, the NL control will give you extra dynamic range in each image due to more open shadows and slightly less saturated colors. If you've ever shot with Fuji NPS film or Kodak Portra negative films and liked them, you'll like this control.
- **VI**, or **Vivid**, is for those of us who love Fuji Velvia slide film! This setting places emphasis on saturating primary colors for intense imagery. The contrast is higher for striking shadow contrast, and the sharpness is higher too. If you are shooting JPEGs and want to imitate a saturated transparency film like Velvia, this mode is for you! If you look at the red block in the VI example in figure 3.13F, you'll see that it's pushed into deep saturation, almost to the point of oversaturation. Plus, the greens and blues are extra strong. That means your nature shots will look saturated and contrasty. Be careful when you are shooting on a high contrast day, such as in direct sunshine in the summer. If you use the VI control under these conditions, you may find that your images are too high in contrast. It may be better to back off to the SD or NL control when shooting in bright sunshine. Of course, with the higher inherent dynamic range in the D810, this is not as much of an issue as with previous Nikons. You will need to experiment with this to see what I mean. On a cloudy or foggy low-contrast day, when the shadows are weak, you may find that the VI control adds pleasing saturation and contrast to the image.

- **MC**, or **Monochrome**, allows the black-and-white lovers among us to shoot in toned black-and-white. The MC control basically removes the color by desaturation. It's still an RGB color image, but the colors have become levels of gray. It does not look the same as black-and-white film, in my opinion. The blacks are not as deep, and the whites are not as bright. To me, it seems that the MC control is fairly low contrast, and that's where the problem lies. Good black-and-white images should have bright whites and deep blacks. To get images like that from a digital camera, you'll have to manually work with the image in a graphics program like Photoshop, using the Channel Mixer (see the upcoming sidebar Note on Photoshop for D810 Black-and-White Images). However, if you want to experiment with black-and-white photography, this gives you a good starting point. Additionally, there are two extra settings in the MC control that allow you to experiment with Filter effects and Toning. We'll look at these settings in the upcoming section called MC Picture Control Filter Effects and Toning. The MC control creates a look that is somewhat like Kodak Plus-X Pan negative film, with blacks that are not as deep.

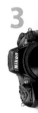

- **PT**, or **Portrait**, is a control that "lends a natural texture and rounded feel to the skin of portrait subjects" (Nikon's description). I've taken numerous images with the PT control and shot the same images with the NL control. The results are very similar. I'm sure that Nikon has included some software enhancements specifically for skin tones in this control, so I would definitely use this control for portraits of people. The results from the PT control look a bit like smooth Kodak Portra or Fuji NPS negative film.

- **LS**, or **Landscape**, is a control that "produces vibrant landscapes and cityscapes," according to Nikon. That sounds like the VI control to me. I shot a series of images using both the LS and VI controls and got similar results. Compared to the VI control, the LS control seemed to have slightly less saturation in the reds and a tiny bit more saturation in the greens. The blues stayed about the same. It seems that Nikon has created the LS control to be similar to, but not quite as drastic as, the VI control. In my test images, the LS control created smoother transitions in color. However, there was so little difference between the two controls that you'd have to compare the images side by side to notice. Maybe this control is meant to be more natural than the super-saturated VI control. It will certainly improve the look of your landscape images. The look of this control is somewhere between Fuji Provia and Velvia. You get great saturation and contrast, with emphasis on the greens and blues in natural settings.

- **FL**, or **Flat**, is a control that allows you to preserve details "over a wide tone range, from highlights to shadows." If you are a JPEG or TIFF shooter and need maximum dynamic range in your image but do not want to use HDR (high dynamic range) imaging (where you shoot several images at different exposures and then combine them), you may be able to use this Picture Control as a substitute. The D810 has very wide dynamic range already, with amazing detail in the shadow areas; therefore, a very low contrast Picture Control setting can help maintain maximum dynamic range in a single image. You may also use this Picture Control when you are shooting video and later want to professionally color grade the results. It is hard to compare this Picture Control to a certain film stock; I have never shot any film with contrast and saturation this low.

MC Picture Control Filter Effects and Toning

The Monochrome, or MC, Picture Control has some added features that are enjoyable for those who love black-and-white photography. As shown in figure 3.13G, there are Filter effects that simulate the effect of yellow (Y), orange (O), red (R), and green (G) filters on a monochrome image. Yellow, orange, and red (Y, O, R) change the contrast of the sky in black-and-white images. Green (G) is often used in black-and-white portrait work to change the appearance of skin tones. You do not have to go buy filters for your lenses; they are included in your D810.

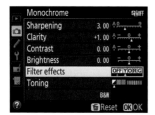

Figure 3.13G – Monochrome Filter effects screen

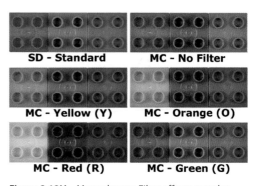

Figure 3.13H – Monochrome Filter effects samples

In figure 3.13H, you'll see an unretouched sample of a color SD Picture Control (for comparison) alongside the five flavors of Monochrome (MC) Filter effects. It is rather interesting how the yellow, orange, red, and green filters affect the RGB Lego blocks.

The Filter effects settings are more pronounced than those you would achieve using a glass filter attached to your lens. Now, let's examine the MC Toning effects.

As shown in figure 3.13I, there are 10 variable Toning effects available—B&W (standard black-and-white), Sepia, Cyanotype, Red, Yellow, Green, Blue Green, Blue, Purple Blue, and Red Purple. Each of the Toning effects is variable within itself, and you can adjust the saturation of the individual tones. In figure 3.13I, I cranked them all the way up to the maximum setting, which tends to oversaturate the toning color. I wanted you to clearly see the maximum potential of the Toning settings.

Note on Photoshop for D810 Black-and-White Images

Since the RGB color channels are still intact in the camera's black-and-white image, you can use Photoshop's Channel Mixer *Image Menu > Adjustments > Channel Mixer…* to manipulate the color channels and improve the blacks and whites. If you use Photoshop to play with the channels, be sure to check the Monochrome box on the Channel Mixer window. If you don't, you'll simply add color back into your black-and-white image. The fact that you must check the Monochrome box proves that a D810 black-and-white image is really just a color image with the colors desaturated to levels of gray. The good thing about this is that you now have room to play with the three color channels, similar to how you use filters when shooting black-and-white film. You can add or subtract contrast by moving the channel sliders until you are happy with the results. There is a lot of discussion of these techniques on the Internet. Why not join the Nikonians.org forum to discuss how to best achieve beautiful black-and-white images? Look for the Nikonians Gold Membership 50% off coupon in the front of this book.

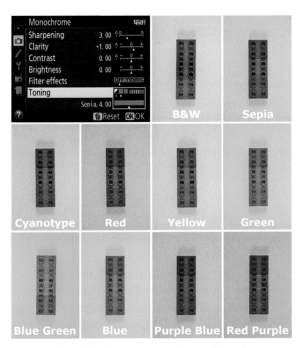

Figure 3.13l – Monochrome Toning screen and samples

Compare how the RGB blocks look under the various toning settings. The red block is on top, green in the middle, and blue on the bottom. Clearly, the toned blocks all look similar in brightness (with only minor variation) to the B&W blocks, showing that the underlying image for each of the color tones is simply black-and-white.

You can shoot a basic black-and-white image, use filters to change how colors appear, or tone the image in experimental ways. Can you see the potential for a lot of fun with these tones?

In the Monochrome menu screen at the top left of figure 3.13I, notice that to the right of the word Toning there is a row of tiny colored rectangles. The first rectangle is half black and half white; that is the normal black-and-white (B&W) selection, and it has no extra toning. Next to that you'll see a golden-brown rectangle; that is the Sepia toning effect (selected). To the right of that is the bluish Cyanotype effect. The smaller rectangles that follow the first three selections are the other available colors for toning.

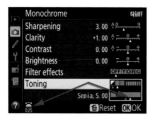

Figure 3.13J – Fine-tuning the Toning setting

Figure 3.13J shows how to adjust the depth of color saturation for each of the colors shown in figure 3.13I. Each color has seven major saturation gradations available, as shown in the little bar tinted the same color as the one you have selected for toning—in this case, Sepia. This saturation adjustment bar allows you to select the depth of saturation for each of the colors. In figure 3.13J, the setting has been moved from 4.00 (default) to 5.00.

Use these steps to adjust the depth of color saturation for toning an image (figure 3.13J):

1. Scroll to Toning on the Monochrome screen, and then press left or right on the Multi selector to select a color (e.g., B&W, Sepia, Cyanotype).
2. To make adjustments to the saturation level of the Toning color, first press down on the Multi selector to select the saturation adjustment bar below the color selections, and then press right or left on the Multi selector to make one-step saturation adjustments. The available saturation adjustment range is from 1.00 to 7.00, with the default being level 4.00 saturation. For adjustments finer than one step, turn the front Sub-command dial in 0.25 increments to select more or less color saturation.
3. Make your Toning saturation-level selection and then press the OK button to lock in the new saturation level.

I'm sure you will agree that Nikon's Picture Control system is very powerful and flexible, especially for those who like to shoot mostly JPEG images. Now, let's see how to go about managing your own Custom Picture Controls in our next section, **Manage Picture Control**.

Manage Picture Control

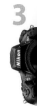

(User's Manual – Page 177)

The *Manage Picture Control* function is designed to allow you to create and store Custom Picture Control settings for future use. You can take an existing Nikon Picture Control (SD, NL, VI, MC, PT, LS, or FL) that is included with the camera, make modifications to it, and then rename it.

If you modify a Picture Control using the Set Picture Control function discussed in the previous section, you simply create a one-off setting. If you'd like to go further and create your own named Custom Picture Controls, the D810 is happy to oblige. There are four choices on the Manage Picture Control screen:

- Save/edit
- Rename
- Delete
- Load/save

Let's look at each of these settings and see how to manage Picture Controls effectively.

Save/Edit a Custom Picture Control

There are six screens used to save/edit a Nikon Picture Control (figure 3.14A) —storing the results for later use as a Custom Picture Control. Here are the steps to edit and save a Picture Control with a modified setting:

1. Select Manage Picture Control from the Shooting Menu and scroll to the right (figure 3.14A, screen 1).
2. Highlight Save/edit and scroll to the right (figure 3.14A, screen 2).
3. Choose a Picture Control that you want to use as a base for your new settings and then scroll to the right (figure 3.14A, screen 3). I am modifying the SD – Standard Picture Control and will save it under a different name.
4. Make your adjustments to Sharpening, Contrast, and so forth. I simply used the Quick adjust setting and added +1 to it, increasing the overall effect of Standard by 1 (out of 2). When you have modified the control in a way that makes it yours, press the OK button (figure 3.14A, screen 4). If you want to abandon your changes and start over, you can simply press the Delete button (garbage can) and it will reset the control to factory specs.

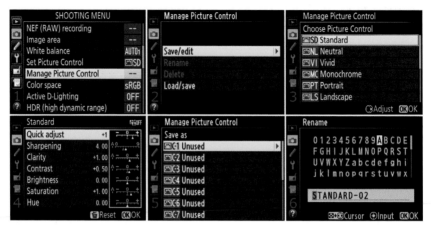

Figure 3.14A – Save/edit a Custom Picture Control

5. Select one of nine storage areas named C-1 to C-9 and scroll to the right (figure 3.14A, screen 5). In figure 3.14A, screen 5, they are all currently marked as Unused. I can save as many as nine different Custom Picture Controls here for later selection with Set Picture Control.

6. You will now see the Rename screen, which works just like the other screens you have used to rename things. Type in a new name by selecting characters from the list at the top of the screen and pressing the Multi selector center button to choose the highlighted character (figure 3.14A, screen 6). To correct an error, hold down the Thumbnail/Playback zoom out button and use the Multi selector to move back and forth along the field that contains the new name. The camera will create a default name for you by appending a dash and two numbers at the end of the current control name. I left it at the default of Standard–02.

7. Press the OK button when you have entered the name of your Custom Picture Control.

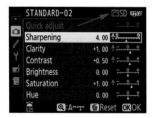

Figure 3.14B – Identifying the base of a Custom Picture Control

Once you have created and saved a Custom Picture Control, you can still tell which control was used as its base, just in case you name it in a way that does not suggest its origins. Notice the red arrow in the upper-right corner of the screen in figure 3.14B. This is the control we just created in the previous steps (Standard–02) and it is derived from an SD Nikon Picture Control, as shown by the SD label at which the arrow is pointing.

Your camera is now set to your Custom Picture Control. You switch between your Custom Picture Controls and the basic Nikon Picture Controls by using Set Picture Control (see previous section titled Set Picture Control). In other words, each of your newly named Custom Picture Controls will appear in the Set Picture Control menu for later selection.

Now, let's look at how to rename an existing Custom Picture Control.

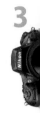

Rename a Custom Picture Control

If you decide to rename an existing Custom Picture Control, you can do so with the following steps:

1. Select Manage Picture Control from the Shooting Menu and scroll to the right (figure 3.14C, screen 1).
2. Select Rename and scroll to the right (figure 3.14C, screen 2).
3. Select one of your Custom Picture Controls from the list (C-1 to C-9) and scroll to the right (figure 3.14C, screen 3). I selected to rename STANDARD-02. This is the Custom Picture Control we created in the preceding section.

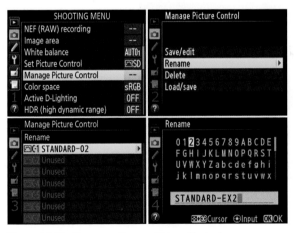

Figure 3.14C – Rename a Custom Picture Control

4. You will now be presented with the Rename screen. To create a different name, hold down the Thumbnail/Playback zoom out button and use the Multi selector to scroll back and forth within the old name. When you have the small gray cursor positioned over a character, you can delete that character with the garbage can Delete button. To insert a new character, position the yellow cursor in the

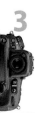

character list above and press the Multi selector center button. The character that is under the yellow cursor will appear on the name line below, at the position of the gray cursor. If there is already a character under the gray cursor, it will be pushed to the right. Please limit the name to a maximum of 19 characters (figure 3.14C, screen 4). I renamed the STANDARD-02 Custom Picture Control STANDARD-EX2.

5. Press the OK button when you have completed the new name.

Note: You can have more than one control with exactly the same name in your list of Custom Picture Controls. The camera does not get confused because each control has a different location (C-1 to C-9) to keep it separate from the rest. However, I don't suggest that you give several custom controls the same name. How would you tell them apart?

When a Custom Picture Control is no longer needed, you can easily delete it.

Delete a Custom Picture Control

You cannot delete a Nikon Picture Control (SD, NL, VI, MC, PT, LS, FL). In fact, they don't even appear in any of the Manage Picture Control menu screens.

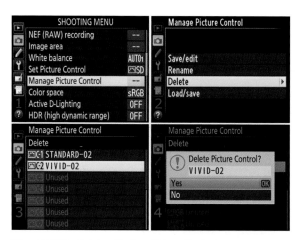

Figure 3.14D – Delete a Custom Picture Control

However, you can delete one or more of your Custom Picture Controls with the following screens and steps:

1. Select Manage Picture Control from the Shooting Menu and scroll to the right (figure 3.14D, screen 1).
2. Select Delete from the Manage Picture Control screen and scroll to the right (figure 3.14D, screen 2).

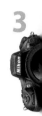

3. Select one of your nine available Custom Picture Controls and scroll to the right (figure 3.14D, screen 3). I selected VIVID-02 for deletion.
4. Choose Yes at the Delete Picture Control? prompt (figure 3.14D, screen 4).
5. Press the OK button and the Custom Picture Control will be deleted from your camera.

Now, let's move to our last menu selection from the Manage Picture Control screen, Load/save.

Load/Save a Custom Picture Control

There are three parts to the Load/save function. They allow you to copy Custom Picture Controls to and from the memory card or delete them from the card.

If you have two memory cards in the camera, the D810 will automatically choose the one assigned as Primary card slot when you save a custom control. You cannot choose to write to the Secondary card slot. However, you could write to the Secondary slot by removing the Primary card, leaving the camera no choice but to write to the only card it can find. (Use *Shooting Menu > Primary slot selection* to set one of the memory card slots to primary).

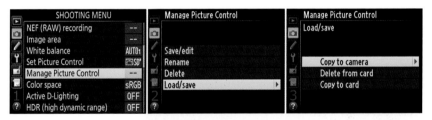

Figure 3.14E – Load/save a Custom Picture Control

Here are the three selections on the Load/save menu, as shown in figure 3.14E, screen 3:

- **Copy to camera** – Loads Custom Picture Controls from the memory card into your camera. You can store up to nine controls in your camera's nine available memory locations (C1–C9).
- **Delete from card** – Displays a list of any Custom Picture Controls found on the memory card. You can selectively delete them.
- **Copy to card** – Allows you to copy your carefully crafted Custom Picture Controls (C1–C9) from your camera to a memory card. You can then share them with others. The camera will display up to 99 control locations (01–99) on any single memory card.

Let's examine each of these selections and see how best to use them.

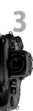

Copy to Camera

You can use the Copy to camera function to copy Custom Picture Controls from your camera's memory card to the camera's Set Picture Control menu. Once you have transferred a Custom Picture Control from your memory card to your camera, it will show up in the *Shooting Menu > Set Picture Control* menu.

Here are the steps to copy a Custom Picture Control from the memory card to the camera itself:

1. Figure 3.14F continues from the last screen shown in figure 3.14E (Load/save on the Manage Picture Control menu). Choose Copy to camera and scroll to the right (figure 3.14F, screen 1).
2. You will be presented with the list of Custom Picture Controls that are currently on the memory card (figure 3.14F, screen 2). If there are no controls on the memory card, the camera will display a screen that says, *No Picture Control file found on memory card.* Figure 3.14F, screen 2, shows two controls—PORTRAIT-02 and LANDSCAPE-02. Select a control from the list and press the OK button. (If you scroll to the right instead, you will be able to examine and adjust the control's settings before saving it to your camera [figure 3.14F, screen 3]. If you don't want to modify it, simply press the OK button.)

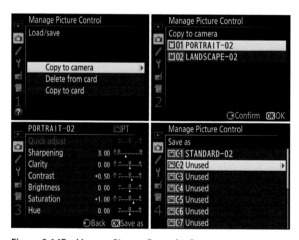

Figure 3.14F – Manage Picture Control – Copy to camera

3. You will now see the Manage Picture Control Save as menu, which lists any Custom Picture Controls already in your camera (figure 3.14F, screen 4). Select one of the Unused memory locations and press the OK button.
4. You'll now be presented with the Rename screen, just in case you want to change the name of the Custom Picture Control (figure 3.14G). If you don't want to change the name, simply press the OK button and the custom control will be added to your camera's Set Picture Control menu. It is okay to have multiple

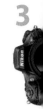

controls with exactly the same name. The camera keeps each control separate in its list of controls (C-1 to C-9). However, I always rename them to prevent future confusion. To create a different name, hold down the Thumbnail/Playback zoom out button and use the Multi selector to scroll back and forth within the old name. Once you have the small gray cursor positioned over a character, you can delete it with the garbage can Delete button. To insert a new character, position the yellow cursor in the character list above and press the Multi selector center button. The character that is under the yellow cursor will appear on the name line below, at the position of the gray cursor. If there is already a character under the gray cursor, it will be pushed to the right. Please limit the name to a maximum of 19 characters. Press the OK button when you have completed the new name.

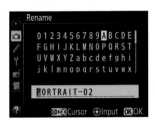

Figure 3.14G – Manage Picture Control – Choose a new name (or Rename)

You can also create Custom Picture Controls in programs like Nikon Capture NX 2, which uses its Picture Control Utility, and load them into your camera using the preceding four steps.

Delete from Card

Once you've finished loading Custom Picture Controls or optional Nikon Picture Controls to your camera, you may be ready to delete a control or two from the memory card. You could format the memory card, but that will blow away all images and Picture Controls on the card. A less drastic method that allows you to be more selective in removing Picture Controls is the Delete from card function.

Here are the steps used to remove Custom Picture Controls from your camera's memory card:

1. Figure 3.14H continues where figure 3.14E left off. Choose Delete from card from the Load/save menu and scroll to the right (figure 3.14H, screen 1).
2. Choose one of the Custom Picture Controls that you want to delete (figure 3.14H, screen 2). I chose PORTRAIT-02. You can confirm that you are deleting the correct control by scrolling to the right, which gives you the fine-tuning screen with current adjustments for that control (figure 3.14H, screen 3). If you are sure that this is the control you want to delete, move on to the next step by pressing the OK button.

3. You will be shown a screen that asks, *Delete Picture Control?* Choose either Yes or No (figure 3.14H, screen 4). If you choose Yes, the Picture Control will be deleted from the memory card. If you choose No, the camera will return to the previous screen.

4. Press the OK button to execute your choice.

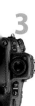

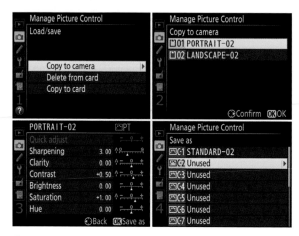

Figure 3.14H – Manage Picture Control – Delete from card

Copy to Card

After you create up to nine Custom Picture Controls using the instructions in the last few sections, you can use the Copy to card function to save them to a memory card. Once they are on a memory card, you can share your custom controls with friends who have compatible Nikon cameras.

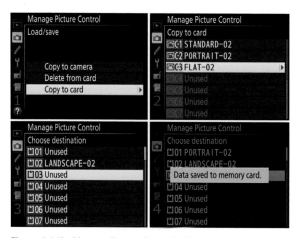

Figure 3.14I – Manage Picture Control – Copy to card

Where Is the Custom Control Stored on the Memory Card?

If you take the time to look at the contents of your camera's memory card with your computer once you've saved a Custom Picture Control, you'll find a new folder called NIKON with a subfolder called CUSTOMPC. This folder contains any Custom Picture Controls you might have saved, each with a filename ending in ".NCP." For instance, the STANDARD-EX4 Custom Picture Control we saved to the memory card in destination 03 is saved to the memory card as PICCON03.NCP in the CUSTOMPC subfolder. If I had used the first destination location (01), the filename would have been PICCON01.NCP. Therefore, you should realize that the memory card destination locations 01–99 are actually individual files in the CUSTOMPC folder, with a range of file names from PICCON01.NCP to PICCON99. NCP. Now you can access the saved custom controls for sharing or for backup to your computer.

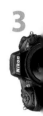

When your Custom Picture Controls are ready to go, use the following steps to copy them to a memory card:

1. Figure 3.14I continues where figure 3.14E left off. Choose Copy to card from the Load/save menu and scroll to the right (figure 3.14I, screen 1).
2. Select one of your current Custom Picture Controls from the Copy to card menu and scroll to the right (figure 3.14I, screen 2). I chose FLAT-02 to copy to the memory card.
3. Now you'll use the Choose destination menu to select the location in which you want to save the custom control (figure 3.14I, screen 3). You have 99 choices; select any Unused location. We previously deleted PORTRAIT-02 from the memory card, leaving card destination number 01 marked as Unused. Just to show that you can save to any of the 99 destination locations, I chose 03 instead of 01.
4. Press the OK button and you'll briefly see a screen that says, *Data saved to memory card*. Your Custom Picture Control is now ready to distribute to the world or load onto another of your compatible Nikon cameras.

Color Space

(User's Manual – Page 296)

Using a *Color space* is an interesting and important part of digital photography. They help your images fit into a much broader range of imaging devices. Software, printers, monitors, and other devices recognize which Color space is attached to your image and use it, along with other color profiles, to help balance the image to the correct output colors for the device in use. The two Color spaces available on

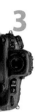

the Nikon D810—sRGB and Adobe RGB—each have a different gamut, or range of color. We'll discuss which might be better after we look into how to select one of the Color spaces.

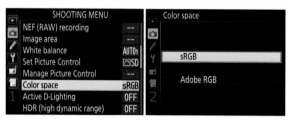

Figure 3.15A – Choosing a Color space

Here's how to select your favorite Color space:

1. Choose Color space from the Shooting Menu and scroll to the right (figure 3.15A, screen 1).
2. Select the Color space setting that you want to use, keeping in mind that Adobe RGB has a larger color gamut (figure 3.15A, screen 2). Adobe RGB is better for commercial printing and publication, while sRGB may be better for snapshots and movies.
3. Press the OK button to lock in your choice.

You can also use the *i* button to open the Quick Menu and select Color space without drilling down in the main camera menus.

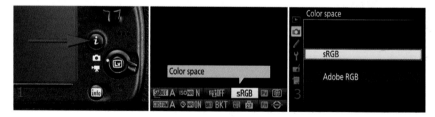

Figure 3.15B – Choosing a Color space from the Quick Menu screen

Use these steps to change Color space quickly:

1. Press the *i* button once (figure 3.15B, screen 1). This will cause the Quick Menu screen to appear.
2. Scroll to the Color space position and press the OK button (figure 3.15B, screen 2).
3. The Color space screen will appear, allowing you to change to a different Color space setting (figure 3.15B, screen 3).

Now, let's look a little more deeply into how Color space works.

Which Color Space Is Best Technically?

There is a large color space used by the graphics industry called CIELAB (figure 3.15C). This particular color space approximates human vision. Adobe RGB covers about 50 percent of the CIELAB color space, while sRGB uses only 35 percent. In other words, Adobe RGB has a wider gamut. That means Adobe RGB gives your images access to significantly higher levels of color, especially cyans and greens.

Another important consideration for those who will be sending their work to companies that use offset printing—such as book and magazine publishers—is that Adobe RGB maps very well to the CMYK offset printing process. If you are shooting commercial work, you may want to seriously consider Adobe RGB. Stock photo shooters are nearly always required to shoot in Adobe RGB.

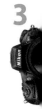

Once a JPEG file is created, in-camera or in-computer, the color gamut for both Adobe RGB and sRGB is compressed into the same number of color levels. A JPEG has only 256 levels for each of its red, green, and blue (RGB) channels. However, since Adobe RGB takes its colors from a wider spectrum, you will have a better representation of reality when there are lots of colors in your image.

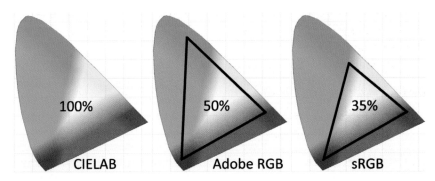

Figure 3.15C – Color space graphs

Of course, when shooting in NEF (RAW), the Color space setting is just a convenience for initial display in your computer before the RAW file is converted to another format, such as JPEG. A RAW file's Color space can be changed after the fact to Adobe RGB, sRGB, or another Color space if one is available in your RAW conversion software. To simplify your RAW workflow, you still may want to consider using Adobe RGB so that you don't have to add Color space conversion to the tasks you must perform for RAW conversion. RAW files can store the maximum number of colors for later reuse. Remember that a NEF (RAW) image file can contain 4,096 levels of color per RGB channel in 12-bit mode and 16,384 levels in 14-bit mode— instead of the 8-bit JPEG's 256 levels. Storing the Adobe RGB Color space in your RAW file's metadata makes a lot of sense because of NEF (RAW)'s capacity to contain more colors as a base storage medium.

For JPEG or TIFF shooters it is much more critical that the best Color space setting is used because once the image is made, the Color space cannot be changed easily without lowering the quality of the image.

There are some drawbacks to using Adobe RGB, though. The sRGB color space is widely used in printing and display devices. Even many local labs print using sRGB because so many point-and-shoot digital camera users bring their pictures to them in that format. If you try to print directly to some ink-jet printers using the Adobe RGB color space, the colors may not be as brilliant as with sRGB. If you aren't going to modify your images in-computer and plan on printing them directly from your camera, you may want to use sRGB. If you shoot JPEGs for computer display only or for Internet usage, it might be better to stay with sRGB for everyday shooting.

If you are a RAW shooter and regularly post-process your images, you should consider using Adobe RGB. You will have a wider gamut of colors to work with and can make your images the best they can be. Later, you can convert your carefully crafted images to print with a good color profile and get great results from ink-jet printers and other printing devices.

So, here's a rough way to look at it:

- Many JPEG shooters use sRGB
- Many RAW shooters use Adobe RGB

These are not hard-and-fast rules but many people follow them, according to their style of shooting. I shoot RAW a lot, so I often use Adobe RGB, if for no other reason than the fact that I don't have to change it later in post-processing. If you are shooting for money, such as for stock images, most places expect that you'll be using Adobe RGB. It has more colors, so it's the quality standard for commercial printing.

Technical Note: If you print to devices that do not support color management, use ExifPrint, or print directly on some household printers or at superstore kiosk printers, the print's colors may not be as vivid when using Adobe RGB. JPEG pictures taken in Adobe RGB color space are DCF compliant. Applications and devices that support the DCF protocol will select the correct color space automatically. If you shoot in TIFF, the camera will imbed an ICC color profile when you shoot in Adobe RGB. Applications and devices that support color management will automatically select the correct color space setting when using the TIFF file. It is a good idea to familiarize yourself with the capabilities of the device you are about to use so you can determine its color space capabilities. Nikon View NX 2 (included with camera) and Nikon Capture NX-D automatically select the correct color space when opening your pictures.

Settings Recommendation: I use Adobe RGB most of the time because I shoot a lot of nature with a wide range of color. I want color that's as accurate as my camera will give me. Adobe RGB has a wider range of colors, so it can be more accurate when a wide range of colors is present in your subject. If you are shooting Optimal quality JPEGs for commercial purposes, I would still carefully consider using Adobe RGB. Even with a JPEG's limited color capacity, the colors in the JPEG represent a broader range of color when you use Adobe RGB. However, if you are just shooting JPEG snapshots or movies, there is no need to worry about this. Leave the camera set to sRGB and have fun.

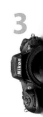

Active D-Lighting

(User's Manual – Page 182)

Active D-Lighting is used to help control contrast in your images. Often, the range of light around the subject is broader than your camera's sensor can capture fully.

Although the D810 has 14.8 EVs (stops) of dynamic range, it is still possible for the range of light in some situations to exceed the range of the sensor's light capturing capability. Or, you may just want to have less image contrast.

The D810 allows you to "D-Light" the image and bring out additional shadow detail, or in other words, lower the image contrast. This extends the dynamic range by opening up the shadows and protecting the highlights. One of the penalties of using Active D-Lighting could be additional noise in shadow details; however, the D810 has excellent noise control, so this is less of a problem than with other cameras.

Active D-Lighting has these six settings:

- Auto (A)
- Extra High (H*)
- High (H)
- Normal (N)
- Low (L)
- Off (no Active D-Lighting)

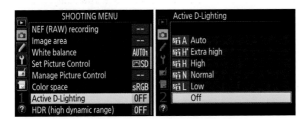

Figure 3.16A – Choosing an Active D-Lighting level

Here are the steps to choose an Active D-Lighting level:

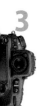

1. Choose Active D-Lighting from the Shooting Menu and scroll to the right (figure 3.16A, screen 1).
2. Select one of the Active D-Lighting levels (figure 3.16A, screen 2). Refer to figure 3.16C to see how each level affects the image.
3. Press the OK button to save your setting.

Additionally, you can open the Active D-Lighting menu without using the Shooting Menu directly. Instead, you can press the *i* button and select it from the Quick Menu screen (figure 3.16B).

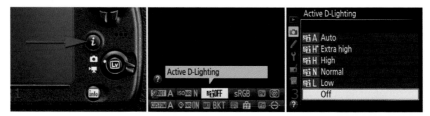

Figure 3.16B – Opening Active D-Lighting from the Quick Menu screen

Use these steps to change Active D-Lighting quickly:

1. Press the *i* button once (figure 3.16B, screen 1). This will cause the Quick Menu screen to appear.
2. Scroll to the Active D-Lighting position and press the OK button (figure 3.16B, screen 2).
3. The Active D-Lighting screen will now appear, allowing you to change quickly to a different level (figure 3.16B, screen 3).

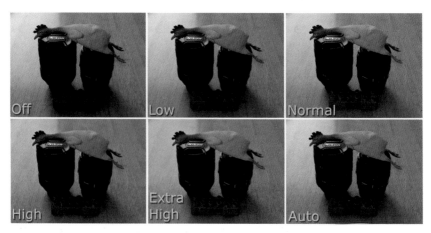

Figure 3.16C – Active D-Lighting samples

Basically, Active D-Lighting will help bring out detail in areas of your image that are hidden in shadow due to excessive image contrast. It also tends to protect the highlights from blowing out, or becoming pure white with no detail. Figure 3.16C shows a series of six images with Active D-Lighting set to its various levels. I chose a backlit scene with heavy shadow to see how these six levels performed.

Settings Recommendation: You'll need to experiment with the Active D-Lighting settings to see which you like best. Active D-Lighting has the effect of lowering contrast, and some people do not like low-contrast images. Also, anytime you recover lost detail from shadows, there may be extra noise in the recovered areas.

This function can be useful for JPEG shooters in particular. Since you really shouldn't modify a JPEG file after shooting it, it's important that the image is created exactly right in the first place. When you are shooting in a high contrast setting, such as in direct sunlight, some degree of Active D-Lighting may help rein in the contrast.

Honestly, before my Nikon D800 and now my D810, I didn't use Active D-Lighting very often because it added noise in the darker areas it opened up. However, things have changed with the D800/D800E/D810 line. I have determined that Active D-Lighting doesn't seem to make as much noise as with previous Nikons. I am quite impressed with the intelligence of the camera, and when I must get a good shot, such as at a wedding ceremony, I am now more open to setting Active D-Lighting to Auto. It has the added benefit of reining in the highlights too, so I keep more detail in a bride's dress, which can be hard to do when shooting with flash in a lowlight room.

Experiment with this by shooting images in a high-contrast and a low-contrast setting at all the various levels of Active D-Lighting. You'll see how the camera reacts and can better decide how you'll use this functionality.

HDR (High Dynamic Range)

(User's Manual – Page 184)

HDR (high dynamic range) asks the camera to combine two JPEG or TIFF exposures into a single image. It is not available in NEF (RAW) modes.

HDR combines details from an underexposed shot and an overexposed shot into one good, normally exposed picture with much greater dynamic range than normal. In figure 3.17A, you can see a sample, with the two images on the left combined, in-camera, to create the third image.

HDR (high dynamic range) in the D810 is a form of simple bracketing that allows you to create an HDR image without setting up a bracketing series using the BKT button. There are three settings under HDR (high dynamic range):

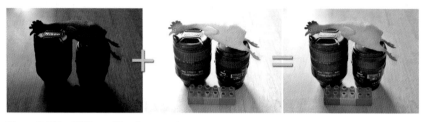

Figure 3.17A – HDR combination sample

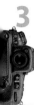

- **HDR mode** – This setting has three options: On (series), On (single photo), and Off. When On (series) is selected, the camera will keep shooting its two-image HDR brackets until you set HDR mode to Off. When On (single photo) is chosen, the camera will take a single HDR bracket for one image. Off means the camera does not create an HDR image.
- **Exposure differential** – You can choose how many stops (EV) there will be between the two images that are later combined. The choices are 1 EV, 2 EV, 3 EV, and Auto. Use 1, 2, or 3 EV when you want to make the decision; choose Auto when you want to let the camera decide. If you control the amount of Exposure differential, be careful to choose only what is needed or you may experience under- or overexposure in the final combined image. If a two-image exposure bracket is insufficient, you may want to investigate the exposure bracketing system connected to the BKT button. We will discuss how to use the camera's primary bracketing system in the chapter titled **Custom Setting Menu**. With it you can do up to a nine-shot bracket.
- **Smoothing** – This allows you to choose smoothing for the boundaries between the two images. There are three choices available: Low, Normal, and High. Each subject's boundaries are different, so you may have to experiment with these settings. Higher values make a smoother combined image. Watch out for uneven shading with some subjects.

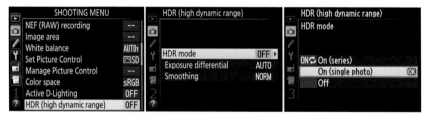

Figure 3.17B – Choosing an HDR mode

First let's examine how to configure the three settings and prepare for HDR shooting. Use these steps to enable HDR mode for a single picture or a series:

1. Choose HDR (high dynamic range) from the Shooting Menu and scroll to the right (figure 3.17B, screen 1).
2. Select HDR mode and scroll to the right (figure 3.17B, screen 2).
3. Decide whether you want to make one or a series of HDR images and choose accordingly: On (single photo) for a single image or On (series) for a series of images (figure 3.17B, screen 3).
4. Press the OK button to prepare the camera for shooting in HDR mode.

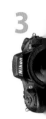

When the D810 is set to HDR mode, you will see an HDR symbol displayed on the camera's Control panel and on the Information display (Monitor). It will go away when HDR mode is set to Off. Now let's look into configuring the Exposure differential setting.

Use the following steps to choose an Exposure differential setting:

1. Choose HDR (high dynamic range) from the Shooting Menu and scroll to the right (figure 3.17C, screen 1).
2. Select Exposure differential and scroll to the right (figure 3.17C, screen 2).
3. Choose one of the four settings, according to how much exposure variance you want between the two images that will be combined into one. Use Auto to let the camera decide, or choose from 1 EV to 3 EV (figure 3.17C, screen 3). If you have a high-contrast subject, you may want to try the 3 EV level first to see if it works best. For low- to medium-contrast subjects, choose 1 EV or 2 EV.
4. Press the OK Button to lock in your choice.

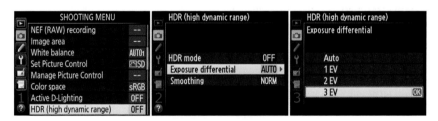

Figure 3.17C – Choosing an Exposure differential setting

Finally, let's see how to configure the Smoothing selection for the best image edge boundary control.

Use these steps to configure Smoothing for the HDR image combination:

1. Choose HDR (high dynamic range) from the Shooting Menu and scroll to the right (figure 3.17D, screen 1).
2. Select Smoothing and scroll to the right (figure 3.17D, screen 2).

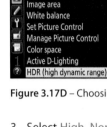
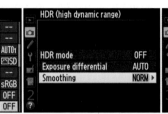
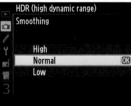
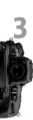

Figure 3.17D – Choosing a Smoothing setting

3. Select High, Normal, or Low. You will need to experiment and observe the differences in image boundaries when you vary this setting.
4. Press the OK button to choose your Smoothing level.

Now it's time to take an HDR picture or three. Here are some things you will need to know during and after the HDR process:

- The camera will take two exposures when you press the Shutter-release button all the way down once. It is a good idea to have the camera on a tripod during low-light HDR operations or you may have some nasty, blurry images as a result. If you do choose to handhold in low light, please brace yourself and do not allow camera movement. When light is very bright, the HDR process can be quite fast. It is much slower when light is low, taking several seconds to deliver a combined image.
- **HDR** will be displayed in the Control panel, on the Information display, and in Live view (Monitor) as soon as you enable HDR (high dynamic range).
- **HDR** will start blinking on the Control panel during the initial exposures.
- **HDR** will display in the lower-right side of the Monitor during Live view HDR shooting. During HDR exposure and image combination, the Live view screen will not display anything.
- **Job HDR** will flash in the viewfinder during image combination.
- **Job HDR** (blinking) will be displayed in the Control panel while the images are being combined.
- The edges of the image may be cropped out, so do not allow important parts of the subject to touch the edges if possible.
- If you detect shadows around bright objects or halos around dark objects, you can reduce this effect by setting Smoothing to a lower level.
- You cannot select any form of NEF (RAW) shooting when you're already using HDR (high dynamic range), only JPEG or TIFF. HDR (high dynamic range) is grayed out on the Shooting Menu when you're using NEF (RAW).

Note: You can assign the BKT button to allow you to select HDR settings with external camera controls (instead of bracketing). See the chapter **Custom Setting Menu**, under the subheading **Custom Setting f8 – Assign BKT button**.

Settings Recommendation: I am a big fan of bracketing and HDR. You'll often find me on top of some Appalachian mountain shooting a five-bracket HDR shot of the valley below. Beautiful things can be done with HDR. I do not like the shadowless HDR that some photographers shoot. To me it looks fake and seems faddish. However, HDR, when used correctly, can help create images that the camera could not normally take due to excessive light range. If you are really into HDR or would like to be, check out the excellent second edition of *Practical HDRI*, by Jack Howard, published by Rocky Nook.

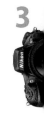

Photoshop has built-in software for HDR, or you can buy a less-costly dedicated package, such as Photomatix Pro by HDRsoft. I've been using Photomatix Pro for several years to combine my bracketed images into carefully tone-mapped HDR images.

There are some limitations to in-camera HDR, which is why people really serious about it use the main bracketing system and combine their images using professional HDR software. However, HDR (high dynamic range) in the D810 is an easy way to knock off a few quick HDRs for those times when only an HDR will do. Give it a try!

Vignette Control

(User's Manual – Page 297)

Vignette control allows you to reduce the amount of vignetting (slight darkening) that many lenses have in the corners at wide-open apertures. The angle at which light strikes a sensor on its edges is greater than the angle at which rays go straight through the lens to the center areas of the sensor. Because of the increased angle, some light falloff occurs at the extreme edges of the frame, especially at wide apertures, because more of the lens element is in use. Full-frame (FX) sensors have microlenses over the pixels that help reduce vignetting, but it is still there in varying degrees with different lenses.

In recognition of this fact, Nikon has provided the Vignette control setting. It can reduce the vignetting effect to a large degree. If more vignette control is required, you can use Photoshop or Nikon Capture NX-D (or other software) to remove it.

Figure 3.18A shows a sample of what the Nikon D810 can accomplish on its own. I shot four pictures of the sky with an AF-S Nikkor 50mm f/1.4G lens at f/1.4 (wide open aperture). Each picture has more Vignette control applied, from Off to High.

Let's see how to configure the Vignette control for edge light falloff reduction with your lenses.

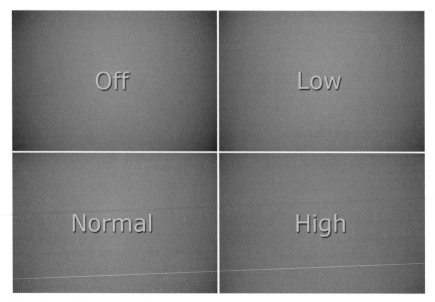

Figure 3.18A – Vignette control range

Here are the steps to choose a Vignette control level for your D810:

1. Choose Vignette control from the Shooting Menu and scroll to the right (figure 3.18B, screen 1).
2. Select a level from the list. I chose Normal in figure 3.18B, screen 2.
3. Press the OK button to lock in the level.

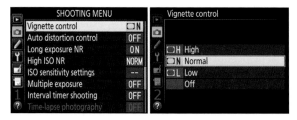

Figure 3.18B – Vignette control choices

Note: The Vignette control does not apply to the following:

- Movies
- Multiple exposures
- FX lenses when *Image area > Choose image area* is set to DX (24x16) crop mode
- DX lenses when *Image area > Auto DX crop* is set to Off and *Image area > Choose image area* is set to any crop mode other than DX (24x16). In other words, the Vignette control will work with DX lenses set to DX (24x16) crop mode only.

Other crop modes have frame boundaries that well exceed the maximum image circle of a DX lens, providing a totally black vignette that cannot be overcome.

The Vignette control will work only with lenses of the G, D, and E types, excluding PC lenses. Nikon warns that you may see noise, fog, or variations in brightness in JPEG and TIFF images "…depending on the scene, shooting conditions, and type of lens." Also, if you are using a Custom Picture Control, or a Nikon Picture Control that has been modified from the factory default values, you may not achieve the "desired effect."

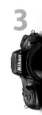

It may be a good idea to test each of your lenses and pixel peep the edges to see if you notice any problems. You will see the best corrective effect at maximum apertures.

Settings Recommendation: The camera defaulted to Normal from the factory, so I have been shooting most of my images with it set to Normal. I like this control. It does help remove vignetting in the corners when I shoot with the aperture wide open. I have not noticed any additional noise or image degradation in the corrected areas. I suggest leaving your camera set to Normal at all times unless you are shooting with a lens that has a greater tendency to vignette, in which case you can increase it to High. Even High does not seem to fully remove the vignetting when a lens is wide open, so this is not an aggressive algorithm that will leave white spots in the corners of your images. Why not shoot a few shots with your lenses at wide aperture and see how Vignette control works with your lens and camera combinations?

Remember, you can remove vignetting in the computer with post-processing software if the camera's Vignette control setting does not entirely remove the problem.

Auto Distortion Control

(User's Manual – Page 298)

Auto distortion control is designed to automatically reduce barrel and pincushion distortion in your images. It will try to keep lines straight but may crop the edges of your image in the process. This function may be best used by architectural photographers who are very concerned about keeping lines and edges straight, for obvious reasons.

Figure 3.19A shows a greatly exaggerated sample of barrel and pincushion distortion. If you have a lens that does this, you might want to dispose of it, unless it is a fisheye or extreme wide angle, of course.

To prevent even mild cases of these two distortion types from ruining images that contain straight lines, you can use this control. Of course, if you are out shooting nature shots or portraits, it is unlikely that you will gain much benefit from this

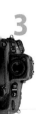

function. If you need automatic barrel and pincushion distortion control, you will already know it from previous work. Most of us will leave this turned off.

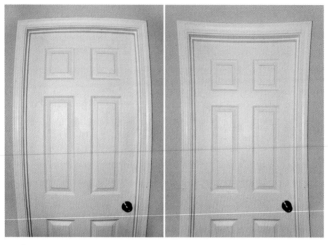

Figure 3.19A – Extreme examples of barrel (left) and pincushion (right) distortion

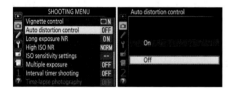

Figure 3.19B – Auto distortion control

Use these steps to enable or disable Auto distortion control:

1. Choose Auto distortion control from the Shooting Menu and scroll to the right (figure 3.19B, screen 1).
2. Select On or Off (figure 3.19B, screen 2).
3. Press the OK button to save the setting.

Settings Recommendation: If you are a photographer who really needs this function, you will already know it. If you question whether it will benefit you, it probably won't. I prefer to remove distortion in software on my computer because I am working with a much larger image and can more easily see what needs to be done. This is an automatic function in the D810 and, like most automatic functions, does great sometimes and not so great other times. However, this may be a handy function for times when you are out in the field shooting and you need some distortion correction immediately. Just watch out and allow for edge cropping as the camera removes the distortion it detects.

Long Exposure NR

(User's Manual – Page 299)

Long exposure NR (noise reduction) is designed to combat visual noise in long exposures. Long-exposure noise is a little different from grainy-looking high-ISO sensitivity noise due to its cause. Nikon says long-exposure noise appears as: "bright spots, randomly-spaced bright pixels, or fog." Why does this happen? During longer exposures, the imaging sensor can start to warm up a little, especially in warm ambient temperatures. This causes a condition called amp noise, in which warmer sections of the imaging sensor start to display more foggy noise than other sections.

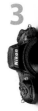

Additionally, when pixels are left turned on for a longer period of time, a few of them may become brighter than normal and record an improper color, often bright red. Those off-color, bright pixels should be removed by the camera. Long exposure NR does just that.

Long-exposure noise is best handled by this Long exposure NR function, while high-ISO noise is well handled by High ISO NR (next section). Sometimes, when you are shooting long exposures at higher ISO settings, both may be needed!

Nikon knows its imaging sensors well. It feels that images taken at shutter speeds longer than 1 second may exhibit more long-exposure noise than is acceptable for normal images. There are two settings for Long exposure NR, as shown in figure 3.20A.

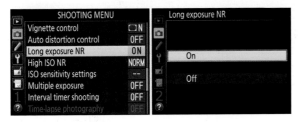

Figure 3.20A – Choosing a Long exposure NR setting

- **On** – When you select On and the exposure goes over 1 second, the camera will take two exposures with the exact same time for each. The first exposure is the normal picture-taking exposure. The second is a dark-frame subtraction exposure, in which a second exposure is made for the same length of time as the first one, but with the shutter closed. The noise in the dark frame image is examined and then subtracted from the original image. It is really quite effective and beats having to blur the image to get rid of noise. I've taken exposures of around 30 seconds and had perfectly usable results. The only drawback is that the exposure time is doubled because two exposures are made. The dark frame exposure is not written to the memory card, so you'll have only one image, with much less noise, in the end. While the dark frame image is being processed, the

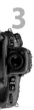

words Job nr will blink on the Control panel and in the Viewfinder. During this second exposure, while Job nr is flashing, you cannot use the camera. If you turn it off while Job nr is flashing, the camera still keeps the first image; it just doesn't do any noise reduction on it. If Long exposure NR is set to On, the frame advance rate may slow down a little in Continuous release mode, and the capacity of the in-camera memory buffer will drop while the image is being processed.

- **Off** – If you select Off, then, of course, you will have no long exposure noise reduction with exposures longer than 1 second.

Here are the steps to choose a Long exposure NR setting:

1. Choose Long exposure NR from the Shooting Menu and scroll to the right (figure 3.20A, screen 1).
2. Select either On or Off (figure 3.20A, screen 2).
3. Press the OK button to save your setting.

You can also open the Long exposure NR menu without using the Shooting Menu directly. Instead, you can select it from the Quick Menu screen by pressing the *i* button.

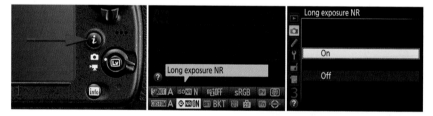

Figure 3.20B – Opening Long exposure NR from the Quick Menu screen

Use these steps to change Long exposure NR quickly:

1. Press the *i* button once (figure 3.20B, screen 1).
2. This will cause the Quick Menu screen to appear. Scroll to the Long exposure NR position and press the OK button (figure 3.20B, screen 2).
3. The Long exposure NR screen will now appear, allowing you to turn it On or Off (figure 3.20B, screen 3).

Settings Recommendation: I like the benefits of Long exposure NR. I shoot a lot of waterfall and stream shots where I often need exposures of several seconds to really blur the water. Also, I like to take midnight shots of the sky and even shots of city scenes at night. Even though it may slow down the frame rate slightly and allow me fewer images in the in-camera memory buffer, I still use it most of the time.

If I were a sports or action shooter using Continuous release mode, I might leave Long exposure NR turned Off. It's unlikely I would be using exposures longer than 1 second, and I would want maximum frames per second as well as the ability to cram as many images into the camera buffer as possible. I wouldn't want my camera to slow down while writing images to the memory card.

Your style of shooting will govern whether this function is useful to you. Ask yourself one simple question: "Do I often shoot exposures longer than one second?" If so, you may want Long exposure NR set to On. Compare how the images look with and without it. I think you'll like Long exposure NR.

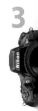

High ISO NR

(User's Manual – Page 299)

High ISO NR (noise reduction) lessens the effects of visual digital noise in your images when you use higher ISO sensitivity (exposure gain) settings. Nikon does not publish the point at which High ISO NR starts working (when enabled) except to say that even when set to Off, "…noise reduction is performed only as required and never at an amount higher than when Low is selected."

With such a high pixel density, the camera probably does some minor noise reduction—if High ISO NR is enabled—at relatively low ISO settings (ISO 800–1600). If so, it is particularly effective.

You can choose the level of High ISO NR you would like to use from one of three active levels: Low, Normal, and High. If you have it set to Off, High ISO NR does nothing to images with low ISO sensitivity values, while at higher ISO values—probably above ISO 1600—the amount of noise reduction is less than the Low setting would provide when enabled.

When High ISO NR is enabled, the higher the setting you use (Low–High), the greater the blurring effect on the image to remove noise. However, the camera compensates after blurring by resharpening to a degree and seems to do a good job at creating very usable high-ISO images. If well exposed, even up to ISO 6400 the camera does a beautiful job, with relatively clean images. You should plan to experiment with the camera to determine your tolerance for noise and the camera's ability to reduce it.

Let's see how to enable or disable High ISO NR.

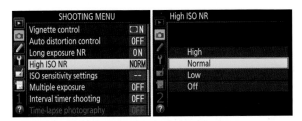

Figure 3.21A – High ISO NR choices

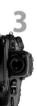

Use these steps to choose a High ISO NR setting:

1. Choose High ISO NR from the Shooting Menu and scroll to the right (figure 3.21A, screen 1).
2. Select one of the noise reduction levels: High, Normal, Low, or Off (figure 3.21A, screen 2).
3. Press the OK button to save your setting.

You can also open the High ISO NR menu without using the Shooting Menu directly. Instead, you can select it from the Quick Menu screen by pressing the *i* button.

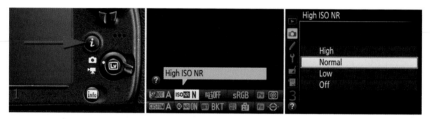

Figure 3.21B – Opening High ISO NR from the Quick Menu screen

Use these steps to change High ISO NR quickly (figure 3.21B):

1. Press the *i* button once (figure 3.21B, screen 1). This will cause the Quick Menu to appear.
2. Scroll to the High ISO NR position and press the OK button (figure 3.21B, screen 2).
3. The High ISO NR screen will now appear, allowing you to choose a level quickly (figure 3.21B, screen 3).

Note: If you are using High ISO NR and the Auto ISO sensitivity control at the same time, or if the ISO is set to 1600 or higher, the memory buffer capacity will be reduced while processing images.

Settings Recommendation: I leave High ISO NR set to Normal at all times. I appreciate a little noise reduction as long as it is not damaging to the sharpness of the images. If you haven't changed your D810, the factory default is Normal (medium). I think Nikon is trying to tell us that we ought to use a little High ISO NR with such a huge camera resolution and so many pixels packed into a 35 mm imaging sensor. While having medium-format resolution, the FX sensor is smaller than other medium-format cameras, so it will need a little noise reduction assistance at higher ISO sensitivity settings. Again, why not shoot a series of high-ISO images with the camera set to all four High ISO NR choices and see which you like best?

ISO Sensitivity Settings

(User's Manual – Page 109)

ISO sensitivity settings give you control over the light sensitivity of the imaging sensor, including whether you manually control it or the camera sets it automatically.

An ISO sensitivity number, such as 200 or 3200, is an agreed-upon sensitivity level for the image-capturing sensor. Virtually everywhere one goes in the world, all camera ISO numbers will mean the same thing. With that fact established, camera bodies and lenses can be designed to take advantage of the ISO sensitivity ranges they will have to deal with.

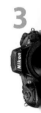

In figure 3.22A we see the external camera controls used to change the ISO sensitivity on the D810. This is a good way to adjust ISO sensitivity quickly. This is also the easiest method to change the camera's ISO sensitivity setting, although it doesn't involve the Shooting Menu, which we are now examining.

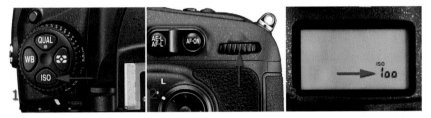

Figure 3.22A – External controls to set ISO manually

Here are the steps you'll use to manually adjust the camera's ISO sensitivity:

1. Hold down the ISO button above the Release mode dial (figure 3.22A, screen 1).
2. Rotate the rear Main command dial counterclockwise to increase the ISO sensitivity or clockwise to decrease sensitivity (figure 3.22A, screen 2).
3. The ISO sensitivity number will show on the Control panel, in the Viewfinder, and at the bottom right of the Live view screen. Figure 3.22A, screen 3, shows the Control panel, which is most often used.

ISO Sensitivity

You can also use ISO sensitivity settings directly from the Shooting Menu to change the camera's ISO sensitivity. Figure 3.22B shows the three screens used. Select your favorite ISO sensitivity for the circumstances in which you find yourself.

Notice in screen 3 of figure 3.22B that you have a scrollable list of ISO sensitivity settings, from Lo 1 (ISO 32) to Hi 1 (ISO 51200). The "normal" ISO range for the D810 is ISO 64 to 12800. Lo 1 to Lo 0.3 represents ISO 32–50, and Hi 0.3 to Hi 2 represents ISO 16000–51200.

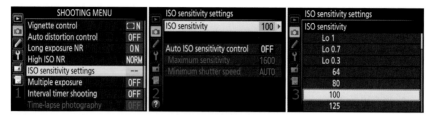

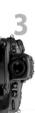

Figure 3.22B – Setting ISO sensitivity from the Shooting Menu

Here are the steps to select an ISO sensitivity setting (figure 3.22B):

1. Choose ISO sensitivity settings from the Shooting Menu and scroll to the right (figure 3.22B, screen 1).
2. Select ISO sensitivity from the menu and scroll to the right (figure 3.22B, screen 2).
3. Scroll up or down in the ISO sensitivity menu until you highlight the ISO value you want to use (figure 3.22B, screen 3).
4. Press the OK button to save the ISO sensitivity setting.

The standard minimum ISO sensitivity for the D810 is ISO 64. You may adjust the camera's ISO sensitivity in a range from ISO 32 to 51200, in 1/3 steps. The ISO step increment is controlled by *Custom Setting Menu > b Metering/exposure > b1 ISO sensitivity step value*, and can be set to 1/3, 1/2, or 1 step. We'll look at this more carefully in the upcoming chapter titled **Custom Setting Menu**.

Select your favorite ISO sensitivity setting, using either the external camera controls or the Shooting Menu's ISO sensitivity settings function. If you'd like, you can simply let your camera decide which ISO it would like to use. Let's consider this often-misunderstood feature in detail.

Auto ISO Sensitivity Control (ISO-AUTO)

You may have noticed in figure 3.22B, screen 2, that there is another setting available, Auto ISO sensitivity control, which defaults to Off. This setting allows the camera to control the ISO sensitivity and shutter speed according to the light levels sensed by the camera. Figure 3.22C shows the Shooting Menu screens used to enable Auto ISO sensitivity control.

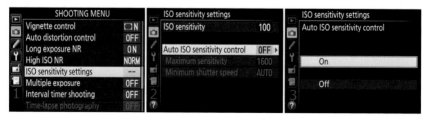

Figure 3.22C – Enabling Auto ISO sensitivity control

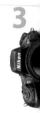

Once you've set Auto ISO sensitivity control to On, you should immediately set two values, according to how you shoot: Maximum sensitivity and Minimum shutter speed. Let's discuss each of them.

Maximum Sensitivity

The Maximum sensitivity setting is a safeguard for you (figure 3.22D). It allows the camera to adjust its own ISO sensitivity from the minimum value you have set in ISO sensitivity (figure 3.22B) to the value set in Maximum sensitivity (figure 3.22D), according to light conditions. The camera will try to maintain the lowest ISO sensitivity it can to get the picture. However, if needed, it can rapidly rise to the Maximum sensitivity level to "get the picture" no matter what.

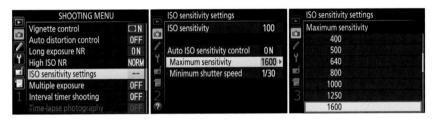

Figure 3.22D – Auto ISO sensitivity control – Maximum sensitivity

If you would prefer that the Maximum sensitivity setting not exceed a certain ISO value, simply select from the list shown in figure 3.22D, screen 3. The Maximum sensitivity default is ISO 12800. This setting will let the camera take the ISO sensitivity all the way up to ISO 12800 in a low-light situation. It is the maximum ISO value the camera will use to get a good exposure when the light drops.

What happens when the camera reaches the Maximum sensitivity setting and there still isn't enough light for a good exposure? Let's find out by examining the second part of the Auto ISO sensitivity control, Minimum shutter speed.

Minimum Shutter Speed

Because shutter speed helps control how sharp an image can be, depending on camera shake and subject movement, you will need some control over the minimum shutter speed allowed while the ISO sensitivity auto control is turned On (figure 3.22E).

The Minimum shutter speed setting allows you to select the minimum shutter speed that the camera will allow when the light diminishes. In exposure modes Programmed auto (P mode – camera controls shutter and aperture) and Aperture-priority (A mode – camera controls shutter and you control aperture), the camera will not go below the Minimum shutter speed unless the Maximum sensitivity setting still won't give you a good exposure.

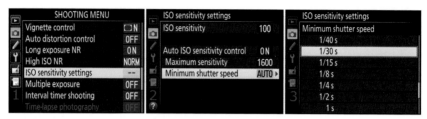

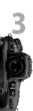

Figure 3.22E – Auto ISO sensitivity control – Minimum shutter speed

This is the answer to our question in the last section about what happens when there is not enough light and the camera has reached the Maximum sensitivity level. Even though you've selected a Minimum shutter speed, the camera will go below the Minimum shutter speed when the Maximum sensitivity ISO number has been reached and the light is still too low for a good exposure.

In other words, in Programmed auto (P) or Aperture-priority (A) exposure modes, if you get into low light and try to take pictures, the camera will try to keep the ISO sensitivity as low as possible until the shutter speed drops to your selected Minimum shutter speed. Once it hits the selected Minimum shutter speed value—like the 1/30s shown in figure 3.22E, screen 3—the ISO sensitivity will begin to rise up to your selected Maximum sensitivity value, like the ISO 1600 shown in figure 3.22D, screen 3.

Once the camera hits the Maximum sensitivity value, if there still isn't enough light for a good exposure, it won't keep raising the ISO sensitivity. Instead, the camera will now go below your selected Minimum shutter speed, dropping below the 1/30s shown in figure 3.22E, screen 3. Be careful, because if the light gets that low, your camera can go all the way down to a shutter speed of 30 seconds to get a good exposure. You had better have your camera on a tripod and have a static subject with shutter speeds that low.

Look at the Minimum shutter speed value as the lowest "safe" speed, after which you'll put your camera on a tripod. Most people can handhold a camera down to about 1/60s if they are careful, and maybe 1/30s if they're extra careful and brace themselves. Below that, it's blur city for your images. It's even worse with telephoto lenses. Camera movement is greatly magnified with a long lens, and a Minimum shutter speed of 1/250s to 1/500s or more may be required.

The next section discusses an excellent solution the Nikon D810 gives us for those times when we are using a longer lens requiring a faster shutter speed to maintain sharp images—the Auto Minimum shutter speed setting.

Auto Minimum Shutter Speed

There is an important principle in photography called the reciprocal of focal length shutter speed rule. You may know the rule; however, a short review won't hurt. This impressive-sounding rule simply means that you should use a tripod (no hand-holding) whenever the shutter speed in use is below the reciprocal of the lens's focal length. For example, if you are using a 50mm zoom position on your lens, you should not use a shutter speed below 1/50s without having the camera on a tripod.

With a 105mm focal length, the minimum handheld shutter speed is 1/100s or 1/125s. There is no 1/105s available, so you can use the closest one. If you are using a 300mm lens, you should not use a shutter speed below 1/300s.

The reason this rule exists is because a longer focal length tends to magnify the subject and any vibrations you introduce when you press the shutter-release button. With a shutter speed below the reciprocal of the lens focal length, you can introduce movement just from your heartbeat, the reflex mirror slap, or natural hand shakiness. If you are going to handhold the camera at slower shutter speeds, you need to learn how to brace yourself properly. The best thing is to use a tripod any time you have to shoot below the reciprocal of the lens's length. Otherwise, you will be known for your well-exposed, yet blurry images (from camera shake). While lenses with vibration reduction (VR) can help, they are not a cure-all for camera shake at slow shutter speeds.

When using the Auto ISO sensitivity control you have an opportunity to implement the reciprocal of focal length shutter speed rule in an automatic fashion. The Nikon D810 has added an Auto setting for Minimum shutter speed, which allows the camera to sense what focal length is currently in use and prohibits the camera from using a minimum shutter speed that would cause camera shake. Let's examine how to use it.

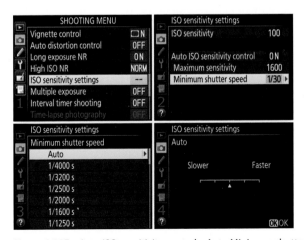

Figure 3.22F – Auto ISO sensitivity control – Auto Minimum shutter speed

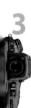

Use these steps to enable Auto Minimum shutter speed:

1. Choose ISO sensitivity settings from the Shooting Menu and scroll to the right (figure 3.22F, screen 1).
2. Select Minimum shutter speed and scroll to the right (figure 3.22F, screen 2).
3. Select Auto from the top of the Minimum shutter speed list and scroll to the right (figure 3.22F, screen 3).
4. Adjust the Auto Minimum shutter speed fine-tuning scale (figure 3.22F, screen 4). Each position on the scale is the equivalent of one stop (1 EV). The camera will use the reciprocal of the focal length of the mounted lens if the yellow pointer is left in the center as seen in figure 3.22F, screen 4. If you move it one notch to the right of center the camera will switch to the reciprocal of the focal length plus one stop. If you are using a 50mm lens, the reciprocal of 50mm plus one stop is 1/100s (1/50s plus 1 EV) for the camera's minimum shutter speed. If you move the scale one notch to the left of center, the camera will use 1/25s instead (1/50s less 1 EV). Here is a list matching what each position on the scale represents if you are using a 50mm lens: 1/13s, 1/25s, 1/50s, 1/100s, 1/200s. Of course, these numbers will vary with the focal length of the lens mounted on the camera.
5. Press the OK button to lock in the fine-tuned Auto Minimum shutter speed.

Settings Recommendation: When I use the Auto ISO sensitivity control with my D810 I set my camera to Auto Minimum shutter speed. Why worry about having to adjust a setting just because I changed lenses? The camera is smart enough to know what to do and tries to protect me from losing sharpness from camera shake.

Note: Shutter-priority (S) and Manual (M) modes allow you to control the camera in a way that overrides certain parts of the Auto ISO sensitivity control.

In Manual mode (M), the camera relinquishes all control of the shutter and aperture. It can adjust only the ISO sensitivity by itself, so it can obey the Maximum sensitivity but the Minimum shutter speed is overridden and does not apply.

In Shutter-priority mode (S), the camera can control the aperture but the shutter speed is controlled only by the camera user. So, the Auto ISO sensitivity control can still control the Maximum sensitivity but has lost control over the Minimum shutter speed.

Also, it may be a good idea to enable High ISO NR—as discussed a few pages back—when you use the Auto ISO sensitivity control. This is especially true if you leave the camera set to the default Maximum sensitivity value of 6400. Otherwise, you may have excessive noise when the light drops.

When a flash unit is used, the value in Minimum shutter speed is ignored. Instead, the camera uses the value found in Custom setting e1 Flash sync speed.

If Auto is selected for Minimum shutter speed, the camera will decide which shutter speed to use as a minimum based on the focal length of the lens in use, if the lens is a CPU type; otherwise, for a non-CPU lens, the camera selects 1/30s as a Minimum shutter speed.

Enabling ISO-AUTO with External Controls

If you like to use external controls to make adjustments when possible (don't we all?), be aware that you can conveniently turn the Auto ISO sensitivity control on and off with the ISO button, the front Sub-command dial, and the Control panel.

Figure 3.22G shows the controls. You will need to configure ISO-AUTO before you use the external controls or the camera will use factory defaults.

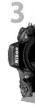

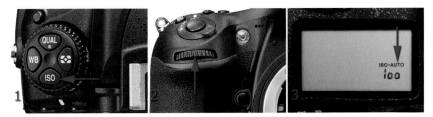

Figure 3.22G – Enabling Auto ISO sensitivity control with external camera controls

Here are the steps you'll use to manually enable or disable ISO-AUTO:

1. Hold down the ISO button above the Release mode dial (figure 3.22G, screen 1).
2. Rotate the front Sub-command dial to enable or disable ISO-AUTO, the Auto ISO sensitivity control (figure 3.22G, screen 2).
3. The ISO-AUTO symbol will show on the Control panel (figure 3.22G, screen 3).

When, Why, and How Should I Use ISO-AUTO?

How much automation do you need to produce consistently excellent images? Let's explore how and when automatic, self-adjusting ISO might improve or degrade your images. What is this feature all about? When and why should I use it? Are there any compromises in image quality when using this mode?

Normally, you set your camera to a particular ISO number, such as 200 or 400, and shoot your images. As the light gets darker, or in the deep shade, you might increase the ISO sensitivity to continue taking handheld images.

If you absolutely must get the shot, the Auto ISO sensitivity control will work nicely. Here are a few scenarios:

- **Scenario # 1**: Let's say you are a photojournalist and you're shooting flash pictures of the president as he disembarks from his airplane, walks into the terminal, and drives away in his limousine. Under these circumstances, you have little

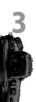

time to check your ISO settings or shutter speeds and are shooting in widely varying light conditions.

- ***Scenario # 2***: You are a wedding photographer in a church that doesn't allow the use of flash. As you follow the bride and groom from the dark inner rooms of the church out into the lobby and finally up to the altar, your light conditions vary constantly. You have no time to deal with the fluctuations in light by changing your ISO because things are moving too quickly.
- ***Scenario # 3***: You are at a party, and you want some great pictures. You want to use flash, but the pop-up Speedlight may not be powerful enough to reach across the room at low ISO settings. You really don't want to be bothered with camera configuration at this time but still want some well-exposed images. Light will vary as you move around the room, talking, laughing, and snapping pictures.

These scenarios present excellent environments for the Auto ISO sensitivity control. The camera will use your normal settings, such as your normal ISO, shutter speed, and aperture, until the light will not allow those settings to provide an accurate exposure. Only then will the camera raise the ISO or lower the shutter speed to keep functioning within the shutter/aperture parameters you have set.

Look at Auto ISO as a failsafe for times when you must get the shot but have little time to deal with camera settings or when you don't want to vary the shutter/ aperture settings but still want to be assured of a well-exposed image.

Unless you are a private detective shooting handheld telephoto images from your car or a photojournalist or sports photographer who must get the shot every time regardless of maximum quality, I personally would not recommend leaving Auto ISO sensitivity control set to On all the time. Use it only when you really need to get the shot under any circumstances!

Of course, if you are unsure of how to use the correct ISO for the light level due to lack of experience, don't be afraid to experiment with this mode. At the very worst, you might get noisier-than-normal images. However, it may not be a good idea to depend on this mode over the long term because noisy images are not very nice.

Are There Any Drawbacks to Using ISO-AUTO?

Maybe! It really depends on how widely the light conditions vary when you are shooting. Most of the time, your camera will maintain the normal range of ISO settings in Auto ISO sensitivity control, so your images will be their normal low-noise, sharp masterpieces. However, at times the light may be so low that the ISO may exceed low-noise range and will start getting into the noisier ranges above ISO 1600.

Just be aware that the Auto ISO sensitivity control can and will push your camera's ISO sensitivity into a range that causes noisier images when light levels drop, if you have allowed it. Use it with this understanding and you'll be fine.

The Auto ISO sensitivity control is yet another feature of our powerful Nikon cameras. Maybe not everyone needs this failsafe feature, but for those who do, it must be there. I will use it myself in circumstances where getting the shot is the most important thing and where light levels may get too low for normal ISO image-making.

Even if you think you might only use it from time to time, do learn how to use it for those times. Experiment with the Auto ISO sensitivity control. It's fun and can be useful!

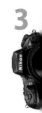

Multiple Exposure

(User's Manual – Page 209)

Multiple exposure is the process whereby you take more than one exposure on a single frame, or picture. Most of us will only do double exposures, which is two exposures on one frame.

Multiple exposure requires you to figure the exposure values carefully for each exposure segment so that in the final picture, all the combined exposures equal one normal exposure. In other words, if you are going to do a non-masked double exposure, your background will need two exposures at half the normal exposure value to equal one normal exposure.

The D810 allows us to figure our own exposure settings and do them manually or gives us Auto gain to help us with exposure calculations.

There are really only four steps to setting up a Multiple-exposure session. However, there are several Shooting Menu screens we'll use to do these four steps. The steps are as follows:

- Select the number of shots you want to take from the Shooting Menu screens.
- Set Auto gain to either On or Off according to how you want to control exposure.
- Choose whether you are shooting one image or a series of images.
- Take the picture.

Use the following steps to configure one or a series of multiple exposures (figure 3.23A):

1. Select Multiple exposure from the Shooting Menu and scroll to the right (figure 3.23A, screen 1).
2. Select Number of shots and scroll right (figure 3.23A, screen 2).
3. Enter the number of shots you wish to take—any number between 2 and 10— and press the OK button (figure 3.23A, screen 3).
4. Select Auto gain and scroll right (figure 3.23A, screen 4).
5. Select On and press the OK button (figure 3.23A, screen 5).

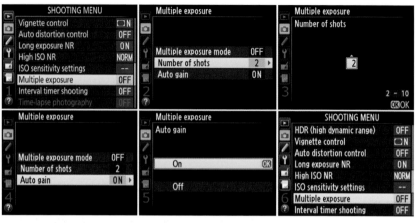

Figure 3.23A – Setting up Multiple exposure basics

6. This brings you back to the beginning and the Multiple exposure selection on the Shooting Menu (figure 3.23A, screen 6). At this point you must reenter the Multiple exposure system and choose whether you want one Multiple exposure or a series (figure 3.23B). Figure 3.23B takes up where figure 3.23A leaves off. It shows the final step of choosing how many multiple exposure images you want to take in this session.

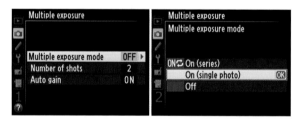

Figure 3.23B – Choosing one multiple exposure or a series of multiple exposures

7. Select Multiple exposure mode and scroll to the right (figure 3.23B, screen 1).
8. Choose On (series) if you want to take more than one distinct Multiple exposure image or On (single photo) for just one Multiple exposure picture.
9. Press the OK button and your camera is ready to take the multiple exposure.

Once you've selected the number of shots (step 2), the camera remembers the value and comes back to it for the next session. To repeat another Multiple exposure series with the same settings, you'll have to use the screens in figure 3.23B again. Start over with step 7 later. That prepares the camera to do the Multiple exposure series (or single photo) in the same way as last time. The camera remembers the previous settings until you reset them using the screens in figure 3.23A.

Understanding Auto Gain

Auto gain defaults to On, so you need to understand it well. Auto gain applies only if you want to make a number of exposure segments with the exact same exposure value for each. If you want to make two exposures, the camera will meter for a normal exposure and then divide the exposure in half for the two shots. For three shots, it will divide the exposure by 1/3, four shots by 1/4, eight shots by 1/8, and so forth.

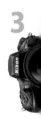

In other words, it will divide the normal exposure for a single shot by the number you entered on the Number of shots screen so that when you are done, you have the equivalent of a single good exposure.

Here's another way of looking at it: If I want a two-shot Multiple exposure, I normally want the background to get 1/2 of a normal exposure in each shot so that it will appear normal in the final image. Auto gain does that automatically. If I need four shots, I want the background to get only 1/4 of a normal exposure for each shot so that I'll have a normally exposed background when the four shots are taken.

The reason I mention this in such a repetitive fashion is that it took me a little while to wrap my brain around the confusing presentation of this fact in the User's Manual. Whoever heard of gain meaning dividing something into parts? What I think the manual writer was trying to say is that each shot "gains" a portion of the normal exposure so that in the end, the exposure is complete and correct.

Auto gain is like an automatic normal-exposure "divider-upper" for multiple exposures. It divides the exposure into appropriate sections—so you won't have to fool with it.

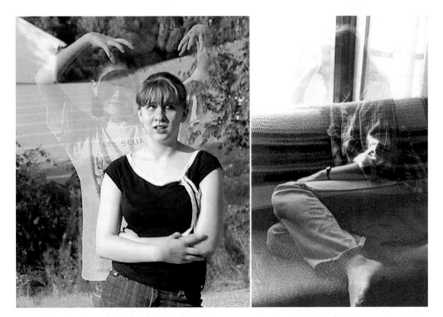

Figure 3.23C – Sample Multiple exposure images

When should one use Auto gain? Only when you have no need for controlling exposure differently for each frame but instead can use an exact division of similar exposures.

Auto gain works fine if you're not using masks, where part of the image is masked off initially and later exposed. When you use a mask, you want a full normal exposure for each of the uncovered (nonmasked) sections of the image, so Auto gain will not work. In this case, you should use manual exposure, with Auto gain turned Off.

Note: You can assign the BKT button to allow you to select Multiple exposure settings with external camera controls (instead of bracketing). We will consider how in the chapter **Custom Setting Menu**, under the subheading **Custom Setting f8 – Assign BKT button**.

Settings Recommendation: Multiple exposure images can be a lot of fun to create (figure 3.23C). I often shoot Multiple exposure images with two people in the frame. One person leaves after the first half of the exposure is taken, while the other stays carefully still. When finished, you will have a normal picture of one person and the background, but the person that left halfway through the Multiple exposure will be ghosted. That means you'll be able to see the background right through her. It's even more fun if you have the person that leaves touch the other person during the first half of the Multiple exposure. Maybe have her put a hand on the other person's shoulder or wrap her arms around him.

If the person that stays for the entire exposure is very careful not to move at all, she will remain sharp and the image will certainly raise eyebrows later.

You can also do this with just one person, as the second picture in figure 3.23C shows. Just make sure she leaves halfway through the Multiple exposure.

Interval Timer Shooting

(User's Manual – Page 216)

Interval timer shooting allows you set up your camera to shoot a series of images over time. Make sure you have a full battery or are connected to a full-time power source, such as the Nikon EH-5b AC adapter, for shooting images over long periods.

Interval timer shooting is different than the setting covered in the next main section, *Time lapse photography*, in that it does not create a movie at the end of the image series. When the camera is done with the Interval timer shooting session, you simply have a series of images taken over a period of time.

There are four steps involved in configuring Interval timer shooting:

- Choose a start time
- Choose an interval

- Choose the number of intervals and the number of shots per interval
- Enable or disable Exposure smoothing

Let's carefully consider how to configure your Interval timer choices.

Configuring an Interval Timer Shooting Session

The screens in figure 3.24A look a little daunting; however, it might help you to realize that the bottom third of screens 2 through 6 are informational in nature. They display the choices you make in the top half of each screen.

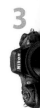

Note: You can start the timer immediately by selecting the Start selection from the menu. However, we will save that step for last because we have configured nothing for the Interval timer. Therefore, we will skip Start at the top of the Interval timer shooting menu (figure 3.24A, screen 2) and begin by setting up Start options (figure 3.24A, screen 3).

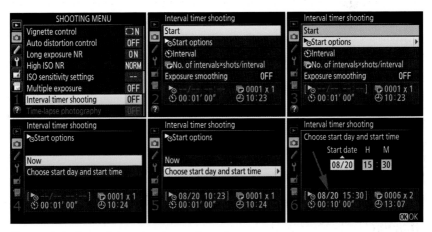

Figure 3.24A – Interval timer shooting configuration

Use the following steps to configure an Interval timer shooting session:

1. Select Interval timer shooting from the Shooting Menu and scroll to the right (figure 3.24A, screen 1).
2. Skip over the Start selection for now because we have not configured any of the Interval timer settings yet (figure 3.24A, screen 2). Later, after you have configured the Interval timer, you can simply come back and select Start to begin the timer. The camera will remember the settings from your last configuration of the Interval timer and you can use them again by selecting Start and pressing the OK button (or the Multi selector center button).
3. Choose Start options and scroll to the right (figure 3.24A, screen 3).

4. The Start options screen will display two choices, Now and Choose start day and start time (figure 3.24A, screen 4). Choose Now if you want to start the timer three seconds after you select Start and press the OK button. If you would rather select a specific date and time to start the timer, simply select Choose start day and start time from the Start options menu and scroll to the right (figure 3.24A, screen 5).

5. The Choose start day and start time screen will now appear (figure 3.24A, screen 6). The Start date is always presented in the Month/Day (MM/DD) format, while the time is presented in a 24-hour (international time) format. If you are not using the Now selection from the previous step, move to the Start date field and enter the month and day, such as:

08/20

Please notice that the Start date (08/20) is highlighted in yellow in the informational section that appears on the lower third of screen 6 (red arrow). As you set the Interval timer functions, you will see each of them appear in this informational area. After the timer is fully configured you can use this section to quickly see whether you want to use current settings or modify them in a future session.

Next, scroll over to the H field and enter an hour in international time format (e.g., 15 = 3 PM). Enter the time at which you want the intervals to begin. The selectable hour (H) range is from 00 (midnight) to 23 (11 PM). After you have entered an hour setting, enter a minute setting. The selectable minute (M) range is from 00 to 59. If you wanted to start at 3:30 PM, you would insert the following:

15:30

Once you've entered the time, press the OK button to lock it in. Check the informational section below, which will show the entry. My camera reflects 08/20 15:30, or August 20th at 3:30 PM in figure 3.24A, screen 6.

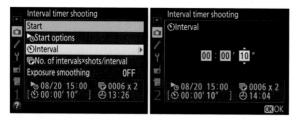

Figure 3.24B – Choosing an Interval

6. The camera will now return to the Interval timer shooting menu. Choose the Interval setting on the Interval timer shooting screen and scroll to the right (figure 3.24B, screen 1).

7. You will now see the Interval selection fields with selections representing Hours : Minutes' Seconds" in the following format (figure 3.24B, screen 2):

00 : 00′ 00″

The first two zeros represent the hours, the second set represents minutes, and the third set seconds. Since we want to start out with an Interval of 10 seconds, let's set the screen to look like this:

00 : 00′ 10″

Once you've entered the time, press the OK button to lock it in.

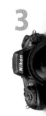

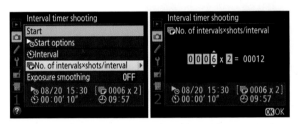

Figure 3.24C – Choosing the number of intervals and number of shots per interval

8. Now we'll choose the number of intervals and shots per interval by selecting No. of intervals×shots/interval and scrolling to the right (figure 3.24C, screen 1).
9. You will be presented with a screen where you can select the number of intervals (No. of intervals) times the number of shots per interval (shots/interval), as seen in figure 3.24C, screen 2. Number of intervals × number of shots = total shots. These values are gathered in this format:

0000 x 0 = 0000

You can set the number of intervals (0000) anywhere between 0001 and 9999. You can set the number of shots taken per interval anywhere between 1 and 9. If, for example, you want to shoot six intervals, and take two pictures during each interval, set your camera so that it looks like this (figure 3.24C, screen 2):

0006 x 2 = 00012

This means that there will be six intervals (0006) of 10 seconds each (set in step 7) and that the camera will take two pictures for each interval (x 2), for a total of 12 pictures (00012). In other words, 2 pictures will be taken every 10 seconds over a period of 60 seconds, for a total of 12 images at the end of the series (0006 intervals x 10 seconds each = 60 seconds). The maximum number of images that can be taken in one Interval timer session is 89991.

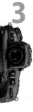

10. Next, you may select Exposure smoothing (figure 3.24D, screen 1), which allows the camera to adjust the exposure of an image so that it matches the exposure of the previous image, when using P, S, and A modes under the Mode button. If you use M mode, you must have *Shooting Menu > ISO sensitivity settings > Auto ISO sensitivity control* set to On, or Exposure smoothing will not work. Choose Exposure smoothing from the Interval timer shooting screen and scroll to the right (figure 3.24D, screen 1).

11. Select On or Off for Exposure smoothing and press the OK button to finish the configuration of the Interval timer shooting system (figure 3.24D, screen 2).

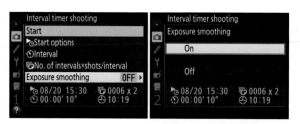

Figure 3.24D – Choosing an Exposure smoothing setting

12. You are now ready to Start the Interval timer using the settings displayed in the informational section on the lower third of the Interval timer shooting screen (figure 3.24E). When you select Start, as shown in figure 3.24E, screen 1, and press the OK button, a *Timer Active* message will briefly appear on your camera's Monitor (figure 3.24E, screen 2). If you look at the top Control panel, you will see the abbreviated word INTVL flashing. INTVL will continue to flash as long as the Interval timer is in operation.

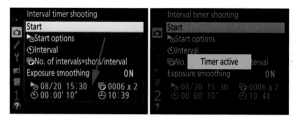

Figure 3.24E – Starting the Interval timer shooting session.

Pause, Cancel, or Restart an Interval Timer Shooting Session

You may need to pause or cancel the Interval timer while it is counting down to the start time you set in Shooting options, or when the timer is already active and taking pictures. The Interval timer will continue to function and count down even if you have switched the camera off. Therefore, once you have activated the timer you will need to use the screens shown in figure 3.24F to pause or cancel it. Let's see how to do it.

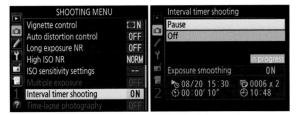

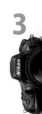

Figure 3.24F – Pausing or canceling an Interval timer shooting session

Use these steps to pause or cancel an Interval timer shooting session:

1. Select Interval timer shooting from the Shooting Menu and scroll to the right (figure 3.24F, screen 1).
2. Choose Pause to temporarily stop the timer, or Off to cancel the session (figure 3.24F, screen 2).
3. Press the OK button to lock in your choice.

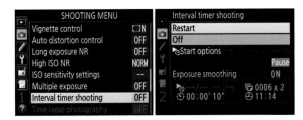

Figure 3.24G – Restarting or canceling an Interval timer shooting session

If you have previously paused the Interval timer and would like to restart or cancel it, use the following steps:

1. Select Interval timer shooting from the Shooting Menu and scroll to the right (figure 3.24G, screen 1).
2. Select Restart, which allows you to continue your Interval timer session, or Off, which lets you cancel the session.
3. Press the OK button to lock in your choice.

Note: If the memory card fills up during a shooting session and has no more room for images, the timer will remain active but the camera will stop taking pictures. You can resume shooting after you have either deleted some pictures or inserted another memory card.

Interval timer shooting will pause if you select the Self-timer position on the Release mode dial. You must turn the dial away from the Self-timer mode position before you can restart the timer.

During pauses, you can replace batteries and memory cards without ending the Interval timer session. To restart the session and continue where it left off, you must use the Shooting Menu screens shown in figure 3.24G.

Please remember that pausing the session does not affect Interval timer settings. If for any reason the camera cannot continue Interval timer photography, it will display a warning on the Monitor.

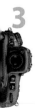

Skipping Intervals: The camera will skip an interval if any of the following occurs for longer than eight seconds:

- Any photographs from the previous session are not yet taken
- The memory card is full
- Single-servo AF is active and the camera is unable to focus (the camera refocuses before each shot)

The camera will then try again at the next interval.

Shooting Menu Banks: Changes to Interval timer shooting apply to all four of the Shooting menu banks (A to D). Therefore, changing to a different Shooting menu bank during a session does not interrupt the Interval timer. However, resetting a Shooting menu bank will cancel the Interval timer and reset the timer to factory default settings.

Bracketing Info: Be sure to adjust any bracketing for the exposure, flash, or Active D-Lighting (ADL) before you start Interval timer shooting. Bracketing overrides the number of shots, so you may not get what you expected if any kind of bracketing is active. Also, according to Nikon, "If White balance bracketing is active during an Interval timer session, the camera will take one shot at each interval and process it to create the number of copies specified in the bracketing program."

Settings Recommendation: Please learn to use this function! It is complicated, but if you read this section carefully and practice using Interval timer shooting as you read, you'll learn it quickly. This type of photography allows you to shoot things like flowers gradually opening or the sun moving across the sky. Have some fun with it!

Time-Lapse Photography

(User's Manual – Page 223)

Time-lapse photography is a close cousin of Interval timer shooting (previous section). The primary difference is that Time-lapse photography is designed to create a silent time-lapse movie obeying the options selected in the final section of this chapter, **Movie Settings**.

During time-lapse photography, the camera automatically takes pictures at intervals you select during setup and later assembles them into a time-lapse movie.

Let's examine how to set up a short time-lapse sequence using Time-lapse photography.

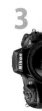

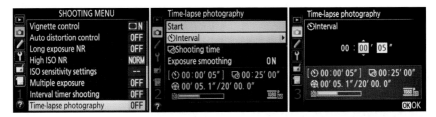

Figure 3.25A – Configuring a Time-lapse Interval

Here are the steps to set up a Time-lapse Interval, Shooting time, and Exposure smoothing:

1. Choose Time-lapse photography from the Shooting Menu and scroll to the right (figure 3.25A, screen 1).

2. We are skipping the Start selection at this time, until we have fully configured the Time-lapse settings. Select Interval from the Time-lapse photography screen and scroll to the right (figure 3.25A, screen 2).

3. Set the picture Interval in minutes and seconds. You can choose from 00:01 second to 10:00 minutes (figure 3.25A, screen 3). The hours column is not available to adjust from the Interval screen. I entered 00′ 05″ in screen 3, which means I have selected a 5 second interval. The camera will take a picture every 5 seconds during the Shooting time period set in Step 4. Press the OK button to lock in your setting and return to the Time-lapse photography screen.

4. Select Shooting time from the Time-lapse photography screen and scroll to the right (figure 3.25B, screen 1).

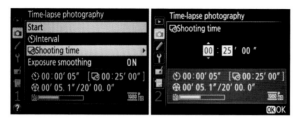

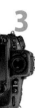

Figure 3.25B – Choosing a Shooting time

5. Choose a Shooting time over which the picture Interval will be executed (figure 3.25B, screen 2). You can choose from 1 minute (00:01) to 7 hours 59 minutes (07:59). The seconds column is not available to adjust from the Shooting time screen. I entered 25 minutes (00 : 25' 00") in screen 2, which means the camera will take a picture every 5 seconds (the Interval set in step 3) over a 25-minute period (the Shooting time). Press the OK button to lock in your setting and return to the Time-lapse photography screen.

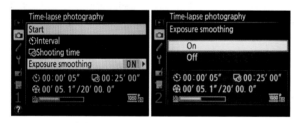

Figure 3.25C – Selecting Exposure smoothing

6. Next, you may select Exposure smoothing (figure 3.25C, screen 1), which prevents abrupt exposure changes between images, when using P, S, and A modes under the Mode button. If you use M mode, you must have *Shooting Menu > ISO sensitivity settings > Auto ISO sensitivity control* set to On, or Exposure smoothing will not work. Choose Exposure smoothing from the Time-lapse photography screen and scroll to the right (figure 3.25C, screen 1).
7. Select On or Off for Exposure smoothing and press the OK button to finish the configuration of the Time-lapse photography system (figure 3.25C, screen 2).
8. Make sure your camera is on a tripod and ready for shooting the Time-lapse sequence, and then select Start from the Time-lapse photography menu (figure 3.25D, screen 1).
9. The camera will display a screen informing you: *Starting time-lapse photography. Press OK to end before shooting is complete.* This screen will be displayed for three seconds and the camera will begin shooting your sequence. During the Time-lapse sequence the abbreviated word INTVL will flash on the upper Control panel. If you choose to end the sequence early, simply press the OK button and

the camera will stop taking pictures. Other than the fact that the camera stops taking pictures and INTVL stops flashing on the Control panel, there is nothing externally visible that lets you know the Time-lapse photography sequence has stopped when you press the OK button. Nothing happens and several seconds later nothing continues to happen!

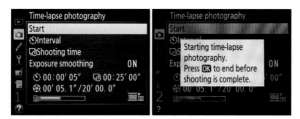
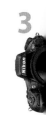

Figure 3.25D – Starting a Time-lapse photography session

Note: Before you start a time-lapse sequence, check the framing and exposure by taking a picture from the position you will use to capture the time-lapse movie. It is often best to shoot in Manual (M) exposure mode with everything preset to a particular aperture, shutter speed, and ISO sensitivity. When shooting in M mode, if you are worried about ambient light changes affecting the exposure during the time-lapse session, simply enable *Shooting Menu > ISO sensitivity settings > Auto ISO sensitivity control*. This will allow the camera to vary the ISO sensitivity within a range you can set, and will prevent inconsistencies in exposure during the sequence. Additionally, it is a good idea to choose a White balance setting other than Auto to keep the colors the same across all the images in the time-lapse movie.

If you have selected a long shooting time, you may want to consider connecting the camera to the optional Nikon EH-5b AC adapter for continuous power (you'll also need the EP-4B power connector if you do).

Time-lapse photography is not available (it's grayed out) if Shutter speed is set to Bulb, when you are in the middle of a bracket sequence, if the camera is connected via an HDMI cable to a device for movie recording, or when HDR, Multiple exposure, or Interval timer shooting is enabled.

Time-sequence length calculation: The total number of frames in the movie can be calculated by dividing the shooting time by the interval. Then you calculate the movie length by dividing the number of frames by the frame rate you've selected in *Shooting Menu > Movie settings > Frame/size/frame rate*. Remember, the Time-lapse photography system makes short movies based on the settings under *Shooting Menu > Movie settings*.

What you will see while shooting: While you're recording the time-lapse sequence, the word INTVL will flash on the Control panel. The time remaining in hours and minutes will be displayed where the shutter speed normally appears, just before each frame is recorded. No matter how you have Auto meter-off delay set, the exposure meter will not turn off during shooting. To stop the sequence outright, press the OK button or turn the camera off.

A movie is made: When the sequence is complete, the camera will automatically assemble a short, silent movie based on the frame rates you selected in *Shooting Menu > Movie settings*. You can identify the time-lapse movie by the fact that it shows a Play button on the screen with the first frame of the movie sequence.

Settings Recommendation: Instead of having to manually assemble frames from Interval time shooting into a movie, Time-lapse photography does it for us, based on normal camera movie settings. It is quite convenient for those of us who would like to experiment with or shoot interesting time-lapse sequences. Try shooting some short sequences of an event and see how easy it is!

Movie Settings

(User's Manual – Page 62)

Movie settings allow you to control how the camera records its main Movies and Time-lapse photography sequences. This set of functions allows you to adjust seven specific things about how the Movie mode works:

- **Frame size/frame rate** – Choose from seven frame size and frame rate combinations, with frame sizes of 720p or 1080p and frame rates from 24p to 60p.
- **Movie Quality** – Select High or Norm quality bit rates from 12 Mbps to 42 Mbps, according to which Frame size/frame rate is chosen.
- **Microphone sensitivity** – Change the sensitivity of the internal or external stereo microphone, or turn it off.
- **Frequency response** – Choose whether the microphone is sensitive to a normal, wide range of frequencies or limited to the vocal frequency range of human voices.
- **Wind noise reduction** – Enable or disable a low-cut filter for the built-in microphone only. This reduces the low-frequency, rumbling noise wind makes when it blows across the built-in stereo mic ports. This setting does not affect external microphones.
- **Destination** – Select which memory card (SD or CF) will receive all Movies and Time-lapse sequences you create. Also, determine how much space there is on a particular card for video recording.

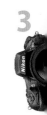

- ***Movie ISO sensitivity settings*** – Choose an ISO sensitivity for shooting in exposure mode M (Manual). You can choose from as low as ISO 64 and as high as Hi 2 (ISO 51200). The function also offers Auto ISO control (mode M), which is similar to the Auto ISO sensitivity control for still images, except it is for use in Movie mode. You can also set a maximum ISO sensitivity to prevent excessive noise in the video.

First let's examine the seven frame rates and how to select your favorite.

Frame Size/Frame Rate
The following steps allow you to select a Frame size/frame rate for your next Movie:

1. Choose Movie settings from the Shooting Menu and scroll to the right (figure 3.26A, screen 1).
2. Select Frame size/frame rate and scroll to the right (figure 3.26A, screen 2).
3. Choose a size and rate for your movie from the list of seven Frame size/frame rate choices (figure 3.26A, screen 3).
4. Press the OK button to lock in the Movie size and rate.

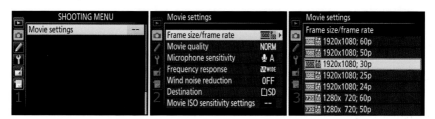

Figure 3.26A – Frame size and rate selection

Movie Quality
Now let's see about selecting High or Normal quality for the Movie. This affects the "bit rate" at which the movie is shot. Table 3.1 on the next page shows a list of Frame size/frame rates, Movie quality Bit rates, and Maximum video lengths controlled by Movie quality (Bit rate).

Use the following steps to choose a Movie quality:

1. Choose Movie settings from the Shooting Menu and scroll to the right (figure 3.26B, screen 1).
2. Select Movie quality from the menu and scroll to the right (figure 3.26B, screen 2).
3. Choose High quality or Normal (figure 3.26B, screen 3).
4. Press the OK button to lock in the Movie quality.

Frame size/ Frame rate	Bit Rate High Quality	Bit Rate Normal	Maximum Length High Quality/Normal
1920x1080; 60p	42 Mbps	24 Mbps	10 min / 20 min
1920x1080; 50p	42 Mbps	24 Mbps	10 min / 20 min
1920x1080; 30p	24 Mbps	12 Mbps	20 min / 29 min 59 sec
1920x1080; 25p	24 Mbps	12 Mbps	20 min / 29 min 59 sec
1920x1080; 24p	24 Mbps	12 Mbps	20 min / 29 min 59 sec
1280x720; 60p	24 Mbps	12 Mbps	20 min / 29 min 59 sec
1280x720; 50p	24 Mbps	12 Mbps	20 min / 29 min 59 sec

Table 3.1 – Frame size/frame rate, Movie quality bit rates, and Maximum movie length

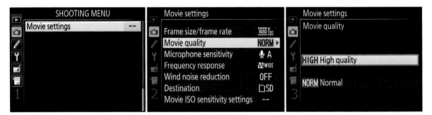

Figure 3.26B – Movie quality selection

Microphone Sensitivity

Now we'll look at choosing the most appropriate Microphone sensitivity setting for your built-in stereo mic, external accessory shoe mic (such as the Nikon ME-1 stereo mic), or external boom-mounted mic.

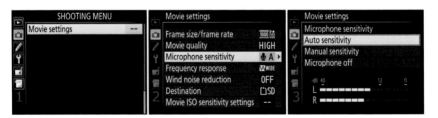

Figure 3.26C – Choosing a Microphone sensitivity setting

The following steps allow you to select a Microphone sensitivity setting for your next Movie:

1. Choose Movie settings from the Shooting Menu and scroll to the right (figure 3.26C, screen 1).

2. Select Microphone sensitivity from the menu and scroll to the right (figure 3.26C, screen 2).
3. Choose Auto sensitivity, Manual sensitivity, or Microphone Off (figure 3.26C, screen 3). These settings are live, so you can test them immediately.
4. Press the OK button to lock in the Microphone sensitivity setting.

If you decide to use Manual sensitivity, you will need to use an extra screen that lets you choose a sound level manually, as seen in figure 3.26D.

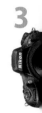

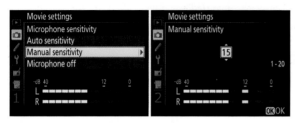

Figure 3.26D – Choosing a Microphone sensitivity setting manually

Use these steps to choose a sound level manually (figure 3.26D). See figure 3.26C to follow the flow to this screen series, which begins where figure 3.26C leaves off:

1. Choose Manual sensitivity from the menu and scroll to the right (figure 3.26D, screen 1).
2. Select a level for the microphone from the box by scrolling up or down with the Multi selector. You can choose from level 1 to level 20. The microphone is set to level 15 currently, the factory default (figure 3.26D, screen 2). These settings are live, so you will be able to test them immediately.
3. Press the OK button to lock in your choice.

Microphone Off: As displayed in figure 3.26D, screen 1, you can also choose to disable the microphone completely and record a silent movie by selecting the Microphone off setting. Use this setting if you are using a clapperboard for synchronization and an external sound-recording device. This will separate sound recording from the camera body or attached mic, removing the little squeaks, clicks, and whines that all cameras make while autofocusing, zooming, and changing apertures.

Frequency Response

Sound is a very important part of video recording. Maybe you want to record a video in the wilds of the jungle and would like to pick up the sound of every bird song, leaf rustle, and buzzing insect. On the other hand, you could be recording a video of a famous lecturer and would rather not pick up the sounds of people walking by, a bird singing outside the window, and road traffic outside.

The Nikon D810 gives you better control of sound quality than any other Nikon before it. With a combination of the Microphone sensitivity and Frequency response functions you can capture some very high-quality sound. Microphone sensitivity affects how sensitive the microphone is, and Frequency response affects which sound frequencies the mic is most sensitive to. We've already considered Microphone sensitivity, so now let's see how Frequency response works.

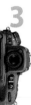
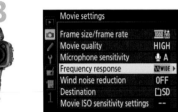
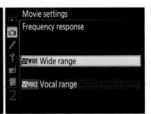

Figure 3.26E – Choosing a microphone frequency response setting

Use the following steps to choose a Frequency response setting for your camera's microphone. This screen series picks up where figure 3.26C leaves off.

1. Select Frequency response from the Movie settings menu and scroll to the right (figure 3.26E, screen 1).
2. Choose a Frequency response setting (figure 3.26E, screen 2). Select Wide range for those times when you want to record every sound near your camera. This setting is best for nature, travel, and general family videos. Choose Vocal range when you are videoing a person or group of people talking. This setting helps eliminate spurious background noises.
3. Press the OK button to lock in your choice.

Wind Noise Reduction

Have you ever recorded a video on a beautiful, breezy spring day, only to later find that you have recorded that distinctive rumbling sound of wind blowing across a microphone instead of the clear sound you desired?

While that sound may not be completely eliminated without using special microphones designed to deal with it, it can be significantly reduced with a low-cut filter, which removes or cuts low frequency noises like wind rumbles.

Fortunately for D810 users, Nikon has included a low-cut filter setting for when you are recording video. If you turn this filter on, you can remove a good portion of that aggravating wind noise when recording outside. However, if you are recording an orchestra, with deep cello and bass parts, a low-cut filter may take away some of the depth in the recording, so maybe it shouldn't be left on all the time. Let's see how to enable and disable the Wind noise reduction low-cut filter.

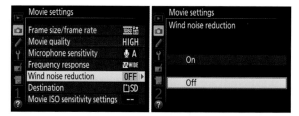

Figure 3.26F – Using the Wind noise reduction low-cut filter

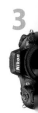

Use the following steps to choose a Wind noise reduction setting for your camera's microphone. This screen series picks up where figure 3.26C leaves off.

1. Select Wind noise reduction from the Movie settings menu and scroll to the right (figure 3.26F, screen 1).
2. Choose On to enable the filter, or Off to disable it (figure 3.26E, screen 2).
3. Press the OK button to lock in your choice.

Settings Recommendation: I use this wind noise filter selectively. Most of the time I am using an external Nikon ME-1 hotshoe microphone, which has a foam screen around the mic to reduce or eliminate any wind noise. I do use Wind noise reduction when I am outside using the built-in stereo mic to record family events, such as a cookout in Great Smoky Mountains National Park.

Destination
Destination lets you choose which memory card will receive and store your camera's video recordings. Just below the card slot selections you will see something like this: 05h 15m 20s (figure 3.26G, screen 2). This is the total recording time a particular card will hold. If you're serious about shooting video with your camera, you'd better buy some high-capacity cards—you'll need them!

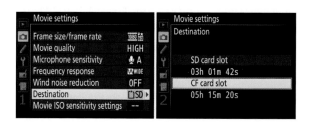

Figure 3.26G – Movie settings – Destination

Here are the steps to select a Destination for your Movies. This screen series picks up where figure 3.26C leaves off.

1. Select Destination from the Movie settings menu and scroll to the right (figure 3.26G, screen 1).
2. Select one of the two cards slots: SD card slot or CF card slot. Your movies will automatically flow to the card slot you have chosen (figure 3.26G, screen 2). My camera has a 64 GB SanDisk Extreme card in both the SD and CF slots. Obviously, there are more pictures and videos already on the SD card because it only has about 3 hours, 1 minute, and 42 seconds of video recording time left (03h 01m 42s). However, the CF card has 5 hours, 15 minutes, and 20 seconds of recording time left (05h 15m 20s). Therefore, for my next video session, I have selected the CF card slot as the Destination for the video file.
3. Press the OK button to use the selected card slot for Movies.

Note: The actual frame rate for 30 fps is 29.97 fps. For 24 fps it's 23.976, and for 60 fps it's 59.94 fps. It is important for you to know this because if you try to interface with some devices using anything but the exact frame rate, the device will not record the video.

The maximum length for any High-quality movie when recording to a memory card is 10 or 20 minutes (see table 3.1). For Normal quality movies, at lower bit rates, the maximum recording length increases to 29 minutes, 59 seconds.

Using HDMI output, you can send an endless stream of uncompressed, clean, broadcast-quality video, with no time limits, to an external recording device such as an Atomos Ninja Star, Ninja 2, or Ninja Blade. I use both a Ninja-2 and a Ninja Blade, and I am looking really hard at the low-cost Ninja Star, which is very small and light and records to an inexpensive Compact Flash (CF) card.

Check out the Atomos external HDMI recorders at **www.Atomos.com**. I highly recommend them! All you need is an Atomos recorder and an HDMI cable to take full advantage of the D810's superior uncompressed video capability.

We will discuss Movies more deeply in the chapter called Movie Live View.

Settings Recommendation: When I shoot a video, I normally select 1920×1080 at 30 fps because I like the superior quality. You have many choices of broadcast-quality video available to you. If you want to save some card space, you may want to drop Frame size/frame rate down to 1920×1080 at 24 fps, the cinematic rate that matches the rate at which most big-screen movies are created.

If you want to shoot slow motion, you can do so by using the camera's new 1080p 60 fps setting and then playing the movie back at a normal speed.

To record in-camera, compressed video (H.264 MPEG-4) successfully, I suggest that you acquire at least some 32 GB cards, and even better, some 64 GB or 128 GB cards. Video uses a lot of storage space!

To make the best video you can possibly make, try one of the Atomos external recorders mentioned in the previous note. You won't believe how excellent the Nikon D810's video output is when shot uncompressed (4:2:2 broadcast quality) through the camera's built-in HDMI port.

Movie ISO Sensitivity Settings

Earlier in this chapter we discussed the ISO sensitivity settings for still images. This included the Auto ISO sensitivity control, which lets the camera adjust ISO on the fly, so you can capture images without worry of under- or overexposure.

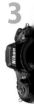

The D810 has a new feature for those who would like to use Manual (M) mode under the Mode button when recording movies. A problem with recording in M mode is that sometimes the light will change faster than a person can smoothly open or close the aperture. Therefore, Nikon added this new feature to allow M mode to be used—with all the manual manipulation of the camera controls that allows—and still prevent exposure issues when the light changes rapidly.

For instance, if you are shooting a video of a person on a bright sunny day walking toward a building, and you follow the person into the building, you will have a massive and immediate drop in ambient light. A situation like this could lead to an underexposure then overexposure oscillation while the videographer scrambles to open the aperture to exactly the right setting, leaving the videographer with amateurish results.

The Nikon D810 overcomes this by allowing the camera to automatically adjust the ISO to compensate for changes in brightness, even when shooting in M mode. This allows the videographer more time to make aperture adjustments for low-noise quality while the video is still being recorded.

There are three settings under the Movie ISO sensitivity settings function:

- *ISO sensitivity (mode M)* – Manually set the ISO sensitivity for when you are using Manual (M) mode video recording only. This separates the ISO sensitivity of the video subsystem from the ISO sensitivity of the still image subsystem. Again, this applies only to M mode video recording. The ISO range from which you can select goes from ISO 64 to ISO 51200 (Hi 2).
- *Auto ISO control (mode M)* – If you set this value to On, the camera will make adjustments to ISO to help control accurate exposure, giving you time to open the aperture to increase the light coming into the camera (or stop down if needed). This will prevent a high ISO value from remaining in effect after a big light change, thereby reducing noise in the video. The camera lets you control depth of field with the aperture and maintains a good exposure in the process. Automatic manual, what a concept!

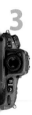

• ***Maximum sensitivity*** – This setting controls the maximum ISO sensitivity the camera will use when there is not enough light for your video. *This setting is not limited to just Manual mode!* It is used when shooting a video in any of the exposure modes, including P, S, A, and M. However, it limits M mode only when Auto ISO control (mode M) is active. If Auto ISO control (mode M) is set to Off, you are responsible for controlling ISO yourself.

Let's examine how to adjust the Movie ISO sensitivity settings.

ISO Sensitivity (mode M)

Use the following steps to choose an ISO value for Manual (M) mode video recording only:

1. Choose Movie settings from the Shooting Menu and scroll to the right (figure 3.27A, screen 1).
2. Select Movie ISO sensitivity settings from the Movie settings menu and scroll to the right (figure 3.27A, screen 2).
3. Highlight ISO sensitivity (mode M) and scroll to the right (figure 3.27A, screen 3).
4. Choose an ISO sensitivity (mode M) value (which will not vary during the video) from the menu (figure 3.27A, screen 4). You can choose from a range of values, from ISO 64 to ISO 51200 (Hi 2). When you use ISO sensitivity (mode M) with Auto ISO control (mode M) set to Off, you will have to watch your exposure carefully when you are using Manual (M) mode under the Mode button. The camera will not adjust ISO for you.
5. Press the OK button to lock in your ISO choice.

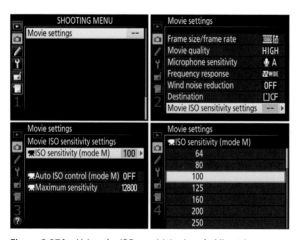

Figure 3.27A – Using the ISO sensitivity (mode M) setting

Auto ISO Control (mode M)

Use the following steps to allow the *camera* to choose an ISO value for Manual (M) mode video recording only:

1. Choose Movie settings from the Shooting Menu and scroll to the right (figure 3.27B, screen 1).
2. Select Movie ISO sensitivity settings from the Movie settings menu and scroll to the right (figure 3.27B, screen 2).
3. Highlight Auto ISO control (mode M) and scroll to the right (figure 3.27B, screen 3).
4. Select either On or Off from the menu (figure 3.27B, screen 4). Normally when using Manual (M) mode you are responsible for controlling the ISO sensitivity value with the settings in the previous subsection, ISO sensitivity (mode M). Choosing On causes the *camera* to take control of the ISO sensitivity and allows it to adjust the ISO from ISO 64 up to the amount you set in Maximum sensitivity (next subsection). When set to the other exposure modes (P, S, and A), the camera controls the ISO all the time anyway. Selecting Off causes the camera to use the normal ISO sensitivity (mode M) value that you have set, and the ISO does not vary unless you change it.
5. Press the OK button to lock in your choice.

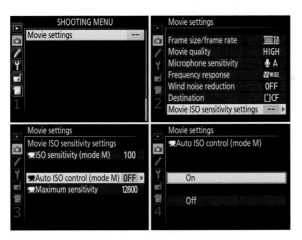

Figure 3.27B – Using the Auto ISO control (mode M)

Maximum Sensitivity

Use the following steps to select a maximum ISO sensitivity value for all video recording exposure modes that have an automatic feature, which includes P, S, A, and even M when Auto ISO control (mode M) is active:

1. Choose Movie settings from the Shooting Menu and scroll to the right (figure 3.27C, screen 1).
2. Select Movie ISO sensitivity settings from the Movie settings menu and scroll to the right (figure 3.27C, screen 2).
3. Highlight Maximum sensitivity and scroll to the right (figure 3.27C, screen 3). You will notice that the factory default value for Maximum sensitivity is ISO 12800, a value that I consider a bit high for maximum video quality. Therefore, I suggest you lower it somewhat.
4. Choose an ISO sensitivity value that will be the maximum value the camera can select when it is controlling the ISO. The range for selection is from ISO 200 to ISO 51200 (Hi 2).

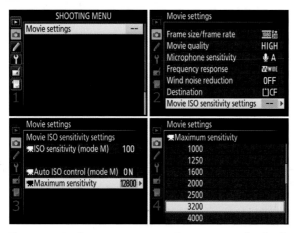

Figure 3.27C – Choosing a maximum ISO sensitivity value for all video recording modes

Settings Recommendation: I normally leave this setting at about ISO 3200, unless there is truly a need for the higher ISO values and the accompanying noise. You will need to experiment in a low-light area to see where your tolerance for high ISO noise stops.

Author's Conclusions

Congratulations! You have fully configured one of the camera's four Shooting menu banks. Now set up the rest of the banks according to your own ideas on how you want them to behave.

Using the four available Shooting menu banks allows you a great deal of flexibility in how your camera operates. You can switch between four different camera types, in a sense.

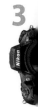

The upcoming information on the Custom setting banks will round out the major configuration of your camera for daily shooting. There are no direct connections between the four Shooting menu banks and the four Custom setting banks. You could create your own connection by naming them similarly. However, the combinations of how you configure this camera, and combine the banks, are virtually endless.

Custom Setting Menu

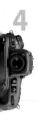

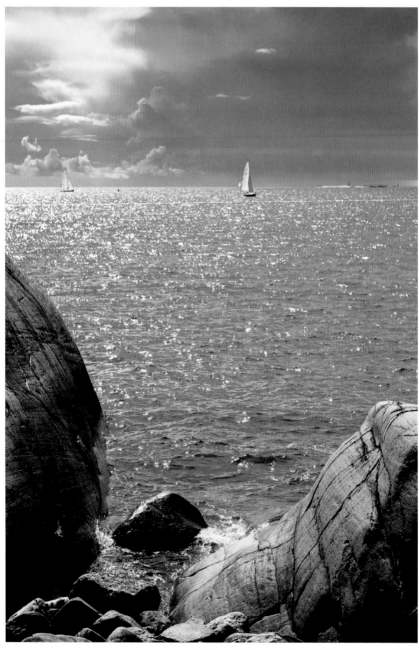

Sailboats by Suomenlinna © Matti Remonen (*MRe*)

In chapter 3 we carefully considered the configurability of the Nikon D810 and its Shooting menu banks. Now we will continue with this process by examining the Custom settings banks in complete detail.

Let me start by clearly stating that the Shooting menu banks and Custom settings banks are separate entities, with different types of functions. I mentioned this in the preceding chapter but wanted to emphasize it here, too. There is no connection between them, although you could create an artificial connection by labeling the banks in a similar manner. However, it's only a label.

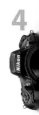

I count no less than 65 Custom Settings in the D810. We've got a lot of ground to cover, and we will, in great detail. When finished with this chapter, you'll have a much deeper knowledge of this camera's inner workings and capabilities.

Without further ado, let's dive right into the settings and see what they do. First, we'll consider the process of renaming Custom settings bank A so that we'll know what style of shooting this bank is configured to support.

In the preceding chapter, we discussed how to rename a Shooting menu bank to describe its functionality. The process for changing the name of a Custom settings bank is exactly the same. If you're familiar with the process, you can just name your bank and skip this first section.

Here are the steps to rename Custom settings bank A:

1. Notice that in the first screen of figure 4.1A, Custom settings bank has an A after it. This means that your camera is using bank A. If any letter other than A is showing, you are in a different Custom settings bank. Select Custom settings bank from the Custom Setting Menu and scroll to the right (figure 4.1A, screen 1).
2. Assuming that you have not yet renamed any of your Custom settings banks, you'll see the four blank default banks called A, B, C, and D, and a selection called Rename (figure 4.1A, screen 2). Set the bank to A, and scroll to the right.
3. Your screen will now look like the third screen in figure 4.1A. This is the bank rename screen. You'll see a series of characters on top, with a line of dashes below. The dashes are where we will put our text to rename the bank. Just after the small letter z there is a blank spot that represents a blank character for insertion in the line of text. Use the Multi selector to scroll through the numbers and letters to find the characters you want to use. Press the Multi selector center button to select a character. Keep selecting new characters until you have the entire bank name in place. If you make a mistake, hold down the Thumbnail/Playback zoom out button while using the Multi selector to move to the position of the error. Press the garbage can Delete button on the back of the camera to remove the bad character. For this example, I have named the bank General Purpose.
4. Press the OK button to save the new name.

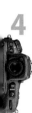

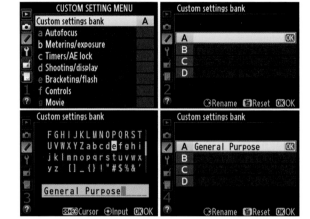

Figure 4.1A – Naming Custom settings bank A

Using the Quick Menu to Access the Custom settings banks

If you would prefer to use a shortcut method for getting to the Custom settings banks, you can use the *i* button and Quick Menu screen.

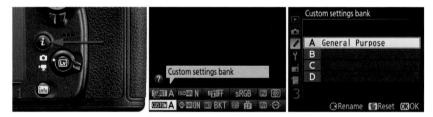

Figure 4.1B – Accessing Custom settings banks with the *i* button and Quick Menu screen

Use these steps to quickly access the Custom settings banks:

1. Press the *i* button once to bring up the Quick Menu (figure 4.1B, screen 1).
2. Use the Multi selector to move to the Custom settings bank position, as shown in figure 4.1B, screen 2.
3. Press the OK button to open the Custom settings bank menu, which will show the main bank label screen (figure 4.1B, screen 3).
4. Press the OK button to select a particular Custom settings bank or scroll to the right to enter the Rename screen. Follow the instructions connected with figure 4.1A, step 3, to rename a Custom settings bank.

Excellent! You've labeled bank A with a more meaningful name so you can quickly recognize this customizable bank of functions. I named bank A General Purpose on my camera to match the Shooting menu bank by the same name. Once again, this is completely optional.

Section One – a Autofocus

Custom Settings a1 to a8

You'll find 12 distinct settings within the *a Autofocus* menu in the D810.

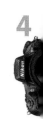

- **a1** – AF-C priority selection
- **a2** – AF-S priority selection
- **a3** – Focus tracking with lock-on
- **a4** – AF activation
- **a5** – Focus point illumination
- **a6** – AF point illumination
- **a7** – Focus point wrap-around
- **a8** – Number of focus points
- **a9** – Store by orientation
- **a10** – Built-in AF assist illuminator
- **a11** – Limit AF-area mode selection
- **a12** – Autofocus mode restrictions

Custom Settings a1–a12 allow you to configure the autofocus system in various ways. The whole process is rather complex—yet important for good photography.

I felt that autofocus and the related functions were important enough to include an entire chapter dedicated to Autofocus (AF), AF-area modes, and Release modes in this book. It covers autofocus and its supporting functions in much deeper detail. Please be sure to read that chapter well.

Custom Setting a1 – AF-C Priority Selection

(User's Manual – Page 306)

AF-C priority selection is designed to let you choose how your autofocus works when using Continuous-servo autofocus mode (AF-C).

Make sure you understand how this function works. If you configure this setting incorrectly for your style of shooting, it's entirely possible that a number of your pictures will be out of focus. Why?

Well, if you'll notice in figure 4.2, screen 3, there are three specific selections:

- ***Release*** – If the image must be taken, no matter what, you will need to set AF-C priority selection to Release. This allows the shutter to fire every time you press the Shutter-release button, even if the image is not in focus. Releasing the shutter has "priority" over autofocus. If you are well aware of the consequences of shooting without a focus guarantee, then use this setting to make your camera take a picture every time you press the Shutter-release button. Your camera will shoot at its maximum frames per second (FPS) rate because it is not hampered by the time it takes to validate that each picture is in correct focus. You'll need

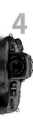

to decide whether taking the image is more important than the image being in focus. We'll discuss why the Release and Release + focus functions exist in an upcoming section titled **Using Custom Settings a1 and a2**.

- *Release + focus* – This function slows the frame rate for improved focus when the light is low or when there is little contrast between the subject and its surroundings, but it still allows the shutter to fire even if it cannot find a good focus point. Release still has priority over focus, but the camera tries to focus before releasing the shutter.

- *Focus* – This setting is designed to prevent your camera from taking a picture when the Viewfinder's green in-focus indicator is off. In other words, if the picture is not in focus, the shutter will not release. It does not mean that the camera will always focus on the correct subject. It simply means that your camera must focus on something before it will allow the shutter to release. Nikon cameras do a very good job with autofocus, so you can usually depend on the AF module to perform well. The Focus setting will drastically increase the chances that your image is in correct focus.

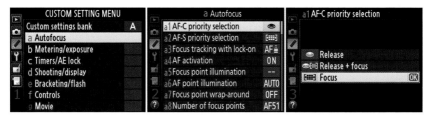

Figure 4.2 – Choosing a shutter-release priority for AF-C mode

Here are the steps to select a shutter-release priority when using AF-C mode:

1. Select a Autofocus from the Custom Setting Menu and scroll to the right (figure 4.2, screen 1).
2. Highlight a1 AF-C priority selection and scroll to the right (figure 4.2, screen 2).
3. Choose one of the three settings from the menu, with full understanding of what may happen if you don't choose Focus. If you have the experience to use depth of field to cover autofocus, in case of slight focusing errors, or if you use the AF-ON button instead of the Shutter-release button for initiating autofocus, you may do well with AF-C priority selection set to Release or Release + focus. Test this carefully.
4. Press the OK button to select your shutter-release priority.

Settings Recommendation: Since I'm not a sports or action shooter, I choose Focus. Even if I were an action shooter, I would choose Focus. Read the section called Using Custom Settings a1 and a2 before you make your final choice. The safe choice is Focus.

However, if you are an action shooter and have enough experience to deal with a camera that will fire the shutter when you press the Shutter-release button, regardless of whether the image is in focus, the Release or Release + focus settings may work better for you.

Custom Setting a2 – AF-S Priority Selection

(User's Manual – Page 307)

AF-S priority selection is very similar to AF-C priority selection. It too allows you to choose whether the camera will take a picture without something in focus. With this function, you set a shutter-release priority for Single-servo autofocus mode (AF-S). Set it wrong and many of your pictures may be out of focus. I choose Focus when using AF-S.

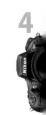

There are two modes to choose from (figure 4.3, screen 3):

- *Release* – A photo can be taken at any time, even if there is nothing in focus. This can lead to images that are out of focus, unless you manually focus each time you take a picture. The camera's priority is releasing the shutter when you press the Shutter-release button.

- *Focus* (default) – The image must be in focus or the shutter will not release. This means that the shutter won't release unless the Viewfinder's green in-focus indicator is on. This is the closest thing to a guarantee that your image will be in focus when you press the Shutter-release button. However, if you are focused on the wrong part of your subject, the camera will still fire.

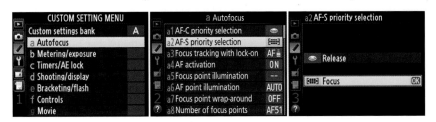

Figure 4.3 – Choosing a shutter-release priority for AF-S mode

Here are the steps to select a shutter-release priority when using AF-S mode:

1. Select a Autofocus from the Custom Setting Menu and scroll to the right (figure 4.3, screen 1).
2. Highlight a2 AF-S priority selection and scroll to the right (figure 4.3, screen 2).
3. Choose one of the two settings from the menu, with full understanding of what may occur if you don't choose Focus (figure 4.3, screen 3).
4. Press the OK button to select your shutter-release priority.

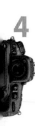

Settings Recommendation: Once again, I choose Focus. I love pictures that are in focus, don't you? When I don't want the camera to care about autofocus over shutter release, I'll just flip the switch to manual on the camera or lens and focus where I want. Up next is the section called **Using Custom Settings a1 and a2**. Read it well!

Using Custom Settings a1 and a2

Before we proceed to the next Custom Setting, please consider the following special information.

Release priority vs. Focus priority – Two of the more important functions in this Custom Settings chapter are a1 and a2. I added this special section so you'll understand why you must pay very close attention to these two settings.

Focus priority simply means that your camera will refuse to take a picture until it can reasonably focus on something. Release priority means that the camera will take a picture when you decide to take it, whether anything is in focus or not!

Now, you might ask yourself, "Why is there such a setting as Release priority?" Well, many professional photographers shoot high-speed events at high frame rates—taking hundreds of images—and use depth of field (or experience and luck) to compensate for less-than-accurate focus. They are in complete control of their camera's systems and have a huge amount of practice in getting the focus right where they want it to be.

There are valid reasons for these photographers to not use Focus priority. However, most of those same photographers do not let pressing the Shutter-release button halfway down start autofocus either because the focus could change every time the Shutter-release button is pressed. They set a4 AF activation so that the autofocus doesn't even activate until the AF-ON button is pressed. They then use the AF-ON button exclusively for autofocus and the Shutter-release button to take the picture. They separate the two functions instead of using the Shutter-release button for both.

You need to ask yourself, "What type of a photographer am I?" If you are a pro shooting hundreds of pictures of fast race cars, Focus priority may not be for you. However, for the average photographer taking pictures of his kids running around the yard, deer jumping a fence, beautiful landscapes, flying birds, or portraits, Focus priority is usually the best choice. For most of us, it's better to have the camera refuse to take the picture unless it's able to focus on our subjects.

When you're shooting at a high frame rate, Focus priority may cause your camera to skip a series of out-of-focus images. It will slow your camera's frame rate so that it will not reach the maximum five frames per second in some cases. But, I have to ask, what is the point of several out-of-focus images mixed with the in-focus pictures?

Why waste the card space, add shutter wear, and then have to weed through the slightly out-of-focus images? Especially with the image sizes the D810 creates!

Pay special attention to these two settings. You will need to decide—based on your style of shooting—whether you want your camera to refuse to take an out-of-focus image. If you set a1 and a2 to Focus priority and you try to take an out-of-focus image, the Shutter-release button will simply not release the shutter. The green in-focus indicator in the Viewfinder will have to be on before the shutter will release.

Settings Recommendation: I set both a1 and a2 to Focus priority. I'm not a high-speed shooter, so I don't need my camera to take a picture "no matter what." What good are out-of-focus images? We'll discuss this even more in the chapter titled Autofocus, AF-Area, and Release Modes.

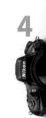

Custom Setting a3 – Focus Tracking with Lock-On

(User's Manual – Page 308)

Focus tracking with lock-on allows you to select the length of time your camera will ignore an intruding object that blocks your subject.

In other words, let's say you are focused on a bird flying past you. As you pan the camera with the bird's movement, the autofocus system tracks it and keeps it in good focus. A road sign briefly interrupts the focus tracking as the bird moves behind it and then reemerges. How would you feel if the bright, high-contrast road sign grabbed the camera's attention and you lost tracking on the bird? That would be quite aggravating, wouldn't it?

The D810 provides Focus tracking with lock-on to prevent this from happening. The "lock-on" portion of this function helps your camera keep its focus on your subject, even if something briefly comes between the camera and subject. The camera locks on to your subject doggedly if this function is enabled.

Without Focus tracking with lock-on, any bright object that gets between you and your subject may draw the camera's attention and cause you to lose focus on the subject.

The camera provides a variable time-out period for the lock-on functionality. Lock-on time-out allows an object that stays between the camera and your subject for a predetermined length of time to attract the camera's attention. You can adjust this time-out according to the delay time period that works best for you. Plan to experiment a bit so that you can determine what is best for your style of shooting. The factory default is Normal, which I've determined from my own testing is about a one-second delay.

Here are the steps to configure Focus tracking with lock-on:

1. Select a Autofocus from the Custom Setting Menu and scroll to the right (figure 4.4, screen 1).
2. Highlight a3 Focus tracking with lock-on and scroll to the right (figure 4.4, screen 2).

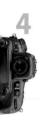

3. Choose one of the six choices from the menu. Figure 4.4, screen 3, shows 3 (Normal), the factory default of about one second. The longest period, 5 (long), seems to provide only about two seconds of delay in my experience. Time each of these for yourself and see what you think.

4. Press the OK button to select the time-out period.

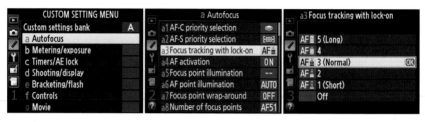

Figure 4.4 – Focus tracking with lock-on

With Single-point AF and Group-area AF, the camera will start the lock-on time-out as soon as the single AF point (Single-area) or small cluster of AF points (Group-area) is unable to detect the subject.

While using Focus tracking with lock-on with Dynamic-area AF, Auto-area AF, or 3D-tracking, I was amused at how adamant the camera was about staying with the current subject. I'd focus on a map on the wall and then cover most of the focusing points with the User's Manual. As long as I allowed at least one or two AF points to remain uncovered so the camera could see the map, the focus did not switch to the manual. I could just hear the D810 muttering, *"Hah, you can't fool me, I can still see a little edge of that map there, so I'm not changing focus!"*

Only when I stuck the D810 manual completely in front of the lens, covering all the AF points, did the camera decide to start timing the Focus tracking with lock-on time-out. After a second or two, the camera would give up on the map and focus on the manual instead.

Try this yourself! It's quite fun and will teach you something about the power of your camera's AF system.

Does Lock-On Cause Autofocus to Slow Down?

Some misunderstanding surrounds this technology. Because it is designed to cause the autofocus to hesitate for a variable time period before seeking a new subject, it may make the camera seem sluggish to some users.

But, this "sluggishness" is really a feature designed to keep you from losing your subject's tracked focus. Once the camera locks on to a subject's area of focus, it tries its best to stay with that subject even if it briefly loses the subject. This keeps the lens from racking in and out and searching for a new subject as soon as the previous subject is no longer under an AF point.

It also causes the camera to ignore other higher-contrast or closer subjects while it follows your original subject. You will have to judge the usefulness of this technology for yourself. I suggest that you go to some event or down to the lake and track moving objects with and without lock-on enabled. Your style of photography has a strong bearing on how you'll use—or whether you'll use—Focus tracking with lock-on.

Focus tracking with lock-on has little to do with how well the camera focuses. Instead, it is concerned with what it is focused on. There are some good reasons to leave Focus tracking with lock-on enabled in your camera.

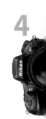

If Focus tracking with lock-on is set to Off, Dynamic-area AF, 3D-tracking, and Auto-area AF will instantly react to something coming between your subject and the camera, even if it only appears in the frame for a moment. A good example of this is when you are tracking a moving subject and just as you are about to snap the picture, a closer or brighter object enters the edge of the frame and is picked up by an outside sensor. The camera may instantly switch focus to the intruding subject. When Focus tracking with lock-on is enabled, the camera will ignore anything that briefly gets between you and your subject.

When using Dynamic-area AF, 3D-tracking, or Auto-area AF mode, I call turning off Focus tracking with lock-on "focus roulette!"

Configuring Custom setting a3 is not difficult. However, you'll need to decide just how long you want your camera to stay locked on to a subject's area before it decides that the subject is no longer available when something intrudes.

Settings Recommendation: I leave Focus tracking with lock-on enabled at all times. When I'm tracking a moving subject, I don't want my camera to be distracted by every bright object that gets in between me and the subject. In fact, the camera defaults to 3 (normal) from the factory. Nikon gives us variable focus lock time-outs so we can change how long the camera will keep seeking the old subject when we switch to a new one. I suggest you play around with this function until you fully understand how it works. Watch how long the camera stays locked on one subject's area before an intruding object grabs its attention.

This is one of those functions that people either love or hate. Personally, I find it quite useful for my type of photography. Try it and see what it does for you.

Custom Setting a4 – AF Activation

(User's Manual – Page 308)

AF activation allows you to choose whether you want the Shutter-release button to cause the camera to autofocus. If you leave this setting at the factory default, the AF system will be activated when you press the Shutter-release button halfway down or when you press the AF-ON button. You can also select the setting that allows only the AF-ON button to initiate autofocus and the Shutter-release button will not activate autofocus.

The primary purpose of this function is to allow a very experienced photographer to separate shutter release and autofocus operations. A sports photographer may only want to autofocus the camera when she presses the AF-ON button and not when she presses the Shutter-release button.

Various styles of photography require the photographer to find a good autofocus point with the AF-ON button, and then fire many frames with the Shutter-release button with no danger of the camera changing the autofocus during shutter release.

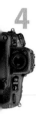

Here's a description of the two selections:

- **Shutter/AF-ON** – Autofocus will be activated if you press the Shutter-release button halfway or if you press the AF-ON button.
- **AF-ON Only** – Autofocus works only when you press the AF-ON button. The Shutter-release button will not activate autofocus; it will only start metering and release the shutter.

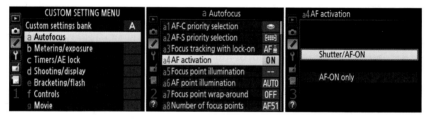

Figure 4.5 – AF activation

Here are the steps used to configure AF activation:

1. Select a Autofocus from the Custom Setting Menu and scroll to the right (figure 4.5, screen 1).
2. Highlight a4 AF activation and scroll to the right (figure 4.5, screen 2).
3. Choose one of the two choices from the menu. In figure 4.5, screen 3, Shutter/AF-ON has been selected.
4. Press the OK button to lock in the setting.

Settings Recommendation: I use Shutter/AF-ON myself because I'm primarily a nature shooter and don't need to separate autofocus from shutter release. I don't have many fast-moving subjects, other than flying birds or leaping deer. And with those, it just feels more natural to me to autofocus and fire the shutter with one button.

However, if I were shooting a high-speed event and wanted to maximize my camera's firing speed (frame rate), I wouldn't hesitate to use AF-ON only, and I would change Custom setting a1 – AF-C priority selection to Release priority. That would let me use my thumb to autofocus with the AF-ON button while my index finger is on the Shutter-release button firing bursts of images—using the Continuous high (CH) frame rate. I would autofocus only when needed and would use depth of field to cover small focus variations. That way, I could get as many pictures into my camera as possible for later publication choices.

Custom Setting a5 – Focus Point Illumination

(User's Manual – Page 309)

Focus point illumination allows you to change how the AF points appear in the Viewfinder. The AF points can be made to disappear while shooting in Manual focus mode. They can be set to appear as dots or small rectangles when not in Manual focus mode.

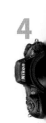

Let's examine each of the three settings to see what they do, and then we will discover how to choose your favorite setting.

Manual focus mode

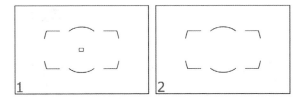

Figure 4.6A – Manual focus mode

If you choose On for this mode, the active focus point will be visible in the Viewfinder (figure 4.6A, screen 1) as a small rectangle that can be moved around among the 51 AF points by pressing the Multi selector's directional sides.

However, if you choose Off, there will be no AF points showing in the Viewfinder until you decide to move the AF point(s) with the Multi selector, which will cause the AF point to appear briefly and then disappear (figure 4.6A, screen 2).

Let's see how to choose one of these two settings.

Use the following steps to choose a Manual focus AF point type:

1. Choose a Autofocus from the Custom Setting Menu and scroll to the right (figure 4.6B, screen 1).
2. Select a5 Focus point illumination from the a Autofocus menu and scroll to the right (figure 4.6B, screen 2).
3. Choose Manual focus mode from the a5 Focus point illumination menu and scroll to the right (figure 4.6B, screen 3).
4. Referring to Figure 4.6A and the information on what On and Off does, select one of the two choices and press the OK button to lock in your choice.

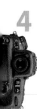

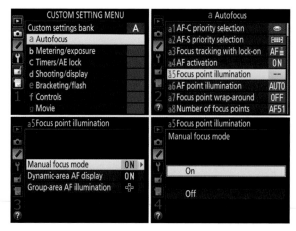

Figure 4.6B – Manual focus mode AF Focus point illumination choices

Now let's examine the next type of Focus point illumination, Dynamic-area AF.

Dynamic-Area AF Display

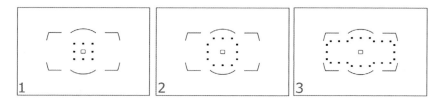

Figure 4.6C – Dynamic-area AF display

There are two choices for Dynamic-area AF display Focus point illumination:

- **On** – The camera will display a series of small dots surrounding one normal AF point (figure 4.6C). All AF points indicated by dots and all AF points inside the dots (invisible) are active. The dots show the borders of the AF points that are active. You can move the dot pattern around the Viewfinder with the Multi selector. There are three modes in Dynamic-area AF, including: 9-point (screen 1), 21-point (screen 2), and 51-point (screen 3).
- **Off** – The camera will simply display a single, moveable AF point—the large point in the center of the screens in figure 4.6C—and you will have to imagine the active points surrounding it. They are there and working but are not visible.

Note: You can change the Dynamic-area AF point pattern (9, 21, 51, and 3D) by holding in the AF-mode button and turning the front Sub-command dial. You must have the camera in AF-C (Continuous-servo AF) to use Dynamic-area AF (or 3D-tracking). Hold in the AF-mode button and turn the rear Main command dial to choose between AF-S (Single-servo AF) and AF-C. We will discuss AF-area modes and Autofocus modes in much more detail in the chapter titled **Autofocus, AF-Area, and Release Modes**.

Now let's examine how to choose a Focus point illumination setting for Dynamic-area AF.

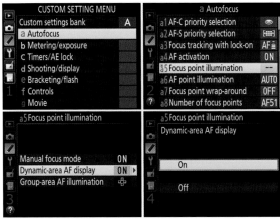
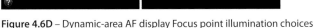
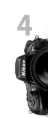

Figure 4.6D – Dynamic-area AF display Focus point illumination choices

Use the following steps to choose a Dynamic-area AF Focus point illumination setting:

1. Choose a Autofocus from the Custom Setting Menu and scroll to the right (figure 4.6D, screen 1).
2. Select a5 Focus point illumination from the a Autofocus menu and scroll to the right (figure 4.6D, screen 2).
3. Choose Dynamic-area AF display from the a5 Focus point illumination menu and scroll to the right (figure 4.6D, screen 3).
4. Referring to Figure 4.6C and the information on what On and Off does, select one of the two choices and press the OK button to lock in your choice.

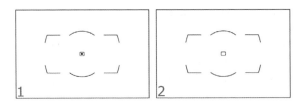

Figure 4.6E – 3D-tracking AF display

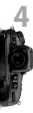

3-D Tracking: Another form of focus that is related to Dynamic-area AF is 3D-tracking. The Focus point illumination for 3D-tracking is controlled by the same steps shown for Dynamic-area AF display (see figure 4.6D and steps 1–4).

If you choose On for Dynamic-area AF display (figure 4.6D, screen 4) when using 3D-tracking, you will see a moveable AF point like the one in figure 4.6E, screen 1, which is a normal AF point with a dot inside of it. If you choose Off for Dynamic-area AF display (figure 4.6, screen 4) you will see a normal AF point, as shown in figure 4.6E, screen 2.

Group-Area AF Illumination

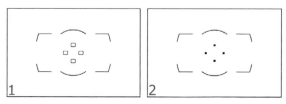

Figure 4.6F – Group-area AF illumination

There are two choices for Group-area AF Focus point illumination. You can choose normal AF point rectangles for Group-area AF, as seen in figure 4.6F, screen 1, or you can choose small dots instead, as shown in screen 2.

Let's see how to choose between the two Focus point illumination types for Group-area AF.

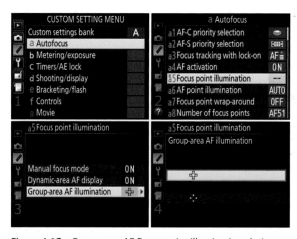

Figure 4.6G – Group-area AF Focus point illumination choices

Use the following steps to choose a Dynamic-area AF Focus point illumination type:

1. Choose a Autofocus from the Custom Setting Menu and scroll to the right (figure 4.6G, screen 1).
2. Select a5 Focus point illumination from the a Autofocus menu and scroll to the right (figure 4.6G, screen 2).
3. Choose Group-area AF illumination from the a5 Focus point illumination menu and scroll to the right (figure 4.6G, screen 3).
4. Referring to Figure 4.6F, select your favorite style (rectangles or dots) from the screen shown in figure 4.6G, screen 4, and press the OK button to lock in your choice.

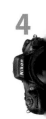

Note: Auto-area AF is not affected by the Focus point illumination settings. You will not see any AF points in the Viewfinder until you have a subject in focus, at which point you will see a varying pattern of AF points displayed briefly. The AF points are always chosen by the camera in Auto-Area AF mode.

Settings Recommendation: This Focus point illumination function is quite helpful. Normally you will not be able to detect any AF points other than the one in the center of the patterns for Dynamic-area AF and 3D-tracking, or the one AF point for Single-point AF. However, with Focus point illumination turned on, it is much easier to detect the outlines of the various AF-area modes and how much of the subject they are covering. I enabled all of the Focus point illumination settings on my D810. I left Group-area AF illumination set to the larger AF points instead of the dots.

Custom Setting a6 – AF Point Illumination

(User's Manual – Page 310)

AF point illumination helps you see the currently active AF points when you first start autofocus. You've seen the little rectangles in the Viewfinder, and dots if Focus point illumination is enabled, which represent the active AF point(s). The AF points briefly appear in red and then turn black. Sometimes the Viewfinder is dark, and it might be difficult to see a black rectangle or dot.

If AF point illumination is set to Off, the black rectangle or dot that represents your selected AF point will still be there, but you may not be able to see it. If you set AF point illumination to Auto or On, the point will flash red when you first start autofocus or when you move the AF point with the Multi selector.

There are three selections on the AF point illumination menu. These affect how the AF points are displayed when active.

Here's a list of each selection and a description of its function:

- ***Auto*** – If the Viewfinder's background is dark, the selected AF point(s) will briefly flash red when you press the Shutter-release button or AF-ON button to start autofocus. If the background is bright, you'll have no trouble seeing the black AF points, so they don't flash red when you start autofocus.

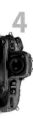

- **On** – The selected AF point is highlighted in red when you start autofocus, regardless of the light level of the background.
- **Off** – The selected AF point does not light up in red when you start autofocus. It is always black.

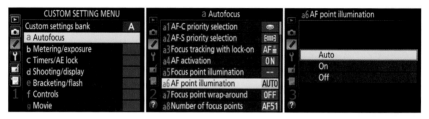

Figure 4.7 – AF point illumination

Here are the steps to configure AF point illumination:

1. Select a Autofocus from the Custom Setting Menu and scroll to the right (figure 4.7, screen 1).
2. Highlight a6 AF point illumination and scroll to the right (figure 4.7, screen 2).
3. Choose one of the three choices from the menu. In figure 4.7, screen 3, Auto has been selected.
4. Press the OK button to lock in the setting.

Settings Recommendation: The simplest setting to use is Auto because that lets the camera determine whether there is enough light coming through the Viewfinder for you to see the AF point(s) at the start of autofocus. If you want to force the AF point(s) to flash each time you start autofocus or move the point(s) with the Multi selector, you can set AF point illumination to On. I wouldn't leave this set to Off unless I was in a consistently lighted studio where the Viewfinder has good contrast.

Custom Setting a7 – Focus Point Wrap-Around

(User's Manual – Pages 310)

Focus point wrap-around allows you to control how AF point scrolling on the Viewfinder works. When you are scrolling your selected AF point to the right or left, or even up and down in the array of 51 points, it will eventually come to the edge of the Viewfinder area. What happens next is controlled by the settings in this function.

Here is a description of the two settings:

- **Wrap** – This setting allows the selected AF point to scroll off of the Viewfinder screen and then reappear on the other side.

- **No wrap** (default) – If you scroll the AF point to the edge of the screen, it stops there! You'll have to use the Multi selector to move the point in the opposite direction, back toward the middle.

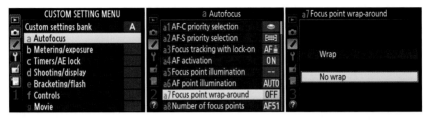
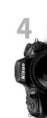

Figure 4.8 – Focus point wrap-around

Here are the steps used to configure Focus point wrap-around:

1. Select a Autofocus from the Custom Setting Menu and scroll to the right (figure 4.8, screen 1).
2. Highlight a7 Focus point wrap-around and scroll to the right (figure 4.8, screen 2).
3. Choose one of the two choices from the menu. In figure 4.8, screen 3, No wrap has been selected.
4. Press the OK button to lock in the setting.

Settings Recommendation: Wrapping the AF point around from one side to the other drives me bonkers. I don't like it on my computer screen or in my camera's Viewfinder. When the AF point gets to the edge, I want it to stop so that I can scroll back the other way with the Multi selector. However, I humbly submit that some people will simply adore having their AF point wrap to the other side of the Viewfinder. If that describes you, simply set it to Wrap. It's always No wrap for me!

Custom Setting a8 – Number of Focus Points

(User's Manual – Page 311)

Number of focus points allows you to adjust the distance the AF point moves when you move it around the screen with the Multi selector.

If you move your AF point often, it might get tiring to scroll through the full 51 focus points, one AF point jump at a time. In older Nikon cameras, we had a maximum of 11 sensors to scroll through, so it wasn't too bad. However, with 51 AF points, it could take longer than you want to scroll from one side of the viewfinder to the other. Or, you might just like the old way better!

Nikon has given you a choice. If you'd rather not scroll through 51 sensors, you can set Number of focus points to 11 sensors instead (figure 4.9A).

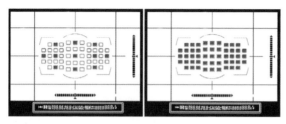

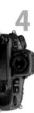

Figure 4.9A – 11 AF points vs. 51 AF points

In Figure 4.9A, the screen on the left shows the 11-point setting, while the right screen shows the 51-point setting.

This does not change the fact that there are 51 sensors available in Dynamic-area AF or Auto-area AF modes. It just means that the Multi selector will make the selected sensor move farther with each press. It skips over sensors when you scroll in Single-area AF and Dynamic-area AF modes. This means that you cannot choose "in-between" sensors as selected AF points, so you have a smaller choice of sensors to start autofocus.

When using Auto-area AF, the camera does not allow you to move the AF points. So this function does not affect the camera when Auto-area AF is selected.

Here is a description of each Number of focus points selection:

- **51 points** (default) – Choose from any of the 51 focus points (AF points) when you are scrolling through them.
- **11 points** – Choose from only 11 focus points (AF points) when you are scrolling through them. The other AF points are still available for autofocus; you just can't scroll directly to them—some are skipped. That means the Multi selector will move the selected AF point around more quickly.

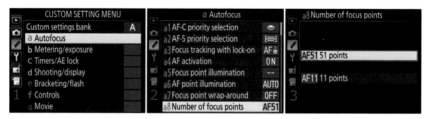

Figure 4.9B – Number of focus points

Here are the steps to select one of the Number of focus points settings:

1. Select a Autofocus from the Custom Setting Menu and scroll to the right (figure 4.9B, screen 1).
2. Highlight a7 Number of focus points and scroll to the right (figure 4.9B, screen 2).

3. Choose one of the two choices from the menu. In figure 4.9B, screen 3, AF51 51 points has been selected.
4. Press the OK button to lock in the setting.

Settings Recommendation: I usually leave my camera set to 51 points for nature work because I have time to scroll among the AF points in an unhurried fashion. The only time I'll change that is when I need to shoot very quickly at an event that moves at a rapid pace, like a graduation ceremony or wedding. At these events I may not have time to scroll through all 51 points to select an AF point on the edge of the Viewfinder, so I'll set Number of focus points to 11 points.

Remember, setting it to 11 points does not change how many AF points are actually used by the camera. It only affects how fast you can move among the AF points when you use the Multi selector to scroll around. Some AF points are skipped during scrolling. You still get the benefit of the other 51 points, if they are set to be active.

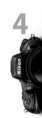

Custom Setting a9 – Store by Orientation

(User's Manual – Page 312)

Store by orientation is a function that allows a photographer who changes the camera from horizontal (landscape) to vertical (portrait) orientation frequently to have separate control over the AF point in use for each orientation. The function also allows you to store a separate AF-area mode for each camera orientation.

There are three settings in the Store by orientation function:

- *Focus point* – You may store up to three separate AF point positions within the 51 AF point grid, one for each camera orientation (figure 4.10A).
- *Focus point and AF-area mode* – As with the previous setting, you may store up to three separate AF point positions within the 51 AF point grid, per the orientation of the camera. You may also select a different AF-area mode (e.g., Group-area AF, Dynamic-area AF, Auto-area AF) for each camera orientation.
- *Off* – The camera does not store a separate AF point position or AF-area mode for different camera orientations.

Figure 4.10A shows the three camera orientations related to the Store by orientation function.

Let's say you are shooting a wedding photo of a group. You moved the selected AF point to the top of the 51 points so that you can focus on faces with the camera in a horizontal orientation (figure 4.10A, left). Afterward, the group leaves, but the bride and groom stay, and you decide to shoot with the camera in a vertical orientation for a nice, full-length portrait (figure 4.10A, middle). If you have the Store by orientation function set to Focus Point, the camera can automatically move the AF point to the left or right side of the 51 AF points, which is now the top of the AF

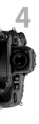

point array because the camera has been rotated into a portrait orientation (figure 4.10A, middle and right). Let's examine how to do it.

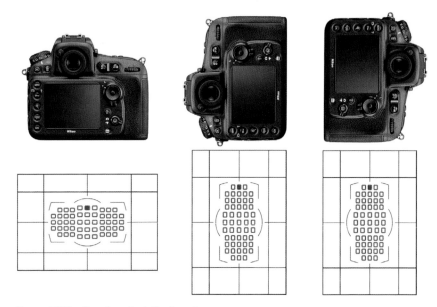

Figure 4.10A – Store by orientation in action

Storing an AF Point Position

First, you will set Custom setting a9 to *Focus point* or *Focus point and AF-area mode* (not *Off*). Next you must set the AF point position for all three available orientations or the camera will not automatically move the AF point when you change the orientation of the D810. Instead, the AF point will stay directly in the middle of the 51 points. You have set each AF point position you want to use for a particular orientation (horizontal or one of the two vertical orientations).

In other words, after enabling Custom setting a9, when you are shooting with the camera in the horizontal orientation, you will select the AF point position you want to use by simply scrolling there with the Multi selector. Afterward, you will switch to each of the vertical orientations and do the same thing—select the AF point you want to use while holding the camera in that orientation. No other action is required to set the AF point position for each camera orientation. Once set, the camera will automatically move the AF point to the correct position for the current camera orientation (figure 4.10A).

The camera will store the position of the AF point for one horizontal and two portrait orientations automatically, without you having to do anything other than select the AF point position for that orientation. You can have separate AF point positions for (1) horizontal; (2) vertical with hand grip up (figure 4.10A, middle); and (3) vertical with hand grip down (figure 4.10A, right). If you shoot with the camera upside down, it will use the AF point for the normal horizontal orientation; there is not a separate upside-down orientation.

This function could save you significant time by preventing you from having to scroll the AF point constantly as you change camera orientations and change AF-area modes for that orientation.

Next let's see how to store an AF-area mode along with your chosen AF point position for each of the three orientations.

Note: The camera's light meter must be active for the D810 to automatically move the AF point to its saved location.

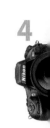

Storing an AF-Area Mode

By selecting the *Focus point and AF-area mode* setting in the Store by orientation function, you can store not only the AF point position, but also a separate AF-area mode for each orientation.

If you decide to store a different AF-area mode for each of the three camera orientations, you can select an AF-area mode by holding in the AF-mode button (found just below the Lens release button on the front of the camera) and turning the front Sub-command dial. You will see the AF-area mode changing on the top Control panel. **Note**: *In order to store an AF-area mode for a specific camera orientation, you must have the camera rotated to that orientation while you select the AF-area mode.*

If you use AF-S (Single-servo AF) you may select Single-point (S), Group-area (GrP), and Auto area (Auto) AF-area modes. When using AF-C (Continuous-servo AF), you can also select Dynamic-area (d9, d21, and d51) and 3D-tracking (3D) AF-area modes. The differences among all these modes are discussed in the chapter titled **Autofocus, AF-Area, and Release Modes**.

Now let's see how to choose one of the three settings found in the Store by orientation function.

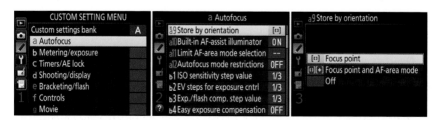

Figure 4.10B – Enabling or disabling Store by orientation

Here are the steps to choose one of the Store by orientation settings:

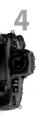

1. Select a Autofocus from the Custom Setting Menu and scroll to the right (figure 4.10B, screen 1).
2. Highlight a9 Store by orientation and scroll to the right (figure 4.10B, screen 2).
3. Choose one of the three choices from the menu. In figure 4.10B, screen 3, Focus point has been selected.
4. Press the OK button to lock in the setting.

Settings Recommendation: I leave my camera set to the Focus point setting because I don't often change both the AF point location and AF-area mode for different camera orientations. However, I do like having the AF point automatically pop to a certain position when I am creating vertical portraits or horizontal group shots. It saves me time!

Custom Setting a10 – Built-In AF-Assist Illuminator

(User's Manual – Page 313)

You've seen the very bright little light on the front of the D810, near the grip (figure 4.11A). Nikon calls this the *Built-in AF-assist illuminator*, and it lights up when the camera senses low-light conditions and when you're using certain AF-area modes (not all) to help with autofocus. Custom setting a8 allows you to control when that powerful little light comes on.

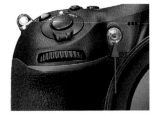

Figure 4.11A – Built-in AF-assist illuminator

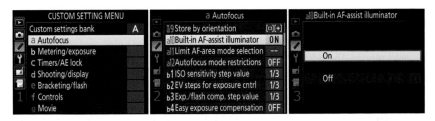

Figure 4.11B – Built-in AF-assist illuminator settings

There are two settings for the Built-in AF-assist illuminator:

- *On* (default) – If the light level is low, the built-in AF-assist illuminator lights up to help illuminate the subject enough for autofocus. This only works with the following Autofocus and AF-area modes:
  a) Auto-area AF-area mode, anytime it's needed
  b) When Single-servo AF (AF-S) Autofocus mode is selected and Single-point AF, Group-area AF, Dynamic-area AF (9, 21, 51 points), or 3D-tracking AF-area modes are in use, and *only* if you have selected the center AF point in the Viewfinder

c) When Continuous-servo AF (AF-C) Autofocus mode is selected the built-in AF-assist illuminator becomes inactive

- **Off** – The AF-assist illuminator does not light up to help you in low-light autofocus situations. The camera may not be able to autofocus in very low light.

Here are the steps to set the Built-in AF-assist illuminator to On or Off:

1. Select a Autofocus from the Custom Setting Menu and scroll to the right (figure 4.11B, screen 1).
2. Highlight a10 Built-in AF-assist illuminator and scroll to the right (figure 4.11B, screen 2).
3. Choose On or Off from the menu. In figure 4.11B, screen 3, On has been selected.
4. Press the OK button to lock in the setting.

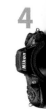

Settings Recommendation: I leave Built-in AF-assist illuminator set to On most of the time. It is activated only when the light is low enough to need it. However, let me qualify this for specific circumstances. If you are trying to take pictures without being noticed, such as from across the room with a zoom lens or while doing street photography, you certainly don't want this extremely bright little light drawing attention when you start autofocus.

Or, you may be shooting wildlife, such as a giant grizzly bear, and surely don't want to call attention to yourself by shining a bright light into the old bear's eyes. Use this feature when you don't mind others noticing you—especially if they are eight feet tall with claws—because it will draw attention immediately.

Custom Setting a11 – Limit AF-Area Mode Selection

(User's Manual – Page 314)

Use *Limit AF-area mode selection* to place limits on which of the available AF-area modes are available when you press the AF-mode button and rotate the front Sub-command dial.

Normally there are seven specific AF-area modes available, including: Single-point AF, Dynamic-area AF (9 point, 21 point, and 51 point), 3D-tracking, Group-area AF, and Auto-area AF. However, if you do not want to use one or more of these modes, you can hide them from the AF-area mode selections you are offered on the camera's LCD screens when selecting an AF-area mode.

Note: Limiting the AF-area modes with this function affects Viewfinder-based photography only. All AF-area modes remain available in Live view (Lv) mode, regardless of how this function is configured. The differences among all these modes are discussed in the chapter titled **Autofocus, AF-Area, and Release Modes**.

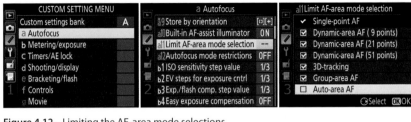

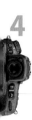

Figure 4.12 – Limiting the AF-area mode selections

Here are the steps to place a limit on the AF-area modes the camera will offer you during Viewfinder-based photography:

1. Select a Autofocus from the Custom Setting Menu and scroll to the right (figure 4.12, screen 1).
2. Highlight a11 Limit AF-area mode selection and scroll to the right (figure 4.12, screen 2).
3. You will be presented with a list of seven AF-area modes. You can uncheck any mode except Single-point AF, which is always available, and that mode will disappear from the AF-area mode selection screens. In figure 4.12, screen 3, Auto-area AF has been unchecked, so it will not be available for selection on the AF-area mode screens. To uncheck or recheck one of the modes, simply highlight it with the yellow bar and press right on the Multi selector.
4. Press the OK button to lock in the setting.

Settings Recommendation: I do not uncheck any of the available AF-area modes because I use each of them at one time or another. If there is an AF-area mode or two that you find useless, simply uncheck it and it will disappear from camera selection screens. You can always recheck it later if you find a use for it.

Custom Setting a12 – Autofocus Mode Restrictions

(User's Manual – Page 314)

Use *Autofocus mode restrictions* to place limits on which Autofocus modes are available when you press the AF-mode button and rotate the rear Main command dial.

Normally there are two specific Autofocus modes available for Viewfinder photography, including: AF-S (Single-servo AF) and AF-C (Continuous-servo AF). However, if you do not want to use one of these modes, you can hide it from the Autofocus mode selections you are offered on the camera's LCD screens when selecting an Autofocus mode.

Note: Limiting the Autofocus modes with this function affects Viewfinder-based photography only. The differences among all these modes are discussed in the chapter titled **Autofocus, AF-Area, and Release Modes**.

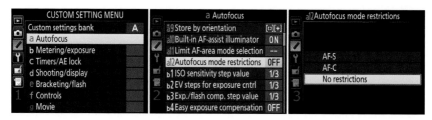

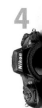

Figure 4.13 – Limiting the Autofocus mode selections

Here are the steps to place a limit on the types of Autofocus modes the camera will offer you during Viewfinder-based photography:

1. Select a Autofocus from the Custom Setting Menu and scroll to the right (figure 4.13, screen 1).
2. Highlight a12 Autofocus mode restrictions and scroll to the right (figure 4.13, screen 2).
3. You will be presented with a list of three choices: AF-S, AF-C, and No restrictions. Choose AF-S or AF-C to eliminate that choice from the Autofocus mode selection screens. Selecting No restrictions will leave both Autofocus mode choices available for selection.
4. Press the OK button to lock in the setting.

Settings Recommendation: I do not uncheck any of the available Autofocus modes because I use each of them frequently. I can't think of any good reasons to limit my camera to only one type of autofocus. However, if you do not need one of them, simply select it in the menu and it will disappear until you come back and select No restrictions.

Section Two – b Metering/Exposure

Custom Settings b1 to b7

You'll find seven settings within the *b Metering/exposure* menu in the D810:

- **b1** – ISO sensitivity step value
- **b2** – EV steps for exposure cntrl
- **b3** – Exp./flash comp. step value
- **b4** – Easy exposure compensation
- **b5** – Matrix metering
- **b6** – Center-weighted area
- **b7** – Fine-tune optimal exposure

What Is EV?

EV simply means exposure value, which is an agreed-upon value of exposure metering. It is spoken of in full or partial EV steps, like 1/3, 1/2, or 1. It simply means different combinations of shutter speeds and apertures that give similar exposures. An EV step corresponds to a standard logarithmic "power-of-2" exposure step, commonly referred to as a stop. So, instead of saying 1 EV, you could substitute 1 stop. EV 0 (zero) corresponds to an exposure time of 1 second at an aperture of f/1.0 or 15 seconds at f/4. EV can be positive or negative. EV -6 equals 60 seconds at f/1.0. EV 10 equals 1/1000 seconds at f/1.0 or 1/60 seconds at f/4. The EV step system was invented in Germany back in the 1950s. Interesting, huh?

The first three settings in the Metering/exposure menu (b1, b2, b3) affect how your camera views steps in its EV range. Most people like to have their camera work very precisely, so they'll use the 1/3 step EV selection for b1, b2, and b3. Others might not be as selective and would prefer to change sensitivity in 1/2 step EV, or even whole steps.

Custom Setting b1 – ISO Sensitivity Step Value

(User's Manual – Page 315)

ISO sensitivity step value allows you to change the way the camera handles its progression of exposure values for ISO. In other words, the camera's ISO "step" value is set with Custom setting b1. You can control the steps with the following values:

- 1/3 step EV (ISO steps 200, 250, 320, 400, etc.)
- 1/2 step EV (ISO steps 200, 280, 400, 560, etc.)
- 1 step EV (ISO steps 200, 400, 800, 1600, etc.)

If you are concerned with maximum ISO control, use the 1/3 step setting. It takes longer to scroll through the ISO selections if you manually set your ISO value in 1/3 steps; however, it gives you greater exposure control. The 1/3 step setting is the factory default value for b1.

Here are the steps to change the ISO sensitivity step value:

1. Select b Metering/exposure from the Custom Setting Menu and scroll to the right (figure 4.14, screen 1).
2. Highlight b1 ISO sensitivity step value and scroll to the right (figure 4.14, screen 2).
3. Choose one of the three items on the menu. In figure 4.14, screen 3, 1/3 step has been selected.
4. Press the OK button to lock in the setting.

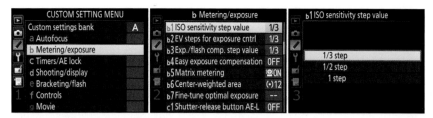

Figure 4.14 – ISO sensitivity step value

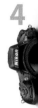

Now, let's talk more about how to use the ISO sensitivity step value setting. With ISO sensitivity step value set to 1/3 step, hold down the ISO button on the top left of the camera and turn the rear Main command dial to the right. If your camera was set to ISO 100 initially, you'll see that the ISO number in the Control panel changes in the following pattern:

ISO sensitivity step value set to **1/3 step**:
64, 80, 100, 125, 160, 200, 250, 320, 400, 500, 640, etc.

ISO sensitivity step value set to **1/2 step**:
64, 72, 100, 140, 200, 280, 400, 560, 800, 1100, 1600, etc.

ISO sensitivity step value set to **1 step**:
64, 100, 200, 400, 800, 1600, 3200, 6400, 12800, etc.

Settings Recommendation: I like the most control I can have over ISO sensitivity increments. I normally leave this set to the factory default of 1/3 step. This allows me to carefully fine-tune the ISO sensitivity value for precise exposures.

Custom Setting b2 – EV Steps for Exposure Cntrl

(User's Manual – Page 315)

EV steps for exposure cntrl refers to the number of steps in the shutter speed and aperture because those are your main exposure controls. It also encompasses the exposure bracketing system. Just as with the ISO sensitivity covered in the previous section, you can control the number of steps in the full range of exposure values.

Here are the three settings available for exposure control:

- 1/3 step (EV is 1/3 step; bracketing can be 1/3, 1/2, or 1 EV)
- 1/2 step (EV is 1/2 step; bracketing can be 1/2 or 1 EV)
- 1 step (EV and Bracketing are 1 step each)

Here are the steps used to adjust EV steps for exposure cntrl:

1. Select b Metering/exposure from the Custom Setting Menu and scroll to the right (figure 4.15, screen 1).

2. Highlight b2 EV steps for exposure cntrl and scroll to the right (figure 4.15, screen 2).
3. Choose one of the three items on the menu. In figure 4.15, screen 3, 1/3 step has been selected.
4. Press the OK button to lock in the setting.

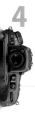
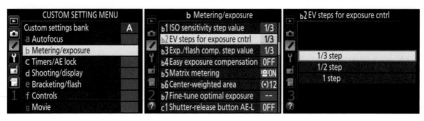

Figure 4.15 – EV steps for exposure cntrl

Now, let's examine the concept in more detail. All EV steps for exposure cntrl really means is that when you are adjusting the shutter speed or aperture manually, each will work incrementally in the following steps.

Shutter and Exposure (starting at a random shutter speed or aperture)

1/3 step EV:
Shutter: 1/100, 1/125, 1/160, 1/200, 1/250, 1/320, etc.
Aperture: f/5.6, f/6.3, f/7.1, f/8, f/9, f/10, etc.

1/2 step EV:
Shutter: 1/90, 1/125, 1/180, 1/250, 1/350, 1/500, etc.
Aperture: f/5.6, f/6.7, f/8, f/9.5, f/11, f/13, etc.

1 step EV:
Shutter: 1/60, 1/125, 1/250, 1/500, 1/1000, 1/2000, etc.
Aperture: f/4, f/5.6, f/8, f/11, f/16, f/22, etc.

Bracketing
1/3 step EV   Bracket: 0.3, 0.7, 1.0 (or 1/3, 2/3, 1 EV steps)
1/2 step EV   Bracket: 0.5, 1.0 (or 1/2 and 1 EV steps)
1 step EV   Bracket: 1.0 (or 1 EV step)

Nikon chose to lump shutter speed, aperture, and bracketing all under Custom setting b2. The factory default value for EV steps for exposure cntrl is 1/3 step.

Settings Recommendation: Similar to ISO sensitivity step value, I keep EV steps for exposure cntrl set to 1/3 step. It's critical to control the EV steps with granularity, especially with exposure. It's best to increment the EV in small steps for use with the histogram.

Custom Setting b3 – Exp./Flash Comp. Step Value

(User's Manual – Page 315)

Exp./flash comp. step value is concerned with the granularity of exposure or flash compensation. Most of us will use the exposure or flash compensation system at one time or another.

Exposure compensation adjustments are made with the +/- Exposure compensation button on the top right of the camera, just behind the Shutter-release button. The Flash compensation button is below the D810 logo on the front of the camera. It has a small lightning bolt arrow icon.

Holding the +/- Exposure compensation button and turning the rear Main command dial allows you to adjust the exposure compensation. Holding the Flash compensation button and turning the front Sub-command dial allows you to adjust flash compensation.

Maybe the camera's light meter or flash is giving your images a little less exposure than you'd like, so you fine-tune by adding a little extra exposure with the +/- Exposure compensation or Flash compensation button. These buttons can be configured by setting b3 so that they allow you to adjust your camera in a finer (1/3 EV) or coarser way (1/2 or 1 EV) for exposure or flash compensation.

Exposure compensation can be added or subtracted in 1/3, 1/2, or 1 EV steps—for up to 5.0 EV (10 stops total adjustment range, or -5.0 to +5.0 EV). Flash is a little less flexible with only +1.0 EV or -3.0 EV in 1/3, 1/2, or 1 EV step.

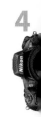

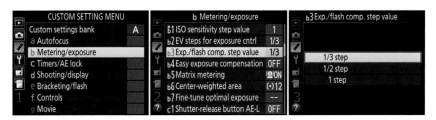

Figure 4.16 – Exp./flash comp. step value

Here are the steps used to adjust Exp./flash comp. step value:

1. Select b Metering/exposure from the Custom Setting Menu and scroll to the right (figure 4.16, screen 1).
2. Highlight Exp./flash comp. step value and scroll to the right (figure 4.16, screen 2).
3. Choose one of the three items on the menu. In figure 4.16, screen 3, 1/3 step has been selected.
4. Press the OK button to lock in the setting.

Here is more information on the step values you can use with exposure or flash compensation, once you've selected your favorite increment (figure 4.16, screen 3):

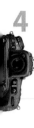

- *1/3 step*: Exposure compensation of up to +/- 5.0 EV: 0.3, 0.7, 1.0, 1.3, 1.7, 2.0, 2.3, 2.7, 3.0, etc. Flash compensation is limited to +1.0 and -3.0 in 1/3 EV steps.
- *1/2 step*: Exposure compensation of up to +/- 5.0 EV: 0.5, 1.0, 1.5, 2.0, 2.5, 3.0, 3.5, 4.0, etc. Flash compensation is limited to +1.0 and -3.0 in 1/2 EV steps.
- *1 step*: Exposure compensation of up to +/- 5.0 EV: 1.0, 2.0, 3.0, 4.0, 5.0. Flash compensation is limited to +1.0 and -3.0 in 1 EV steps.

Settings Recommendation: The factory default for Exp./flash comp. step value is 1/3 step. Most shooters will leave it set to 1/3 step because that allows fine control over the amount of exposure or flash compensation. Like the two previous Custom settings (b1 and b2), b3 allows you to have fine or coarse control over compensation values. The 1/3 step EV setting seems to be the best for most of us.

Custom Setting b4 – Easy Exposure Compensation

(User's Manual – Page 316)

Easy exposure compensation lets you set the camera's exposure compensation without using the +/- Exposure compensation button. Instead, you can use the Command dial of your choice to dial in exposure compensation.

There are three settings in Easy exposure compensation: On (Auto reset), On, and Off. If you set the camera to On (Auto reset) or simply to On, you can use the Command dials to set exposure compensation instead of the +/- Exposure compensation button. Off means what it says; you will have to use the +/- Exposure compensation button.

Each exposure mode (P, S, A, M) reacts somewhat differently to Easy exposure compensation. Let's consider how the Program (P), Shutter-priority (S), and Aperture-priority (A) modes act when you use the three settings. The Manual (M) mode is not affected by Custom setting b4, although it does allow compensation with the normal +/- Exposure compensation button.

Here are the values and how they work:

- *On (Auto reset)* – Using the Sub-command dial in Program (P) or Shutter-priority (S) mode or the Main command dial in Aperture-priority (A) mode, you can dial in exposure compensation without using the normal +/- Exposure compensation button. The other Command dial will control the aperture or shutter speed, as it normally would. Once you allow the meter to go off, or turn the camera off, the compensation value you dialed in is reset back to 0. That's why it's called Auto reset. If you have already set a compensation value using the normal +/- Exposure compensation button, then the process of dialing in compensation with the Command dial simply adds or substracts compensation from the value you added with the normal +/- Exposure compensation button. When the meter resets, it returns back to the compensation value you added with the +/- Exposure compensation button and not to 0.

- **On** – This works the same way as On (Auto reset), except that the compensation you've dialed in does not reset but stays in place, even if the meter or camera is turned off.
- **Off** – Only the normal +/- Exposure compensation button applies exposure compensation.

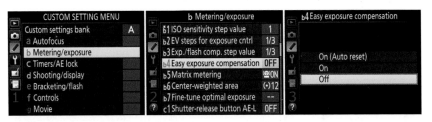
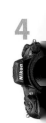

Figure 4.17 – Easy exposure compensation

Here are the steps used to configure Easy exposure compensation:

1. Select b Metering/exposure from the Custom Setting Menu and scroll to the right (figure 4.17, screen 1).
2. Highlight b4 Easy exposure compensation and scroll to the right (figure 4.17, screen 2).
3. Choose one of the three items on the menu. In figure 4.17, screen 3, Off has been selected.
4. Press the OK button to lock in the setting.

Note: The granularity of Easy exposure compensation's EV step fine-tuning is affected by Custom setting b3, with 1/3, 1/2, or 1 step EV settings. Also, the Command dials used to set compensation and change shutter speed and aperture can be swapped in *Custom Setting Menu > f9 Customize command dials > Change main/sub*, which we will consider later in this chapter.

When you adjust exposure compensation with either the normal +/- Exposure compensation button or with Easy exposure compensation, a +/- symbol will appear on the Control panel, in the Information display (open with info button), in the Viewfinder, and in Live view mode while exposure compensation is active.

Settings Recommendation: The normal +/- Exposure compensation button works fine for me. However, I have read in forums that some people really like this functionality because they can change the shutter speed and aperture with one Command dial, and dial in exposure compensation with the other.

I think I will keep on using what I am used to; however, why not experiment with this for a few minutes and see if you like dialing in compensation with the Command dials instead of the +/- Exposure compensation button? Nikon gives us a lot of choices!

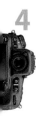

Custom Setting b5 – Matrix Metering

(User's Manual – Page 317)

Use the *Matrix metering* function to enable or disable Face detection when using the Matrix meter for Viewfinder-based photography. The camera is capable of detecting faces and metering for them when Face detection is enabled. In a sense, setting this function to On enables face-priority metering when the Matrix meter is active and you are looking through the Viewfinder to take pictures.

This function does not affect Spot or Center-weighted metering. Let's examine how to enable or disable Face detection for Matrix metering.

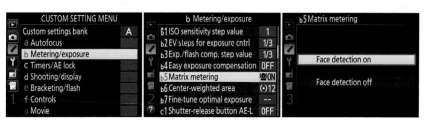

Figure 4.18 – Using Face detection when the Matrix meter is active

Here are the steps used to configure Face detection for Viewfinder-based Matrix metering:

1. Select b Metering/exposure from the Custom Setting Menu and scroll to the right (figure 4.18, screen 1).
2. Highlight b5 Matrix metering and scroll to the right (figure 4.18, screen 2).
3. Choose one of the two items on the menu. In figure 4.18, screen 3, Face detection on has been selected, which allows the camera to use Matrix metering Face detection when shooting with the Viewfinder. If Face detection is turned off, Matrix metering works normally, with no special interest in faces.
4. Press the OK button to lock in the setting.

Settings Recommendation: I used this function during a wedding shoot immediately upon buying my Nikon D810. I found it really helped keep my subjects' faces well exposed. Of course, this function would have little value for any type of photography that does not involve people. However, it certainly seems reasonable to leave Matrix metering set to Face detection on when photographing people so that their faces will have priority over the surroundings.

Custom Setting b6 – Center-Weighted Area

(User's Manual – Page 317)

Center-weighted area allows you to control the area on the Viewfinder that has the greatest weight in metering a subject when the camera is using Center-weighted metering mode. Years ago our cameras didn't have Matrix metering. Back in the good old days, we all had averaging meters, partially averaging meters, or none at all.

If you prefer not to use Nikon's built-in database of image scenes, otherwise known as Matrix metering, and you use Spot metering only as needed, you are most likely using the Center-weighted meter. It's cool that Nikon gives us a choice. You have four meter styles in your camera, adding to its flexibility.

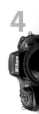

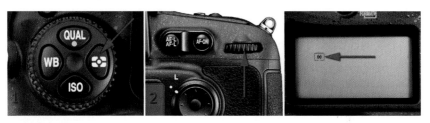

Figure 4.19A – Metering button, Main command dial, and Control panel

On top of the camera, next to the QUAL, WB, and ISO buttons, you will find a button with a Matrix metering symbol on it (figure 4.19A, image 1). This is the Metering button, and it is used to select the type of meter you want to use. Hold the Metering button down and turn the rear Main command dial (figure 4.19A, image 2) while watching the Control panel on top of the camera. It will display one of the four metering symbols (figure 4.19A, image 3). In this case, we have the Center-weighted meter selected because this section considers how it works.

The Center-weighted meter can be configured to use a central area of the Viewfinder to do most of its metering, with less attention paid to subjects outside this area, or it can be set up to simply average the entire frame.

Here are the five area-size settings used by the Center-weighted metering mode:

- 8 or 8 mm   • 12 or 12 mm   • 15 or 15 mm
- 20 or 20 mm   • Avg or Average

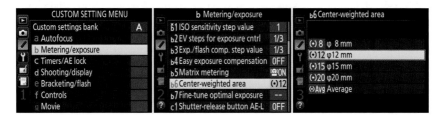

Figure 4.19B – Center-weighted metering mode area

Here are the steps used to choose a Center-weighted metering mode area:

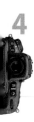

1. Select b Metering/exposure from the Custom Setting Menu and scroll to the right (figure 4.19B, screen 1).
2. Highlight b5 Center-weighted area and scroll to the right (figure 4.19B, screen 2).
3. Choose one of the five items on the menu. In figure 4.19B, screen 3, 12 mm has been selected.
4. Press the OK button to lock in the setting.

Let's see how each setting works. Figure 4.19C shows the approximate size of the most sensitive area in the Viewfinder for each area size of the Center-weighted meter. The pink circle is the most sensitive area for metering, and it gets larger for each setting. In the final frame of figure 4.19C, all areas of the frame are equally sensitive and average the light values of everything seen in the Viewfinder.

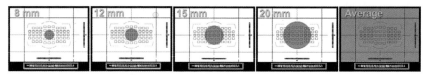

Figure 4.19C – Center-weighted and Average-weighted areas shown in pink

When you are using the Center-weighted metering mode, the metering system uses an invisible circle in the center of the Viewfinder to meter the subject (figure 4.19C). When it's set down to 8 mm, it's almost small enough to be a spot meter because the real Spot metering mode of the camera uses a 4 mm circle surrounding the currently selected AF point.

The Center-weighted meter does not move around with the currently selected AF point as the Spot meter does. Instead, it assigns the greatest weight to the center of the Viewfinder frame, and everything outside the circle in the center is not as important.

Each size increase from 8, 12, 15, to 20 mm will increase the sensitivity of the center of the Viewfinder so that more emphasis is given to a larger area in the middle. If you select the Avg – Average setting, the entire Viewfinder frame is used to meter the scene. The camera takes an average of the entire frame by including all light and dark areas mixed together for an averaged exposure.

Note: If you use a non-CPU lens with the Center-weighted meter, the camera selects the 12 mm circle automatically and it cannot be changed. The Average weighting works for both CPU and non-CPU lenses.

Settings Recommendation: When I use the Center-weighted meter, I generally use the 20 mm setting to make the largest area of the center of the Viewfinder be the most sensitive section. Personally, I use 3D Matrix metering most of the time and have my camera's Fn button set up to switch to the Spot meter temporarily. That way, I am using Nikon's incredible 3D Color Matrix Metering III, with its ability to consider brightness, color, distance, and composition. Matrix gives me the best metering I've had with any camera yet! The Center-weighted meter is still included in our modern cameras to make people who are used to using the older style meter more comfortable. Most of us will use Matrix metering these days.

Custom Setting b7 – Fine-Tune Optimal Exposure

(User's Manual – Page 318)

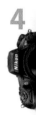

Nikon has taken the stance that users should be allowed to fine-tune most major camera systems. The exposure system is no exception. *Fine-tune optimal exposure* allows you to fine-tune the Matrix, Center-weighted, Spot, and Highlight-weighted metering systems by +1/-1 EV in 1/6 EV steps, independently.

In other words, you can force each of the four metering systems to add or deduct a little exposure from what it normally would use to expose your subject.

This stays in effect with no further notice until you set it back to zero. It is indeed fine-tuning because the maximum 1 EV step up or down is divided into six parts (1/6 EV). If you feel that your camera is too conservative with the highlights, mildly underexposing, and you want to force it to add 1/2 step exposure, you simply add 3/6 EV to the compensation system for that metering system. (Remember basic fractions—where 1/2 equals 3/6?)

This works like the normal compensation system except it allows you only 1 EV of compensation. As screen 3 of figure 4.20A shows, an ominous-looking warning appears telling you that your camera will not show a compensation icon, as it does with the normal +/- Exposure compensation button, when you use the Fine-tune optimal exposure system. This simply means that while you have this fine-tuning system dialed in for your light meter, the camera will not remind you that it is fine-tuned by showing you a compensation icon. If it did turn on the compensation icon (+/- on the Control panel and in the Viewfinder), how could it show you the same icon when you are using normal compensation at the same time as meter fine-tuning?

This light meter fine-tuning applies only to the Custom setting bank you are currently working with. If you are working in bank A, banks B, C, and D are not changed.

Use the following steps to fine tune any of the four metering systems:

1. Select b Metering/exposure from the Custom Setting Menu and scroll to the right (figure 4.20A, screen 1).
2. Select b6 Fine-tune optimal exposure and scroll to the right (figure 4.20A, screen 2).
3. Select Yes from the warning screen and scroll to the right (figure 4.20A, screen 3).
4. Select the metering system you want to adjust. In figure 4.20A, screen 4, you can see that I selected Matrix metering. Now, scroll to the right. All four meter fine-tuning operations work exactly the same way, and each meter can

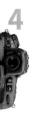

be adjusted independently of the other three. If you want to adjust a different meter besides Matrix metering, simply substitute one of the other three meter types in this step (Center-weighted metering, Spot metering, or Highlight-weighted metering).

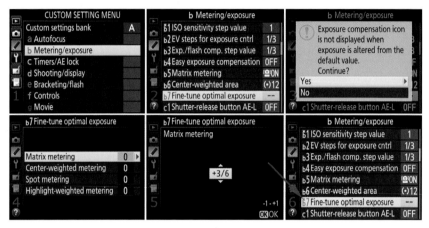

Figure 4.20A – Fine-tune optimal exposure

5. Scroll up or down in 1/6 EV steps until you reach the fine-tuning value you would like to use (figure 4.20A, screen 5). I set +3/6, which is the equivalent of adding +1/2 EV of extra exposure to the Matrix metering system.

6. Press the OK button to lock in the fine-tuning value for the metering system you selected in step 4 only. *You must fine-tune each metering system separately.* Notice the red arrow in figure 4.20A, screen 6. It is pointing to an asterisk that shows, at a glance, that something in this menu has been fine-tuned. If you go into the menu system to see what is changed, it will show the fine-tuning fraction next to the meter that has been fine-tuned, as shown at the red arrow in figure 4.20B.

That's all there is to it! Just remember that you have Fine-tune optimal exposure turned on because the camera will not remind you. Watch your histogram to make sure you're not regularly underexposing or overexposing images once you have the fine-tuning adjustment in place. If so, just go back in and adjust the fine-tuning up or down, or turn it off.

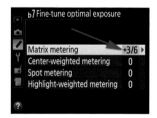

Figure 4.20B – Fine tuning the Matrix meter

Settings Recommendation: Unless you have a good reason to adjust this, most of us will leave it alone. It certainly won't hurt anything to make a fine-tuning adjustment, if you feel confident that you really need it. I used to run +3/6 on my Nikon D300 a few years back, to force a brighter exposure. However, the D810 has the most accurate light metering systems I have ever used; therefore, it may not be necessary to fine tune any of the four meter types in your camera.

We have the ability to fine-tune our cameras to an amazing degree. Whether you need this now or not, you might later. Learn how it works and, as always, experiment with it to see if fine-tuning your light meter gives you better exposures.

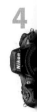

Section Three – c Timers/AE Lock

Custom Settings c1 to c4

You'll find four settings within the *c Timers/AE lock* menu in the D810:

- **c1** – Shutter-release button AE-L
- **c2** – Standby timer
- **c3** – Self-timer
- **c4** – Monitor off delay

Let's examine each of them and learn how to control various timers in the camera. We will also explore how to use auto-exposure lock (AE-L).

Custom Setting c1 – Shutter-Release Button AE-L

(User's Manual – Page 319)

Shutter-release button AE-L is designed to allow you to lock your camera's exposure when you press the Shutter-release button halfway down. Normally that type of exposure lock happens only when you press and hold the AE-L/AF-L button. However, when you have Shutter-release button AE-L set to On, your camera will act like you've pressed the AE-L/AF-L button every time you start autofocus and take a picture.

This function allows you to meter from one area of the scene and then recompose to another area without losing the meter reading from the first area, as long as you hold the Shutter-release button halfway down.

Looking at this another way, when you have Shutter-release button AE-L set to Off, exposure will lock only when you hold down the AE-L/AF-L button.

Here are the steps used to configure Shutter-release button AE-L:

1. Select c Timers/AE lock from the Custom Setting Menu and scroll to the right (figure 4.21, screen 1).
2. Highlight c1 Shutter-release button AE-L and scroll to the right (figure 4.21, screen 2).

3. Choose one of the two choices on the menu. In figure 4.21, screen 3, Off has been selected.
4. Press the OK button to lock in the setting.

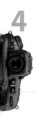
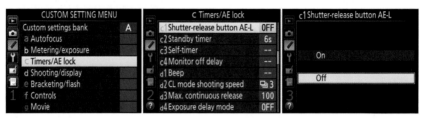

Figure 4.21 – Shutter-release button AE-L

Settings Recommendation: I use this feature only when I really need it, then I turn it off. The rest of the time, I just use the AE-L/AF-L button to lock my exposure. I don't think I'd leave Shutter-release button AE-L turned on all the time because I might be holding the Shutter-release button halfway down to track a moving subject through light and dark areas.

For sunset shooters (or something similar) who like to include the sun in their image, this is a nice function. You can meter from an area of the sky that has the best color and then swing the camera around to include the sun in the shot. The camera will expose for the originally metered area as long as you hold the Shutter-release button halfway down. Normally, you'd just do this with the AE-L/AF-L lock button.

Custom Setting c2 – Standby timer

(User's Manual – Page 319)

Standby timer controls the amount of time your camera's light meter stays on after you press the Shutter-release button halfway and then release it. The default value is 6 seconds.

When the light meter goes off, the various displays—like shutter speed and aperture—in the Control panel and Viewfinder do also.

If you would like your light meter to stay on longer for whatever reason, such as for multiple exposures, you can adjust it to the following settings:

- **4 s** – 4 seconds
- **6 s** – 6 seconds (default)
- **10 s** – 10 seconds
- **30 s** – 30 seconds
- **1 min** – 1 minute
- **5 min** – 5 minutes
- **10 min** – 10 minutes
- **30 min** – 30 minutes
- **No limit** – meter stays on until camera is turned off

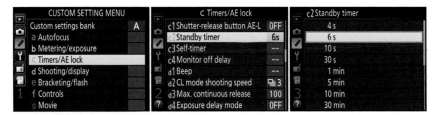

Figure 4.22 – Selecting a Standby timer setting

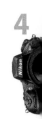

Here are the steps to set the Standby timer:

1. Select c Timers/AE lock from the Custom Setting Menu and scroll to the right (figure 4.22, screen 1).
2. Highlight c2 Standby timer and scroll to the right (figure 4.22, screen 2).
3. Choose one of the nine choices on the menu. In figure 4.22, screen 3, 6 s has been selected. You can't see all the available selections in screen 3. Scroll down on your camera to find one more setting, No limit.
4. Press the OK button to lock in the setting.

Settings Recommendation: There are times when you want the light meter to stay on for a longer or shorter period of time than it normally does. When I'm shooting multiple exposures, I leave Standby timer set to No limit. However, when I'm shooting normally, it stays at either 6 s or 10 s. The longer the light meter stays on, the shorter the battery life, so extend the meter time only if you really need it. You can adjust it from 4 s to No limit. Easy enough!

Custom Setting c3 – Self-Timer

(User's Manual – Page 319)

The *Self-timer* setting allows you to take pictures remotely or without touching the camera except to start the Self-timer operation. Hands-off shooting on a tripod can reduce vibrations so that you have sharper pictures. Additionally, it gives you time to place yourself in group shots so there will be some pictures of you to look at later. Put yourself in front of the camera from time to time, or no one will remember what you look like!

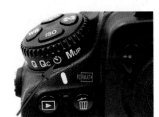

Figure 4.23A – Self-timer selection on Release mode dial

To set the Self-timer, hold down the Release mode dial lock button and turn the Release mode dial until the little timer symbol (figure 4.23A) is directly above the white dash. When you press the Shutter-release button, the Self-timer will start its timed countdown and will flash the little AF-assist illuminator light (figure 4.11A) until just before the shutter fires. Additionally, if you have Custom setting d1 Beep

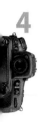

set to On, the camera will beep about twice per second while counting down and speed up to about four times per second just before it fires the shutter.

Here are the three choices you have when configuring the Self-timer:

- **Self-timer delay** – This setting allows you to specify a delay before the camera's shutter fires so you have time to position yourself for the shot or allow vibrations to settle down. The time delay ranges from 2 to 20 seconds. This setting can be used instead of a remote release, and you won't have cables to trip over.
- **Number of shots** – Use this setting to choose how many shots will be taken for each cycle of the Self-timer. You can choose from one to nine shots in a row.
- **Interval between shots** – If you are taking more than one shot during a Self-timer cycle, this setting allows you to choose a time interval between each shot ranging from 1/2 second to 3 seconds. This lets you select a time that allows vibrations from the previous shot to settle down.

Now let's look at the screens and steps used to adjust each of these settings. First, we'll look at the Self-timer delay. Here is a list of the four available Self-timer delay settings:

- **2 s** – 2 seconds
- **5 s** – 5 seconds
- **10 s** – 10 seconds (default)
- **20 s** – 20 seconds

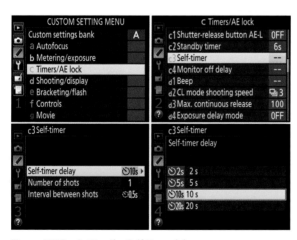

Figure 4.23B – Setting the Self-timer delay

Use the following steps to configure the Self-timer delay (figure 4.23B):

1. Select c Timers/AE lock from the Custom Setting Menu and scroll to the right (figure 4.23B, screen 1).
2. Highlight c3 Self-timer and scroll to the right (figure 4.23B, screen 2).

3. Select Self-timer delay from the menu and scroll to the right (figure 4.23B, screen 3).
4. Choose one of the four options from the menu (2 s to 20 s). Figure 4.23B, screen 4, shows that I selected 10 s.
5. Press the OK button to lock in the setting.

Next, let's look at how to configure the Number of shots for each Self-timer cycle.

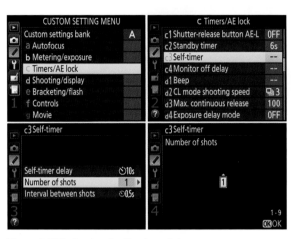
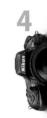

Figure 4.23C – Setting the Number of shots

Use the following steps to configure the Number of shots:

1. Select c Timers/AE lock from the Custom Setting Menu and scroll to the right (figure 4.23C, screen 1).
2. Highlight c3 Self-timer and scroll to the right (figure 4.23C, screen 2).
3. Select Number of shots from the menu and scroll to the right (figure 4.23C, screen 3).
4. Choose the Number of shots, from 1 to 9, by scrolling up or down with the Multi selector. Figure 4.23C, screen 4, shows that I selected 1 shot.
5. Press the OK button to choose the setting.

Finally, let's look at how to configure the Interval between shots for each Self-timer cycle. Here is a list of the four available Interval between shots settings:

- **0.5 s** – 1/2 second (default)
- **1 s** – 1 second
- **2 s** – 2 seconds
- **3 s** – 3 seconds

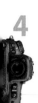

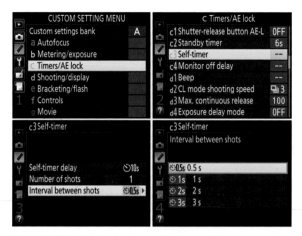

Figure 4.23D – Setting the Interval between shots

Use the following steps to configure the Interval between shots:

1. Select c Timers/AE lock from the Custom Setting Menu and scroll to the right (figure 4.23D, screen 1).
2. Highlight c3 Self-timer and scroll to the right (figure 4.23D, screen 2).
3. Select Interval between shots and scroll to the right (figure 4.23D, screen 3).
4. Choose the Interval between shots, from 0.5 s to 3 s, by scrolling up or down with the Multi selector. Figure 4.23D, screen 4, shows that I selected 0.5 s (1/2 second).
5. Press the OK button to choose the setting.

Settings Recommendation: Often, if I don't want to take the time to plug in a remote release cable, I just put my camera on a tripod and set the Self-timer delay to 2 or 5 seconds. This lets the D810 make a hands-off exposure so I don't shake the camera or the tripod. If I must run to get into position for a group shot, I often increase the delay to at least 10 seconds to keep from looking like an idiot as I trip while running for position.

I can also control how many shots to take each time I use the Self-timer and how long to delay between those shots to allow vibrations to go away. I'm sure you'll agree that the Self-timer in your D810 is one of the most flexible timers in a DSLR camera.

Custom Setting c4 – Monitor Off Delay

(User's Manual – Page 320)

Monitor off delay lets you set a time-out for the Monitor on the back of the camera. You can select a variable timing for five individual functions that use the Monitor to display various screens. The Monitor will stay on until the time-out period expires. Here is a list of the individual functions:

- Playback
- Menus
- Information display
- Image review
- Live view

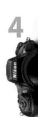

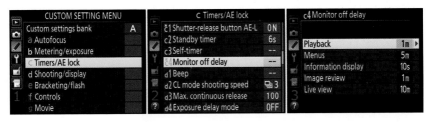

Figure 4.24A – Monitor off delay

Here are the steps to get to the screen for adjusting the time-outs. We'll consider each function individually.

1. Select c Timers/AE lock from the Custom Setting Menu and scroll to the right (figure 4.24A, screen 1).
2. Highlight c4 Monitor off delay and scroll to the right (figure 4.24A, screen 2).
3. Choose one of the five choices on the menu, as shown in figure 4.24A, screen 3. You can set the Monitor off delay for each specific display type. Let's examine each one.

Playback

First, let's look at setting a time-out for *Playback*. This is used when you are "playing back" images you have taken previously. This is not the Image review time-out, which is used when the camera displays a picture on the Monitor immediately after taking it. Playback is for when you are looking at a series of images on the Monitor for your own enjoyment and quality verification or when you are showing images to another person. The available time-out is from 4 s to 10 min.

Use the following steps to choose a Monitor off delay for viewing images on the Monitor after pressing the Playback button:

1. Figure 4.24B picks up where figure 4.24A leaves off. Select Playback from the c4 Monitor off delay screen (figure 4.24B, screen 1).
2. Choose from 4 seconds (4 s) to 10 minutes (10 min) delay time. The factory default of 10 s is selected (figure 4.24B, screen 2).
3. Press the OK button to lock in the setting.

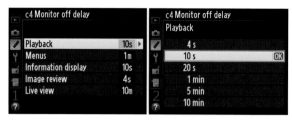

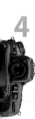

Figure 4.24B – Monitor off delay – Playback

Menus

Second, let's look at setting a time-out for using the *Menus* when you make adjustments to camera settings. How long do you want the time-out to be before the Monitor shuts off (4 s to 10 min)?

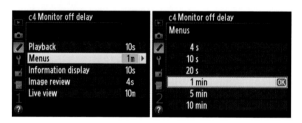

Figure 4.24C – Monitor off delay – Menus

Use the following steps to choose a Monitor off delay for viewing screens on the Monitor after pressing the Menu button:

1. Figure 4.24C picks up where figure 4.24A leaves off. Select Menus from the c4 Monitor off delay screen (figure 4.24C, screen 1).
2. Choose from 4 seconds (4 s) to 10 minutes (10 min) delay time. The factory default of 1 min is selected (figure 4.24C, screen 2).
3. Press the OK button to lock in the setting.

Information Display

Third, let's look at configuring a time-out for the *Information display* that shows up when you press the info button. This time-out also applies to the Quick Menu that is accessed by pressing the *i* button, which allows you to adjust several camera settings quickly. You can select from 4 s to 10 min as a timeout for both screens.

Use the following steps to choose a Monitor off delay for viewing screens on the Monitor after pressing the info or *i* button:

1. Figure 4.24D picks up where figure 4.24A leaves off. Select Information display from the c4 Monitor off delay screen (figure 4.24D, screen 1).

2. Choose from 4 seconds (4 s) to 10 minutes (10 min) delay time. The factory default of 10 s is selected (figure 4.24D, screen 2).
3. Press the OK button to lock in the setting.

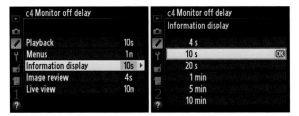

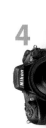

Figure 4.24D – Monitor off delay – Information display and Quick Menu

Image Review

Fourth, let's look at setting a time-out for *Image review*. When you take a picture and have *Playback Menu* > *Image review* set to On, the camera will display a picture on the Monitor for a specific period of time, controlled by the Image review timeout (2 s to 10 min).

Please note that Image review is not the same as Playback, which is concerned with viewing a series of images, maybe even hours after they were taken. Image review sets the time-out for how long an image appears on the Monitor immediately after you take it.

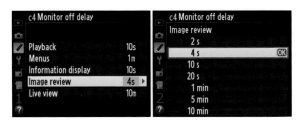

Figure 4.24E – Monitor off delay – Image review

Use the following steps to choose a Monitor off delay for viewing images immediately after taking them:

1. Figure 4.24E picks up where figure 4.24A leaves off. Select Image review from the c4 Monitor off delay screen (figure 4.24E, screen 1).
2. Choose from 2 seconds (2 s) to 10 minutes (10 min) delay time. The factory default of 4 s is selected (figure 4.24E, screen 2).
3. Press the OK button to lock in the setting.

Live View

Finally, let's look at setting a time-out for *Live view* (Lv). This time-out is used when you are taking still pictures or videos with the Monitor instead of the Viewfinder.

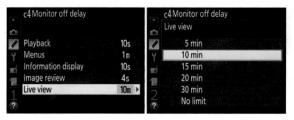

Figure 4.24F – Monitor off delay – Live view

Use the following steps to choose a Monitor off delay for viewing subjects on the Monitor after pressing the Lv button:

1. Figure 4.24F picks up where figure 4.24A leaves off. Select Live view from the c4 Monitor off delay screen (figure 4.24F, screen 1).
2. Choose from 5 minutes (5 min) to No limit delay time. The factory default of 10 min is selected (figure 4.24F, screen 2).
3. Press the OK button to lock in the setting.

Settings Recommendation: I set Monitor off delay to 1 min for Playback, Information display, and Image review on my D810.

If you want to conserve battery power, leave the Monitor off delay set to a low value like 4 to 20 seconds. The longer the Monitor stays on, the shorter the battery life, so extend the Monitor time only if you really need it. Like a small notebook computer screen, that big, luxurious 3.2-inch VGA resolution Monitor pulls a lot of power. The Monitor and Control panel backlights are probably the biggest power drains in the entire camera. However, you don't need to be overly concerned about this. With as much image review (chimping) as I do, I can still shoot most of a day on one battery charge.

Live view uses the Monitor full time, which of course drains the battery rather quickly. Therefore, it's not a good idea to have a long Live view Monitor off delay. Therefore, the 10 minute time-out seems reasonable to me, or even the 5 minute time-out if you use Live view often for taking still pictures. The timeout starts when you stop using the camera. Why leave it sitting there for a long time draining the battery?

Section Four – d Shooting/Display

Custom Settings d1 to d13

Within the *d Shooting/display* menu, you'll find 13 settings in the D810, as follows:

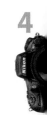

- **d1** – Beep
- **d2** – CL mode shooting speed
- **d3** – Max. continuous release
- **d4** – Exposure delay mode
- **d5** – Electronic front-curtain shutter
- **d6** – File number sequence
- **d7** – Viewfinder grid display
- **d8** – ISO display and adjustment
- **d9** – Screen tips
- **d10** – Information display
- **d11** – LCD illumination
- **d12** – MB-D12 battery type
- **d13** – Battery order

Custom Setting d1 – Beep

(User's Manual – Page 321)

The *Beep* setting allows your camera to make a beeping sound (if enabled) to alert you during the following events:

- Focus lock while in Single-servo AF (AF-S) mode
- Focus lock while in Live view mode
- Countdown in Self-timer mode operations
- At the end of Time-lapse photography
- If you try to take a picture with the memory card locked
- While using Mirror-up (Mup) mode, if you press the Shutter-release button a second time to release the shutter

You can set the camera to beep with a high- or low-pitched tone, and you can adjust the volume at which that tone sounds—or you can turn the beep sound off. When Beep is active, you'll see a little musical note displayed in the top Control panel and also in the Information display on the Monitor.

First let's examine how to set the Volume or disable Beep. It defaults to Off in the D810. The Volume settings under Beep in the Custom Setting Menu are 3, 2, 1, and Off (figure 4.25A).

Use the following steps to select one of the d1 Beep Volume choices:

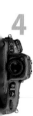

1. Select d Shooting/display from the Custom Setting Menu and scroll to the right (figure 4.25A, screen 1).
2. Highlight d1 Beep and scroll to the right (figure 4.25A, screen 2).
3. Select Volume from the menu and scroll to the right (figure 4.25A, screen 3).
4. Choose one of the four options from the list (1, 2, 3, or Off). In figure 4.25A, screen 4, Off is selected (factory default). You will hear a sample beep in each volume level as you choose it. The level 1 beep is rather quiet, so you may not hear it unless you hold your ear closer to the camera, while the level 3 beep is almost obnoxiously loud.
5. Press the OK button to lock in the setting.

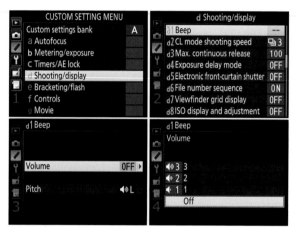

Figure 4.25A – Choosing a Volume level for the camera's Beep

Next let's consider how to change the pitch of the beep. You have two pitch levels available: High (H) and Low (L). I compared them to my piano, and the Low (L) sound is F# just above middle C. The High (H) sound is almost three octaves higher. It is the B just before three octaves above middle C.

(You probably don't need that much information; however my somewhat compulsive personality requires that I give it to you. Notice that I didn't give you the decibel level of the three Beep volume levels. Wouldn't that be excessively excessive? Of course, with my trusty Radio Shack digital sound level meter, I do have that information. If you really want it, send me an e-mail.)

Getting back on track, here are the screens and steps to select a pitch for the beep.

Use the following steps to select a Beep Pitch:

1. Select d Shooting/display from the Custom Setting Menu and scroll to the right (figure 4.25B, screen 1).

2. Highlight d1 Beep and scroll to the right (figure 4.25B, screen 2).
3. Select Pitch from the menu and scroll to the right (figure 4.25B, screen 3).
4. Choose one of the two options from the list (High or Low). In figure 4.25B, screen 4, Low is selected. You will hear a sample beep in each pitch (B or F#) as you choose it.
5. Press the OK button to lock in the setting.

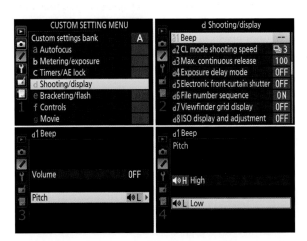
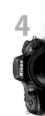

Figure 4.25B – Choosing a Pitch for the camera's Beep

Settings Recommendation: I don't use Beep; it's turned Off on my D810. If I were using my camera in a quiet area, why would I want it beeping and disturbing those around me? I can just imagine me zooming in on that big grizzly bear, pressing the Shutter-release button, and listening to the grizzly roar his displeasure at my camera's beep. I want to live, so I turn off Beep. This is another function that you either love or hate. You can have it either way, but be careful around big wild animals when Beep is enabled. They might think you're calling them to supper, and you may be the main course.

However, you might want the reassurance of hearing a beep when AF has been confirmed or when the Self-timer is counting down. If so, turn it on. The AF-assist illuminator flashes during Self-timer operations, so I generally use that instead of Beep.

By the way, Beep is automatically disabled when you're using the new Q, or Quiet, shutter-release mode on the Release mode dial, regardless of how this setting is configured.

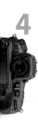

Custom Setting d2 – CL Mode Shooting Speed

(User's Manual – Page 321, 104)

CL mode shooting speed controls how many frames-per-second (fps) the camera can take when set to Continuous low speed (CL) on the Release mode dial.

CL mode is for those of us who would like to use a conservative frames-per-second (fps) rate. With the proper power in Continuous high speed (CH) mode, the camera can record 5 fps in FX mode, and up to 7 fps in DX mode. However, unless you are shooting race cars that are driv-

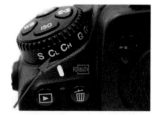

Figure 4.26A – CL mode on Release mode dial

ing 200 mph, and unless you have large memory cards, you may not want a large number of frames of the same subject a few hundredths of a second apart. Therefore, Nikon has given you CL mode to rein in the number of images you will capture in a burst, while still giving you multiple-image capture capability.

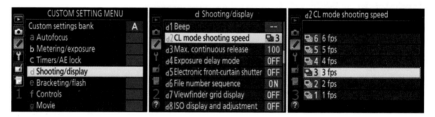

Figure 4.26B – CL mode shooting speed

Here are the steps used to configure CL mode shooting speed:

1. Select d Shooting/display from the Custom Setting Menu and scroll to the right (figure 4.26B, screen 1).
2. Highlight d2 CL mode shooting speed and scroll to the right (figure 4.26B, screen 2).
3. Choose one of the six choices on the list. In figure 4.26B, screen 3, 3 fps has been selected. If you set this setting to 5 fps, it will equal the CH setting on the Release mode dial. 6 fps is not available unless you have *Shooting Menu > Image area > Choose image area* set to DX mode.
4. Press the OK button to lock in the setting.

As the last screen in figure 4.26B, screen 3, shows, you can adjust CL mode shooting speed so that your camera shoots at any frame rate from 1 to 6 fps. The default is 3 fps. Remember, you always have CH mode for when you want to blast off images like there's no end to your memory card(s), or when you want to impress bystanders with that extra-cool Nikon shutter-clicking sound.

Note: When you are shooting Interval timer photography, this setting also sets the frame advance rate for single-frame.

Settings Recommendation: Use your favorite CL mode shooting speed, and grab a few, or many, frames with each press and hold of the Shutter-release button. I leave mine set at the default of 2 fps because that is reasonably fast yet not wasteful of card space. If you'd like, you can slow it all the way down to 1 fps and take only one picture each second that you hold the Shutter-release button down. You'll need to play around with this setting and decide for yourself what speed you like.

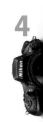

Again, remember that you have both low (CL) and high (CH) speeds for the camera's shooting rate. This function is for the low speed setting (CL) found on the Release mode dial.

The D810 is not a very fast camera when it comes to frames per second, especially compared to a blazing-speed camera like the Nikon D4s. In all honesty, this CL mode shooting speed function is not all that useful to me. If I need to shoot a series of images in rapid sequence, 5 fps (CH mode) is usually barely enough. However, for consistency's sake and for those who really need slower speeds, Nikon makes this function available.

Custom Setting d3 – Max. Continuous Release

(User's Manual – Page 322, 489)

Max. continuous release sets the maximum number of images you can shoot in a single burst. It sounds like you can just start blasting away with your camera, shooting in a single burst until you have reached number specified in figure 4.27, screen 3, which is up to 100 images. While it is possible that you could reach 100 images in a single burst, it is improbable. Your camera is limited by the size of its internal memory buffer and the image format you are shooting.

There's a list in your camera User's Manual that specifies how large your camera's buffer is for each image type. In case you're interested in the raw buffer capacity data, the list is on page 489. Here is a summary of what the User's Manual reports concerning FX mode (there is some variation for changes in *Shooting Menu > Image area*):

- **NEF (RAW) files** – In FX mode (36×24 Image area), while using an FX lens, the memory buffer holds from 18 to 58 images. These same numbers also apply if you are using an FX lens in DX mode. While using a DX lens in DX mode (24×16 Image area), the buffer holds 23 to 100 images. The number varies for both FX and DX shooting, according to whether you are shooting with 12- or 14-bit color-or-depth and whether or not you are using compression.
- **TIFF files** – In FX mode (36×24 Image area), while using an FX lens, the memory buffer holds from 25 to 72 images. The same numbers apply if you are using an FX lens with the camera set to DX mode. While using a DX lens in DX mode

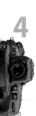

(24×16 Image area), the buffer holds 39 to 100 images. The number varies for both FX and DX shooting, according to whether you are shooting L, M, or S size images.

- **JPEG files** – In both FX (36×24 Image area) and DX (24x16) mode, the camera will hold up to 100 images in its internal buffer, regardless of the image size, compression level, or type of lens used.

Note: All the preceding figures are approximate and will vary with the complexity of the subject matter in the image. The maximum number of images stored in the buffer may drop to a lower number in the following situations:

- JPEG Optimal quality compression is On
- ISO sensitivity is set to Hi 0.3 or higher
- Enabling High ISO NR when Auto ISO sensitivity control is On
- Enabling High ISO NR when ISO sensitivity is set to ISO Hi 0.3 or higher
- Long exposure noise reduction is On
- Auto distortion control is On

Unless you are shooting with JPEG Size priority compression, you may fill up your camera buffer before you reach the maximum of 100 shots specified by Max. continuous release.

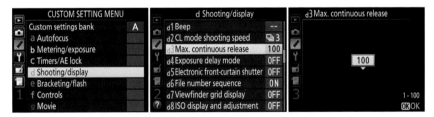

Figure 4.27 – Max. continuous release

Here are the steps used to configure Max. continuous release:

1. Select d Shooting/display from the Custom Setting Menu and scroll to the right (figure 4.27, screen 1).
2. Highlight d3 Max. continuous release and scroll to the right (figure 4.27, screen 2).
3. Use the Multi selector to scroll up or down and set the number of images you want in each burst. In figure 4.27, screen 3, 100 has been selected.
4. Press the OK button to lock in the setting.

Settings Recommendation: If you have a need to limit your camera to a maximum number of images in each shooting burst, simply change this number from its default of 100 images to whatever you feel works best for you. Personally, I want

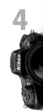

the buffer to hold as many images as it possibly can when I am blasting away in high-speed shooting modes, so I leave Max. continuous release set to 100.

However, you may want to artificially limit the camera to a maximum number of frames in one burst. If so, simply select the maximum number of images in figure 4.27, screen 3, and the camera will stop when it reaches that number. This allows you to maintain some control over your enthusiastic high-speed shooting. Do you really want dozens and dozens (and dozens) of pictures of those flying seagulls?

Custom Setting d4 – Exposure Delay Mode

(User's Manual – Page 322)

Exposure delay mode introduces a delay of 1 to 3 seconds after the Shutter-release button is pressed—and the reflex mirror raised—before the shutter is actually released. Hopefully, during the 1-second delay, camera vibrations will die down and the image will be sharper.

The following settings are available in Exposure delay mode (figure 4.28).

- *1 s*, *2 s*, or *3 s* – The camera first raises the reflex (viewing) mirror and then waits 1, 2, or 3 seconds before firing the shutter, depending on the selection you choose, as shown in figure 4.28, screen 3. This allows the vibrations from the mirror movement to dissipate before the shutter fires. Of course, this won't be useful at all for shooting anything moving or for any type of action shots. But for slow shooters of static scenes, this is great and keeps you from having to use Mirror-up (MUP), which requires you to press the Shutter-release button twice to take a picture. It has the same effect as MUP but requires only one Shutter-release button press and a 1- to 3-second delay.
- *Off* – The shutter has no delay when this setting is turned off.

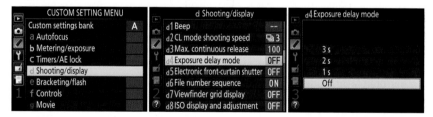

Figure 4.28 – Exposure delay mode

Here are the steps used to configure Exposure delay mode:

1. Select d Shooting/display from the Custom Setting Menu and scroll to the right (figure 4.28, screen 1).
2. Highlight d4 Exposure delay mode and scroll to the right (figure 4.28, screen 2).

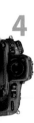

3. Choose one of the four choices on the list. In figure 4.28, screen 3, Off has been selected.
4. Press the OK button to lock in the setting.

Settings Recommendation: Exposure delay mode is very important to me. As a nature shooter, I use it frequently for single shots. When I'm shooting handheld—or even on a tripod—and want a really sharp image, I use this mode to prevent the camera's internal reflex mirror movement from vibrating my camera and blurring my pictures.

If you handhold your camera, shoot mostly static subjects, and want sharper pictures, this will help. On a tripod, this is a time-saver compared to Mirror-up (MUP) mode, which requires two Shutter-release button presses, or a 30-second delay.

Custom Setting d5 – Electronic Front-Curtain Shutter

(User's Manual – Page 323)

Use *Electronic front-curtain shutter* when you have selected MUP (mirror up) mode (on the Release mode dial; figure 4.29A) to minimize camera vibrations.

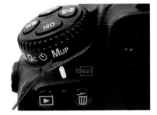

The D810 has two mechanical curtains in its shutter assembly, a front curtain and a rear one. Normally, it uses both of these shutter curtains during an exposure in all Release modes, includ-ing MUP.

Figure 4.29A – Selecting mirror up (MUP) mode

However, when you enable the Electronic front-curtain shutter and are using MUP mode, the camera withdraws the mechan-ical first curtain before the exposure starts. The exposure is then initiated by simply turning on the sensor to receive light, for whatever shutter speed time is selected. At the end of the exposure, the rear curtain closes to block light from hitting the sensor, ending the exposure. This removes the vibration caused by the mechani-cal front curtain moving out of the way, and since the camera has already raised the mirror in MUP mode, there are no vibrations created by the shutter during the exposure. Using this mode will let you create some of the sharpest images you have ever made.

To use this mode, enable the Electronic first-curtain shutter setting and then set your camera to MUP mode. The Electronic first-curtain shutter does not work in any other exposure mode besides MUP and while using Live view.

Here are the steps used to configure Exposure delay mode:

1. Select d Shooting/display from the Custom Setting Menu and scroll to the right (figure 4.29B, screen 1).
2. Highlight d5 Electronic front-curtain shutter and scroll to the right (figure 4.28, screen 2).

3. Choose Enable to withdraw the mechanical first-curtain shutter during MUP exposures (only). Select Disable to turn the Electronic first-curtain shutter off. In figure 4.29B, screen 3, Enable has been selected.
4. Press the OK button to lock in the setting.

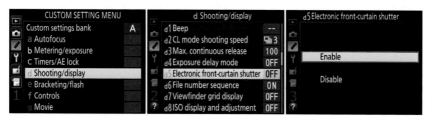
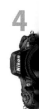

Figure 4.29B – Enabling or disabling the Electronic front-curtain shutter setting

Settings Recommendation: I leave d5 Electronic first-curtain shutter (EFCS) set to Enable at all times. Since it is only active for MUP mode exposures, and I always want to reduce vibrations in MUP mode, it seems reasonable to leave it enabled so that the camera is prepared to take the sharpest pictures.

Nikon recommends that you use a type G, D, or E lens with the EFCS. Nikon limits the shutter speed to 1/2000 second when the EFCS is active. If you are using lenses other than G, D, or E and notice lines or fogging in the image, it may be best to Disable the EFCS or switch lenses to a recommended type.

One of the concerns that some people have had with an EFCS is that due to the lack of delay from the mechanical shutter, there may not be enough time for the lens iris (aperture) to close down fast enough, thereby affecting the exposure. However, one of the side benefits of using MUP mode is that it stops down the aperture at the same time it raises the mirror. Therefore, when using MUP and the EFCS, it is safe to use even old lenses with slower iris blades on the D810 without worry.

Some have reported (on other camera brands besides Nikon) that they have seen some underexposure issues when using an EFCS with very high shutter speeds, which, I suppose, is why Nikon limits the shutter speed to 1/2000 second. Others have reported some distortion with a subject moving at a very high speed. Therefore, you should test your camera in MUP mode with the EFCS to see if you detect any problems when using it for your style of photography.

Custom Setting d6 – File Number Sequence

(User's Manual – Page 324)

File number sequence allows your camera to keep count of the image file numbers for each picture you take, in a running sequence from 0001 to 9999. After 9999 pictures, it rolls back over to 0001. Or, you can cause it to reset the image number to 0001 when you format or insert a new memory card.

Here are the three settings, and an explanation of how each works:

- **On** (default) – Image file numbers start at 0001 and continue running in a sequence until you exceed 9999, at which point the image numbers roll over to 0001 again. The File number sequence continues even if a new folder is created, a new memory card is inserted, or the current memory card is formatted. If the file number exceeds 9999 during a shoot, the camera will create a brand-new folder on the same memory card and start writing the new images in numbered order from 0001 into the new folder. Similarly, if you accumulate 999 images in the current folder, the next image capture will result in the camera creating a new folder, but the file numbering will not be reset to 0001 unless that 999th image had a file number of 9999. No matter what you do with your memory cards, or how many folders you or the camera create, the File number sequence will continue incrementing until 9999 images have been taken. Only then will the File number sequence reset to 0001. In other words, file numbering continues from the last number used or the largest file number in the current folder, whichever is bigger, until 9999 images are reached, at which point the camera starts the numbering sequence over at 0001.
- **Off** – Whenever you format or insert a new a memory card, the number sequence starts over at 0001. If you exceed 999 images in a single folder, the camera creates a new folder and starts counting images at 0001 again.
- **Reset** – This is similar to the On setting. However, it is not a true running total to 9999 because the image number is dependent on the folder in use. The camera simply takes the last number it finds in the current folder and adds 1 to it, up to 999. If you switch to an empty folder, the numbering starts over at 0001. Because a folder cannot hold over 999 pictures, you will not exceed 999 images in any one folder. Each folder has its own number series and causes a File number sequence Reset.

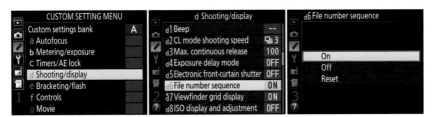

Figure 4.30 – File number sequence

Here are the steps used to configure File number sequence:

1. Select d Shooting/display from the Custom Setting Menu and scroll to the right (figure 4.30, screen 1).
2. Highlight d6 File number sequence and scroll to the right (figure 4.30, screen 2).

3. Choose one of the three choices on the list. In figure 4.30, screen 3, On has been selected. On is the best choice for most of us.
4. Press the OK button to lock in the setting.

Settings Recommendation: I heartily recommend that you set File number sequence to On, if it has been turned off. After much experience with Nikon DSLR cameras, and many years of storing thousands of files, I've found that the fewer number of files with similar image numbers, the better. Why take a chance on accidentally overwriting the last shooting session when copying files on your computer just because they have the same image numbers?

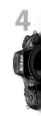

Custom Setting d7 – Viewfinder Grid Display

(User's Manual – Page 325)

A few years ago, the 35mm film Nikon N80/F80 was released with a *Viewfinder grid display*, and I was hooked. Later, as I bought more professional cameras, I was chagrined to find that they did not have the on-demand gridlines that I had grown to love.

With the D810, you have not only a Viewfinder grid display, but also Live view (LV) gridlines. The best of both worlds! There are only two selections in Viewfinder grid display:

- **On** – Gridlines are displayed in the Viewfinder and on the Monitor in LV mode.
- **Off** – No gridlines are displayed.

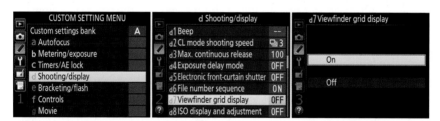

Figure 4.31 – Viewfinder grid display

Here are the steps used to enable/disable the Viewfinder grid display:

1. Select d Shooting/display from the Custom Setting Menu and scroll to the right (figure 4.31, screen 1).
2. Highlight d7 Viewfinder grid display and scroll to the right (figure 4.31, screen 2).
3. Choose On or Off from the list. In figure 4.31, screen 3, On has been selected.
4. Press the OK button to lock in the setting.

Settings Recommendation: I use these gridlines to line up things as I shoot so that I won't have weird tilted horizons and such. Many of us tend to tilt the camera one way or another, and gridlines help us see that we've tilted the frame.

I especially enjoy shooting with gridlines enabled when I'm down at the beach. Who needs tilted ocean views? When you're shooting architecture, the gridlines are invaluable for making sure buildings, walls, and doors are correctly oriented with the edge of the frame. There are lots of ways to use the Viewfinder grid display.

If you set Viewfinder grid display to On, I doubt you'll turn it back Off. The nice thing is that you can turn the gridlines On and Off at will. You don't have to buy an expensive viewfinder replacement screen for those times you need gridlines. Good stuff, Nikon!

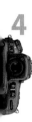

Custom Setting d8 – ISO Display and Adjustment

(User's Manual – Page 325)

The *ISO display and adjustment* setting modifies how the D810 shows you the ISO sensitivity in the Control panel and Viewfinder, where you can normally see the frame count, or how many pictures you have left to take before the memory card is full. You can use ISO display and adjustment to modify the readout so the ISO sensitivity is shown instead of the frame count. There are three settings:

- **Show ISO sensitivity** – This setting displays the ISO sensitivity, instead of the frame count, in the Control panel.
- **Show ISO/Easy ISO** – This setting affects how you adjust the ISO sensitivity as well as how it is displayed. It works like Show ISO sensitivity in that it replaces the frame count with the ISO sensitivity value. It also adds a way to change the ISO sensitivity while taking pictures. Normally you would use *Shooting Menu > ISO sensitivity settings* or press the ISO button and turn the rear Main command dial to change the ISO sensitivity. However, when you enable Show ISO/Easy ISO, the camera lets you adjust the ISO sensitivity with either the rear Main command dial or front Sub-command dial alone, without using the ISO button, according to which exposure mode you are using. This applies only when you use the P, S, or A modes on the Mode dial.

  Normally, when you have the camera in P or S mode, you control the aperture (P mode) or shutter speed (S mode) with the rear Main command dial. The front Sub-command dial does nothing. When you set the camera to Show ISO/Easy ISO, the front Sub-command dial now sets the ISO sensitivity when the P or S mode is set. Likewise, when the camera is set to A mode, you normally control the aperture with the front Sub-command dial, and the rear Main command dial does nothing. When you enable Show ISO/Easy ISO in A mode, the camera lets you adjust ISO sensitivity with the unused rear Main command dial, and you continue to control the aperture with the front Sub-command dial. Basically, for photographers who need to adjust ISO sensitivity quickly while shooting, this can be very convenient. M mode on the Mode dial is not affected by this setting.

- ***Show frame count*** (default) – This is the default setting and leaves the camera functioning as normal, with the frame count showing in the Control panel and Viewfinder.

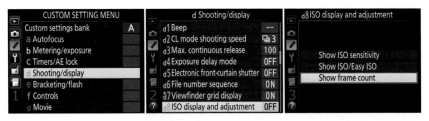
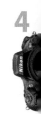

Figure 4.32 – Using ISO display and adjustment

Use the following steps to select an ISO display and adjustment setting:

1. Select d Shooting/display from the Custom Setting Menu and scroll to the right (figure 4.32, screen 1).
2. Highlight d8 ISO display and adjustment and scroll to the right (figure 4.32, screen 2).
3. Choose one of the three settings from the menu. In figure 4.32, screen 3, Show frame count is selected.
4. Press the OK button to lock in the setting.

Settings Recommendation: I find little use for this setting because the ISO button is so easily available. My slow and deliberate tripod-based style of nature shooting rarely requires changing ISO sensitivity from its low settings (ISO 64–100). However, I recognize that many people need to change ISO sensitivity on the fly and may not want to use the Auto ISO sensitivity control, which adjusts ISO sensitivity automatically, within bounds, to get the shot.

This feature shows how interested Nikon is in giving us very fine control over our cameras. You can use automatic methods or control everything manually. ISO display and adjustment basically gives you manual control over a feature that most people would manage with Auto ISO sensitivity control.

If you are an action shooter and find yourself in varying light levels where you want to maintain fast manual control over ISO sensitivity, maybe you should learn to use this feature.

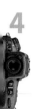

Custom Setting d9 – Screen Tips

(User's Manual – Page 325)

Screen tips allows you to enable small, helpful tips on the camera's Quick Menu screen, which is accessed by pressing the camera's *i* button. The Quick Menu allows you to change several important settings. It's a shortcut screen with settings that are accessed frequently, such as the Shooting menu bank and Custom settings bank.

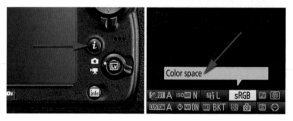

Figure 4.33A – The Quick Menu with Screen tips enabled

Figure 4.33A, screen 1, shows the *i* button that you'll use to access the Quick Menu, where the Screen tips are displayed, and screen 2 shows the Quick Menu. I have Screen tips enabled on my camera, so you can see the small Screen tip for selecting the Color space (figure 4.33A, screen 2). Screen tips help you identify what the otherwise cryptic symbols on the Quick Menu screen represent.

If you press the OK button when you have one of the settings highlighted on the Quick Menu screen—as figure 4.33A, screen 2, shows for Color space—the camera will switch to a normal text menu and allow you to modify the setting. If you disable Screen tips, the little white tip bar shown at the red arrow in screen 2 will not be displayed.

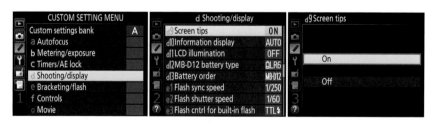

Figure 4.33B – Enabling Screen tips

Here are the steps to configure Screen tips:

1. Select d Shooting/display from the Custom Setting Menu and scroll to the right (figure 4.33B, screen 1).
2. Highlight d9 Screen tips and scroll to the right (figure 4.33B, screen 2).

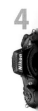

3. Choose On or Off from the list. In figure 4.33B, screen 3, On has been selected.
4. Press the OK button to lock in the setting.

Settings Recommendation: This is a helpful function that gives you "tool tips" for using the Quick Menu screen. I leave this set to the factory default of On. These little tips don't get in the way of anything, and they help remind you which setting you are looking at on the Quick Menu.

Custom Setting d10 – Information Display

(User's Manual – Page 326)

The *Information display* setting allows your camera to automatically sense how much ambient light there is in the area where you are shooting and adjust the color and brightness of the Information display screen accordingly. If the ambient light is bright, the color of the physical Information display screen will also be bright so it can overcome the ambient light.

To open the Information display screen, press the info button. The Information display screen shows the current shooting information.

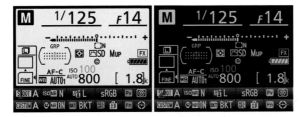

Figure 4.34A – (1) Dark-on-light and (2) Light-on-dark display screens

Figure 4.34A shows the difference between the light and dark screens, which you can select by using one of the two Manual settings or by using Auto to allow the camera to select a screen automatically. In figure 4.34A, screen 1 is the Dark-on-light screen and screen 2 is the Light-on-dark screen.

Try this: With your lens cap off, your camera turned on, and nothing displayed on the rear Monitor, press the info button. If there's dim to bright ambient light, you'll see a white information screen with black characters. Now, go into a dark area or put your lens cap on and cover the Viewfinder eyepiece with your hand. You'll see that anytime there is very little ambient light, the camera changes the Information display screen to light gray characters on a dark background. This assures that you won't be blinded when you need to see the shooting information in a dark area.

In screen 2 of figure 4.34A, I have actually brightened the screen's gray text so that it is clear in the printed book. In real life it is somewhat dimmer than displayed to allow you to keep your night vision.

As shown in figure 4.34B, image 3, there are two available selections for the Information display setting:

- **Auto** – The D810 decides through its capless lens or uncovered Viewfinder eyepiece how much ambient light there is and changes the color and contrast of the Information display screen accordingly.
- **Manual** – The Manual setting allows you to select the light or dark version of the Information display screen manually. If you choose Manual, you can see in figure 4.34C, screen 4, that you have two options: B Dark on light (white screen) and W Light on dark (dark screen).

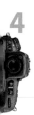

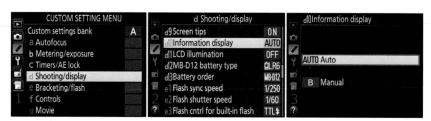

Figure 4.34B – Setting Information display to Auto

Use the following steps to configure the Information display setting for Auto:

1. Select d Shooting/display from the Custom Setting Menu and scroll to the right (figure 4.34B, screen 1).
2. Highlight d10 Information display and scroll to the right (figure 4.34B, screen 2).
3. In figure 4.34B, screen 3, Auto is selected. The camera will choose the light or dark screen depending on the ambient light level.
4. Press the OK button to lock in the setting.

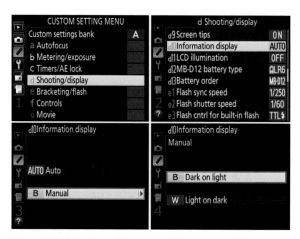

Figure 4.34C – Setting Information display to Manual

If you want to manually select the screen color for your camera's Information display screen, use the following steps:

1. Select d Shooting/display from the Custom Setting Menu and scroll to the right (figure 4.34C, screen 1).
2. Highlight d10 Information display and scroll to the right (figure 4.34C, screen 2).
3. Choose B Manual and scroll to the right (figure 4.34C, screen 3).
4. The next screen shows the B Dark on light and W Light on dark choices. In figure 4.34C, screen 4, B Dark on light is selected, so the light screen will be displayed when I press the info button.
5. Press the OK button to lock in the setting.

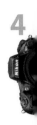

Settings Recommendation: I leave Information display set to Auto because it seems to work very well at automatically selecting the proper screen for current light conditions.

If you want to impress your friends and make your enemies envious, just show them how cool your camera is when it's smart enough to adjust its screen color to the current light conditions.

Custom Setting d11 – LCD Illumination

(User's Manual – Page 326)

The *LCD illumination* setting gives you a simple way to set how the illumination of the Control panel LCD backlight works. When it's on, the Control panel lights up in yellowish green. Here are the two choices and how they work:

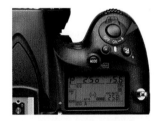

Figure 4.35A – Backlight position of the Power and backlight switch

- **Off** (default) – If you leave LCD illumination set to Off, the Control panel will not turn on its backlight unless you tell it to by moving the Power switch to the backlight setting (figure 4.35A). If you move the Power switch all the way to the right, the Control panel will light up. The length of time the Control panel backlight stays on is controlled by the delay value selected in *Custom Setting Menu > c Timers/AE lock > Standby timer*, which also controls how long the light meter stays on after activation.
- **On** – This setting makes the Control panel illumination come on anytime the exposure meter is active. If you shoot in the dark and need to refer to the Control panel often, then switch this setting to On. This setting will cause a greater battery drain.

Use the following steps to configure the LCD illumination setting:

1. Select d Shooting/display from the Custom Setting Menu and scroll to the right (figure 4.35B, screen 1).
2. Highlight d11 LCD illumination and scroll to the right (figure 4.35B, image 2).
3. Choose either On or Off from the menu. In figure 4.35B, image 3, Off is selected.
4. Press the OK button to lock in the setting.

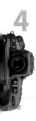
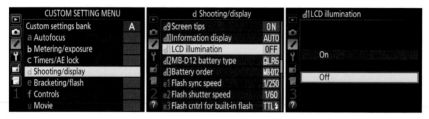

Figure 4.35B – LCD illumination

Settings Recommendation: This setting will affect the camera's battery life because backlights pull a lot of power, so I don't suggest using the On setting unless you really need it. You have the Power switch (On/Off/Backlight)—surrounding the shutter-release button—to manually turn on the Control panel light when needed.

Custom Setting d12 – MB-D12 Battery Type

(User's Manual – Page 327)

MB-D12 battery type applies only when you choose to use AA-sized batteries of various types in your optional MB-D12 battery pack. It does not apply when you are using normal Nikon EN-EL3e, EN-EL4, or EN-EL4a li-ion batteries because they're intelligent and communicate with the camera.

If you have an MB-D12 and plan on using cheap AA batteries, then you'll need to tell the camera what type of AA batteries you're using for this session. It certainly is not a good idea to mix AA battery types.

These are the battery types the camera will accept (figure 4.36):

- LR6 (AA alkaline)
- HR6 (AA Ni-MH)
- FR6 (AA lithium)

Here are the steps used to configure the MB-D12 battery type:

1. Select d Shooting/display from the Custom Setting Menu and scroll to the right (figure 4.36, screen 1).
2. Highlight d12 MB-D12 battery type and scroll to the right (figure 4.36, screen 2).
3. Choose one of the three choices on the list. In figure 4.36, screen 3, LR6 (AA alkaline) has been selected.

4. Press the OK button to lock in the setting.

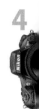

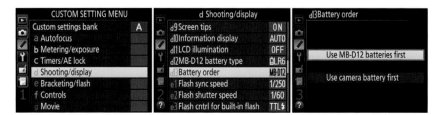

Figure 4.36 – MB-D12 battery type

Settings Recommendation: Nikon allows but does not recommend using certain AA batteries, such as alkaline (LR6). Its primary objection to this type is that they do not work well at lower temperatures. In fact, once the ambient temperature drops below 68 degrees F (20 degrees C), an alkaline battery starts losing its ability to deliver power and will die rather quickly. You may not get as many shots out of a set of AA batteries, so your cost of shooting may rise.

However, AA batteries are readily available and relatively low cost, so some people like to use them, especially in an emergency. If you do choose to use AA batteries, I recommend sticking with lithium types (FR6). That is the same type of cell used in the normal Nikon EN-EL15 batteries and is not affected as much by a low ambient temperature. You can also use the Ni-MH (HR6, nickel-metal hydride) batteries safely because they are not as temperature sensitive and provide consistent power.

Custom Setting d13 – Battery Order

(User's Manual – Page 328)

Battery order lets you choose the order in which you want the available batteries to be used—camera's battery first or those in the MB-D12 battery pack first.

Here are the two menu choices:

- Use MB-D12 batteries first
- Use camera battery first

Figure 4.37 – Battery order

Here are the steps used to configure the Battery order:

1. Select d Shooting/display from the Custom Setting Menu and scroll to the right (figure 4.37, screen 1).
2. Highlight d12 Battery order and scroll to the right (figure 4.37, screen 2).
3. Choose one of the two settings on the list. In figure 4.37, screen 3, Use MB-D12 batteries first has been selected.
4. Press the OK button to lock in the setting.

Settings Recommendation: Which battery do you want to draw down first? Personally, I like to use the MB-D12 batteries first and have my camera's internal battery available as a backup. That way, if I remove the MB-D12, my camera won't suddenly go dead due to a depleted battery. Nikon thinks the same way, evidently, because the camera defaults to Use MB-D12 batteries first.

Section Five – e Bracketing/Flash

Custom Settings e1 to e7

Within the *e Bracketing/flash* menu, you'll find eight settings in the D810:

- **e1** – Flash sync speed
- **e2** – Flash shutter speed
- **e3** – Flash cntrl for built-in flash
- **e4** – Exposure comp. for flash
- **e5** – Modeling flash
- **e6** – Auto bracketing set
- **e7** – Auto bracketing (Mode M)
- **e8** – Bracketing order

Custom Setting e1 – Flash Sync Speed

(User's Manual – Page 329)

Flash sync speed lets you select a basic flash synchronization speed from 1/60 s to 1/250 s. The D810 has a more flexible Flash sync speed than many cameras. Or, if you prefer, you can use the two Auto FP modes of your camera—1/250 s (Auto FP) or 1/320 s (Auto FP). These Auto FP modes are available only with certain external Speedlights and not with the built-in pop-up Speedlight. The built-in flash is limited to 1/250 s.

At press time, seven Nikon Speedlights can be used with the D810 in Auto FP high-speed sync mode:

- SB-910
- SB-900
- SB-800
- SB-700
- SB-600
- SB-500
- SB-R200

Auto FP high-speed sync enables the use of fill flash even in bright daylight with wide aperture settings. It allows you to set your camera to the highest shutter speed available, up to 1/8000s, and still use the external flash unit to fill in shadows. See the upcoming section titled **Auto FP High-Speed Sync Review**, where we discuss how this works. Here are your choices (figure 4.38, screen 3):

- 1/320 s (Auto FP)
- 1/250 s (Auto FP)
- 1/250 s

- 1/200 s
- 1/160 s
- 1/125 s

- 1/100 s
- 1/80 s
- 1/60 s

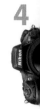

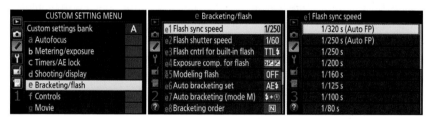

Figure 4.38 – Flash sync speed

Here are the steps used to adjust your camera's Flash sync speed:

1. Select e Bracketing/flash from the Custom Setting Menu and scroll to the right (figure 4.38, screen 1).
2. Highlight e1 Flash sync speed and scroll to the right (figure 4.38, screen 2).
3. Choose one of the nine choices on the list—1/60 s to 1/320 s (Auto FP). In figure 4.38, screen 3, 1/320 s (Auto FP) has been selected.
4. Press the OK button to lock in the setting.

When you're using Auto FP mode, the output of your flash is reduced but doesn't cut off the frame for exposures using a shutter speed higher than the normal flash sync speed (X Sync). Why? Let's review.

Auto FP High-Speed Sync Review

In a normal flash situation, with shutter speeds of 1/250 of a second and slower, the entire shutter is fully open and the flash can fire a single burst of light to expose the subject. It works like this: There are two shutter curtains in your camera. The first shutter curtain opens, exposing the sensor to your subject. The flash fires, providing correct exposure, and then the second shutter curtain closes. For a very brief period, the entire sensor is uncovered. The flash fires during the time when the sensor is fully uncovered.

However, when your camera's shutter speed goes above 1/250 of a second, the shutter curtains are never fully open for the flash to expose the entire subject in one burst of light. The reason is that at higher shutter speeds, the first shutter curtain starts opening and the second shutter curtain quickly starts following it. In effect, a slit of light is scanning across the surface of your sensor, exposing the subject. If the flash fired normally, a flash of light would expose the width of that slit between the shutter curtains, but the rest of the sensor would be blocked by the curtains. You would have a band of correctly exposed image, and everything else would be underexposed.

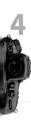

What happens to your external Nikon Speedlight to allow it to follow that slit of light moving across the sensor? It changes from a normal flash unit into a pulsing strobe unit. Have you ever danced under a strobe light? A strobe works by firing a series of light pulses. Similarly, when your camera's shutter speed is so high that the Speedlight cannot fire a single burst of light for correct exposure, it can use its Auto FP high-speed sync mode and fire a series of light bursts over and over as the shutter curtain slit travels in front of the image sensor. The Speedlight can fire thousands of bursts per second. To a photographer or subject, it still looks like one big flash of light, even though in reality it is hundreds or thousands of bursts of light, one right after the other.

When the camera is set to Auto FP mode, you'll see something like this on the Speedlight's LCD monitor:

- TTL FP
- TTL BL FP

This tells you that the camera and Speedlight are ready for you to use any shutter speed you'd like and still get a good exposure. Even with wide open apertures!

You can safely leave your camera set to 1/320 s Auto FP or 1/250 s Auto FP all the time because the high-speed sync mode does not kick in until you raise the shutter speed above the maximum setting of 1/250 s. Below that shutter speed, the flash works in normal mode and does not waste any power by pulsing the output.

This pulsing of light reduces the maximum output of your flash significantly but allows you to use any shutter speed you'd like while still firing your external Speedlight. The higher the shutter speed, the lower the flash output. In effect, your camera is depending on you to provide enough ambient light to offset the loss in power. I've found that even my powerful SB-910 Speedlight can provide only enough power to light a subject out to about 8 feet (2.4 m) when using a 1/8000s shutter speed. With shutter speeds that high, there needs to be enough ambient light to help the flash light the subject, unless you are very close to the subject.

However, now you can use wide apertures to isolate your subject in direct sunlight—which requires high shutter speeds. The flash will adjust and provide great fill light if you're using Auto FP high-speed sync mode.

Note: If your flash fires at full power in normal modes, it will blink the flash indicator in the Viewfinder to let you know that all available flash power has been used and that you need to check to see if the image is underexposed. When the camera is

> ### Which Flash Units for Auto FP High-Speed Sync Mode?
>
> If you are using the camera's built-in pop-up Speedlight, or the small Nikon SB-300 or SB-400, your camera's maximum flash shutter speed is limited to 1/250 s. If you use the external Speedlights SB-910, SB-900, SB-800, SB-700, SB-600, SB-500, and SB-R200, you can use any shutter speed and the flash will adjust (pulse) to match lighting needs. With the larger Speedlights, you'll need to learn how to balance ambient light with light from the flash when using shutter speeds higher than 1/250 s. Just remember that your flash unit's range will be seriously reduced at higher shutter speeds.

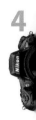

firing in Auto FP high-speed sync mode, that doesn't happen. You'll get no warning in the Viewfinder if the image does not have enough light. Check the camera's histogram often to validate your exposures when using Auto FP.

Special Shutter Speed Setting X + Flash Sync Speed

When using Manual (M) or Shutter-priority auto (S) exposure modes, there is still one more setting below 30 seconds and bulb, named X + Flash sync speed. This special setting allows you to set the camera to a known shutter speed and shoot away. You will see X 250 if Custom Setting Menu > e1 Flash sync speed is set to 1/250 s. Whatever Flash sync speed you select will show up after the X. If you select a Flash sync speed of 1/125 s, then X 125 will show up as the next setting below bulb. Selecting a Flash sync speed of 1/60 s means that X 60 will show up below bulb.

The shutter speed will not vary from your chosen setting. The camera will adjust the aperture and flash when in Shutter-priority auto (S) mode, or you can adjust the aperture while the flash controls exposure in Manual (M) mode.

This special X-Sync mode is not available in Aperture-priority auto (A) or Programmed auto (P) modes because the camera controls the shutter speed in those two settings. Primarily, you'll use this setting when you are shooting in Manual or in Shutter-priority auto and want to use a known X-Sync speed.

Settings Recommendation: I leave my camera set to 1/320 s (Auto FP) as shown in figure 4.38, screen 3, all the time. The camera works just as it normally would until one of my settings takes it above 1/250 s shutter speed, at which time it starts pulsing the light to match the shutter curtain travel. Once again, you won't be able to detect this high-frequency strobe effect because it happens so fast it seems like a single burst of light.

Just remember that the flash loses significant power (or reach) at higher shutter speeds because it is forced to work so hard. Be sure you experiment with this to get the best results. You can use a big aperture like f/1.4 to have very shallow depth of

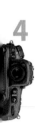

field in direct bright sunlight because you can use very high shutter speeds. This will allow you to make images that many others simply cannot create. Learn to balance the flash and ambient light in Auto FP high-speed sync mode. All this technical talk will make sense when you see the results. Pretty cool stuff!

Custom Setting e2 – Flash Shutter Speed

(User's Manual – Page 331)

Flash shutter speed controls the minimum shutter speed your camera can use in various flash modes. You can select between 30 seconds (30 s) and 1/60 of a second (1/60 s). Whereas the previous function, Flash sync speed, controls the fastest shutter speed available, Flash shutter speed controls the slowest shutter speed available in specific modes.

Let's consider each mode and its minimum shutter speed:

- ***Front-curtain sync, Rear-curtain sync,* or *Red-eye reduction*** – In Programmed auto (P) mode or Aperture-priority auto (A) mode, the slowest shutter speed can be selected from the range of 1/60 second (1/60 s) to 30 seconds (30 s) (figure 4.39). Shutter-priority (S) mode and Manual (M) mode cause the camera to ignore Flash shutter speed, and the slowest shutter speed can be as slow as 30 seconds (30 s) if the photographer chooses a speed that slow.
- ***Slow sync, Red-eye reduction with slow sync,* or *Slow rear-curtain sync*** – These three modes ignore Flash shutter speed, and the slowest shutter speed can be as slow as 30 seconds (30 s) if the camera or photographer chooses a shutter speed that slow.

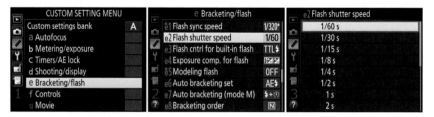

Figure 4.39 – Flash shutter speed

Here are the steps to set the Flash shutter speed minimum:

1. Select e Bracketing/flash from the Custom Setting Menu and scroll to the right (figure 4.39, screen 1).
2. Highlight e2 Flash shutter speed and scroll to the right (figure 4.39, screen 2).
3. Choose one of the settings on the list—1/60 s to 30 s. In figure 4.39, screen 3, 1/60 s has been selected. Remember that slower shutter speeds can cause subject ghosting when flash is used in high ambient light conditions.
4. Press the OK button to lock in the setting.

Custom setting e2 is only partially used by the flash modes because the default is preset to as slow as 30 seconds in Shutter-priority and Manual modes.

Settings Recommendation: I normally use 1/60 s. Shutter speeds lower than 1/60 s can cause ghosting if the ambient light is too high. The subject can move after the flash fires but with the shutter still open and with enough ambient light to record a blurred ghost effect. You'll have a well-exposed picture of the subject with a ghost of him also showing in the image. Use slower shutter speeds only when you are sure that you'll be in dark conditions and the flash will provide the only lighting—unless you're shooting special effects, like a blurred aftereffect following your subject to imply movement.

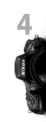

Custom Setting e3 – Flash Cntrl for Built-in Flash

(User's Manual – Page 331)

Flash cntrl for built-in flash provides four distinct ways to control the pop-up Speed-light's flash output. This setting does not apply to flash units you attach via the Accessory shoe (hotshoe) on top of the camera. It is only for the pop-up flash.

Additionally, the built-in flash can be used to control multiple groups or banks of standalone Speedlight flash units. When you use the flash in this manner, you are using it in Commander mode, which we will also discuss.

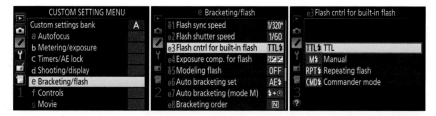

Figure 4.40A – Flash cntrl for built-in flash – TTL mode

Here are the steps used to configure Flash cntrl for built-in flash:

1. Select e Bracketing/flash from the Custom Setting Menu and scroll to the right (figure 4.40A, screen 1).
2. Highlight e3 Flash cntrl for built-in flash and scroll to the right (figure 4.40A, screen 2).
3. Choose one of the four choices on the list. In figure 4.40A, screen 3, TTL has been selected. The other choices will be detailed in figures 4.40B, 4.40C, and 4.40D. Those three figures start where figure 4.40A leaves off.
4. Press the OK button to lock in the setting.

Let's consider each of these modes.

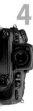

TTL

Also known as i-TTL, this mode is the standard way to use the camera for flash pictures (figure 4.40A). TTL (through the lens) allows very accurate and balanced flash output using a pre-flash method to determine correct exposure before the main flash burst fires. This is a completely automatic mode and will adjust to distances along with the various shutter speeds and apertures your camera is using.

M – Manual

This mode allows you to manually control the output of your flash (figure 4.40B). The range of settings can go from Full power to 1/128. At full power, the built-in Speedlight has a Guide Number of 12/39 (m/ft, ISO 100, 20°C/68°F).

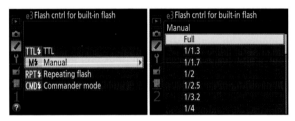

Figure 4.40B – Flash cntrl for built-in flash – Manual mode

This setting turns your flash into a strobe unit that you can see pulsing (unlike Auto FP high-speed sync mode), allowing you to get creative with stroboscopic multiple flashes. Using screen 2 in figure 4.40C, you can use the Multi selector to scroll up and down to set the values or left and right to move between Output, Times, and Frequency. Press the OK button when you have it configured.

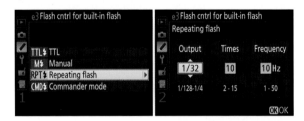

Figure 4.40C – Flash cntrl for built-in flash – Repeating flash mode

There are three settings, as shown in Figure 4.40C, screen 2:

- **Output** – You can vary the power of the flash from 1/4 to 1/128 of the full power. The more power the flash uses, the fewer times it can fire. Here is a table of how many times the built-in pop-up flash can fire using the different Output levels:

> ## How Does Repeating Flash Work, Technically?
>
> If you have Output set to 1/128, Times set to 5, and Frequency set to 50, that means the camera will fire its built-in pop-up Speedlight at 1/128 of the full power, five times, with each flash burst divided into 50 pulses. Therefore, the flash will pulse a total of 250 times at 1/128 power for a 1-second exposure, or 4 times for a 1/60-second exposure.

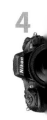

1/4: 2 times
1/16: 2–10 times
1/64: 2–10, 15, 20, 25 times

- **1/8**: 2–5 times
- **1/32**: 2–10 or 15 times
- **1/128**: 2–10, 15, 20, 25, 30, 35 times

- **Times** – This setting controls the number of times the flash will strobe per second, between 2 and 10 in one-step increments and then from 10 to 35 (at 1/128) in five-step increments. Refer to the preceding table to set the number of times the flash can fire. Increasing the flash power output (going toward 1/4) will lower the number of times, while decreasing the power (going toward 1/128) will increase the number of times the flash can fire. As you change the Output amount, you'll see the Times maximum change.
- **Frequency** – This lets the flash fire a series of pulses for each of the times it fires, from 1 pulse to 50 pulses.

C – Commander Mode

This mode allows your camera to become a commander, or controller, of up to two banks of an unlimited number of external CLS-compatible Speedlight flash units, with four available channels (figure 4.40D).

In figure 4.40D, screen 2, you'll see Built-in flash, Group A and B, and a Channel setting. Following Built-in flash and Group A and B, you'll see Mode and Comp. settings. Use the Multi selector to move around and modify settings on this screen.

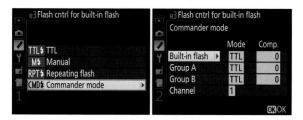

Figure 4.40D – Flash cntrl for built-in flash – Commander mode

Built-in flash – This lets you set the pop-up flash to one of three settings. The settings do not affect any of the flash units the Commander mode is controlling in Group A or B:

- **TTL** – Otherwise known as i-TTL mode, this is a completely automatic mode that does monitor pre-flashes to determine correct exposure for the pop-up flash. You can set compensation (Comp.) from +3.0 to -3.0 EV in 1/3 EV steps.
- **M** – This allows you to choose a manual flash level from 1/1 (full power) to 1/128 (1/128 of the full power).
- **- - -** I call this the double-dash mode. This disables the pop-up flash from adding light to the image. The primary light burst from the pop-up flash will not fire. However, the pop-up flash still must fire the monitor pre-flashes to determine a correct exposure and to communicate with any flash units out there in Group A or Group B that it is "commanding."

Group A and B – These banks represent groups of an unlimited number of remote mode (slaved) Speedlights that your camera can control and fire under the Nikon Creative Lighting System (CLS). Each group has four settings that apply to each flash unit in the bank:

- **TTL** – This works like Built-in flash except that it causes all flash units being controlled in each group to use TTL (i-TTL) for the group. You can also set compensation (Comp.) between +3.0 and -3.0 EV in 1/3 EV steps. Comp. will affect all flash units in the group, or bank.
- **AA** – This stands for Auto aperture and is only available when your D810 is controlling a top-end Speedlight flash unit in slave mode on a bank. This is an older technology that does not use the newer i-TTL exposure technology. It is included for those who are used to using the older style of exposure. You can safely ignore this mode and use TTL instead and you'll get better exposures. If you really want to use AA mode, that's fine. It works like TTL mode but with less accurate exposures. You can set compensation (Comp.) between +3.0 and -3.0 EV in 1/3 EV steps. Comp. will affect all flash units in that group or bank.
- **M** – This allows you to choose a manual flash level between 1/1 (full power) and 1/128 (1/128 of the full power) for each of the flash units being controlled by a particular group. If you like to shoot manually for ultimate control, the camera gives you a way to control multiple groups of flash units manually.
- **- - -** The flash units in the group do not fire. Double-dash mode disables an entire group so that you can concentrate on configuring the other group. Then you can turn the disabled group back on and configure it too. Or, you can just use one group of slaved Speedlights (A or B) and disable the other.

Channel – This one channel controls all slaved flash units. You must match the Channel number for the camera and each flash unit. This is the channel on which communications flow to all grouped, remote flashes. You have a choice of four Channel numbers, 1 to 4. This allows you to use your flash units near another photographer who is also controlling groups without firing the other person's flash units accidentally. You just each choose a different channel.

An upcoming chapter of this book, Speedlight Flash, is devoted to using Nikon's Creative Lighting System (CLS) and covers each of the Commander modes and flash unit types in more detail than the summary found here.

Commander Mode Notes

When you're using multiple flash units under the control of your camera in Commander mode, it is important that you understand the following points.

First, the camera communicates with the remote slaved flash groups (A and B) during the monitor pre-flash cycle, so the pop-up flash must be raised in Commander mode in order to communicate with the remote flash units.

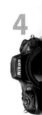

Second, each remote flash unit has a little round photocell sensor on its side that picks up the monitor pre-flashes from your camera's pop-up flash. Make sure those little sensors are not blocked or exposed to direct, very bright light while in use or they may not be able to see the monitor pre-flashes from your camera.

Third, if you want to prevent the monitor pre-flashes from appearing in photographs, or causing people to squint, you need to purchase the optional SG-3IR infrared panel for the pop-up flash. This infrared panel makes the monitor pre-flashes mostly invisible to humans and imaging sensors, yet the remote flash units can still see them and react properly. Nikon says this in the User's Manual (page 337) about using the built-in flash in Commander mode: *"To prevent timing flashes emitted by the built-in flash from appearing in photographs taken at short range, choose low ISO sensitivities or small apertures (high f-numbers) or use an optional SG-3IR infrared panel for the built-in flash. An SG-3IR is required for best results with rear-curtain sync, which produces brighter timing flashes."*

Fourth, don't position any of the remote flash units more than 33 feet (10.05 m) from the camera. That's the maximum distance Nikon supports for the D810 pop-up flash in Commander mode.

If these issues bother you, then invest in the Nikon SU-800 Wireless Infrared Controller unit that replaces the pop-up flash/Commander mode combo. You mount it onto the Accessory shoe and let it control the remote slaves out to 66 feet (20.10 m) without some of the issues just mentioned.

Custom Setting e4 – Exposure Comp. for Flash

(User's Manual – Page 338)

The Exposure comp. for flash function allows you to treat the subject and background differently when you use flash. You can separate the normal exposure compensation function (for the background) and the flash compensation function (for the subject). Exposure compensation can be applied to the background only, or to the background and subject (the entire frame) with flash. There are two available settings:

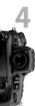

- *Entire frame* – Both the flash and the exposure compensation work normally.
- *Background only* – The nonflash exposure compensation (that you adjust with the Exposure compensation button) and the flash compensation (that you apply with the Flash compensation button) are separate. Flash compensation applies to the subject only, and nonflash exposure compensation applies to the background only.

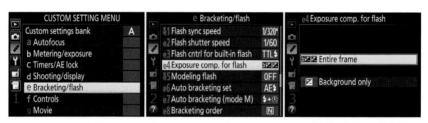

Figure 4.41 – Exposure comp. for flash

Use the following steps to choose a flash and exposure compensation combination:

1. Select e Bracketing/flash from the Custom Setting Menu and scroll to the right (figure 4.41, screen 1).
2. Highlight e4 Exposure comp. for flash and scroll to the right (figure 4.41, screen 2).
3. Choose either Entire frame or Background only. If you choose Background only, the nonflash and flash compensation functions are applied separately (figure 4.41, screen 3).
4. Press the OK button to lock in your choice.

Settings Recommendation: I leave my D810 set to Entire frame for most shooting. If I need to change the light level relationship between the subject and the background, I set the camera to Background only and experiment until I find the best compensation for balance or to emphasize one or the other. Why not spend some time experimenting and learning how to use this new technology?

Custom Setting e5 – Modeling Flash

(User's Manual – Page 338)

Modeling flash lets you fire a pulse of flashes to help you see how the light is wrapping around your subject. It works like modeling lights on studio flash units except it pulses instead of shines. You can press the Depth-of-field preview button to see the effect if you set Modeling flash to On.

This function works with Nikon's main Speedlight flash unit group: SB-910, SB-900, SB-800, SB-700, SB-600, SB-500, and SB-R200. It also works with the pop-up flash for limited periods. The SB-400 flash unit does not work with Modeling flash.

Here's what each of the settings for Modeling flash accomplishes:

- **On** – This setting allows you to see (somewhat) how your flash will light the subject. If you have this setting turned On, you can press the Depth-of-field preview button to strobe the pop-up flash, or any attached/controlled external Speedlight unit, in a series of rapid pulses. These pulses are continuous and simulate the lighting that the primary flash burst will give your subject. The Modeling flash can be used for only a few seconds at a time to keep from overheating the flash unit, so look quickly.
- **Off** – This means that no Modeling flash will pulse when you press the Depth-of-field preview button.

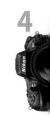

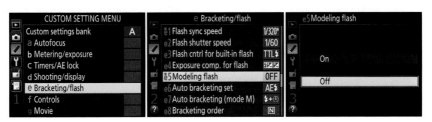

Figure 4.42 – Modeling flash

Here are the steps used to configure Modeling flash:

1. Select e Bracketing/flash from the Custom Setting Menu and scroll to the right (figure 4.42, screen 1).
2. Highlight e4 Modeling flash and scroll to the right (figure 4.42, screen 2).
3. Choose one of the two settings on the list. In figure 4.42, screen 3, Off has been selected.
4. Press the OK button to lock in the setting.

Settings Recommendation: I used to forget that Modeling flash was turned on and when I checked my actual depth of field on a product shot by pressing the Depth-of-field preview button, I would get the modeling light instead of depth of field. I didn't find this feature to be particularly useful, and it often startled me. I now leave it set to Off.

However, you might like it if you do a lot of studio-style flash photography that requires a modeling light. Give it a try, but be prepared—the pulsing of the flash sounds like an angry group of hornets about to attack your face.

Custom Setting e6 – Auto Bracketing Set

(User's Manual – Pages 338)

Auto bracketing set lets you choose how bracketing works for each of the camera's bracketing methods. You can set up bracketing for the exposure system (AE), flash, White balance, and Active D-Lighting.

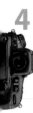

Let's start by reviewing the five types of bracketing on the D810. I'll explain how to use bracketing in an upcoming section:

- **AE & flash** – When you set up a session for bracketing, the camera will cause any type of normal pictures you take to be bracketed, whether they are standard exposures or you are using flash. See how to bracket in the next section.
- **AE only** – Your bracketing settings will affect only the exposure system and not the flash.
- **Flash only** – Your bracketing settings will affect only the flash system and not the exposure.
- **WB bracketing** – White balance bracketing works the same as exposure and flash bracketing, except it is designed for bracketing color in mired values, instead of bracketing light in EV step values. WB bracketing is not available with image quality settings of NEF (RAW) or NEF (RAW) + JPEG.
- **ADL bracketing** – In this case, you are bracketing Active D-Lighting (ADL) in up to five separate exposures. The next higher level of ADL is used on each selected exposure.

External Camera Controls for Bracketing

First let's examine the controls used to set up your camera for all five bracketing methods.

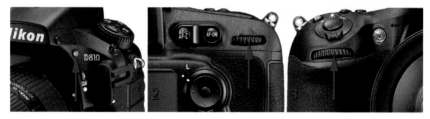

Figure 4.43A – Controls for Auto bracketing: (1) BKT button, (2) Main command dial, (3) Sub-command dial

You'll use the BKT button (1) and the Main command dial (2) or Sub-command dial (3) to change the bracketing values. Use figure 4.43A as an external control guide for the rest of the **Custom Setting e6 – Auto Bracketing Set** section.

Now let's consider each of the bracketing methods that use the controls shown in figure 4.43A.

AE & Flash Bracketing (Includes AE Only and Flash Only)

(User's Manual – Page 133)

Exposure bracketing (*AE & flash*) allows you to bracket a series of images using ambient light and/or a Speedlight flash unit. You can later combine these images into a high dynamic range (HDR) image with greater than normal dynamic range, as seen in figure 4.43B.

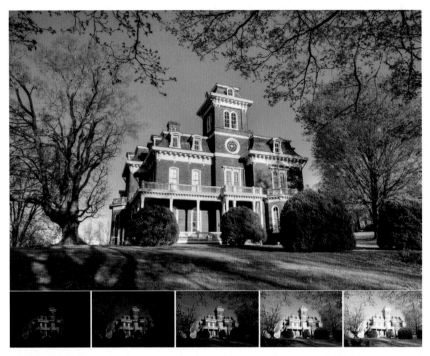

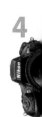

Figure 4.43B – Five-image bracket combined in Photomatix Pro to a single HDR image

In figure 4.43B you will find a sample five-image bracket with 1.0 EV step between each exposure. I combined the five images using Photomatix Pro software (**http://www.hdrsoft.com**) and was pleased with the final result. The main image was created with a bracketed series of five shots—the pictures underneath the main image—using the same settings shown on the Control panel in figure 4.43D, screen 1, as discussed in step 4 of the bracketing step-by-step method.

AE & flash, AE only, and Flash only all use bracketing in exactly the same manner and are all considered in this one section.

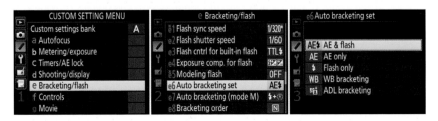

Figure 4.43C – AE and flash bracketing (top three types in screen 3)

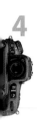

Here are the steps to configure AE and flash bracketing for results similar to what is seen in figure 4.43B:

1. Select e Bracketing/flash from the Custom Setting Menu and scroll to the right (figure 4.43C, screen 1).
2. Highlight e6 Auto bracketing set and scroll to the right (figure 4.43C, screen 2).
3. Choose AE & flash and press the OK button to lock in the setting (figure 4.43C, screen 3).
4. Next, press and hold the BKT button (figure 4.43A, image 1). You can identify that bracketing is active by the BKT symbol on the Control panel.

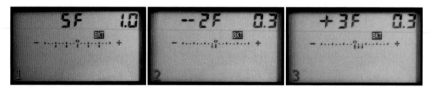

Figure 4.43D – Auto bracketing (AE & flash)

When you hold down the BKT button, you will see symbols on your camera's Control panel similar to the ones shown in figure 4.43D. The symbols will initially be 0F and 1.0 (if not previously changed) and there may be no lines hanging below the -/+ scale. You will set both of those values as you create the bracket. The number of shots in the bracket appears on the top center of the Control panel, as shown in each screen in figure 4.43D as 5F, --2F, and +3F. You can shoot up to 9 frames (9F) in an AE & flash, AE only, or Flash only bracket. The number of small vertical lines hanging below the - ...... 0 ...... + scale equals the number of shots in the bracket. The position of those lines represents the EV spread of the shots in the bracket. In figure 4.43D, screen 1, for instance, you can count five lines hanging below the -/+ scale, and there is one stop of exposure between each line. Those five shots are represented by the 5F in screen 1.

While holding the BKT button, turn the rear Main command dial (figure 4.43A, image 2) to select the number of shots in the bracket (up to 9). The number of shots can have a plus sign, minus sign, or no sign next to it (figure 4.43D). Select a number with a plus sign if you want the bracket to take only normal and overexposed shots. Select a number with a minus sign if you want the bracket to take only normal and underexposed shots. If you want the bracket to take exposures that are evenly distributed on both sides of the scale, select a number that has no plus or minus sign in front of it.

5. The front Sub-command dial (figure 4.43A, number 3) controls the EV steps between each exposure in the bracket. This value appears on the top right of each screen in figure 4. 43D as 1.0, 0.3, and 0.3. While holding the BKT button,

rotate the front Sub-command dial to select the EV step value between each image in the bracket, in steps of 1/3, 1/2, or 1 EV. (The EV step value is set in *Custom Setting Menu b2 > EV steps for exposure cntrl*. You can use *Custom Setting Menu > e8 Bracketing order* to set the order of the exposures. We'll discuss this in a later section titled **Custom Setting e8 – Bracketing Order**. The default order is *normal > underexposed > overexposed*. You can change it to *underexposed > normal > overexposed* if you'd like.) Following are detailed explanations of the values on screens 1, 2, and 3 of figure 4.43D:

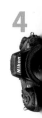

Figure 4.43D, screen 1, shows a five-shot bracket on the camera's Control panel with 1.0 EV step between each image. You can tell there are five shots by the 5F at the top center of the Control panel along with the number of lines hanging below the scale. The 1.0 means that there is 1.0 EV step (1 stop) between each exposure in the bracket. The fact that the 5F has no plus or minus sign in front of it tells us that the bracket uses exposures that are normal, overexposed, and underexposed.

Figure 4.43D, screen 2, shows a two-image bracket with 0.3 EV steps (1/3 stop) between each exposure. Notice the minus signs before the 2F symbol (--2F). This means that the bracket is configured to take only normal and underexposed shots—no overexposed ones. The bracketed images are on the minus side of the -/+ scale.

Figure 4.43D, screen 3, represents a three-image bracket with 0.3 EV steps between each exposure. The bracket is configured to take only normal and overexposed shots (+3F).

6. Once you have configured your bracket, press the Shutter-release button to take each bracketed picture in the series. As you take each image, one of the lines that hang down below the -/+ scale will disappear. When they are all gone, your bracket is complete. If you have your camera set to one of the Continuous release modes (CL or CH), you can shoot the number of frames in your bracket by holding down the Shutter-release button. Once the bracket is complete, the camera will stop firing.

Note about flash bracketing: If you are using a Speedlight flash unit to light the bracketed series, it may or may not be able to keep up with bracketed shots taken in Continuous-release mode. If you fully dump the flash power between shots, you'll have to wait for the next shot. Also, the pop-up flash simply does not recycle fast enough to be able to shoot continuously while flash bracketing, so you'll have to take each shot individually.

Here's a short review:

- BKT button plus rear Main command dial = number of exposures
- BKT button plus front Sub-command dial = EV step value of bracketed exposures (1/3, 1/2, or 1 EV step)

Settings Recommendation: I normally bracket with a 1 EV step value (1 stop) so that I can get a good spread of light values in high dynamic range (HDR) images. In most cases, I will do a three- to five-image bracket, with one or two images over-exposed and one or two images underexposed by 1 stop. This type of bracketing allows me to combine detail from the highlight and dark areas in-computer for the HDR exposures everyone is experimenting with these days.

WB Bracketing

(User's Manual – Page 139)

The process for *WB bracketing* (white balance bracketing) is similar to the process for flash or exposure bracketing; you even use the same controls (figure 4.43A). No form of AE or flash bracketing will work during the time that Custom setting e6 is set to WB bracketing.

WB bracketing does not work when your camera is in NEF (RAW) and NEF (RAW) + JPEG modes. White balance information is stored with the RAW image but is not directly applied to the image. You can change the White balance after the fact when you are shooting RAW, so bracketing a RAW image does not make sense.

Now let's examine how to select WB bracketing, and then bracket the white balance.

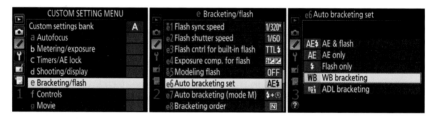

Figure 4.43E – Auto bracketing set – WB bracketing

Here are the steps to configure WB bracketing:

1. Select e Bracketing/flash from the Custom Setting Menu and scroll to the right (figure 4.43E, screen 1).
2. Highlight e6 Auto bracketing set and scroll to the right (figure 4.43E, screen 2).
3. Choose WB bracketing (figure 4.43E, screen 3) and press the OK button.

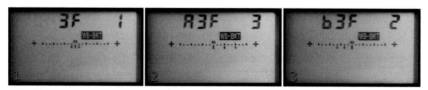

Figure 4.43F –WB bracketing (White balance)

4. You will use the controls shown in figure 4.43A to choose the number of shots in the bracket, which is displayed at the top center of the Control panel (3F, A3F, or b3F in figure 4.43F). Press and hold the BKT button while turning the rear Main command dial left or right to select the number of shots, up to nine shots total (9F). In figure 4.43F, the 3F symbol shows the number of images (3), as do the lines hanging below the -/+ scale, just below the WB-BKT symbol.

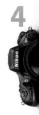

Control Panel	No. of Shots	WB Increment	Bracketing Order
0F	0	1	0
b3F	3	1B	0 > 1B > 2B
A3F	3	1A	0 > 2A > 1A
b2F	2	1B	0 > 1B
A2F	2	1A	0 > 1A
3F	3	1A, 1B	0 > 1A > 1B
5F	5	1A, 1B	0 > 2A > 1A > 1B > 2B
7F	7	1A, 1B	0 > 3A > 2A > 1A > 1B > 2B > 3B
9F	9	1A, 1B	0 > 4A > 3A > 2A > 1A > 1B > 2B > 3B > 4B

Table 4.1 – Control panel symbols, no. of shots, Amber/blue increments, and bracketing order

5. You control the white balance color differences by bracketing toward amber or blue (A or B), using the symbols on the Control panel, as described in Table 4.1. Each increment of color difference is called a *mired* and is controlled by the number at the top right of the Control panel screens in figure 4.43F. Change the mired number by holding the BKT button while turning the front Sub-command dial left or right, up to three maximum. Each number represents multiple mired. Choose 1, 2, or 3, where 1=5 mired, 2=10 mired, and 3=15 mired. Figure 4.43F, screen 1, shows a 5 mired difference (1), screen 2 shows a 15 mired difference (3), and screen 3 shows a 10 mired difference (2). Following are detailed explanations of the values on screens 1, 2, and 3 of figure 4.43F:

Figure 4.43F, screen 1, shows a three-image bracket on the camera's Control panel, with a 5 mired difference (1) in color between each image. One has more amber, one is normal, and one has more blue (3F).

Figure 4.43F, screen 2, shows a three-image bracket with a 15 mired difference (3) between each image, in the amber direction only (A3F).

Figure 4.43F, screen 3, shows a three-image bracket with a 10 mired color difference (2) in the blue direction only (b3F). If you do not see an A (A3F) or b (b3F)

What Is Mired?

Changes to mired simply modify the color of your image, in this case toward amber (reddish) or blue. In effect, changing mired toward amber or blue warms or cools the image. The color changes are applied directly to the image by the camera when shooting JPEGs or are saved as markers when shooting RAW images. You don't have to worry about mired values unless you are a color scientist.

You can just determine whether you like the image the way it is or would prefer that it be warmer or cooler and bracket accordingly. WB bracketing toward the A direction warms the image, while the b direction cools it. Technically, a mired is calculated by multiplying the inverse of the color temperature by 106.

I'd rather let my camera figure mired values and then judge them with my eye, wouldn't you? Remember, if you shoot in RAW, you can modify color values later in your computer. Otherwise, they are applied permanently to JPEG files.

---

in the image number position at top center, it simply means that the bracket goes in both directions, such as *amber > normal >blue* or *normal>amber >blue*, according to how you have *Custom Setting Menu > e Bracketing/flash > e8 Bracketing order* set.

6. Press the Shutter-release button to take the bracketed picture series. Interestingly, you do this by taking **one** picture. The camera takes that picture, reapplies the color filtration for each image in the bracket, and then saves each image as a separate image file with a new consecutive file number and bracketed color value. This works very differently from AE or flash bracketing, where you have to fire off each individual frame of the bracket. WB bracketing is very easy because you only have to set the bracket in the Control panel and take one picture. The series of images in the bracket (up to nine) simply appears on your memory card. Nikons are fun!

ADL Bracketing

(User's Manual – Page 143)

ADL bracketing (ADL stands for Active D-Lighting) is designed to let you shoot a normal image and then a series of up to four additional images with Active D-Lighting applied to each at progressively higher levels.

As you set ADL bracketing from two to five shots, you are setting the camera to switch to a higher ADL level for each consecutive shot. The progressive levels are Off, Low, Normal, High, and Extra High.

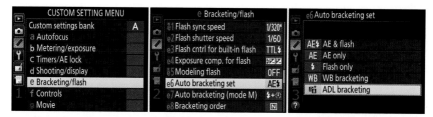

Figure 4.43G – Auto bracketing set – ADL bracketing

Here are the steps to use ADL bracketing:

1. Select e Bracketing/flash from the Custom Setting Menu and scroll to the right (figure 4.43G, screen 1).

2. Highlight e6 Auto bracketing set and scroll to the right (figure 4.43G, screen 2).

3. Choose ADL bracketing (figure 4.43G, screen 3) and press the OK button.

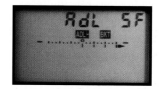

Figure 4.43H – ADL bracketing

4. Using the controls shown in figure 4.43A, hold down the BKT button and turn the rear Main command dial to select the number of frames you want in the bracket (two to five images). You'll see AdL at the top center of the Control panel and the number of frames in the bracket series at the top right (5F).

5. **Figure 4.43H** shows a bracket of five frames (5F), which means that the camera will use all five available levels of Active D-Lighting (Off, Low, Normal, High, and Extra high) as the five images are taken (Auto Active D-Lighting is ignored). You'll be able to see hanging lines under the +/- scale for only four of the shots—an arrow points to the right for the fifth. *Custom Setting Menu > e Bracketing/flash > e8 Bracketing order* does not apply to ADL bracketing.

6. Press the Shutter-release button to take each shot in the bracketed series. As each shot is taken, you'll see one of the vertical lines just under the -/+ scale disappear. If you have your camera set to one of the Continuous-release modes (CL or CH), you can shoot the number of frames in your bracket by holding down the Shutter-release button. Once the bracket is complete, the camera will stop firing.

Settings Recommendation: This is a great way to capture very important shots and try to get extra shadow detail and highlight protection in some of them. You may not need ADL bracketing on all shots, but on very important images where you are slightly off on your exposure selection, ADL will help to open shadows and mildly protect the highlights.

Of course, if you shoot in RAW mode, you can apply ADL in-computer. I don't bracket ADL very often, but I'm glad to know it's there when I need it.

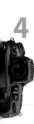

One final note about bracketing of any type: Turn it off when you're done! I often forget and then wonder why my camera keeps under- and overexposing a series of images. Only after wasting several images do I realize that I left bracketing turned on. You'll see what I mean if you use AE & flash bracketing often, as I do.

Custom Setting e7 – Auto Bracketing (Mode M)

(User's Manual – Page 339)

Auto bracketing (Mode M) is a series of four selections that let you, or the camera, control the flash, shutter speed, and aperture in various ways during a bracketing operation, but only when the camera is set to Manual (M) exposure mode. This gives you a little finer control over manual camera settings while you are taking several exposures within a bracket of images.

Here is a list of the four settings under Auto bracketing (Mode M) and what each does. The camera controls the selected setting when you are using Manual (M) exposure mode while bracketing. These functions are dependent on how *Custom Setting Menu > e Bracketing/flash > e6 Auto bracketing set* is configured.

- *Flash/speed* – This setting allows you to control the aperture for best depth of field while still using bracketing. The camera will control the shutter speed. If *Custom Setting Menu > e Bracketing/flash > e6 Auto bracketing set* is configured to AE & Flash, the camera will vary the shutter speed and flash level to expose the bracketed images while you control the aperture. If e6 Auto bracketing set is set to AE only, the camera will vary only the shutter speed to get the exposures.
- *Flash/speed/aperture* – This setting is for those who want the camera to control the shutter speed, aperture, and flash while still using bracketing. If *Custom Setting Menu > e Bracketing/flash > e6 Auto bracketing set* is configured to AE & Flash, the camera will vary the shutter speed, aperture, and flash level to expose the bracketed images. If e6 Auto bracketing set is set to AE only, the camera will vary the shutter speed and aperture to get the exposures.
- *Flash/aperture* – This setting is for those who want to control the shutter speed for best action shots while still using bracketing. The camera will control the aperture and flash. If *Custom Setting Menu > e Bracketing/flash > e6 Auto bracketing set* is configured to AE & Flash, the camera will vary the aperture and flash level to expose the bracketed images. If e6 Auto bracketing set is set to AE only, the camera will vary only the aperture to get the exposures.
- *Flash only* – This setting is for those who want to control only the flash while using bracketing. The camera will only vary the flash level to get the bracketed exposures. AE only obviously does not apply with this setting.

Note: Flash bracketing is performed only with i-TTL or AA flash control. If any setting other than Flash only is selected and the flash is not used, the ISO sensitivity will be fixed at the value for the first shot regardless of the setting selected for Auto ISO sensitivity control.

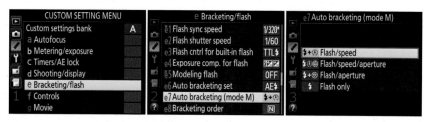
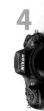

Figure 4.44 – Auto bracketing (Mode M)

Here are the steps used to configure Auto bracketing (Mode M):

1. Select e Bracketing/flash from the Custom Setting Menu and scroll to the right (figure 4.44, screen 1).
2. Highlight e7 Auto bracketing (Mode M) and scroll to the right (figure 4.44, screen 2).
3. Choose one of the four settings on the list. In figure 4.44, screen 3, Flash/speed has been selected.
4. Press the OK button to lock in the setting.

Settings Recommendation: Because I am mostly a nature shooter, I often leave my camera set to Flash/speed so that the camera will control the shutter speed when I take a series of bracketed images, but I'll control the aperture. That way I can choose how much depth of field I want to allow in my images.

If I were shooting important action shots and wanted to bracket, I'd select Flash/aperture so that the camera would control the aperture and flash while I controlled the shutter speed for action.

If I were letting only my Speedlight flash control the exposure, as with indoor shots, I might use Flash only during the bracket.

Finally, if I wanted to let the camera alone decide how to get the best exposure during the bracket, I might use Flash/speed/aperture. Then all I have to do is take pictures and let the camera do the rest. This seems to me to be a small violation of the principle of manual exposure, though.

Custom Setting e8 – Bracketing Order

(User's Manual – Page 340)

Bracketing order allows you to choose the order of your exposure settings (normal, overexposed, and underexposed) during a bracketing operation. There are two bracketing orders available in the D810. They allow you to control which images are taken first, second, and third in the bracketing series.

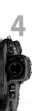

Here are the three values in the bracket order and what they each mean:

- **MTR** = Metered value (normal exposure)
- **Under** = Underexposed
- **Over** = Overexposed

Next, let's see how these are used during bracketing:

- *MTR > under > over* – With this setting, the normal exposure (MTR) is taken first, followed by the underexposed image, and then the overexposed image. If you are taking a group of five images in your bracket (Custom setting e5), the camera will take the images like this: *normal exposure > most underexposed > least underexposed > least overexposed > most overexposed*. For WB bracketing, the pattern is *normal > amber > blue*. This does not apply to ADL bracketing.
- *Under > MTR > over* – Using this order for bracketing means that a five-image bracket will be exposed in the following manner: *most underexposed > least underexposed > normal exposure > least overexposed > most overexposed*. For WB bracketing, the pattern is *amber > normal > blue*. This does not apply to ADL bracketing.

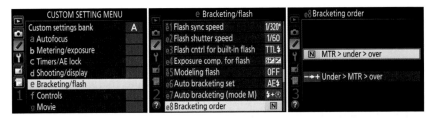

Figure 4.45 – Bracketing order

Finally, let's look at the steps to actually configure the Bracketing order:

1. Select e Bracketing/flash from the Custom Setting Menu and scroll to the right (figure 4.45, screen 1).
2. Highlight e8 Bracketing order and scroll to the right (figure 4.45, screen 2).
3. Choose one of the two bracketing orders on the list. In figure 4.45, screen 3, MTR > under > over has been selected.
4. Press the OK button to lock in the setting.

Settings Recommendation: I leave Bracketing order set to *MTR > under > over*, so that when the images are displayed in series by the camera, I can see the normal exposure (MTR) first and then watch how it varies as I scroll through the bracketed images. It gets confusing to me if there are nine images in a bracket and I am trying to figure out which one is the MTR image, as I would with the other bracketing order.

If that doesn't suit you, change it to the other direction, *Under > MTR > over*. The normal exposure will be in the middle of the bracket instead of at the beginning. Some prefer the more natural flow of that bracketing order (under to over).

Section Six – f Controls

Custom Settings f1 to f13

Within the *f Controls* menu you'll find 17 settings in the D810:

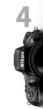

- **f1** – Switch (Backlight)
- **f2** – Multi selector center button
- **f3** – Multi selector
- **f4** – Assign Fn button
- **f5** – Assign preview button
- **f6** – Assign AE-L/AF-L button
- **f7** – Shutter spd & aperture lock
- **f8** – Assign BKT button
- **f9** – Customize command dials
- **f10** – Release button to use dial
- **f11** – Slot empty release lock
- **f12** – Reverse indicators
- **f13** – Assign movie record button
- **f14** – Live view button options
- **f15** – Assign MB-D12 AF-ON
- **f16** – Assign remote (WR) Fn button
- **f17** – Lens focus function buttons

Custom Setting f1 – ☀ Switch (Backlight)

(User's Manual – Page 341)

The *Backlight switch* control position has been on the Power switch for many generations of Nikon cameras—controlling the backlight for the Control panel. However, the D810's Power switch's Backlight position can potentially control two functions. One is for the Control panel backlight, and the other is for the Information display (rear Monitor) backlight.

When you push the switch (figure 4.46A) you'll turn on the backlight for just the Control panel or both the Control panel and the Information display, according to how you have the Backlight switch function configured. In figure 4.46A, the top red arrow shows the direction to push the Power switch for the backlight position, and the bottom red arrow points to the tiny icon on the camera's Power switch.

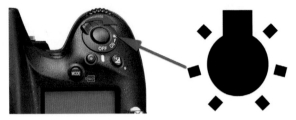

Figure 4.46A – Backlight switch position around Shutter-release button

The Control panel and Information display have different backlight time-outs controlled by separate functions. The Control panel backlight time-out is controlled by *Custom Setting Menu > c Timers/AE lock > c2 Standby timer*. The Information display backlight time-out is controlled by *Custom Setting Menu > c Timers/AE lock > c4 Monitor off delay > Information display*. You can set these two time-outs first, and when you activate the Backlight switch, both timers will start counting down separately, with one important caveat. When you are using the Information display screen on the rear Monitor, it keeps the light meter active for as long as it displays. Therefore, if you have *Custom Setting Menu > c Timers/AE lock > c4 Monitor off delay > Information display* set to a long value, such as 1 min (one minute), the Information display will time-out first at the end of its 1 min delay, and then the Control panel backlight will start its countdown, using the delay set in *Custom Setting Menu > c Timers/AE lock > c2 Standby timer*.

This sounds a bit confusing, but think of it this way: Because the Control panel time-out is tied in with the light meter time-out, the Control panel backlight will stay on longer than the Information display by the amount you have set in *Custom Setting Menu > c Timers/AE lock > c2 Standby timer*. If that value is the default of 6 s (six seconds), that means the Control panel backlight will time-out six seconds after the Information display times out.

Here is a list of the two settings and explanations of what they accomplish:

- **LCD backlight** (☀) – When you select the Backlight position on the Power switch, only the Control panel LCD will light up.
- **☀ and information display** – When you select the Backlight position on the Power switch, both the Control panel LCD and the Information display will light up.

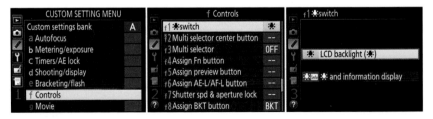

Figure 4.46B – Backlight switch

Here are the steps to select what the Backlight switch controls:

1. Select f Controls from the Custom Setting Menu and scroll to the right (figure 4.46B, screen 1).
2. Highlight f1 ☀ switch and scroll to the right (figure 4.46B, screen 2).
3. Choose one of the two types on the list. In figure 4.46B, screen 3, LCD backlight (☀) has been selected.
4. Press the OK button to lock in the setting.

Settings Recommendation: While this function could be useful if you use the Information display frequently, I suspect that many D810 users do not depend on the Information display as often as those who own lower-cost Nikons. The lower-end cameras are more and more Information display-centered, since many of their users came over from the point-and-shoot world and expect that easy, shortcut style of camera configuration.

Only recently has Nikon added more functionality to the Information display on the D810-level cameras, which sets a pattern that will only grow in future cameras.

In any case, I still mostly use the Backlight switch setting to turn on the backlight for the Control panel only. I would rather simply press the info button when I want access to the Information display on the rear Monitor.

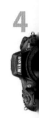

Custom Setting f2 – Multi Selector Center Button

(User's Manual – Page 341)

Multi selector center button determines how the unlabeled button in the center of the Multi selector works in three different camera modes.

The three modes that affect how the Multi selector center button works are as follows:

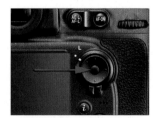

Figure 4.47A – Multi selector center button

- **Shooting mode** is in force when you are actually using the camera to take pictures through the Viewfinder.
- **Playback mode** is in use when you are examining pictures you've already taken on the rear Monitor.
- **Live view** is used when you are in Live view mode taking pictures with the Monitor instead of the Viewfinder.

Figure 4.47A shows an arrow pointing to the Multi selector center button on the back of the camera. Let's examine each mode in detail.

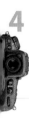

Shooting Mode

First let's see how pressing the Multi selector center button works in the Viewfinder-based Shooting mode. Following are the screens and steps used to configure what the Multi selector center button does (figure 4.47B).

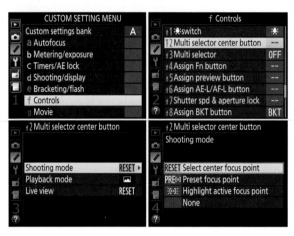

Figure 4.47B – Multi selector center button (Shooting mode)

Use these steps to begin configuration of the Multi selector center button:

1. Select f Controls from the Custom Setting Menu and scroll to the right (figure 4.47B, screen 1).
2. Highlight f2 Multi selector center button and scroll to the right (figure 4.47B, screen 2).
3. Select Shooting mode and scroll to the right (figure 4.47B, screen 3).
4. Choose one of the four choices, according to the upcoming descriptions of each selection. In figure 4.47B, screen 4, Select center focus point has been chosen.
5. Press the OK button to lock in the setting.

The four Shooting mode selections are as follows (figure 4.47B, screen 4):

- **Select center focus point** – Often when shooting, you'll be using the Multi selector with your thumb to move the selected focus point (AF point) around the Viewfinder to focus on the most appropriate area of your subject. When you are done, you have to scroll the AF point back to the center. Not anymore! If Select center focus point is chosen, the focus point pops back to the center point of the Viewfinder when you press the Multi selector center button. This is the default action of the button.
- **Preset focus point** – This setting allows you to select a specific AF point that the camera will return to when you press the Multi selector center button. You can select separate AF points for vertical (portrait) and horizontal (landscape)

shooting if you have *Custom Setting Menu > a Autofocus > a9 Store by orientation* set to either *Focus point* or *Focus point and AF-area mode*.

a) To select one of the 51 AF points that the camera will return to immediately upon pressing the Multi selector center button, you will do the following: 1. look through the viewfinder; 2. select the AF point you want to use; 3. hold down the AF-mode button (the button just under the lens release button); and 4. hold down the Multi selector center button until the selected AF point flashes in the Viewfinder. Now when you press the Multi selector center button in Shooting mode, the AF point will jump to your preset position.

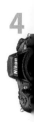

b) To select an AF point for horizontal shooting and a different AF point for vertical shooting, you must do the following: 1. set your camera's *Custom Setting Menu > a Autofocus > a9 Store by orientation* to either *Focus point* or *Focus point and AF-area mode*; 2. repeat step a) for each direction (horizontal and vertical).

- **Highlight active focus point** – Sometimes when the Viewfinder is showing a confusing subject, it may be a little hard to see the small black AF point bracket. When Highlight active focus point is selected and you press the Multi selector center button, the AF point lights up in red for easy viewing in its current location.

- **Not used** – This does what it says—nothing happens when you press the Multi selector center button in Shooting mode.

Playback Mode

Now let's examine how the Multi selector center button can be used in Playback mode. Playback mode is used when you are examining images on the camera's Monitor after you have taken them.

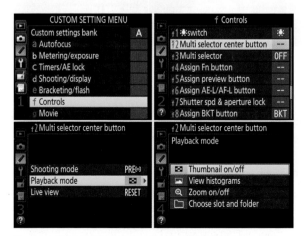

Figure 4.47C – Multi selector center button (Playback mode)

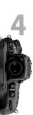

Use these steps to set up the Multi selector center button:

1. Select f Controls from the Custom Setting Menu and scroll to the right (figure 4.47C, screen 1).
2. Highlight f2 Multi selector center button and scroll to the right (figure 4.47C, screen 2).
3. Select Playback mode and scroll to the right (figure 4.47C, screen 3).
4. Choose one of the four options on the list, according to the upcoming instructions. In figure 4.47C, screen 4, Thumbnail on/off has been chosen. If you choose Zoom on/off, you'll need to scroll to the right and select one of the three subsettings (use figure 4.47F in the upcoming section called **Zoom on/off**). If you select Choose slot and folder, you'll also need to be aware of some additional screens your camera will present (use figure 4.47G in the upcoming section called **Choose slot and folder**).
5. Press the OK button to lock in the setting.

There are four selections in Playback mode, as follows (figure 4.47C, screen 4):

Thumbnail on/off

This feature allows you to switch from viewing one image on your camera's Monitor to viewing multiple thumbnails instead. It's a toggle, so you can press the Multi selector center button to turn thumbnail view on and off. In figure 4.47D, screen 1, Thumbnail on/off has been selected.

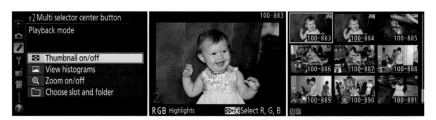

Figure 4.47D – Multi selector center button (Playback mode – Thumbnail on/off)

Use the following steps to configure and use Thumbnail on/off:

1. Figure 4.47D continues where figure 4.47C leaves off. Select Thumbnail on/off from the Playback mode menu (figure 4.47D, screen 1) and press the OK button to select the setting.
2. Now when you press the Playback button and view a picture on the Monitor, like the cute baby girl picture shown in figure 4.47D, screen 2, you can then press the Multi selector center button to get a thumbnail view of that image along with the eight subsequent images (figure 4.47D, screen 3). If you press the button repeatedly, the camera will toggle between normal view and thumbnail view.

View histograms

I discovered this really cool View histograms feature while I was writing another book, and now I immediately switch my Nikons to this setting when I get a new one.

When the Multi selector center button function is set to View histograms, I can have an image open on my Monitor, and then press and hold the Multi selector center button to view a luminance histogram. This saves a lot of scrolling around through the data, RGB histograms, and information screens. It's a quick histogram view that disappears when the Multi selector center button is released. Great feature! Let's see how to configure and use it.

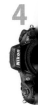

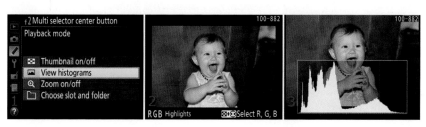

Figure 4.47E – Multi selector center button (Playback mode – View histograms)

Use the following steps to configure and use View histograms:

1. Figure 4.47E continues where figure 4.47C leaves off. Select View histograms from the Playback mode menu (figure 4.47E, screen 1) and press the OK button to select the setting.
2. Now when you press the Playback button and view a picture on the Monitor, like another cute baby picture shown in figure 4.47E, screen 2, you can then press the Multi selector center button to get a luminance histogram of that image (figure 4.47D, screen 3). This is an extremely convenient setting for those who use the histogram regularly.

Zoom on/off

If you want to zoom into your image on the Monitor without using the normal zoom in and out buttons, this is a good feature for you. If you have an image showing on the Monitor and Zoom on/off is selected, you can press the Multi selector center button to jump immediately to one of three levels of zoom. It works like a toggle switch—pressing the Multi selector center button a second time takes you back to a normal full-screen view.

Here is a description of the three levels of zoom available under this setting (Low to High):

- **Low magnification** seems to be the same as viewing the image at about 50 percent pixel-peeping level. Pressing the Playback zoom in button seven times brings you to the same 50 percent level.

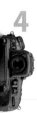

- *Medium magnification* is for viewing the image at about 100 percent. This is like pressing the Playback zoom in button nine times.
- *High magnification* is around the 200 percent viewing level. This is like pressing the Playback zoom in button 10 times.

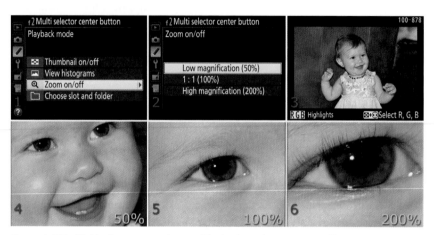

Figure 4.47F – Multi selector center button (Playback mode – Zoom on/off settings)

Use the following steps to configure and use Zoom on/off:

1. Figure 4.47F continues where figure 4.47C leaves off. Select Zoom on/off from the Playback mode menu (figure 4.47F, screen 1).
2. Select Low magnification (50%), 1:1 (100%), or High magnification (200%) from the Zoom on/off list (figure 4.47F, screen 2) and press the OK button to select the setting.
3. Press the Playback button to display a picture on the Monitor (as shown in figure 4.47F, screen 3, where you see little Miss cute baby face again in RGB Highlights screen mode).
4. Now press the Multi selector center button and the camera will immediately zoom in to view the picture on the Monitor at whatever magnification level you chose in step 2. Screens 4, 5, and 6 in figure 4.47F match the zoom levels selectable in screen 2: Low magnification (50%), 1:1 (100%), and High magnification (200%).

Note: The zoom display centers on the focus point used to take the image. If you are using Thumbnail view, you can select from a series of images on the Monitor. When you have one of the images selected, even though it is not full size, you can press the Multi selector center button and the image will be enlarged to whatever magnification level you previously selected. When you press the button again, the camera switches back to Thumbnail view.

Choose slot and folder

When you select Choose slot and folder, you will have a memory card slot selection screen available while you are examining an image in Playback mode. To open the slot selection screen, press the Multi selector center button.

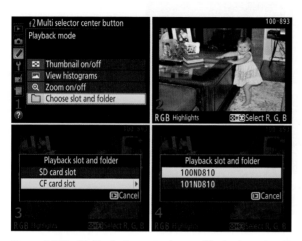
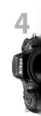

Figure 4.47G – Multi selector center button (Playback mode – Choose slot and folder)

Use the following steps to configure and use Choose slot and folder:

1. Figure 4.47G continues where figure 4.47C leaves off. Select Choose slot and folder from the Playback mode menu (figure 4.47G, screen 1).
2. Press the OK button to select the setting.
3. Press the Playback button to display a picture on the Monitor.
4. When you press the Multi selector center button (figure 4.47G, screen 2), you will be presented with the screen shown in figure 4.47G, screen 3. Choose a card type, SD card slot or CF card slot, and then scroll to the right.
5. You will see a screen showing you the folders that can be found on the card in the slot you selected in the previous step (figure 4.47G, screen 4). Select one of the folders, if there is more than one available, and press the OK button.
6. The camera will now show images from the folder you have selected. If you have Playback Menu > Playback folder set to All or ND810, the camera will switch folders, and even memory cards, when it gets to the end of the current folder. If Playback Menu > Playback folder is set to Current, the camera will show only the images in the current folder and will display no other images from any other folder or card.

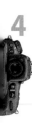

Live View

When shooting still images in Live view mode, you can assign one of three different settings to the Multi selector center button.

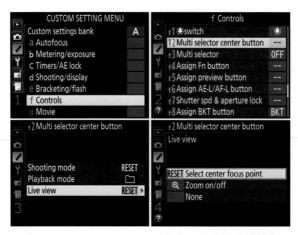

Figure 4.47H – Multi selector center button (Live view mode)

Use the following steps to choose how the Multi selector center button functions in Live view mode:

1. Select f Controls from the Custom Setting Menu and scroll to the right (figure 4.47H, screen 1).
2. Highlight f2 Multi selector center button and scroll to the right (figure 4.47H, screen 2).
3. Select Live view and scroll to the right (figure 4.47H, screen 3).
4. Choose one of the three settings, according to the upcoming descriptions. In figure 4.47H, screen 4, Select center focus point has been chosen. Please refer to the list following these steps to decide which functionality you like best. If you select Zoom on/off, there will be another screen presented to you so that you can choose a magnification level for the Zoom on/off function. Figure 4.47I shows the screen with magnification choices.
5. Press the OK button to lock in the setting.

Here are descriptions of each of the functions available:

- **Select center focus point** – When you are using Live view, you can scroll the little contrast-detection focus square to any point of the Monitor for excellent focusing with the AF-ON button or Shutter-release button (halfway down). Unfortunately, moving the little focus square around the screen is time-consuming. If you want to return the focus square to the center of the screen at any time and have this Select center focus point mode selected, just press the Multi selector center button and the focus square pops to the middle of the Monitor.

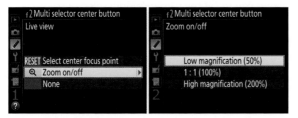

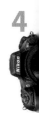

Figure 4.47I – Multi selector center button (Live view mode – Zoom on/off)

- **Zoom on/off** – The Live view contrast-detection autofocus system allows you to zoom into your subject quite deeply so that you can focus very accurately. You could use the Playback zoom in button or Thumbnail/Playback zoom out button to zoom in and out, or you can configure this function and use the Multi selector center button to zoom in and out instead. With Zoom on/off, you can select one of three levels of magnification for focusing in Live view mode. When you want to zoom into the live image to focus on your subject in a very accurate way, simply press the Multi selector center button and the camera will immediately jump to a zoom position of 50 percent for Low magnification, 100 percent for Medium magnification (1:1), and 200 percent for High magnification. Use the screens found in figure 4.47I to select a magnification level (Low, Medium, or High magnification). Figure 4.47I starts where figure 4.47H leaves off. This works similarly to functions found under *Playback mode > Zoom on/off* (figure 4.47F) except it is working with a live subject on the Monitor in Live view.
- **None** – If you press the Multi selector center button while in Live view, it has no effect.

Settings Recommendation: I have my camera set so that when I press the Multi selector center button in Shooting mode, it jumps to the center AF point. It saves time because I don't have to scroll back manually.

When I press the Multi selector center button in Playback mode, I have the camera show me a luminance histogram. I absolutely adore being able to see a histogram for an image I just took by pressing the Multi selector center button instead of scrolling to the histogram screen. This saves time by letting me see my camera's histogram when I need it most, right after taking the picture.

When using Live view mode, I leave my camera set to Select center focus point because it takes so long to scroll the little focus square around the Monitor. I find it quite nice to be able to pop the focus square to the center by pressing the Multi selector center button.

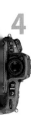

Custom Setting f3 – Multi Selector

(User's Manual – Page 343)

The *Multi selector* function allows you to set the camera's Multi selector so that any usage of it turns the exposure meter on or resets its delay back to the value found in *Custom Setting Menu > c Timers/AE lock > c2 Standby timer*. This allows the light meter to stay on after you've used the Multi selector until the Auto meter-off delay time-out expires.

Here are descriptions of the two available settings:

- **Reset standby timer** – This setting is a handy way to turn on the exposure meter without pressing the Shutter-release button halfway down. Maybe you'd like to meter the subject but not cause autofocus to start, so instead of using the Shutter-release button to turn the meter on, you can use the Multi selector. I find this to be a useful function for another reason. I'll often want to move an AF point around the Viewfinder, but the light meter has gone off, so it won't move. I have to press the Shutter-release button halfway down to activate the meter and then scroll the AF point around the Viewfinder. When Reset standby timer is selected, any usage of the Multi selector causes the light meter to come on. Custom setting c2 (Auto meter-off delay) controls how long it stays on; the default is 6 seconds.
- **Do nothing** – If the light meter is off, it stays off when you press the Multi selector.

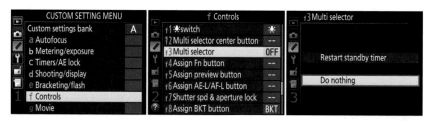

Figure 4.48 – Multi selector

Here are the steps used to configure the Multi selector function:

1. Select f Controls from the Custom Setting Menu and scroll to the right (figure 4.48, screen 1).
2. Highlight f3 Multi selector and scroll to the right (figure 4.48, screen 2).
3. Choose one of the two selections. In figure 4.48, screen 3, Do nothing has been selected.
4. Press the OK button to lock in the setting.

Settings Recommendation: I have been leaving my camera set to Reset standby timer so that any use of the Multi selector will keep my camera's meter from going off. The only drawback is shorter battery life because this will tend to keep the meter on longer. Of course, the D810 is quite good at managing its battery. It has to be, now that the Japanese Electrical Appliance and Material Safety Law requires smaller batteries in our cameras.

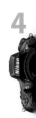

Custom Setting f4 – Assign Fn Button
Custom Setting f5 – Assign Preview Button
Custom Setting f6 –Assign AE-L/AF-L Button

(User's Manual – Pages 343, 349)

Assign Fn button, *Assign preview button*, and *Assign AE-L/AF-L button* are all discussed in this one section. All three work exactly the same way, so instead of repeating the same instructions three times, I chose to explain them once.

When I speak of the **Selected button**, I am talking about the camera button you want to configure—Fn, Preview, or AE-L/AF-L. When you see the words **Selected button** in bold italics, please mentally replace this with the button name you want to configure.

You can assign various camera functions to any of the three buttons mentioned. After we consider each of the screens used to assign the various functions, we'll look at each function in detail in the section **Assignable Function List**. There are a lot of different functions to select from.

The screens, steps, and settings we are about to review are designed to let you customize the usage of the Selected button alone or the Selected button + Command dials.

Here are the screens and steps used to configure Assign Fn button, Assign preview button, and Assign AE-L/AF-L button (figures 4.49A, 4.49B, and 4.49C):

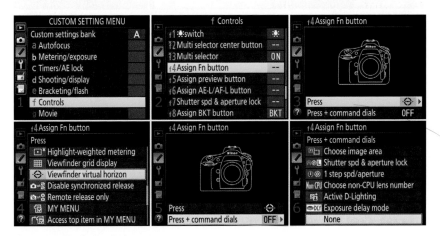

Figure 4.49A – Assign Fn button

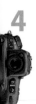

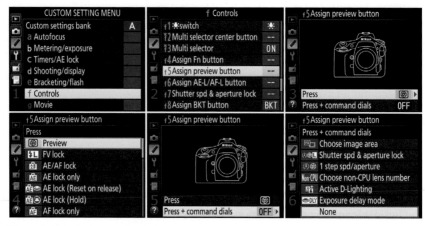

Figure 4.49B – Assign preview button

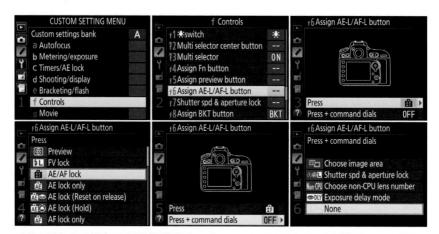

Figure 4.42C – Assign AE-L/AF-L button

Remember that the next nine steps are designed to explain any of the three buttons to which you can assign a function. **Selected button** represents the button you are currently assigning. For example, Preview button press is represented by **Selected button** press.

1. See figures 4.49A, 4.49B, and 4.49C for individual button assignment screens:
    figure 4.49A = Fn button
    figure 4.49B = Preview button (a.k.a., Depth-of-field preview button)
    figure 4.49C = AE-L/AF-L button
2. Select f Controls from the Custom Setting Menu and scroll to the right (figure 4.49A, 4.49B, or 4.49C, screen 1).

3. Highlight (f4, f5, f6) Assign **Selected button** (Fn, Preview, or AE-L/AF-L) and scroll to the right (figure 4.49A, 4.49B, or 4.49C, screen 2). This is where you choose which button you are working with and select it for function assignment.
4. Choose Press and scroll to the right (figure 4.49A, 4.49B, or 4.49C, screen 3). The next step makes an assignment for when you simply press the button.
5. Select one of the functions from the list. This will assign the function you choose to a single press of the **Selected button** you are configuring (figure 4.49A, 4.49B, or 4.49C, screen 4). See the upcoming section **Assignable Function List** for an explanation of each function.
6. Press the OK button to lock in the assignment for **Selected button** Press.
7. Now highlight Press + command dials and scroll to the right (figure 4.49A, 4.49B, or 4.49C, screen 5). The next step makes an assignment for when you press and hold the button and then rotate one of the Command dials.
8. Choose one of the functions to assign to Press + command dials (figure 4.49A, 4.49B, or 4.49C, screen 6). The upcoming section **Assignable Function List** will explain what each one does.
9. Press the OK button to lock in the setting for **Selected button** Press + command dials.

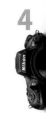

Important note: The upcoming **Assignable Function List** is composed of two parts: The **Press** list of items, and the **Press + Command Dials** list of items.

Many items in the **Press** list cannot be used in combination with items in the **Press + Command dial** list. If you select one of these mutually exclusive Press functions, the camera will disable the Press + command dials function (if already selected) for that particular button. You'll see a warning on the screen that says, *"No function assigned to button + command dial."* Then, as soon as you select the Press function, the camera will set the Press + command dials function to None.

If you then go back and try to reset the value under Press + command dials, the camera will give you a warning that says, *"No function assigned to button press,"* and will set the Press function to None. The two functions cannot be used at the same time.

The only way to know which Press and Press + command dials functions cannot be used at the same time is to try and set them and see what happens. If they cannot be used at the same time, the camera will warn you, and you should select the one most important to you.

Now let's look at the Assignable Function List to see what amazing powers we can give each of the assignable buttons on our cameras.

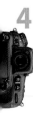

Assignable Function List

(User's Manual – Pages 344–346)

Let's review each of the functions you can assign to the **Selected button** Press. Then we'll look at the ones you can assign to the **Selected button** Press + command dials.

Press

- **Preview** – Normally, the depth of field function is controlled by the Depth-of-field preview button. Some users may not like the location of the Depth-of-field preview button, and—since it is also configurable—decide to switch the Fn button (for instance) with the Depth-of-field preview button. Then, when Preview is selected in one of these Custom settings, the Fn button will activate Depth-of-field preview instead.
- **FV lock** – If you set **Selected button** to FV lock, the button will cause the built-in Speedlight or the external Speedlight to emit a monitor pre-flash and then lock the flash output to the level determined by the pre-flash until you press the **Selected button** a second time.
- **AE/AF lock** – Enabling this function causes AE (exposure) and AF (focus) to lock on the last meter and autofocus system reading while the Selected button is held down.
- **AE lock only** – This allows you to lock AE (exposure) on the last meter reading when you hold down the Selected button.
- **AE lock (Reset on release)** – Enabling this function causes AE (exposure) to lock on the last meter reading when the **Selected button** is pressed once. It stays locked until you press the **Selected button** again. Releasing the shutter resets the AE Lock just as pressing the **Selected button** a second time does. If the light meter goes off, it will also reset this function.
- **AE lock (Hold)** – Enabling this function causes AE (exposure) to lock on the last meter reading when the **Selected button** is pressed once. It stays locked until you press the **Selected button** again. In other words, the **Selected button** toggles AE lock. This is similar to AE lock (Reset on release) except that releasing the shutter does not reset the AE lock hold. You must press the **Selected button** again to release AE lock.
- **AF lock only** – When set, this function locks the AF system (focus) on the last autofocus reading while you hold down the **Selected button**.
- **AF-ON (Assign AE-L/AF-L button only)** – If you set AE-L/AF-L button press to AF-ON, then the AE-L/AF-L button duplicates the functionality of the AF-ON button and will initiate autofocus. AF-ON cannot be assigned to the other two buttons (Fn and Preview). It doesn't even appear in their lists of functions.
- **Flash Disable/enable** – This is a temporary way to disable the flash when you want to leave your flash turned on and still be able to take a non-flash picture.

While you hold down the **Selected button**, the flash is disabled. If you press and hold the button while the flash is physically turned off, the camera will change to front-curtain sync while you hold down the **Selected button**.

- **Bracketing burst** – Normally, during a bracketing sequence with the shutter's Release mode set to Single Frame Release Mode—the S next to CL and CH on the Release mode dial—you have to press the Shutter-release button once for each of the images in the bracket. The only way to shoot all the images in the bracketed series without letting up on the Shutter-release button is to set the Release mode dial to CH, CL, or Qc. If you set Bracketing burst, you can hold down the **Selected button** while also holding down the Shutter-release button and the camera will take all the images in the bracket without letup. This seems a bit redundant to me. I think I'd rather just set the Release mode to CL–Continuous-low or CH–Continuous-high release mode and take the bracketed burst. This applies to AE, Flash, and ADL bracketing, which each take one image for each shutter release. WB bracketing is mentioned in the manual too, but because it takes the entire bracket in one shutter release, what's the point? If you use this function for WB bracketing and hold down the Shutter-release button, you'll create multiple groups of bracketed images on your memory card. Remember, WB bracketing takes the entire bracket in one shutter press. Multiple shutter releases will capture numerous multi-image WB brackets. Be careful with this function when using WB bracketing.

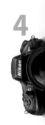

- **+NEF (RAW)** – If you are a regular JPEG shooter and have JPEG fine, normal, or basic selected as your normal image capture format, you can use the **Selected button** to temporarily switch to NEF (RAW) mode. Once you take the RAW format picture, the camera switches back to JPEG. If you decide not to take the NEF (RAW) picture, just press the **Selected button** again to return to JPEG mode.

- **Matrix metering** – If you do not use Matrix metering as your primary metering system but want to use it occasionally, this setting allows you to turn on Matrix metering by holding down the **Selected button**. When you release the **Selected button**, the camera returns to your customary meter type, such as Spot, Center-weighted, or Highlight-weighted metering.

- **Center-weighted** – If you do not use Center-weighted metering as your primary metering system but want to use it occasionally, you can turn on Center-weighted metering by holding down the **Selected button**. When you release the button, the camera returns to your customary meter type, such as Spot, Matrix, or Highlight-weighted metering.

- **Spot metering** – If you do not use Spot metering as your primary metering system but want to use it occasionally, you can turn on Spot metering by holding down the **Selected button**. When you release the button, the camera returns to your customary meter type, such as Center-weighted, Matrix, or Highlight-weighted metering.

- *Highlight-weighted metering* – If you do not use Highlight-weighted metering but want to use it occasionally, you can turn on Highlight-weighted metering by holding down the *Selected button*. When you release the button, the camera returns to your customary meter type, such as Center-weighted, Matrix, or Spot metering.
- *Viewfinder grid display* – When you press the *Selected button*, the camera will turn the framing grid display on or off in the Viewfinder.
- *Viewfinder virtual horizon* – You can press the *Selected button* to display a Virtual horizon indicator on the right and bottom sides of the Viewfinder.
- *Disable synchronized release* – When using a wireless remote controller for remote synchronized release of multiple cameras, you can press and hold the *Selected button* to take pictures with the master camera only (not with the remote cameras).
- *Remote release only* – When using a wireless remote controller for remote synchronized release, you can press and hold the *Selected button* to take pictures with the remote cameras only (not with the master camera).
- *MY MENU* – Pressing the *Selected button* opens the My Menu display on the Monitor. This is convenient for using favorite settings from My Menu without having to scroll through menus to activate the My Menu display.
- *Access top item in MY MENU* – You can press the *Selected button* to jump directly to the top item in My Menu. This allows you to quickly modify a frequently used menu item.
- *Playback* – This function causes the *Selected button* to act as if you had pressed the Playback button. Nikon included this so that you could play back images when using a big telephoto lens that requires two hands to use.
- *None* (default) – When this setting is enabled, the *Selected button* does nothing.

Press + Command Dials

- *Choose image area* – You may press the *Selected button* and rotate either of the Command dials to choose from the camera's various image areas. Your choices are FX (36x24) 1.0x, 1.2x (30x20) 1.2x, DX (24x16) 1.5x, and 5:4 (30x24). Use the menu shown in figure 4.49D, screen 3, to choose which Image area selections you want to appear on the camera's Control panel at selection time. To add or remove a check mark next to one of the image areas, highlight the image area and scroll to the right. You cannot uncheck the FX mode. The check marked image areas will be available on the Control panel in the following formats as you hold down the *Selected button* and turn either one of the Command dials:
  36 - 24 equals FX (36x24) 1.0x
  30 - 20 equals 1.2x (30x20) 1.2x
  24 - 16 equals DX (24x16) 1.5x
  30 - 24 equals 5:4 (30x24)

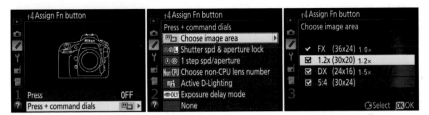

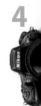

Figure 4.49D – Choose image area by menu selection

Figure 4.49E shows the 5:4 (30×24) image area on the Control panel, represented by the numbers 30 – 24.

- **Shutter speed & aperture lock** – Simply press the **Selected button** and rotate the front Main command dial to lock in the camera's shutter speed when you are using Shutter-priority (S) and Manual (M) modes. Or, you can press the **Selected button** and turn the front Sub-command dial to lock in the aperture setting when using Aperture-priority (A) and Manual (M) modes.

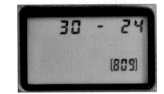

Figure 4.49E – Choose image area – 30x24 mm (5:4) is selected

- **1 step spd/aperture** (not available for AE-L/ AF-L + command dials) – If you set *Custom Setting Menu > b Metering/exposure > b2 EV steps for exposure cntrl* to 1/3 step you can change your camera's shutter speed and/or aperture in 1/3 EV steps while in Aperture-priority (A), Shutter-priority (S), and Manual (M). However, you may want to use larger EV steps occasionally. By setting 1 step spd/aperture, you can hold down the Selected button and the camera will allow you to change the shutter speed or aperture in 1 step increments instead of the normal 1/3 step. Example shutter speeds in 1/3 EV steps are 1/60, 1/80, 1/100, 1/125, 1/160. Example shutter speeds in 1 EV step are 1/60, 1/125, 1/250, 1/500, 1/1000.

- **Choose non-CPU lens number** – If you have configured non-CPU lenses under Setup Menu > Non-CPU lens data you'll be able to hold down the **Selected button** while rotating the front Sub-command dial to scroll through a list of up to nine non-CPU lenses. Figure 4.49F shows the Control panel icons you will see when you use Choose non-CPU lens number. The number 35 shown in figure 4.49F is the focal length of one of my registered non-CPU lenses—my AI Nikkor 35mm f/2—and the F2 represents the maximum aperture. The n-1 represents the lens numbers (n-1 through n-9) that are registered with the camera.

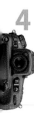

- *Active D-Lighting* – Press the *Selected button* and rotate either of the Command dials to adjust Active D-Lighting (ADL) to one of its six settings: Off (oFF), Low (L), Normal (n), High (H), Extra high (HP), and Auto. Figure 4.49G shows the Control panel icons you will see when you use Active D-Lighting as described here. You will see the symbols that represent the various settings, such as Auto, H, and HP, scroll by as you turn either of the Command dials.

- *Exposure delay mode* – Press the *Selected button* and rotate either of the Comand dials to choose an exposure delay of 1, 2, or 3 second(s). This is the same as setting an exposure delay with Custom setting d4 Exposure delay mode. Figure 4.49H shows the Control panel with Exposure delay mode selected. The dLY symbol stands for delay and the number in the bottom right corner is the delay time. In figure 4.49H, you can see that I selected 3 seconds of exposure delay. Therefore, when I press the Shutter-release button, my camera will raise the mirror and then wait three seconds to fire the shutter. This allows vibrations to die down, resulting in a sharper picture.

- *None* – Nothing happens when you hold down the *Selected button* and rotate the Command dials.

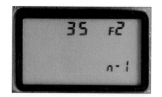

Figure 4.49F – Choose non-CPU lens number

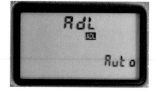

Figure 4.49G – Active D-Lighting – Auto

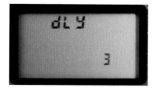

Figure 4.49H – Exposure delay mode – 3 seconds

Using the Quick Menu to Assign Buttons

Interestingly, you can also use the camera's *i* button and Quick Menu to initiate assignments to the Fn button, Preview button, and AE-L/AF-L buttons. Use the following screens to do it, referring back to the **Assignable Function List** for selections.

Use the following steps to access the Quick Menu and initiate changes to the *Selected button* assignments:

1. Press the *i* button to open the Quick Menu.

2. You will see selectable settings as shown in figure 4.49I. Scroll around with the Multi selector and choose the button you want to assign (positions shown in figure 4.49I).

3. When you have selected the correct button assignment screen, simply press the OK button to open the actual assignment menus, which are identical to the menus covered in figures 4.49A, 4.49B, and 4.49C (starting with screen 3 in each) and include all the functions listed in the **Assignable Function List**. Basically, the Quick Menu allows you to skip the first two menu items on the Custom Setting Menu and jump directly to the assignment screens (screens 3–6) in figures 4.49A, 4.49B, and 4.49C. This may save you a little time in the field.

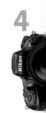

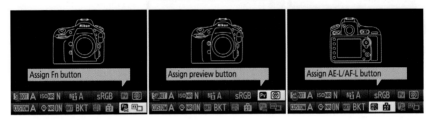

Figure 4.49I – Selected button assignment from the Quick Menu

Settings Recommendation: There are so many available functions here that I'm loathe to recommend anything definitively. However, I will tell you how I set mine, and you can experiment and see if that suits your style. If not, you've got a lot of choices!

Darrell's favorites:

• *Assign Fn button press* – Spot metering (my normal meter is Matrix)
• *Assign Fn button + command dials* – Not used
• *Assign preview button press* – Preview (Depth-of-field preview)
• *Assign preview button + command dials* – Not used
• *Assign AE-L/AF-L button press* – AE lock only
• *Assign AE-L/AF-L button + command dials* – Exposure delay mode

Custom Setting f7 – Shutter Spd & Aperture Lock

(User's Manual – Page 350)

Shutter spd & aperture lock is an interesting function that allows you to lock the shutter speed at the currently selected value when shooting in Shutter-priority (S) or Manual (M) mode. You can also lock the aperture at its current value when you are shooting in Aperture-priority (A) or Manual (M) mode. This function does not apply to and will not work when shooting in Programmed auto (P) mode.

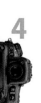

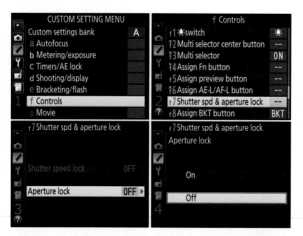

Figure 4.50 – Selecting Shutter spd & aperture lock

Use the following steps to keep your shutter speed or aperture from changing, according to which exposure mode you are using:

1. Select f Controls from the Custom Setting Menu and scroll to the right (figure 4.50, screen 1).

2. Highlight f7 shutter spd & aperture lock and scroll to the right (figure 4.50, screen 2).

3. When you are using Aperture-priority (A) mode, Shutter speed lock will be grayed out and unavailable (as you see in figure 4.50, screen 3). When you are using Shutter-priority (S) mode, Aperture lock will be grayed out and unavailable. If you have the camera set to Manual (M) mode, Shutter speed lock and Aperture lock are both available. When the camera is set to Programmed-auto (P) mode, the entire Shutter spd & aperture lock function is grayed out and non-selectable. Select Shutter speed lock or Aperture lock (according to which exposure mode you are currently using) and scroll to the right (figure 4.50, screen 3).

4. Choose either On or Off from the list. In figure 4.50, screen 4, Off has been chosen for Aperture lock. On locks the setting (Shutter speed or Aperture), while Off allows you to continue adjusting that setting. (The screens for Shutter speed lock are not shown in figure 4.50. They work exactly the same way as Aperture lock.)

5. Press the OK button to lock in the setting.

Settings Recommendation: If I were shooting in a studio, under carefully controlled lighting, and wanted to lock the shutter speed or aperture to a value that will not change throughout the session, this function will do the job well. It can be a protection for when you do not want a value to change.

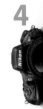

Custom Setting f8 – Assign BKT button

(User's Manual – Pages 350, 133, 211, 184)

Assign BKT button allows you to either leave bracketing assigned to the BKT button or to assign Multiple exposure or HDR (high dynamic range), instead of bracketing, to the BKT button. Bracketing is fully described in the previous section **Custom Setting Menu – e6 Auto bracketing set**, in case you want to review it.

In the chapter titled **Shooting Menu**, we covered how to do multiple exposures and shoot HDR (high dynamic range) images based on Shooting Menu settings.

Let's see how to change BKT button's assignment to initiate one of these functions.

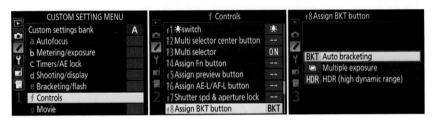

Figure 4.51A – Assign BKT button

Use these steps to change the assignment of the BKT button from Bracketing to Multiple exposure or HDR:

1. Choose f controls from the Custom Setting Menu and scroll to the right (figure 4.51A, screen 1).
2. Select f8 Assign BKT button from the menu and scroll to the right (figure 4.51A, screen 2).
3. Choose Auto bracketing, Multiple exposure, or HDR (high dynamic range) from the list (figure 4.51A, screen 3).
4. Press the OK button to select the setting.

You can manage all three of these functions—Auto bracketing, Multiple exposure, and HDR (high dynamic range)—using external camera controls and the Control panel. We covered the normal use of the BKT button (exposure bracketing) in a previous section of this chapter, **Custom Setting e6 – Auto bracketing set**, so we won't review it here. However, we need to examine the Control panel screens for Multiple exposure and HDR (high dynamic range).

Multiple Exposure

First let's look into the Control panel icons and what they mean for Multiple exposure (figure 4.51B). You may want to review the section titled **Multiple Exposure** in the **Shooting Menu** chapter to make sure you understand what each part of this function does.

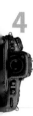

Press the BKT button and rotate the rear Main command dial until you see the symbols shown in figure 4.51B. Here is what each symbol means, and how to use it, referenced by the numbers in red:

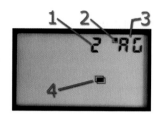

1. This symbol shows the number of shots in the Multiple exposure. Hold down the BKT button and turn the front Sub-command dial to select between 2 and 10 exposures for the Multiple exposure.

2. The tiny symbol L informs you that you have selected On (series), meaning you will take a series of multiple-exposure images, not just one. If the L is not displayed, you have selected On (single photo) and will take only a single Multiple exposure. Hold down the BKT button and turn the rear Main command dial to toggle the symbol—and the functionality it represents—On or Off.

Figure 4.51B – Multiple exposure using the BKT button

3. The symbol AG stands for Auto Gain. It is displayed if you have Auto gain set to On in Shooting Menu > Multiple exposure > Auto gain. You cannot turn AG on or off by using external camera controls. You must use the Shooting Menu instead.

4. This symbol is displayed to let you know you have enabled Multiple exposure. Hold down the BKT button and rotate the rear Main command dial until the symbol appears on the Control panel. Now, we will examine how you can use external camera controls to enable and change the HDR (high dynamic range) function.

Next let's consider how to use the HDR functionality on the fly, without using menus.

HDR (High Dynamic Range)

This function is simply a shortcut to the *Shooting Menu > HDR (high dynamic range)* function. You can use it to quickly shoot a single two-shot HDR bracket, or a series of two-frame HDR shots, without using the camera's menus. You can set the exposure difference between each frame in the two-shot HDR bracket to 1, 2, or 3 stops, or you can select Auto and let the camera decide.

Why not review the section titled **HDR (High Dynamic Range)** in the **Shooting Menu** chapter to make sure you understand what each part of this function does.

Following is a description of what each symbol means, and how to use it, referenced by the numbers in red (figure 4.51C):

1. The Hdr of (off) symbol appears when you hold down the BKT button, unless you already have HDR enabled. If you rotate the rear Main command dial, you can enable or disable HDR (high dynamic range). The Hdr on or Hdr of symbols will appear, indicating whether HDR is on or off. Figure 4.51C shows that HDR is enabled. Additionally, a small HDR symbol will appear near the center of the Control panel when HDR is enabled.

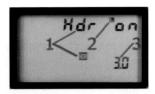

Figure 4.51C – HDR using the BKT button

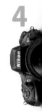

2. A little L symbol will appear and disappear as you rotate the rear Main command dial. When the L is showing, it means that the camera will take multiple HDR shots, one after the other, as you press the Shutter-release button. Please allow the camera some time for HDR processing between shots. If the little L is not showing, the camera will take only one HDR shot and automatically set itself to Hdr of (off). In other words, if the L is showing, HDR mode is set to On (series). If the L is not showing, HDR mode is set to On (single photo). (See *Shooting Menu > HDR (high dynamic range) > HDR mode*).

3. This number 3.0 represents the exposure differential between the shots in the two-shot bracket. In this case there will be a 3-stop exposure difference between the two pictures that will later be combined into one HDR image. You can select: Auto, 1, 2, or 3 (stops). Hold down the BKT button and rotate the front Sub-command dial to change the exposure differential. If you select Auto, the camera decides how much exposure differential to allow between the two HDR frames.

Settings Recommendation: I usually leave the BKT button set to bracketing because I do a lot of bracketing when I'm out shooting high-contrast landscape scenes. However, if you do more multiple exposures or two-picture HDR than bracketing, why not assign the BKT button to one of those two alternate functions? Nikon gives us some excellent personal customizability with this camera.

Custom Setting f9 – Customize Command Dials

(User's Manual – Page 351)

Customize command dials does exactly what it sounds like—it lets you change how the Command dials operate. There are several operations you can modify:

- Reverse rotation
- Change main/sub
- Aperture setting
- Menus and playback
- Sub-dial frame advance

Let's examine each of these items and the screens and steps used to change them.

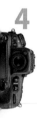

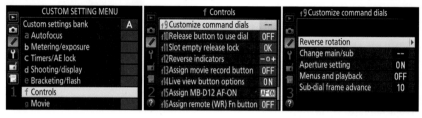

Figure 4.52A – Customize command dials

Use the following steps to change the functionality of the Command dials:

1. Select f Controls from the Custom Setting Menu and scroll to the right (figure 4.52A, screen 1).
2. Highlight f9 Customize command dials and scroll to the right (figure 4.52A, screen 2).
3. Choose one of the five selections from the list. In figure 4.52A, screen 3, Reverse rotation has been selected.
4. Scroll to the right and use the screens and steps under each of the following sections to configure the various functions (figures 4.52B to 4.52G).

Reverse Rotation

Reverse rotation allows you to change what happens when you rotate the Command dials in a certain direction, including those on a mounted MB-D12 battery pack. You can reverse Command dial operations with this setting. There are two selections:

- **Exposure compensation** – When you press and hold the Exposure compensation button and turn the Sub-command dial clockwise, it decreases the amount of compensation. If you place a check mark in this box and select Done, the camera will increase the amount of compensation when you turn the Sub-command dial clockwise.
- **Shutter speed/aperture** – Normally, when the D810 is set to Aperture-priority (A) or Manual (M) mode and you rotate the Sub-command dial clockwise, the aperture gets smaller. If you put a check mark next to Shutter speed/aperture and select Done, the aperture will instead get larger when you turn the Sub-command dial clockwise. The same goes for shutter speed in Shutter-priority (S) and Manual (M) modes. Normally, turning the rear Main command dial clockwise slows down the shutter speed. If you put a check mark next to Shutter speed/aperture and select Done, the shutter speed will instead get faster when you turn the Main command dial clockwise. Finally, when you override the

aperture setting in Programmed auto (P) mode by turning the Main command dial clockwise, instead of decreasing the size of the aperture, it increases it.

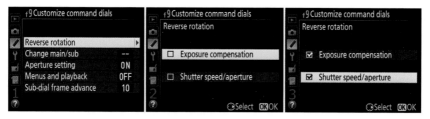

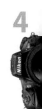

Figure 4.52B – Customize command dials (Reverse rotation)

Here are the steps to change the rotation direction of the Command dials:

1. Continuing from figure 4.52A, screen 3, select Reverse rotation and scroll to the right (figure 4.52B, screen 1).
2. Using the Multi selector, highlight Exposure compensation or Shutter speed/ aperture and scroll to the right to set a check mark in the corresponding small check box (figure 4.52B, screen 2). In figure 4.52B, screen 3, I have placed a check mark in both of the selections.
3. Press the OK button to lock in the setting.

Settings Recommendation: I leave the Command dials rotation set to factory default. I find life confusing enough without my camera working backwards. Of course, if you come from a different camera brand than Nikon—having been drawn by the siren call of 36 megapixels—and are used to the dials working in the opposite direction, you may feel more comfortable reversing them on your D810.

Change Main/Sub

Change main/sub allows you to swap the functionality of the two Command dials. The rear Main command dial will take on the functions of the front Sub-command dial and vice versa.

You can configure the camera so that this reversal of the Main and Sub command dials applies to both the Exposure setting (aperture and shutter speed) and the Autofocus setting (Autofocus modes and AF-area modes).

Exposure Setting

The Exposure setting subfunction allows you to switch the Main and Sub functionality of the Command dials for changing the aperture and shutter speed. Normally, the aperture is controlled by the front Sub-command dial, and the shutter speed is controlled by the rear Main command dial. However, when switched, that is reversed.

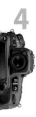

Let's consider the three settings you can choose under this subfunction and see how they each affect the actions of the Command dials.

Here are the three setting variations:

- **On** – By selecting On, you reverse the functionality of the two Command dials so that the Sub-command dial controls shutter speed while the Main command dial controls aperture.
- **On (Mode A)** – This special mode sets the camera so that the Main command dial controls the aperture when using Aperture-priority (A) mode only.
- **Off** – The functionality of the Command dials is set to the factory default. The Main command dial controls the shutter speed while the Sub-command dial controls the aperture.

Let's examine how to choose one of these settings.

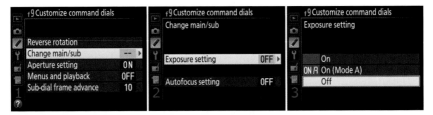

Figure 4.52C – Customize command dials (Change main/sub – Exposure setting)

Here are the steps to swap the functionality of the Command dials for the Exposure setting:

1. Continuing from figure 4.52A, screen 3, select Change main/sub and scroll to the right (figure 4.52C, screen 1).
2. Choose Exposure setting from the Change main/sub menu and scroll to the right (figure 4.52C, screen 2).
3. Select one of the three settings: On, On (Mode A), or Off (figure 4.52C, screen 3).
4. Press the OK button to lock in the setting.

Settings Recommendation: I leave the Command dials set to factory default (Off). I've been using Nikons for too many years to change Command dial functionality now. However, you may have valid reasons for swapping the Command dial functionality. If so, it's very easy.

Autofocus Setting

When adjusting the Autofocus setting you will hold in the AF-mode button (just under the Lens release button) and turn one of the Command dials while watching the modes change on the Control panel. Normally, the rear Main command dial controls the Autofocus mode (i.e., AF-S, AF-C) and the front Sub-command dial controls the AF-area mode (e.g., Single-point AF, Group-area AF, Dynamic-area AF). However, you can reverse that with the *Change main/sub > Autofocus setting* subfunction.

Here is a list of the two settings within this subfunction and what each does:

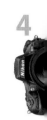

- **On** – By selecting On, you reverse the functionality of the two Command dials so that the front Sub-command dial controls the Autofocus mode (i.e., AF-S, AF-C) and the rear Main command dial controls the AF-area mode (e.g., Single-point AF, Group-area AF, Dynamic-area AF).
- **Off** – The functionality of the Command dials is set to the factory default. The the front Sub-command dial controls the AF-area mode (e.g., Single-point AF, Group-area AF, Dynamic-area AF) and the rear Main command dial controls the Autofocus mode (i.e., AF-S, AF-C).

Let's see how to choose one of these settings.

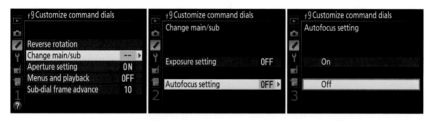

Figure 4.52D – Customize command dials (Change main/sub – Autofocus setting)

Here are the steps to swap the functionality of the Command dials for the Autofocus setting:

1. Continuing from figure 4.52A, screen 3, select Change main/sub and scroll to the right (figure 4.52D, screen 1).
2. Choose Autofocus setting from the Change main/sub menu and scroll to the right (figure 4.52D, screen 2).
3. Select On or Off (figure 4.52D, screen 3).
4. Press the OK button to lock in the setting.

Settings Recommendation: Again, I see no reason to reverse the functionality of the Command dials because I have trained my muscle memory over the last several years to work with the normal Main and Sub command dial functions. However, if you have recently come from a different camera brand over to the new Nikon D810 and are used to the dials working in reverse, or you just prefer it that way, by all means reverse how the Command dials work.

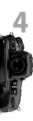

Aperture Setting

There are two selections that allow you to modify how the camera treats CPU lenses that have aperture rings on them (non-G lenses):

- **Sub-command dial** – This is the factory default setting. The aperture is set using the Sub-command dial. If you select this setting and are using a non-G lens with an old-style aperture ring, you will need to set and lock it (if available) to the smallest aperture and then use the Sub-command dial to change apertures.
- **Aperture ring** – This setting allows those with older non-G type lenses with a CPU to use the lens's aperture ring to adjust the aperture instead of using the Sub-command dial. The EV increments will be displayed in only 1 EV steps when this is active. If you are using a G-type lens with no aperture ring, you clearly can't set the aperture with a nonexistent aperture ring, so the camera ignores this setting.

Note: When a non-CPU lens is used, the aperture ring must always be used to set the aperture instead of the Sub-command dial.

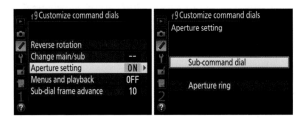

Figure 4.52E – Customize command dials (Aperture setting)

Here are the steps to change the style of Aperture setting:

1. Continuing from figure 4.52A, screen 3, select Aperture setting and scroll to the right (figure 4.52E, screen 1).
2. Select Sub-command dial or Aperture ring from the list (figure 4.52E, screen 2).
3. Press the OK button to lock in the setting.

Settings Recommendation: I leave Aperture setting set to Sub-command dial. I have some older AF Nikkors that I still like using, so I keep them locked at their smallest aperture settings and use the Sub-command dial to change their apertures. I don't adjust apertures with the old aperture ring on the lens unless I'm using older non-CPU, manual focus AI or AI-S lenses.

Menus and Playback

Menus and playback is designed for those who do not like to use the Multi selector for viewing image Playback or Info screens. It also allows you to use the Command

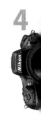

dials for scrolling though menus. There are two selections for how the menus and image playback work when you would rather not use the Multi selector:

- **On** – While viewing images during playback, turning the Main command dial to the left or right scrolls through the displayed images. Turning the Sub-command dial left or right scrolls through the data and histogram screens for each image. While viewing menus, turning the Main command dial left or right scrolls up or down in the screens. Turning the Sub-command dial left or right scrolls left or right in the menus. The Multi selector button works normally, even when this is set to On. This setting simply allows you two ways to view your images and menus instead of one. Also, when you are using thumbnail viewing of multiple images on the Monitor, turning the rear Main command dial moves left and right in the list of thumbnail images, while the front Sub-command dial moves up and down in the list of thumbnails.

- **On (image review excluded)** – This works exactly the same as On, with one exception. When you use On alone (previous setting) and take a picture, the picture will show up on the Monitor and you can then use the Command dials to review images other than the one you just took. However, if you select On (image review excluded) instead of just On, you will not be able to examine other images with the Command dials when an image pops up for review after you take it. In other words, image review with the Command dials is excluded just after you take a picture. You can view only the picture you just took unless you use the Multi selector, not the Command dials, to scroll through the other images taken previously. You can still use the Command dials for Playback image review (after pressing the Playback button)—just not immediately after taking an image, when it first pops up on the Monitor.

- **Off** – This is the default action. The Multi selector is used to scroll through images and menus.

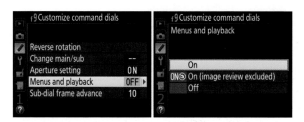

Figure 4.52F – Customize command dials (Menus and playback)

Here are the steps used to configure Menus and playback:

1. Continuing from figure 4.52A, screen 3, select Menus and playback and scroll to the right (figure 4.52F, screen 1).

2. Select one of the three settings (figure 4.52F, screen 2). On is selected in screen 2.
3. Press the OK button to lock in the setting.

Settings Recommendation: I have my camera set to On for Menus and playback. I like the fact that I can use the Multi selector or the Command dials to move around in my camera's menus and images. Try this one out; you may like it too!

Sub-Dial Frame Advance

With the huge memory cards available today, you may find yourself having hundreds or even thousands of images on a single memory card. Have you ever had to scroll through a large number of images to find an image you want to look at more closely?

Nikon has come to our rescue with a function that lets you move around more efficiently within a large number of images, or even multiple folders, on a memory card.

This function is closely tied to the previous function, Menus and playback. Please review that function for details. If you have On or On (image review excluded) enabled under Menus and playback, you can use the following functionality:

- **10 frames** – When you rotate the front Sub-command dial during full-frame playback, the camera will jump forward or backward 10 frames at a time, skipping over the frames in between.
- **50 frames** – When you rotate the front Sub-command dial during full-frame playback, the camera will jump forward or backward 50 frames at a time, skipping the frames in between.
- **Folder** – When you rotate the front Sub-command dial during full-frame playback, the camera will move between folders. If there is only one folder on the memory card, the Sub-command dial does nothing.

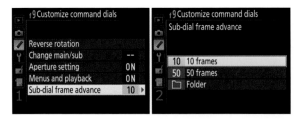

Figure 4.52G – Customize command dials (Sub-dial frame advance)

Use these steps to choose a Sub-dial frame advance setting:

1. Continuing from figure 4.52A, screen 3, select Sub-dial frame advance and scroll to the right (figure 4.52G, screen 1).

2. Select one of the three settings: 10 frames, 50 frames, or Folder (figure 4.52G, screen 2).
3. Press the OK button to lock in the setting.

Note: If you do not have On or On (image review excluded) set in Menus and play-back (previous subheading), the camera will not respond to any settings in the Sub-dial frame advance function. When you rotate the front Sub-command dial during full-frame playback, nothing will happen.

Settings Recommendation: I have my camera set to Folders because I often use different folders to separate the images on my camera's memory card. I currently shoot with 64GB Sandisk cards and they will hold hundreds of RAW images and thousands of JPEGs. As memory cards increase in size and the larger ones become more affordable, I can foresee a time when this function will become even more important.

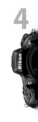

Custom Setting f10 – Release Button to Use Dial

(User's Manual – Page 353)

Release button to use dial allows those who don't like to or cannot hold down but-tons and turn a Command dial at the same time to change to an easier method. This function may be very useful to people with limited hand strength, allowing them to operate the camera more easily.

The function works with the following buttons only:

- MODE button
- +/- Exposure compensation button
- +/- Flash compensation button
- BKT button
- ISO button
- QUAL button
- WB button
- Metering button
- AF-mode button
- Fn button
- Pv (Preview) button
- AE-L/AF-L button
- Movie-record button

There are two settings under this function. Let's examine them and then look at the screens and steps to modify Release button to use dial:

- **Yes** – This setting changes a two-step operation into a three-step operation. Normally, you would press and hold down a button while rotating a Command

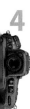

dial. When you select Yes under Release button to use dial, the camera allows you to press and release a button, rotate the Command dial, then press and release the button again. The initial button press locks the button so that you do not have to hold your finger on it while turning the Command dial. Once you have changed whatever you are adjusting, you must press the button a second time to unlock it.

- **No** – This is the default setting. You must press and hold a button while rotating the Command dials in order to change camera functionality.

If the exposure meter turns off or you press the Shutter-release button halfway while the Yes operation is active, you must press the original button again to restart the action. You can set the exposure meter to No limit or a longer time-out in *Custom Setting Menu > c Timers/AE lock > c2 Standby timer* to prevent the exposure meter from turning off after a few seconds. This may make the function more useful if you have weak hands or must move slowly.

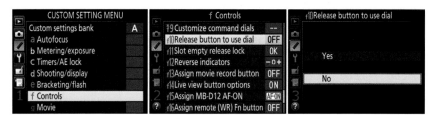

Figure 4.53 – Release button to use dial

Here are the steps to configure Release button to use dial:

1. Select f Controls from the Custom Setting Menu and scroll to the right (figure 4.53, screen 1).
2. Highlight f10 Release button to use dial and scroll to the right (figure 4.53, screen 2).
3. Choose Yes or No. In figure 4.53, screen 3, No has been selected.
4. Press the OK button to lock in the setting.

Settings Recommendation: I haven't found this function useful for myself. However, a person with certain physical disabilities may find this to be a very useful function.

Custom Setting f11 – Slot Empty Release Lock

(User's Manual – Page 354)

Slot empty release lock defaults to locking the shutter when you try to take an image without a memory card inserted in the camera. By enabling it, you can take pictures without a memory card but cannot save them later.

This function exists so that when you have your camera tethered to your computer using Nikon Camera Control Pro 2 software (not included), you can send pictures directly to the computer, bypassing the memory card.

You can allow the camera to take pictures with no card inserted when you select the OK Enable release setting. Here is a description of both settings:

- **LOCK Release locked** – When you choose this default setting, your camera will refuse to release the shutter when there is no memory card present.
- **OK Enable release** – Use this setting if you want to use the optional Camera Control Pro 2 software to send images from the camera directly to the computer.

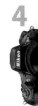

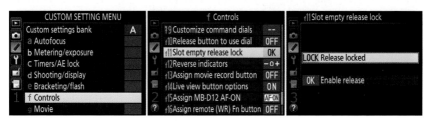

Figure 4.54 – Slot empty release lock

Here are the steps used to configure Slot empty release lock:

1. Select f Controls from the Custom Setting Menu and scroll to the right (figure 4.54, screen 1).
2. Highlight f11 Slot empty release lock and scroll to the right (figure 4.54, screen 2).
3. Choose one of the two settings from the list. In figure 4.54, screen 3, LOCK Release locked has been selected.
4. Press the OK button to lock in the setting.

Settings Recommendation: I tried using the OK Enable release setting as an experiment. I found that there is no real reason to use this setting other than when the camera is tethered to a computer. You cannot save the images in the memory buffer to a memory card later.

Custom Setting f12 – Reverse Indicators

(User's Manual – Page 354)

Reverse indicators lets you change the direction of your camera's exposure displays. Normally, anytime you see the exposure indicators in your camera's Control panel, Viewfinder, or the Information display, the - is on the left and the + is on the right. See Figure 4.55A, where I show the Information display and the exposure indicator therein. The first image shows the normal direction. The second image shows the Information display with the exposure indicators reversed (see red arrows).

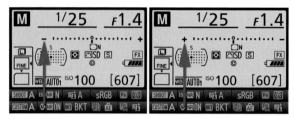

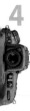

Figure 4.55A – Reversed indicators on the Information display (see red arrows)

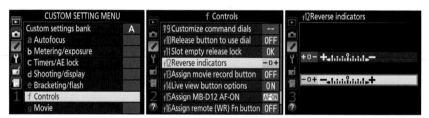

Figure 4.55B – Reverse indicators

Here are the steps to reverse the direction of all camera exposure indicators:

1. Select f Controls from the Custom Setting Menu and scroll to the right (figure 4.55B, screen 1).
2. Highlight f12 Reverse indicators and scroll to the right (figure 4.55B, screen 2).
3. Choose one of the two selections from the list. In figure 4.55B, screen 3, the reversed exposure indicator direction has been selected. Set it back to factory default with the other selection.
4. Press the OK button to lock in the setting.

Settings Recommendation: If you have been using an older Nikon SLR or DSLR you may find the reversed exposure indicator scale on your D810 somewhat jarring.

Having used Nikons since way back in 1980, I was quite used to my camera's exposure scale having the plus on the left and the minus on the right. When I first started using a Nikon that reversed this scale, it aggravated me to no end, and I changed it back to the "normal" +/- setting.

However, after thinking about it for a while, I realized that the histogram works in a -/+ direction, with dark on the left and bright on the right. I use the histogram frequently, so I changed the indicator direction back to the factory default of -/+. I have now used it this way for some time and it is beginning to make sense and feel more natural.

However, if you feel uncomfortable seeing the meter indicator working "backwards," you may want to change the exposure indicator to the "correct" direction. If you do change it, you may also want to reverse the Exposure compensation direction with *Custom Setting Menu > f controls > f9 Customize command dials > Reverse rotation > Exposure compensation* (see the previous section **Custom Setting f9 – Customize Command Dials**). Otherwise, you will notice that the Exposure compensation setting works backwards from the reversed direction of the exposure indicator. It's a good thing we still have a choice about reversing things!

Custom Setting f13 – Assign Movie Record Button
(User's Manual – Page 355)

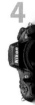

Assign movie record button allows you to assign various functions to the Movie-record button for use during still-image shooting. When you are using your camera to take still pictures in Viewfinder or Live view photography mode, the Movie-record button has no functionality. It just sits there looking pretty with its exciting red dot. Normally, the only time the button has a function to perform is when you press it to start recording a video in Movie live view mode.

However, by assigning a function to the Movie-record button with this setting, you can use it to make adjustments when you are taking still images. This function becomes disabled when you set the Live view selector switch on the back of the camera to the Movie live view position. It is only active when taking stills.

There are five available subfunctions for the Movie-record button, as follows:

- **White balance** – Press the button and rotate a Command dial to choose a White balance setting (e.g., Flash, Cloudy, Shade).
- **ISO sensitivity** – Press the button and rotate a Command dial to choose an ISO sensitivity setting (e.g., 64, 125, 250)
- **Choose image area** – Press the button and rotate a Command dial to choose an Image area setting (FX, DX, 5:4, 1.2x)
- **Shutter spd & aperture lock** – Press the button and rotate the Main command dial to lock the shutter speed in Shutter-priority (S) and Manual (M) modes. Press the button and rotate the Sub-command dial to lock the aperture in Aperture-priority (A) and Manual (M) modes.
- **None** – The Movie-record button does nothing when taking still pictures in Viewfinder or Live view photography mode.

The Movie-record button maintains normal functionality for during video recordings, regardless of how this setting is configured. Let's examine how to choose one of the listed settings.

Use these steps to choose a role for the Movie-record button when you are taking still pictures:

1. Select f Controls from the Custom Setting Menu and scroll to the right (figure 4.56A, screen 1).
2. Highlight f13 Assign movie record button and scroll to the right (figure 4.56A, screen 2).

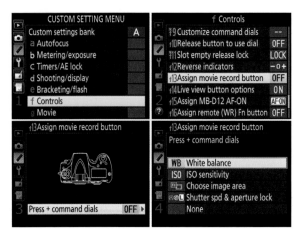

Figure 4.56A – Assign movie record button

3. Press + command dials will automatically be selected. Scroll to the right (figure 4.56A, screen 3).

4. Choose one of the five selections from the list (figure 4.56A, screen 4). To select White balance, ISO sensitivity, Shutter spd & aperture lock, or None, simply high-light it and press the OK button to lock in the setting. Skip steps 5 and 6.

5. If you select Choose image area, you will be directed to an additional screen that lists the four Image area formats (figure 4.56B, screen 2). Follow the remaining directions to select and use Choose image area:

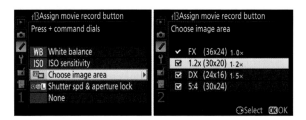

Figure 4.56B – Choose image area

Select Choose image area and scroll to the right (figure 4.56B, screen 1). Strangely enough, you do not use this selection to immediately choose an Image area, despite the name. Instead, you use the list of Image areas (figure 4.56B, screen 2) to choose which modes will be available when you hold down the Movie-record button and rotate either of the Command dials.

To actually select the Image areas you want to appear on the Control panel, you must check or uncheck the items you see in figure 4.56B, screen 2. You cannot uncheck the FX mode. To check or uncheck an item, highlight it and scroll to the right (screen 2). The check-marked image areas will be available for selection when you hold down the Movie-record button and turn either one of the Command dials. They appear on the Control panel in the following formats:

36 - 24 equals FX (36x24) 1.0x

30 - 20 equals 1.2x (30x20)

24 - 16 equals DX (24x16) 1.5x

30 - 24 equals 5:4 (30x24)

6. Press the OK button to lock in the Image area selections for later use.

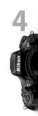

Settings Recommendation: I wish Nikon had broadened our choices a bit for functions to assign to the Movie-record button. We already have buttons on the camera's top plate for White balance and ISO sensitivity, and they cannot be reassigned. Therefore, it seems like an additional White balance or ISO sensitivity button is a poor choice.

I set my camera to Choose image area so that I can easily select from one of the four image areas without having to look through the Shooting Menu for the *Image area > Choose image area* function. However, since I shoot mostly in RAW, I rarely need to change Image area modes.

I do not need to lock my shutter speed or aperture with the Shutter spd & aperture lock function, so for me, this is a fairly useless function. Maybe a firmware update will give us more choices later?

Custom Setting f14 – Live View Button Options

(User's Manual – Page 356)

Live view button options allows you to disable the Lv button. If you do not use Live view at all for still images and/or video, or you frequently hit the Lv button by accident and enter Live view when you really don't want to, the camera offers you a solution.

When the Lv button is disabled, the camera will not use any form of Live view. Therefore, pressing the Lv button in either Live view photography mode or Movie live view mode does nothing.

Let's see how to enable or disable the Live view button.

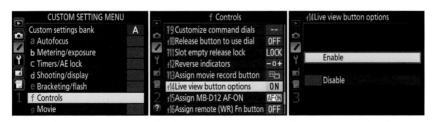

Figure 4.57 – Live view button options

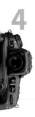

Use the following steps to enable or disable the Lv button, thereby enabling or disabling the camera's Live view functionality for both still shooting and video recording:

1. Select f Controls from the Custom Setting Menu and scroll to the right (figure 4.57, screen 1).
2. Highlight f14 Live view button options and scroll to the right (figure 4.57, screen 2).
3. Choose one of the two selections from the list (figure 4.57, screen 3). Enable allows the Lv button to open up Live view for shooting still images or videos. Disable turns off all Live view functionality, rendering the D810 a Viewfinder-based, stills-only camera.
4. Press the OK button to lock in the setting.

Settings Recommendation: If you don't need or want Live view mode, you can now turn it off completely by disabling the Lv button. I use Live view for both still image shooting and video recording at times, so I leave this function set to Enable.

Custom Setting f15 – Assign MB-D12 AF-ON

(User's Manual – Page 356)

The *Assign MB-D12 AF-ON* setting lets you assign a different function to the AF-ON button built into the optional MB-D12 battery pack than the button on the camera's body. There are eight distinct functions you can assign to the MB-D12's AF-ON button, as follows:

- *AF-ON* – This causes the camera to initiate autofocus when you press the AF-ON button on the MB-D12. This is the normal setting for the AF-ON button.
- *AF lock only* – This function locks the AF (focus) system on the last autofocus reading while you hold down the AF-ON button on the MB-D12.
- *AE/AF lock* – Enabling this function causes AE (exposure) and AF (focus) to lock on the last meter and autofocus system reading while the AF-ON button on the MB-D12 is held down.
- *AE lock only* – This allows you to lock AE (exposure) on the last meter reading when you hold down the AF-ON button on the MB-D12.
- *AE lock (Reset on release)* – AE (exposure) locks when the MB-D12's AF-ON button is pressed once and released. AE remains locked until the AF-ON button is pressed and released a second time, the exposure meter turns off, or the shutter is released.
- *AE lock (Hold)* – Enabling this function causes AE (exposure) to lock on the last meter reading when the AF-ON button on the MB-D12 is pressed and released once. It stays locked until you press the AF-ON button again or the exposure meter goes off.

- *FV lock* – If you set the AF-ON button on the MB-D12 to FV lock, the button will cause the built-in Speedlight or an external Speedlight to emit a monitor pre-flash. It will lock the flash output to the level determined by the preflash until you press the AF-ON button on the MB-D12 a second time.
- *Same as Fn button* – This setting allows you to set the AF-ON button on the MB-D12 so it executes whatever function you assigned to the camera's Fn button in *Custom Setting Menu > f controls > f4 Assign Fn button*.

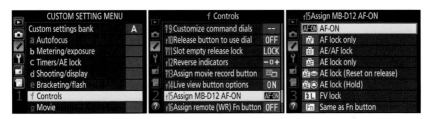
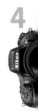

Figure 4.58 – Assign MB-D12 AF-ON

Use the following steps to assign various functions to the Nikon MB-D12 battery pack's AF-ON button:

1. Select f Controls from the Custom Setting Menu and scroll to the right (figure 4.58, screen 1).
2. Highlight f15 Assign MB-D12 AF-ON and scroll to the right (figure 4.58, screen 2).
3. Choose one of the eight selections from the list of functions (figure 4.58, screen 3).
4. Press the OK button to lock in the setting.

Settings Recommendation: If you use an MB-D12 battery pack and don't use back button focus, you can choose one of the other seven functions to assign to the AF-ON button on the MB-D12. As a nature photographer, I rarely use back button focus, and I often lock my exposure using AE lock, so I assigned AE lock only to my MB-D12's AF-ON button.

Custom Setting f16 – Assign Remote (WR) Fn Button
Assign remote (WR) Fn button allows you to assign various functions to the Fn button found on a Nikon WR-T10 Wireless Remote Controller. The WR-T10 controller is used to operate your camera through a Nikon WR-R10 Wireless Remote Transceiver.

You can assign one of 11 subfunctions to the Fn button on the controller, as follows:

- *Preview* – While you are using the Viewfinder, you can press the Fn button on the WR-R10 controller to preview depth of field. During Live view photography you can use the button as a toggle to open the aperture (maximum aperture) or stop it down (current aperture setting).

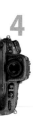

- **FV lock** – Press the Fn button on the WR-R10 controller to lock the flash value for the built-in flash and compatible accessory-shoe mounted Speedlights.
- **AE/AF lock** – Press and hold the Fn button on the WR-R10 controller to lock both the focus and exposure.
- **AE lock only** – Press and hold the Fn button on the WR-R10 controller to lock the exposure only.
- **AE lock (Reset on release)** – Press the Fn button on the WR-R10 controller once to lock the exposure and a second time to unlock the exposure.
- **AF lock only** – Press and hold the Fn button on the WR-R10 controller to lock the focus.
- **AF-ON** – Press the Fn button on the WR-R10 controller to initiate autofocus.
- **Flash Disable/enable** – Press the and hold the Fn button on the WR-R10 controller to disable the active flash unit. Release the Fn button to enable the flash. If there is no flash present or turned on, the camera will use Front-curtain sync mode while you press and hold the Fn button.
- **+ NEF (RAW)** – If you are shooting in any of the JPEG modes (Fine, Normal, or Basic) and press the Fn button on the WR-R10 controller, the camera will immediately switch to NEF (RAW) mode for the next picture only. The original picture quality mode will be restored as soon as you release pressure on the Shutter-release button. If you decide not to take a RAW picture after pressing the WR-R10's Fn button, simply press the button again to cancel.
- **Live view** – Pressing the Fn button on the WR-R10 controller starts and ends Live view.
- **None** – Pressing the Fn button on the WR-R10 controller has no effect.

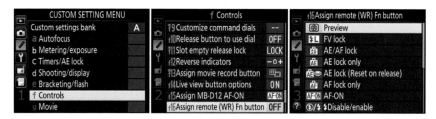

Figure 4.59 – Assign remote (WR) Fn button

Use the following steps to assign a function to the Nikon WR-R10 controller's Fn button:

1. Select f Controls from the Custom Setting Menu and scroll to the right (figure 4.59, screen 1).
2. Highlight f16 Assign remote (WR) Fn button and scroll to the right (figure 4.59, screen 2).

3. Choose one of the 11 selections from the list (figure 4.59, screen 3). The camera defaults to None.
4. Press the OK button to lock in the setting.

Settings Recommendation: Choose the function that best fits your current use of the camera. If you are standing near the camera and using the WR-R10 controller as a remote release, nearly all of the functions listed are beneficial.

Custom Setting f17 – Lens Focus Function Buttons

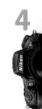

(User's Manual – Page 359)

The *Lens focus function buttons* setting allows you to use the Focus function buttons on Nikkor lenses. (Please note that most Nikkor lenses do not have these buttons). You can assign one of the following eight subfunctions to the buttons on the lens:

*   ***AF lock only*** – Press and hold a Focus function button on your Nikkor lens to lock focus on your subject.
*   ***AE/AF lock*** – Press and hold a Focus function button on your Nikkor lens to lock both the focus and exposure.
*   ***AE lock only*** – Press and hold a Focus function button on your Nikkor lens to lock the exposure only.
*   ***Preset focus point*** – The *a9 Store by orientation* function (*Custom Setting Menu > a Autofocus > a9 Store by orientation > Focus point*) allows you to choose two preset AF point positions based on how you hold the camera, horizontally (landscape) or vertically (portrait). Press and hold a Focus function button on your Nikkor lens to use one of the preset focus points, according to how you are holding the camera. Release the button to restore your original AF point position.
*   ***AF-area mode*** – Press and hold a Focus function button on your Nikkor lens to use an AF-area mode that is different than the mode currently configured on the camera. You must select the AF-area mode that the camera will switch to before using this function. We will consider how to select the AF-area mode in the step-by-step instructions accompanying figure 4.60B (3D-tracking mode is excluded).
*   ***Flash Disable/enable*** – Press and hold a Focus function button on your Nikkor lens to disable the active flash unit. Release the Focus function button to reenable the flash. If there is no flash present or turned on, the camera will use Front-curtain sync mode while you press and hold a Focus function button.
*   ***Disable synchronized release*** – When you are using a wireless, master/remote camera setup—where a master camera wirelessly causes remote cameras to fire their shutters—you can press and hold a Focus function button on your Nikkor lens to disable synchronized release. The master camera will take a picture but the remote cameras will not. Releasing the Focus function button restores synchronized release.

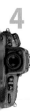

• **Remote release only** – When you are using a wireless, master/remote camera setup—where a master camera wirelessly causes remote cameras to fire their shutters—you can press and hold a Focus function button on your Nikkor lens to disable synchronized release. The remote cameras will take a picture but the master camera will not. Releasing the Focus function button restores synchronized release.

Note: You must have the Memory Recall switch on your Nikkor lens set to AF-L (not AF-ON) in order to use the Focus function buttons with any of the assignable subfunctions.

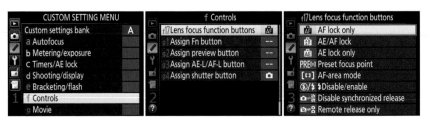

Figure 4.60A – Assigning a function to the Focus function buttons on a Nikkor lens

Use the following steps to assign a function to the Lens focus function buttons:

1. Select f Controls from the Custom Setting Menu and scroll to the right (figure 4.60A, screen 1).
2. Highlight f17 Lens focus function buttons and scroll to the right (figure 4.60A, screen 2).
3. Choose one of the eight selections to assign to the lens Focus function buttons from the list of subfunctions (figure 4.60A, screen 3). Refer to the subfunction list to see what each setting does. If you have chosen any subfunction other than AF-area mode, simply press the OK button to set the function, and then skip the rest of these steps. This completes the assignment process.
   AF-area mode assignment: If you have chosen AF-area mode, there is an extra screen you must use to choose a specific AF-area mode (figure 4.60B, screen 2). Continue with step 4.
4. Figure 4.60B, screen 1, continues where figure 4.60A, screen 3, leaves off. Choose AF-area mode and scroll to the right (figure 4.60B, screen 1).
5. There are six available AF-area modes (e.g., Single-point AF, Group-area AF), as seen in figure 4.60B, screen 2. Choose one of these AF-area modes as the alternate mode the camera will switch to when you press and hold a lens Focus function button.
6. Press the OK button to lock in the setting.

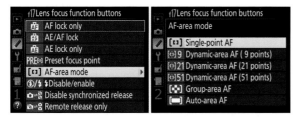

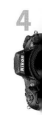

Figure 4.60B – Choosing an AF-area mode for the Focus function buttons

Settings Recommendation: I love to be able to switch very quickly between AF-area modes when using a long lens. Therefore, I assign my Focus function buttons to AF-area mode.

However, there are seven more functions available for assignment, one of which may match your needs more closely. Learn how to set this function properly if you have a Nikkor lens with Focus function buttons.

Be sure to set the Memory Recall switch on your Nikkor lens to AF-L (not AF-ON) in order to use the Focus function buttons with any of the assignable subfunctions!

Section Seven – g Movie

Custom Settings g1 to g4

Within the *g Movie* menu you'll find four Custom settings in the D810:

- **g1** – Assign Fn button
- **g2** – Assign preview button
- **g3** – Assign AE-L/AF-L button
- **g4** – Assign shutter button

Custom Setting g1 – Assign Fn Button

(User's Manual – Page 361)

Assign Fn button lets you choose how the Fn button works in Movie live view mode only. Following are the four choices:

- ***Power aperture (open)*** – The power aperture function works while a movie is being recorded, unlike the power aperture function on the D810's ancestors. By selecting this function, you ask the camera to open the aperture to a larger setting when you press and hold the Fn button. This is accomplished automatically without you having to turn any dials; just pressing and holding the Fn button "powers" the aperture open smoothly.

This function works in conjuction with Power aperture (close) under Custom setting g2 (*Custom Setting Menu > g Movie > g2 Assign preview button > Preview button press*). When you set the camera to Power aperture (open) in Custom setting g1, the D810 automatically selects the Power aperture (close) setting in Custom setting g2 (Assign preview button). You will see an on-screen message that says, *"Power aperture has been assigned to the Fn and Preview buttons."* At that point, Custom settings g1 and g2 are paired. If you try to change Custom setting g2 to another function, the camera will give you a terse warning: *"Fn button power aperture assignment has been canceled."*

During a movie recording session in Aperture-priority (A) mode, you can press the Fn button to open the aperture or the Preview button to close (stop down) the aperture, and the camera will adjust the ISO sensitivity to keep the exposure accurate. While shooting a movie in Manual (M) mode, the camera lets you control everything, including the ISO sensitivity. If you press the info button a few times you will find the live histogram screen for your convenience. **Note**: Power aperture is available only in Aperture-priority (A) and Manual (M) modes.

- *Index marking* – If you have Index marking enabled while you are recording a movie, you can set an index mark at the current frame position by pressing the Fn button. This index mark does not actually appear in the movie itself. It is, however, available when you are viewing and editing movies.

- *View photo shooting info* – This function allows you to view shooting information for still images when using Movie live view mode. The resulting still images have a slightly reduced image size and a different ratio, which we will discuss in a moment. Normally, when in Movie live view mode, the camera displays the shutter speed, aperture, and ISO sensitivity (recording information) for a potential movie at the bottom of the Monitor. When you press the Fn button, the camera displays the shutter speed, aperture, and ISO sensitivity (shooting information) for still image creation instead. The camera will happily take still images when you are using Movie live view mode. However, please note that there are some image size and ratio differences when taking a still image using Movie live view instead of Live view photography mode. When you are using Live view photography mode, a normal Large FX image is 7,360 × 4,912 (36.2 MP); however, while in Movie live view, a Large still image is 6,720 × 3,776 (25.3 MP). When using Movie live view, the camera switches its thinking and formats over to the HD world, which is one of the reasons this camera is called an HD-SLR, not just a D-SLR. Instead of the 3:2 aspect ratio used by Live view photography mode, the still image from Movie live view uses a 16:9 ratio. It is still a fully usable image at 25.3 MP. The ratio matches the look of an HDTV (16:9) instead of a normal picture format. You could use this mode for still images when you know the pictures will be displayed on an HDTV because it will match the HD ratio without the blank space on the sides you will find when displaying a normal 3:2 image on a modern monitor. Test this for yourself on a newer LCD or LED computer monitor and you will see how much more closely the 16:9 format matches the monitor's display size. See the section **Image Area** in the chapter titled **Shooting Menu** for more detail on image aspect ratios.

- **None** – Pressing the Fn button when in Movie live view mode does nothing.

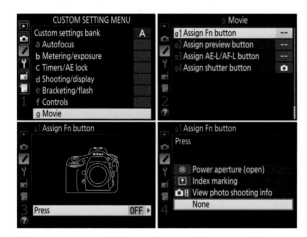
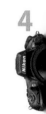

Figure 4.61 – Assign Fn button for Movie live view mode

Use these steps to assign the previously mentioned functions to the Fn button (figure 4.61):

1. Select g Movie from the Custom Setting Menu and scroll to the right (figure 4.61, screen 1).
2. Highlight g1 Assign Fn button and scroll to the right (figure 4.61, screen 2).
3. Press will already be highlighted, so scroll to the right (figure 4.61, screen 3).
4. Choose one of the four selections from the list. In figure 4.61, screen 4, None is selected.
5. Press the OK button to lock in the setting.

Settings Recommendation: I enjoy using the Power aperture (open) setting because it is a useful function to quietly open or close the aperture while shooting a movie.

However, if I didn't shoot many movies but used the 25.3 MP 16:9 still images provided by Movie live view mode, I would select View photo shooting info so I could easily validate my exposure information. The Index marking function is very useful for those who want to mark certain locations in a movie for future editing purposes.

Custom Setting g2 – Assign Preview Button

(User's Manual – Page 362)

Assign preview button lets you choose how the Preview button works in Movie live view mode only. Following are the four choices:

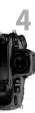

- **Power aperture (close)** – By selecting this function, you ask the camera to close (stop down) the aperture to a smaller setting when you press and hold the Preview button. This is accomplished automatically without you having to turn any dials; just pressing the Preview button closes the aperture smoothly.

  This function works in conjuction with Power aperture (open) under *Custom Setting Menu > g Movie > g1 Assign Fn button > Fn button press*. When Power aperture (open) is assigned to Custom setting g1, the D810 automatically assigns the Power aperture (close) setting to Custom setting g2. If you break that partnership by trying to assign one of the other selections (e.g., Index marking, None) to Custom setting g2, the camera will give you the following message: *"Fn button power aperture assignment has been canceled."*

  In a similar fashion, when you set the camera to Power aperture (close) in Custom setting g2, the D810 automatically selects the Power aperture (open) setting in Custom setting g1 (Assign Fn button), and gives you an on-screen notice that says, *"Power aperture has been assigned to the Fn and preview buttons."* At that point, Custom settings g1 and g2 are paired. If you try to change Custom setting g1 to another function, the camera will give you a terse warning: *"Preview button power aperture assignment has been canceled."* **Note**: Power aperture is available only in Aperture-priority (A) and Manual (M) modes.

- **Index marking** – If you have Index marking enabled while you are recording a movie, you can set an index mark at the current frame position by pressing the Preview button. This index mark does not actually appear in the movie itself. It is, however, available when you are viewing and editing movies.

- **View photo shooting info** – This function allows you to view shooting information for still images when using Movie live view mode. Normally, the camera displays the shutter speed, aperture, and ISO sensitivity (recording information) for a potential movie at the bottom of the Monitor. When you press the Preview button, the camera displays the shutter speed, aperture, and ISO sensitivity (shooting information) for still image creation instead.

- **None** – Pressing the Fn button when in Movie live view mode does nothing.

Use these steps to assign the previously mentioned functions to the Preview button:

1. Select g Movie from the Custom Setting Menu and scroll to the right (figure 4.62, screen 1).

2. Highlight g2 Assign preview button and scroll to the right (figure 4.62, screen 2).

3. Press will already be highlighted, so scroll to the right (figure 4.62, screen 3).
4. Choose one of the four selections from the list. In figure 4.62, screen 3, Index marking is selected.
5. Press the OK button to lock in the setting.

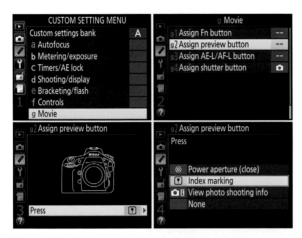
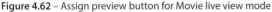
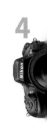

Figure 4.62 – Assign preview button for Movie live view mode

Settings Recommendation: Because I use the sister function (g1 Assign Fn button) with an assignment of Power aperture (open), the Power aperture (close) function is a natural complement. I enjoy using the Power aperture (close) setting because it is a useful function for adjusting the aperture during video recording.

However, as I mentioned in the preceding section, if I didn't shoot many movies but used the 25.3 MP 16:9 still images provided by Movie live view mode, I would select View photo shooting info so I could easily validate my exposure information. Again, the Index marking function is very useful for those who want to mark certain locations in a movie for future editing purposes.

Custom Setting g3 – Assign AE-L/AF-L Button

(User's Manual – Page 363)

Assign AE-L/AF-L button lets you choose how the AE-L/AF-L button works in Movie live view mode only. Following are the seven choices:

- **Index marking** – If you have Index marking enabled while you are recording a movie, you can set an index mark at the current frame position by pressing the AE-L/AF-L button. This index mark does not actually appear in the movie itself. It is, however, available when you are viewing and editing movies.
- **View photo shooting info** – This function allows you to view shooting informa-tion for still images when using Movie live view mode. Normally, the camera

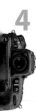

displays the shutter speed, aperture, and ISO sensitivity (recording information) for a potential movie at the bottom of the Monitor. When you press the AE-L/AF-L button, the camera displays the shutter speed, aperture, and ISO sensitivity (shooting information) for still image creation instead.

- **AE/AF lock** – Enabling this function causes AE (exposure) and AF (focus) to lock on the last meter and autofocus system reading while the AE-L/AF-L button is held down.
- **AE lock only** – This allows you to lock AE (exposure) on the last meter reading when you hold down the AE-L/AF-L button.
- **AE lock (Hold)** – This function causes AE (exposure) to lock on the last meter reading when the AE-L/AF-L button is pressed and released once. It stays locked until you press the AE-L/AF-L button again or the exposure meter goes off.
- **AF lock only** – This function locks the AF (focus) system on the last autofocus reading while you hold down the AE-L/AF-L button.
- **None** – Pressing the AE-L/AF-L button when in Movie live view mode does nothing.

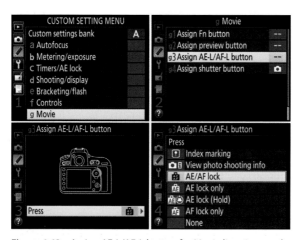

Figure 4.63 – Assign AE-L/AF-L button for Movie live view mode

Use these steps to assign the previously mentioned functions to the AE-L/AF-L button:

1. Select g Movie from the Custom Setting Menu and scroll to the right (figure 4.63, screen 1).
2. Highlight g3 Assign AE-L/AF-L button and scroll to the right (figure 4.63, screen 2).
3. Press will already be highlighted, so scroll to the right (figure 4.63, screen 3).
4. Choose one of the seven selections from the list. In figure 4.63, screen 3, AE/AF lock is selected.
5. Press the OK button to lock in the setting.

Settings Recommendation: Sometimes when you are making movies, the light will suddenly change levels drastically when the subject moves near a window or a bright lamp in the room. The surroundings will go dark, including the subject, while the camera adjusts to the much brighter light source. To prevent that from happening, it is a good idea to use AE lock (hold). With a single touch of the AE-L/AF-L button, I can lock the camera at a correct exposure for the subject. If the subject walks in front of a bright window, the details outside the window will be blown out but the subject will still be properly exposed. The camera does not change exposure levels when a sudden bright light is temporarily introduced.

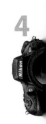

However, what if I need to walk from a darker room into a bright room, or even go outside with my subject? I simply press the AE-L/AF-L button again, allow the camera to adjust to the new light source, and then press it once more to lock the exposure again. Many videographers use a similar method. I find AE lock (Hold) to be the most useful function to assign to the AE-L/AF-L button.

Of course, since there are seven functions, you should read about each one and experiment with when and why you might use it. You will likely need all of them at one time or another.

Custom Setting g4 – Assign Shutter Button

(User's Manual – Page 364)

Assign shutter button lets you choose how the Shutter-release button works in Movie live view mode only. Following are the two choices:

- *Take Photos* – If you are in the middle of recording a movie and you absolutely must have a Large FX still image of something going on in the frame, you can acquire a 16:9 aspect ratio image by pressing the Shutter-release button all the way down. The camera will stop recording the movie and take a still image with a pixel ratio of 6,720 × 3,776 (25.3 MP). This image will closely match the format of an HDTV and modern computer monitor, being shorter and wider than a normal 3:2 aspect ratio FX image.
- *Record movies* – If you are going to shoot movies for a while instead of taking still images, you can select this setting and the camera will enter Movie live view mode whenever you press the Shutter-release button halfway down. Once in Movie live view mode, you can focus by pressing the Shutter-release button halfway down again. Then press the Shutter-release button all the way down to start recording the movie. To stop recording the movie, simply press the Shutter-release button all the way down again. To stop Movie live view mode, press the LV button. When you have this function selected, the camera behaves more like a true movie camera than a still camera. You cannot, of course, take still images when using this function because the Shutter-release button is set to enter, focus, start, and stop movie recording.

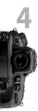

CUSTOM SETTING MENU		g Movie		g4 Assign shutter button
Custom settings bank	A	g1 Assign Fn button	--	
a Autofocus		g2 Assign preview button	--	
b Metering/exposure		g3 Assign AE-L/AF-L button	--	📷 Take photos
c Timers/AE lock		g4 Assign shutter button	📷	
d Shooting/display				🎥 Record movies
e Bracketing/flash				
f Controls				
g Movie				

Figure 4.64 – Assign shutter button for Movie live view mode

Use these steps to assign the previously mentioned functions to the Shutter-release button:

1. Select g Movie from the Custom Setting Menu and scroll to the right (figure 4.64, screen 1).
2. Choose g4 Assign shutter button and scroll to the right (figure 4.64, screen 2).
3. Choose one of the two selections from the list. In figure 4.64, screen 3, Take photos is selected.
4. Press the OK button to lock in the setting.

Settings Recommendation: If you use the Record movies function, the camera's brain becomes focused on recording video and turns off almost everything that has to do with still image creation. You can't take pictures, measure preset white balance, take dust off reference photos, do interval timer photography, or do most other things related to still imagery. If you think you might need to stop a movie and take a picture, don't use Record movies; use Take photos instead. You can still shoot a video, but you have the ability to stop the video and get a quick still image.

If you bought the Nikon D810 to take advantage of its superior, clean, uncompressed, broadcast-quality video, you will most likely set the Record movies function and never look back. However, if you are like most of us and want the D810 for both video and still images, Take photos is the best setting.

Author's Conclusions

Using the Shooting Banks and Custom Banks Together

Now that you have set up and named one of the Custom settings banks, you are ready to make your camera act like a chameleon (or herd of chameleons). It is time to configure all the Custom settings banks with different shooting styles in mind. Once you have each Shooting menu bank and Custom settings bank configured, you can use them together.

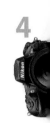

Often, I use a combination of Shooting menu bank A and Custom settings bank A. But nothing prevents you from using Shooting menu bank B with Custom settings bank D, or Shooting menu bank C with Custom settings bank A. Choose whatever combination you'd like to use. That's where the camera's extreme flexibility comes in.

Maybe you have Shooting menu bank A set for Best Quality JPEGs and are shooting them with Custom settings bank A, which is set for no focus tracking. Suddenly, a flock of geese flies by and you realize you must use focus tracking to accurately capture the one big fat goose you like. You simply press the MENU button, scroll to Custom settings bank B, and you are set. (You did configure Custom settings bank B for focus tracking, right?)

Or, maybe while you're using Shooting menu bank A for Fine-quality JPEGS, an incredibly beautiful rainbow appears. You quickly switch to Shooting menu bank C, where you've previously set lossless RAW mode for maximum quality.

Get the point? Your camera can change the way it shoots on the fly, in much less time than it takes to talk about it. Now that you've read this over, set up a few banks on your camera. Give it some serious thought and then do it. Think of the ways you most often take pictures, and configure your D810 for each of those ways. Your camera will be customized to you!

Now, let's move into the next menu system—the Setup Menu—and configure the camera's basic setup. This menu is very important for initial camera configuration, but only a few of its functions are used after initial setup.

Setup Menu

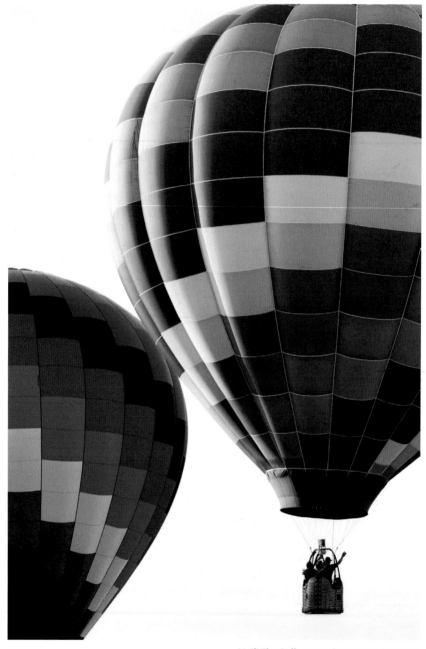

5

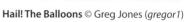

Hail! The Balloons © Greg Jones (*gregor1*)

The Setup Menu contains a series of settings for basic camera configuration not directly related to taking pictures. It covers things like how bright you'd like the Monitor, battery information, firmware version, the default language, image sensor cleaning, and many other basic settings.

These menus are most likely the first you'll use when you prepare your new D810. You'll have to set the Time zone and date, Language, and Copyright information (for embedding in images), among other things.

Following is a list of the 22 functions available in the Setup Menu:

- **Format memory card** – This function allows you to delete all images from your camera's memory card(s).
- **Monitor brightness** – Choose the brightness level for the Monitor on the back of your camera.
- **Monitor color balance** – Use this function to adjust the color balance of the Monitor. You can use a reference shot taken by the camera, such as a picture of a color chart, to calibrate the Monitor's color balance.
- **Clean image sensor** – This function allows immediate cleaning of the imaging sensor to remove dust spots, or you can configure the camera to clean the sensor at startup and shutdown.
- **Lock mirror up for cleaning** – You can safely lock the mirror up and open the shutter so you can manually clean the sensor with a brush, blower, or chemicals and swabs.
- **Image Dust Off ref photo** – You can create a dust off reference photo to help remove a dust spot from images accidentally taken with some dust on the sensor. This requires the use of a program like Nikon Capture NX-D to actually remove the dust with the reference photo as a guide.
- **Flicker reduction** – If you often shoot under fluorescent or mercury-vapor lights while making a movie, this function allows you to choose a frequency that matches the local electrical power supply to reduce flickering.
- **Time zone and date** – Set the Time zone, Date and time, Date format, and Daylight saving time in your camera.
- **Language** – Choose the language you would like your camera to use from a list of 36 languages. Menus and screens will be displayed in the chosen language.
- **Auto image rotation** – This function adds camera orientation information to each image so it will display correctly on your camera's Monitor and later on your computer's monitor.
- **Battery info** – This function gives you information about the battery's current charge, the number of pictures taken with the battery on the current charge, and the useful life remaining in the battery (battery age) before you should dispose of it.

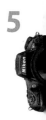

- **Image comment** – Add a comment (up to 36 characters) that embeds itself in the internal metadata of each image. This can help you protect yourself from image theft or simply add pertinent personal or location information to each image.
- **Copyright information** – You can add two items of information, including Artist (36 characters) and Copyright (54 characters). This function is designed for those who use their images commercially. It allows you to embed specific identity information into the picture's internal metadata.
- **Save/load settings** – This function allows you to save the current menu configuration of most internal camera settings to a memory card for transfer to a computer. You can back up complex configurations and restore them to the camera when needed.
- **Virtual horizon** – This function displays a virtual horizon on the camera's Monitor. This display shows tilt to the left or right and forward or backward. This is an excellent tool for leveling the camera on a tripod and prevents having to use an Accessory-shoe mounted bubble level.

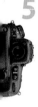

- **Non-CPU lens data** – This function lets you select from a series of nine non-CPU lenses, such as AI and AI-S Nikkor lenses from the late 1970s to now. Each lens is registered within the camera with its own number so you can select it and use it later.
- **AF fine-tune** – You can fine-tune the autofocus for up to 20 of your AF-S lenses. The camera will detect which lens you have mounted and correct for front or back focus according to your settings.
- **HDMI** – You can select various HDMI sync rates for interfacing with an HDTV or monitor.
- **Location data** – If you own a GPS that can be connected to the Nikon D810— such as the Accessory-shoe mounted Nikon GP-1 or another GPS unit—this function allows you to record Latitude, Longitude, Altitude, Heading, and UTC (Coordinated Universal Time) into the metadata of each image.
- **Network** – Allows photographers who own a Nikon UT-1 communication unit to set up a physical Ethernet network connection with the Nikon D810 via the USB port.
- **Eye-Fi upload** – You can use an Eye-Fi Mobi, Connect, Mobile, or Pro wireless SD card to transmit images from your D810 to your home computer and/or online services (e.g., Flickr). Or you can use the Eye-Fi Pro X2 cards to transmit images directly to your Wi-Fi–enabled computer using Ad hoc transfer. You'll have menu access to enable or disable uploading along with connectivity information.
- **Firmware version** – Discover the current firmware version installed in your camera. Firmware is the camera's operating system software that is embedded on in-camera memory chips. It can be upgraded when Nikon releases new firmware specific to your camera.

Let's examine each of these settings in detail.

Format Memory Card

(User's Manual – Page 366)

Format memory card allows you to prepare your memory card(s) for use in your camera. This is the best way to prepare the memory card, and it should be done before using a new one.

Interestingly, formatting a memory card doesn't actually remove any images from the card. Instead, it removes their entries in the memory card's file allocation table (FAT) so they can no longer be seen or found by the camera. However, you could use card recovery software to rescue the images if you do not write anything new to the card after you format it. That's a good thing to remember in case you ever accidentally format a card with images you wanted to keep.

The D810 has two memory card slots, the CF card slot and SD card slot. You have to format each of them separately. There are two ways to format a memory card. First, you can use the *Setup Menu > Format memory card* function; second, you can use external camera controls. We'll look at both methods in this section.

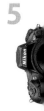

Let's see how it is done with the Setup Menu by looking at the screens and steps for card formatting.

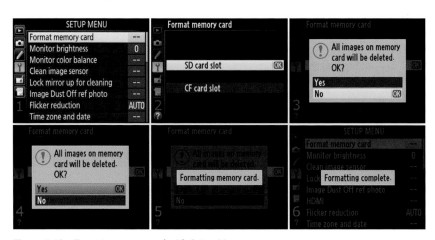

Figure 5.1A – Format memory card with Setup Menu screens

Use the following steps to format a memory card (figure 5.1A):

1. Select Format memory card from the Setup Menu and scroll to the right (figure 5.1A, screen 1).
2. Next, you'll see a screen that asks you to select the card you want to format (figure 5.1A, screen 2). You have a choice of SD card slot or CF card slot. Choose the one you want to format, and scroll to the right. You'll need to repeat this action to format the second card.

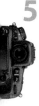

3. The next screen makes it very clear with an ominous-sounding message that you are about to delete all the images on the card you have selected for formatting. The screen presents a big red exclamation point and the message *All images on memory card will be deleted. OK?* If you have decided not to format the card, just select No and press the OK button; otherwise, continue with step 4 (figure 5.1A, screen 3).

4. Select Yes from the screen with the warning that all images will be deleted (figure 5.1A, screen 4).

5. Press the OK button to start the format. When you press the OK button, you'll see two screens in quick succession (figure 5.1A, screens 5 and 6). The first will say, *Formatting memory card*. A few seconds later—when the card has been successfully formatted—you'll briefly see a final screen that says, *Formatting complete*. Then the camera switches back to the Setup Menu's first screen. The card is now formatted and you can take lots of pictures.

Camera Button Format Method

This is the fastest method to format the memory card, and it is not very difficult. The camera defaults to formatting the primary card slot, not the secondary slot. You can select the secondary slot instead, as I'll describe in the upcoming step-by-step method. Figure 5.1B shows the buttons and Control panel screens used to format the card. Notice how the two buttons are marked with the red FORMAT symbol.

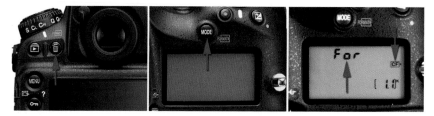

Figure 5.1B – Format memory card with camera controls

To complete the memory card formatting process, follow these steps (figure 5.1B):

1. Hold down the Delete/Format button and MODE/Format button at the same time for more than two seconds (figure 5.1B, screens 1 and 2), until *For* starts flashing on the Control panel (figure 5.1B, screen 3, red arrow on left).

2. While you're still holding down the two buttons and *For* is flashing, you can rotate the Main command dial with your thumb to select either CF or SD on the Control panel (screen 3, red arrow on right). It's a three-finger operation, but it's easier than it sounds. You can see in figure 5.1B, screen 3, that I selected the CF card slot.

3. While *For* is still flashing in the Control panel, quickly release and instantly repress the Delete/Format button and MODE/Format button together. You'll see *For* showing on the Control panel where the image count normally appears (figure 5.1B, screen 3, bottom right corner where my camera says [1.1]^K). The format operation is in process while *For* appears in the image count location. Do not turn your camera off during a format. When *For* changes back to the image count number, the format operation is complete. You can repeat the operation for the other slot on the D810 if needed.

Settings Recommendation: Both the *Setup Menu > Format memory card* and camera button format methods are easy to use. Most people learn to use the button press method because it's so fast. However, I sometimes use the *Setup Menu > Format memory card* method immediately after viewing images on the Monitor for verification of previous transfer to my computer. If it's safe to format the card, I quickly switch to the Setup Menu to format because I'm already looking at the Monitor. It's a good idea to learn how to use both methods.

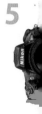

Monitor Brightness

(User's Manual – Page 367)

Monitor brightness is more important than many people realize. If the Monitor is too dim, you'll have trouble seeing your images in bright light. If it is too bright, you might allow some images to be underexposed because they look fine on the Monitor. Even a seriously underexposed image may look okay on a screen that is too bright.

The D810 allows you to adjust the brightness of the Monitor manually. You can select from 10 levels of brightness, varying from -5 to +5. If you want to adjust this frequently, just add this function to My Menu in your camera. We will discuss how to add items to My Menu in the chapter **My Menu and Recent Settings**.

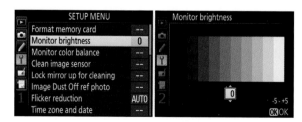

Figure 5.2A – Monitor brightness level adjustment

Use the following steps to adjust the brightness of the camera Monitor (figure 5.2A):

1. Select Monitor brightness from the Setup Menu and scroll to the right (figure 5.2A, screen 1).
2. Use the Multi selector to scroll up or down through the values -5 to +5, scrolling to the minus side to dim the Monitor or to the plus side to brighten it (figure 5.2A, screen 2). Now, use the gray-level bars (dark to light) as a guide to adjust the brightness. Adjust until you can make a distinction between the last two dark bars on the left. That may be the best setting for your camera in the current ambient light. The brightness defaults to 0 (zero), which is right in the middle.
3. Press the OK button when you've found the value you like best.

Settings Recommendation: I generally leave Monitor brightness set to the zero setting unless I need the extra brightness on a sunny day. If you choose to set your camera to a level brighter than 0, be sure to check the histogram frequently to validate your exposures. Otherwise, you may find that you are mildly underexposing images because they look fine on the Monitor due to the extra brightness. That's one reason I examine the histogram often.

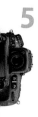

Some photographers run their monitor at -1 to keep the images from appearing artificially bright. This is a setting where experimentation is required. Letting the Monitor run too brightly might mask those times when the camera needs help. The bright screen can fool you. Use your histogram!

Monitor Color Balance

(User's Manual – Page 394)

Monitor color balance is a function that allows you to control the tint of the camera's Monitor. If you feel the Monitor has, let's say, a greenish tint, you can add a little bit of a complimentary color to change the color to one that is more acceptable to you.

There are four color axes you can use for adjustment: green (G), amber (A), magenta (M), and blue (B). By moving the small black indicator toward a certain axis you will add a tint for that color. You can blend the colors to arrive at nearly any tint you prefer by moving the indicator between axes.

The effect is not extremely strong, so you will not make your monitor look garish with this function. However, the color tinting is strong enough that you can overcome any tint you perceive on the Monitor.

This effect does not change the color of the camera's images in any way. It only tints the color of the Monitor, allowing you to balance it against other known color sources.

In figure 5.3A there is a sample image from a normal Monitor coloration (screen 2) and four others with the tint shifted (screens 3–6).

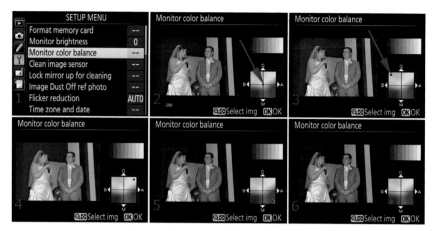

Figure 5.3A – Changing the color balance of the camera Monitor

Use the following steps to adjust the color balance of the camera's rear Monitor:

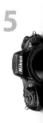

1. Select Monitor color balance from the Setup Menu and scroll to the right (figure 5.3A, screen 1).

2. At the point of the red arrow in figure 5.3A, screen 2, you will notice a small black square directly at the cross point of the color axes. You can move this small square directly along either of the color axis lines, or within the quadrants, as shown in screen 3 (red arrow). Notice how the small square has been moved into the corner of the quadrants in screens 3–6?

3. As you move the small black square around the color quandrants, you will see the tint of the small sample image change. Be sure you have a good sample showing on the screen so that you can choose the best balance. Maybe get an X-Rite color checker chart and take a picture of it under a neutral light source and use that picture for your sample. Remember that the ambient light will affect your perception of colors under that light, so make sure you balance the Monitor under the light source you use most often.

Note: Again, this adjustment does absolutely nothing to the picture the camera captures. It is merely for user comfort. If the memory card contains no images, a gray square will be displayed in place of the sample picture.

Settings Recommendation: Since I do not often adjust images in-camera, I will not be influenced by the way the Monitor looks. I mostly use the Monitor to make composition choices and to check the histogram. I think the Monitor on my D810 is excellent the way it is and have no need for this Monitor color balance function.

However, if I were shooting in a studio, with carefully controlled lighting, and needed to do careful color matching for a product shot, maybe I would be more concerned about Monitor color balance.

Clean Image Sensor

(User's Manual – Page 445)

Clean image sensor is Nikon's helpful answer to dust spots on your images that are due to a dirty imaging sensor. Dust is everywhere and will eventually get on your camera's sensor. The D810 cleans the sensor by vibrating the entire sensor unit. These high-frequency vibrations will hopefully dislodge dust and make it fall off the filter so you won't see it as spots on your pictures.

The vibration cleaning method seems to work pretty well. Of course, if sticky pollen or other moist dust gets into the camera, the vibration system won't be able to remove it. Then it may be time for brush or wet cleaning.

Clean Now

Clean now allows you to clean the imaging sensor at any time. If you detect a dust spot, or just get nervous because you are in a dusty environment with your D810, you can simply select Clean now and the camera will execute a sensor cleaning cycle.

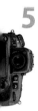

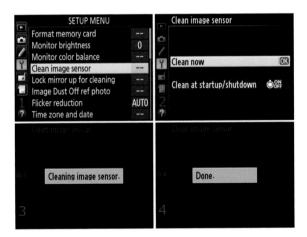

Figure 5.4A – Clean now screens

Use the following steps to clean the camera's sensor immediately:

1. Select Clean image sensor from the Setup Menu and scroll to the right (figure 5.4A, screen 1).
2. Select Clean now from the menu and press the OK button (figure 5.4A, screen 2).
3. Step 2 starts the automatic cleaning process. A screen will appear that says, *Cleaning image sensor* (figure 5.4A, screen 3). When the process is complete, another screen will appear that says, *Done* (figure 5.4A, screen 4). Then the camera switches back to the Setup Menu.

Now, let's look at how to select an active method for regular sensor cleaning.

Clean at Startup/Shutdown

For preventive dust control, many people set their cameras to clean the sensor at startup, shutdown, or both. There are four selections for startup/shutdown cleaning:

- Clean at startup
- Clean at shutdown
- Clean at startup & shutdown
- Cleaning off

These settings are self-explanatory. I find it interesting that I don't detect any startup or shutdown delay when using the startup/shutdown cleaning modes. I can turn my camera on and immediately take a picture. The cleaning cycle seems to be very brief, or at least interruptible, in this mode.

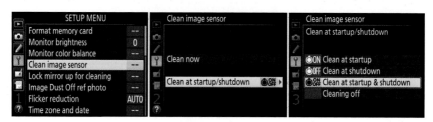
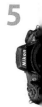

Figure 5.4B – Clean at startup/shutdown screens

Use the following steps to choose a Clean at startup/shutdown method:

1. Select Clean image sensor from the Setup Menu and then scroll to the right (figure 5.4B, screen 1).
2. Choose Clean at startup/shutdown from the menu and scroll to the right (figure 5.4B, screen 2).
3. Select one of the four methods shown in figure 5.4B, screen 3. I chose Clean at startup & shutdown.
4. Press the OK button to lock in your choice.

Nikon suggests that you hold the camera at the same angle as when you are taking pictures (bottom down) when you use these modes to clean the sensor.

Settings Recommendation: I leave my camera set to Clean at startup & shutdown. That way it will do a cleaning cycle every time I turn the camera on or off. It doesn't seem to slow down shooting; I can still turn on the camera and immediately begin taking photographs. A little sensor cleaning in this dusty world seems like a good idea to me.

Lock Mirror Up for Cleaning

(User's Manual – Page 448)

Lock mirror up for cleaning is for those times when the high-frequency vibration method of cleaning your D810's sensor does not dislodge some stickier-than-normal dust. You may have to clean your sensor more aggressively.

In many cases, all that's needed is to remove the dust with a puff of air from a dust blower. The D810 helps out by providing the Lock mirror up for cleaning mode so you can more safely blow a stubborn piece of dust off the sensor.

Using this function is much safer for blowing dust off the sensor; you can use both hands while the battery power holds the reflex mirror up and the shutter open.

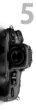

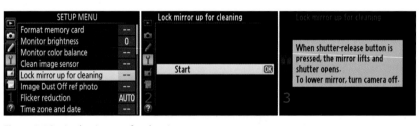

Figure 5.5A – Lock mirror up for cleaning

Use the following steps to select this mode for manual sensor cleaning (figure 5.4A):

1. Select Lock mirror up for cleaning from the Setup Menu and scroll to the right (figure 5.5A, screen 1).
2. Press the OK button with Start highlighted (figure 5.5A, screen 2).
3. You'll see a message screen telling you that as you press the Shutter-release button the camera will raise the mirror and open the shutter (figure 5.5A, screen 3).
4. Remove the lens and press the Shutter-release button once. The sensor will now be exposed and ready for cleaning. Be careful not to let new dirt in while the sensor is open to air.
5. Clean the sensor with proper fluids and pads (i.e., Eclipse fluid and PEC*PADs).
6. Turn the camera off and put the lens back on.

Make sure you have a fresh battery in the camera because that's what holds the shutter open for cleaning. It must have a 60 percent or greater charge or the camera will refuse to allow you to start the process.

Settings Recommendation: You'll need a good professional sensor-cleaning blower, such as my favorite, the Giottos Rocket-air blower with a long tip for easy insertion (figure 5.5B). I bought my Rocket-air blower from the Nikonians Photo Pro Shop (**http://www.PhotoProShop.com**).

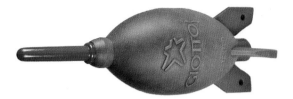

Figure 5.5B – Giottos Rocket-air blower

If an air blower fails to remove stubborn dust or pollen, you will have to either have your sensor professionally cleaned or do it yourself. Nikon states that you will void your warranty if you touch the sensor. However, many people still wet or brush clean their D810's sensor.

If all of this makes you nervous, then send your camera off to Nikon for approved cleaning, or use a professional service. Fortunately, a few puffs of air will often remove dust too stubborn for the high-frequency vibration methods. It helps to have the proper tools, such as the Giottos Rocket-air blower from the Nikonians PhotoProShop.

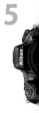

Image Dust Off Ref Photo

(User's Manual – Page 369)

You may go out and do an expensive shoot only to return and find that some dust spots have appeared in the worst possible places in your images. If you immediately create an *Image Dust Off ref photo*, you can use it to remove the dust spots from your images and then clean the camera's sensor for your next shooting session.

When you use the following instructions to create the Image Dust Off ref photo, you'll be shooting a blank, unfocused picture of a pure white or gray background. The dust spots in the image will then be readily apparent to Nikon Capture NX-D software. Yes, you must use Nikon's software to automatically batch-remove dust spots from a large number of images.

When you load the image to be cleaned into Capture NX-D, along with the Image Dust Off ref photo, the software will use the Image Dust Off ref photo to remove the spots in your production image.

The position and amount of dust on the sensor may change. You should take Image Dust Off ref photos regularly and use one that was taken within one day of the photographs you wish to clean up.

Finding a Subject for the Dust-Off Reference Photo

First, you'll need to select a featureless subject to make a photograph for the Image Dust Off ref photo. The key is to use a material that has no graininess, such as a bright, well-lit white card. I tried using plain white sheets of paper held up to a bright window, but the resulting reference photo was unsatisfactory to Capture NX-D. It gave me a message that my reference photo was too dusty when I tried to use it.

After some experimentation, I finally settled on three different subjects that seem to work well:

- A slide-viewing light table with the light turned on
- A computer monitor with a blank white word processor document
- A plain white card in the same bright light in which your subject resides

All of these were bright and featureless enough to satisfy both my camera and Capture NX-D. The key is to photograph something fairly bright, but not too bright. You may need to experiment with different subjects if you don't have a light table or computer.

Now, let's prepare the camera for the actual reference photo.

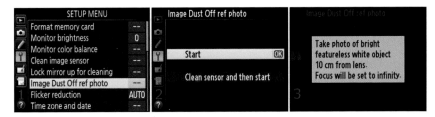

Figure 5.6A – Image Dust Off ref photo settings

Here are the steps you'll use to create an Image Dust Off ref photo:

1. Select Image Dust Off ref photo from the Setup Menu and scroll to the right (figure 5.6A, screen 1).
2. Choose Start and press the OK button (figure 5.6A, screen 2). Afterward, you'll see the characters *rEF* in the Viewfinder and on the Control panel. This simply means that the camera is ready to create the image. (There is also a Clean sensor and then start selection. However, since I want to remove dust on current pictures, I won't use this setting. It might remove the dust bunny that is imprinted on the last 500 images I just shot! I'll clean my sensor after I get a good Image Dust Off ref photo. Choose Clean sensor and then start only if the Image Dust Off ref photo will not be used with existing images!)
3. When the camera is ready, hold the lens about 4 inches (10 cm) away from the blank subject. The camera will not try to autofocus during the process, which is good because you want the lens at infinity. You are not trying to take a viewable picture; you're creating an image that shows where the dust is on the sensor. Focus is not important, and neither is minor camera shake. If you try to take the picture and the subject is not bright enough, too bright, or too grainy (not

---

White Card Tip

Remember, all your camera needs to create an Image Dust Off ref photo is a good look at its imaging sensor so it can map the dust spots into an NDF file (ref photo file). If you get the warning screen shown in figure 5.6B that says exposure settings are not appropriate, change the exposure settings and try again with a nice bright, clean, white surface. Put the lens very close to the surface, and make sure it is not in focus. Nikon recommends less than 4 inches (10 cm). You might even want to manually set the lens to infinity if you are having problems with this. When you've found your favorite white or gray surface for Image Dust Off ref photos, keep it safe and use it consistently.

---

featureless), you will see the screen shown in figure 5.6B. If you are having problems with too much brightness, use a gray surface instead of white. Most of the time this error is caused by insufficient light.

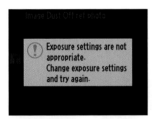

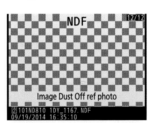

Figure 5.6B – Image Dust Off ref photo failure

Figure 5.6C – Successful Image Dust Off ref photo

If you don't see the screen in figure 5.6B and the shutter fires, you have successfully created an Image Dust Off ref photo. You will find the image shown in figure 5.6C on your camera's Monitor. A file that's approximately 7 MB—mine was 6718 KB (6.7 MB)—is created on your camera's memory card with a filename extension of .ndf instead of the normal .nef, .tif, or .jpg (an example filename is DSC_1234.NDF). This NDF file is basically a small database of the millions of clean pixels in your imaging sensor and a few dirty ones. You cannot display the Image Dust Off ref photo on your computer. It will not open in Nikon Capture NX-D or any other graphics program that I tried. It is used only as a reference by Capture NX-D when it's time to clean images.

Where to Store the Reference Photo

Copy the NDF file from your camera's memory card to the computer folder containing the images that have dust spots on them, the ones for which you created this Image Dust Off ref photo. You can now use Nikon Capture NX-D to remove the dust spots from all of the images represented by the Image Dust Off ref photo. Let's examine how to do just that.

Using Capture NX-D to Remove Dust Spots

Copy the NDF file (figure 5.6C) from your camera's memory card to the computer folder containing the images that have dust spots on them, the ones for which you created this Image Dust Off ref photo. You can use the Image Dust Off function (figure 5.6D) in Nikon Capture NX-D to remove the dust spots from all of the images represented by the Image Dust Off ref photo.

In figure 5.6D, the red-rimmed cutout in the middle is an enlargement of the Camera and Lens Corrections window in the control bar on the right side of Capture NX-D.

Here are the steps to use the Image Dust Off functions in Nikon Capture NX-D to remove dust from a group of images, using an Image Dust Off ref photo (figure 5.6D):

1. Copy your images into a folder on your computer, along with the Image Dust Off ref photo. It is best if they are in the same folder to make sure they represent the images you recently shot. You can browse to a different folder if you want to store the dust off photo elsewhere.

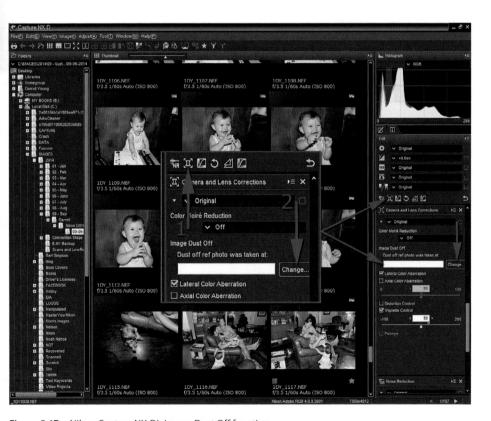

Figure 5.6D – Nikon Capture NX-D's Image Dust Off function

2. Now, open Capture NX-D and use the folder browser on the left side of the screen to browse to the folder that contains your images and the dust off photo.
3. Press the Camera and Lens Corrections button (figure 5.6D, arrow 1) on the right side of the screen.
4. Select the image you want to process from the picture(s) shown in the center section of Nikon Capture NX-D. Wait a moment. When the software detects a dust off ref photo in the folder, the Change button (figure 5.6D, arrow 2) will become available.
5. Press the Change button. If there is only one dust off ref photo in the folder with the images, a query window will open with the following question: "Do you want to use a Dust off ref photo that is in the same folder as the active image?" If there is more than one dust off photo in the folder, Capture NX-D will show you all the dust off photos available and ask the following question: "More than one suitable Dust off ref photos have been found. Please select the one you wish to use based on its shooting date and time." Choose the date-and-time-stamped dust off photo you want to use. Your choices will look like this:

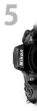

2015/04/30 13:45:05 DSC_1150.ndf
2015/04/30 15:50:10 DSC_1185.ndf

6. Click the Yes button and Capture NX-D will process the images in the folder against the Image Dust Off ref photo, removing the dust spots from all the images in the folder. It will take some time to process the image—the computer will show a wait indicator until the picture is processed. Capture NX-D does not inform you that it is done, but when the hourglass or other wait indicator goes away the process is complete.
7. In the text field next to the Change button, you will see the date-and-time stamp of the Image Dust Off ref photo used to correct the image. It will look like this: "2015/04/30 15:50:10".

Settings Recommendation: Nikon Capture NX-D is free, and it's a good form of insurance, even if you use it for nothing more than removing dust from your images. Whenever you find yourself out in nature or shooting in an environment that might be dusty, why not create an Image Dust Off ref photo as the last photo of the day? That dust off photo may save you a lot of dust removal work. Let Capture NX-D do it for you!

Download the free Nikon Capture NX-D at the following website:

http://imaging.nikon.com/lineup/microsite/capturenxd/

If for some reason the link does not work, just Google "Download Nikon Capture NX-D" and I'm sure you will find it.

Flicker Reduction

(User's Manual – Page 371)

Flicker reduction allows you to attempt to match the camera's recording frequency to that of the local AC power supply so that when you use Live view photography or Movie live view modes under fluorescent or mercury-vapor lighting, you can minimize flickering.

Start out by trying the Auto setting to see if the camera can determine the best setting. If not, there are two things you can do. First, try using the 50 Hz and 60 Hz settings individually to see if one helps. If the subject is especially bright, which makes flicker worse, Nikon recommends closing down the aperture.

Second, use a shutter speed that is close to the frequency of the local power supply. For a 60 Hz supply, use 1/30 s, 1/60 s, or 1/125 s. For a 50 Hz supply, use 1/25 s or 1/50 s.

In some cases, flicker can be impossible to remove completely; however, these methods may help you reduce it. Let's see how to choose a Flicker reduction frequency.

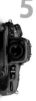

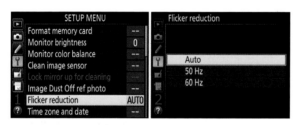

Figure 5.7 – Selecting a Flicker reduction frequency

Use the following steps to select a setting in hopes of reducing flicker:

1. Select Flicker reduction from the Setup Menu and scroll to the right (figure 5.7, screen 1).
2. Choose Auto, 50 Hz, or 60 Hz from the menu (figure 5.7, screen 2).
3. Press the OK button to lock in your setting.

Settings Recommendation: This function is somewhat limited because there are only two settings: 50 Hz or 60 Hz. However, it could help to control the flickering that looks like dark horizontal bands moving through the movie. Experiment to see if it helps to switch between the two settings when you detect flickering under fluorescent or mercury-vapor lighting. The best solution is to stay away from those types of lighting when shooting videos.

Time Zone and Date

(User's Manual – Page 372)

Time zone and date allows you to configure the Time zone, Date and time, Date format, and Daylight saving time for your camera.

If you haven't set the time and date, you'll see the word CLOCK flashing on the Control panel. In addition to the main li-ion battery pack, the camera has a built-in clock battery that is not user replaceable. The built-in battery charges itself from the main camera battery pack. If CLOCK is blinking in the Control panel, it can also mean that the internal battery is exhausted and the clock has been reset.

It takes about two days of having a charged battery in the camera to fully charge the separate built-in clock battery. When the clock battery is fully charged, the clock will remain active without a main camera battery for up to three months.

Let's examine how to set the various parts of Time zone and date. You may have already done this when you first received your camera. We discussed this briefly in the first chapter.

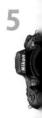

Time Zone

The *Time zone* screen used to set the local time zone displays a familiar world map from which you will select the area of the world where you are using the camera. Figure 5.8A shows the Time zone configuration screens.

As an example, New York is in the Eastern Time zone (ET). You'll need to select your Time zone by choosing it from the map (figure 5.8A, screen 3). I hope you remember your geography lessons! Fortunately, the camera displays some major city names below the Time zone map in case you don't recognize your location.

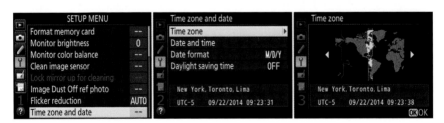

Figure 5.8A – Time zone settings

Use the following steps to set the Time zone:

1. Select Time zone and date from the Setup Menu and scroll to the right (figure 5.8A, screen 1).
2. Choose Time zone from the menu and scroll to the right (figure 5.8A, screen 2).

3. To set the Time zone, use the Multi Selector to scroll left or right until your location is under the vertical yellow bar or you see the nearest city marked with a small red dot (figure 5.8A, screen 3).
4. Press the OK button to lock in the Time zone.

Date and Time

Figure 5.8B shows the three *Date and time* configuration screens. The final screen allows you to select the year, month, and day (Y, M, D) and the hour, minute, and second (H, M, S).

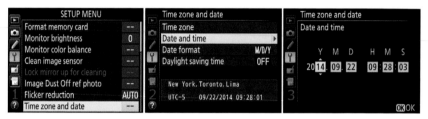

Figure 5.8B – Date and time settings

Use the following steps to set the Date and time (figure 5.8B):

1. Select Time zone and date from the Setup Menu and scroll to the right (figure 5.8B, screen 1).
2. Choose Date and time from the menu and scroll to the right (figure 5.8B, screen 2).
3. Using the Multi Selector, scroll left or right until you've selected the value you want to change. Then scroll up or down to change the value. The Y M D settings on the left in 5.8B, screen 3, are for the year, month, and day. The H M S settings on the right are for the hour, minute, and second.
4. Press the OK button to lock in the Date and time.

Note: The international time format (ISO) is used for the time setting. To set the clock to 3 p.m., you would set the H and M settings to 15:00. Please refer to the following 12 - to 24-Hour Time Conversion Chart.

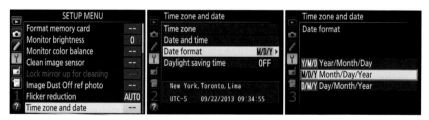

Figure 5.8C – Date format settings

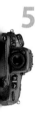

12- to 24-Hour Time Conversion Chart

A.M. Settings:

12:00 a.m. = 00:00 (midnight)	06:00 a.m. = 06:00
01:00 a.m. = 01:00	07:00 a.m. = 07:00
02:00 a.m. = 02:00	08:00 a.m. = 08:00
03:00 a.m. = 03:00	09:00 a.m. = 09:00
04:00 a.m. = 04:00	10:00 a.m. = 10:00
05:00 a.m. = 05:00	11:00 a.m. = 11:00

P.M. Settings:

12:00 p.m. = 12:00 (noon)	06:00 p.m. = 18:00
01:00 p.m. = 13:00	07:00 p.m. = 19:00
02:00 p.m. = 14:00	08:00 p.m. = 20:00
03:00 p.m. = 15:00	09:00 p.m. = 21:00
04:00 p.m. = 16:00	10:00 p.m. = 22:00
05:00 p.m. = 17:00	11:00 p.m. = 23:00

Note: There is no 24:00 time (midnight). After 23:59 comes 00:00.

Date Format

Date format gives you three different ways to format the camera's date, as follows:
- *Y/M/D* – Year/Month/Day (2013/12/31)
- *M/D/Y* – Month/Day/Year (12/31/2013)
- *D/M/Y* – Day/Month/Year (31/12/2013)

Here are the steps to set the Date format (figure 5.8C):

1. Select Time zone and date from the Setup Menu and scroll to the right (figure 5.8C, screen 1).
2. Choose Date format from the menu and scroll to the right (figure 5.8C, screen 2).
3. Choose your favorite Date format from the menu (figure 5.8C, screen 3). I selected M/D/Y Month/Day/Year.
4. Press the OK button to lock in the Date format.

Daylight Saving Time

Many areas of the world observe daylight saving time. On a specified day in spring of each year, many people set their clocks forward by one hour. Then in the fall they set them back, leading to the clever saying "spring forward, fall back."

If you set *Daylight saving time* to On, the camera will move the time forward by one hour. In the fall, you will need to remember to change this setting to Off so that the camera will move the time back by one hour. Otherwise the time stamp on your images will be off by one hour for half the year.

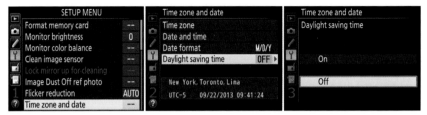

Figure 5.8D – Daylight saving time settings

Here are the steps to enable or disable Daylight saving time (figure 5.8D):

1. Select Time zone and date from the Setup Menu and scroll to the right (figure 5.8D, screen 1).
2. Choose Daylight saving time from the menu and scroll to the right (figure 5.8D, screen 2).
3. Figure 5.8D, screen 3, shows you the two choices for Daylight saving time: On or Off. If you select On, your camera will move the time forward by one hour from its current setting. Select Off and the camera will move the time back by one hour. This is not an automatic function. You must remember to change the time if you are concerned with having a correct time stamp in your picture metadata. If you don't observe daylight saving time, just leave this setting set to Off and make sure the camera time matches your local time.
4. Press the OK button to lock in the setting.

Settings Recommendation: This series includes the first settings you'll modify when you get a brand-new D810 camera. It is important that all these items are set correctly because this information is written into the metadata of each image you make. Daylight saving time is optional, but if you use it, you must remember to change it in the fall and spring of each year so your camera's time will match the local time. I have a reminder set up on my smart phone so that I won't forget. When you are setting all of your clocks and watches for the semi-annual time change, just remember to set your camera's internal clock too.

Language

(User's Manual – Page 372)
Language is a function that lets the camera know what language you prefer for the camera's menus, screens, and messages. Nikon is an international company that

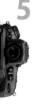

sells cameras and lenses around the world. For that reason, the D810 can display its screens and menus in 36 languages.

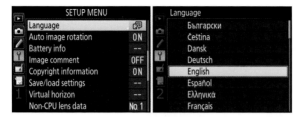

Figure 5.9 – Language selection

Use the following steps to select your preferred Language (figure 5.9):

1. Select Language from the Setup Menu and scroll to the right (figure 5.9, screen 1).
2. Choose your preferred Language (figure 5.9, screen 2).
3. Press the OK button to lock in your choice.

The camera should come preconfigured for the main language that is spoken where you live. If you prefer a different one, use this setting to select it.

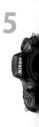

Auto Image Rotation

(User's Manual – Page 373)

Auto image rotation is concerned with how vertical images are displayed on your camera's Monitor and later on your computer. Horizontal images are not affected by this setting. The camera has a direction-sensing device, so it knows how the camera was oriented when a picture was taken.

Depending on how you have Auto image rotation set, how the *Playback Menu > Rotate tall* setting is set, and the direction in which you hold your camera's hand grip, the camera will display a vertical image either as an upright portrait image, with the top of the image at the top of the Monitor, or lying on its side in a horizontal direction, with the top of the image to the left or right on the Monitor. The two selections in the menu are as follows:

- **On** – With Auto image rotation turned On, the camera stores orientation information within each image, primarily so the image will display correctly in computer software such as Nikon Capture NX-D, Lightroom, and Photoshop. In other words, the camera records, as part of the image metadata, whether you were holding your camera horizontally or vertically (hand grip down) or even upside-down vertically (hand grip up). The image will display in the correct orientation on your camera's Monitor only if you have *Playback Menu > Rotate tall* set to On.

Auto image rotation lets the image speak for itself as to orientation, while Rotate tall lets the camera listen to the image and display it in the proper orientation.

- ***Off*** – If Auto image rotation is turned Off, the vertical image will be displayed as a horizontal image lying on its side in your computer software. The top of the image will be on the left or right according to how you held the hand grip—up or down—when you took the picture. The camera does not record orientation information in the image metadata. It will display images horizontally even if you have the *Playback Menu > Rotate tall* function set to On.

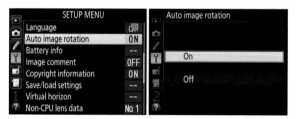

Figure 5.10 – Auto image rotation settings

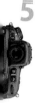

Use the following steps to set the Auto image rotation function:

1. Select Auto image rotation from the Setup Menu and scroll to the right (figure 5.10, screen 1).
2. Choose On or Off from the menu (figure 5.10, screen 2).
3. Press the OK button to lock in your selection.

If you're shooting in one of the Continuous frame advance modes (CL or CH), the position in which you hold your camera for the first shot sets the direction in which images are displayed.

Settings Recommendation: If you want your images to be displayed correctly on your camera's Monitor and in your computer, you need to be sure that Auto image rotation is set to On. I always keep mine set that way.

Battery Info

(User's Manual – Page 332)

The *Battery info* screen (figure 5.11A, screen 2) will let you know how much battery charge has been used (Charge), how many images have been taken with this battery since the last charge (No. of shots), and how much life the battery has before it will no longer hold a good charge (Battery age).

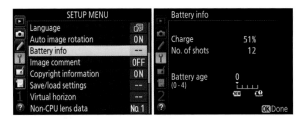

Figure 5.11A – Battery info screen

Here are the steps to examine the Battery info:

1. Select Battery info from the Setup Menu and scroll to the right (figure 5.11A, screen 1).
2. The next screen is the Battery info screen. It is just for information, so there's nothing to set (figure 5.11A, screen 2).
3. When you've finished examining your camera's Battery info, press the OK button to exit.

The D810 goes a step further than most cameras. Not only does it inform you of the amount of charge left in your battery, it also lets you know how much life is left. After some time, all batteries weaken and won't hold a full charge. The Battery age meter will tell you when the battery needs to be completely replaced. It shows five stages of battery life, from 0 to 4, so you'll be prepared to replace the battery before it gets too old to take many shots.

Battery Info When Using an MB-D12 Battery Pack

If you are using a battery in your MB-D12 battery pack in addition to the one in the camera, the Battery info screen will display as a split screen. The left side of the screen shows information for the battery in the camera, and the right side shows information for the battery in the MB-D12 battery pack (figure 5.11B).

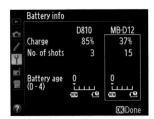

Figure 5.11B – Battery info screen with MB-D12 mounted

Additionally, when you are using a larger Nikon D4 EN-EL18 battery in the MB-D12, you will see a fourth item—besides Charge, No. of shots, and Battery age—on the Battery info screen. You will see calibration information (not shown). Calibration

(CAL) shows up on the screen when the battery needs to be recalibrated with a Nikon MH-26 battery charger. This ensures that the battery's Charge level can be reported accurately after repeated use and recharging. When Calibration is not required, a long dash (—) will appear instead of CAL.

Settings Recommendation: It's important to use Nikon brand batteries in your D810 so they will work properly with the camera. Aftermarket batteries may not charge correctly in the D810 battery charger. In addition, they may not report correct Battery age information. There may be an aftermarket brand that works correctly, but I haven't found it. Instead, I use the batteries designed by Nikon to work with this camera. I am a bit afraid to trust a camera that costs this much to a cheap aftermarket battery of unknown origin.

Image Comment

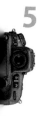

(User's Manual – Page 375)

Image comment is a useful setting that allows you to attach a 36-character comment to each image you shoot. The comment is embedded in the picture's internal metadata and does not show up on the image itself. I attach the comment "Photo by Darrell Young" to my images.

You could include information containing your copyright here even though the camera has a place to put Copyright information (next section).

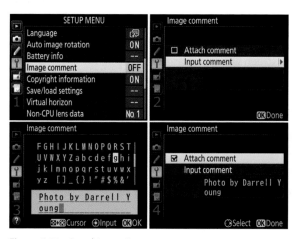

Figure 5.12 – Attaching an Image comment

Use the following steps to create an Image comment:

1. Select Image comment from the Setup Menu and scroll to the right (figure 5.12, screen 1).
2. Select Input comment from the menu and scroll to the right (figure 5.12, screen 2).
3. In figure 5.12, screen 3, you'll see a series of letters, numbers, and symbols on top and a rectangle with tiny lines in the gray area at the bottom. Add your Image comment text there, up to 36 characters. The camera will attach the text in the comment field to the image. There is a blank spot just after the lowercase z, which represents a blank space that you can insert in the line of text. Notice that lowercase letters follow the uppercase letters. Use the Multi Selector to scroll through the numbers and letters to find the characters you want to use, and press the Multi Selector center button to insert a character. If you make a mistake, hold down the checkered Thumbnail/Playback zoom out button while using the Multi Selector to move to the position of the error. Push the Delete button and the character will disappear.
4. Press the OK button when you are finished entering the comment.
5. The camera will switch back to the Image comment screen (figure 5.12, screen 4). You need to put a check mark in the Attach comment check box so the comment will attach itself to each image. To check the box, highlight the Attach comment line and scroll to the right with the Multi selector to place a check mark in the box.
6. Press the OK button to save the new comment.

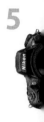

Settings Recommendation: You can use this comment field for any text you want to add to the internal metadata of the image (up to 36 characters). There is another Setup Menu selection called Copyright information (next section) that allows you to add your personal copyright. I added basic "who took it" information here because I am worried about image theft. You may want to add other text—since the camera provides a specific Copyright information screen—such as information to identify the shoot. Remember, you are limited to 36 characters in the comment.

Copyright Information

(User's Manual – Page 376)
Copyright information allows you to embed Artist and Copyright data into each image. Refer to figure 5.13 and use the following steps to add personal information to your camera. Your Artist name and Copyright information will then be written into the metadata of each of your images.

Here are the steps to enter your Artist and Copyright information:

1. Select Copyright information from the Setup Menu and scroll to the right (figure 5.13, screen 1).

2. Scroll down to Artist and scroll to the right (figure 5.13, screen 2).
3. You'll now see the Artist data input screen with all the available characters to choose from (figure 5.13, screen 3). Add your name here, with a maximum of 36 characters. Use the Multi Selector to scroll around within the characters. Lowercase characters follow the uppercase letters. Select a character by pressing the Multi selector center button. Correct errors within the text you've already entered by holding down the Thumbnail/Playback zoom out button and scrolling left or right with the Multi Selector. Remove a character that's already in the name area by scrolling to it and pressing the Delete button. Press the OK button when you have entered your name.

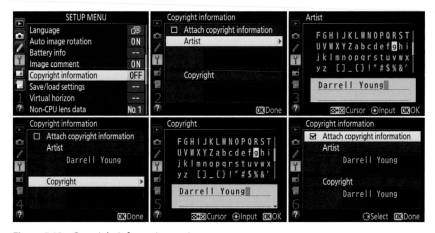

Figure 5.13 – Copyright information settings

4. Now scroll down to the Copyright line on the Copyright information screen and scroll to the right (figure 5.13, screen 4).
5. Add your name using the method and controls described in step 3 (figure 5.13, screen 5).
6. Scroll up to the Attach copyright information line (figure 5.13, screen 6). Initially there will be no check mark in the little box. You need to place one there. Scroll to the right with the Multi selector and you'll see a tiny check mark appear in the box.
7. Press the OK button to save your Artist and Copyright information.

Settings Recommendation: Be sure to add your name in both the Artist and Copyright sections of this function. With so much intellectual property theft going on these days, it's a good idea to identify each of your images as your own. Otherwise, you may post an image on Flickr or Facebook to share with friends and later find it on a billboard along the highway. With the Artist and Copyright information embedded in the image metadata, you will be able to prove that the image is yours and charge the infringer.

Embedding your personal information is not a foolproof way to identify your images because unscrupulous people may steal them and strip the metadata out of them. However, if you do find one of your images on the front page of a magazine or on someone's website, you can at least prove that you took the image and have some legal recourse under the Digital Millennium Copyright Act (DMCA). When you've taken a picture, you own the copyright to that image. You must be able to prove you took it. This is one convenient way.

You'll have even more power to protect yourself if you register your images with the US Copyright Registry at the following web address: **http://copyright.gov/eco/**.

If you sell your camera, or loan it to someone, be sure to remove the Artist and Copyright information to prevent misuse of your name.

Save/Load Settings

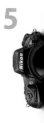

(User's Manual – Page 377)
Do you have your D810 set up exactly the way you like it? Have you spent hours and hours reading this book and the User's Manual, or simply exploring menus, and finally got all the settings in place? Are you worried that you might accidentally reset your camera or that it could lose its settings in one way or another? Well, worry no more! *Save/load settings* writes configuration settings to the memory card, allowing you to back up camera settings to your computer.

When you have your camera configured to your liking, or at any time during the process, simply use the Save/load settings function to save the camera configuration to your memory card. It creates a 2 KB file named NCSETUPF.BIN in the root directory of your memory card. You can then save that file to your computer's hard drive and have a backup of your camera settings.

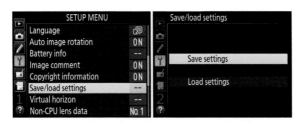

Figure 5.14 – Save/load settings

Here are the steps to save or load the camera's settings:

1. Choose Save/load settings from the Setup Menu and scroll to the right (figure 5.14, screen 1).
2. Select Save settings or Load settings from the Save/load settings menu, and then follow one of these two easy procedures (figure 5.14, screen 2):

   a) **Save settings** – Select Save settings and press the OK button. Your most important camera settings will be saved to your memory card. Afterward, copy the settings file (NCSETUPF.BIN) to your computer for safekeeping. **Warning**: You may notice in the screen display in figure 5.14, screen 2, that the Load settings selection is grayed out on your camera. If Load settings is not grayed out when you get ready to save the settings, be careful—you are about to overwrite previously saved settings that are currently on the memory card. The only time you'll see Load settings not grayed out is when an NCSETUPF.BIN file already exists on the memory card.

   b) **Load settings** – Insert a memory card with a previously saved NCSETUPF.BIN file in the card's root directory, select Load settings, and press the OK button. The settings you previously saved will be reloaded into the D810 and will overwrite your current settings without prompting you for permission, so be sure that you are ready to have the settings overwritten. If you change the name of the NCSETUPF.BIN file, the D810 will not be able to reload your settings.

Here is a list of settings that are saved or loaded when you make use of one of these functions. It doesn't save or load every setting in the D810, only the ones listed here:

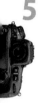

Playback Menu
- Playback display options
- Image review
- After delete
- Rotate tall

Shooting Menus (all four banks included)
- Shooting menu bank
- Extended menu banks
- File naming
- Primary slot selection
- Secondary slot function
- Image quality
- JPEG/TIFF recording
- NEF (RAW) recording
- Image area
- White balance (includes fine-tuning adjustments and presets d-1 to d-6)
- Set Picture Control (Custom Picture Controls are saved as Standard)
- Color space

- Active D-Lighting
- Vignette control
- Auto distortion control
- Long exposure NR
- High ISO NR
- ISO sensitivity settings
- Movie settings

Custom Settings (all four banks included)
- All Custom Settings

Setup Menu
- Clean image sensor Flicker reduction
- Time zone and date (except Date and time)
- Language
- Auto image rotation
- Copyright information
- Non-CPU lens data
- HDMI
- Location data Eye-Fi upload

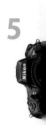

My Menu and Recent Settings
- My Menu (includes all items you've entered)
- All Recent Settings
- Choose tab

Settings Recommendation: This function is a great idea. After using my camera for a few days and getting it set up just right, I save the settings file to my computer for safekeeping. Later, if I change things extensively for some reason and then want to reload my original settings, I just put the backed-up settings file on a memory card, pop it into the camera, select Load settings, and I'm back in business.

Virtual Horizon

(User's Manual – Page 379)

Virtual horizon is a function that allows you to level your camera when it's on a tripod. This particular Virtual horizon function is not for Live view photography or Movie live view still image or video use. All this function does is bring up the Virtual horizon indicator on the camera's Monitor so that you can use it to help level your camera on a tripod or other stable shooting base.

Let's see how to use the convenient Virtual horizon to level your camera. No more need for those Accessory-shoe mounted bubble levels!

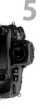

SETUP MENU				
Language	🌐			
Auto image rotation	ON			
Battery info	--			
Image comment	ON			
Copyright information	ON			
Save/load settings	--			
Virtual horizon	--			
Non-CPU lens data	No 1			

Figure 5.15A – Virtual horizon

Here are the steps to use the Virtual horizon:

1. Choose Virtual horizon from the Setup Menu and scroll to the right (figure 5.15A, screen 1).
2. The next two screens (figure 5.15A, screens 2 and 3) show the Virtual horizon indicator. You can use it to level the camera on your tripod or even handheld if you would like. The indicator shows left and right tilts, along with forward and backward tilts. Figure 5.15, screen 2, indicates that the camera is tilted to the right with the lens point slightly downward. Screen 3 shows that the camera is level.

Note: The Live view photography and Movie live view modes have a similar, translucent version of this Virtual horizon that you can see through during live usage. That Virtual horizon is available by pressing the info button repeatedly until it shows up as one of several overlays available in either of those Live view modes.

Settings Recommendation: This is a very convenient function because it allows me to level my camera when I am using a tripod without breaking out the old Accessory-shoe bubble level. I suggest adding this function to the My Menu section of your camera. That way, you will have it available whenever you want to use it, without digging through menus to find it. We will discuss how to add items to My Menu in the chapter titled **My Menu and Recent Settings**.

Viewfinder Virtual Horizon

Although not directly related to the graphical Virtual horizon function for the camera's Monitor, there is another function called *Viewfinder virtual horizon* that is available to you. You can use it to see a somewhat different-looking Virtual horizon indicator in the camera's Viewfinder by assigning one of the assignable buttons to Viewfinder virtual horizon. Let's use the Fn button as an example. We covered how to assign different functionality to the Fn button in the chapter **Custom Setting Menu** in the section **Custom Setting f4 – Assign Fn button**.

If you go to *Custom Setting Menu > f Controls > f4 Assign Fn button > Press* and choose Viewfinder virtual horizon, you will see another type of Virtual horizon on the bottom and the right side of your camera's Viewfinder when you press the button you've assigned it to (figure 5.15B, red arrows). If you prefer not to assign the Viewfinder virtual horizon to the Fn button, you can assign it to other buttons instead (e.g., Preview button).

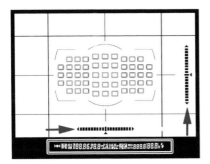

Figure 5.15B – Viewfinder virtual horizon

The Viewfinder virtual horizon is showing level in figure 5.15B. Once it's assigned to a button, you can activate the Viewfinder virtual horizon with a press of that button. When it shows in the Viewfinder, it will register left and right tilt, along with forward and backward tilt, by changing the look of the two indicators at the red arrows' tips.

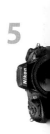

Non-CPU Lens Data

(User's Manual – Page 229)

Non-CPU lens data helps you use older non-CPU Nikkor lenses with your camera. Do you still have several older AI or AI-S Nikkor lenses? I do! The image quality from the older manual-focus (MF) lenses is excellent.

Since the D810 is positioned as a pro-level camera, it must have the necessary controls to use both auto focus (AF) and manual focus (MF) lenses. Many photographers on a budget use the older MF lenses to obtain professional-level image quality without having to break the bank on expensive lens purchases. You can buy excellent AI and AI-S Nikkor lenses on eBay for US$100–$300 and have image quality that only the most expensive zoom lenses can produce.

Lens manufacturers like Zeiss and Nikkor are still making MF lenses, and because some of them do not have a CPU (electronic chip) that communicates with the camera, it's important to have a way to let the D810 know something about the lens in use.

This Non-CPU lens data function allows you to do exactly that. You can store information for up to nine separate non-CPU lenses within this section of the D810.

Here is a detailed analysis of the Non-CPU lens data screen selections (figure 5.16A, screen 2):

- **Lens number** – Using the Multi Selector, you can scroll left or right to select one of your lenses. There are nine lens records available. When you select a Lens number here, the focal length and maximum aperture of that lens will show up in the Focal length and Maximum aperture fields. If you haven't stored information for a particular Lens number, you'll see double dashes (– –) in the Focal length and Maximum aperture fields.
- **Focal length (mm)** – This field contains the actual focal length in millimeters (mm) of the lens in use. You can select focal lengths from 6 mm to 4000 mm. Hmm, I didn't know they even made a 4000 mm lens. I want one!
- **Maximum aperture** – This field is for the Maximum aperture of the lens. You can enter an f-stop number from F1.2 to F22. Remember, this is for the maximum aperture only (largest opening or f-stop). When you've entered a maximum aperture, the camera will be able to determine the other apertures by your use of the aperture ring on the lens. (Remember those?)

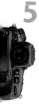

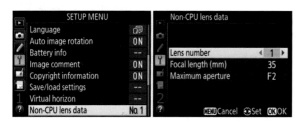

Figure 5.16A – Non-CPU lens data

Use the following steps to configure (save) each of your non-CPU lenses for use with your D810:

1. Select Non-CPU lens data from the Setup Menu and scroll to the right (figure 5.16A, screen 1).
2. Choose Lens number and scroll left or right until you find the number you want to use for this particular lens (figure 5.16A, screen 2).
3. Scroll down to Focal length (mm) and scroll left or right to select the focal length of the lens. If you are configuring a non-CPU zoom lens, select the widest setting. This works because the meter will adjust for any light falloff that may occur as the lens is zoomed out.
4. Scroll down to Maximum aperture and scroll left or right to select the maximum aperture of the lens. If you are configuring a variable-aperture zoom lens, select the largest aperture the lens can use. This works because the meter will adjust for the variation in the aperture.
5. Press the OK button to store the setting.

The screen shown in figure 5.16A, screen 2, allows you to either select a lens or save changes to one or all nine of your lenses. In other words, you can use the set of screens in figure 5.16A to both input and select a non-CPU lens.

When you have selected a lens for use, the *Setup Menu > Non-CPU lens data* selection will show the number of the lens you've selected. It will be in the format of No. 1 to No. 9. In figure 5.16A, screen 1, you can see the lens selection (No. 1) at the end of the Non-CPU lens data line. That's my beloved AI Nikkor 35mm f/2 lens!

Selecting a Non-CPU Lens with External Camera Controls

The D810 allows you to customize its buttons to do things the way you want them to be done. You may have only one or two non-CPU lenses, so it may be sufficient to use the Non-CPU lens data menu to select a lens. However, if you have a large selection of non-CPU lenses, you may wish Nikon had provided more than nine lens selections in the Non-CPU lens data menu.

Since I use several older manual-focus AI Nikkor lenses, I use the Custom Setting Menu's assign button functions to assign *Custom Setting Menu > f Controls > f4 Assign Fn button > Press + command dials* to Choose non-CPU lens number, for selecting Non-CPU lens data on the fly. Then I can simply hold down the Fn button and turn either of the Command dials to select one of the nine non-CPU lenses I have already registered with the camera.

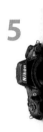

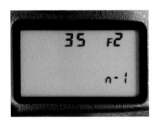

Figure 5.16B – Non-CPU lens data with external controls

Here are the steps to select a non-CPU lens using external camera controls, after making an assignment to one of the camera's buttons (e.g., Fn button):

1. On the bottom right of figure 5.16B, you will see n – 1. That is where you choose the actual lens by its assigned number. You'll see n–1 to n–9 scroll by as you rotate whichever Command dial is most convenient to you.
2. In figure 5.16B, the number in the top center applies to the focal length of the currently selected lens, in this case, 35mm (35).
3. The number on the top right of figure 5.16B shows the maximum aperture of the currently selected non-CPU lens (F2).

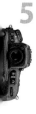

4. Hold down the button you've assigned (I use Fn) and turn a Command dial until the number of your lens appears (n -1 to n - 9), and then release the button. Now your camera knows which lens is mounted.

This is a really quick way to change the camera's Non-CPU lens data settings after you mount a different non-CPU lens.

Settings Recommendation: I like using the *f4 Assign Fn button > Press + command dial* setting to select my non-CPU lenses. This is very fast and easy in the field. Or, you can simply use the *Setup Menu > Non-CPU lens data* function to select a lens with menus. Play with both and learn how to use each. They'll both come in handy at different times.

AF Fine-Tune

(User's Manual – Page 380)

One thing that really impresses me about the D810 is its ability to be fine-tuned in critical areas like metering and autofocus. With many older cameras, if an AF lens had a back focus problem, you just had to tolerate it or send it off to be fixed. Now, with *AF fine-tune*, you can adjust your camera so the lens focuses where you want it to focus.

Nikon has made provisions for keeping a table of up to 20 lenses you have fine-tuned for better focus. The idea behind fine-tuning is that you can push the focus forward or backward in small increments, with up to 20 increments in each direction.

When the little round, green AF indicator comes on in your camera's Viewfinder and AF fine-tune is enabled for a lens you've already configured, the actual focus is moved from its default position forward or backward by the amount you've specified. If your lens has a back focus problem and you move the focus a little forward, the problem is solved. There are four selections on the AF fine-tune menu:

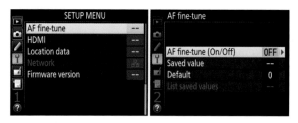

Figure 5.17A – Fine-tuning the focus of a lens

- AF fine-tune (On/Off)
- Saved value
- Default
- List saved values

Use the following steps to start the process of fine-tuning a lens (figure 5.17A):

1. Choose AF fine-tune from the Setup Menu and scroll to the right (figure 5.17A, screen 1).
2. Select AF fine-tune (On/Off) from the menu and scroll to the right (figure 5.17A, screen 2).
3. The next four subsections show the screens to configure AF fine-tune (figures 5.17B to 5.17E). Each of the following figures continues where figure 5.17A, screen 2, left off.

AF Fine-Tune (On/Off)

Figure 5.17B shows the AF fine-tune (On/Off) screen and its selections. The two values you can select are as follows:

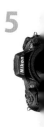

- **On** – This setting turns the AF fine-tune system on. Without this setting enabled, the D810 focuses like a factory default D810. Set AF fine-tune (On/Off) to On if you are planning to fine-tune a lens now. Press the OK button to save the value.
- **Off** – This default setting disables the AF fine-tune system.

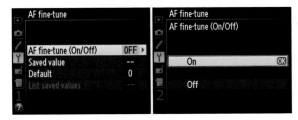

Figure 5.17B – Enabling or disabling AF fine-tune

Saved Value

With an autofocus lens mounted, *Saved value* allows you to control the amount of front or back focus fine-tuning you would like to input for the listed lens. At the top left of figure 5.17C, screen 2, just under the words Saved value, you'll see the focal length of the lens that is mounted on your camera, the maximum aperture, and the number assigned to the lens. If you're configuring a lens for the first time, you'll see No. – –. You can fine-tune a maximum of 20 lenses. After you save a lens configuration, a number will appear in place of the dashes (No. 1 to No. 20).

To the right of the lens information is a scale that runs from +20 on the top to -20 on the bottom. The yellow pointer on the right starts out at 0. You can move this yellow pointer up or down to change the amount of focus fine-tuning you need

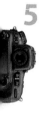

for this lens. Moving the pointer up on the scale pushes the focal point away from the camera, and moving it down pulls the focal point toward the camera. I set my 50mm F1.4 lens to +5 forward focus, as shown in figure 5.17C, screen 2. When you set the fine-tuning amount you need, press the OK button.

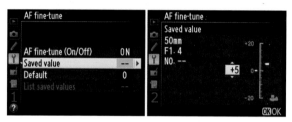

Figure 5.17C – Fine-tuning a lens with a Saved value

Default

The *Default* configuration screen looks a lot like the Saved value screen, except there is no lens information listed. This Default value will be applied to all AF lenses you mount on your camera. If you are convinced that your particular camera (not a lens) always has a back or front focus problem and you are not able or ready to ship it off to Nikon for repair, you can use the Default value to push the autofocus in one direction or the other until you are satisfied that your camera is focusing the way you'd like. *Again, this will affect all autofocus lenses you mount on your camera.*

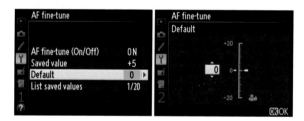

Figure 5.17D – Setting a Default fine-tune adjustment for all lenses

As shown in figure 5.17D, screen 2, to set an *AF fine-tune > Default*, use the scale that runs from +20 on the top to -20 on the bottom. The yellow pointer starts at 0. You can move this yellow pointer up or down to change the amount of focus fine-tuning you need for whatever lens you currently have on the D810 if no value already exists in the Saved value for the lens. Moving the pointer up on the scale pushes the focal point away from the camera (front focus), and moving it down pulls the focal point toward the camera (back focus). When you are done, press the OK button.

Note: You could use this Default value as a value for any of your AF lenses that do not have a Saved value. I tested this with a different lens (not shown) by setting a

Saved value of +1 for my AF-S Nikkor 24-120 mm lens. While the 24-120 mm lens was still mounted, I set a value of -2 for the Default value. When I removed the 24-120 mm lens and mounted an AF Nikkor 60 mm micro lens, the +1 in the Saved value field disappeared, but the -2 in the Default field stayed put. So it appears that you can use the Default field either for all AF lenses that have no Saved value or for a currently mounted AF lens that you want to adjust but not save a value for.

List Saved Values

Notice in figure 5.17E that there are several screens used to configure the list of saved values. *List saved values* helps you remember which lenses you've fine-tuned. It also allows you to set an identification number (00–99) for a particular lens out of the 20 lenses you can register.

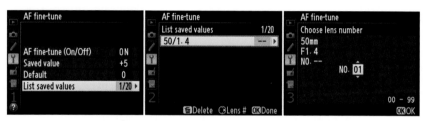
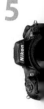

Figure 5.17E – Assigning an AF fine-tune lens number to one of your 20 lenses

Many people use the last two digits of the lens's serial number as the List saved values number for that lens. Alternatively, you can select a sequential number from 00–99. In figure 5.17E, screen 2, you'll see the 50/1.4 lens listed; this screen will show a list of all lenses for which you have saved values. Notice in the third screen that there is a little box in the middle after No. Use the Multi Selector to scroll up or down in that box, from 00 to 99. That way, you can set whatever number you want to use for each particular lens.

Note: With AF fine-tune enabled, the lens may not be able to focus at the minimum focus distance or at infinity. Test this carefully! Fine-tuning is not applied to any lenses when you're using Live view photography mode. If you use teleconverters, you will need to store a value for the lens itself and the lens with the teleconverter mounted.

Settings Recommendation: AF fine-tune is good to have. If I buy a new lens and it has focus problems, I don't keep it. Back it goes to the manufacturer for a replacement. However, if I buy a used lens or have had one long enough to go out of warranty and it later develops front or back focus problems, the camera allows me to fine-tune the autofocus for that lens. A pro-level camera has these little necessities to keep you out of trouble when shooting commercially.

HDMI

(User's Manual – Page 269)

HDMI (high-definition multimedia interface) allows you to display your images and video on a high-definition television (HDTV), external video monitor, or computer monitor with an HDMI connection. You can also use the HDMI port to stream clean, uncompressed, broadcast-quality video to an external video recording device, such as one of the recorders found on **www.Atomos.com** (my favorite is the Ninja Blade).

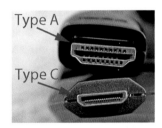

Figure 5.18A – HDMI connectors

You'll need an HDMI Type-A to HDMI Type-C cable, which is not included with the camera but is available from many electronics stores. This cable is also known as a mini-HDMI–to–HDMI A/V HD cable.

Figure 5.18A gives you a closeup look at both ends of the cable. The smaller end (mini-HDMI Type-C) goes into the HDMI port under the rubber flap on your camera, and the other end (HDMI Type-A) plugs into your HD device. The HDMI setting has two options, Output resolution and Advanced, which we'll discuss next.

Output Resolution

You can select one of the following formats for output to your HDMI device:

- *Auto (default)* – This allows the camera to select the most appropriate format for displaying your image on the currently connected device.
- *1080p (progressive)* – 1920 × 1080 progressive format.
- *1080i (interlaced)* – 1920 × 1080 interlaced format.
- *720p (progressive)* – 1280 × 720 progressive format.
- *576p (progressive)* – 720 × 576 progressive format.
- *480p (progressive)* – 640 × 480 progressive format.

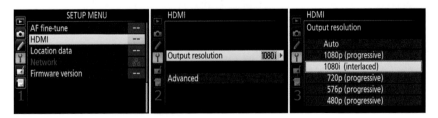

Figure 5.18B – Selecting an HDMI Output resolution

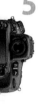

Use the following steps to select an Output resolution (figure 5.18B):

1. Select HDMI from the Setup Menu and scroll to the right (figure 5.18B, screen 1).
2. Choose Output resolution from the menu and scroll to the right (figure 5.18B, screen 2).
3. Select one of the five output resolutions (figure 5.18B, screen 3) or Auto. I chose 1080i (interlaced) as an example. You might want to try Auto at first to see if the camera and display device will interface by themselves. If not, read the user's manual for the display device to find out what output resolution works best with it. Set the camera accordingly.
4. Press the OK button to lock in your selection.

Advanced

With the large variety of display and recording devices available, your camera has to deal with all sorts of video standards. Here is a brief list of the controls available for modifying the HDMI video output:

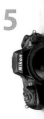

- **Output range** controls how color is displayed on the receiving device. You can limit the RGB video output to a Limited range of 16 to 235, or a Full range of 0 to 255.
- **Output display size** sets frame coverage for horizontal and vertical output. Your choices are 95% or 100%. This allows you to fit the video display on monitors with a reduced display area, or a full display area.
- **Live view on-screen display** controls whether the camera outputs clean HDMI video or video with the shooting information overlaid on the video signal (e.g., aperture, shutter speed, ISO).
- **Dual Monitor** allows you to mirror the video stream from the HDMI port on the camera's Monitor, in addition to an external monitor. This uses more battery power but gives you dual monitors.

Let's examine each setting on the Advanced menu in more detail.

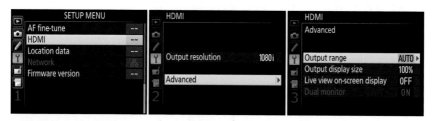

Figure 5.18C – Using Advanced HDMI settings

Use the following steps to open the Advanced menu (figure 5.18C):

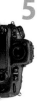

1. Select HDMI from the Setup Menu and scroll to the right (figure 5.18C, screen 1).
2. Choose Advanced from the menu and scroll to the right (figure 5.18C, screen 2).
3. Select one of the three settings from the Advanced menu and scroll to the right (figure 5.18C, screen 3).
4. Refer to figures 5.18D through 5.18G for details on the configuration of each item.

Output Range

Output range allows you to adjust the level of colors sent to a recording or display device. When you are outputting video to a device, such as an HDTV or recorder, the device may not accept normal *Full range* RGB with a color range of 0 to 255 correctly. Some devices accept only *Limited range* RGB input in the range of 16 to 235 color levels (YCbCr). If you try to send Full range RGB video output to a Limited range YCbCr device, you may end up with washed-out, grayish blacks and blown-out, featureless whites.

The solution is to match the correct output to the correct device type. If you see the problems just described when the camera is set to Full range (RGB), try the Limited range (YCbCr) setting instead. Or, you could try the Auto setting to see if the camera can detect what the display or recording device requires.

Again, we will discuss this in deeper detail in the upcoming chapter **Movie Live View**.

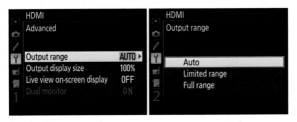

Figure 5.18D – Selecting an Output range

Use the following steps to select Full range or Limited range output (figure 5.18D continues from figure 5.18C):

1. Select Output range from the Advanced menu and scroll to the right (figure 5.18D, screen 1).
2. Select Auto, Limited range, or Full range from the Output range menu. Auto (factory default) is selected in figure 5.18D, screen 2.
3. Press the OK button to select the Output range.

Output Display Size

At times, the *Output display size* may not match the display device well. In that case, you can reduce the Output display size from 100% to 95%, to help the display fit better. I plugged my D810 into a Vizio 32-inch HDTV and found that the output from the camera on the TV was a little bit too tall. I changed Output display size to 95% and it fit perfectly.

You can do this while viewing the live output on the HDTV by opening the *Setup Menu > HDMI > Output display size* setting and making the change. Let's see how to modify the Output display size.

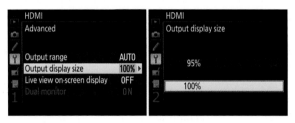

Figure 5.18E – Changing the Output display size

Use the following steps to change the Output display size (figure 5.18E continues from figure 5.18C):

1. Select Output display size from the Advanced menu and scroll to the right (figure 5.18E, screen 1).
2. Select 95% or 100% from the Output display size menu. 100% (factory default) is selected in figure 5.18E, screen 2).
3. Press the OK button to select the Output display size.

Live View On-Screen Display

Live view on-screen display is the setting you'll use when you want the streaming video output from the camera to have no shooting information overlays. Here are your two choices:

- **Off** – When Live view on-screen display is set to Off, the camera outputs a clean, uncompressed, 4:2:2 video stream with no distracting overlays.
- **On** – If you choose On, the camera will stream video with the same information you see on the Monitor, which may include shooting information such as aperture, shutter speed, ISO sensitivity, metering mode, gridlines, sound input levels, focus mode, Picture Control type, image size, image quality, image area, and so forth.

If you want to output clean, overlay-free, uncompressed, broadcast-quality video, choose Off for this setting.

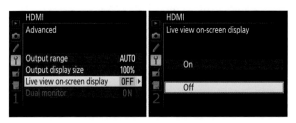

Figure 5.18F – Choosing a Live view on-screen display mode

Use the following steps to change the Live view on-screen display, enabling or disabling pure video output (figure 5.18F continues from figure 5.18C):

1. Select Live view on-screen display from the Advanced menu and scroll to the right (figure 5.18F, screen 1).
2. Select On or Off from the Live view on-screen display menu. Off (factory default) is selected in figure 5.18F, screen 2.
3. Press the OK button to lock in the setting.

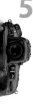

We have examined only how to select and set the modes, with some basic reasons why we decided to use each mode. Shooting video is new to many photographers, so the chapter **Movie Live View** will provide much-needed detail.

Dual Monitor

The Nikon D810 can send an HDMI video output signal to two monitors simultaneously: an external monitor and the Monitor on the camera. You can use a basic external monitor merely to see the output more clearly, or you can use an external recorder, such as my favorite, the Atomos Ninja Blade. Unlike its ancestors, the D810 can also show the same signal you see on the external monitor on the camera's Monitor. Let's see how it works.

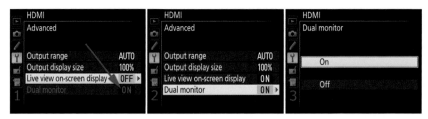

Figure 5.18G – Use an external monitor and the camera's Monitor

Use the following steps to enable or disable the Dual monitor capability built into the Nikon D810 (figure 5.18G continues from figure 5.18C):

1. Please notice at the arrow in figure 5.18G, screen 1, that the Dual monitor feature defaults to On. Therefore, if you want to use dual monitors, the camera is ready immediately. Also, please notice that, in screen 1, Live view on-screen display is set to Off, meaning that the camera will output no shooting information overlays with the clean video signal. But, what if you want to disable the Dual monitor capability? It is grayed out and unavailable!

2. You can disable Dual monitor, but first you have to set Live view on-screen display to On. Once you have done so, the Dual monitor function becomes available. Figure 5.18G, screen 2 shows that Live view on-screen display is enabled (On), also un-graying the Dual monitor feature. To enable or disable Dual monitor, choose Dual monitor and scroll to the right.

3. Select On or Off from the menu, which enables or disables Dual monitor. Press the OK button to lock in the Dual monitor setting. Once you have made your selection, you will once again need to decide whether you want the Live view on-screen display to suppress shooting information overlays (set to Off). Use the step-by-step method attached to figure 5.18F (previous subsection) to change the Live view on-screen display back to the way you want it.

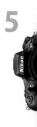

Settings Recommendation: Please spend some time familiarizing yourself with the features of this function. Later in this book, in the chapter titled Movie Live View, you will need to have an understanding of using HDMI output. The D810 camera has enhanced video output compared to its predecessors. Therefore, if you have not been fond of video with an HD-SLR in the past, you may want to reconsider now that you are using the Nikon D810. It is a portable home movie studio, with full broadcast-quality commercial capabilities!

Location Data

(User's Manual – Page 233)

Nikon has wisely included the ability to geotag your images with global positioning system (GPS) location data by providing an easy-to-use interface for various GPS devices.

Now when you shoot a spectacular travel image, you can rest assured that you'll be able to find that exact spot next year. With the Nikon GP-1 or GP-1A GPS units (or an aftermarket brand), the D810 will record the following GPS information about your location into the metadata of each image:

- Latitude
- Longitude
- Altitude
- Heading (aftermarket only)
- UTC (time)

Using a GPS Unit with Your D810

The GPS unit you choose must be compatible with the National Marine Electronics Association NMEA0183 data format version 2.01 or 3.0.

I use a Nikon GP-1 GPS unit on my D810. It's small, easy to carry and store, and works very well. I have other Nikon DSLRs too, and this GPS unit works on all of them, with the proper cables. The Nikon GP-1A GPS unit is also fully compatible with the D810.

In figure 5.19A, you can see a Nikon GP-1 attached to the camera's Accessory shoe. You can also see the GP1-CA10 cable plugged into the 10-pin connector on the front of the camera. I deliberately put the curl in the cable to keep it from sticking out awkwardly.

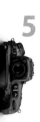

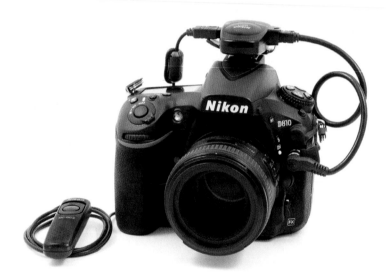

Figure 5.19A – Nikon D810 with a Nikon GP-1 GPS unit, GP1- CA10 cable, and MC-DC2 remote release cable

The GP1-CA10 cable will interface with Nikon cameras that have a 10-pin port on the body, such as the D200, D300, D300S, D700, D800, D800E, D810, D2X, D3, D3S, D3X, D4, and D4S.

The GP-1 GPS unit also comes with a GP1-CA90 cable to interface with Nikon cameras such as the D3000, D3100, D3200, D3300, D5000, D5100, D5200, D5300, D90, D7000, D7100, D600, D610, Df, and D750, so it is a useful device for almost any of your newer Nikons.

You can also get an optional Nikon MC-DC2 remote release cable that plugs directly into the GP-1 GPS unit for hands-off, vibration-free photography. The MC-DC2 remote release cable can be used to fire the shutter on any Nikon DSLR or

HD-SLR that can interface with the GP-1 GPS unit. You can see the MC-DC2 remote release cable on the left side of the camera in figure 5.19A. It is plugged into the GP-1 GPS unit on the opposite side of where the GP1-CA10 cable plugs in.

The mentioned cables are compatible with both the Nikon GP-1 and GP-1A GPS units.

Note: The Nikon GP-1 and GP-1A GPS units do not have a built-in digital compass, so they will not report heading information to the camera. Other GPS units do have the built-in compass and will report the heading. If that is important to you, please investigate the Geotagger Pro GPS unit at **https://www.photoproshop.com/**.

Preparing the Camera for GPS Usage

There are several screens used in setting up the D810 for GPS use. First, you have to make a decision about the exposure meter when a GPS unit is plugged into the camera. While the GPS is plugged in, the camera's exposure meter must be active to record GPS data to the image. You should do one of two things:

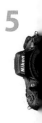

- Set the exposure meter to stay on for the entire time that a GPS is plugged in. This, of course, will increase battery drain, but it keeps the GPS locked to the satellites (no seeking time).
- Press the Shutter-release button halfway down to activate the exposure meter before finishing the exposure. If you push the Shutter-release button down quickly and the GPS is not active and locked, it won't record GPS data to the image. The meter must be on before the GPS will seek satellites.

Standby Timer

Figure 5.19B shows the screens used to set the meter to either stay on the entire time the GPS is connected or shut down after Custom setting c2 Standby timer delay expires.

Interestingly, the Location data function also has a subfunction named *Standby timer*. You can select either Enable or Disable for this Standby timer to control whether or not the GPS unit stays on continuously or shuts down when the timeout occurs for Custom setting c2 Standby timer.

The Custom setting c2 Standby timer function is for all aspects of the camera. The Location data's Standby timer subfunction applies only to an attached GPS unit.

Here's what each setting in Standby timer does:

- ***Enable*** (default) – The meter turns off after the *Custom Setting Menu > c Timers/ AE lock > c2 Standby timer* delay expires (default 6 seconds). GPS data will be recorded only when the exposure meter is active, so allow some time for the GPS unit to reacquire a satellite signal before taking a picture. This is hard to do when c2 Standby timer is set to Enable. You just about have to stand around with your finger on the Shutter-release button trying to keep the meter active. I suggest using Disable, as described next.

- **Disable** – The exposure meter stays on the entire time a GPS unit is connected. As long as you have a good GPS signal, you will be able to record GPS data at any time. This is the preferred setting for using the GPS for continuous shooting. It does use extra battery life, so you may want to carry more than one battery if you're going to shoot all day. Turn the camera off between locations.

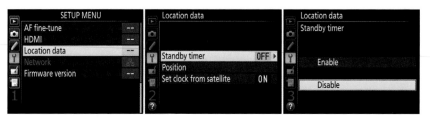

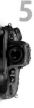

Figure 5.19B – Setting an Auto meter off delay for GPS usage

Here are the steps to configure the GPS settings (figure 5.19B):

1. Choose Location data from the Setup Menu and scroll to the right (figure 5.19B, screen 1).
2. Select Standby timer and scroll to the right (figure 5.19B, screen 2).
3. Select Enable or Disable (figure 5.19B, screen 3). Use Disable for more reliable GPS usage, with somewhat greater battery drain. It is a good idea to carry multiple batteries if you are shooting all day with a Nikon GP-1, GP-1A, or an aftermarket GPS unit attached.
4. Press the OK button to lock in the setting.

Position

There is also a *Position* setting, as shown in figure 5.19C, screen 2. If your GPS unit is not attached to the camera, the Position selection is grayed out. When a GPS is attached, the next screen after Position shows the actual GPS location data being detected by the D810 (figure 5.19C, screen 3).

To validate that the GPS is picking up GPS location data, examine the Position screen by using the following steps (figure 5.19C):

1. Choose Location data from the Setup Menu and scroll to the right (figure 5.19C, screen 1).
2. Select Position from the Location data menu and scroll to the right (figure 5.19C, screen 2).

3. Examine the Position screen to see the five items provided from the GPS satellite data (figure 5.19C, screen 3). Notice that my Nikon GP-1 GPS unit did not
give me Heading information. Other GPS units will give you that information,
as discussed previously.

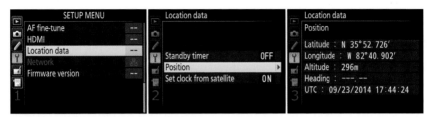

Figure 5.19C – GPS Position information screen

When the camera establishes communication with your GPS unit, three things
happen:

- Position information appears on the GPS Position screen (figure 5.19C, screen 3).
- A small GPS satellite symbol will display on the Control panel, just under the
aperture indicator. The same symbol will be shown on the Information display,
just to the left of the battery charge indicator. It will blink when acquiring a GPS
signal lock and stop blinking when at least three global positioning satellites
are acquired.
- An additional data information display screen will be displayed when you are
using the Playback button to review images captured while the GPS was active.
You can press up or down with the Multi Selector button to scroll through the
image data screens on the Monitor. One of them will be similar to the screen
shown in figure 5.19D, which is a picture of the GPS data screen from a picture
I took of a tree.

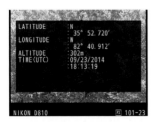

Figure 5.19D – GPS Information display screen (Playback)

Note: The Nikon GP-1 GPS unit will blink its rear LED light in red while acquiring
satellites and shine solid green when locked onto three satellites. Allow a few seconds for the GPS to acquire satellites when the camera has been turned off. If you

are a significant distance from where you last used the GP-1 GPS unit, it may require up to a minute or two to acquire a satellite lock. Once the GP-1 has a local satellite lock and you turn the camera off, the GPS unit will reacquire the signal in just a few seconds when the camera is turned back on.

Use GPS to Set Camera Clock

The D810 has a cool feature designed to let the GPS satellite keep your camera's time accurate: the *Set clock from satellite* function. The camera can query the GPS satellite and set the camera's clock. If you use GPS a lot, you might want to leave this on. The clock in the Nikon D810 is not as accurate as a wristwatch, for instance, and will tend to lose accuracy more quickly. It's a good idea to set the camera's clock from time to time. This is an easy way to accomplish that for GPS users.

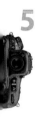

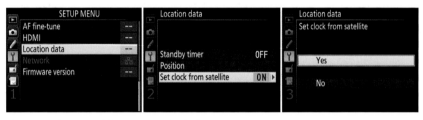

Figure 5.19E – Using GPS to set camera clock

Here are the steps to enable Set clock from satellite:

1. Choose Location data from the Setup Menu and scroll to the right (figure 5.19E, screen 1).
2. Select Set clock from satellite and scroll to the right (figure 5.19E, screen 2). Select Yes to enable the setting or No if you want to check the clock yourself from time to time (figure 5.19E, screen 3).
3. Press the OK button to save the setting.

Using the GPS

If the GPS icon is flashing on the Control panel and Information display screen, it means that the GPS is searching for a signal. If you take a picture with the GPS icon flashing, no GPS data will be recorded. If the GPS icon is not flashing (solid), it means that the D810 is receiving good GPS data and is ready to record data to a picture. If the D810 loses communication with the GPS unit for more than two seconds, the GPS icon will disappear. Make sure the icon is displayed and isn't flashing before you take pictures!

If you want the GPS Heading information to be accurate, keep your GPS unit pointing in the same direction as the lens. Some aftermarket GPS units also contain a digital compass, unlike the Nikon GP-1. Point the GPS in the direction of your subject and give it enough time to stabilize before you take the picture or the Heading information will not be accurate. This does not apply to the Nikon GP-1 or GP-1A GPS unit, which has no digital compass. It records only Latitude, Longitude, Altitude, and UTC time, not the Heading.

The Nikon GPS units mount either onto the camera's Accessory shoe (figure 5.19A) or on the camera's strap, with the included GP1-CL1 strap adapter.

Note: You can also attach some external handheld GPS units through an optional (and pricey) Nikon MC-35 cable, which uses a D-sub 9-pin connector. You must find a handheld GPS unit with a cable that will connect to the 9-pin connector on the MC-35, which is not as easy as it used to be because many handheld units use USB cable connections now.

A handheld unit I have personally used successfully is the Garmin eTrex Legend GPS unit. You can pick up a new Garmin eTrex Legend GPS unit for around US$170 on Amazon.com. It can be used with the Nikon MC-35 cable to interface with your camera, and when it's disconnected from the camera, it can keep you from getting lost while hiking to and from that special scenic spot. To interface a handheld unit with the Nikon D810, you will need to use NMEA mode at 4800 baud. Refer to the GPS unit's user's manual for more information on setting the mode and baud rate. As mentioned previously, the GPS unit you choose must be compatible with the National Marine Electronics Association NMEA0183 data format version 2.01 or 3.0.

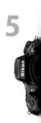

Settings Recommendation: Get the Nikon GP-1 or GP-1A GPS unit from one of many vendors, or get the Geotagger Pro GPS from the Nikonians PhotoProShop (www.PhotoProShop.com). Either unit is easy to use, foolproof, and has all the cables you need for interfacing with your camera.

If you choose one of the Nikon GPS units, the only other cable you'll need to buy is the optional MC-DC2 shutter-release cable (coiled on the left in figure 5.19A). I use the tiny Nikon GP-1 GPS unit constantly when I'm shooting nature images so I can remember where to return in the future. After you start using a GPS unit, you'll find it hard to stop.

Network

(User's Manual – Page 261)
Network allows you to interface the Nikon D810 with an Ethernet network cable for use on a local area network. You must own the Nikon UT-1 communication unit, which has an Ethernet port and a USB connector that plugs into the camera's USB port. When using the UT-1 communication unit to connect with a network, you can use the following functions:

- **FTP upload** – Transfer your images to an FTP server, or upload new images as they are taken.
- **Image transfer** – Transfer your images to a computer, or upload new images as they are taken.
- **Camera control** – Use the optional Camera Control Pro 2 software to save new images and videos directly to your computer.
- **HTTP server** – View and take pictures remotely, using a computer web browser or iPhone.

Professional studio and sports shooters may be using the UT-1 communication unit on an Ethernet network or attached to a WT-5A wireless transmitter. The majority of Nikon shooters transfer images via USB cable or a card reader.

Using this UT-1 communication unit is beyond the scope of this book. Please refer to the Nikon UT-1 User's Manual for more information.

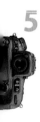

Eye-Fi Upload

(User's Manual – Page 382)

Eye-Fi upload allows you to use an Eye-Fi card to send images you take from your camera to your computer, either through a local Wi-Fi Internet connection or directly to the computer with an Ad hoc Wi-Fi connection.

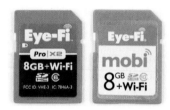

Figure 5.20A – Eye-Fi Pro X2 8 GB and mobi 8GB Wi-Fi cards

Eye-Fi upload appears on the Setup Menu of your D810 *only* when you have an Eye-Fi card inserted. Otherwise, the camera does not even show the Eye-Fi Upload menu selection between Network and Firmware version on the Shooting Menu.

The Eye-Fi company makes several of these SD cards with built-in Wi-Fi transmitters. Figure 5.20A shows two of my Eye-Fi cards: the Pro X2 8 GB high-speed Class 6 SDHC card and the mobi 8GB Class 10 SDHC card.

With an Eye-Fi card inserted and Eye-Fi software installed on a computer with a wireless network connection, you can take pictures that are automatically transferred to your computer. You can also simultaneously transfer images to file-sharing websites like Flickr and Facebook (and many more).

Most lower-cost Eye-Fi cards require a wireless network to transfer the images. However, Eye-Fi's X2 Pro cards will do Ad hoc transfers, meaning that they don't need a wireless network connection and will send pictures directly to a computer with wireless capability. In effect, the Eye-Fi card becomes a wireless (Wi-Fi) transmitter that can talk directly to a Wi-Fi–enabled computer, without an intervening network. At the time of this writing, only the Eye-Fi Pro X2 cards will transfer images directly to a computer without a wireless network as an intermediary. The other cards cost less but require a wireless network connection to move images.

The current Eye-Fi card for the majority of users is called mobi. It uses the latest technology for those who want to connect their Nikon to a tablet or smartphone through the Eye-Fi Mobile App. The app is available as a free download from the iTunes store (Apple), Google Play store (Android), and Kindle store (Amazon).

Older Eye-Fi cards that may still be available in some places include Connect, Explore, Mobile, and Geo X2. For more information on Eye-Fi cards, see the following website: **http://www.eyefi.com**.

Enabling Eye-Fi Uploads on the D810

An Eye-Fi card does not use any more battery life than a normal SD card until you enable Wi-Fi. Unless you are currently shooting images for transfer, I wouldn't leave the Eye-Fi upload feature (Wi-Fi) enabled. Why waste battery life out in the woods where there are no wireless networks? To make it really convenient to access the Eye-Fi upload function for quick enabling—only when needed—I simply added it to My Menu in the D810. We'll examine how to add functions to My Menu in the chapter, **My Menu and Recent Settings**.

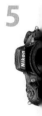

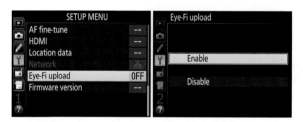

Figure 5.20B – Enabling Eye-Fi (Wi-Fi)

Here are the steps to Enable or Disable Eye-Fi upload (figure 5.20B):

1. Choose Eye-Fi upload from the Setup Menu and scroll to the right (figure 5.20B, screen 1).
2. Select Enable or Disable from the Eye-Fi upload screen (figure 5.20B, screen 2).
3. Press the OK button to lock in the setting.

On page 383 of the Nikon D810 User's Manual, there is a discussion of various Eye-Fi card status symbols. If you are a frequent user of Eye-Fi card technology, you may want to learn what the symbols mean.

Settings Recommendation: An Eye-Fi card doesn't give you the large wireless range and multiple modes that the powerful Nikon WT-4A transmitter offers, but it allows you to shoot an event within 50 to 90 feet of a notebook computer and have immediate wireless Ad hoc file transfer capability.

Because even the low-priced Eye-Fi cards have the ability to use an existing Wi-Fi connection to transfer images through the Internet to a home computer, you could do a photographic walkabout downtown, stop in at a McDonalds for a burger or Starbucks for a coffee, and use its wireless connection to transfer images to your home computer while you eat. I really like this little Eye-Fi card!

Finally, the mobi card is great if you want to transfer your files from your D810 to your tablet (and they are quite affordable).

Firmware Version

(User's Manual – Page 383)

Firmware version is a simple informational screen, like the Battery info screen. It shows you which version of the camera's operating system (firmware) you are running. My camera is currently running version C1.00 and L2.005.

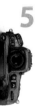

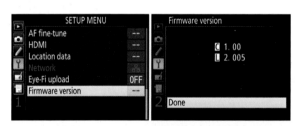

Figure 5.21 – Viewing the camera's Firmware version

Here are the steps to see the Firmware version of your camera (figure 5.21):

1. Choose Firmware version from the Setup Menu and scroll to the right (figure 5.21, screen 1).
2. Examine the Firmware version (figure 5.21, screen 2).
3. Select Done and press the OK button.

When it's time to do a Firmware update, you will use this same Firmware version menu to update the camera. An extra menu item will appear below the Done selection, allowing you to update the Firmware. Follow the instructions provided on Nikon's website for each Firmware update.

Author's Conclusions

Whew! The D810 may seem like a complicated little beast, but that's what you get when you fold medium-format, pro-level functionality into a relatively small DSLR body. For as complex as it is, I'm certainly delighted with it.

Next, we'll consider how to use the camera's Retouch Menu to adjust images without using a computer. If you are in the field shooting RAW files and you need a quick JPEG, black-and-white version of a file, or red-eye reduction, the Retouch Menu has you covered.

You can even do things like image distortion and perspective control, color balance changes, filtration, cropping, and image resizing—all without touching a computer. Let's see how!

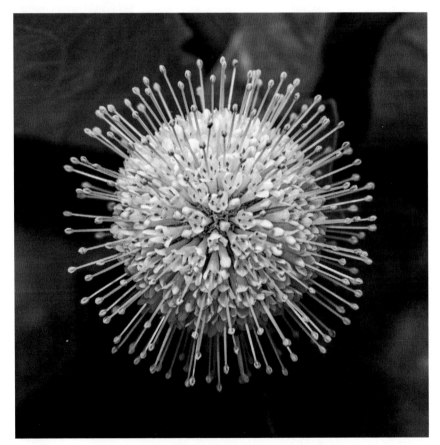

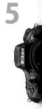

Buttonbush Plant in the Gardens at Buttonwood Park in New Bedford, Massachusetts
© Robert Smith (*greyface*)

Shot with a Nikon D810 and Tamron 150-600 f/5-6.3 lens at
600mm, 1/500 sec at f/8, ISO 220, -2/3 EV compensation.

Retouch Menu

6

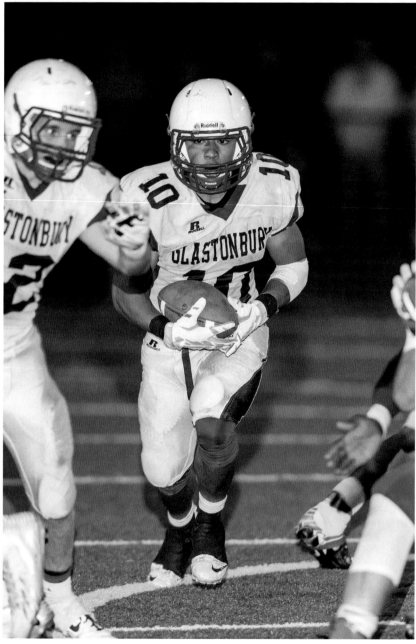

Running Back Carries the Football through the Line © Jonathan Bloom (*jbloom*)

Retouching allows you to modify your images in-camera. If you like to do digital photography but don't particularly like to adjust images on a computer, these functions are for you! Obviously, the camera's Monitor is not large enough to allow you to make heavily creative changes to an image—as you could do within Nikon Capture NX-D, Lightroom, Aperture, or Photoshop—but it's surprising what you can accomplish with the Retouch Menu.

The D810 has 20 Retouch Menu selections. The following is a list of each function and what it does:

- **D-Lighting** – This feature opens up detail in the shadows and tends to protect highlight details from blowing out. This is similar to the *Shooting Menu > Active D-Lighting* function, but it's applied *after* the image is taken.
- **Red-eye correction** – This removes the unwanted red-eye effect caused by light from a flash reflecting back from the eyes of your human subjects.
- **Trim** – This feature creates a trimmed (cropped) copy of a selected photograph. You can crop the image according to several aspect ratios, including 1:1, 3:2, 4:3, 5:4, and 16:9.
- **Monochrome** – You can convert your color images into monochrome. There are three tints available, including Black-and-white (grays), Sepia (golden), and Cyanotype (bluish).
- **Filter effects** – There are seven filter effects that can be applied to an image to change its appearance. The seven filters are Skylight, Warm filter, Red intensifier, Green intensifier, Blue intensifier, Cross screen, and Soft.
- **Color balance** – To change the color balance of your image, you can increase or decrease the amount of Green, Blue, Amber, and Magenta.
- **Image overlay** – This creates a new image by overlaying two existing NEF (RAW) files. Basically, you can combine two RAW images to create special effects—such as adding an image of the moon into a separate landscape picture.
- **NEF (RAW) processing** – You can create highly specialized JPEG images from your NEF (RAW) files without using your computer.
- **Resize** – You can take a full-size image and convert it into several smaller sizes. This is useful if you would like to send an image via e-mail or if you need a smaller image for other reasons.
- **Quick retouch** – The camera automatically tweaks the image with enhancements to saturation and contrast. In addition, when a subject is dark or is backlit, the camera applies D-Lighting to open up shadow detail.
- **Straighten** – You can straighten an image with crooked horizons by rotating it in-camera. The camera will trim (crop) the edges of the image to create a normal image perspective, without the tilt.

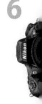

- **Distortion control** – You can remove barrel and pincushion distortion that affects the edges of the image. You can cause the camera to make automatic adjustments or you can do it manually. The camera automatically trims (crops) the edges of the image after adjustment.
- **Fisheye** – This feature allows you to incrementally bulge images from their centers to get that strange fisheye effect you often see while looking through a door peephole. It provides a very distorted image that will make your friends either laugh or chase you.
- **Color outline** – This creates an outline effect, as if you had traced an underlying image on paper with a pencil. The effect is in monochrome, contrary to the name of the function. Nikon provides this effect to "create an outline of a photograph to use as a base for painting."
- **Color sketch** – This effect is very similar to Color outline; the main difference is that it is in pastel color. It sketches the edges of the subjects in your image and colorizes them in a way similar to using colored pencils or crayon. You can control the vividness of the color and the contrast of the line edges.
- **Perspective control** – This is a useful control that helps adjust perspective distortion out of an image. It's useful for pictures of things like buildings, which can have a falling-over-backward effect when shot with a wide-angle lens. The camera automatically crops the edges of the image to allow the distortion to be removed.

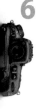

- **Miniature effect** – This effect allows you to create a reverse diorama (an image taken from a high vantage point of a real scene with a very limited band of sharpness) to make the image look fake. The image may be of a real subject, like a city shot from the top of a tall building; however, the Miniature effect causes the scene to look artificial, as if small models of reality were used.
- **Selective color** – You can use this function to create photographs with certain elements in color and the rest black-and-white. Imagine a bright red rose with nothing in the image in color except the rose petals. You can selectively choose a color with an eyedropper icon, and only that color will show in the image.
- **Edit movie** – You can shorten a movie by cropping out a small section from a large movie file.
- **Side-by-side comparison** – You can compare a retouched image—created via the Retouch Menu—with the original image. The images are presented side by side so you can see before and after effects.

The Retouch Menu is the fifth menu down the menu selection bar, just below the Setup Menu. Its icon resembles a palette and paintbrush. Unless you have some images on one of the camera's memory cards, the Retouch Menu is grayed out and unavailable, for obvious reasons. No images, no retouching!

Figure 6.1 shows a sample of the results from only one of the 20 functions available in the Retouch Menu. I was shooting RAW files in the Great Smoky Mountains in Tennessee and decided to create a JPEG from one of my images immediately. Having no computer handy, I simply used the NEF (RAW) processing function to convert the image to JPEG. Fast and easy!

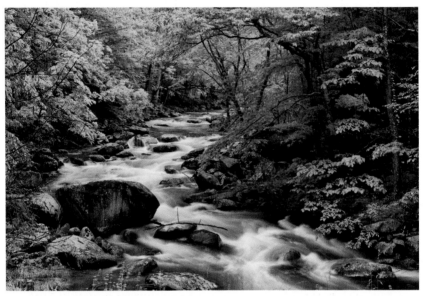

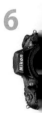

Figure 6.1 – Cascades in Great Smoky Mountains National Park, Tennessee, United States. An image converted from NEF (RAW) to JPEG using the Retouch Menu. Nikon D800, AF-S Nikkor 50mm f/1.4G lens at f/13, on tripod, Aperture-priority mode, LS (Landscape) Picture Control, 1-second exposure at ISO 50. Hoya circular polarizer used to remove reflections from the water. Active D-Lighting set to Normal.

Retouched Image File Numbering

When you use Retouch Menu items, the D810 does not overwrite your original file. It always creates a JPEG file with the next available image number. The retouched image will be numbered as the last image on the memory card. If you have 100 images on your card and you are retouching image number DSC_0047, the new JPEG image will be numbered DSC_0101 (it will be the 101st image).

Accessing the Retouch Functions – Two Methods

There are two methods for accessing the Retouch Menu. You can use the main Retouch Menu—under the MENU button—to choose an image to work with, or you can display an image on the Monitor in Playback mode and press the OK button to open the Retouch Menu.

They work basically the same, except the Playback Retouch Menu leaves out the step of choosing the image (since there is already an image on the screen), and it has fewer retouch selections. The most comprehensive retouch selections are available under the Retouch Menu.

Since both the Playback Retouch Menu and Retouch Menu methods have the same functions, we'll discuss them as if you were using the Retouch Menu. However, in case you decide to use the Playback method, let's discuss it briefly.

Playback Retouching

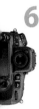

Use the following steps if you want to work with an image that you are viewing on your camera's Monitor—what I call Playback retouching:

1. Press the Playback button and choose a picture by displaying it on the Monitor (figure 6.2A, images 1 and 2). You now have a picture ready for retouching.
2. Press the OK button to open an abbreviated Retouch Menu (figure 6.2A, screen 3).
3. Select one of the Playback Retouch Menu items (figure 6.2A, screen 4).

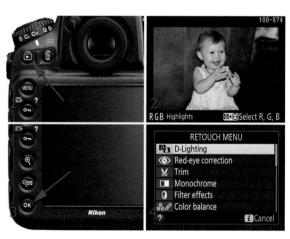

Figure 6.2A – Playback Retouch Menu

Remember that some of the Retouch Menu options are not available under the Playback Retouch Menu.

The following descriptions require that you select a Retouch Menu function and then select an image to which you want to apply the effect.

Limitations on Previously Retouched Images

Sometimes there are limitations imposed when you are working on an image that has already been retouched. You may not be able to retouch a previously retouched image with another Retouch Menu function.

When using the Playback retouch method, certain menu items will be grayed out because they cannot be applied to an already retouched image. If you use the Retouch Menu directly, any images that are overlaid with a box containing a yellow X cannot be retouched again with the current retouch function (figure 6.2B, red arrows).

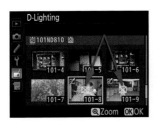

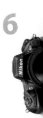

Figure 6.2B – Cannot be retouched

Using Retouch Menu Items Directly

D-Lighting

(User's Manual – Page 388)

D-Lighting allows you to reduce the shadows in an image and maybe even rein in the highlights a bit, lowering the overall image contrast. It works like Active D-Lighting except that it is applied to the image after it is taken.

Remember that Retouch Menu effects are applied to a copy of the image, so your original picture is safe and untouched. In figure 6.3, you can see that I retouched a wedding image that was about one stop underexposed. I used High D-Lighting and brought out the shadow detail.

Use the following steps for applying D-Lighting to an image:

1. Select D-Lighting from the Retouch Menu and scroll to the right (figure 6.3, screen 1).
2. Select the image you want to modify and press the OK button (figure 6.3, screen 2).
3. Using the Multi selector to scroll left or right, choose the amount of D-Lighting you want for the chosen image. You'll choose from Lo to Hi (figure 6.3, screen 3, red arrow). When the image on the right of the side-by-side comparison images looks the way you want it to, press the OK button to save the new file. I selected the Hi setting to bring out shadow detail on the underexposed image of the groom getting dressed before the wedding.
4. The D810 will display a brief *Image saved* notice between screens 3 and 4, and then display the new file on the Monitor. The retouched image will have a small palette-and-paintbrush icon to show that it has been retouched (figure 6.3, screen 4, red arrow). The original image is still available for future retouching.

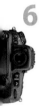

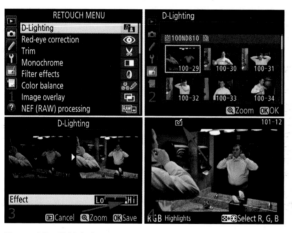

Figure 6.3 – D-Lighting

Settings Recommendation: There is no one setting that is correct for all images. I often use the middle setting between Lo and Hi to see if an image needs more or less D-Lighting, and then change to Hi or Lo if needed. Remember that any amount of D-Lighting has the potential to introduce noise in the darker areas of the image, so the less D-Lighting you use, the better.

Red-Eye Correction

(User's Manual – Page 389)

Red-eye correction attempts to change bright red pupils—caused by flash exposure reflection—back to their normal dark color. Red-eye makes a person look like one of those aliens with glowing eyes from a science fiction show.

If you've used flash to create a picture, the Red-eye correction function will work on the image if it can detect any red-eye. If it can't detect red-eye in the image, you will briefly see a screen that says *Unable to detect red-eye in selected image*.

The camera will not let you select an image that was not taken with flash. Each image not taken with flash will have a box with a yellow *X*, signifying that the image cannot be selected for this function.

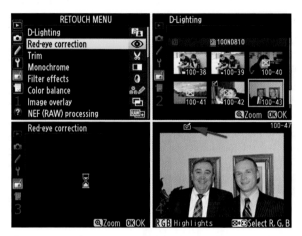

Figure 6.4 – Red-eye correction

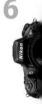

Use the following steps to execute the Red-eye correction function:

1. Select Red-eye correction from the Retouch Menu and scroll to the right (figure 6.4, screen 1).
2. Select the image you want to modify and press the OK button (figure 6.4, screen 2).
3. You'll see an hourglass on the Monitor while the camera detects and removes red-eye (figure 6.4, screen 3). This can take several seconds.
4. Press the OK button to save the file with a new file number as a retouched image (figure 6.4, screen 4, red arrow) or press the Playback button to cancel. After Red-eye correction is complete, you can use the Playback zoom in button to zoom in on the image and see how well it worked. Zoom back out with the checkered Thumbnail/Playback zoom out button.

Settings Recommendation: I've found that the Red-eye correction function works pretty well as long as the subject is fairly large in the frame. I have tried Red-eye correction on smaller subjects, such as in larger groups of people, and sometimes it works and other times it doesn't. When the subject is smaller, the eyes are much smaller too. The camera may struggle to find red-eye in very tiny subjects. I've had it correct one eye that was closer to the camera (and therefore larger) and not the other. I would rate this function as quite helpful but not always completely effective. It's a good function to have for quick red-eye correction on critical images you need to use immediately.

Trim

(User's Manual – Page 390)

The *Trim* function allows you to crop an image in-camera, change its aspect ratio, and save the file as a new image. Your original image is not modified. This is a useful function if you need to remove distracting elements from the background.

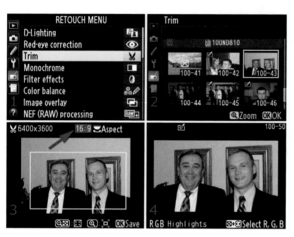

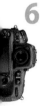

Figure 6.5 – Trim function

Use the following steps to Trim an image in-camera:

1. Select the Trim function from the Retouch Menu and scroll to the right (figure 6.5, screen 1).
2. Select the image you want to modify and press the OK button (figure 6.5, screen 2).
3. You'll see a screen that has an area of the image outlined in yellow (figure 6.5, screen 3). Use the checkered Thumbnail/Playback zoom out button to make the size of the yellow crop outline smaller or the Playback zoom in button to enlarge the outline. Use the Multi selector to move the yellow selection rectangle in any direction within the frame until you find the best crop.
4. Select the aspect ratio of the cropped image by rotating the rear Main command dial. Your choices are 3:2, 4:3, 5:4, 1:1 (square), or 16:9. Figure 6.5, screen 3 (red arrow), shows that the 16:9 aspect ratio is selected.
5. When you have the cropped area correctly sized and the aspect ratio set, press the OK button to save the image with a new file name (figure 6.5, screen 4).

Settings Recommendation: This is a very useful function for cropping images without a computer. The fact that you have multiple aspect ratios available is just icing on the cake. The D810 has some useful aspect ratios, including a square (1:1) and an HD format (16:9).

Monochrome

(User's Manual – Page 392)

The *Monochrome* function in the D810 is fun to play with and can make some nice images. Converting the images to one of the three monochrome tones is a good starting point for creative manipulation.

The three options for the Monochrome function are as follows:

- Black-and-white (grays)
- Sepia (golden tone)
- Cyanotype (blue tone)

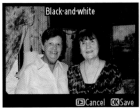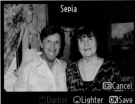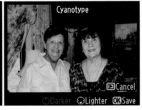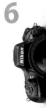

Figure 6.6A – Monochrome images

Figure 6.6A shows a sample of the three monochrome tones you can use to convert a normal color photo. I chose the Darker setting on the Sepia and Cyanotype versions to show their maximum effects. Notice in screen 1 that the Black-and-white version has no darkness or lightness setting because the D810 provides only one level. However, for Sepia and Cyanotype, you can fine-tune the tint from lightly saturated to very saturated in three levels. The Sepia and Cyanotype images in figure 6.6A are at the Darker (most saturated) maximum.

Use the following steps to create a Monochrome image from one of your color images:

1. Select Monochrome from the Retouch Menu and scroll to the right (figure 6.6B, screen 1).
2. Select a Monochrome tone—Black-and-white, Sepia, or Cyanotype (figure 6.6B, screen 2). I selected Black-and-white.
3. Select the image you want to modify (figure 6.6B, screen 3).

4. For a Black-and-white image, you cannot adjust the level of lightness or darkness. For Sepia and Cyanotype, you can use the Multi selector to saturate or desaturate the tone. Scroll up or down and watch the screen until the tint is as dark or light as you want it to be. You can cancel the operation by pressing the Playback button. Figure 6.6B, screen 4 displays the final, adjusted image.

5. Press the OK button to save the new image with a new file name. A screen that says *Image saved* will appear briefly, and then the final image will appear with a retouch icon in the top left of the Monitor (not shown).

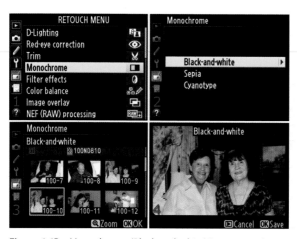

Figure 6.6B – Monochrome (Black-and-white) image creation

Settings Recommendation: I normally use the Black-and-white conversion when I need an immediate Monochrome image. However, it's a lot of fun to make the image look old-fashioned with either Sepia or Cyanotype. New Sepia-toned images can look very old if you dress people accordingly (figure 6.6C).

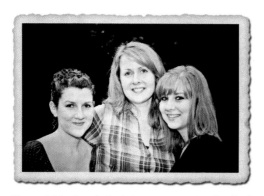

Figure 6.6C – Sample Sepia image conversion (border from Photoshop manipulation)

Filter Effects

(User's Manual – Page 393)

The D810 allows you to add various *Filter effects* to any image. You can intensify the image colors in certain ways and add starburst effects to points of light. You can even experiment with a soft filter effect for a dreamy look.

Here is a list of the effects that are available:

- Skylight
- Red intensifier
- Blue intensifier
- Soft

- Warm filter
- Green intensifier
- Cross screen (starburst filter)

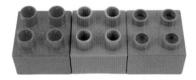

Figure 6.7A – RGB test subject: my Lego blocks again

Figure 6.7A shows a red, green, and blue (RGB) test subject. Let's use this subject to compare the changes made by each filter effect, and in the end we will look at the changes all together.

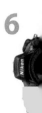

Skylight Filter Effect

The *Skylight* filter effect is rather mild and removes the blue effect caused by atmospheric diffraction in distant scenes. Basically, by using this effect you will make the image slightly less blue.

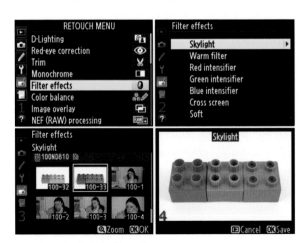

Figure 6.7B – Skylight filter effect

Use the following steps to choose the Skylight filter effect:

1. Select Filter effects from the Retouch Menu and scroll to the right (figure 6.7B, screen 1).
2. Select Skylight and scroll to the right (figure 6.7B, screen 2).
3. Choose an image and press the OK button (figure 6.7B, screen 3).
4. You will see the image with the Skylight effect added (figure 6.7B, screen 4). Press the OK button to save the image with a new file name or press the Playback button to cancel.

Warm Filter Effect

The *Warm filter* filter effect adds a mild red cast to the image to make it appear a little warmer.

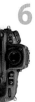

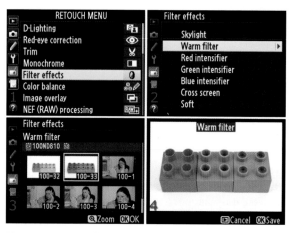

Figure 6.7C – Warm filter effect

Here's how to set the Warm filter effect:

1. Select Filter effects from the Retouch Menu and scroll to the right (figure 6.7C, screen 1).
2. Select Warm filter and scroll to the right (figure 6.7C, screen 2).
3. Choose an image and press the OK button (figure 6.7C, screen 3).
4. You will see the image with the Warm filter effect added (figure 6.7C, screen 4). Press the OK button to save the image with a new file name or press the Playback button to cancel.

Red Intensifier Filter Effect

The *Red intensifier* filter effect intensifies the reds in an image. There are three levels of intensity.

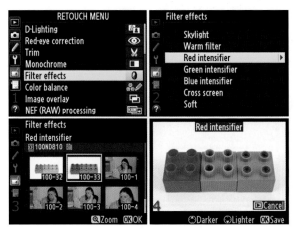

Figure 6.7D – Red intensifier filter effect

Here's how to set the Red intensifier filter effect:

1. Select Filter effects from the Retouch Menu and scroll to the right (figure 6.7D, screen 1).
2. Select Red intensifier and scroll to the right (figure 6.7D, screen 2).
3. Choose an image and press the OK button (figure 6.7D, screen 3).
4. You will see a new image with the Red intensifier effect added (figure 6.7D, screen 4). You can control the intensity of this effect by using the Multi Selector to scroll up or down when the image is on the screen. The default level of intensity is applied first. You can scroll up for the maximum effect and scroll down for the minimum effect.
5. Press the OK button to save the image with a new file name or press the Playback button to cancel.

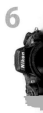

Green Intensifier Filter Effect

The *Green intensifier* filter effect intensifies the greens in an image. There are three levels of intensity.

Here's how to set the Green intensifier filter effect:

1. Select Filter effects from the Retouch Menu and scroll to the right (figure 6.7E, screen 1).
2. Select Green intensifier and scroll to the right (figure 6.7E, screen 2).

3. Choose an image and press the OK button (figure 6.7E, screen 3).

4. You will see a new image with the Green intensifier effect added (figure 6.7E, screen 4). You can control the intensity of this effect by using the Multi Selector to scroll up or down when the image is on the screen. The default level of intensity is applied first. You can scroll up for the maximum effect and scroll down for the minimum effect.

5. Press the OK button to save the image with a new file name or press the Playback button to cancel.

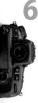

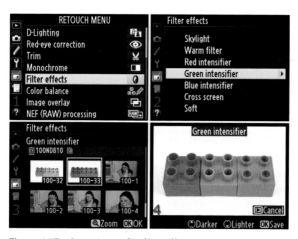

Figure 6.7E – Green intensifier filter effect

Blue Intensifier Filter Effect

The *Blue intensifier* filter effect intensifies the blues in an image. There are three levels of intensity.

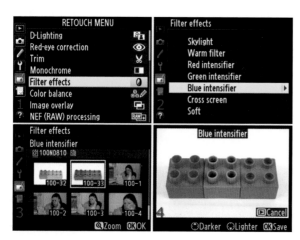

Figure 6.7F – Blue intensifier filter effect

Here's how to set the Blue intensifier effect:

1. Select Filter effects from the Retouch Menu and scroll to the right (figure 6.7F, screen 1).
2. Select Blue intensifier and scroll to the right (figure 6.7F, screen 2).
3. Choose an image and press the OK button (figure 6.7F, screen 3).
4. You will see a new image with the Blue intensifier effect added (figure 6.7F, screen 4). You can control the intensity of this effect by using the Multi Selector to scroll up or down when the image is on the screen. The default level of intensity is applied first. You can scroll up for the maximum effect and scroll down for the minimum effect.
5. Press the OK button to save the image with a new file name or press the Playback button to cancel.

Let's take a look at the filters side by side to compare their effects (figure 6.7G).

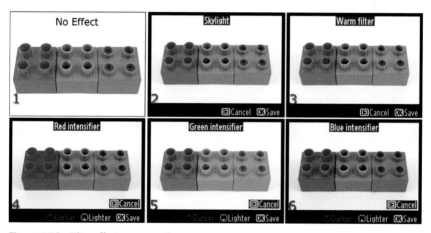
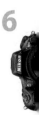

Figure 6.7G – Filter effects compared

I increased the filter effects to their maximum settings (Darker) in screens 4 through 6 to give you a better view of the effect. It can be hard to show effects like this in a book due to the subtlety of the color shift. I can say from personal observation that there is a distinct effect for each of the intensifier filters in particular. They do intensify the individual color without adding a strong cast to the overall image.

Cross Screen Filter Effect

The *Cross screen* filter effect adds a starburst to any points of light. There are four adjustments for this effect, along with Confirm and Save commands.

To create the Cross screen filter effect, use the following steps:

1. Select Filter effects from the Retouch Menu and scroll to the right (figure 6.7H, screen 1).
2. Select Cross screen and scroll to the right (figure 6.7H, screen 2).

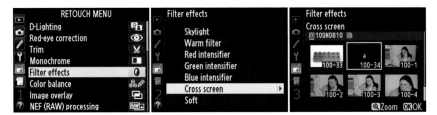

Figure 6.7H – Cross screen filter effect

3. Choose an image with the Multi selector and press the OK button to select it (figure 6.7H, screen 3).
4. Now follow steps 5 through 10. Step 5 and figure 6.7I starts where figure 6.7H, screen 3, leaves off.
5. **Note:** Through this upcoming series of Cross screen effect pictures (figures 6.7I–6.7M), you will not see a change in the appearance of the candle until the end when I apply the Confirm step. At that point, all the settings are applied and the appearance changes to its final form, ready for the Save step.
6. The first adjustment is the Number of points (4, 6, or 8) in the starburst (figure 6.7I). Scroll to the right to select the Number of points. In the image on the right, you can see that an icon with the number of rays in the starburst is provided along with a numeral. I selected 8 points. Press the OK button to lock in your selection. You will follow the same procedure for the next three adjustments, which are Filter amount, Filter angle, and Length of points.

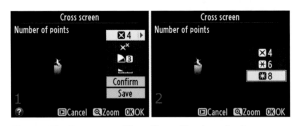

Figure 6.7I – Cross screen filter effect – Number of points

7. The second adjustment is the Filter amount (figure 6.7J). This adjustment affects the brightness of the light source(s). The more *X*s, the brighter the light source. I selected the maximum level, as you can see in screen 2.

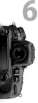

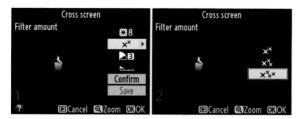

Figure 6.7J – Cross screen filter effect – Filter amount

8. Select the angle of the starburst rays with the Filter angle adjustment (figure 6.7K). You can rotate the rays in a clockwise direction until the starburst is at the angle you prefer.

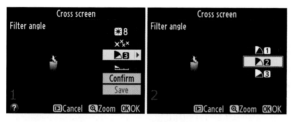

Figure 6.7K – Cross screen filter effect – Filter angle

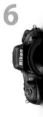

9. Select the length of the starburst rays with the Length of points adjustment (figure 6.7L). I wanted the longest rays, so I selected the bottom setting, shown in screen 2.

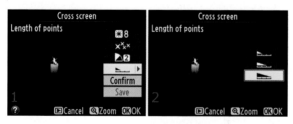

Figure 6.7L – Cross screen filter effect – Length of points

10. Select Confirm to see the effect applied to your image (figure 6.7M). This is like an update button. You can change the adjustments in steps 5 through 8 multiple times and Confirm them each time to see the updated image until you're happy with the effect. Screens 1 and 2 of figure 6.7M show the image before and after I selected Confirm.

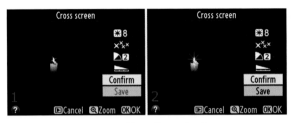

Figure 6.7M – Cross screen filter effect – Confirm

11. Select Save and press the OK button (figure 6.7N, screen 1). After a moment you'll see a screen that says *Image saved* (figure 6.7N, screen 2). Then you'll see the full-size image in normal Playback mode (figure 6.7N, screen 3). Notice the retouch icon at the top left of the image, which tells you that the image has been retouched. This is the final, fully retouched version of the image (screen 3).

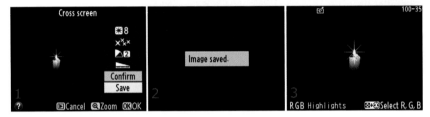

Figure 6.7N – Cross screen filter effect – Save

Soft Filter Effect

The *Soft* filter effect is designed to give your subject that dreamy look popularized by old movies, where the beautiful woman looks soft and sweet. You can select from three levels of softness: Low, Normal, and High.

Figure 6.7O shows small versions of the original image and the three softness settings. The images are in this order: 1 = Original, 2 = Low (Lo), 3 = Medium, 4 = High (Hi).

This is an interesting effect. Even though the overall image has a softness to it after the effect has been applied, the subject is still somewhat sharp. It doesn't look like the image is soft because it's not in focus or the camera moved. It's like a softness has been overlaid on the image, and the original image is still sharp. You'll have to see this misty look in a full-size image to see what I mean.

Use the following steps to select one of the Soft filter levels for your image:

1. Select Filter effects from the Retouch Menu and scroll to the right (figure 6.7P, screen 1).
2. Choose Soft from the menu and scroll to the right (figure 6.7P, screen 2).

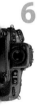

3. Select the image to which you want to apply the Soft filter effect and press the OK button (figure 6.7P, screen 3).

4. You'll see the word Effect surrounded by yellow (figure 6.7P, screen 4). Use the Multi selector to scroll left or right and select one of the softness levels (Lo to Hi). The small image on the left is the original image, and the one on the right has been adjusted using the medium setting. You can easily see the softness vary as you select different levels.

5. Press the OK button to save the new image and display it on the Monitor.

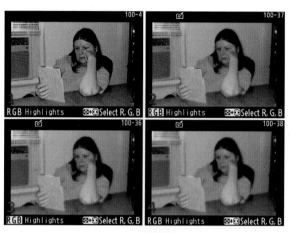

Figure 6.7O – Soft filter effect samples

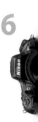

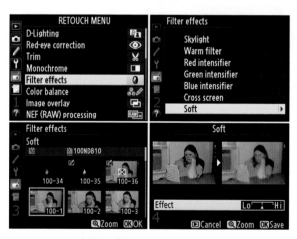

Figure 6.7P – Soft filter effect settings

Settings Recommendation: In comparing the levels of softness, I tend to like the medium setting best. Low looks like I made a mistake, and High is too soft. Compare the three levels and see which works best for you.

Color Balance
(User's Manual – Page 394)

Color balance lets you deliberately add various tones to your pictures. You can visually add a mild or strong color cast. You might want to warm things up a bit by adding a touch of red or cool things down with a touch of blue. Or you could get creative and add various color casts to an image for special effects.

You can tone the image with the following color casts:

- Green
- Blue
- Amber
- Magenta

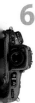

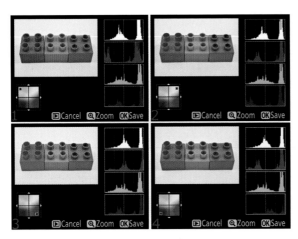

Figure 6.8A – Color balance samples

Figure 6.8A shows four samples of the colors used for tinting. Notice the red arrow in screen 1 that points to the color box. You move the little black square around in the color box to add tints to the image. In screens 1 though 4 you can see that I moved the tiny black square into different areas of the color box. The small picture above the color box shows how the final image will look. You can return the square to the center of the color box to neutralize any tints.

On the right side of each screen you can see the RGB histograms for the image. As you make color changes, you will see the color shift in the histograms. Be careful not to over- or underexpose any of the colors (clip them off on the right or left) or you will lose detail in that particular color channel (R, G, or B). We'll discuss the histogram in more detail in the chapter **Metering, Exposure Modes, and Histogram**.

Use the following steps to modify the Color balance in your image:

1. Select Color balance from the Retouch Menu and scroll to the right (figure 6.8B, screen 1).
2. Select the image you want to modify and press the OK button (figure 6.8B, screen 2).

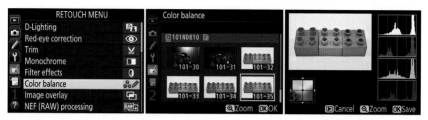

Figure 6.8B – Color balance settings

3. Use the Multi selector to move the black indicator square in the center of the color box toward whatever color makes you happy (figure 6.8B, screen 3). Watch the histograms as they display the changing color relationships between the red, green, and blue color channels. You can see the color changes or casts as they are applied to the small version of your image in the upper-left corner of the screen (screen 3).
4. Press the Playback button to cancel or the OK button to save the image with a new file name (figure 6.8B, screen 4).

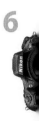

Note: If you zoom in with the Playback zoom in button, the camera will update the histogram to reflect only what can be seen on the Monitor. This is a nice way to get a histogram for only a portion of your subject.

Settings Recommendation: This is a cool function for persnickety people, and I'm one of them! If you like to fine-tune the color of your pictures—but hate using the computer—here's your control. You can introduce almost any color tint into the image by moving the black square in any direction within the color box, using combinations of colors to arrive at one that pleases you. This also allows you to overcome current color casts caused by various lighting-source color temperatures. Very flexible camera, eh?

Image Overlay

(User's Manual – Page 395)

The *Image overlay* function is a nice way to combine two RAW images as if they were taken as a multiple exposure. Basically, you can select a couple of NEF (RAW) shots and combine them into a new overlaid image.

The results can be a lot like what you get when using *Shooting Menu > Multiple exposure*, but Image overlay gives you a visual way to overlay two separate images instead of shooting multiple exposures on one picture.

The results can be high quality because the overlay is done using RAW image data. You can vary the density of each image, with a review display (overlay) showing how the combined image will appear, before you make the final combination of the two images.

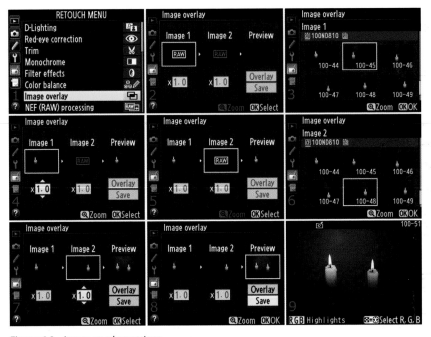

Figure 6.9 – Image overlay settings

Use the following steps to do an Image overlay:

1. Select Image overlay from the Retouch Menu and scroll to the right (figure 6.9, screen 1).
2. Select the RAW Image 1 box (outlined in yellow in figure 6.9, screen 2) from the combination screen and press the OK button to open the selection screen.
3. Select an image from the selection screen (figure 6.9, screen 3). Press the OK button again to return to the combination screen with an image selected in the Image 1 position (figure 6.9, screen 4). You can vary the gain of the first image by using the Multi selector to scroll up or down in the X1.0 field (figure 6.9, screen 4). The X1.0 setting is variable from X0.1 to X2.0. It lets you control how bright or dark (dense) an image is so it can more closely match the density of the other image in the overlay. X1.0 is normal image density, as shown.
4. Use the Multi selector to move the yellow box to the RAW Image 2 position (figure 6.9, screen 5). Press the OK button again and select the second picture from the image selection screen (figure 6.9, screen 6).

5. Press the OK button to insert the image into the Image 2 position (figure 6.9, screen 7). As mentioned in step 3, you can use the X1.0 field to vary the density of an image, in this case the second image in the overlay (figure 6.9, screen 7). Try to match the density of Image 1 as much as possible to provide a realistic overlay.

6. Use the Multi selector to move the yellow box to the Preview area. You will see two selections below it: Overlay and Save. Choose one of them and press the OK button (figure 6.9, screen 8).

   a. If you select Overlay, the D810 will temporarily combine the images and you will see another screen that displays a larger view of the new image (not shown). You can press the OK button to save the image with a new file name, or you can press the checkered Thumbnail/Playback zoom out button to return to the previous screen.

   b. If you choose Save instead of Overlay and press the OK button, the D810 immediately combines the two images and saves the image with a new file name without letting you review the image first. Basically, the Save selection saves now, and Overlay gives you a preview of the combination so you can modify or save it.

Settings Recommendation: This is an easy way to overlay images without a computer. There are some drawbacks, though. One image may have a strong background that is impossible to remove no matter how much you adjust the gain or image density (X0.1 to X2.0). This is a situation in which a computer excels because you can use software tools like masking in Photoshop to remove parts of the background and make a more realistic overlay. However, if you must combine two images in the field, you have a way to do it in-camera.

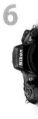

NEF (RAW) Processing

(User's Manual – Page 399)

NEF (RAW) processing is a function that allows you to convert a RAW image into a JPEG inside the camera. If you normally shoot in RAW but need a JPEG quickly, this is a great function. It works only on images taken with the D810, so you can't insert a card from a different Nikon and expect to process its images.

There is quite a comprehensive catalog of things you can do to an image during NEF (RAW) processing. A RAW file is not yet an image, so the camera settings you used when you took the picture are not permanently applied. In effect, when you use NEF (RAW) processing, you are applying camera settings to the JPEG image after the fact, and you can change the settings you used when you originally took the picture.

You can apply settings just before you take a picture through the Shooting Menu or by using external camera controls. However, with NEF (RAW) processing, the settings are applied to the image after the fact instead of while shooting. See the chapter titled **Shooting Menu** for a thorough explanation of each setting.

Here's a list of post-shooting adjustments you can make with NEF (RAW) processing, with basic explanations of each function:

- *EXE* – This simply means execute. When you select this and press the OK button, all your new settings will be applied to a new JPEG image, and it will be saved to the memory card with a separate file name.
- *Image quality* – With NEF (RAW) processing, you are converting a RAW file to a JPEG file, so the camera gives you a choice of FINE, NORM, or BASIC. These are equivalent to the *Shooting Menu > Image quality* settings called JPEG fine, JPEG normal, or JPEG basic.
- *Image size* – This lets you select how large the JPEG file will be. Your choices are L, M, or S, which are equivalent to the Large (36.2 megapixels), Medium (20.3 megapixels), and Small (9.0 megapixels) *Shooting Menu > Image size* settings.
- *White balance* – This lets you change the White balance of the image after you have already taken the image. You can select from a series of symbols that represent various types of White balance color temperatures. As you scroll up or down in the list of symbols, notice that the name of the corresponding White balance type appears just above the small picture. You can see the effect of each setting as it is applied.

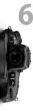

- *Exposure compensation* – This function allows you to brighten or darken the image by applying -/+ Exposure compensation to it. You can apply compensation up to 2 EV in either direction (+2.0 to -2.0 EV).
- *Picture control* – With this setting you can apply a different Picture Control than the one with which you took the image. It shows abbreviations for each Nikon Picture Control (SD, NL, VI, MC, PT, or LS) plus any Custom Picture Controls you might have created with the designations of C-1, C-2, C-3, and so forth.
- *High ISO NR* – You can change the amount of High ISO noise reduction applied to the image. The camera offers you H, N, L, and Off settings, which are equivalent to the *Shooting Menu > High ISO NR* settings called High, Normal, Low, and Off.
- *Color space* – You can change which Color space is applied to the image. You can choose from the camera's two Color space settings, sRGB or Adobe RGB. Adobe RGB is abbreviated as Adobe in this setting. This is equivalent to the *Shooting Menu > Color space* setting.
- *Vignette control* – This allows you to reduce the light falloff on the corners and edges of the frame, common when using a full-frame sensor with certain lenses. You have four choices: Off, Low (L), Normal (N), and High (H).
- *D-Lighting* – This lets you manage the level of contrast in the image by brightening the shadows and protecting the highlights. You have four choices: Off, Low (L), Normal (N), and High (H).

Now, let's look at the steps you can use to convert a file from NEF (RAW) to JPEG in-camera (figures 6.10A–6.10N):

1. Select NEF (RAW) processing from the Retouch Menu and scroll to the right (figure 6.10A, screen 1).
2. Select a RAW image with the Multi selector and press the OK button (figure 6.10A, screen 2). Only NEF (RAW) images will show in the list. Now we'll look at each setting shown in figure 6.10A, screen 3. The following steps and figures (6.10B to 6.10N) begin where figure 6.10A, screen 3 leaves off.

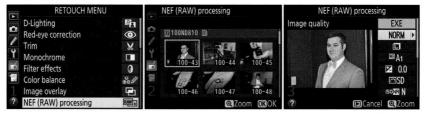

Figure 6.10A – NEF (RAW) processing

3. Select one of the Image quality settings—FINE, NORM, or BASIC—from the Image quality menu (figure 6.10B, screen 2). FINE gives you the best possible quality in a JPEG image. Press the OK button to save the setting and return to the main NEF (RAW) processing configuration screen. You can cancel the operation with the Playback button. You can zoom in to check the image quality with the Playback zoom in button.

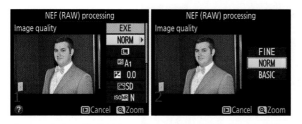

Figure 6.10B – NEF (RAW) processing – Image quality

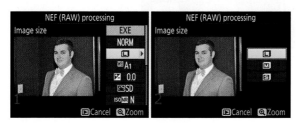

Figure 6.10C – NEF (RAW) processing – Image size

4. Select one of the Image size settings from the Image size menu (figure 6.10C, screen 2):

- L – Large (7360×4912; 36.2 MP)
- M – Medium (5520×3680; 20.3 MP)
- S – Small (3680×2456; 9.0 MP)

When you've selected a setting, press the OK button to return to the main NEF (RAW) processing configuration screen. You can cancel the operation with the Playback button or zoom in to check the image quality with the Playback zoom in button.

5. Select one of the White balance settings for your new JPEG (figures 6.10D to 6.10G). You can choose from AUTO, Incandescent, Fluorescent, Direct sunlight, Flash, Cloudy, Shade, K - Choose color temp., or PRE - Preset manual. Please review the chapter titled **White Balance** for detailed information on each of these selections. The Auto (A1 or A2), Fluorescent, K, and PRE settings have additional screens with choices you must select. A1 (Auto 1) is selected in this example (figure 6.10D, screens 2 and 3). We won't consider how to select each individual White balance setting because they work basically the same way. However, because Auto (A1 or A2), Fluorescent, K, and PRE are different, we will look at each of those settings individually (they each have extra screens). A1 is the normal auto setting, while A2 is designed for warm lighting (somewhat warmer pictures).

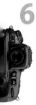

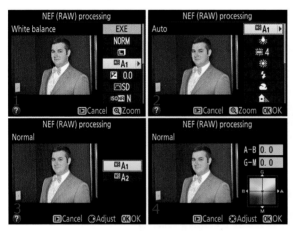

Figure 6.10D – NEF (RAW) processing – White balance

a. **Fluorescent** – You must choose a type of fluorescent light. There are seven choices, with names like Sodium-vapor lamps, Warm-white fluorescent, Cool-white fluorescent, etc. Each choice has a number assigned to it. Figure 6.10E, screen 3, shows Cool-white fluorescent, which is number 4 on the list. Scroll to the right to move to the fine-tuning screen, where you can adjust the color tint of the image by moving the black dot in the color box (figure 6.10E, screen 4). Press the OK button to save the setting, or press the Playback button to cancel.

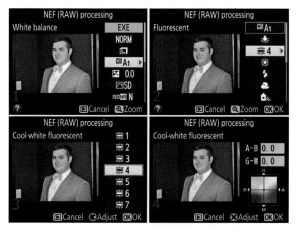
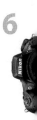

Figure 6.10E – NEF (RAW) processing – White balance – Fluorescent

b. **K - Choose color temp.** – You can choose a color temperature from the list shown in figure 6.10F, screen 3. Remember that color temperatures change how the image color looks by warming it (reddish) or cooling it (bluish). The list ranges from 2500K (cool) to 10000K (warm). You can also use the fine-tuning screen to modify the color's base, if you'd like (figure 6.10F, screen 4). Press the OK button to save the setting or the Playback button to cancel.

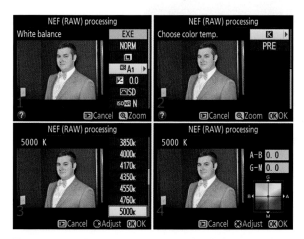

Figure 6.10F – NEF (RAW) processing – White balance – K-Choose color temp.

c. ***PRE - Preset manual*** – With this setting you can choose an already-saved White balance that you previously obtained while letting the camera measure the ambient light reflected from a gray or white card (the PRE method). See the chapter titled **White Balance** for information on doing ambient light (PRE) readings. You can choose from up to six previous PRE readings that are stored in memory locations d-1 to d-6 (figure 6.10G, screen 3). As you scroll through the list of settings, you'll be able to see the color temperature of the image change. Select the setting you want to use and press the OK button to return to the main NEF (RAW) processing configuration screen. You can fine-tune the colors of the individual White balance by using the settings shown in figure 6.10G, screen 4. You'll see your fine-tuning adjustment change the color temperature of the image. If you don't want to fine-tune the White balance, simply press the OK button when you get to the fine-tuning screen. The camera will return to the main NEF (RAW) processing configuration screen. You can cancel the operation with the Playback button.

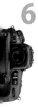
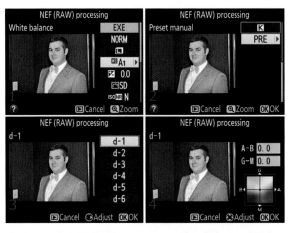

Figure 6.10G – NEF (RAW) processing – White balance – PRE-Preset manual

6. Now you have an opportunity to lighten or darken the image by selecting an Exposure compensation value of +/- 2.0 EV steps (figure 6.10H, screen 2). In screen 1 of figure 6.10H, you can see that the image is a little overexposed. In screen 2, you can see that I removed one stop of light (-1.0 EV). The image looks about right at that setting. When your image looks just right, press the OK button to save the setting and return to the main NEF (RAW) processing configuration screen. You can cancel the operation with the Playback button.

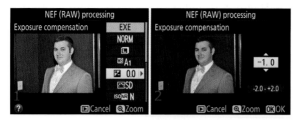

Figure 6.10H – NEF (RAW) processing – Exposure compensation

7. Next, you can apply a Nikon Picture Control or one of your own Custom Picture Controls, if you have created any (figure 6.10I, screen 2). You can make the image sharper and give it more contrast, give it more or less color saturation, or even change it to monochrome. In fact, you can even modify the current Picture Control's settings by using the fine-tuning screen (figure 6.10I, screen 3). Choose from SD-Standard, NL-Neutral, VI-Vivid, MC-Monochrome, PT-Portrait, LS-Landscape, FL-Flat, or any of your custom controls (C-1 to C-9) that appear farther down the list than this screen shot shows (figure 6.10I, screen 2).

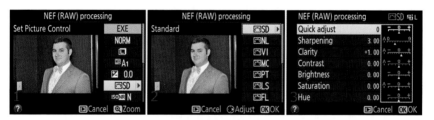
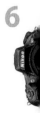

Figure 6.10I – NEF (RAW) processing – Picture Control

8. You can scroll to the right with the Multi selector if you want to fine-tune the image (figure 6.10I, screen 3). Scroll up or down to select one of the settings— Sharpening, Contrast, Brightness, and so forth—and then scroll left or right (-/+) to modify the selected setting. If you make a mistake and want to start over, press the Delete button and the camera will display a screen that says *Selected Picture Control will be reset to default settings. OK?* Choose Yes or No and press the OK button. When a Picture Control is adjusted so that it's different from the factory default, an asterisk will appear next to its name in all menus. The Monochrome (MC) Picture Control not only lets you adjust things like Sharpening, Contrast, and Brightness in the fine-tuning screen, it also gives you toning (tint) controls like the *Shooting Menu > Set Picture Control* function.

9. When the image looks just right, press the OK button to save the setting and return to the main NEF (RAW) processing configuration screen. You can cancel the operation with the Playback button.

10. If the image needs high ISO noise reduction, you can apply it now (figure 6.10J, screen 1). You have a choice of four settings: High (H), Normal (N), Low (L), or Off (figure 6.10J, screen 2). Choose one and press the OK button to save the setting and return to the main NEF (RAW) processing configuration screen. You can cancel the operation with the Playback button.

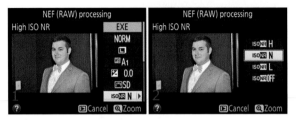

Figure 6.10J – NEF (RAW) processing – High ISO NR

11. Color space lets you choose one of the camera's two color space settings, sRGB or AdobeRGB (figure 6.10K, screen 2). Choose one and press the OK button to save the setting and return to the main NEF (RAW) processing configuration screen. You can cancel the operation with the Playback button. As a comparative test, why not look carefully at your picture while you switch back and forth between sRGB and AdobeRGB. You will find that AdobeRGB has a smoother look when your subject has a good range of colors. AdobeRGB has a wider color gamut and is best for commercial printing, whereas sRGB may do better with computer and Internet display and home printing on basic inkjet printers.

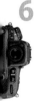

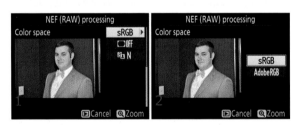

Figure 6.10K – NEF (RAW) processing – Color space

12. Vignette control lets you choose a level for edge and corner light falloff correction (figure 6.10L, screen 2), as is sometimes needed on an FX-sized imaging sensor with certain lenses. You have a choice of four settings: High (H), Normal (N), Low (L), or Off. Choose one and press the OK button to save the setting and return to the main NEF (RAW) processing configuration screen. You can cancel the operation with the Playback button.

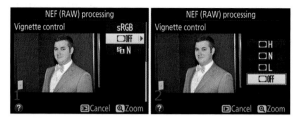

Figure 6.10L – NEF (RAW) processing – Vignette control

13. D-lighting (figure 6.10M) is very similar to *Shooting Menu > Active D-Lighting* in that it restores shadow detail and protects highlights in your images. However, D-Lighting is applied after the fact. Active D-Lighting is applied at the time the image is taken. Otherwise, they are basically the same thing. You can select from high (H), normal (N), low (L), or Off (figure 6.10M, screen 2). Press the OK button to set the D-Lighting level, or press the Playback button to cancel.

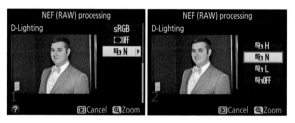

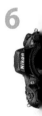

Figure 6.10M – NEF (RAW) processing – D-Lighting

14. When you are finished with NEF (RAW) processing, scroll down to the EXE (execute) selection and press the OK button (figure 6.10N, screen 1). An hourglass will appear for a few seconds while the new JPEG is being created with your carefully crafted settings. An *Image saved* screen will appear briefly (figure 6.10N, screen 2), indicating that the new JPEG has been saved on the memory card with a new file name, and the image will be displayed on the Monitor (figure 6.10N, screen 3). You can cancel the operation with the Playback button.

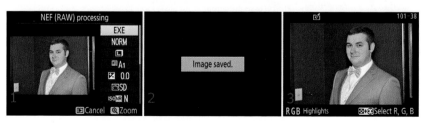

Figure 6.10N – NEF (RAW) processing – EXE

This is a nice way to create specialized JPEG images from NEF (RAW) files without using a computer. How much longer will it be until our cameras come with keyboard, monitor, and mouse ports? They are powerful graphics processing computers after all! (Hmmm, Minecraft on a 3.2-inch Monitor wouldn't be too bad.)

Settings Recommendation: NEF (RAW) processing is a complex, multistep process because you're doing a major conversion from NEF (RAW) to JPEG in-camera, without using your computer. You're in complete control of each level of the conversion and can even replace the camera settings you originally used when you took the picture. If you want to simply convert the image without going through all these steps, just choose the EXE selection first and press the OK button. That will convert the image immediately with the camera settings you used to take the picture.

Resize

(User's Manual – Page 401)

The *Resize* function allows you to convert an image from a full-size 36.2M (7360×4912) picture to a smaller one, with four available megapixel sizes. This function seems to be designed so you can create images that can easily be e-mailed or used on a website or blog. There are three selections:

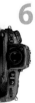

- **Select image** – This selection allows you to choose one or more images for resizing.
- **Choose destination** – This selection allows you to choose a destination for the resized pictures.
- **Choose size** – You can choose from four image sizes:
- 1920×1280; 2.5M
- 1280×856; 1.1M
- 960×640; 0.6M
- 640×424; 0.3M

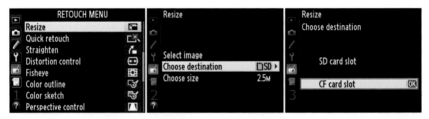

Figure 6.11A – Resize – Choose destination

Let's examine the steps for resizing images (figure 6.11A):

1. Select Resize from the Retouch Menu and scroll to the right (figure 6.11A, screen 1). Although it seems out of order, select Choose destination and scroll to the right (figure 6. 11A, screen 2). Select either SD card slot or CF card slot to be a destination for the resized images and press the OK button (figure 6.11A, screen 3). This selection will be grayed out if one of the memory card slots is empty. In that case, the destination will be the single card slot that contains a card. Skip this step if you are using only one memory card.

2. Next, select Choose size and scroll to the right (figure 6.11B, screen 2). You will see four sizes, from 2.5M to 0.3M (figure 6.11B, screen 3). These are the actual megapixel sizes available for images after you save them. Select a size and press the OK button.

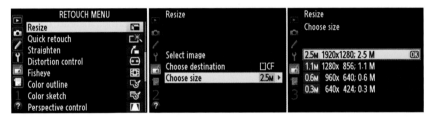

Figure 6.11B – Resize – Choose size

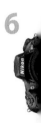

3. Next, choose Select image and scroll to the right (figure 6.11C, screen 2). You'll see six image thumbnails. Use the Multi selector to scroll around in this group of thumbnails and press the Multi selector center button to select an image you want to resize. You can select as many images as you'd like, and each of them will be resized. A tiny resize symbol will appear in the top-right corner of each thumbnail you select (figure 6.11C, screen 3, red arrow).

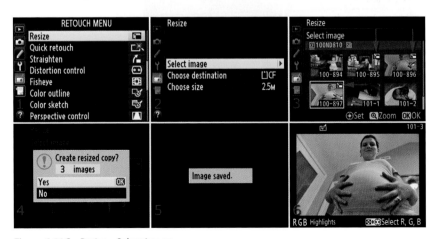

Figure 6.11C – Resize – Select image

4. When you have selected the images, press the OK button. A screen will appear with a message asking, *Create resized copy? N images* (figure 6.11C, screen 4). Select Yes and press the OK button to create the resized images. An hourglass will be displayed on the Monitor while the images are resized, and then an *Image saved* screen will briefly appear (figure 6.11C, screen 5). The last image in the group of resized images will appear on the Monitor (figure 6.11C, screen 6). The resized images will look just like the originals except they'll each have a retouch icon in the top-left corner (figure 6.11C, screen 6).

Settings Recommendation: I use this function when I'm in the field and want to make a small image to send via e-mail. The full-size JPEG file is too large to send through some e-mail systems. It's nice to have a way to reduce image size without having to find a computer. Please notice that this function does not reduce the image size by cropping, like the Trim function we studied earlier. Instead, it simply reduces the image size in the same aspect ratio as the original, except it has fewer megapixels.

Quick Retouch

(User's Manual – Page 404)

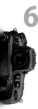

If you want to adjust an image without much effort so that all parameters are within viewable range, use the *Quick retouch* function. It creates a new copy of an existing image with "enhanced saturation and contrast," according to the User's Manual. D-Lighting is automatically applied to your old image, and the new image is supposed to look better. You can scroll up and down in the preview screen to see the range of enhancements that can be applied when the new image is created.

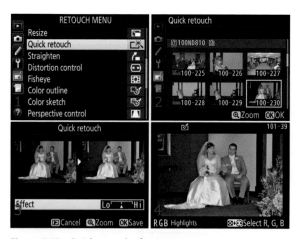

Figure 6.12 – Quick retouch of an image

Here are the steps to use Quick retouch:

1. Select Quick retouch from the Retouch Menu and scroll to the right (figure 6.12, screen 1).
2. You'll see the images on your memory card(s) that are eligible for Quick retouch. Use the Multi selector to scroll to an image you want to retouch, and press the OK button to select it (figure 6.12, screen 2).
3. Use the Multi selector to scroll up or down, and then move the slider between Lo and Hi (figure 6.12, screen 3). You can preview the effect of your changes on the image by looking at the before and after images. I chose a medium setting.
4. Press the OK button when you're satisfied with the look. The new image will be created and displayed on the Monitor (figure 6.12, screen 4).

Settings Recommendation: This function can give some images a little more snap. I use Quick retouch only if I am going to give someone an image directly out of the camera and want to enhance it a little first. This function can be used for quick saturation and contrast enhancements.

Straighten

(User's Manual – Page 404)

Straighten is another excellent and useful function. Often, I'll be shooting a landscape or ocean view handheld, and in my excitement I'll forget to level the horizon. With Straighten I can adjust the image to level before anyone else sees it.

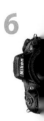

You can rotate an image up to 5 degrees clockwise or counterclockwise. You use the Multi selector to scroll right or left through a graduated scale line. Each increment is equal to about 0.25 degrees. As you rotate the image, the camera will automatically trim the edges so that the picture looks normal. Of course, this means you are throwing away some of the image and making it smaller. However, it's better for the image to be a little smaller and have a nice level horizon, don't you think?

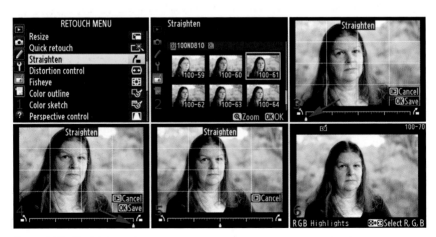

Figure 6.13 – Straighten an image

Here are the steps to straighten an image:

1. Select Straighten from the Retouch Menu and scroll to the right (figure 6.13, screen 1).
2. You'll see the images on your memory card(s). Use the Multi selector to scroll to the one you want to straighten and press the OK button to select it (figure 6.13, screen 2).
3. Now, rotate the image to the left (counterclockwise) or right (clockwise) in 0.25 degree increments using the Multi selector. The little yellow pointer moves as you press the Multi selector to the left or right (figure 6.13, screens 3 and 4, red arrows).
4. When you are happy with the new image, press the OK button to save it or the Playback button to cancel (figure 6.13, screen 5).
5. An *Image saved* screen will briefly appear between screens 5 and 6 (not shown).
6. Finally, you will see the newly saved image on the Monitor (figure 6.13, screen 6).

Settings Recommendation: This is a handy function to level an image—as long as it is not tilted more than 5 degrees—without using a computer. Some of us tend to tilt our cameras just a little when we take pictures. Use this function to save embarrassment later.

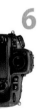

Distortion Control

(User's Manual – Page 405)

The *Distortion control* function is a companion to the Straighten function. Whereas the Straighten function is concerned with leveling the image left to right, the Distortion control function is concerned with barrel and pincushion distortion. Barrel distortion causes the edges of a subject to bow outward, like a barrel. Pincushion distortion is the opposite: the edges bow inward, like an hourglass. Using this control will remove some of the edge of the image as distortion compensation takes place. There are two settings in the Distortion control function: Auto and Manual.

Auto Distortion Control

You can use this setting only if you have a D or G lens on your D810. Select Auto when you want the camera to automatically make rough distortion adjustments. Then you can fine-tune the adjustments yourself if you think the new image needs it.

Here are the steps to let the camera make an Auto distortion adjustment:

1. Select Distortion control from the Retouch Menu and scroll to the right (figure 6.14A, screen 1).
2. Choose Auto from the menu to let the camera make automatic distortion adjustments (figure 6.14A, screen 2).

3. Next you'll see the images on your memory card. Use the Multi selector to select the one you want to fix and press the OK button (figure 6.14A, screen 3).

4. The camera will automatically make its best adjustment and then display the adjusted image (figure 6.14A, screen 4). The red arrow in screen 4 points to the yellow adjustment pointer, which will be centered. If you are not satisfied with the camera's Auto adjustment, use the Multi selector to move the yellow pointer along the scale to the left to remove pincushion distortion (add barrel) or to the right to remove barrel distortion (add pincushion). Screens 5 and 6 in Figure 6.14A show the maximum settings (red arrows).

5. When you are happy with the appearance of the image, press the OK button to save it or the Playback button to cancel (not shown).

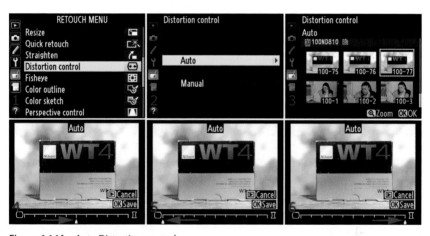
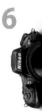

Figure 6.14A – Auto Distortion control

The effect is not easy to see in these small images or on the Monitor of the camera. However, if you look closely at figure 6.14A, screen 5, and compare it to screen 6, you can see a slight difference. Greater adjustments should be made on a computer with full-sized images.

Manual distortion adjustments work the same way, except the camera does not make an Auto adjustment before displaying an image that you can manually adjust.

Manual Distortion Control

You are in control of this operation. You can adjust the image until you think it looks good, without interference from the camera. It makes no initial distortion adjustment as Auto does.

Here are the steps to manually correct distortion:

1. Select Distortion control from the Retouch Menu and scroll to the right (figure 6.14B, screen 1).

2. Choose Manual from the menu and scroll to the right (figure 6.14B, screen 2).

3. You'll see the images on your memory card. Use the Multi selector to scroll to the one you want to fix and press the OK button (figure 6.14B, screen 3). You can zoom in to check the image with the Playback zoom in button.

4. The image will be displayed with the yellow pointer centered under the scale (figure 6.14B, screen 4, red arrow). No adjustment has been made at this point. Move the yellow pointer along the scale to the left to remove pincushion distortion (add barrel) or to the right to remove barrel distortion (add pincushion). Full barrel distortion correction is applied in figure 6.14B, screen 5 (red arrow). As with the Auto distortion adjustment, the Manual distortion adjustment is rather minor.

5. When you are happy with the appearance of the image, press the OK button to save it or the Playback button to cancel. You'll see the new adjusted image on the Monitor.

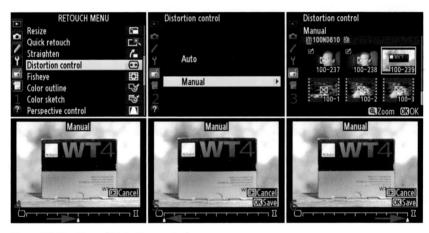

Figure 6.14B – Manual Distortion control

Settings Recommendation: This function is only somewhat useful because it does not allow for larger corrections. However, it does allow minor distortion correction for images with just a little distortion. If you have no computer available and need to use an image with a touch of distortion quickly, this function may be helpful.

Fisheye

(User's Manual – Page 406)

The *Fisheye* function is quite fun! You can distort your friends and make hilarious pictures that will make everyone laugh (well, maybe not everyone). Although the results are not true circular fisheye images, they do have a similar distorted appearance.

Figure 6.15A shows a few samples of the Fisheye setting. Notice the small yellow pointer at the bottom under the scale. When it's all the way to the left, the image appears normal. The farther right you move it, the more distorted the image.

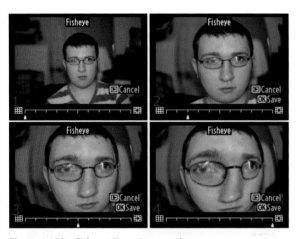

Figure 6.15A – Fisheye distortion samples

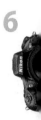

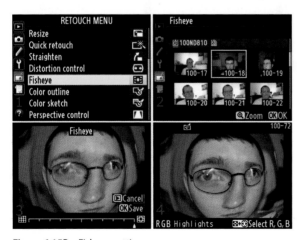

Figure 6.15B – Fisheye settings

Here are the steps to use Fisheye to distort one of your images:

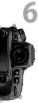

1. Select Fisheye from the Retouch Menu and scroll to the right (figure 6.15B, screen 1).
2. You'll see the images on your camera's memory card(s). Scroll to the one you want to distort and press the OK button to select it (figure 6.15B, screen 2).
3. Now press the Multi selector to the right and watch the yellow pointer move and the distortion grow (figure 6.15B, screen 3).
4. When you have found the perfect distortion amount (to the max, right?), simply press the OK button to save the image or the Playback button to cancel (figure 6.15B, screen 4).

Settings Recommendation: Be careful with this one! If you publish many pictures of your friends with this effect, I'm afraid they'll start running when they see you with your camera.

Color Outline

(User's Manual – Page 406)

Have you ever wanted to convert one of your images to a cartoon or a line drawing? This retouch setting creates an interesting outline effect on the distinct lines or color changes in your image. Figure 6.16A shows an original image and the image after Color outline was applied. The final image is not actually in color; it is black-and-white to allow an artist to fill (computer), draw (colored pencils and crayons), or paint (oil and watercolor) a print's colors.

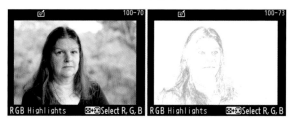

Figure 6.16A – Color outline sample

You can convert an image to a color outline, open it in Photoshop, and use the fill functions to add cartoon colors between the lines (like the Color sketch function, coming up next). Or you can post-process the image into a fine-art line tracing. This is an unusual functionality and shows the direction that our highly computerized cameras are going. They have computer power built in, so why not make use of it in new and fun ways?

Notice in figure 6.16A that the camera did not pick up the background. This is because the background is blurred from my using a large aperture. There are no strong edges in the background for an outline to be applied to. From this you can see that if you want to eliminate the background in your image, you can use a large aperture or telephoto lens to blur the background and the camera will ignore it.

Here are the steps to create a Color outline:

1. Choose Color outline from the Retouch Menu and scroll to the right (figure 6.16B, screen 1).
2. Select an image from the list of thumbnails. You can either press the OK button to start the conversion to outline form or press the Playback zoom in button to check the image (figure 6.16B, screen 2). If you press the OK button, you will see an hourglass for a few seconds while the image is converted.
3. After conversion, press the OK button to save the new image or the Playback button to cancel (figure 6.16B, screen 3). The new image will appear on the Monitor (figure 6.16B, screen 4).

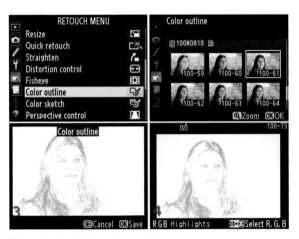
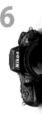

Figure 6.16B – Color outline settings

Settings Recommendation: The Color outline setting gives you the opportunity to be creative and have some fun with your images. It creates a very sparse image that resembles a line drawing. You could use this as a basis for a painting, hand coloring, or just to have a cool-looking image that most cameras won't make.

Color Sketch

(User's Manual – Page 407)

With the *Color sketch* function, you can create a copy of your image that looks (somewhat) like a sketch made with colored pencils or crayons. This function is similar to Color outline except it uses pastel colors instead of a gray scale. Figure 6.17A shows an image before and after Color sketch was applied.

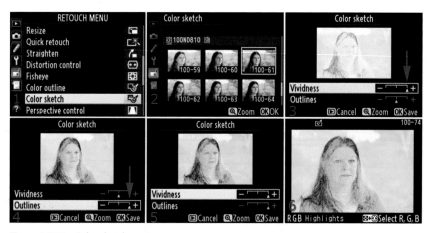

Figure 6.17A – Color sketch sample

You can convert an image to a Color sketch and change the Vividness (pastel color saturation) and Outlines (line and color contrast) until you get the look you want. The converted image in figure 6.17A uses both settings set to maximum.

Figure 6.17B – Color sketch settings

Use the following steps to create a Color sketch:

1. Choose Color sketch from the Retouch Menu (figure 6.17B, screen 1).
2. Select an image and press the OK button (figure 6.17B, screen 2).
3. You can now set the Vividness, or color saturation, of the pastel colors (figure 6.17B, screen 3).
4. Next, you will choose an Outlines setting, which will change the contrast of the lines and colors (figure 6.17B, screen 4).
5. I set both Vividness and Outlines to the plus side, or maximum (figure 6.17B, screen 5). Press the OK button to make the new image or press the Playback button to cancel.
6. You will see an *Image saved* screen between screens 5 and 6 (not shown), and then the new image will appear on the Monitor (figure 6.17B, screen 6).

Settings Recommendation: Like Color outline, the Color sketch function lets you play around with the post-processing computer in your camera. Occasionally, I like to play with these functions. Are they really useful? Well, I guess it depends on how often you need a Color outline or Color sketch. Maybe you have a great use for them in mind?

Perspective Control

(User's Manual – Page 408)

When you use a wide-angle lens to take a picture from the base of a tall object, like a building, the object will look like it is falling over backward. You can correct the problem with large-format view cameras using their rise, fall, shift, tilt, and swing controls. Nikon makes perspective-control lenses that perform some of the functions of a view camera, namely tilt and shift—for a significant investment, of course.

Nikon has given D810 users some image correction capability with the Straighten, Distortion control, and *Perspective control* functions. We discussed the first two earlier in this chapter. Now let's see how to use Perspective control.

Perspective control allows you to stretch the left, right, top, or bottom of an image in a way that tends to twist leaning objects so they appear straighter in the corrected image. Figure 6.18A, screen 3, shows yellow pointers and their indicators (identified by the red arrows). You can move these pointers to change the perspective of the image by tilting the top toward or away from you or rotating the image to the left or right. This is a powerful control because it can help give certain images a much better perspective.

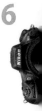

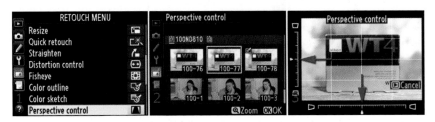

Figure 6.18A – Adjusting an image with Perspective control

Use the following steps to configure Perspective control:

1. Select Perspective control from the Retouch Menu and scroll to the right (figure 6.18A, screen 1).
2. Choose an image from the list of thumbnails and press the OK button (figure 6.18A, screen 2).
3. You will see gridlines for edge comparison and two slider controls that are operated by the Multi selector (figure 6.18A, screen 3). Move the yellow pointer on the vertical scale up or down to tilt the top of the image toward you or away

from you. Slide the yellow pointer on the horizontal scale to the left or right to turn the left or right edge toward you or away from you.

4. When the image looks the way you want it, press the OK button to save the image or the Playback button to cancel.

Figure 6.18B shows what happens to the image when you use the vertical slider on the left side. Notice how the top of the subject leans either toward you or away from you (forward-to-backward tilt) according to how the vertical slider is positioned.

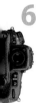

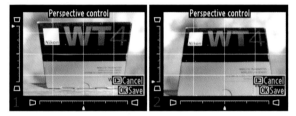

Figure 6.18B – Tilting the top of the image

Figure 6.18C shows how the image swings to the left or right as you move the horizontal slider on the bottom. Can you see how powerful this functionality is to control perspective? The camera automatically crops off the top and bottom of the stretched ends to keep the image looking like a normal rectangle, so the final image will be smaller.

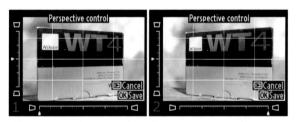

Figure 6.18C – Rotating the sides of the image

Settings Recommendation: Learn to use this rather powerful function! You now have excellent Perspective control, with no additional lens purchases! Add Straighten for leveling horizons (rotating the image), Distortion control for removing barrel and pincushion distortion, and finally Perspective control to remove angle distortion, and you have the basics of a graphics software program built right into the camera.

Remember that you can convert RAW files to JPEG with NEF (RAW) processing and use Print set (DPOF) to create a print order and print directly to a PictBridge printer. Why do we need a computer? What an amazing camera!

Miniature Effect

(User's Manual – Page 409)

Miniature effect is unusual because it allows you to create a reverse diorama. A diorama is a small 3-D model that looks like the real thing. You may have seen a city diorama, where there are tiny detailed houses and cars and even figures of people. A diorama is often used to make a movie when the cost would be too high to use real scenes.

The reason I call the Miniature effect a reverse diorama is that the camera takes a real image and uses a very narrow band of sharpness with a very shallow depth of field to make the subject look like a diorama.

Figure 6.19A is a sample Miniature effect image I took while looking at a train depot from a bridge over the tracks. It's best to shoot this type of image from a high vantage point so it looks like a real miniature.

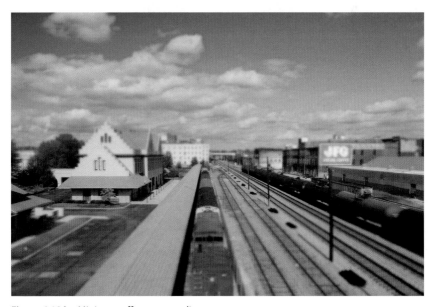
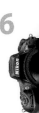

Figure 6.19A – Miniature effect reverse diorama

The camera added extra saturation to the image to make the train cars look unreal. Notice how there is a band of sharpness running horizontally across the middle of the image on this Miniature effect application. That very shallow depth of field in a full-sized image makes it look fake. Depth of field is usually that narrow in closeup and macro shots only.

Here are steps to create your own Miniature effect reverse diorama:

1. Select Miniature effect from the Retouch menu and scroll to the right (figure 6.19B, screen 1).
2. Choose an image shot from a high vantage point that would make a good reverse diorama and press the OK button (figure 6.19B, screen 2).

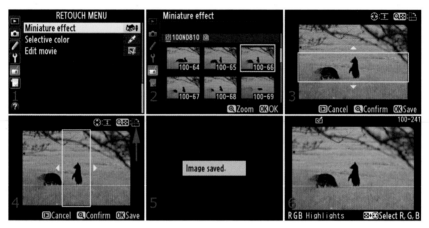

Figure 6.19B – Miniature effect settings

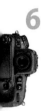

3. Notice the yellow rectangle in figure 6.19B, screen 3. This band represents a horizontal, movable band of sharpness. You can move it up or down on the screen with the Multi selector until you find the optimum place to put the sharpness. Everything above and below the band is blurry. If you are working with a vertical image, the band will be vertical instead of horizontal. In other words, it is across the image, left to right, no matter what direction you hold the camera when using the horizontal setting. You can change the band of sharpness from horizontal to vertical by pressing the Thumbnail/Playback zoom in button (figure 6.19B, screen 4, red arrow). After you position the band where you want it, press the OK button to save the image.
4. An hourglass will appear while the Miniature effect is applied, and then an *Image saved* screen will appear briefly. You will now see the new Miniature effect image on the Monitor (figure 6.19B, screen 6). It is saved with a new file name on your memory card.

Settings Recommendation: To get good use out of this function, you'll need to be looking down on your subject—for example, from a bridge, the top of a building, or an airplane (unless you are shooting a vertical reverse diorama). It's a lot of fun to make these images, although it's difficult to make one look realistic. Next time you are high above a real scene with lots of detail, try shooting a Miniature effect image for fun.

Selective Color

(User's Manual – Page 410)

Selective color allows you to create black-and-white still images with selective colors left in. We have all seen pictures of a lovely red rose with only the petals having color while the rest of the image is black-and-white. Well, the Nikon D810 goes a step farther than that and allows you to create black-and-white images with up to three selective colors. Let's see how to do it.

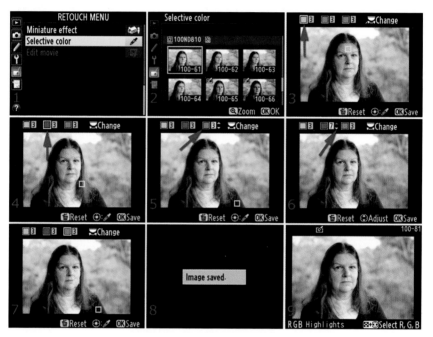

Figure 6.20 – Using Selective color

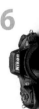

Use these steps to create black-and-white images with up to three selective colors included:

1. Select Selective color from the Retouch menu and scroll to the right (figure 6.20, screen 1).
2. Choose an image to use as a base and press the OK button (figure 6.20, screen 2).
3. Turn the rear Main command dial to select one of the color boxes, as shown at the top left of figure 6.20, screen 3, where you will store the colors you want to remain in your black-and-white image. You will need to turn the Main command dial multiple times in either direction to get it to skip over a color box with its up/down adjustments and move to the next box.

4. Use the Multi selector to scroll the yellow selection box to the location from which you want to choose a color and then press the Multi selector center button to choose it. You can zoom in with the Playback zoom in button to select a color more precisely from a small section of the subject. Zoom back out with the Thumbnail/Playback zoom out button.

5. In figure 6.20, screen 3, you will note that I have chosen the color of my subject's forehead for one of the available color choices. The first color box contains the selected color (see arrow). In figure 6.20, screen 4, you can see that I chose a second color to keep in the image, based on her brown hair. Pressing the Multi selector center button captured the hair color and stored it in the second color box (red arrow). Figure 6.20, screen 5, shows that I chose the color of the subject's blouse (red arrow), storing it in the third color box (red arrow).

6. As shown in figure 6.20, screen 6, you can adjust the range of similar colors in any of the color boxes by highlighting its up/down selector with the rear Main command dial and then using the Multi selector to raise or lower the number from as low as 1 to as high as 7. The higher the number, the more similar colors—to the shade in the color box—the camera will allow into the image. In my opinion, the interface for moving around among the color boxes needs improvement. It is slow and clunky.

7. Once you have finished configuring the Selective color system, you can press the OK button to save the image. Figure 6.20, screen 7, shows the hourglass that stays on the screen for a few seconds while the camera removes the colors you have disallowed. A screen with the words *Image saved* will appear briefly (figure 6.20, screen 8). The final image will then appear on the Monitor, having been saved under a new file name (figure 6.20, screen 9).

Settings Recommendation: Selective color still images are a lot of fun. You can shoot images and later remove most of the colors for fine art black-and-white images. Other than the clunky interface surrounding the color boxes, this function is a useful one. You may want to spend a few minutes learning to use it and then see if you can make some art.

Edit Movie
(User's Manual – Page 67)

Edit movie gives you a two-step process to cut a section out of the middle of a movie created with your D810, or you can remove a beginning or ending segment. In addition, you can save an individual frame as a still image from anywhere in the movie.

There are two individual parts to the process of editing a movie—choosing a start point and choosing an end point. You can use one or the other, or both. When you finalize one of the Start point and/or End point selections, the camera saves the file as a new movie with a new file name. This tends to create a bunch of smaller movies on your memory card that you'll need to delete, taking care that you don't delete the wrong one.

There are two parts to Edit movie:

- **Choose start/end point** – This allows you to delete frames from the beginning or the end of your movie and choose a new starting or ending point.
- **Save selected frame** – You can take a low-resolution 16:9 ratio (up to 2.07 megapixel) JPEG snapshot of any frame in the movie.

Choose Start/End Point
Method 1 – Editing a Movie from the Playback Retouch Menu

Let's examine the steps to remove a portion—select the start or end—of a movie segment (figure 6.21A). I refer to these steps as Method 1 because we will later look at an even more precise but slow variation, which I call Method 2.

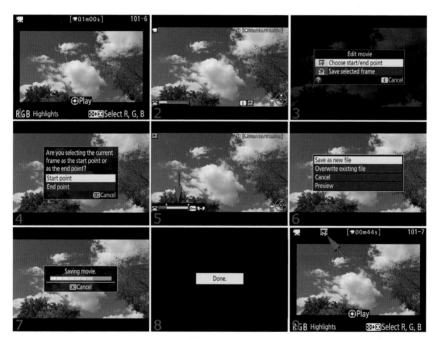
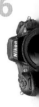

Figure 6.21A – Edit movie

Here are the steps to use Method 1:

1. Choose a movie to play by pressing the Playback button and scrolling with the Multi selector until a movie is showing on the Monitor (figure 6.21A, screen 1).

2. Press the Multi selector center button to play the movie (figure 6.21A, screen 2). When the movie gets to the point where you want to cut it, press down on the Multi selector, which pauses the movie. Press the *i* button to open the Choose start/end point menu.

3. Select Choose start/end point and scroll to the right (figure 6.21A, screen 3).

4. Choose Start point or End point from the menu (figure 6.21A, screen 4). If you choose Start point, you will be removing a segment from the front of the movie file. Choosing End point lets you cut off the end of the movie file.

5. When you choose a Start point or End point to cut the movie and press the OK button, a screen showing the new length of the movie will appear. In the bottom-left corner, you will see the length indicator showing the new length (figure 6.21A, screen 5, red arrow). When this screen is active, you can toggle between the Start point and End point selections by pressing the Protect/Picture Control/Help button (looks like a key, right below the MENU button). This allows you to cut both ends of the movie in one operation by toggling the Start point/End point selection to End point and scrolling backward with the Multi selector until you have removed some of the end of the movie.

6. Press up on the Multi selector to cut the movie to the new length. A screen offering to Save as new file, Overwrite existing file, Cancel, or Preview will appear (figure 6.21A, screen 6). Choose one of the options. Here is a list of what each option on the menu does:

   - **Save as new file** – If you choose Save as new file, the camera will both retain the old, longer movie and create the new, shorter movie with its own new file name.
   - **Overwrite existing file** – If you choose Overwrite existing file (be careful), the camera will overwrite the older, long movie with the new, shorter one.
   - **Cancel** – If you choose Cancel, the camera returns to the location shown in figure 6.21A, screen 5, and awaits further input from you.
   - **Preview** – If you select Preview, the camera will play the movie from or to the position of the new cut point. In other words, it plays what would become the new, shorter movie if you save it. When the Preview movie is finished playing, the camera will return to the menu as shown in figure 6.21A, screen 6, and await further input.

7. Figure 6.21A, screen 6, shows that I chose Save as new file, and the camera saved the file. Screen 8 appears briefly with the word *Done*, and then the camera displays the new, shorter movie on the Monitor. You can tell it is a cut movie by the frame and scissors symbol in the left corner, after the movie camera icon (figure 6.21A, screen 9, red arrow).

Method 2 – Editing a Movie Directly from the Main Retouch Menu

You can start this entire process directly from the Retouch Menu. The steps are basically the same except that you choose a movie from a list of movies in the Retouch Menu instead of starting with a movie on the Monitor.

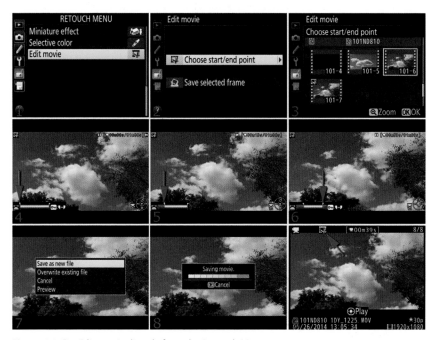

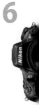

Figure 6.21B – Edit movie directly from the Retouch Menu

Following are the steps to choose a new start and end point for a movie directly from the Retouch Menu:

1. Choose Edit movie from the Retouch Menu and scroll to the right (figure 6.21B, screen 1).
2. Select Choose start/end point from the Edit movie menu and scroll to the right (figure 6.21B, screen 2).
3. Choose a movie from the list of movies and press the OK button to select it. You can briefly zoom in on the movie to make sure it is the one you want to edit by pressing and holding the Playback zoom in button (figure 6.21B, screen 3).
4. When a screen similar to the one in figure 6.21B, screen 4, appears, either press the Multi selector center button to start playing the movie or manually scroll to the right with the Multi selector to move the left Start point selector to the right (figure 6.21B, screen 4, red arrow).
5. The Start point selector will move to the right as you select footage to remove by either letting the movie play or by manually scrolling with the Multi selector

(figure 6.21B, screen 5, red arrow). If you are playing the movie, simply press down on the Multi selector to pause the video once it has reached the position you want to be the new beginning of the movie. If you are scrolling through frames manually with the Multi selector, stop when you find the frame you want to use as the beginning frame for the new shorter movie (figure 6.21B, screen 5).

6. If you want to remove footage from the end of the movie, press the Protect/ Picture Control/Help button to toggle to the End point selector (figure 6.21B, screen 6, red arrow). Press left on the Multi selector to scroll the End point selector to the left until you have found the frame you want to use as the last frame of the movie.

7. Press up on the Multi selector and the menu will pop open, allowing you to save the new, shorter movie. See step 6 in the steps for Method 1 for a full explanation of what each menu choice does.

8. Once you have chosen to save the file, screens 8 and 9 of figure 6.21B will appear in rapid sequence. The final screen, screen 9 in the figure, is the new, shorter movie, saved under a new file name—as shown by the frame and scissors symbol at the red arrow point.

Note: Your movie must be at least two seconds long when you're done or the camera will refuse to cut any more frames; it will give you a terse message informing you that it cannot edit the movie. Also, if you try to clip a movie by pressing up on the Multi selector when a movie is displayed for edit and the Start point or End point selectors have not been moved, the camera will refuse to let you edit and you will see the message Cannot edit movie.

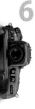

Settings Recommendation: I have presented the two main methods of editing or trimming a movie. Method 1 is what the User's Manual proposes, and it seems somewhat easier and faster. Method 2 is more precise; however, it takes significantly longer because you may have to scroll through thousands of frames. I generally use Method 2 because I like to be precise. You should shoot some junk movies and practice using both of these methods until you decide which you like best. It will take some practice to remember how the methods work because they are a bit complicated. Keep this book handy!

Save Selected Frame

You can save an individual low-resolution frame from anywhere in the movie. The still image frame size is based on the format of the movie (1080p or 720p), which is set in *Shooting Menu > Movie settings > Movie quality*:

- A still image created from a 1920×1080 movie is a little larger than 2 megapixels.
- A still image created from a 1280×720 movie is about 921 KB, or smaller than a 1-megapixel image.

Method 1 – Save Selected Frame by Using Movie Playback

Similar to the methods in the previous section about editing movies, there are multiple ways to cut a single frame out of the movie. Method 1 is the method shown in the User's Manual.

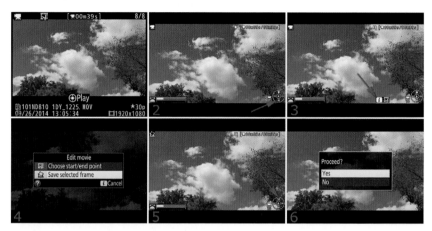

Figure 6.21C – Save an individual frame from a movie

Use these steps to save a single frame from the movie as a still image, using playback:

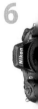

1. Press the Playback button and scroll to the movie that contains the frame you want to save. Press the Multi selector center button to play the movie (figure 6.21C, screen 1).
2. Let the movie play until you reach the point where you want to grab the frame from the movie, and then press down on the Multi selector to pause the movie (figure 6.21C, screen 2).
3. The screen shown in figure 6.21C, screen 3, will now appear. You can scroll left or right with the Multi selector to move one frame at a time while the movie is paused. This allows you to find the exact frame that best suits your purposes. The red arrow points to an icon that appears to let you know you can access the Retouch Menu by pressing the *i* button. Press the *i* button now to open the Retouch Menu.
4. Figure 6.21C, screen 4, shows the Retouch Menu with the same two choices we discussed earlier. Select Save selected frame and press the OK button.
5. The movie will now appear again, still paused (figure 6.21C, screen 5), and the camera's Memory card access lamp will be shining brightly. Nothing will happen until you press up on the Multi selector (red arrow) or press the Playback button to cancel. (This was confusing to me until I did it several times!)

6. Press up on the Multi selector, and a message that says *Proceed?* will appear (figure 6.21C, screen 6). Highlight Yes on the menu and press the OK button again.
7. The camera will now cut out the frame you selected, a screen will show briefly saying *Done*, and the new, saved low-res image will appear on the Monitor (not shown).

Method 2 – Save Selected Frame by Using the Retouch Menu Directly

This method of saving a frame from somewhere in the movie is a bit more direct. You select your movie from a list of movies brought up directly by the Retouch Menu instead of choosing one from the playback screen on the Monitor. Let's see how.

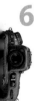

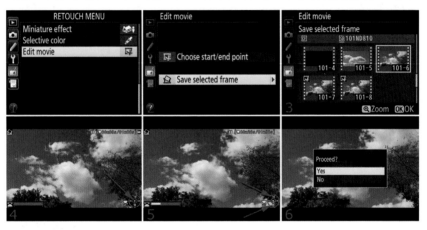

Figure 6.21D – Save an individual frame from a movie using the Retouch Menu

Use these steps to save an individual frame from a movie by using the Retouch Menu directly:

1. Choose Edit movie from the Retouch Menu and scroll to the right (figure 6.21D, screen 1).
2. Select Save selected frame and scroll to the right (figure 6.21D, screen 2).
3. Choose one of the available movies and press the OK button. You can briefly zoom in on the movie to make sure it is the one that contains the frame you want to save by pressing and holding the Playback zoom in button (figure 6.21D, screen 3).
4. Press the Multi selector center button to start playing the movie (figure 6.21D, screen 4, red arrow). When you reach the point that contains the frame you want to save, press down on the Multi selector to pause the movie (figure 6.21D, screen 5, lower red arrow).

5. Scroll to the left or right with the Multi selector until the exact frame you want is showing on the screen. Press up on the Multi selector toward the little scissors icon (figure 6.21D, screen 5, upper red arrow).

6. A screen with a small box will appear that says *Proceed?* (figure 6.21D, screen 6). Choose Yes from the menu and the camera will make a copy of the frame as a separate image. While the selected frame is being extracted and saved, you will see an hourglass, then a screen that says *Done*, and a final screen showing the saved, low-res image with a new file name (not shown). The still frame will have the same 16:9 ratio of an HD movie and will generally be less than 1 megabyte in size.

Settings Recommendation: I like to use Method 2, even though the User's Manual recommends Method 1. Both get the job done, but I find Method 2 more satisfactory because I can select the movie from a list of several movies instead of scrolling through the playback. The camera displays movies only when you use Method 2, narrowing down your choices by hiding any image files.

Side-by-Side Comparison

(User's Manual – Page 412)

Side-by-side comparison allows you to compare an image you've retouched with its original source image. Interestingly, this function is not available from the main Retouch Menu. You'll find it on the Playback Retouch Menu only, which you access by pressing the OK button when a picture is displayed on the Monitor.

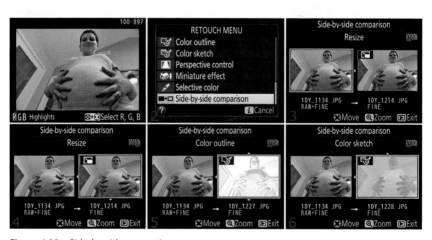

Figure 6.22 – Side-by-side comparison

Here are the steps to compare an original and retouched image side by side on the camera's Monitor:

1. Press the Playback button and find the image you want to compare (figure 6.22, screen 1).
2. Press the OK button to access the Playback Retouch Menu. Scroll all the way down to the bottom of the menu, select Side-by-side comparison, and scroll to the right (figure 6.22, screen 2). The original image will appear on the left, and one of the retouched versions will appear on the right (figure 6.22, image 3).
3. If you retouched an original image more than once, a tiny yellow arrow will appear above and below the retouched image. This means that you can scroll up or down to see the other retouched images. The right-side pictures of the pregnant woman in figure 6.22, screens 4, 5, and 6, are three different retouched images; the left-side picture is the original image. Screen 4 shows a Resize operation, screen 5 shows the Color outline filter effect, and screen 6 shows the Color sketch filter effect.

Settings Recommendation: I often use this function when I want to see how images to which I've added a color cast compare to the original. It's very convenient because you can choose the original image or one of the retouched images, and the camera is smart enough to place them in the proper position in the Side-by-side comparison. You can tell an image has been retouched by looking for the retouch icon in the upper-left corner of the image when it's displayed on the Monitor.

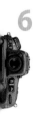

Author's Conclusions

Nikon has given camera users who dislike computers many ways to work with their images in-camera. Although the Retouch Menu is not as fully featured as a computer graphics program, it does allow you to do quick one-off conversions for convenience.

I didn't think this group of Retouch Menu functions would be all that useful to me when I first read about them. However, in the field I find myself using them more than I expected. Whether you use them often or not, it's good to know you have them for emergency use.

Next, we'll move into the final menu system in the camera. It's called My Menu, and it may become very valuable to you as you learn how it works. It's a place to put your often-used, favorite settings so you can get to them very quickly. Let's see how My Menu and its cousin, Recent Settings, work in the next chapter.

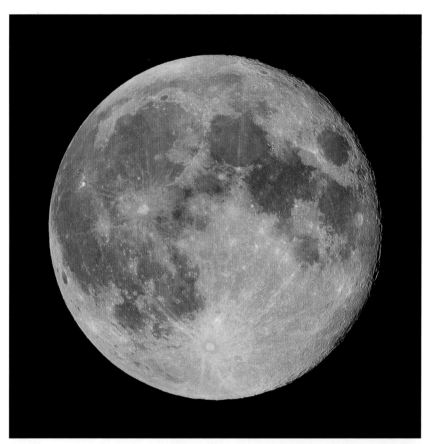

Supermoon in Devon England © Brian Tilley (*briantilley*)

This image of the supermoon (when the full moon is at its closest to Earth) was taken at my home in Devon, England. After failed attempts to get a good shot the previous month, I'd been hoping for a clear night, and this time I was rewarded with a cloudless sky. I focused manually and took bursts of three shots to give me a decent chance of capturing a sharp image. This was the best one, and I processed it in Lightroom to remove a little chromatic aberration and adjust the contrast.
Shot with Nikon D810, Tamron SP 150-600mm f/5-6.3 Di VC USD lens at 600mm, 1/250 sec at f/9, ISO 200, on a Gitzo monopod with VC turned on.

My Menu and Recent Settings

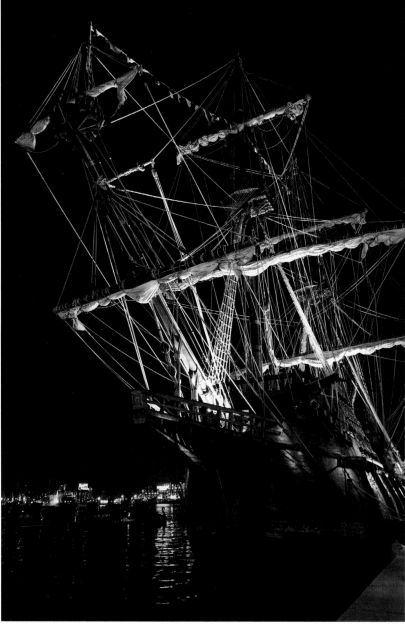

El Galeón Andalucía at Baltimore Port © Jackie Donaldson (*bhpr*)

As you have read through this book and experimented with your camera, you've surely noticed that the D810 has a large number of menus, screens, functions, and settings. When I took pictures of the camera's menus and screens for this book, I ended up with hundreds of images. That many screens can be somewhat complex to navigate. We need a shortcut menu for our most-used settings—a place to keep the functions we're constantly changing.

Nikon has given us two specialty menus in the D810: My Menu and Recent Settings. These are both designed to give us exactly what we need—a menu that can be customized with only the most-used functions, and a menu of recent changes to functions.

For instance, I often turn Exposure delay mode on and off. Instead of having to search through all the Custom settings, trying to remember exactly where Exposure delay mode lives, I simply added that Custom setting to My Menu. Now, whenever I want to add a 1- to 3-second exposure delay after pressing the Shutter-release button so that mirror vibrations can settle down, I can just go to My Menu and enable Exposure delay mode. I can do it quickly and without searching.

I rarely use Recent Settings. I prefer the control I get with my own personally customizable menu—My Menu. The Recent Settings menu has very little flexibility because it's an automatically updated, camera-controlled menu system. You really can't do much in the way of configuring it. You'll just select and use it. On the other hand, My Menu is a personal collection of links to my most-used settings. It is completely configurable.

We'll consider both menus in this chapter, with heavy emphasis on configuring My Menu.

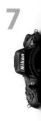

What's the Difference between My Menu and Recent Settings?

You can add up to 20 settings from the Playback Menu, Shooting Menu, Custom Setting Menu, Setup Menu, and Retouch Menu to My Menu. Recent Settings will automatically show the last 20 settings you've modified in the other menus, but it's not configurable. The most important difference between the two menus is the level of control you have over what appears on them. My Menu is completely customizable and does not change unless you change it, and, as mentioned previously, Recent Settings simply shows the last 20 changes you've made to your camera's settings. Recent Settings will change every time you change a setting in your camera. However, because it shows the last 20 changes, you ought to be able to find the ones you change most often somewhere in the list. The two menus are mutually exclusive and cannot appear on the D810 at the same time. One takes the place of the other when you select the Choose tab setting at the end of each menu and choose your favorite.

My Menu

(User's Manual – Page 414)

My Menu is *my* menu! I can add or remove virtually any camera setting found on one of the primary menus. When I use My Menu, I don't have
to spend time looking for the function buried
in the main menu system. Because I often use
each function on My Menu, I'm glad to have it
immediately available.

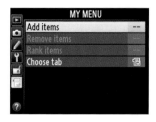

Figure 7.1 – My Menu

   My Menu is the last selection on the D810's
menu system (figure 7.1). Its icon looks like a file
folder tab turned sideways, with a check mark on it.

   When you first look at My Menu, you'll see nothing but the following menu
options:

* Add items
* Rank items

* Remove items
* Choose tab

Let's examine each of these menu choices in detail.

Add Items

To add an item to My Menu, you'll need to locate the item first. Search through the
menus until you find the setting you want to add, and then make note of where it's
located. You could do this from within the Add items menu, but I find that it's harder
to locate what I'm looking for if I haven't already confirmed where it lives. Is it under
the Custom Setting Menu or the Shooting Menu or maybe the Setup Menu? Make
a note of where items you want to add to My Menu are located before you start
adding them, or it may take longer than necessary.

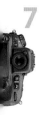

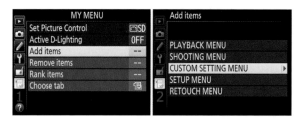

Figure 7.2 – Adding items to My Menu

After you've found the item you want to add and made note of its location, use the
following steps:

1. Select Add items from My Menu. Notice that I already have Set Picture Control and Active D-Lighting added to My Menu (figure 7.2, screen 1). I want to add something else.

2. Use the Multi selector to scroll right, and you'll find a list of menus to choose from. The Add items screen shows all the menus available in the D810 except My Menu and Recent Settings (figure 7.2, screen 2). Let's add one of my favorites, Exposure delay mode (figure 7.3).

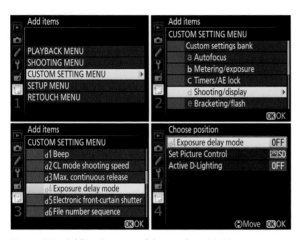

Figure 7.3 – Adding Exposure delay mode to My Menu

3. Figure 7.3 picks up where figure 7.2 left off. We already know that Exposure delay mode is under the Custom setting menu, so let's scroll down to it and scroll to the right (figure 7.3, screen 1).

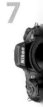

4. We now see the Custom setting menu and Custom settings a through e (figure 7.3, screen 2). Scroll down to d Shooting/display and then scroll to the right. **Note**: There are more Custom settings than appear on screen 2. If you scroll down, you will also find Custom settings f and g.

5. Figure 7.3, screen 3, shows the d4 Exposure delay mode function that we want to add. All we have to do is highlight it and press the OK button. Once that is done, the D810 switches to the Choose position screen (figure 7.3, screen 4).

6. Figure 7.4 begins where figure 7.3 ends. Since I've already added a couple of other items to My Menu, I now have to decide the order in which I want them to be presented. The new d4 Exposure delay mode setting is on top because it is the newest entry (figure 7.4, screen 1). I think I'll move it down two rows and put Set Picture Control in the top position.

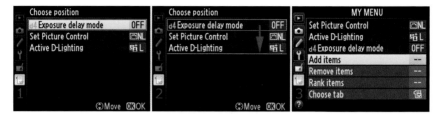

Figure 7.4 – Choosing a position for Custom setting d4 Exposure delay mode on My Menu

7. To move the position of the selected item, simply scroll down. The d4 Exposure delay mode setting has a yellow box around it (figure 7.4, screen 2). As you scroll down, a yellow underline moves down the list (figure 7.4, screen 2, red arrow). This yellow underline represents the place to which I want to move d4 Exposure delay mode. When I've decided on the position and have the yellow underline in place, I just press the OK button. The screen pops back to the first My Menu screen, with everything arranged the way I want it (figure 7.4, screen 3). Notice that d4 Exposure delay mode is now at the bottom of the list.

Remove Items

Now that I've shown you how to Add items, let's examine how to Remove items. The D810 allows me to open the Set Picture Control menu by pressing the Protect/ Picture Control/Help button when nothing is showing on the Monitor. I think I'd rather just press the Picture Control button than use My Menu, so I'll remove it from My Menu and save one of the 20 slots for something else.

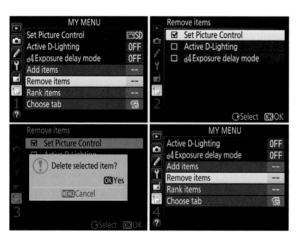

Figure 7.5 – Removing an item from My Menu

Use the following steps to Remove items from My Menu:

1. Select Remove items from My Menu and scroll to the right (figure 7.5, screen 1).
2. The Remove items screen presents a series of selections with check boxes. Whichever boxes you check will be deleted when you press the OK button (figure 7.5, screen 2). You can check the boxes by highlighting the line item you want to delete and scrolling right. You can also press the Multi selector center button to place a check mark in a setting's box. Pressing the Multi selector center button acts like a toggle and will check or uncheck a line item.
3. When you've checked the settings you want to remove, simply press the OK button. A small white box pops up and asks, *Delete selected item?* (Figure 7.5, screen 3.)
4. Pressing the OK button signifies Yes and removes the Set Picture Control setting from My Menu. A screen displaying *Done* shows briefly, and then the D810 switches back to the My Menu screen. You can press the MENU button to cancel if you decide you don't want to remove an item. You will notice, in screen 4, that the Set Picture Control setting is now gone.

Rank Items

Ranking items is similar to positioning new additions in My Menu. All the Rank items selection does is move an item up or down in My Menu. You can switch your most-used My Menu items to the top of the list.

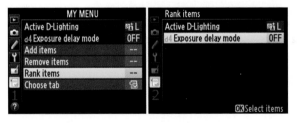
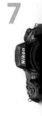

Figure 7.6 – Ranking items in My Menu

Use the following steps to Rank items:

1. Select Rank items from My Menu and scroll to the right (figure 7.6, screen 1).
2. Now you'll see the Rank items screen and all the current My Menu items (figure 7.6, screen 2). I've decided that I use d4 Exposure delay mode more than Active D-Lighting, so I'll move it to the top.
3. Highlight d4 Exposure delay mode and press the OK button. A yellow box will appear around that item. Move appears at the bottom of the screen (figure 7.7, screen 1).
4. Next, scroll up with the Multi selector (figure 7.7, screen 2). This action moves the yellow positioning underline to the top of the list (figure 7.7, screen 2, red arrow).

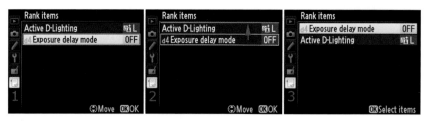

Figure 7.7 – Ranking items in My Menu (continued)

5. Press the OK button to select the new position and d4 Exposure delay mode will move to the top of the list (figure 7.7, screen 3).

Choose Tab

Choose tab allows you to switch between My Menu and Recent Settings. Both menus have the Choose tab selection as their last menu choice.

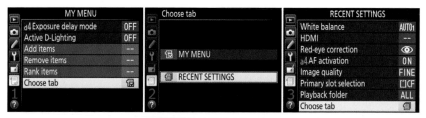

Figure 7.8 – Selecting My Menu or Recent Settings (Choose tab)

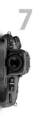

Use the following steps to switch between My Menu and Recent Settings:

1. At the bottom of My Menu, select Choose tab and scroll to the right (figure 7.8, screen 1).
2. You'll now have a choice between My Menu and Recent Settings. Choose Recent Settings and press the OK button (figure 7.8, screen 2).
3. The Recent Settings screen will now appear, completely replacing My Menu on the main menu screen (figure 7.8, screen 3). Notice that it has a Choose tab selection at the bottom, just as My Menu does. The items you see on the Recent Settings menu are items I have recently adjusted. Your camera will display a different list of items. The last 20 items adjusted will be displayed when you scroll up or down on the Recent Settings menu.
4. Select Choose tab and press the OK button to return to My Menu (figure 7.8, screen 3).

Clearly, this is a circular reference. You can use the Choose tab selection as a toggle between the two menus. When you do, one menu replaces the other as the last selection on the camera's main menu screen.

Settings Recommendation: You can see how My Menu gives you nice control over a customized menu that is entirely yours. Configure it however you want by choosing from selections in the primary menus. My Menu will save you significant time when you look for your 20 most-used selections.

If you're inclined to use Recent Settings, just remember that after you pass 20 camera setting adjustments, the next setting you use will jump to the top of the list, moving everything down by one position. The last item on the list will simply disappear.

Now, let's take a look at Recent Settings in a little more detail.

Recent Settings

(User's Manual – Page 418)

Recent Settings is very simple. This menu remembers the last 20 changes you've made to your D810 camera. Each menu selection that was modified is stored in a temporary place called Recent Settings.

If you change something in your camera that's not already on the Recent Settings menu, it will be added to the menu, replacing the old-est change with your new one—at the top of the list—if there is no room left at the bottom (i.e., you've exceeded 20 items).

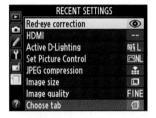

Figure 7.9 – Recent Settings

This can be a convenient way to find something you've changed recently but whose location you have trouble remembering on the main menu systems.

Settings Recommendation: If you want a more permanent menu for your favor-ite changes to the D810, you'll need to enable the My Menu system instead of the Recent Settings Menu. The Recent Settings Menu is fine, but I want to directly con-trol what settings I have quick access to without searching. My Menu is my choice!

Author's Conclusions

This is the last of the text-based menus we'll cover in the D810. We've been through all the menu screens in the last several chapters!

Now it's time to see how to use the controls we've carefully configured. Our next chapter takes up the subjects of exposure metering, exposure modes, and the histogram. Please pay extra attention to the section on the histogram if you want excellent exposures every time.

Metering, Exposure Modes, and Histogram

8

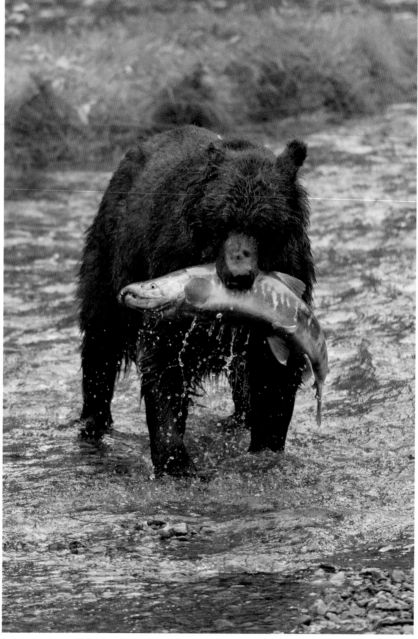

I've been using Nikon cameras since 1980. It seems that with each new camera, there have been improvements in metering and exposure modes. The Nikon D810 is no exception. Within this camera, Nikon has designed metering and exposure to work not only with still images, but also with broadcast-quality video (D-Movies).

In this chapter, you'll learn how the exposure metering system and modes work. We'll look at how each of four different light meter types is best used. We'll examine the various modes you can use when taking pictures, and finally, we'll look in detail at how the histogram works on the Nikon D810. This little readout gives you great control over metering and will help you make the most accurate exposures you've ever made. It is very important that you understand the histogram, so we'll look at it in detail. This chapter is divided into three parts:

- *Section 1 – Metering* – The Nikon D810 provides four major light metering systems: 3D Color Matrix Metering III, Center-weighted, Highlight-weighted, and Spot.
- *Section 2 – Exposure Modes* – The camera's MODE button allows access to various shooting or exposure modes, such as Programmed auto (P), Shutter-priority auto (S), Aperture-priority auto (A), and Manual (M).
- *Section 3 – Histogram* – The histogram is a digital bell-curve readout that shows how well an image is exposed. It's an important tool for advanced photographers. This chapter discusses how to read the histogram and better control your exposures.

Let's get started by looking more deeply into the four exposure metering systems.

Section 1 – Metering

(User's Manual – Page 114)

The basis for the Nikon D810's exposure meter is a 91,000-pixel RGB sensor that meters a wide area of the frame. Figure 8.1 shows a close-up of that sensor, which is used to meter the light and provide a correct exposure.

When used with a Nikkor G, E, or D lens that contains a CPU, the camera can set the exposure based on the distribution of brightness, color, distance, and composition. Most people leave their light meter set to Matrix metering and enjoy excellent results.

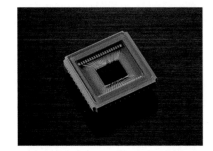
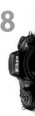

Figure 8.1 – D810's 91,000-pixel RGB sensor (light meter)

The Nikon D810 uses a newly developed Advanced Scene Recognition System that includes the 91,000-pixel RGB sensor that measures each scene's light properties, color spectrum, and brightness levels. It then compares your subject against the camera's built-in image database to provide even more accurate autoexposure. With a metering sensor this sensitive, the D810 can do things with ease that other cameras struggle to accomplish.

Figure 8.2 shows the controls used to select a Metering mode—the Metering button and rear Main command dial—along with the four Metering mode symbols on the top Control panel.

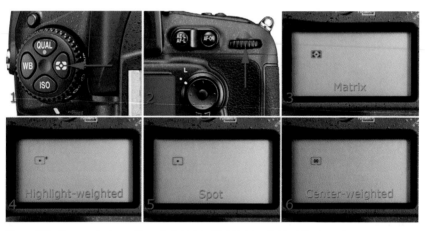

Figure 8.2 – Four meter types (in order): Matrix, Highlight-weighted, Spot, and Center-weighted

To switch among the four exposure meter types, simply hold down the Metering button and rotate the rear Main command dial. You will see a series of four metering symbols on the Control panel, as shown in figure 8.2.

Figure 8.3 shows the Information display screen with the four metering symbols and all the other icons you'll normally see. These same symbols, shown at the point of the red arrows, can be seen at the bottom-left corner when you look through the Viewfinder. Learn to recognize what each Metering symbol means.

Figure 8.3 displays the four meter types in the order you will find them when you hold down the Metering button and rotate the rear Command dial counterclockwise. Match the screen number and metering symbols to these metering types:

1. Matrix metering
2. Highlight-weighted metering (notice the asterisk)
3. Spot metering
4. Center-weighted metering

Now, let's examine the four meter types to see which you will use most often.

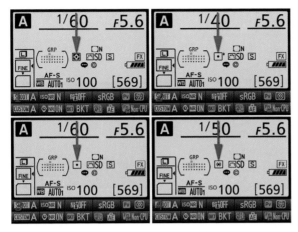

Figure 8.3 – Metering mode symbols on the Information display

3D Color Matrix III Metering

The Nikon D810 contains the 3D Color Matrix III metering system, one of the most powerful and accurate automatic exposure meters in any camera today.

In figure 8.4, you can see the Matrix metering symbol. This is the factory default meter.

How does Matrix metering work? There are characteristics for many thousands of images stored in the camera. These characteristics are used along with proprietary Nikon software and

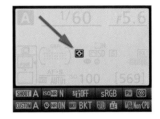

Figure 8.4 – Matrix metering mode symbol

complex evaluative computations to analyze the image that appears in your Viewfinder or in Live view. The meter is then set to provide accurate exposures for the greatest majority of your images.

Whether you are taking a scenic picture with the bright sky above and the darker earth below, or a group shot with one or several human faces, the metering system evaluates the image and compares it to hundreds of similar images in the camera's database; then it automatically selects and inputs a meter setting for you.

The meter examines four critical areas of each picture. It compares the levels of *brightness* in various parts of the scene to determine the total range of EV values. It then notices the *color* of the subject and surroundings. If you are using a G, E, or D lens with a CPU chip, it also determines how far away your lens is focused so it can determine the *distance* to your subject. Finally, it looks at the *compositional* elements of the subject.

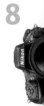

When it has all that information, it compares your image to tens of thousands of image characteristics in its image database, makes complex evaluations, and comes up with an exposure value that is usually right on target, even in complex lighting situations.

Highlight-Weighted Metering

Some types of photography, such as theater, concert, or other types of event photography, may have a bright subject against a dark background. Since most other meter types tend to average the light in the frame, you may see a burned-out, overly bright subject as the camera tries to compensate for the extreme contrast between the subject and the background.

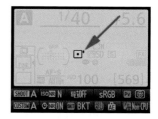

Figure 8.5 – Highlight-weighted metering mode symbol

Highlight-weighted metering causes the camera to pay more attention to the highlights of your subject than to its darker surroundings, often giving you a much better exposure for the subject.

In figure 8.5 you can see the Highlight-weighted metering symbol: the small square with the asterisk on the top right corner.

If you are photographing a concert singer at a microphone under a spotlight, for instance, this type of metering will give you a better exposure of the singer, at the expense of letting the background and surroundings go dark.

I can imagine all types of situations where the subject is bright and the surroundings are dark. This meter type should help you create better images under those circumstances.

Spot Metering

Often only a spot meter will do. In situations where you must get an accurate exposure for a very small section of the frame, or if you must get several meter readings from various small areas, the D810 can be adjusted to fit your needs. The Spot meter evaluates only 1.5 percent of the frame, so it is indeed a *spot* meter.

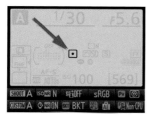

Figure 8.6A – Spot metering mode symbol

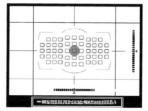

Figure 8.6B – Spot metering size

In figure 8.6A, you can see the Spot metering symbol. The D810's Spot meter consists of a 4 mm circle (0.16 inch) surrounding the currently active AF point in both Single and Continuous AF modes (AF-S and AF-C)

How big is the 4 mm spot? The Spot meter barely surrounds the AF point square in your viewfinder (figure 8.6B). It is a little larger than the brackets that appear around the active AF sensor when you slightly press the Shutter-release button. In fact, the Spot meter follows the currently active AF point around the Viewfinder, so you can move the Spot meter around the frame with the Multi selector.

When your D810 is in Spot meter mode and you move the AF point to some small section of your subject, you can rest assured that you're getting a true spot reading. In fact, you can use your Spot meter to determine an approximate EV range of light values in the entire image by taking multiple manual spot readings from different parts of the subject and comparing the values. If the values exceed 8 or 9 EV steps, you have to decide which part of your subject is most important and meter for it.

On an overcast day, you can usually get by with no worries since the range of light is often within the recording capability of the sensor. On a bright, sunny day, the range of light can be more than a single image can record, and you might have to use a graduated neutral-density filter or HDR imaging to rein in the excessive light range.

Just remember that spot metering is often a trade-off. Either you have the highly specific ability to ensure that a certain portion of an image is exposed with spot-on accuracy (Spot meter) or you can use the camera's multiple averaging skills (Matrix meter) to generally get the correct exposure throughout the frame. The choice is yours, depending on the shooting situation.

If you spot meter the face of someone who is standing in the sun, the shadows around the person will usually be underexposed and have little or no data. If you spot meter the areas in the shadows instead, the person's face is likely to be blown out and lose detail. We'll discuss this more in section 3 of this chapter, which explores the histogram.

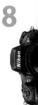

Center-Weighted Metering

If you're a bit old-fashioned, raised on a classic center-weighted meter and still preferring that type, the D810's exposure meter can be transformed into a flexible center-weighted meter with variable-sized weighting that you can control.

In figure 8.7, you can see the Center-weighted metering symbol. The Center-weighted meter in the D810 meters the entire frame but

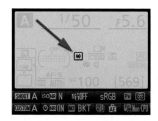

Figure 8.7 – Center-weighted metering mode symbol

concentrates 75 percent of the metering into an adjustable circle in the middle. The 25 percent of the frame outside the circle provides the rest of the metering. If you'd like, you can make the circle as small as 8 mm or as large as 20 mm. You can even completely eliminate the circle and use the entire Viewfinder frame as a basic averaging meter.

Let's examine the Center-weighted meter more closely. Using *Custom Setting Menu > b Metering/exposure > b6 Center-weighted area*, you can change the size of the circle where the camera concentrates the meter reading. (See **Custom Setting b6 – Center-weighted Area** in the chapter **Custom Setting Menu**.)

The default circle is 12 mm in the center of your camera's Viewfinder (figure 8.8, screen 2). However, by changing Custom setting b6 Center-weighted area, you can adjust this size to one of the following:

- 8 mm (0.31 inch)
- 12 mm (0.47 inch) (default)
- 15 mm (0.59 inch)
- 20 mm (0.79 inch)
- Average (full frame)

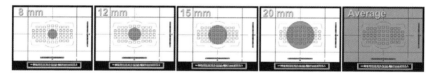

Figure 8.8 – Center-weighted metering

Again, the Center-weighted meter is a pretty simple concept. The part of your subject that's in the center of your D810's Viewfinder influences the meter more than the edges of the frame, on a 75/25 basis. The circle gets 75 percent importance. The red circles shown in figure 8.8 are just rough approximations. Simply meter the subject with the center of the Viewfinder, and you should have good results.

Note: If you are using a non-CPU lens, the Center-weighted meter defaults to 12 mm and cannot be changed. Adjustments to Custom setting b6 Center-weighted area have no effect.

Where's the Circle?

You can't actually see any indication of circles in the Viewfinder, so you'll have to imagine them, as I did in figure 8.8.

Locate your current autofocus (AF) sensor in the middle of your Viewfinder. Now imagine the smallest circle, 8 mm, which is about one-third of an inch. The largest circle is 20 mm, which is a little bigger than three-quarters of an inch. This unseen

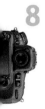

circle in the center area of the Viewfinder provides the most important 75 percent metering area.

Settings Recommendation: If I used the Center-weighted meter often, I would stay with the 8 mm setting. That's a pretty small circle—almost a spot meter—so it should give you good readings. I would point the circle at the most important part of my subject, get a meter reading, use the AE-Lock button to lock the exposure, recompose the picture, and then release the shutter.

The most sensitive area is large enough at 8 mm to see more than a pure spot meter, though, so you have the best of both worlds. There is so little difference between 8 mm and 15 mm that it probably makes little difference which one you use. If you are concerned, then experiment with the settings and see which one works best for you.

Using the Average Setting

If you set your meter to Average (Avg) in Custom setting b6 Center-weighted area, the light values of the entire Viewfinder are averaged to arrive at an exposure value. No particular area of the frame is assigned any greater importance (figure 8.8, screen 5).

This is a little bit like Matrix metering but without the extra smarts. In fact, on several test subjects, I got similar meter readings from the Average and Matrix meters. However, Matrix metering should do better in difficult lighting situations because it has a database of image characteristics to compare with your current image—including color, distance, and where your subject is located in the frame.

Settings Recommendation: Use your Spot meter to get specific meter readings of small areas on and around your subject; then make some exposure decisions yourself and your subject should be well exposed. Just remember that the Spot meter evaluates only for the small area that it sees, so it cannot adjust the camera for anything except that one tiny area. Spot metering requires some practice, but it is a very professional way to expose images.

On cameras previous to the D810, I often used the Spot meter on a person's face when I was taking pictures in darker surroundings so that the person's face was not blown out (due to the meter being influenced by the dark surroundings). However, the D810 is much better at locating and exposing for faces accurately, especially with Highlight-weighted metering, even when using the Viewfinder instead of Live view. I now use the Spot meter much less than I did before.

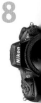

Section 2 – Exposure Modes

(User's Manual – Page 116)

My first Nikon was an FM, which I remember with fondness because that was when I first got serious about photography. It's hard for me to imagine that it has already been 34 years since I used my first Nikon. Things were simpler back then. When I say simple, I mean that the FM had a basic center-weighted light meter, a manual exposure dial, and manual aperture settings. I had to decide how to create the image in all aspects. It was a camera with only one mode—M, or manual.

Later on, I bought a Nikon FE and was amazed to use its A mode, or Aperture-priority auto. I could set the aperture manually and the camera would adjust the shutter speed for me. The FE had two modes, M-manual and A-Aperture-priority.

A few more years went by and I bought a Nikon F4 that was loaded with features and was much more complex. It had four modes, including the two I was used to (M and A) and two new ones, Shutter-priority auto (S) and Programmed auto (P). I had to learn even more stuff! The F4 was my first P, S, A, M camera.

Does this sound anything like your progression? If you're older than 40 years, maybe so; if not, I ought to stop reminiscing and get to the point.

Today's cameras are amazingly complex compared to cameras only a few years ago. Let's examine how we can use that flexibility for our benefit. The D810 is also a P, S, A, M camera. That's the abbreviated progression of primary shooting modes that allow you to control the camera's shutter speed and aperture yourself.

To select the P, S, A, or M mode, simply hold down the MODE button (found just above the Control panel) and turn the rear Main command dial in either direction. The mode changes will be displayed in the upper-left corner of the Control panel and Information display screen. You will also see a tiny P, S, A, or M at the bottom middle of the Viewfinder. Let's examine each exposure mode in detail.

Programmed Auto Mode (P)

Programmed auto mode (P) is designed for those times when you just want to shoot pictures and not think much about camera settings but still want emergency control when needed. The camera takes care of the shutter speed and aperture for you and uses your selected exposure meter type to create the best pictures it can without human intervention. You can override the aperture by turning the rear Main command dial.

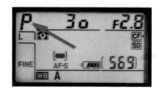

Figure 8.9 – Programmed auto (P) mode on the Control Panel

The big **P** in the upper-left corner of the Control panel in figure 8.9 shows that the camera is set to Programmed auto mode (P). This mode is called Programmed

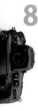

auto because it uses a software program built into the camera. It tries its best to create optimal images in most situations.

However, even the User's Manual calls this a "snapshot" mode. P mode can handle a wide variety of situations well, but I wouldn't depend on it for my important shooting. It can be great at a party, for example, when I want some nice snapshots. I don't have to think about the camera then, and I can just enjoy the party. P mode to me is "P for Party."

It's a good mode to use when you want to let the camera control the aperture and shutter while you control the flash. In a sense, it's like auto mode on lesser cameras, except that you decide when to use the pop-up Speedlight instead of letting the camera decide.

Programmed auto mode also lets you override the camera's aperture in an emergency. You may need more depth of field and decide to use a smaller aperture. The camera allows you to do that by turning the rear Main command dial. When you do, the aperture is under your control, and the camera controls the shutter.

P mode actually comes in two parts: Programmed auto and Flexible program. Flexible program is similar to Aperture-priority auto (A) mode. Why do I say that? Let me explain with an example.

Get Down, Uncle Ben!

You're shooting at a family reunion and suddenly you see a perfect shot of a somewhat tipsy Uncle Ben dancing on the dinner table and Aunt Myrtle standing on the floor behind him with her hand over her mouth. You (being a well-trained photographer) glance down at your camera and realize that the f/4 aperture showing on the Control panel won't give you enough depth of field to focus on Uncle Ben and still have a sharp image of Aunt Myrtle, who by this time is tugging at Ben's pants leg. With only seconds to spare, you turn your rear Main command dial to the left. The D810 realizes that it is being called upon to leave snapshot mode and give you some control. It displays a small P* (P with an asterisk, as seen in figure 8.10) on the Control panel to let you know it realizes you are taking over control of the aperture. Since you are turning the dial to the left, it obligingly starts cranking down the aperture. A few clicks to the left and your aperture is now at f/8. As soon as the D810 detected you were turning the Main command dial, it started adjusting the shutter speed to match the new aperture. With only seconds before Aunt Myrtle starts dragging Uncle Ben off the dinner table, you get the camera to your eye, compose the shot, press the Shutter-release button, and the D810 starts grabbing frames. You get several frames off in the few seconds it takes Aunt Myrtle to get Uncle Ben down from the table. A "priceless" family memory, captured!

What you did in this imaginary scenario was invoke the Flexible program mode (P*) in your D810. How? As soon as you turned the rear Main command dial, the D810 left normal P mode and switched to Flexible program. Before you turned

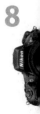

the Main command dial, the D810 was happily controlling both shutter speed and aperture for you. When you turned the dial, the D810 immediately switched to Flexible program mode and let you have control of the aperture. It then controlled only the shutter speed. In effect, the D810 allowed you to exercise your knowledge of photography very quickly and only assisted you from that point.

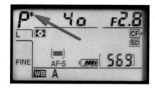

Figure 8.10 – Flexible program (P*) mode on the Control panel

When you enter Flexible program (P*) and turn the rear Main command dial to the left, the aperture gets smaller. Turn it to the right and the aperture gets larger. Nothing happens if you turn the front Sub-command dial. Nikon gives you control of the aperture only in Flexible program mode. Can you see why I say Flexible program mode acts like Aperture-priority auto mode (A)?

Beware the Extra Clicks

If you turn the rear Main command dial to the right until the aperture reaches its maximum size, the camera starts counting clicks but does nothing else. The same thing happens if you try to go smaller than the minimum aperture. In order to start making the aperture change again, you have to turn back the same number of clicks (up to 15). I have no idea why Nikon does it this way, but it has for many years—maybe to allow for lenses with more aperture range.

It's confusing to have the camera stop letting you control the aperture just because you turned the Main command dial past wide open by several clicks and then give you control again when you turn it back the same number of clicks. It's no big deal, really; just be aware that this will happen so you won't think the camera is not working correctly.

Shutter-Priority Auto Mode (S)

Shutter-priority auto is for those who need to control their camera's shutter speed while allowing the camera to maintain the correct aperture for the available light. You'll turn the rear Main command dial to adjust the shutter speed, while the camera controls the aperture.

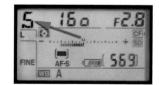

Figure 8.11 – Shutter-priority auto (S) mode on the Control panel

In Figure 8.11, the Control panel shows that Shutter-priority auto (S) mode is set. If you find yourself shooting action, you'll want to keep the shutter speed high enough to capture an image without excessive blurring.

Shooting sports, air shows, auto races, or any quickly moving subject requires careful control of the shutter. If you shoot a bird in flight, you may want to use a fast shutter speed that allows for just a tiny bit of motion blur in its wings, while completely stopping the body of the bird, or a faster shutter speed to eliminate all blur.

Sometimes you'll want to set your shutter speed to slow settings for special effects or time exposures, such as a small waterfall in a beautiful mountain stream. See figure 8.12 for both stop-motion and blurring effects.

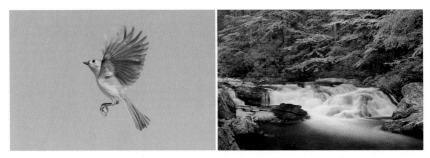

Figure 8.12 – Fast shutter speed to stop bird and slow shutter speed to blur water

To change the shutter speed, simply rotate the rear Main command dial to any value between 30 seconds and 1/8000 of a second. Turn the dial to the left (counterclockwise) for faster shutter speeds and right (clockwise) for slower. The camera will adjust your aperture to maintain a correct exposure and will warn you when it can't.

Watch Out for Camera Shake!
Be careful when the shutter speed is set below 1/125 second. Camera shake becomes a problem for many people at 1/60 second and slower. If you are careful to stand still, brace your arms against your chest, and spread your feet apart with one in front of the other, you'll probably be able to make sharp images at 1/60 to 1/30 second (figure 8.13, image on the left).

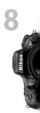

Surprisingly, your heartbeat and breathing is reflected in your hands during slow shutter speed photography. At 1/15 second and slower, most people cannot take sharp pictures without having the camera on a tripod (figure 8.13, image on the right). If you are going to shoot at slow shutter speeds, buy yourself a solid tripod. You'll make much nicer pictures. You can also use a monopod for a very portable device to steady the camera, with results in between handholding and tripod use.

The picture of the small waterfall in Great Smoky Mountains National Park in figure 8.12 was taken at a shutter speed of several seconds. It is virtually impossible to hold a camera perfectly still for several seconds, so a shot like that would be unachievable without a tripod.

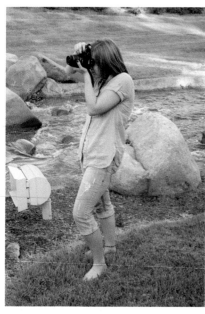
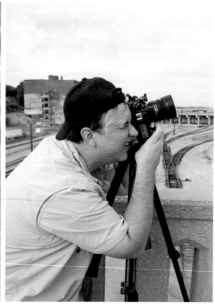

Figure 8.13 – Woman holding camera for steady shooting, and pro photographer using a tripod

Aperture-Priority Auto Mode (A)

Nature, macro, and portrait shooters, and anyone concerned with carefully controlling depth of field, will often leave their cameras set to Aperture-priority auto (A) mode. This mode allows you to control the aperture while the camera takes care of the shutter speed for optimal exposures. To select an aperture, you'll use the front Sub-command dial. Turn the dial to the right (clockwise) for smaller apertures and to the left (counterclockwise) for larger apertures.

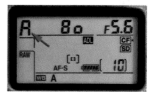

Figure 8.14 – Aperture-priority auto (A) mode on the Control panel

The Control panel in Figure 8.14 shows that Aperture-priority auto (A) mode is set. The minimum and maximum aperture settings are limited by the minimum and maximum aperture available on the lens you've mounted on the camera. Most consumer lenses run from f/3.5 to f/22. More expensive, pro-style lenses may have apertures as large as f/0.95 or f/1.4, but they generally start at f/2.8 and end at f/22–f/32.

For those new to digital photography, the aperture directly controls the depth of field (DOF)—or zone of sharpness—in an image. DOF is an extremely important concept for photographers to understand. Simply put, it allows you to control the range or depth of sharp focus in your images. In the bird image in figure 8.15, the DOF is very shallow, and in the scenic shot it is very deep.

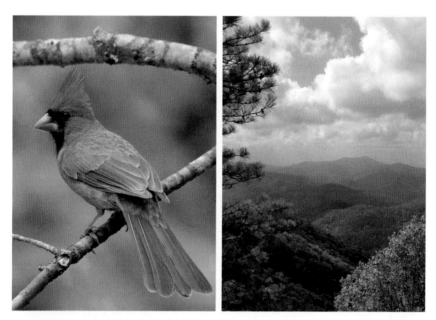

Figure 8.15 – Large aperture to blur background (left) and small aperture for deep depth of field (right)

Manual Mode (M)

Manual mode takes a big step backward to days of old. It gives you complete control of your camera's shutter and aperture so that you can make all the exposure decisions, with suggestions from the light meter.

The big *M* in the upper-left corner of the Control panel in figure 8.16, screen 1, and the Information display in screen 3 shows that the camera is in Manual (M) mode. You can't see it in the figure, but there is a tiny M showing in the Viewfinder just above the Exposure indicator.

You should have no problem knowing when you have the camera in Manual mode.

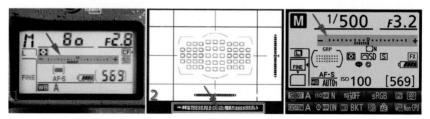

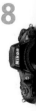

Figure 8.16 – Manual (M) showing along with the -/+ Exposure indicator on all display screens (Control panel, Viewfinder, and Information display)

Also in figure 8.16, notice the analog Exposure indicator display (red arrows on the Control panel, Viewfinder, and Information display). The Exposure indicator display has a minus sign (-) on the left and a plus sign (+) on the right. Each tiny square on the scale represents 1/3 EV step, and each slightly larger tiny rectangle represents 1 EV step. You can control how sensitive this scale is by changing Custom setting b2 EV steps for exposure cntrl. You can set Custom setting b2 to 1/3, 1/2, or 1 EV step. The camera defaults to 1/3 step from the factory.

When you are metering your subject, a bar will appear underneath the analog Exposure indicator and extend from the zero in the center toward the plus side to indicate overexposure or toward the minus side to indicate underexposure.

You can gauge the amount of over- or underexposure by the number of dots and lines the bar passes as it heads toward one side or the other. The goal in Manual mode is to make the bar disappear. In figure 8.16, screens 1 and 3, the Exposure indicator shows that the scene is underexposed by 1 EV step (1 stop). The Viewfinder is showing the same thing, except you can't see it in the tiny graphic. Check your camera's Viewfinder in Manual mode to see how it looks. You should zero the Exposure indicator for a good exposure.

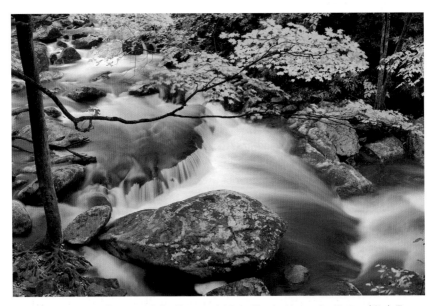

Figure 8.17 – A cascading waterfall at Tremont in Great Smoky Mountains National Park, Tennessee, in springtime. Shot with an AI Nikkor 35mm f/2 non-CPU, manual focus lens with aperture of f/11, shutter speed of 5 seconds, Manual (M) mode, SD picture control, circular polarizer to remove reflections, on a tripod with an Exposure delay of 3 seconds (d4).

You can adjust the aperture with the front Sub-command dial, and you can adjust the shutter speed with the rear Main command dial. When you put the camera in Manual mode (M), you have control over the aperture for depth of field and the shutter speed for motion control. If your subject needs a little more depth of field, just make the aperture smaller, but be sure to slow down the shutter speed as well (or your image may be underexposed). If you need a faster shutter speed, then set it faster, but be sure to open the aperture to compensate.

The point is, you are in complete control of the camera and must make decisions for both the shutter speed and aperture. The camera makes suggestions with its meter, but you make the final decision about how the exposure will look. Manual mode is for taking your time and enjoying your photography. It gives you the most control over how the image looks but also expects you to have a higher level of knowledge to get correct exposures.

Most people who use the D810 are advanced photographers, reflecting the purpose of this feature-laden camera, and they fully understand things like depth of field, shutter speed, and aperture. If you're new to the world of DSLRs, you can find in-depth coverage of these important concepts in my book *Beyond Point-and-Shoot* (Rocky Nook, 2012).

Settings Recommendation: As a nature photographer, I am mostly concerned with getting a nice sharp image with deep depth of field. About 90 percent of the time, my camera is set to Aperture-priority auto (A) and f/8. I control the aperture opening, and the camera controls the shutter speed. I started using this mode in about 1986 when I bought my Nikon FE, and I've used it ever since.

However, if I were shooting sports or action, I would set my camera to Shutter-priority auto (S) most often, which would allow me to control the speed of the shutter and capture those fast-moving subjects without a lot of blur. The camera controls the aperture so that I only have to concentrate on which shutter speed best fits my subject's movement.

I use the other two modes, Programmed auto (P) and Manual (M), only for special occasions.

Manual mode is for when I have time to just enjoy my photography. When I want to control the camera absolutely, I go to Manual. I've even been known to carry a small blanket with me so that when I'm shooting in Manual mode I can toss it over the back of the camera and my head. That way I can feel like Ansel Adams or another view camera artist. I do admit that people (especially kids) seem to find that hilarious. Well, I bet they don't know how to use Manual mode!

I probably use Programmed auto (P) mode least of all. I might use it when I am at a party and just want to take nice pictures for my own use. I'll let the camera make most of the decisions by using P mode and still have the ability to quickly jump into Flexible program (P*) mode when events call for a little more aperture control.

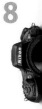

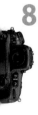

Bad Exposure Warning

If the light changes drastically and the camera cannot maintain a correct exposure due to your current settings, the offending setting will blink in the Viewfinder, Control panel, and Information display. The camera will also display the -/+ Exposure indicator (as you use in Manual mode) with an approximate number of EV steps of over- or underexposure.

If you see the aperture or shutter-speed setting blinking in any of the displays along with the -/+ Exposure indicator displaying a -/+ EV value, please validate your exposure before taking the picture.

Section 3 – Histogram

Back in the good old film days, we didn't have a histogram, so we had to depend on our experience and light meter to get a good exposure. Because we couldn't see the exposure until after we had left the scene, we measured our success by the number of correctly exposed images we were able to create. With the exposure meter/histogram combination found in the D810, and the ability to zoom in to our images with the high-resolution Monitor on the back, our success rate is much higher than ever before.

The histogram can be as important as the exposure meter, or even more so. The meter sets up the camera for the exposure, and the histogram verifies that the exposure is a good one.

If your exposure meter stopped working, you could still get perfect exposures using only the histogram. In fact, I gauge my efforts more by how the histogram looks than anything else. The exposure meter and histogram work together to make sure you get excellent results from your photographic efforts.

Figure 8.18 shows the D810's three histogram screens.

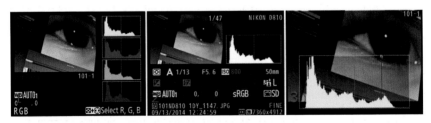

Figure 8.18 – The D810's three histogram screens

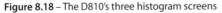

RGB Histogram, Screen 1 – Figure 8.18, screen 1, is the RGB histogram screen. It shows an individual histogram for each color channel. On the top is a luminance histogram followed by the red, green, and blue (RGB) channels.

If your camera does not display the RGB histogram screen shown in figure 8.18, screen 1, you'll need to select the check box found at *Playback Menu > Playback display options > RGB histogram*. This setting enables or disables the RGB histogram screen, which you can then find by displaying an image on the Monitor and then scrolling up or down with the Multi selector.

One important reason to examine the RGB histogram is to see if any one color channel has lost all detail in the dark or light areas. Later in this chapter, we will examine how you can determine when detail has been lost.

Luminance Histogram, Screen 2 – Figure 8.18, screen 2, shows a slightly larger luminance histogram along with image information.

If your camera does not display the Luminance histogram screen shown in figure 8.18, screen 2, you'll need to select the check box found at *Playback Menu > Playback display options > Overview*. This setting enables or disables the Overview screen, which you can then find by displaying an image on the Monitor and then scrolling up or down with the Multi selector.

This is a basic luminance histogram, which is a weighted view of the brightness and color in a scene based on how the human eye perceives light. How does the luminance histogram differ from the RGB histograms? The luminance histogram is a representation of the perceived brightness (luminosity) from a combination of the red, green, and blue channels.

In other words, the luminance histogram tries to accurately reflect the light you see by weighting its color values in a particular way. Since the human eye sees green most easily, the luminance histogram is heavily weighted toward green. Notice in figure 8.18, screen 1, how the luminance histogram at the top (the white one) looks very similar to the green channel histogram below it.

Red and blue are also represented in the luminance histogram but in lesser quantities (59 percent green + 30 percent red + 11 percent blue = luminance). The luminance histogram measures the perceived brightness in 256 levels (0–255).

The luminance histogram is an accurate way of looking at the combined color levels in real images. Because it more accurately reflects the way our eyes actually see color brightness, it may be the best histogram for you to use, most of the time.

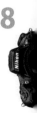

Luminance Histogram, Screen 3 – The white histogram shown in figure 8.18, screen 3, is exactly the same as the white luminance histogram seen in screen 2 and the top white histogram in screen 1.

This particular histogram (figure 8.18, screen 3) is available only by assigning one of the camera's buttons to open it. In *Custom Setting Menu > f Controls > f2*

Multi selector center button > Playback mode, I assigned View histograms to the Multi selector center button.

Now whenever I am viewing an image on the camera's Monitor, I can press the Multi selector center button and the camera will display the histogram seen in figure 8.18, screen 3, as long as I hold down the button. This works only when you're using Playback mode (viewing images). It is a fast and convenient way to get a histogram open without scrolling through a bunch of image data screens.

Now that we have discussed how to open the various histogram screens in the D810, let's discuss how a histogram works.

Understanding the Histogram

Using your D810's histogram screens will guarantee you a much higher percentage of well-exposed images. It is well worth spending time to understand the histogram. It's not as complicated as it looks.

I'll cover this feature with enough detail to give you a working knowledge of how to use the histogram to make better pictures. If you are deeply interested in the histogram, there is a lot of research material available on the Internet. Although this overview is brief, it will present enough knowledge to improve your technique immediately.

Best Dynamic Range Ever

The D810's sensor can record a certain range of light values—according to DxO Labs, 14.8 EV steps, which is an amazing amount of dynamic range. In fact, the D810 has one of the widest dynamic range capabilities of any digital camera tested by DxO Labs.

Unfortunately, even with the massive potential dynamic range the D810 has, many of the higher-contrast subjects we shoot contain more light range than the camera can capture in one exposure.

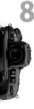

It is important to understand how your camera records light so you can better control how the image is captured. Even though the dynamic range of the D810 is superior to other cameras, it still can't handle the range of light captured by the human eye.

Let's look into the histogram so you can determine how well you have captured the light in the scene before your lens. The gray rectangular area in figure 8.19 represents an in-camera histogram. Examine it carefully! Think about it for a minute before reading on.

The histogram is basically a graph of 256 steps that represents the maximum range of light values your camera can capture (0 = pure black and 255 = pure white). In the middle of the histogram are the midrange values that represent middle colors like grays, light browns, and greens. The values from just above zero and just below 255 contain detail.

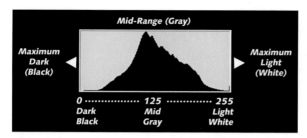

Figure 8.19 – A basic histogram

The actual histogram looks like a mountain peak, or a series of peaks, and the more there is of a particular color, the taller the peak that represents that color. In some cases the graph will be rounder on top, and in other cases it will be flattened or have several peaks.

The left side of the histogram represents the maximum dark values that your camera can record. The right side represents the maximum light values your camera can capture. On either end of the histogram (0 or 255), the light values contain no detail. They are either completely black (0) or completely white (255).

The height of the histogram (top of mountain peaks) represents the amount of individual colors. You cannot easily control this value in-camera, other than changing to a Picture Control with more or less saturated color, so it is for your information only.

We are mostly concerned with the left- and right-side values of the histogram because we do have much greater control over those (dark versus light). In figure 8.20, we see a basic histogram tutorial with three separate histograms that have different exposures. Refer to figure 8.20 as we discuss the histogram further.

Simply put, the histogram's horizontal scale is related to the darkness and lightness of the image, and the vertical scale of the histogram (valleys and peaks of the mountains) have to do with the amount of color information.

The left (dark) and right (light) directions of the horizontal scale are very important for your picture taking. If the image is too dark, the light values will be clipped off on the left side; if it's too light, the light values will be clipped off on the right side. This will become easier to understand as we look at well-exposed and poorly exposed images.

When you see the three histograms next to each other (figure 8.20), does it make more sense? See how the underexposed histogram is all the way to the left of the histogram window and is clipped midpeak? Note how both edges of the well-exposed histogram just touch the horizontal edges of the histogram window. Finally, notice how the overexposed histogram is crammed toward the right and clipped. Now, let's look at some histogram details.

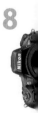

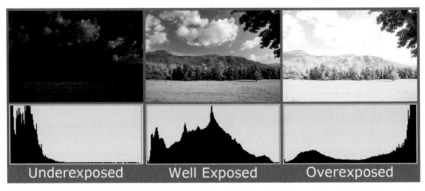

Figure 8.20 – Three histograms: underexposed, well exposed, and overexposed

Histogram Shape

The image in figure 8.21 is well exposed with no serious problems. The entire light range of this particular image fits within the histogram window, which means that it's not too light or too dark and will need very little or no adjustment to view or print. This image is similar to the well-exposed image in figure 8.20. It contains no more than 6 or 7 stops (EV steps) of light. To finalize the image, I might increase the brightness in the trees a little, but otherwise it's a sound image with potential for immediate usage.

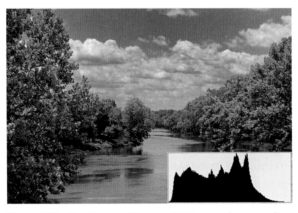

Figure 8.21 – Good image with normal histogram shape, no clipping

Compare the histogram in figure 8.21 to the histogram in figure 8.22. Notice that the histogram in figure 8.21 is not crammed against the dark value side (left side) like the histogram in figure 8.22. In other words, the dark values in figure 8.21 are not clipped on the left. This means that the camera recorded all the dark values in this image with no loss of shadow detail.

Now look at the right side of the histogram in figure 8.21 and note that it is not completely against the light value side (right side), although it is quite close. The image contains all the available light values. Everything between the right and left sides is exposed quite well, with full detail. A histogram does not have to cover the entire window for the exposure to be correct. When there is a very limited range of light, the histogram may be rather narrow.

The image in figure 8.21 is a relatively bland image with smooth gradations of tone, so it makes a smooth mountain-shaped histogram. This will not occur every time because most images contain quite a bit more color information. Each prominent color will be represented with its own peak on the histogram. The most prominent colors will have higher peaks, and the less prominent colors will have lower or no peaks.

As we progress into images with more color or light information, we'll see that the corresponding histograms look quite different.

Look at the image in figure 8.22. This image slightly exceeds the range of the camera's digital sensor.

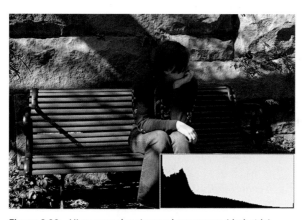

Figure 8.22 – Histogram showing underexposure (dark side)

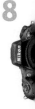

Notice that, overall, this image is dark and looks underexposed. The histogram is crammed to the left and is clipped. There are no gradual climbs as on a mountain range, from valley to peak and back to valley. Instead, the image shows up on the left side in midpeak.

The most important thing to understand when you see a histogram like the one in figure 8.22, with part of the peak clipped off on the left, is that some or all of the image is significantly underexposed.

In figure 8.23 a larger aperture was used and more light was allowed in. We can now see much more detail. But once again, the range of light is too great for the sensor to fully capture, and both sides of the histogram display (dark and light) are clipped.

The image in figure 8.23 shows more detail but is not professional-looking and will win no awards. The range of light is simply too great to be recorded fully. Many of the details are overly light, and that can be seen by the clipping of the histogram on the right side. The most important thing to remember is that when you see a histogram that is crammed all the way to the right and clipped, some or all of the image is significantly too light. A portion of the image in figure 8.23 is recorded as pure white and is permanently gone, or blown out.

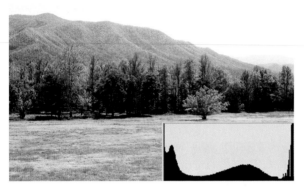

Figure 8.23 – Histogram showing overexposure (light side)

From the clipping on the left, you can see that some dark detail has been lost in the image, too. Looking at the base of the closest trees in the picture, you can clearly see dark shadows with little or no detail. This image simply has too much light range for the camera to record it all. We will discuss what to do about this later in the chapter.

It is important that you try to center the histogram without clipping either edge. This is not always possible, as shown in figure 8.23, because the light range is often too great and the sensor or histogram window can't contain it. If you center the histogram, your images will be better exposed. If you take a picture and the histogram is shifted toward the left or right, you can retake the photograph and adjust the exposure.

If there is too much light to allow the histogram to be centered, you must decide which part of the image is more important—the light or dark values—and expose for those values.

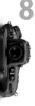

How Does the Eye React to Light Values?
With its imaging sensor and glass lenses, the D810 is only a weak imitation of our marvelously designed eye and brain combination. There are very few situations in which our eyes cannot adjust to the available light range. So, as photographers, we are always seeking ways to record a portion of what our eyes and mind can see.

Since our eyes tend to know that shadows are black, and we expect that, it is usually better to expose for the highlights. If you see dark shadows, that seems normal. We're simply not used to seeing light so bright that all detail is lost. An image exposed for the dark values will look weird because most highlight detail will be burned out.

Your eyes can see a huge range of light in comparison to your digital sensor. The only time you will ever see light values that are so bright that detail is lost is when you are looking directly at an overwhelmingly bright light, like the sun. In a worst-case scenario, if you expose the image so the right side of the histogram just touches the right side of the histogram window, and the image will look more normal.

Since photography's beginnings, we have always fought with being able to record only a limited range of light. But with the digital camera and its histogram, we can now see a visual representation of the light values. We can immediately review the image, reshoot it emphasizing lighter or darker values, or use a graduated neutral-density filter to hold back part of the light in the scene.

Many of today's digital photographers prefer to use high dynamic range (HDR) imaging, where multiple images are exposed with different values to capture a much broader range of light. The images are then combined into one image with a much greater range of light displayed.

Computer Adjustment of Images

Looking at the image in figure 8.24, taken in midday with overhead sunshine, we see an example of a range of light too great to be captured by a digital sensor but exposed in such a way that we can get a usable photo later.

Notice how the dark values are clipped and the dark detail is lost. But look to the right side of the histogram and notice how the light values are not clipped. The camera recorded all of the light values but lost some dark values.

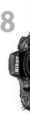

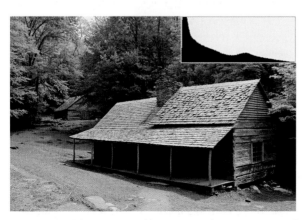

Figure 8.24 – Cabin picture and histogram with correct exposure but dark shadows

Since our eyes see this as normal, this image looks okay. If we were standing there looking at the cabin ourselves, our eyes would be able to see much more detail in the front porch area. But the camera just can't record that much light range. If we want to get a bit more detail in the shadows than this image seems to contain, we can do it. Normally, a camera does not give us enough control to add light values on the fly, so we use the histogram to get the best possible exposure and then adjust the image later in the computer. Some cameras can be profiled to capture light ranges more effectively in one direction or the other, but when you push one area, the opposite area must give. So we need a way to take all this light and compress it into a more usable range.

We are now entering the realm of post-processing, or in-computer image manipulation. Look at the image in figure 8.25. This is the same image as figure 8.24, but it has been adjusted in Photoshop to cram more image detail into the histogram by compressing the midrange values. Notice that the mountain peak of the histogram is farther right, toward the light side, than the histogram for figure 8.24, and that the whole histogram fits within the histogram window without any clipping. We removed a good bit of the midrange, but since there was already a lot of midrange there, our image did not suffer greatly.

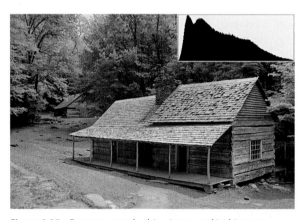

Figure 8.25 – Post-processed cabin picture and its histogram

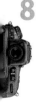

How this computer post-processing was done is outside the scope of this book, but it is not very difficult. Buy a program like Nikon Capture NX-D, Photoshop, Photoshop Elements, Lightroom, Aperture, or another fine graphics program designed for photographers. Your digital camera and your computer are a powerful imaging combination—a digital darkroom, where you are in control from start to finish, from releasing the shutter to printing the image. Retreating from philosophy, let's continue with our histogram exploration.

Notice in figure 8.25 that the histogram edge is just touching the highlight side of the histogram window. If it had gone a tiny bit past the right edge and clipped a small amount, the image would not have been damaged too badly or at all, for a reason we will discuss in a moment. Sometimes a very small amount of clipping does not seriously harm the image, especially when you are shooting in RAW mode.

The photographer must be the judge. The greater apparent detail in the image in figure 8.25 is the result of compressing the midrange of the light values a bit in the computer. If you compress or make the midrange light values smaller, that will tend to pull the dark values toward the light side and the light values toward the dark side. It's like cutting a section out of the middle of a garden hose. If you pull both of the cut ends together, the other two ends of the hose will move toward the middle, and the hose will be shorter overall. If you compress or remove the midrange of the histogram, both ends of the graph will move toward the middle. If one end of the graph is beyond the edge of the histogram window (clipped), it will be less so when the midrange is compressed.

We are simply trying to make the histogram fit into the frame of its window. We can cut out some of the middle to bring both ends into the window because there is usually plenty in the middle to cut out, so the image rarely suffers. Remember, this is done outside of the camera in a computer. You can't really control the in-camera histogram to compress values, but you need to be aware that it can be done in a computer so that you can expose accordingly with your camera's histogram. Then you will be prepared for later post-processing of the image. Now that we have compressed the midrange values, figure 8.25 more closely resembles what our eye normally sees, so it looks more normal to us.

Shooting in RAW Can Benefit Your Images

In many cases, your progression from the shooting site to your digital darkroom can benefit if you shoot NEF (RAW) images. A RAW digital image contains an adjustable range of light, in a sense. With a RAW image, you can use controls in Capture NX-D, Lightroom, Photoshop, or even the basic Nikon View NX 2 software included with the D810 to select from the range of light within the big RAW image file. It's like moving the histogram window to the left or right over all that wide range of RAW image data. You select a final resting place for the histogram window, capture the underlying RAW data, and your image is ready for use.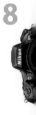

This is a serious oversimplification of the process, but I hope it is more understandable. In reality, the digital sensor records a wider range of light than you can use in one image. You always have that extra information available to you in a RAW image, but it is thrown away when you shoot or convert to JPEG.

Although you can't get all of that range into the final image without special processing, it is there in the RAW file as a selectable range. I prefer to think of it as a built-in bracket because it works in a similar way.

In reality—and this is an important point—the histogram we use in our D810 cameras (and other Nikons) is based on a camera-processed JPEG file. Therefore, when you are shooting in RAW mode, there is a little more headroom for clipping on the dark and light sides of the histogram than what the histogram window shows. You can over- and underexpose by a slight amount when shooting in RAW mode and still pull out good detail, where the detail would be gone had you been shooting in JPEG mode.

In my experience with the D810, the dark detail contains an *amazing* amount of information that can be recovered, with a little added noise as a penalty. The bright values do not have quite the same amount of headroom, so be careful not to seriously overexpose your images or nothing will recover the light detail.

Using Active D-Lighting for Expanded Dynamic Range

Interestingly, the Active D-Lighting function on the D810 is a good example of what I mean by there being extra detail available in a RAW file. Where do you suppose Active D-Lighting gets its detail? From the extra headroom in the RAW sensor data, of course. A JPEG file especially benefits from Active D-Lighting in many cases.

When you have Active D-Lighting turned on, the JPEG is created from RAW sensor data, with expanded dynamic range from Active D-Lighting applied as the JPEG file is created and saved to the memory card. The D810 is especially powerful when it comes to using Active D-Lighting. It is the first digital camera I have ever used where I will leave this function turned on most of the time. It does a simply marvelous job at extending the range of light your images can contain.

Highlights Blink Mode

There are also other Monitor viewing modes that you can use along with the histogram, such as the Highlights (blink) mode for blown-out highlights (see the *Playback Menu > Playback display options* and select Highlights, as shown in figure 8.26).

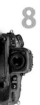

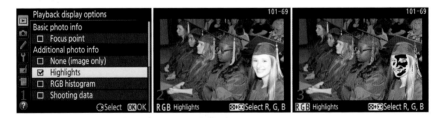

Figure 8.26 – Selecting the Highlights blink mode

This mode will cause your image to blink from light to dark in the blown-out highlight areas, as seen in the young graduate's face in figure 8.26, screens 2 and 3.

This white-to-black blinking is a rough representation of a histogram in which the highlight value is clipped, and it is quite useful for quick shooting. Using your camera's light meter, histogram, and Highlights (blink) mode together is a very powerful way to control your exposures.

Why Master the Histogram?

If you master using the histogram, you will have a fine degree of control over where you place the light range of your images. This is sort of like using the famous Ansel Adams black-and-white Zone System, but it is represented visually on the Monitor of your D810.

The manipulation of histogram levels in-computer is a detailed study in and of itself. It's part of having a digital darkroom. Learn to use your computer to tweak your images, and you'll be able to produce superior results most of the time. Even more important, learn to use your histogram to capture a nice image in the first place!

Your histogram is simply a graph that lets you see at a glance how well your image is contained by your camera. If it's too far left, the image is too dark; if it's too far right, the image is too light. If clipped on both ends, there is too much light for one image to contain. Learn to use the histogram well and your images are bound to improve!

Settings Recommendation: The camera's light meter should be used to get the initial exposure only. Then you can look at the histogram to see if the image's light range is contained within the limited range of the sensor. If the histogram is clipped to the right or the left, you may want to add or subtract light with the +/- Exposure compensation button or use Manual mode. Let your light meter get you close, then fine-tune with the histogram.

Author's Conclusions

This camera certainly gives you a lot of choices for light meters and exposure modes. You can start using this camera at whatever level of photographic knowledge you have. If you are a beginner, use the P mode. If you want to progress into partial automation, use the S or A mode. And if you are a dyed-in-the-wool imaging fanatic, use the M mode for full manual control of the camera. You have a choice with the D810!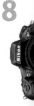

The next chapter is about a subject of great importance to digital photographers—white balance (WB). Understanding WB gives you an edge over other photographers. Learning about the histogram and white balance will place you in a spot occupied by relatively few people. When you have mastered those two subjects and learned about color spaces, you will indeed be an advanced digital photographer. Let's proceed!

White Balance

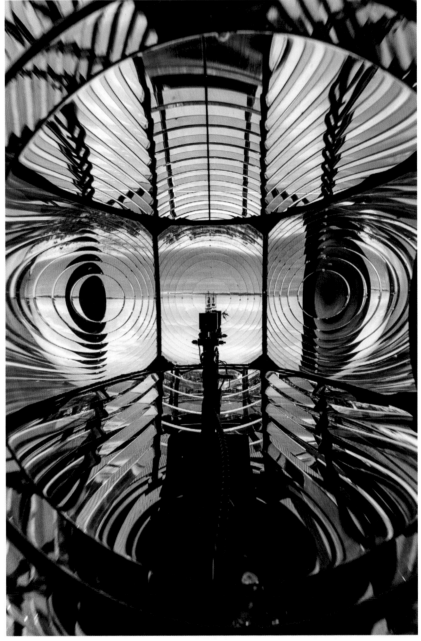

9

Giant Fresnel Lens in Pensacola Lighthouse © Larry Loar (*folkloar*)

Back in the good old days, photographers bought special rolls of film or filters to meet the challenges of color casts that come from indoor lighting, overcast days, or special situations.

The D810's method for balancing the camera to the available light comes with the White balance (WB) controls. Fortunately, the D810's two Auto White balance settings do a great job for general shooting. However, discerning photographers learn how to use the White balance controls so they can achieve color consistency in special situations.

How Does White Balance (WB) Work?

(User's Manual – Page 148)

Normally White balance is used to adjust the camera so that whites are truly white and other colors are accurate under whatever light source you are shooting. You can also use the White balance controls to deliberately introduce color casts into your image for interesting special effects.

Camera WB color temperatures are exactly the opposite of the Kelvin scale we learned in school for star temperatures. Remember that a red giant star is cool, while a blue/white star is hot. The WB color temperatures are the opposite because the WB system adds color to make up for a deficit of color in the original light of the subject.

For instance, under a fluorescent light, there is a deficit of blue, which makes the subject appear greenish yellow. When blue is added, the image is balanced to a more normal appearance.

Another example might be shooting on a cloudy, overcast day. The cool, ambient light could cause the image to look bluish if it's left unadjusted. The White balance control in your camera sees the cool color temperature and adds some red to warm the colors a bit. Normal camera White balance on a cloudy, overcast day might be about 6000K.

Just remember that we use the real kelvin temperature range in reverse and that red colors are considered warm and blue colors are cool. Even though this is the opposite of what we were taught in school, it fits our situation better. To photographers, blue seems cool and red seems warm! Just don't let your astronomer friends convince you otherwise.

Understanding WB in a fundamental way is simply realizing that light has a range of colors that go from cool to warm. We can adjust our cameras to use the available light in an accurate and neutral, balanced way that compensates for the actual light source. Or we can allow a color cast to enter the image by unbalancing the settings. In this chapter, we will discuss this from the standpoint of the D810's camera controls and how they deal with WB.

9

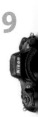

Color Temperature

(User's Manual – Page 150)

The D810 WB range can vary from a very cool 2500K to a very warm 10,000K. Figure 9.1A shows the same picture adjusted in Photoshop, with the use of photo filters, to three WB settings. Notice how the image in the center is about right; the image on the left is cooler (bluish cast) and the image on the right is warmer (reddish cast).

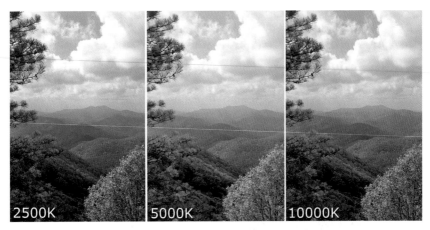

2500K   5000K   10000K

Figure 9.1A – Same image with three different WB Color Temperature settings

The same adjustments we made with film and filters can now be achieved with the White balance settings built into the D810. To achieve the same effect as daylight film and a warming filter, simply select the Cloudy White balance setting while shooting in normal daylight. This sets the D810 to balance at about 6000K, which makes nice, warm-looking images. If you want to really warm up the image, choose the White balance setting called Shade, which sets the camera to 8000K. Or you could set the D810's White balance to Auto2 (A2), which warms up the colors and automatically adjusts for current light sources.

On the other hand, if you want to make the image appear cool or bluish, try using the Fluorescent (4200K) or Incandescent (3000K) setting in normal daylight.

Remember, the color temperature shifts from cool values to warm values. The D810 can record your images with any color temperature from 2500K (very cool or bluish) to 10,000K (very warm or reddish) and any major value in between. There is no need to carry different film emulsions or filters to deal with light color range. The D810 has very easy-to-use color temperature controls and a full range of color temperatures available.

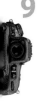

There are two separate methods for setting the White balance on the D810:

- Manual WB using the WB button and selecting options
- Manual WB using the Shooting Menu and selecting options

We'll consider each of these techniques because you may prefer to use different methods according to the amount of time you have to shoot and the color accuracy you want.

Camera Control Locations for WB Adjustment

In this chapter we will often use the WB button, Main and Sub-command dials, and Control panel when adjusting White balance (figure 9.1B). You may want to place a bookmark here for future reference if you are not sure where these controls are.

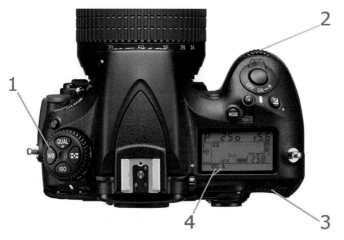

Figure 9.1B – Camera controls for White balance adjustment

Figure 9.1B shows the following controls:

1. WB button
2. Sub-command dial
3. Main command dial
4. Control panel with WB symbols

Remember these control names and locations for use in this chapter and later in the field.

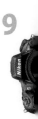

> ### What Is Mired?
>
> Often in this chapter I will talk about adjusting White balance in mired incre-ments. *Mired* stands for *micro reciprocal degree*. It is a unit of measurement used to express color temperature value differences. It is based on a just-noticeable difference between two light sources and founded on the difference of the recip-rocal of their kelvin color temperatures (not the temperatures themselves). The use of mired values dates back to 1932 when Irwin G. Priest invented the method. It is based on a mathematical formula, as follows: **M = 1,000,000 / T**, where M is the desired mired value and T is the color temperature in units of kelvin. Most of us don't need to be concerned about understanding the term mired. Just realize that it means a visual difference between color values.

Manual White Balance Using the WB Button

(User's Manual – Page 149)

Sometimes you might want to control the WB in a totally manual way. This and the next section's methods accomplish the same thing, except this first method config-ures the WB using a button and dial and the next uses the camera's menu system.

Each of these methods will allow you to set a particular WB temperature. If you want your image to appear cool, medium, or warm, you can set the appropriate color temperature, take the picture, and then look at the image on the Monitor.

Here is how to manually choose a WB type using the WB button, Main command dial, and Control panel (figure 9.1B and figure 9.2):

1. Press and hold the WB button on top of your D810 (figure 9.1B #1).
2. Rotate the rear Main command dial (figure 9.1B #3).
3. The symbols in the following list will appear one at a time on the Control panel (figure 9.2, red arrow, and figure 9.1B, #4)). Each click of the dial will change the display to the next WB setting. These symbols, options, and their kelvin values are as follows:

A Auto White Balance – 3500K to 8000K (A on Control panel, Auto in camera menus, and AUTO1 (A1) or AUTO2 (A2) on Informa-tion display)
- Incandescent – 3000K
- Fluorescent – 2700K to 7200K
- Direct sunlight – 5200K
- Flash – 5400K
- Cloudy – 6000K

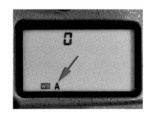

Figure 9.2 – Manual White Balance with Control panel

☘ Shade – 8000K

⏻ K – Choose a color temperature (2500K–10,000K)

PRE PRE (Preset manual) – White balance measured from actual ambient light

Manual White Balance Using the Shooting Menu

(User's Manual – Page 149)

This method uses the Shooting Menu screens to select the appropriate White balance.

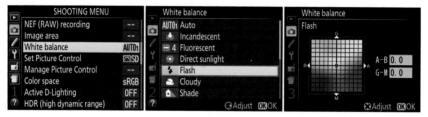

Figure 9.3A – Manual White balance with Shooting Menu screens

Here are the steps used to select a White balance setting:

1. Select White balance from the Shooting Menu and scroll to the right (figure 9.3A, screen 1).
2. Select one of the preset values, such as Flash, and scroll to the right (figure 9.3A, screen 2).
3. Press the OK button immediately, without moving the little square from its center position, unless you want to fine-tune the White balance setting (figure 9.3, screen 3). Fine-tuning is discussed in detail in the upcoming section **Fine-Tuning White Balance**.

Normally, you'll use only the first two screens in figure 9.3A to select one of the preset WB values, such as Cloudy, Shade, or Direct sunlight. Then you'll press the OK button on the final screen without changing anything. If you'd like, you can fine-tune the white balance with the third screen. As mentioned in step 3, we'll discuss how later in the chapter.

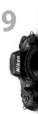

9

Additional Screen for Auto and Fluorescent WB

If you choose Auto or Fluorescent, you will find an additional screen before you get to the final fine-tuning screen.

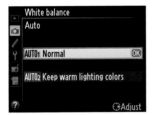

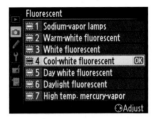

Figure 9.3B – Extra Auto WB screen before fine-tuning screen

Figure 9.3C – Extra Fluorescent WB screen before fine-tuning screen

Auto White balance has two values from which to choose: AUTO1 Normal and AUTO2 Keep warm lighting colors (figure 9.3B). AUTO2 can make a somewhat warmer image than AUTO1.

Fluorescent includes seven types of Fluorescent lighting: Sodium-vapor lamps, Warm-white fluorescent, White fluorescent, Cool-white fluorescent, Day white fluorescent, Daylight fluorescent, and High temp. mercury-vapor (figure 9.3C).

Manual Color Temperature with the WB Button

(User's Manual – Page 157)

The K selection on the Control panel is flexible and allows you to manually select a WB value between 2500K and 10,000K.

Here are the steps to select a specific kelvin (K) White balance value using external camera controls (figure 9.1B and figure 9.4):

1. Select the K symbol on the Control panel by holding down the WB button and rotating the rear Main command dial (figure 9.1B and 9.4).
2. While still holding down the WB button, rotate the front Sub-command dial to select the actual WB kelvin temperature you desire, from 2500K to 10,000K. In figure 9.4, I used the front Sub-command dial to select 5000K.

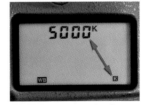

Figure 9.4 – Manual Color temperature (K) with external camera controls

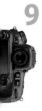

Manual Color Temperature with the Shooting Menu

(User's Manual – Page 155)

You can also manually select a color temperature using the Shooting Menu screens.

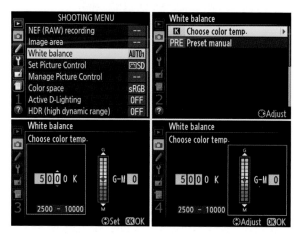

Figure 9.5 – Manual Color temperature (K) with Shooting Menu screens

Here are the steps to select a specific kelvin (K) White balance value using Shooting Menu screens:

1. Choose White balance from the Shooting Menu and scroll to the right (figure 9.5, screen 1).
2. Select Choose color temp. from the White balance menu and scroll to the right (figure 9.5, screen 2).
3. Using the Multi selector to scroll up or down in the color temperature box, you can choose a number from 2500K to 10,000K. In figure 9.5, screen 3, you can see that I selected 5000K. Notice how a large yellow rectangle is surrounding the Choose color temp. area of the screen? This screen has two sides, one for color temperature selection and the other for fine-tuning. Scroll to the right to move the yellow triangle to the fine-tuning area.
4. Now you can fine-tune the color temperature to include more green or magenta in six steps, G1–G6 or M1–M6. You simply press up or down on the Multi selector to fine-tune. Up adds green (G) and down adds magenta (M).
5. Once you have fine-tuned the color temperature to your liking, press the OK button.

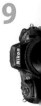

When you have selected an exact White balance temperature, all images you shoot from that point forward—until you change to another WB—will have that setting. You can have very consistent White balance from image to image by using this method. For in-studio product shoots, or in any circumstance where you need a constant White balance, this is a desirable function.

Measuring Ambient Light by Using PRE

(User's Manual – Page 158)
This method allows you to measure ambient light values and set the camera's WB. It's not hard to learn and is very accurate because it's an actual through-the-lens measurement of the source light's kelvin temperature.

You'll need a white or gray card to accomplish this measurement. Figure 9.6A shows the popular WhiBal white balance reference cards, which are available at **http://michaeltapesdesign.com/whibal.html**. The WhiBal card set is very convenient because it contains card versions that will easily fit in your pocket or camera bag.

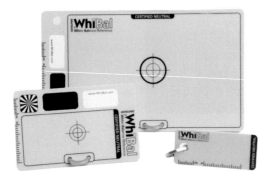

Figure 9.6A – WhiBal cards

Here's how to select the PRE White balance measurement method (figures 9.1B, 9.6B, and 9.6C):

1. Press and hold the WB button (figure 9.1B).
2. Rotate the rear Main command dial until PRE shows at the lower-right of the Control panel (figure 9.6B). You'll also see d-1 at the top of the Control panel.
3. While still pressing the WB button, turn the front Sub-command dial and select one of the preset memory locations, d-1 to d-6. Your measured White balance reading will be stored in that location.
4. Release the WB button.

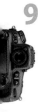

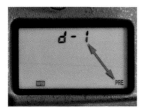

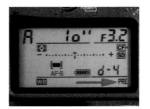

Figure 9.6B – PRE White balance measurement method

Figure 9.6C – PRE White balance measurement method

5. Press and hold the WB button again until PRE starts blinking* in the lower-right corner of the Control panel (figure 9.6C, red arrow). You will see the preset memory location number just above the flashing PRE (figure 9.6C shows that we are adjusting d-4).

6. Point the camera at a white or neutral gray card lit by the same light source you will be using to take pictures. The camera does not have to focus on the card, but the card should fill the frame, so try to get close without making a shadow.

7. Press the Shutter-release button fully, as if you were photographing the card. The shutter will fire, but nothing will appear on the Monitor.

8. Check the Control panel to see if *Good* is flashing and PrE (with lowercase r) appears on the lower-right portion of the Control panel (above the tiny PRE). If *Good* is flashing, you have successfully measured for a correct White balance under the light in which you are shooting. If you see *no Gd* flashing (instead of *Good*), the operation was not successful. Your available light may not be bright enough to take an accurate reading.

*Note: Once PRE starts blinking on the Control panel, you must take the new White balance measurement (step 6) within about six seconds, or you will have to repeat steps 4 and 5. If you have Custom Setting c2 Auto meter-off delay set to longer than six seconds, the PRE measurement time-out (how long PRE flashes) will match it. The PRE measurement time-out is tied directly to the Auto meter-off delay.

The PRE measurement is very sensitive because it uses the light coming through the lens to set the WB. Unless you are measuring in extremely low light it will virtually always be successful.

Fine-Tuning White Balance

(User's Manual – Page 151)

You can fine-tune White balance using the camera's external WB controls or the Shooting Menu. Fine-tuning with external controls allows for adjustment of only amber or blue. The Shooting Menu allows you to fine-tune not only amber and blue, but also green and magenta.

Fine-Tuning with External Controls

Only certain White balance values can be fine-tuned with external controls, including Auto, Incandescent, Fluorescent, Direct sunlight, Flash, Cloudy, and Shade. Basically, you select one of the White balance values provided by the camera and add amber or blue in 5-mired increments. You can add or subtract amber or blue in up to six steps—A1 to A6 or b1 to b6. That means you can change the color from

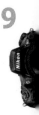

a minimum of 5 mired to a maximum of 30 mired. Remember, a 1-mired step is equivalent to a barely perceptible change in color.

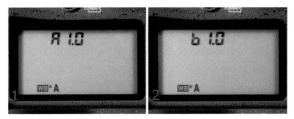

Figure 9.7A – Fine-tuning White balance with external controls

Here is how to add or subtract amber or blue from a Nikon-provided White balance value, using external camera controls (figures 9.1B and 9.7A):

1. Press and hold the WB button and turn the rear Main command dial (figure 9.1B) until you select a White balance value you would like to fine-tune. In figure 9.7A, you can see the results of selecting a WB value; I selected auto (A) White balance.
2. While still holding down the WB button, turn the front Sub-command dial to the left (counterclockwise) for amber values (A1–A6) or to the right (clockwise) for blue values (b1–b6). Remember that each Sub-command dial click is a 5-mired value. In figure 9.7A, there are two Control panel screens showing the two color types that I selected (A1 and b1). Screen 1 is one 5-mired step of additional amber, and screen 2 is one 5-mired step of extra blue added to the current WB value.
3. Release the WB button, and you're ready to take pictures with your fine-tuned WB value. It stays fine-tuned until you change it back. You'll see a small asterisk next to the WB symbol on the Control panel when you are using a fine-tuned WB value. You can see the asterisk in both images in figure 9.7A between WB and A. If you select a different White balance that has not been fine-tuned, the asterisk goes away.

Unfortunately, external control fine-tuning is not a visual process. You'll need to examine the images taken with your new WB* value to determine if you like the results of your fine-tuning effort.

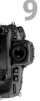

Fine-Tuning with the Shooting Menu
You can use the Shooting Menu to fine-tune even more effectively than you can with the camera's external controls. Instead of two colors (amber and blue), you can adjust four colors (amber, blue, green, and magenta).

If you want to fine-tune a previously saved White balance value, you can do it with the Shooting Menu screens, too. The value in any of the d-1 to d-4 memory locations can be manually fine-tuned. The color balance can be moved toward G (green), A (amber), M (magenta), or B (blue), or it can be moved toward intermediate combinations of those colors.

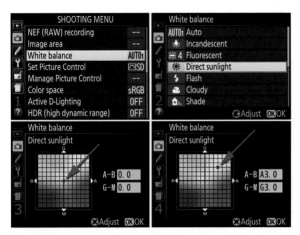

Figure 9.7B – Fine-tuning White balance with Shooting Menu screens

Here are the steps used to fine-tune a White balance setting using Shooting Menu screens:

1. Select White balance from the Shooting Menu and scroll to the right (figure 9.7B, screen 1).
2. Choose one of the White balance types. I chose Direct sunlight. Now scroll to the right or press the OK button (figure 9.7B, screen 2).
3. You will now see the fine-tuning screen with its color box. In the middle of the color box is a small black square (figure 9.7B, screen 3, red arrow). When this square is in the middle, as shown in screen 3, nothing has been changed. Each press of the Multi selector in a given direction is equal to one 5-mired step in that direction—up is green (G), down is magenta (M), left is blue (B), and right is amber (A). You can see in figure 9.7B, screen 4, that I have added 3.0 to both G and A by moving the little square to a position in between those two values (see red arrow in screen 4).
4. Press the OK button to save your change. An asterisk will appear after the name of the fine-tuned White balance selection on the Shooting Menu screen (figure 9.7C, screen 6, red arrow). To remove the fine-tuning adjustment, simply return to the screen with the color box and center the little square, as in figure 9.7B, screen 3.

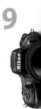

Note: If you aren't familiar with adjusting the preset's default color temperature, or if you don't want to change it (most people don't), then simply press the OK button without moving the little square from the center (figure 9.7B, screen 3).

Fine-Tuning a PRE Measured White Balance

Previously we examined how to take a PRE measurement from a white or gray card to balance the camera to the available light. What if you want to fine-tune one of the d-1 to d-6 Preset values? Let's do it!

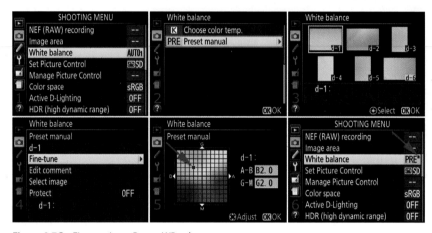

Figure 9.7C – Fine-tuning a Preset WB value

Use these steps to fine-tune a Preset White balance value:

1. Select White balance from the Shooting Menu and scroll to the right (figure 9.7C, screen 1).
2. Choose Preset manual from the menu and scroll to the right (figure 9.7C, screen 2).
3. Use the Multi selector to scroll to the memory location you want to fine-tune, d-1 to d-6 (figure 9.7C, screen 3). Press the Multi selector center button to select it.
4. Choose Fine-tune from the Preset manual menu and scroll to the right (figure 9.7C, screen 4).
5. Use the Multi selector to adjust the color balance in 5-mired increments (figure 9.7C, screen 5). Scroll around in the color box toward whatever color you want to add to the currently stored White balance (red arrow). You'll see the color-mired values change on the right side of the screen in the fields next to A–B and G–M. Each increment (click) of the Multi selector is equal to about 5 mired.
6. Press the OK button to save your adjustments to the stored White balance. The camera will return to the main Shooting Menu screen and PRE* will appear next to White balance (figure 9.7, screen 6). The asterisk shows that this particular Preset White balance has been fine-tuned.

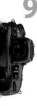

Editing the PRE WB Comment Field

(User's Manual – Page 169)

You can edit (add text to) the comment field of the memory location (d-1 to d-6) in which you just stored a White balance setting. Change the comment to something that will remind you of this measured WB setting's purpose.

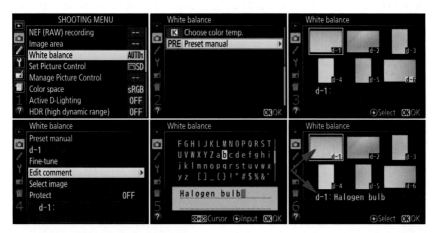

Figure 9.8 – Editing the comment field

Here are the steps to edit a WB setting's comment field:

1. Select White balance from the Shooting Menu and scroll to the right (figure 9.8, screen 1).
2. Choose Preset manual from the menu and scroll to the right (figure 9.8, screen 2).
3. Select the memory location for which you want to edit the comment (d-1 to d-6) and press the Multi selector center button (figure 9.8, screen 3). This will open the Preset manual menu.
4. Choose Edit comment from the menu and scroll to the right (figure 9.8, screen 4).
5. The character-selection panel will now appear (figure 9.8, screen 5). Use the Multi selector to navigate among the letters and numbers. Press the Multi selector center button to add a character to the comment line at the bottom of the screen. To scroll through characters already added, hold down the Thumbnail/playback zoom out button while navigating to the left or right with the Multi selector. Press the Delete button to delete the current character. Press the OK button to save the memory location comment.
6. The White balance memory location screen will now appear with the new memory location comment displayed (figure 9.8, screen 6, red arrow). I changed the comment field for memory location d-1 to Halogen bulb.

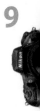

Using the White Balance from a Previously Captured Image

(User's Manual – Page 158)

You can also select a White balance setting from an image you have already successfully taken. This value can be applied to the picture you are about to take, or it can be copied to memory locations d-1 to d-6 (using the function described previously) for later use.

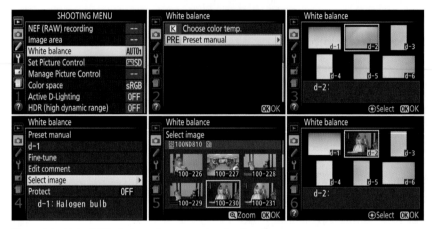

Figure 9.9 – Using White balance from a previously taken image

Here are the steps to recover the White balance setting from an image stored on your camera's memory card:

1. Select White balance from the Shooting Menu and scroll to the right (figure 9.9, screen 1).
2. Choose Preset manual from the menu and scroll to the right (figure 9.9, screen 2).
3. Choose a memory location to which you want to save the White balance setting from an existing picture. I chose d-2 (figure 9.9, screen 3). Press the Multi selector center button to select the Preset memory location. This opens the Preset manual menu.
4. Choose Select image from the Preset manual menu and scroll to the right (figure 9.9, screen 4). Select image will be grayed out if there are no images on your current memory card.
5. You will now see the Select image screen (figure 9.9, screen 5). Navigate through the available images until you find the one you want to use for white balance information. You can zoom in to look at a larger version of the image by pressing the Playback zoom in button. Press the OK button to select the image.

6. A small picture of the image will appear in your selected Preset White balance memory location and is saved there for future use (figure 9.9, screen 6). The White balance setting from that picture is now the White balance setting for the camera, until you change it.

Note: If you attempt to overwrite an existing PRE White balance setting (e.g., d-1) the camera will warn you with a screen that says: "d-1 already in use. Overwrite d-1? Yes/No"

Protecting a White Balance Preset

(User's Manual – Page 169)

You may have gone to great efforts to create a particular White balance Preset value that you will use frequently. Maybe you have a studio with a certain type of lighting that does not vary, and you want to have a dependable Preset value available for it. Let's see how to protect a Preset (d-1 to d-6) value.

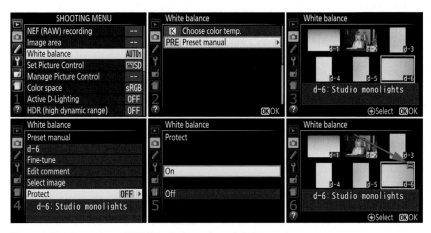

Figure 9.10 – Protecting a PRE White balance from deletion or change

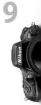

Here are the steps to protect a White balance Preset value:

1. Select White balance from the Shooting Menu and scroll to the right (figure 9.10, screen 1).

2. Choose the memory location you want to protect (d-1 to d-6). I chose d-3 (figure 9.10, screen 3). Press the Multi selector center button to select the Preset memory location. This opens the Preset manual menu.

3. Choose Protect from the Preset manual menu and scroll to the right (figure 9.10, screen 4).

4. Choose On to protect or Off to remove protection from a White balance memory location. I am protecting d-6, so I chose On (figure 9.10, screen 5).

5. The camera will now display the White balance screen with a protection symbol showing on the memory location you protected. The key symbol at the point of the red arrow in figure 9.10, screen 6, shows that memory location d-6 is locked from deletion and change. You cannot modify the protected value in any way, including fine-tuning or editing the comment field (d-6: Studio monolights), until you remove the protection.

Auto White Balance

(User's Manual – Page 148)

Auto White balance works pretty well in the D810. As the camera's RGB meter senses colors, it does its best to balance to any white or midrange grays it can find in the image. However, the color will vary a little on each shot. If you shoot only in Auto WB mode, your camera considers each image a new WB problem and solves it without reference to the last image taken.

The Auto WB setting also has the White balance fine-tuning screen, as discussed in the section **Fine-Tuning White Balance** earlier in this chapter. I don't see how this is particularly useful because each image is likely to have slightly different color temperatures. That would mean the fine-tuning would have little value for more than an image or two. If you were shooting in the exact same light for a period of time, I suppose the fine-tuning would be useful; however, wouldn't it make more sense to do a PRE reading of the light for exact WB? This choice will depend on your shooting style and personal preferences.

Using Auto WB (AUTO1 and AUTO2)

Auto White balance comes in two flavors: AUTO1 and AUTO2. The difference is that AUTO2 uses warmer colors in comparison to AUTO1.

For general shooting, AUTO1—or AUTO2, if you prefer warm colors—is all that's needed.

Here are the steps to select one of the Auto White balance options:

1. Choose White balance from the Shooting Menu and scroll to the right (figure 9.11, screen 1).

2. Select Auto from the menu and scroll to the right (figure 9.11, screen 2).

3. Choose AUTO1 Normal or AUTO2 Keep warm lighting colors (according to your color warmth preference) and scroll to the right (figure 9.11, screen 3).

4. Press the OK button to lock in the WB setting, or scroll to the right to fine-tune if you'd like (figure 9.11, screen 4). See the section Fine-Tuning White Balance earlier in this chapter.

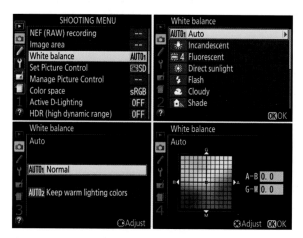

Figure 9.11 – Auto White balance choices

Settings Recommendation: I often use AUTO1 White balance on my D810. The only time I use anything but AUTO1 is when I am shooting special types of images. For instance, if I am shooting an event with flash and I want consistent image color, I often choose the Flash White balance setting. Or, if I am shooting landscapes under direct sunlight, I often shoot with the Direct sunlight White balance setting. Other than special occasions, Auto White balance works very well for me. Give it a try, along with each of the others in their respective environments. This is all part of improving our digital photography. A few years back, we carried different film emulsions and colored filters to get these same effects. Now it's all built in!

Should I Worry about White Balance If I Shoot in RAW mode?

The quick answer is no, but that may not be the best answer. When you take a picture using NEF (RAW) mode, the sensor image data has no White balance, sharpening, or color saturation information applied. Instead, the information about your camera settings is stored as markers along with the RAW black-and-white sensor data. Color information, including White balance, is applied permanently to the image only when you post-process and save the image in another format, like JPEG, TIFF, or EPS.

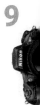

When you open the image in Nikon Capture NX 2, or another RAW conversion pro-gram, the camera settings are applied to the sensor data in a temporary way so you can view the image on your computer screen. If you don't like the White balance or almost any other setting you used in-camera, you can simply change it in the conversion software, and the image will look as if you used the new setting when you took the picture.

Does that mean I am not concerned about my WB settings because I shoot RAW most of the time? No. The human brain can quickly adjust to an image's colors and perceive them as normal, even when they are not. This is one of the dangers of not using correct WB. Because an unbalanced image on your computer screen is not compared to another correctly balanced image side by side, there is some danger that your brain may accept the slightly incorrect camera settings as normal, and your image will be saved with a color cast.

As a rule of thumb, if you use your WB correctly at all times, you'll consistently produce better images. You'll do less post-processing if the WB is correct in the first place. As RAW shooters, we already have a lot of post-processing work to do. Why add WB corrections to the workflow? It's just more work, if you ask me!

Additionally, you might decide to switch to JPEG mode in the middle of a shoot, and if you are not accustomed to using your WB controls, you'll be in trouble. When you shoot JPEGs, your camera will apply the WB information directly to the image and save it on your memory card—permanently. Be safe; always use good WB technique!

White Balance Tips and Tricks

When measuring WB with a gray or white card, keep in mind that your camera does not need to focus on the card. In PRE mode, it will not focus anyway because it is only trying to read light values, not take a picture. The important thing is to put your lens close enough to the card to prevent it from seeing anything other than the card. Three or four inches (about 75 mm to 100 mm) away from the card is about right for most lenses.

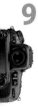

Be careful that your lens does not cast a shadow onto the card in a way that lets your camera see some of the shadow. This will make the measurement less accu-rate. Also, be sure that your source light does not produce glare on the card. This problem is not common because most cards have a matte surface, but it can hap-pen. You may want to hold the card at a slight angle to the source light if the light is particularly bright and might cause glare.

Finally, when the light is dim, use the white side of the card because it is more reflective. This may prevent a no Gd reading in low light. The gray card may be more accurate for color balancing, but it might be a little dark for a good measurement in dim light. If you are shooting in normal light, the gray card is best for balancing. You might want to experiment in normal light to see which you prefer.

Author's Conclusions

With these simple tips and some practice, you can become a D810 WB expert. Starting on page 148 of your D810 User's Manual, you'll find extensive WB information if you want another perspective on Nikon WB.

Learn to use the color temperature features of your camera to make superior images. You'll be able to capture very accurate colors or make pictures with color casts to reflect how you feel about the images. Practice a bit, and you'll find it easy to remember how to set your WB in the field.

Now, let's turn our attention to the autofocus (AF) system in the D810. Many people find the various modes hard to remember and even a bit confusing. In the upcoming chapter, we'll examine how the AF modes work and how they relate to other important camera functions, such as the AF-area and Release modes.

9

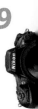

Autofocus, AF-Area, and Release Modes

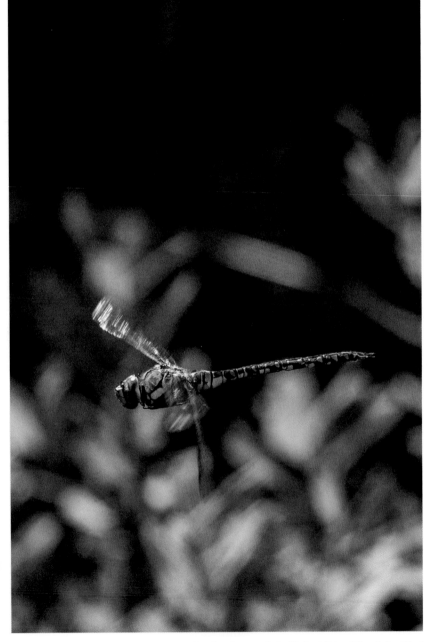

Hawker Dragonfly in Flight © Brian Tilley (*briantilley*)

10

Autofocus (AF) and Release modes are active settings that you'll deal with each time you use your camera. Unlike adjusting settings in the menus, which you'll do from time to time, you'll use Autofocus and Release modes every time you make an image or movie. You will adjust AF-area modes less often; however, these critical functions affect how and where the camera focuses on your subject.

To take pictures and make movies, you need to be very familiar with these settings, so this is a very important chapter for your mastery of the Nikon D810. Grab your camera and let's get started!

This chapter is divided into three sections:

- Section 1 – Autofocus in Viewfinder Photography
- Section 2 – Autofocus in Live View Photography
- Section 3 – Release Modes

Section 1 – Autofocus in Viewfinder Photography

The Nikon D810 has two types of autofocus built in, with different parts of the camera controlling AF in different shooting modes (figure 10.1). When you take pictures through the Viewfinder, one type of autofocus is used, and when you shoot a picture or movie using Live view, a different type is used. They are as follows:

- *TTL phase detection autofocus* – The Multi-CAM 3500 FX autofocus module provides through-the-lens (TTL) phase detection autofocus, with 51 AF points in a grid-like array in the central area of the Viewfinder (figure 10.1, image 1). This type of AF is known simply as *phase detection AF*. It is a very fast type of autofocus and is used by the camera only when you are taking pictures through the Viewfinder.
- *Focal plane contrast AF* – The camera's imaging sensor provides focal plane contrast AF, which uses pixel-level contrast detection (figure 10.1, image 2). A simple name for this is *contrast-detect AF*. The entire surface of the imaging sensor can be used to detect contrast between light and dark boundaries to provide autofocus. This is a relatively slow form of autofocus, but it is extremely accurate because it is done at the pixel level. This form of autofocus is used only while you are shooting in Live view mode.

What Is the Multi-CAM 3500 FX Autofocus Module?

The Multi-CAM 3500 FX AF module is a very accurate autofocus system that controls where and how your camera's AF and AF-S lenses achieve the sharpest focus on your subject.

10

The Nikon D810 offers a significant boost in the number of Viewfinder AF points over lesser cameras, with a total of 51. What do we gain from all these extra AF points and more powerful modes? As we progress through this chapter, we will discuss these things in detail, along with how your photography will benefit most from using all the features of the Multi-CAM 3500 FX AF system.

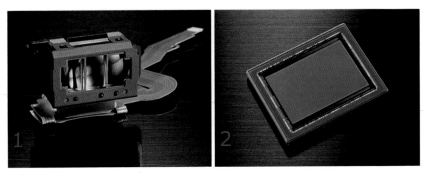

Figure 10.1 – (1) Multi-CAM 3500 FX AF module and (2) CMOS FX format imaging sensor

Three Mode Groups

There are three specific mode groups that you should fully understand: Autofocus modes, AF-area modes, and Release modes.

Many people get these modes confused and incorrectly apply functions from one mode to a completely different mode. It *is* a bit confusing at times, but if you read this carefully and try to wrap your brain around the different functionalities provided, you'll have much greater control of your camera later.

Note: The Nikon User's Manual page numbers are provided in case you want to see what the manual has to say. Using the manual is entirely optional because this book covers the information in more explicit detail.

First, let's consider how autofocus works when using the Viewfinder. The three mode groups for Viewfinder shooting are as follows:

Autofocus modes (User's Manual – Page 87):
- Single-servo (AF-S)
- Continuous-servo (AF-C)

AF-area modes (User's Manual – Page 90):
- Single-point AF
- Dynamic-area AF (9, 21, and 51 AF points)
- 3D-tracking AF
- Group-area AF
- Auto-area AF

10

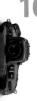

Custom Settings for Viewfinder AF and Live view/Movie AF
The AF module has 12 configurable Custom settings, a1–a12. We've examined each of those Custom settings in the chapter titled **Custom Setting Menu**. You may want to review each of them.

Release modes (User's Manual – Page 102):

- Single frame (S)
- Continuous low speed (CL)
- Continuous high speed (CH)
- Quiet shutter-release (Q)
- Quiet continuous shutter-release (Qc)
- Self-timer
- Mirror up (MUP)

What is the difference between these modes? Think of them like this: The AF-area modes control *where* the AF module focuses, the Autofocus modes control *how* it focuses, and the Release modes control *when* focus happens and how often a picture is taken.

While the Release modes are not technically Autofocus modes, it is a good idea to consider them at the same time because they control when Autofocus functions.

In upcoming sections, we'll look into all of these mode types and see how they work together to make the D810's autofocus and subject tracking system one of the world's best.

With the controls built into the D810 body, you'll be able to select whether the AF module uses 1 or many of its 51 AF points to find your subject. You'll also select whether the camera simply locks focus on a static subject or whether it continuously seeks a new focus if your subject is moving, and how fast (in frames per second) it captures the images.

Settings Recommendation: If you are having trouble remembering what all these modes do—join the club! I've written multiple books about Nikon cameras and I still get confused about what each mode does. I often refer back to my own books to remember all the details. I have both the print and e-book versions of my books so they are always nearby (I love my iPad).

You'll become familiar with the modes you use most often, and that is usually sufficient. Try to associate the type of mode with its name, and that will make it easier. Learn the difference between an AF-area mode (focus *where*), an Autofocus mode (focus *how*), and a Release mode (focus *when*).

10

Using Autofocus and AF-Area Modes for Viewfinder Photography

(User's Manual – Pages 87)

The D810 has distinct modes for how and where to focus. We'll examine each of those modes as a starting point in our understanding of autofocus with the Multi-CAM 3500 FX AF module. We'll tie together information about the AF-area modes, Autofocus modes, and Release modes since they work together to acquire and maintain good focus on your subject. Release modes are covered in the last section of this chapter because both Viewfinder and Live view photography use the same Release modes.

Figure 10.2 shows the controls we'll use in combination to change how the camera focuses and captures images. The caption helps you identify each control.

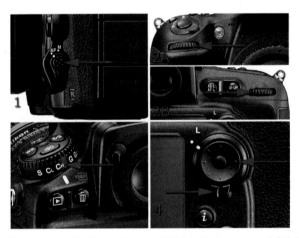

Figure 10.2 – (1) AF-mode button, (2A) Front Sub-command dial, (2B) Rear Main command dial, (3) Release mode dial, and (4) Multi selector, with AF-lock switch below

Notice in figure 10.2, image 4, that the Multi selector has a lock switch below it. You can see a white dot and an L to the left side of the switch. Move the switch to the dot setting (as shown), which unlocks the internal AF point movement capability. Otherwise, you won't be able to move the AF point around the Viewfinder within the 51 available points.

Settings Recommendation: I leave my D810's AF-lock switch unlocked all the time, but I check as the camera is focusing to make sure I am using the AF point I want to use. I can use the Multi selector to move a single AF point around the array of 51 available points when using Single-point AF, or a group of points when using Group-area AF or Dynamic-area AF. We'll discuss this in more detail later.

10

Cross-Type AF Sensors at Various Apertures

Cross-type AF sensors will initiate autofocus in either a horizontal or a vertical direction, unlike standard AF sensors, which work only in a horizontal direction. The ability of the AF system to function properly is dependent on the maximum aperture of the lens in use (or of the lens and teleconverter combination). Lenses normally autofocus at maximum aperture and only stop down to the aperture you have selected when you take a picture. Most cameras are designed to autofocus with lenses having a maximum aperture of f/5.6 or larger (e.g., f/1.4, f/2.8, f/4).

The Nikon D810 is in a special class of camera since its autofocus can work with lenses that have a maximum aperture smaller than f/5.6. The camera can autofocus using lenses or teleconverter/lens combos that have maximum apertures from f/5.6 to f/8.

Figure 10.3 shows the various arrangements of cross-type and extra-sensitive AF sensors the camera can use when you are working with small maximum apertures. You must be sure to select one of the AF sensors shown in figure 10.3 if you are using a lens or teleconverter/lens combo that has a maximum aperture smaller than f/5.6. The camera will not prevent or warn you if you try to use an AF sensor inappropriate to the small maximum aperture.

You cannot in some way select one of the overall patterns shown in figure 10.3. You simply move your active AF sensor into one of the locations in the patterns, according to how small the maximum aperture happens to be. Study this carefully if you regularly use teleconverters on telephoto lenses with autofocus.

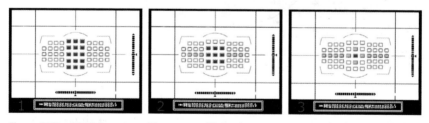

Figure 10.3 – (1) 15 Cross-type AF sensors at f/5.6 or larger aperture in red; (2) 9 Cross-type AF sensors in red and 6 AF sensors that work between f/5.6 and f/8 in blue; (3) 1 Cross-type AF sensor in red and 12 AF sensors that work at f/8 in blue.

- ***Figure 10.3, image 1***, shows the 15 AF points (in red) that are cross-type AF points. The center three columns of AF points are cross-type and work with lenses that have a maximum aperture of f/5.6 or larger.
- ***Figure 10.3, image 2***, shows the arrangement of 9 cross-type AF sensors (in red), along with 6 extra-sensitive AF sensors (in blue) that are not cross-type, all of which work with lenses that have a maximum aperture between f/5.6 and f/8.

- *Figure 10.3, image 3*, shows the arrangement of 1 cross-type sensor (in red), along with 12 extra-sensitive AF sensors (in blue) that are not cross-type, all of which work with lenses that have a maximum aperture of f/8.

The remaining 51 AF sensors not marked in red or blue in figure 10.3 are standard AF sensors that work only at apertures between wide open and f/5.6. You may be able to get the standard-sensitivity AF sensors to respond at smaller apertures, but you shouldn't depend on consistency of autofocus when a standard AF sensor is in use at maximum apertures smaller than f/5.6.

Autofocus Modes in Detail

(User's Manual – Page 87)

The focus modes allow you to control how the autofocus works with static and moving subjects. They allow your camera to lock focus on a subject that is not moving or is moving very slowly. They also allow your camera to follow focus on an actively moving subject. Let's consider the two servo-based focus modes to see when and how you might use them best.

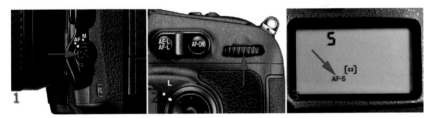

Figure 10.4 – Selecting an Autofocus mode

Here are the steps to select an Autofocus mode (figure 10.4):

1. Hold in the AF-mode button (figure 10.4, image 1).
2. Turn the rear Main command dial (figure 10.4, image 2).
3. The Control panel will show each of the two modes (AF-S and AF-C) as you turn the rear dial (figure 10.4, image 3, red arrow). Single-servo Autofocus mode (AF-S) is selected.
4. Let go of the AF-mode button when the mode you want to use is displayed on the Control panel.

Let's consider what each of the two modes does.

10

Single-Servo AF Mode (AF-S)

Single-servo AF (AF-S) works best when your subject is stationary—like a house or landscape. You can use AF-S on slowly moving subjects if you'd like, but you must be careful to keep autofocus adjusted as the subject moves. The two scenarios listed next may help you decide:

- **Subject is not moving** – When you press the Shutter-release button halfway down, the AF module quickly locks focus on your subject and waits for you to fire the shutter. If your subject starts moving and you don't release and reapply pressure on the Shutter-release button to refocus, the focus will be obsolete and useless. When you have focus lock, take the picture quickly. This mode is perfect for stationary subjects or, in some cases, very slowly moving subjects.
- **Subject is regularly moving** – This will require a little more work on your part. Since the AF system locks focus on your subject, if the subject moves even slightly, the focus may no longer be good. You'll have to lift your finger off the Shutter-release button and reapply pressure halfway down to refocus. If the subject continues moving, you'll need to continue releasing and pressing the Shutter-release button halfway down to keep the focus accurate. If your subject never stops moving, is moving erratically, or stops only briefly, AF-S is probably not the best mode to use. In this case, AF-C is better because it never locks focus and the camera is able to track your subject's movement, keeping it in constant focus.

Continuous-Servo AF Mode (AF-C)

Using Continuous-servo AF (AF-C) is slightly more complex because it is a focus-tracking function. The camera looks carefully at whether the subject is moving, and it even reacts differently if the subject is moving from left to right, up and down, or toward and away from you. Read these three scenarios carefully:

- **Subject is not moving** – When the subject is standing still, Continuous-servo AF acts a lot like Single-servo AF with the exception that the focus never locks. If your camera moves, you may hear your lens chattering a little as the autofocus motor makes small adjustments in the focus position. Because focus never locks in this mode, you'll need to be careful that you don't accidentally move the AF point off the subject because it may focus on something in the background instead.
- **Subject is moving across the Viewfinder** – If your subject moves from left to right, right to left, or up and down in the Viewfinder, you'll need to keep your AF point on the subject when you are using Single-point AF area mode. If you are using Dynamic-area AF or Auto-area AF mode, your camera can track the subject across a few or all of the 51 AF points. We'll cover this in more detail in the upcoming section called AF-Area Modes in Detail.
- **Subject is moving toward or away from the camera** – If your subject is coming toward you, another automatic function of the camera kicks in. It is called *predictive focus tracking*, and it figures out how far the subject will move before the shutter fires. After you've pressed the Shutter-release button all the way down, predictive focus tracking moves the lens elements slightly to correspond to

10

where the subject should be when the shutter fires a few milliseconds later. In other words, if the subject is moving toward you, the lens focuses slightly in front of your subject so that the camera has time to move the mirror up and get the shutter blades out of the way. It takes 42 milliseconds for the camera to respond to a press of the Shutter-release button.

Predictive Focus Tracking

Let's talk about the practical use of these Autofocus modes. If you are shooting an air show, for instance, a fast-moving airplane can move enough to slightly change the focus area by the time the shutter opens. If you press the Shutter-release button all the way down until the shutter releases, autofocus occurs first, and then the mirror moves up and the shutter starts opening. That takes about 52 milliseconds in the D810. In the time it takes for the camera to respond to your press of the Shutter-release button, the airplane has moved slightly, which just barely throws the autofocus off. With predictive focus tracking, the camera predicts where the airplane will be when the image is actually exposed, and it adjusts the focus accordingly.

Let's say you're playing a ball game and you throw the ball to a running player. You would have to throw the ball slightly in front of the receiving player so that the player and the ball arrive in the same place at the same time. Predictive focus tracking does something similar for you. It saves you from trying to focus your camera in front of your subject and waiting 52 milliseconds for it to arrive. The timing would be a bit difficult!

Effect of Lens Movement

Lens movement (especially with long lenses) can be misinterpreted by the camera as subject movement. In that case, predictive focus tracking follows your camera movement while simultaneously trying to track your subject.

Attempting to handhold a long lens will drive your camera crazy. Use a vibration reduction (VR) lens or a tripod for best results. Nikon says that there are special algorithms in predictive focus tracking that allow it to notice sideways or up-and-down movement, and the camera shuts down the predictive focus tracking. That is, predictive focus tracking is not activated by the D810 for sideways or up-and-down subject movement or panning.

Settings Recommendation: I leave my camera's Autofocus mode set to AF-S most of the time because I shoot a lot of static nature images and portraits. If I am shooting sports, though, I switch to AF-C mode so that the camera will keep updating its autofocus as the subject moves very quickly. Wildlife photography is another type of imaging that begs for AF-C and its continuously updating autofocus.

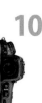

AF-Area Modes in Detail

(User's Manual – Page 90)

The AF-area modes are designed to let you control how many Viewfinder AF points or sensors—the area of focus attention—are in use at any one time. Three of the four modes will track subject movement.

You can use 1 AF point in Single-point AF mode; 5 AF points in Group-area AF; and 9, 21, or 51 AF points in Dynamic-area AF mode. You can even use 3D-tracking mode (51 AF points), which uses the color of the subject to help track it, keeping it in focus while it moves around.

If you don't want to think about the autofocus area, you can let the camera automatically control the AF-area mode by selecting the Auto AF-area mode setting.

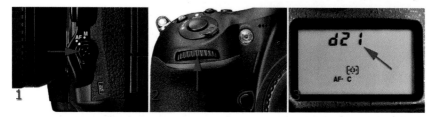

Figure 10.5 – Controls to set AF-area mode

Here are the steps to choose an AF-area mode:

1. Hold in the AF-mode button (figure 10.5, image 1).
2. Turn the front Sub-command dial (figure 10.5, image 2) as you watch the four available modes scroll by on the Control panel (figure 10.5, screen 3), which shows the camera set to 21-point Dynamic-area AF mode (red arrow).
3. Release the AF-mode button when the mode you want to use is displayed on the Control panel.

Note: Some of the AF-area modes will not show up if you have your camera set to Single-servo AF mode (AF-S), which allows only these AF-area modes: Single-point AF and Auto-area AF. You cannot use the following AF-area modes unless you switch the Autofocus mode to Continuous-servo AF mode (AF-C): 9-point Dynamic-area AF, 21-point Dynamic-area AF, 51-point Dynamic-area AF, and 3D-Tracking.

In other words, to use most of the AF-area modes, you must make sure your camera's Autofocus mode is set to AF-C.

Remember, you adjust the Autofocus mode with the rear Main command dial and the AF-area mode with the front Sub-command dial, while holding in the AF-mode button. Let's discuss each AF-area mode in detail.

10

Single-Point AF

Single-point AF uses 1 AF point out of the array of 51 points to acquire good focus. As mentioned earlier, you can control which AF point is used by selecting it with the Multi selector. In figure 10.6, notice that the center AF point (of the 51 sensor points) is the one that provides focus information.

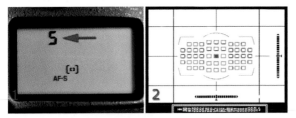

Figure 10.6 – Single-point AF mode

If two people are standing next to each other, with a gap in the middle, the single center AF point will examine the space between the two subjects. You can do one of two things to overcome this problem:

- You can get the focus first by pointing the center AF point at the face of one of the subjects, pressing the Shutter-release button halfway to focus, and then holding it down while recomposing the image. When you have recomposed the shot—without releasing the button—press the Shutter-release button the rest of the way down and take the picture.
- You can compose the picture first by centering it however you'd like, then use the Multi selector to move the single AF point until it rests on the face of one of the subjects. With the AF point repositioned, press the Shutter-release button halfway down to get good focus and the rest of the way down to take the picture.

Either of these methods will solve the age-old autofocus problem of having a perfectly focused background with out-of-focus subjects, caused by the center AF point concentrating on the background between the subjects.

Single-Point AF Example

If a subject is not moving—like a tree or a standing person—then Single-point AF and Single frame (S) Release mode will allow you to acquire focus. When the focus is acquired, the AF module will lock focus on the subject and the focus will not change. If the subject moves, your focus may no longer be perfect and you'll need to recompose while releasing and then pressing the Shutter-release button halfway down.

10

Release Priority Settings

When you switch your D810 out of Single frame (S) Release mode, you must be aware of how Custom settings a1 and a2 are configured. These two Custom settings allow you to choose focus or release priority when shooting in AF-S and AF-C Autofocus modes. It's important that you understand these two priorities before you start using your camera on critical shoots, or some of your images may not be in focus at all. I won't cover that information in this chapter, but we've looked at Custom settings a1 and a2 in detail in the chapter titled **Custom Setting Menu**. Please be very sure that you understand what they do! (Hint: Use Focus priority.)

Often, if the subject is moving very slowly or sporadically, I don't use Continuous low speed (CL) Release mode. Instead I leave the camera in Single frame (S) Release mode. I tap the Shutter-release button halfway to acquire focus when the subject moves and tap it again as needed. When I'm ready, I simply press the Shutter-release button the rest of the way down, and I've got the shot!

Group-area AF

Group-area AF is designed to give you an autofocus safety factor over using a single AF point. Instead of just one AF point, as discussed in the previous subsection, Group-area AF gives you a cross-pattern of 5 AF points, only four of which are visible in the Viewfinder (figure 10.6A).

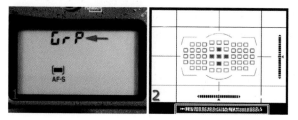

Figure 10.6A – Group-area AF mode

When there is a risk of the camera focusing on the background by sensing the area between or around your subject(s), the cross-pattern of AF points will tend to make AF points fall on some part of your subject without recomposing. Use this pattern when you are photographing subjects that are difficult to shoot with a single AF point.

A powerful feature of Group-area AF mode is the fact that, if you have Face detection on set in *Custom Setting Menu > b Metering/Exposure > b5 Matrix metering*

10

and are using Matrix metering, the camera will detect human faces in the View-finder. Therefore, this is a great mode to use for human subjects in events such as a wedding, graduation, or portrait session.

The cross-pattern appears in the Viewfinder as a group of four AF points sur-rounding an invisible AF point (figure 10.6A, screen 2). However, the invisible AF point in the center is active. You can move the group of five AF points to any loca-tion within the 51 AF points in the Viewfinder by scrolling with the Multi selector. The five points work in unison.

The five-point cross-pattern makes it easier to detect a subject's eyes in Matrix metering mode. In my experience, it is very accurate. I think you will come to enjoy this mode. I use it most of the time.

Dynamic-Area AF

This mode is best used when your subject is moving. Instead of using a single AF point for autofocus, several sensors surrounding the one you have selected are also active.

Again, this mode is available only if you have the AF-C autofocus mode (Contin-uous-servo AF) selected. It won't even appear on the Control panel if you have AF-S autofocus mode (Single-servo AF) selected.

The top row of figure 10.7 shows the Control panel with Dynamic-area AF selected in 9, 21, and 51 point modes. You must select one of the three AF-point patterns using the controls shown in figure 10.5. In figure 10.5, screen 3, 21-point Dynamic-area AF has been selected.

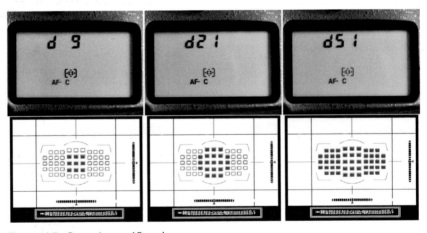

Figure 10.7 – Dynamic-area AF mode

The bottom row of figure 10.7 shows the three AF point patterns (9, 21, and 51) in the Viewfinder. While taking pictures, you will not actually see all these extra AF points light up, only when you first select a pattern (see the upcoming subsection, **Viewing Autofocus Patterns**). Instead you will see only the AF point in the center of the pattern. You will have to imagine the other points surrounding the single point you can see. You can move the 9- and 21-point patterns around the Viewfinder with the Multi selector.

The AF point you can see in the Viewfinder provides the primary autofocus; however, the surrounding points in the pattern you've selected are also active. If the subject moves and the primary AF point loses its focus, one of the surrounding points will quickly grab the focus.

If the subject is moving slowly or predictably, you can use a smaller pattern, such as the 9-point selection. If the subject's movement is more erratic or unpredictable, you might want to increase the number of AF points involved. If 9 won't do it, try 21, or even 51, for subjects that are very unpredictable and move quickly.

One caution is that the more AF points you use, the slower the initial autofocus may be, especially in low light. However, when the initial focus is acquired, the camera can track the subject quite well with all three patterns.

Can you see how flexible Dynamic-area AF could be for you, especially when you adjust the patterns? If your subject will move only a short distance—or is moving slowly—you can simply select a pattern of 9 points. Maybe you're doing some macro shots of a bee on a flower and the bee is moving around the blossom. Or you might be photographing a tennis game, in which case you could use 21 or 51 points to allow for more rapid side-to-side movement without losing focus. You'll have to decide which pattern best fits your needs for the current shooting situation.

Using Dynamic-area AF, you can more accurately track and photograph all sorts, sizes, and speeds of moving subjects. The initial focus reaction speed of the AF system is somewhat slower when you use 51 points because the camera needs to process a lot more information. Take that into consideration when you are shooting events. However, I have used 51-point Dynamic-area AF at both weddings and graduation ceremonies with great success. The D810 is faster than my previous Nikons at acquiring the initial focus.

Viewing Autofocus Patterns

You can actually see the autofocus patterns if you use the camera's Viewfinder or Information display (info button) while choosing the setting. The pattern display on the top Control panel is not very detailed.

In the Viewfinder and on the Information display, the 9-, 21-, and 51-point patterns are shown accurately. However, when seen in the Viewfinder, the patterns for Auto-area AF and 3D-tracking do not actually reflect the pattern the camera uses. Instead, the camera shows an outline surrounding all 51 AF points when displaying the Auto-area AF mode in the Viewfinder. In reality, when in Auto-area, the camera chooses any combination of the 51 AF points it deems necessary to use. The camera

10

spells out "3 D," using the AF points, when you select 3D-tracking, which, like Auto-area, uses whatever AF point it needs to track the moving subject.

You may notice that the 9-, 21-, and 51-point AF-area patterns shown on the Information display have tiny + signs on each active AF point in the pattern. The little + signs represent the fact that each AF point in the pattern can actively seek focus on your subject, and you can select which AF point(s) to use. On the other hand, when showing Auto AF-area on the Information display, the tiny + signs are missing. This simply means the camera will choose which AF point(s) it likes best.

3D-Tracking AF

The mode called *3D-tracking* (shown as 3D on the Control panel, Information display, and in the Viewfinder) adds color-detection capability to the tracking system (figure 10.8). The camera not only tracks by subject area, but also remembers the color of the subject and uses it to track even more accurately.

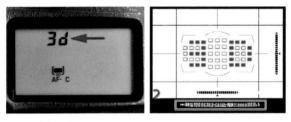

Figure 10.8 – 3D-tracking AF mode

3D-tracking works like the 51-point pattern except that it is more intelligent. Often your subject will be a different color from the background, and the D810's color-based system will provide more accuracy in difficult conditions. Be careful if the subject is a similar color to the background because this may reduce the autofocus tracking accuracy.

3D-tracking is a good mode for things like action sports, air shows, races, and so on. It allows the camera to become a color-sensitive, subject-tracking machine.

Note: As mentioned in an earlier section, you will see "3 D" in the Viewfinder only when you first select 3D-tracking AF. After that, you will just see the AF point move around the Viewfinder as it tracks your subject.

Auto-Area AF

Auto-area AF turns the D810 into an expensive point-and-shoot camera. Use this mode when you simply have no time to think and would still like to get great images. The AF module decides what the subject is and selects the AF points it thinks will work best.

10

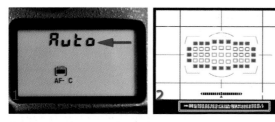

Figure 10.9 – Auto-area AF mode

If you are using a D, E, or G lens, there is "human recognition technology" built into this mode. Using Auto-area AF, your D810 can usually detect a human face and help you avoid shots with perfectly focused backgrounds and blurry human subjects. Additionally, the D810 specifically tries to expose for faces when it can find them. This is great for when you are using flash with people against dark backgrounds. The camera tries its best to keep the exposure accurate for the faces.

Previous to the D810, I rarely used Auto-area AF for anything except snapshots. However, I have been trying it when shooting quickly at events such as weddings and graduations, and am finding the camera quite accurate at finding and exposing for people. This is a great people mode. Give it a try!

Now, let's talk about how the camera uses the mode groups in unison. See the sidebar **Capturing a Bird in Flight** for an example of how the camera uses the three mode groups—AF-area, Autofocus, and Release modes—to track a flying bird.

Settings Recommendation: Many people use Single-point AF-area mode quite often. It works particularly well for static or slowly moving subjects. When I'm out shooting beautiful nature images, I use Single-point AF-area mode along with Single frame (S) Release mode almost exclusively.

If I'm shooting a wedding where the bride and groom are walking slowly up the aisle, Single-servo Autofocus mode (AF-S), Group-area AF-area mode, and Continuous low speed (CL) Release mode seem to work well for me, although recently, I have been successfully experimenting with Continuous-servo Autofocus mode (AF-C), Auto-area AF mode, and Continuous-high (CH) Release mode. The D810 is uncannily accurate at finding and tracking human faces in Auto-area AF mode. You must use AF-C along with Auto-area to let the camera track a face. If you use AF-S and Auto-area, the camera will quickly find the face but not track it. That's okay when you're taking a group shot, but it's not so good when you're tracking a moving face, such as a bride walking up the aisle.

I suggest experimentation with all these modes. You will need to use them all for different types of photography, so take the time necessary to learn how each mode functions for your styles of shooting.

10

Capturing a Bird in Flight

Let's imagine that you are photographing a colorful bird perched in a tree but you want some shots of it in flight. You are patiently waiting for it to fly. Your camera is set to 3D-tracking (51-point) AF-area mode and Continuous high speed (CH) Release mode. You are using Continuous-servo (AF-C) Autofocus mode so that autofocus never locks and will track the bird instantly when it starts flying. You've already established focus with the AF point you selected with the Multi selector, and you are holding the Shutter-release button halfway down to maintain focus. Since you've set the Release mode to CH (Continuous high), you can fire off rapid bursts of images (up to four per second). Suddenly, and faster than you can react, the bird takes flight. By the time you can get the camera moving, the bird has moved to the left in the Viewfinder, and the focus tracking system has adjusted by instantly switching away from the primary AF point you used to establish focus. It is now using other AF points in the pattern of 51 points to maintain focus on the bird. You press the Shutter-release button all the way down, and the images start pouring into your memory card. You are panning with the bird, firing bursts until it moves out of range. You've got the shot!

Now, let's examine how the camera uses autofocus in Live view photography mode (non-Viewfinder).

Section 2 – Autofocus in Live View Photography

(User's Manual – Page 39)

Live view (Lv) mode is one of the new features that many old-timers love to hate. New DSLR users generally like to use it because they are accustomed to composing on the LCD screen of a point-and-shoot camera.

Both types of users should reconsider Live view. An old-timer who is used to using only the Viewfinder to compose images might find that some types of shooting are easier with Live view. Point-and-shoot graduates may want to see if they can improve image sharpness by using the Viewfinder.

I've been using SLR, DSLR, rangefinder, and point-and-shoot cameras for more than 45 years, and with the D810 I'm now using a powerful HD-SLR. When Live view mode first came out, my initial thought was "gimmick." However, since I've been shooting macro shots with Lv mode, the ease of use has changed my thinking. When I need extreme, up-close focusing accuracy, Lv mode can be superior to the Viewfinder. If you're an experienced DSLR photographer, try shooting some macros

10

with Lv mode. I think you'll find that your work improves, and your back feels much better, too.

If you've come over from the point-and-shoot world with your new D810, then use Lv mode if it makes you comfortable—at first. However, please realize that it is difficult to make sharp images when you are waving a heavy HD-SLR around at arm's length while composing a picture on the Monitor, especially with the 36-megapixel D810 having such massive image resolution. Also, the extra weight of the DSLR will tire your arms needlessly. Learn to use the Viewfinder for most work and Lv mode for specialized pictures. Both image composition tools are useful.

Using Autofocus and AF-Area Modes for Live View Photography

Live view mode is a little different than the Viewfinder when it comes to autofocus. In some ways it is simpler, and in other ways it is more complex. The Autofocus modes have only two settings, and the AF-area modes have four.

The Release modes that we will discuss in **Section 3 – Release Modes** are the same whether you're using Live view mode or the Viewfinder.

The three mode groups available in Live view mode are as follows:

Autofocus modes (User's Manual – Page 39):
- Single-servo (AF-S)
- Full-time-servo AF (AF-F)

AF-area modes (User's Manual – Page 40):
- Face-priority AF
- Wide-area AF
- Normal-area AF
- Subject-tracking AF

Release modes (User's Manual – Page 102):
- Single frame (S)
- Continuous low speed (CL)
- Continuous high speed (CH)
- Quiet shutter-release (Q)
- Quiet continuous shutter-release (Qc)
- Self-timer
- Mirror up (MUP)

Autofocus in Live View Mode

In some instances, a live view through the Monitor is quite useful. For instance, what if you want to take an image of a small flower growing very close to the ground? You can lie down on the ground and get your clothes dirty, or you can use Lv mode instead. Live view photography mode allows you to see what your camera's lens sees without using the Viewfinder. Anytime you need to take pictures up high or down low, or even on a tripod, the D810 will happily give you that power with Lv mode.

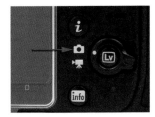

To set your camera to Live view photography mode, simply flip the little Live view selector switch on the back of the camera to the top position so that the white dot lines up with the small camera icon, as shown in figure 10.10A.

Most of the Autofocus mode, AF-area mode, and Release mode information discussed in this chapter for Live view photography mode also applies to Movie live view mode (bottom movie-camera-on-tripod position in figure 10.10A). We will discuss Movie live view mode in a later chapter.

Once you have chosen Live view photography mode, press the Lv button, and you are ready to start taking well-focused still pictures.

A Difference in Live View Mode Compared to Earlier Nikons

The Nikon D810 differs from previous Nikons when using Live view mode. Whereas previous semi-pro Nikons had Handheld and Tripod modes, the D810 combines the two modes, sort of. In previous Nikons, the reflex mirror would drop during an autofocus operation in Handheld mode so the camera could use standard phase-detection autofocus. The mirror stayed up in Tripod mode only with contrast-detection autofocus.

The D810 is different in that it raises the reflex mirror at the beginning of Live view mode and does not lower it for autofocus operations. Therefore, the Nikon D810 always uses mirror-up shooting when in Live view. That means the camera cannot use the fast phase-detection autofocus provided for shooting with the Viewfinder. The primary problem is that contrast-detection AF is usually slower than phase-detection AF. However, the contrast-detection AF in the Nikon D810 is vastly improved over previous Nikons.

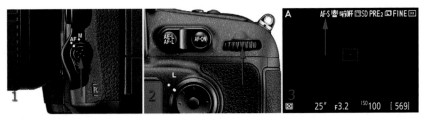

Figure 10.10B – Choosing an Autofocus mode under Live view

Many photographers were initially confused by the sounds coming from the D810 when taking a picture in Live view. It sounds like the mirror is dropping when you take a picture, but it isn't. The Monitor blacks out briefly, as on previous Nikons, while the camera fires the physical shutter. However, the Monitor blackout happens only while the shutter is firing. It has nothing to do with movement of the reflex mirror.

Now, let's examine the two Autofocus modes. Remember, the Autofocus modes tell the camera *how* to focus. Use the following steps to change the Autofocus mode (figure 10.10B):

1. Press and hold the AF-mode button (figure 10.10B, image 1).
2. Rotate the rear Main command dial (figure 10.10B, image 2).
3. AF-S and AF-F will appear on the Monitor as you turn the dial. Release the AF-Mode button when your chosen mode appears. Singe-servo AF (AF-S) is selected in figure 10.10B, image 3.

The two Autofocus mode selections are covered next. I photographed the screen with the lens cap on so you can clearly see the selections on a black background.

Single-Servo AF

Figure 10.11 has a red arrow pointing to the Single-servo AF (AF-S) mode symbol on the Live view screen. You control the focus by pressing the Shutter-release button halfway down or the AF-ON button all the way down. When focus is acquired, it locks and does not update unless you deliberately update it. You will have to refocus if you or your subject moves by releasing pressure on the button and then reapplying pressure to refocus.

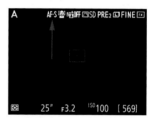

Figure 10.11 – Single-servo AF (AF-S) mode

A single red or green AF point square (with a dot) will appear in the middle of the Monitor. It will be red when the scene is not in focus and green when the scene is in good focus. You can move the square around the screen to select the area of your subject on which the camera will focus. If your subject doesn't move or moves very slowly, use this AF mode.

Full-Time Servo AF

Figure 10.12 has a red arrow pointing to the Full-time servo AF (AF-F) mode symbol on the Live view screen. The red or green AF point square appears in the middle of the Monitor, as in Single-servo AF mode. It blinks on and off in red as the camera focuses, then turns green and stops blinking when good focus is acquired. As focus changes and is reacquired, you will see

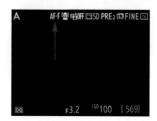

Figure 10.12 – Full-time-servo AF (AF-F) mode

10

it blink green a few times. You can move the focus square around the Monitor to select a focus area.

This mode provides constantly updating autofocus that is tempered by the AF-area mode (discussed next) you have selected. The size and shape of the focus square changes with the AF-area mode you have selected.

The focus doesn't lock on the subject initially, which simply means it updates continuously (like AF-C) until you press the Shutter-release button halfway down, at which time the camera locks focus. If you release pressure from the Shutter-release button, the camera unlocks the focus and resumes continuous autofocus. The camera acts as if it is in AF-S mode when you have pressure on the Shutter-release button and AF-C mode when you remove pressure.

In Movie live view mode, you won't press the Shutter-release button at all, except to force a refocus. The camera will maintain focus on your subject automatically.

Settings Recommedation: Unless I am going to do some very specialized macro shooting, I leave Live view mode's Autofocus mode set to AF-F, or Full-time servo AF. That way, the camera will automatically attempt to keep a good focus on my subject.

If I am shooting a macro shot, I want to control exactly where the focus falls for depth of field control, so I use AF-S, or Single-servo AF.

Professional video shooters will invariably focus manually to prevent the frequent and sometimes noisy refocus operations of the camera when it detects changes in subject distance or contrast.

AF-Area Modes

The AF-area mode lets you choose *where* the camera senses your subject. Autofocus works differently for each of the four AF-area modes. You can cause the camera to look for people's faces, track a moving subject, widen out for landscapes, or pinpoint the focus on a small area of the frame.

Let's look at how to select the four AF-area modes, then examine what each one does.

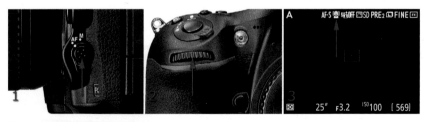

Figure 10.13 – Choosing an AF-area mode under Live view

Use the following steps to change the AF-area mode (figure 10.13):

1. Press and hold the AF-mode button (figure 10.13, image 1).
2. Rotate the front Sub-command dial (figure 10.13, image 2).
3. Various symbols will appear on the Monitor as you turn the dial. They represent four choices: Face-priority AF, Wide-area AF, Normal-area AF, and Subject-tracking AF. Release the AF-Mode button when your chosen mode appears. Face-priority AF is selected in figure 10.13, image 3.

Face-Priority AF

The red arrow in figure 10.14 points to the *Face-priority AF* symbol. When you are taking portraits in Live view mode or shooting movies with people in Movie mode, you may want to consider using Face-priority AF. The camera has the ability to track focus on the faces of several people at the same time. It is quite fun to watch as the little green and yellow AF point squares find faces and stay with them as they move—green squares are for focused faces and yellow squares are for unfocused faces.

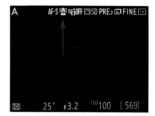

Figure 10.14 – Face-priority AF

Nikon claims the camera can detect up to 35 faces at the same time. That's a lot of people! According to Nikon, "When multiple faces are detected, the camera will focus on the subject recognized to be the closest. Alternatively, you can also choose a different subject with the Multi selector."

Wide-Area AF

The red arrow in figure 10.15 points to the *Wide-area AF* symbol. If you are a landscape shooter who likes to use Live view mode or shoot movies of beautiful scenic areas, this is your mode. The camera will display the AF point square on the Monitor, and it will be red when out of focus, green when in focus. You can move this AF point around until it rests exactly where you want the best focus to be. The camera will sense a wide area and determine the best focus, with priority on the area under the focus square.

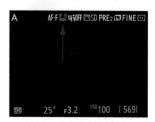

Figure 10.15 – Wide-area AF

Nikon says, "Suitable for hand-held shooting such as landscape."

10

Normal-Area AF

The red arrow in figure 10.16 points to the *Normal-area AF* symbol. This mode is primarily for shooters who need to get very accurate focus on a small area of the frame.

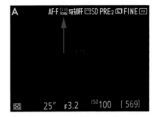

Figure 10.16 – Normal-area AF

If you are shooting a butterfly up close and want to focus on one of the antennae, use Normal-area AF. This is a great mode to use with a macro lens because it gives you a much smaller AF point square that you can move around the frame. Compare it to the AF point in Wide-area AF mode and you'll see that it is about 25 percent of the size. You can pinpoint the exact area of the subject that you want to have the sharpest focus.

Nikon says, "Suitable for tripod shooting with pinpoint focus such as close up."

Subject-Tracking AF

The red arrow in figure 10.17 points to the *Subject-tracking AF* symbol. When autofocus is locked in—either by using the Shutter-release button in AF-S mode or automatically in AF-F mode (discussed previously)—this mode lets you start subject tracking with the Multi selector center button. When the subject is selected (after you press the Multi selector center button), the camera locks its attention on the subject and tracks it whether the subject or the camera moves.

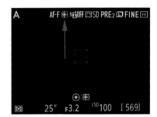

Figure 10.17 – Subject-tracking AF

If you are making a movie of a black bear in the Great Smoky Mountains, you just move the focus point to the bear, focus, and press the Multi selector center button, and focus will stay with the bear. It is amazing to watch the camera do this.

I suggest that you try AF-F, or Full-time servo AF, with this mode. Full-time autofocus allows your camera to fully track the subject without you worrying about keeping it in focus yourself.

Nikon says, "Suitable for a moving subject."

Settings Recommendation: Why not leave the AF-area mode set to Face-priority AF if you photograph people a lot? If you are using Live view for macro shooting, Normal-area AF gives you the smallest, most accurate mode for detailed, up-close focusing. Landscape shooters should use Wide-area AF, and wildlife or sports shooters should use Subject-tracking AF.

Now, let's carefully examine the Release modes, which affect the camera for Viewfinder and Live view shooting.

10

> **Using Focus Lock**
>
> Focus lock is a tool for those times when you need to lock the focus on a certain area of the subject and recompose for a different composition. If the AE-L/AF-L button is configured correctly, you can lock the focus on your subject whenever you want to. The Custom setting that controls the AE-L/AF-L button is Custom setting f6: *Custom Setting Menu > f Controls > f6 Assign AE-L/AF-L button > AE-L/ AF-L button press*. It defaults from the factory to AE/AF lock. You can leave the setting at the default, which locks both the exposure and autofocus, or choose AF lock only so you can lock just the autofocus at any time. This is convenient when you are using the AF-C Autofocus mode, which never locks focus on the subject but keeps updating. For a picture or two, you may want to lock the focus and recompose without the focus changing. Assign AE/AF lock or AF lock only to the AE-L/AF-L button so that whenever you press the button, the focus is locked until you release it.

Section 3 – Release Modes

(User's Manual – Page 102)

The D810 has several *Release modes*, which apply to both Viewfinder and Live view photography.

Release modes involve *when* images will be taken and how fast you can take them. In figure 10.18, we see the Release mode dial with its lock release button. Press the lock release button (left red arrow) and turn the Release mode dial (right red arrow) to select a mode. CH is selected in figure 10.18.

Now, let's look at each of the seven release modes in more detail.

- S – Single frame
- CL – Continuous low speed
- CH – Continuous high speed
- Q – Quiet shutter-release
- Qc – Quiet continuous shutter-release
- Self-timer
- MUP – Mirror up

In the "good-old" film days, the first three release modes would have been called motor-drive settings because they are concerned with how fast the camera is allowed to take pictures.

We've already talked about these modes to some degree in the sections on the AF-area modes.

10

Single Frame (S) Release Mode

Single-frame Release mode is the simplest frame rate because it takes a single picture each time you press the Shutter-release button fully. There is no speed here. This is for photographers shooting a few frames at a time. Nature shoot-ers often use this mode because they are more concerned with correct depth of field and excel-lent composition than blazing speed (which the D810 is incapable of anyway at only 5 fps with-out a battery pack).

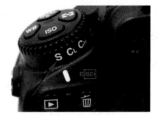

Figure 10.19 – Single frame (S) Release mode

Continuous Low Speed (CL) Release Mode

Continuous low speed Release mode allows you to select a frame rate between one and six frames per second (fps). When you hold down the Shutter-release button, the camera will fire at the chosen frame rate continuously until you let up on the button or the internal memory buf-fer gets full. Choose CL on the Release mode dial to select this mode (figure 10.20).

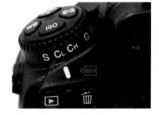

Figure 10.20 – Continuous low speed (CL) Release mode

The default CL frame rate from the factory is 3 fps. If you want more or less speed, simply open *Custom Setting Menu > d Shooting/display > d2 CL mode shooting speed* and select your favorite frame rate (figure 10.21).

The D810 will attempt to capture 5 fps in FX mode (36.2 MP), and 6 fps in 1.2x mode (25.1 MP) or DX mode (15.4 MP). The D810 can manage 7 fps in DX mode with an MB-D12 battery pack and an EN-EL18 battery (or AA batteries) powering the camera.

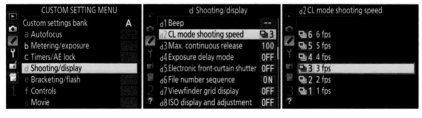

Figure 10.21 – Choosing a Continuous low speed Release mode frame rate

Requirements for Fast Frame Rates
All of the settings for fast frame rates (high fps) are based on the assumption that you are shooting with at least a 1/250s shutter speed, have a fully charged battery, and have some buffer space left in your camera's memory.

Continuous High Speed (CH) Release Mode

Continuous high speed Release mode is designed for when you want to shoot at the highest frame rate the camera can manage (figure 10.22).

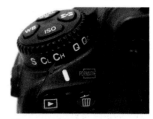

The normal frame rate for the Nikon D810 is 5 fps. When set to CL mode, the camera cannot exceed 5 fps unless you select DX or 1.2x mode, at which point it can manage 6 fps when powered by an EN-EL15 battery. With an MB-D12 battery pack and an EN-EL18 battery (or AA batteries) powering the D810, the camera can manage 7 fps in DX mode or 6 fps in 1.2x mode.

Figure 10.22 – Continuous high speed (CH) Release mode

Note: There is a chart on page 104 of the Nikon User's Manual that lists the frames-per-second rate the camera can achieve when using various power sources.

Internal Memory Buffer

The camera's internal memory buffer limits how many frames you can take. When shooting in JPEG mode, you will be able to shoot 100 frames in one burst. You can control this maximum by adjusting *Custom Setting Menu > d Shooting/Display > d3 Max. continuous release*.

In lossless compressed NEF (RAW) mode, you can shoot 28 images at 14 bits or 47 pictures at 12 bits before the memory buffer is full. You'll have to wait for the camera to offload some buffered images to the memory card before you can shoot another long burst.

See the "Buffer capacity" column in the chart on page 489 of your Nikon User's Manual for a list of Image quality/Image size modes and buffer capacity.

10

Quiet Shutter-Release (Q) Release Mode

When not using Live view mode, *Quiet shutter-release* (Q) Release mode is designed to help the camera make as little noise as possible when you fire the shutter (figure 10.23). Instead of raising the reflex mirror, taking the picture, then lowering the mirror in one smooth step, the D810 ties the raising and lowering of the mirror to the position of the Shutter-release button.

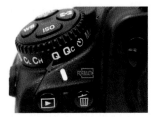

Figure 10.23 – Quiet shutter-release (Q) Release mode

When you press the Shutter-release button down and take a picture in Q mode, the mirror raises and the shutter fires. However, the mirror does not lower until you fully release the Shutter-release button.

If you want to reduce noise, you can hold the Shutter-release button down longer than normal and separate the raising and lowering of the mirror into two steps. This tends to draw out the length of the mirror/shutter action and reduces the perception of noise volume. In reality, the noise is not much quieter, but since it is broken into two parts, it sounds quieter.

In Live view mode the mirror is always raised; therefore, Q mode does nothing special for the mirror when using Live view. However, in Live view mode, the camera's focal-plane shutter is always open for viewing (obviously) and closes only long enough to time the image exposure. When you press the Shutter-release button in Q mode, the camera's shutter closes, reopens for the exact length of the selected shutter speed, then closes again. It does not reopen for viewing until you release pressure from the Shutter-release button. That breaks the shutter action into four parts when you fully press the Shutter-release button: shutter closes > shutter opens for shutter speed time length > shutter closes at the end of shutter speed time > shutter reopens for Live view. The final step, shutter reopens for Live view, happens only after finger pressure is released from the Shutter-release button. This quiets the shutter a tiny bit.

What makes this a little confusing is that the camera seems to act in a similar manner even when you are not using Q mode. In non-Q mode, the Monitor does not come back on when you are taking a Live view picture until you release pressure from the Shutter-release button, even though the shutter has already reopened. The only real difference between Q and non-Q mode is the fact that the final click of the shutter reopening is delayed until you let go of the Shutter-release button. You'll have to take a few pictures in Q and non-Q modes while counting the clicks to see what I mean.

10

Quiet Continuous Shutter-Release Mode

The *Quiet continuous shutter-release* (Qc) Release mode is an additional Quiet (Q) mode with the added feature of continuous shutter firing at 3 frames per second (fps), as long as you hold the Shutter-release button down all the way (figure 10.23A).

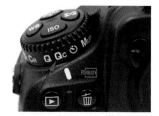

Figure 10.23A – Quiet continuous shutter-release (Q) Release mode

Where the Q mode simply fires one shot when you press the Shutter-release button—allowing you to control the timing of the mirror's return to the down position—the Qc mode lengthens the time between the mirror being raised with the shutter firing and the mirror being dropped back down, somewhat reducing the snappiness of the sound.

If you will compare the camera in CL mode at 3 fps to the Qc mode's 3 fps, you will hear a somewhat more muted sound due to the separation of the shutter and mirror slap.

Self-Timer Release Mode

Use the *Self-timer* Release mode to cause your camera to take pictures a few seconds after you press the Shutter-release button (figure 10.24). The camera will autofocus when you press the Shutter-release button halfway down and start the Self-timer when you press it all the way down.

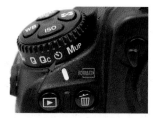

Figure 10.24 – Self-timer Release mode

The factory default time-out for the Self-timer is 10 seconds. You can use *Custom Setting Menu > d Shooting/display > c3 Self-timer* to set the time-out to 2, 5, 10, or 20 seconds. You can also use c3 Self-timer to control the number of shots taken for each self-timer cycle (up to 9), and the amount of time between each shot (up to 3 seconds).

If you like to hear that little *beep beep beep* when the Self-timer is counting down the seconds before firing the shutter, you can control that sound with *Custom Setting Menu > d Shooting/display > d1 Beep*.

After you press the Shutter-release button in Self-timer mode, the AF-assist illuminator will blink about twice per second and the beeping will start. When the last two seconds arrive, the AF-assist illuminator will shine continuously and the beeping will double in speed. You are out of time when the beeping speeds up! The image is taken at about the time the beeping stops.

If you want to stop the self-timer, all you have to do is press the MENU or Playback button.

10

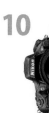

Mirror Up (MUP) Release Mode

Use *Mirror up* Release mode to raise the camera's mirror, allowing vibrations to die down before releasing the shutter (figure 10.25). The camera will first autofocus when you press the Shutter-release button halfway down and then raise the mirror when you press it all the way down.

You can then use a remote release to fire the shutter, or even press the Shutter-release button again (not recommended because it cancels out the benefit of using MUP mode by introducing new vibrations). If you do nothing after raising the mirror, the camera will fire by itself after about 30 seconds.

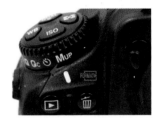

Figure 10.25 – Mirror up (MUP) Release mode

In Live view mode, the mirror is already raised. Therefore, the primary benefit from MUP mode is the fact that the camera delays firing the shutter until you press the Shutter-release button a second time. That means you can allow camera vibrations to die down before the final shutter release happens, even when shooting in Live view mode.

Electronic front-curtain shutter: If you are really serious about sharpness, which you probably are since you are using MUP in the first place, why not also enable Custom setting d5 – Electronic front-curtain shutter. This causes the camera to disengage the mechanical front shutter curtain and use an electronic action instead—simply turning the sensor on to start the exposure, which seriously reduces vibrations. The Electronic front-curtain shutter is controlled by Custom Setting Menu > d Shooting/display > d5 Electronic front-curtain shutter. It works only in MUP mode and is designed to give you maximum image sharpness.

The MUP mode is very simple and very effective. I use this constantly when I am doing nature photography.

Don't Touch That Shutter Release!

Please buy an electronic shutter release (Nikon MC-30 or MC-DC2) so you don't have to use your finger to press the Shutter-release button when the camera is on a tripod and in MUP mode. Touching the camera seems a bit silly after going to all that trouble to stabilize the camera and raise the mirror. A finger press could shake the entire tripod! If you do not have a wireless or cabled shutter release, simply wait 30 seconds after pressing the Shutter-release button in MUP mode, and the camera will fire on its own. This could be used as a slow but high-quality self-timer.

10

Custom Settings for Autofocus (a1–a8)

For a complete discussion of the autofocus-related Custom settings a1 through a12, please see the chapter titled **Custom Setting Menu**. When considering autofocus issues, it is very important that you read the information in that chapter concerning Custom settings a1 and a2. If you don't read and understand that section, you may get quite a few out-of-focus images as a result.

Also, please consider using Focus tracking with lock-on when you are using any mode that does focus tracking (9-point, 21-point, 51-point, or 3D-tracking). This will prevent your camera from losing focus on the subject if something comes between the camera and the subject while the subject is moving. Otherwise, the camera may switch the focus to the intruding object and lose the tracked subject. To enable Focus tracking with lock-on, go to *Custom Setting Menu > a Autofocus > a3 Focus tracking with lock-on* and choose a tracking delay time-out.

With lock-on enabled, the camera remembers the subject you are tracking for up to a couple of seconds after it loses contact with it. If the subject reappears, the camera will continue tracking it.

Author's Conclusions

I've followed the development of Nikon autofocus systems since the late 1980s. Autofocus with the Nikon D810 is a real pleasure. It has a more powerful AF system than many cameras before it, and yet it is somewhat simplified in its operation by comparison. The system can still seem complex, but if you spend some time with this chapter, you should come away with a much greater understanding of the D810's AF module. You'll better understand how you can adapt your camera to work best for your style of photography. Enjoy your D810's excellent Multi-CAM 3500 FX autofocus system!

10

Live View Photography

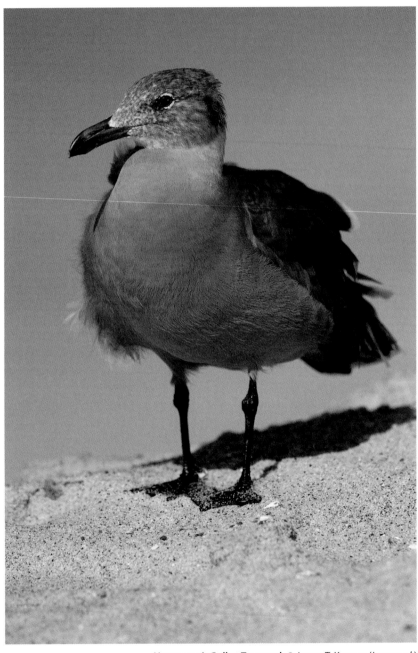

Heermann's Gull at Tamarack © James T. Keenan (*Lomcevak*)

Live view photography mode in the Nikon D810 is a mature still-imaging system that's easy to use and full featured. It allows you to take your eye away from the camera and use the Monitor on the back as your viewfinder.

If you need to shoot with your camera at arm's length, such as in a crowd while taking pictures over the top of people's heads, the big 3.2-inch (8.13 cm) Monitor makes it easy to see your subject. If you need to take pictures that require you to bend over, such as when shooting closeups (macros) of plants or insects, the Live view mode will save your back a lot of pain.

The contrast-detection autofocus used by Live view photography mode detects contrast at the pixel level, providing literally microscopic focus accuracy. Additionally, you can move the focus square to any point on the Monitor that will give you the most accurate autofocus.

Live view is divided into two parts in the Nikon D810, Live view photography mode and Movie Live view mode. In this chapter, we will examine Live view photography mode, which is used exclusively for shooting still images. You cannot shoot video in Live view photography mode; the Movie-record button will not respond.

In the next chapter, we'll investigate Movie live view mode for special format (16:9) still images and broadcast-quality HD movies.

Live View Mode

(User's Manual – Page 35)

To enter *Live view photography* mode you'll flip the Live view selector lever to its top position (figure 11.1A, image 1) and press the Lv button. To exit Live view photography mode, simply press the LV button again. Figure 11.1A, screen 2, shows the Live view screen you'll see first. Normally, this screen would show the subject you are about to photograph, but I left the lens cap on to provide maximum contrast for all the controls we will discuss.

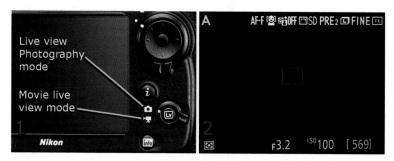

Figure 11.1A – Entering and exiting Live view mode

Opening Notes on Using Live View Photography Mode

As discussed in the previous chapter, Live view photography mode uses contrast-detection autofocus, which is activated by the Shutter-release or AF-ON button if you are using Single-servo AF (AF-S) mode, or automatically if you selected Full-time servo AF (AF-F) mode.

You can move the red focus square to any location on the screen to select off-center subjects. When you have good focus, the red square turns green. You are not limited to the central 51-point AF area as you are when you're looking through the Viewfinder.

Screen Blackout During Exposure

The screen doesn't black out while autofocus is active because the camera focuses by detecting contrast changes on the imaging sensor. When you fire the shutter, the Monitor will black out briefly while the picture is taken. The blackout is necessary to allow the camera to fire the shutter, which blocks light to the imaging sensor briefly. The reflex mirror does not drop when you are taking a picture in Live view photography mode, therefore the blackout period is brief.

Extreme Focusing Accuracy

Use Live view photography mode when you need extreme autofocus accuracy. Contrast-detection AF is slower than phase-detection AF but very accurate. You can zoom in to pixel-peeping levels with the Playback zoom in button before starting autofocus. This is great for macro shooting because you can select very specific sections of the subject for focusing (figure 11.1B).

Taking Pictures in Live View Photography Mode

Hold the Shutter-release button down all the way and wait a moment for the camera to take the picture. It's usually slower than taking a picture with the Viewfinder because autofocus takes more time. When you take a picture in Live view photography mode, it appears on the Monitor. To return to Live view photography to take more pictures, just press the Shutter-release button halfway down.

According to Nikon, one important consideration in Live view photography mode is to close the Eyepiece shutter when using Live view. Very bright external light coming in the eyepiece of the Viewfinder may influence the exposure detrimentally.

However, I experimented with this by shining an *extremely* bright LED flashlight directly into the Viewfinder eyepiece while I was metering the subject with Live view and saw absolutely no change in exposure. I then switched to standard Viewfinder-based photography mode and found that shining the flashlight in the Viewfinder eyepiece had an immediate and large effect on exposure.

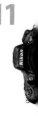

You may want to test this for yourself and see if your D810 reacts to light through the Viewfinder during Live view photography. Or, you can play it safe and close the Eyepiece shutter.

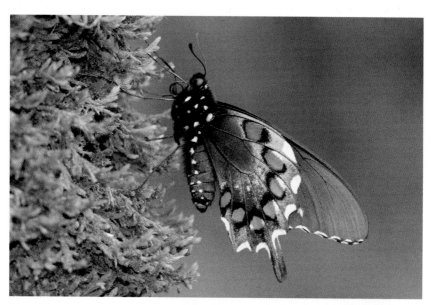

Figure 11.1B – Pipevine Swallowtail (*Battus philenor*) captured in Great Smoky Mountains National Park with a mid-70s AI Nikkor 200 mm f/4 on a bellows for macro, from about six feet (two meters) away.

Settings Recommendation: You can use Live view photography mode on or off your tripod. I normally use Live view for macro images (figure 11.1B), for which I especially need the extra accuracy and focus positioning capability. With older Nikons, I was not all that interested in Live view photography because it didn't feel mature or complete. However, the Nikon D810 has a very refined Live view photography mode. It can be used in almost any situation where standard Viewfinder-based photography will work.

One exception is action shooting. Live view photography is not as good for many types of action shots because the autofocus method is slower and the shutter lag seems longer. If you are prefocused in Live view, maybe you could capture some action, but I wouldn't try it for action shots that require rapid autofocus.

Live view photography mode is for when you have the time and inclination to stand back from your camera and take excellent photos in a more contemplative manner. To my way of thinking, it is like using a small view camera instead of an HD-SLR. If you've not been in the habit of using Live view, I would suggest you give it a try. The D810 makes it a lot easier and more effective to use.

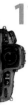

Live View Photography Mode Screens

(User's Manual – Pages 35–48)

There are five screens available in Live view photography mode. You move between these screens by pressing the info button repeatedly.

Note: One of the screens will not be visible unless you have selected Exposure preview mode with the OK button. We will discuss how when examining screen 4.

Live View Photography – Screen 1

Figure 11.2 shows numerous symbols that allow you to see how various features are configured. To help examine the small symbols shown, I have numbered them and provided an explanation.

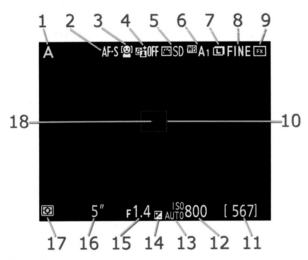

Figure 11.2 – Live view photography, screen 1

1. **Shooting mode** – Selected by holding down the MODE button on top of the camera while turning the rear Main command dial. The available selections you will see on the Monitor are Programmed auto (P), Shutter-priority auto (S), Aperture-priority auto (A), and Manual (M).
2. **Autofocus mode** – Set with AF-mode button and rear Main command dial. Available settings are AF-S and AF-F.
3. **AF-area mode** – Set with AF-mode button and front Sub-command dial. Available settings are Face-priority AF, Wide-area AF, Normal-area AF, and Subject-tracking AF (uses graphical symbols).

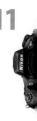

11

4. ***Active D-Lighting*** – Controlled by *Shooting Menu > Active D-Lighting*, with settings Low to Extra High and Auto or Off (L = Low, N = Normal, H = High, H* = Extra high, A = Auto, Off).

5. ***Picture Control*** – Controlled by *Shooting Menu > Set Picture Control*. You can also control this setting by pressing the Protect/Picture Control/Help button and selecting a Picture Control from the Monitor with the Multi selector. See the upcoming subsection **Selecting a Picture Control in Live View** for more detail.

6. ***White balance*** – Set the camera's White balance by holding down the WB button and rotating the rear Main command dial. Select from nine white balance settings, including Auto (A1), Incandescent, Fluorescent, Direct sunlight, Flash, Cloudy, Shade, Choose color temp., and Preset manual (uses graphical symbols).

7. ***Image size*** – Controlled by *Shooting Menu > Image size* with settings Large (L), Medium (M), and Small (S). You can also hold down the QUAL button on top of the camera and rotate the front Sub-command dial to select this value.

8. ***Image quality*** – Controlled by *Shooting Menu > Image quality*, with settings NEF (RAW) + JPEG, NEF (RAW), JPEG, and TIFF. You can also hold down the QUAL button on top of the camera and rotate the rear Main command dial to select this value. The abbreviations you'll see on the Monitor for these settings are FINE, NORM, BASIC, RAW+F, RAW+N, RAW+B, RAW, and TIFF.

9. ***Image area*** – Controlled by the *Shooting Menu > Image area* setting. You can select any of the available image areas, including: FX, 1.2x, DX, and 5:4. The Monitor will display an image cropped to the various sizes selected in Image area. This value must be selected before you enter Live view photography mode. It cannot be changed during an active Live view photography session.

10. ***AF point (focus)*** – Can be moved around the screen with the Multi selector to select the subject for autofocus. This focus rectangle will vary in size and color according to the AF-area mode selected (#3) and whether the subject is in focus.

11. ***Frame count (remaining pictures)*** – Approximately how many more pictures can be taken and stored on the currently selected memory card.

12. ***ISO sensitivity*** – Controlled by *Shooting Menu > ISO sensitivity settings*, with choices of ISO values from Lo 1 (ISO 50) to Hi 2 (ISO 25,600). You can also control this value by holding down the ISO button and turning the rear Main command dial. The ISO values will change on the Monitor.

13. ***ISO mode*** – Controlled by *Shooting Menu > ISO sensitivity settings > Auto ISO sensitivity control*, with the choice of On or Off. You can also control this value by holding down the ISO button and turning the front Sub-command dial to select from ISO or ISO AUTO on the Monitor.

14. ***Exposure compensation*** – This symbol will appear only when +/- exposure compensation has been dialed into the camera. Adjust this value with the +/- Exposure compensation button near the Shutter-release button.

15. ***Aperture*** – Set by turning the front Sub-command dial, with aperture minimum and maximums that vary according to the mounted lens. Manual change is available only in Aperture-priority auto (A) and Manual (M) modes. The Camera controls this value in Shutter-priority auto (S) and Programmed auto (P) modes.

16. ***Shutter speed*** – Set with the rear Main command dial, with settings from 30 seconds to 1/8000 second (8000). Manual change is available only in Shutter-priority auto (S) and Manual (M) modes. The Camera controls this value in Aperture-priority auto (A) and Programmed auto (P) modes.

17. ***Metering mode*** – Set by holding down the Metering button and turning the rear Main command dial, with the following choices: Matrix, Center-weighted, Highlight-weighted, and Spot.

18. ***Center of Frame Dot*** – This small dot appears when the AF point rectangle is directly in the middle of the frame. It will be red when out of focus and green when in focus, following the color of the surrounding AF point.

Live View Photography – Screen 2

Figure 11.3 shows a much cleaner screen with an almost blank area at the top and a single line of information along the bottom, which matches the descriptions #10 through #18 for figure 11.2. This is for users who prefer an uncluttered screen while shooting still pictures.

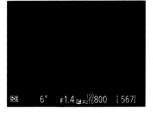

Figure 11.3 – Live view photography, screen 2

Live View Photography – Screen 3

Figure 11.4 shows a screen that is similar to the previous screen except that gridlines are added. Use these gridlines to level your subject in the Viewfinder, as is necessary when photographing things like a horizon in scenic photography or buildings, doors, and walls in architectural photography.

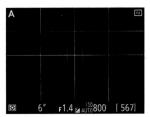

Figure 11.4 – Live view photography, screen 3

Live View Photography – Screen 4

Figure 11.5 shows a live histogram and Exposure preview screen that you will not see unless you have pressed the OK button and turned on the Exposure preview indicator before you start scrolling through the overlay screens with the info button.

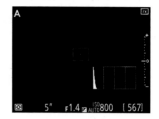

Figure 11.5 – Live view photography, screen 4

When you press the OK button, a small exposure indicator will appear on the right side of the Monitor, allowing you to manually adjust exposure compensation with the Exposure compensation button until the exposure looks good to you on the Monitor.

Once you have enabled the Exposure preview, the +/- indicator will stay on the right side of each screen in the entire series of overlay screens. In order to see and use the live histogram, the Exposure preview must be active. Otherwise, the camera will skip the Histogram screen shown in figure 11.5 and go directly to the Virtual horizon screen (next section).

The little rectangle between the red AF point and the Exposure compensation indicator is a Live histogram. Currently it is crammed all the way to the left—signifying a very dark image—because the lens cap was on while capturing the graphic for this book. Having a live histogram is a powerful tool in Live view photography. Use it for very accurate live exposures.

How to Use the Exposure Preview

To adjust the exposure, hold down the Exposure compensation button and turn the rear Main command dial. You will see the small exposure indicator displaying your exposure compensation changes, up to three stops plus or minus. You can actually adjust exposure up to five stops +/- but the little indicator shows only an arrow point when you have exceeded three stops in either direction.

Note: Exposure in Live view may differ from exposure in Viewfinder-based photography. The exposures in Live view are automatically adjusted to better work with the Live view display. What you see in the Live view display will closely match the final exposure.

Live View Photography – Screen 5

The final screen, shown in figure 11.6, displays a Virtual horizon that allows you to level the camera in a dual-axis horizontal and vertical direction. If you are an aviation pilot, you'll feel right at home with this new tool because it resembles the artificial horizon used to keep an airplane's wings and nose level.

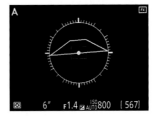

Figure 11.6 – Live view photography, screen 5

Selecting a Picture Control in Live View

Picture Controls are easy to change in Live view photography mode. Interestingly, you can see their effects on the subject actually displayed on the Monitor as you select each Picture Control. You can see some samples in figure 11.7A applied to my Copper Top and Lego blocks image.

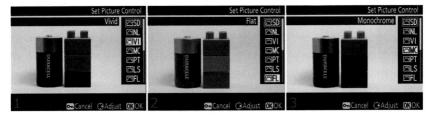

Figure 11.7A – Samples of Vivid, Neutral, and Monochrome Picture Controls

To choose a Picture Control in Live view photography mode, you can press the MENU button and select *Shooting Menu > Set Picture Control* while a Live view session is active, or you can use external camera controls as described in the following steps. (See the **Set Picture Control** subheading in the chapter titled **Shooting Menu** for more detail on how picture controls work.) Your Picture Control choices are as follows:

- **SD** – Standard
- **NL** – Neutral
- **VI** – Vivid
- **MC** – Monochrome
- **PT** – Portrait
- **LS** – Landscape
- **FL** – Flat

The camera displays a special screen when you press the Protect/Picture Control/Help button, as seen in figure 11.7B, screen 2.

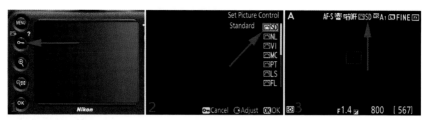

Figure 11.7B – Selecting a Picture Control while in Live view photography mode

Use these steps to select a Picture Control while in a Live view photography session (figure 11.7B):

1. With the camera already in Live view photography mode, press the Protect/ Picture Control/Help button (figure 11.7B, image 1, red arrow). The button has a key symbol.

2. The Picture Control screen will appear while the camera is still in Live view photography mode (figure 11.7B, screen 2). The current Picture Control in use will be highlighted in yellow. Select a different Picture Control by scrolling up or down with the Multi selector and highlighting one of the others; then press the Multi selector center button (or OK button). Notice on your camera's Monitor how the sharpness, clarity, contrast, brightness, saturation, and hue of the subject being viewed changes when you select different Picture Controls.

3. The camera will switch back to the Live view photography screen with the new Picture Control now providing services. It will be listed at the top of the screen (figure 11.7B, screen 3, red arrow).

Note: Any Picture Control you select while using Live view photography mode will still be selected when you exit Live view.

Using the *i* Button Menu in Live View Photography Mode

Pressing the *i* button while in Live view photography mode gives you access to six convenient control functions, including:

- ***Image area*** – Use this function to change the size and shape of the pictures you take in Live view photography mode. This is the same as the *Shooting Menu > Image area* function, and includes the following Image areas: FX (36x24) 1.0x; 1.2x (30x20); DX (24x16) 1.5x; and 5:4 (30x24).

- ***Active D-Lighting*** – Use this function to enable various levels of increased image dynamic range (contrast reduction) with shadow and highlight detail enhancement (D-Lighting). Your choices are: Off, Low (L), Normal (N), High (H), Extra high (H*), and Auto (A). This is the same as the *Shooting Menu > Active D-Lighting* function.

- **Electronic front-curtain shutter** – Since Live view is similar to Mirror up (MUP) mode—because the mirror is always raised when you are using Live view photography mode—you have the Electronic front-curtain shutter feature available. This allows you to disable the camera's mechanical front shutter curtain and use the electronic version instead for less vibration and sharper images.
- **Monitor brightness** – When using Live view there are times when bright ambient light may interfere with your ability to see details on the Monitor. At other times, when shooting in dark areas, the brightness of the Monitor could be blinding. You may want to use this function to change the backlight intensity of the Monitor from quite bright to very dim.
- **Photo live view display WB** – Use this setting to apply a separate White balance (WB) to the *Live view monitor only*, not the images captured by the camera. In other words, this function only applies to the preview image shown on the Monitor. It does not affect the image the camera captures, which is governed instead by the *Shooting Menu > White balance* setting. Your choices are: None (--), which uses the camera's assigned WB on the monitor, A1 (or A2, Auto mode), Incandescent, Fluorescent, Direct sunlight, Flash, Cloudy, Shade, Choose color temp (K), and Preset manual (PRE). You cannot modify adjustable WB values with this function (e.g., K or PRE); it is for selection only.
- **Split-screen display zoom** – Use this function to split the view on the monitor into two parts, left and right. You can then view two separate areas of the subject to check focus or image alignment. You can also zoom in all the way to pixel-peeping levels. By switching back and forth between the two sides of the split screen, you can scroll to separate parts of the subject for viewing details.

Let's discuss each of these functions in detail.

Image Area

This convenient function allows you to choose one of the four Image area selections found in the *Shooting Menu > Image area* setting.

You can select from the following values:

- **FX** – 36 x 24mm (1.0x)
- **1.2x** – 30 x 20mm (1.2x)
- **DX** – 24 x 16mm (1.5x)
- **5:4** – 30 x 24mm

Use the following steps to choose one of the Image area settings:

1. Select Live view photography mode with the Live view selector switch. Press the Lv button to enter Live view.
2. Press the *i* button and the Live view photography menu will open (figure 11.8A, screen 1), or press the *i* button again to cancel.

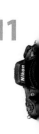

3. Choose the first item on the menu and Image area will be displayed on the top right of the screen. Scroll to the right (figure 11.8A, screen 1).
4. The Image area menu on the right side of the screen will allow you to select the Image area you want to use for this Live view session. Scroll up or down with the Multi selector and choose one of the four Image area values.
5. Press the OK button or Multi selector center button to lock in the Image area.

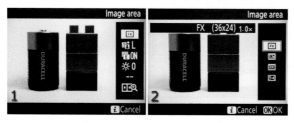

Figure 11.8A – Setting the Image area

When you choose an Image area value, you will see the rear Monitor adjust to the new image area. It will immediately reflect the new image size and shape.

Note: The Image area you select while in Live view will remain the same when you close Live view and go back to shooting with the Viewfinder.

Active D-Lighting

This function provides an easy way to change the Active D-Lighting value (for extending the dynamic range of your images) while using Live view photography mode.

For more information on how Active D-Lighting works, please see the **Active D-Lighting** subheading in the chapter titled **Shooting Menu**.

Your Active D-Lighting choices are as follows:

- *A* – Auto
- *H** – Extra high
- *H* – High
- *N* – Normal
- *L* – Low
- *Off*

Use the following steps to select one of the Active D-Lighting settings:

1. Select Live view photography mode with the Live view selector switch. Press the Lv button to enter Live view.
2. Press the *i* button to open the Live view photography menu (figure 11.8B, screen 1), or press the *i* button again to cancel.

3. Choose the second item on the menu and Active D-Lighting will be displayed on the top right of the screen. Scroll to the right (figure 11.8B, screen 1).
4. Select one of the five Active D-Lighting values or Off (figure 11.8B, screen 2). Low (L) is selected in screen 2.
5. Press the OK button or Multi selector center button to lock in the value.

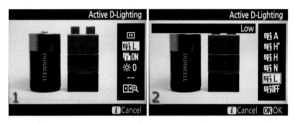

Figure 11.8B – Configuring Active D-Lighting

Note: Whatever Active D-Lighting value you select while in Live view photography mode will still be active for Viewfinder shooting when you close Live view.

Electronic Front-Curtain Shutter

The Electronic front-curtain shutter (EFCS) is available only in camera modes where the mirror is raised, such as the Viewfinder mode's MUP setting on the Release mode dial, and when you have selected Live view photography mode. This function is the same as the *Custom Setting Menu > d Shooting/display > d5 Electronic front-curtain shutter* function.

The EFCS allows the camera to disable the first curtain of the camera's two-curtain mechanical shutter (it has front and rear curtains). With the mechanical front curtain disabled, all the camera must do to start the exposure is turn on the sensor for the time specified by the Shutter-speed setting and then stop the exposure by closing the mechanical rear curtain.

By not using any mechanical parts until the very end of the exposure (the mirror is already raised), camera vibration is seriously reduced, leading to sharper pictures.

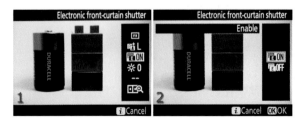

Figure 11.8C – Using the Electronic front-curtain shutter

Use the following steps to enable or disable the EFCS:

1. Select Live view photography mode with the Live view selector switch and press the Lv button to enter Live view.
2. Press the *i* button and the Live view photography menu will open (figure 11.8C, screen 1), or press the *i* button again to cancel.
3. Choose the third item on the menu and Electronic front-curtain shutter will be displayed on the top right of the screen. Scroll to the right (figure 11.8C, screen 1).
4. Select On or Off to enable or disable the EFCS (figure 11.8C, screen 2). On is selected in screen 2.
5. Press the OK button or Multi selector center button to lock in the value.

Note: If you enable the EFCS in Live view photography mode it will remain enabled for the next time you use either the Viewfinder's MUP mode or switch back to Live view photography mode.

Monitor Brightness

You can change the brightness of the Monitor while you are in Live view photography mode. These changes do nothing to the pictures you are taking. If you are shooting in a very bright or dark area, you may need to quickly adjust the Monitor brightness. You can do that with this function.

In figure 11.8D, screens 2–4 show examples of the medium, high, and low screen brightness settings. The difference in brightness between the low and high settings is striking.

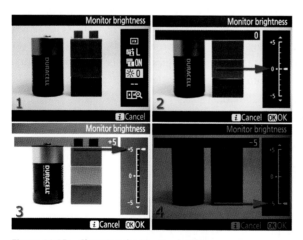

Figure 11.8D – Changing the Monitor brightness

Use the following steps to adjust the Monitor's brightness level:

1. Select Live view photography mode with the Live view selector switch and press the Lv button to enter Live view.
2. Press the *i* button to open the Live view photography menu (figure 11.8D, screen 1), or press the *i* button again to cancel.
3. Choose the fourth item on the menu and Monitor brightness will be displayed on the top right of the screen. Scroll to the right (figure 11.8D, screen 1).
4. You have 10 steps of Monitor brightness available (-5 to +5). Use the Multi selector to move the tiny yellow pointer up toward high (+5) or down to low (-5), as shown by the red arrows in figure 11.8D, screens 2–4. The default is the medium (0) setting shown in screen 2. Screens 3 and 4 show the large range of Monitor brightness adjustment you can make.
5. Press the OK button or Multi selector center button to lock in the value.

Note: Changing the Monitor's brightness in Live view photography mode does not affect the Monitor brightness after leaving Live view, such as when viewing pictures on the Monitor, adjusting menu items, and viewing the Information display or Quick Menu. However, this setting does affect how bright the Monitor appears when you are using Movie live view mode to record videos (see next chapter). Live view photography mode and Movie live view mode are both affected by this setting, but not Viewfinder mode. Movie live view mode also allows you to adjust Monitor brightness in a similar way.

If you cannot select Monitor brightness on your camera, you have Exposure preview enabled. If you enable the Exposure preview indicator, as discussed at the beginning of this main chapter section, the Monitor brightness setting becomes grayed out and unavailable. Exposure preview is enabled and disabled by pressing the OK button just after entering Live view photography mode. You can tell when Exposure preview is enabled because an Exposure preview indicator will appear on the right side of the Monitor. You can use this indicator to see how much +/- Exposure compensation you have dialed into the camera (+/- 5.0 EV steps).

Photo Live View Display WB

While taking pictures in Live view photography mode, you may have reason for the Monitor to display a different White balance (Hue) than the actual image the camera will take, which is governed by the *Shooting Menu > White balance* function. Use the Photo Live View Display WB function to select a White balance (WB) value *for the monitor only*.

Why use this function? You might be shooting outdoors in NEF (RAW) mode, knowing that RAW mode does not write WB information into the actual image. It only stores it within the image metadata. RAW allows you to change the WB of the image after the fact.

You would like to preview what the image will look like if Direct sunlight WB (5200 K) is selected. You could leave the camera set to Auto WB (A1 or A2) and then shoot your RAW images with the Monitor set to Direct sunlight. All images taken will display on the Monitor as if you were shooting with Direct sunlight WB, when in fact the camera is using Auto WB (A1). Later, when you view the RAW image on your computer monitor, you can modify the RAW file to use whatever WB you would like and then save it as JPEG or TIFF.

There may be other reasons to have the Monitor display a certain WB color and capture the image with a different one, such as having one light source to frame the image (Incandescent) and another to actually take the picture (Flash). If so, you have the means to separate the image and Monitor's WB values.

However, be careful when shooting JPEG or TIFF files while using this function because the true camera WB information is written directly into the image file and cannot be easily changed later. It would be a shame to have the Monitor WB set to display in Fluorescent (4200 K) and the camera WB set to capture images using Cloudy (6000 K), not realizing that you were actually creating much warmer JPEG images than the camera's Monitor was showing you.

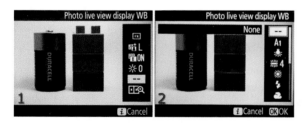

Figure 11.8E – Adjusting the White balance (WB)

Use the following steps to set the Monitor's White balance to a different value than the camera is using to capture images:

1. Select Live view photography mode with the Live view selector switch. Press the Lv button to enter Live view.
2. Press the *i* button to open the Live view photography menu (figure 11.8E, screen 1), or press the *i* button again to cancel.
3. Choose the fifth item on the menu and Photo live view display WB will become visible on the top right of the screen. Scroll to the right (figure 11.8E, screen 1).
4. Select one of the nine WB values to change the hue of the monitor (figure 11.8E, screen 2). Select None (- -) if you want the camera and Monitor to use the same WB value.
5. Press the OK button or Multi selector center button to lock in the value.

11

Note: Using this function does not affect Viewfinder mode screens or Movie live view. However, the camera will remember your Monitor WB setting for when you return to Live view photography mode.

Split-Screen Display Zoom

This function allows you to view two separate areas of the subject in two side-by-side frames. You could use this function to align your subject, such as a building, with the horizon. Or, you could simply use it to zoom in and check the focus on two separate areas of the subject.

Let's see how it works.

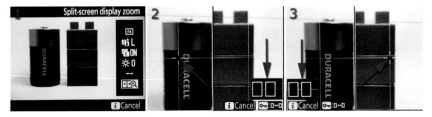

Figure 11.8F – Using the Split screen

Use the following steps to split the camera's Monitor into two side-by-side sections:

1. Select Live view photography mode with the Live view selector switch and press the Lv button to enter Live view.
2. Press the *i* button to open the Live view photography menu (figure 11.8F, screen 1), or press the *i* button again to cancel.
3. Choose the sixth item on the menu and Split-screen display zoom will be displayed on the top right of the screen. Scroll to the right (figure 11.8F, screen 1).
4. There are several things you should take note of in figure 11.8F, screens 2 and 3 (at the red arrows). First, notice that you can use the Protect/Picture Control/ Help button (key symbol) to switch between the two sides of the split screen. You will see a small cross on the screen that has the focus (screen 2, left arrow, and screen 3, right arrow). That cross is the target that you can use to focus and select the area of the subject you want. Next, notice that on the screen without the target, there is a small black horizontal rectangle with smaller yellow vertical rectangles (screen 2, right arrow, and 3, left arrow). The size of the small yellow vertical rectangle shows the amount of zoom, as discussed in the next step (figure 11.8G).

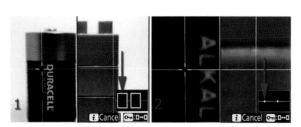

Figure 11.8G – Using the Split screen zoom in feature

5. The small yellow rectangle in figure 11.8G, screen 1, is full size and shows that the camera is not zoomed in on the subject. Screen 2 shows the same subject, but zoomed all the way in. Notice how the yellow rectangle in screen 1 is reduced in size to a mere yellow dot, signifying that the camera is zoomed in. As you zoom in with the Playback zoom in button, or zoom out with the Thumbnail/Playback zoom out button, you will see the subject and the yellow vertical rectangle change sizes to reflect whether you are zooming in or out. You can zoom in or out in four steps. Next, let's examine how you can scroll left or right in each side-by-side window (figure 11.8H).

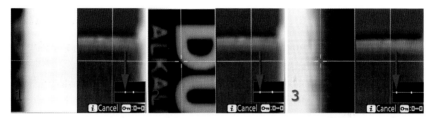

Figure 11.8H – Scrolling one side while zoomed in

6. In figure 11.8H, you'll notice several things. First, the split screen on the left is selected in all three screens. Notice that the small vertical yellow boxes are very tiny, indicating that the camera is zoomed in on the subject. Now, look at the position of the arrow in each of the three screens. Each arrow is pointing at the small yellow rectangle that represents the left side of the split screen. In screen 1, you can just see the right edge of the Copper Top battery on the left of the screen. If you scroll to the left with the Multi selector (as seen in screen 2) you'll see that the camera is scrolling across the face of the battery. Notice how the yellow rectangle (indicated by the red arrow) in screen 2 has moved toward the left edge of the black box, indicating the relative position of the zoomed image. In screen 3, you will see the left edge of the battery and that the yellow rectangle (indicated by the red arrow) is all the way to the left. This shows that you have scrolled as far left as possible.

7. Use the previous six steps to position the split screens on various parts of your subject to align them or check focus. Use the Protect/Picture Control/Help button (key symbol) to switch between the two sides of the split screen, and then scroll around. Zoom in or out with the Playback zoom in and Thumbnail/Playback zoom out buttons. The zoom function affects both sides of the split screen. You cannot zoom each side separately. When you have the subject focused and positioned the way you want, take your picture.

Closing Notes on Live View Photography Mode

Movie Live View Still Images

An important fact to note is that when you first place your camera in Movie live view mode, before you press the Movie-record button, it can take 25.4 megapixel still pictures in a 16:9 format (6720×3776 pixels). The Movie live view still image size matches most HD devices, so if you are shooting stills for display on HD devices closely matching the 16:9 format, use Movie live view to take some pictures.

Nearly all the information we have considered in this chapter applies to Movie live view still images, too. Just flip the Live view selector switch to the bottom position, press the Lv button, and start taking excellent 25.4 MP still images for HD devices (e.g., tablets, HDTVs, and newer computer monitors). We will consider more about Movie live view in the next chapter.

Using Autofocus in Live View

Nikon strongly recommends using an AF-S lens when you are shooting in Live view modes. According to Nikon, "The desired results may not be achieved with other lenses or teleconverters."

You may see darkening or brightening in the Monitor as autofocus takes place, and autofocus will be slower than it is with Viewfinder-based photography. From time to time, the focus indicator square may remain green (instead of red) when the camera is not actually in focus. Simply refocus when that occurs.

There are several issues that may cause the camera to have difficulty focusing in Live view, as follows (according to Nikon):

- The subject contains lines parallel to the long edge of the frame.
- The subject lacks contrast.
- The subject under the focus point contains areas of sharply contrasting brightness or includes spotlights, a neon sign, or another light source that changes in brightness.
- There is flickering or banding under fluorescent, mercury-vapor, sodium-vapor, or similar lighting.
- A cross-screen (star) filter or other special filter is used.

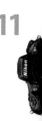

- The subject appears smaller than the focus point.
- The subject is dominated by regular geometric patterns (e.g., window blinds or a row of windows in a skyscraper).
- The subject is moving.

There are several issues that may cause focus tracking to fail in Live view mode:

- The subject is moving too fast.
- Another object gets between the camera and the subject, obscuring it.
- The subject changes visibly in size.
- The subject's color changes.
- The subject gets brighter or dimmer.
- The subject gets too small, too close, or too light or dark.
- The subject is the same color as the background.

Live View Camera Protection System

If conditions may harm the camera when using Live view, such as using Live view for extended periods on a hot day, causing the camera to overheat, the D810 will protect itself by automatically shutting down Live view. A countdown will show on the Monitor 30 seconds before the Live view system shuts down. If conditions warrant, the countdown timer may appear immediately upon entering or reentering Live view. This countdown allows your expensive camera to protect its internal circuits from overheating and causing damage.

Author's Conclusions

Live view photography mode in the D810 is a mature and very usable way to shoot still images. Using the Monitor is not just for point-and-shoot photographers any more. There are several good reasons for using the Live view system, such as extreme focusing accuracy when shooting macro images and when composing the image on the Monitor gives you a better feel for the subject than the Viewfinder.

The next step in learning about the Nikon D810 is to examine Movie live view mode. This mode can be used for special HD-format still images, but it's primarily designed for shooting excellent, broadcast-quality HD movies. Let's examine the powerful video subsystem in your D810 and see how it works.

Movie Live View

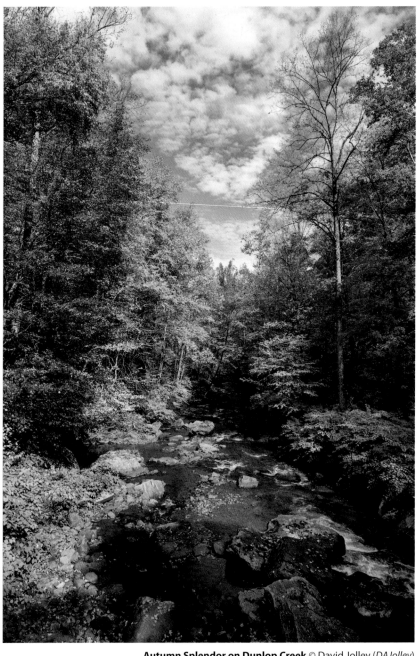

Autumn Splendor on Dunlop Creek © David Jolley (*DAJolley*)

12

With each new DSLR camera released, Nikon has advanced the capability of the video recording system. The Nikon D810 is no exception. In fact, this camera has achieved a level of video capability that few other cameras can claim, even outside the 35 mm form factor. Due to the power and flexibility of its Movie live view video mode, it has led the way in establishing a new type of camera, the *hybrid digital single-lens reflex* camera, or HD-SLR. Where previous Nikon DSLR cameras were primarily still-image producers that happened to have video recording capability, the new HD-SLR D810 was constructed with a video system just as capable as the still-image system.

When you use the still-imaging side of the Nikon D810, you are taking extreme-resolution images that no other 35 mm form-factor DSLR can match (at the time of writing). When you create videos with the D810, again you can create video that few cameras can match. The Nikon D810 has the ability to stream broad-cast-quality, uncompressed, HD (720p) or Full HD (1080p) video with no camera control overlays—called clean video—from its HDMI port.

In a sense, the Nikon D810 has two video subsystems. One is for recording high-quality, compressed home videos in MOV format, up to 29 minutes and 59 seconds long each, to the camera's CF and SD memory cards. The second is for out-putting a clean, uncompressed 1080p video stream from the HDMI port with no time constraints. The second video type allows true commercial use of the Nikon D810 for shooting Full HD video.

This camera is so appealing and powerful in both its still-image and video modes that it is causing a large influx of other-brand users to come over to Nikon. And why not? The Nikon D810 has the most dynamic range of any production digital camera ever created (14.8 EV), the highest-quality medium-format imaging sensor ever seen in a 35 mm camera, and a video system that is more capable than most cam-eras in its class. And the nice thing is—you own a Nikon D810!

High Definition vs. Hybrid Digital

You will find quite a bit of discussion on the Internet about what HD-SLR truly stands for. Some claim it stands for *High Definition Single Lens Reflex* and others claim *Hybrid Digital Single Lens Reflex*. In fact, the *HD* in HD-SLR stands for hybrid digital. The camera is a hybrid that shoots both stills and video.

Honestly, though, where do the abbreviations stop? What new abbreviations will the next generation of cameras bring? If you want to go all out on abbrevi-ation usage, the Nikon D810 is a high-definition, video-enabled, hybrid, digital single-lens reflex camera (HDVEHDSLR?). Now that's a satisfying abbreviation. ☺

Selecting Movie Live View Mode

12

(User's Manual – Page 49)

Just in case you are a new HD-SLR user and have never used Nikon's Live view modes, let's see how to switch the camera into Movie live view mode. In figure 12.1, the camera is set to Movie live view mode, which is just below the setting for Live view photography mode (previous chapter) on the Live view selector switch.

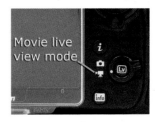

Figure 12.1 – Selecting Movie live view mode

Once you have entered Movie live view mode, you can take HD-ratio (16:9) still images and HD videos in the 16:9 aspect ratio only. No matter how you have the camera set in *Shooting Menu > Image area*, the still images and video are still in 16:9 ratio.

If you are shooting in DX mode or with a DX lens attached, the images and movies are still in the 16:9 aspect ratio; however, the camera creates a cropped, DX-sized 16:9 ratio image or video that gives the appearance of pulling the subject in closer. It isn't really magnifying the image, just using less of the imaging sensor to capture the subject, so it appears larger in the image or video when displayed.

It is apparent from experimentation that the 1.2x and 5:4 formats under *Shooting Menu > Image area* do not influence the image or video in Movie live view mode. When you are shooting in the 1.2x or 5:4 formats, the camera simply creates an FX-sized 16:9 ratio image or movie.

Movie Live View Still Images

As mentioned at the end of chapter 11, the Nikon D810 provides a still-image capability in Movie live view mode that is very similar to that of Live view photography mode. In fact, most of what is written in the chapter **Live View Photography** applies equally to Movie live view mode's 16:9 ratio still images.

For that reason, we will not discuss all the capability of the Movie live view still-imaging function because that would merely be a repeat of the previous chapter. When you decide to take a picture (instead of a movie) using Movie live view mode, let the information in chapter 11 govern how you shoot, tempered by the differences discussed in this chapter.

I know this seems a little odd, and I wish that Nikon had simply included a 16:9 aspect ratio format in the *Shooting Menu > Image area* menu. However, that is not

12

Figuring Print Sizes in Inches and Centimeters

The print sizes listed in table 12.1 are based on printing the image at 300 dpi. The print size will be different at different dots per inch (dpi) settings. The formula to figure print sizes at various dpi settings is as follows (1 inch = approximately 2.54 cm):

Print size (in) = Pixel size (one dimension) / dpi

Therefore, a pixel size of 6720 pixels / 300 dpi = 22.4 inches (56.9 cm), as shown in table 12.1. That means the same pixels at 240 dpi would provide a larger image, as the formula shows: 6720 pixels / 240 dpi = 28 inches (71.12 cm). For metric system users, the formula would have one more step:

Print size (cm) = (Pixel size / dpi) x 2.54

So, a pixel size of (6720 pixels / 300 dpi) × 2.54 = 55.89 cm. Remember this useful formula, whether in inches or centimeters, if you use dots per inch as the standard for printing. This formula works for any pixel-to-print size conversion (in dots per inch), not just in Movie live view mode. Use the pixel size for each dimension (height and width) of the image to determine an overall print size.

the case and some may enjoy shooting in the 16:9 aspect ratio, so let's consider the available options and sizes listed in the following table.

Image Area	Image Size	Pixel Size	Print Size (in/cm)
FX	L	6720×3776	22.4×12.6 / 56.9×32.0
FX	M	5040×2832	16.8×9.4 / 42.7×24.0
FX	S	3360×1888	11.2×6.3 / 28.4×16.0
DX	L	4800×2704	16.0×9.0 / 40.6×22.9
DX	M	3600×2024	12.0×6.7 / 30.5×17.1
DX	S	2400×1352	8.0×4.5 / 20.3×11.4

Table 12.1 – Movie live view mode 16:9 still Image area and Image size with pixel and print dimensions

Image Area in table 12.1 represents the values found in *Shooting Menu > Image area > Choose image area* but includes only values from FX and DX because those are the only formats supported for the 16:9 aspect ratio of Movie live view mode. You must select the Image area before you enter Movie live view mode. The Image area choice is grayed out on the Shooting Menu when you are in Movie live view.

Image Size in table 12.1 represents the values found in *Shooting Menu > Image size*. The table reflects the Large (L), Medium (M), and Small (S) Image sizes available in Movie live view mode. You can select these values from the Shooting Menu by pressing the MENU button while in Movie live view mode.

A still image taken in Movie live view in FX mode is approximately 91 percent of the width of a normal FX image.

Movie Live View Screens

Let's start out by examining each of the five screen overlays you can use while taking stills or shooting movies in Movie live view mode. You can scroll through each of the five screens by pressing the info button repeatedly.

Movie Live View – Screen 1

The Nikon D810 has two screens for each overlay in Movie live view. The first screen is available when you are shooting still images and the second when you are recording video. I am using the first screen as a guide initially so that we can examine each of the controls on the screen. Once you start recording movies, some of the controls in the overlay disappear. Figure 12.2 shows the first screen you should see when you enter Movie live view. Let's examine each of the controls displayed in the overlay.

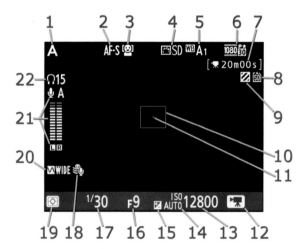

Figure 12.2 – Movie live view screen overlay 1

Here is a list of controls shown on the first screen. Each number in figure 12.2 has a corresponding entry in the list that follows:

12

1. ***Exposure mode*** – Selected by holding down the MODE button on top of the camera while turning the rear Main command dial. The available selections you will see on the Monitor are Programmed auto (P), Shutter-priority auto (S), Aperture-priority auto (A), and Manual (M).

2. ***Autofocus mode*** – Set with the AF-mode button and rear Main command dial. Available settings are AF-S and AF-F. AF-S uses single autofocus that locks on your subject; AF-F provides continuous autofocus.

3. ***AF-area mode*** – Set with the AF-mode button and front Sub-command dial. Available settings are Face-priority AF, Wide-area AF, Normal-area AF, and Subject-tracking AF (uses graphical symbols).

4. ***Picture Control*** – Controlled with *Shooting Menu > Set Picture Control*. You can also control this setting by pressing the Protect/Picture Control/Help button and selecting a Picture Control from the Monitor with the Multi selector.

5. ***White balance*** – Set the camera's White balance by holding down the WB button and rotating the rear Main command dial. Select from nine white balance settings, including Auto (A1), Incandescent, Fluorescent, Direct sunlight, Flash, Cloudy, Shade, Choose color temp., and Preset manual (uses graphical symbols).

6. ***Frame size/frame rate*** – This is controlled with *Shooting Menu > Movie settings > Frame size/frame rate*. It shows the frame size and frame rate to which your Movie mode is currently set. The choices are 1080p at 60, 50, 30, 25, or 24 fps, or 720p at 60 or 50 fps. You can also adjust this setting before you start shooting a video with the Frame size/frame rate setting in the *i* Button Menu, as described in the upcoming **Preparing to Make Movies** section.

7. ***Time remaining*** – When you are recording a movie, this feature shows you how much time is left before the camera automatically stops recording. Here is a list of the recording times:
    *   1080p60 and 1080p50 both have a maximum recording time of 10 minutes with the High quality bit rate and 20 minutes with the Normal quality bit rate.
    *   1080p30, 1080p25, 1080p24, 720p60, and 720p50 all have maximum recording times of 20 minutes with the High quality bit rate and 29 minutes 59 seconds with the Normal quality bit rate.
    *   When you use the HDMI port to send uncompressed video to an external video recording device, there is no limit on the recording time.

8. ***Movie destination*** – This setting reflects the configuration stored in *Shooting Menu > Movie Settings > Destination*. You can also adjust this setting before you start shooting a video with the Destination setting in the *i* Button Menu, as described in the upcoming **Preparing to Make Movies** section. You have a choice of the SD card slot or the CF card slot. Movies will be recorded only to the selected destination card unless it has been removed from the camera, at which time the D810 will record video to the only available card.

12

9. ***Highlight display*** – Also known as Zebra mode, the Highlight display places alternating black and white stripes, like a zebra, on areas that are blown out to pure white and have lost all highlight detail. You must enable or disable this setting before you start shooting a video with the Highlight display setting in the *i* Button Menu, as described in the upcoming **Preparing to Make Movies** section.

10. ***AF point (focus)*** – This AF point rectangle can be moved around the screen with the Multi selector to select the subject for autofocus. This focus rectangle will vary in size and color according to the AF area mode selected (#3) and whether or not the subject is in focus.

11. ***Center of Frame Dot*** – This small dot appears when the AF point rectangle is directly in the middle of the frame. This dot, as well as the surrounding AF point rectangle (#10), will be red when the subject is out of focus and green when it is in focus.

12. ***Movie live view symbol*** – This symbol is merely a label to let you know you have the camera set to Movie live view mode.

13. ***ISO sensitivity*** – Controlled by *Shooting Menu > Movie settings > ISO sensitivity (mode M)*, with ISO values choices from Lo 1 (ISO 32) to Hi 2 (ISO 51,200). You must choose an ISO sensitivity setting before you start shooting the movie. If this value needs to vary, you will need to use ISO Auto Mode as discussed in #14. Also, see the chapter titled **Shooting Menu** under the subheading **Movie Settings** for more information on this setting.

14. ***ISO Auto mode*** – Controlled by *Shooting Menu > Movie settings > Movie ISO sensitivity settings > Auto ISO control (mode M)*, with the choice of On or Off. You must choose and adjust this setting before you start recording a video. See the chapter titled **Shooting Menu** under the subheading **Movie Settings** for more information on this setting.

15. ***Exposure compensation*** – This symbol will appear only when +/- exposure compensation has been dialed into the camera. Adjust this value with the +/- Exposure compensation button near the Shutter-release button.

16. ***Aperture*** – Set by turning the front Sub-command dial, with aperture minimum and maximums that vary according to the mounted lens. Manual change is available only in Aperture-priority auto (A) and Manual (M) modes. The camera controls this value in Shutter-priority auto (S) and Programmed auto (P) modes.

17. ***Shutter speed*** – Set shutter speed with the rear Main command dial. Settings range from 1/30 second to 1/8000 second (8000) when using Manual mode (M) only. The camera controls this value in Aperture-priority auto (A), Shutter-priority auto (S), and Programmed auto (P) modes. Even in Shutter-priority auto (S) mode, the camera forces you to use the ISO Auto setting (#14). Only in Manual mode (M) do you have limited control over the shutter speed (1/30 to

1/8000 sec). (**Note:** You can enable or disable ISO Auto in Manual (M) exposure mode by setting Auto ISO control (mode M) to On or Off with *Shooting Menu > Movie settings > Movie ISO sensitivity settings > Auto ISO control (mode M)*. That's right, you can use ISO Auto in Manual (M) mode in case the light changes too quickly for you to manage it with manual controls. This is a powerful feature and safety factor for the Nikon D810 camera.)

18. *Wind noise reduction* – This symbol will appear when Wind noise reduction is enabled. This function attempts to remove the worst of the rumbling sound you hear when wind strikes an unprotected microphone. This function is controlled by the *Shooting Menu > Movie settings > Wind noise reduction* setting, or by the Wind noise reduction setting in the *i* Button Menu, as described in the upcoming **Preparing to Make Movies** section.

19. *Metering mode* – Movie live view allows you to use three of the four metering modes the camera offers: Matrix metering, Highlight-weighted metering, and Center-weighted metering. Hold down the Metering button and rotate the rear Main command dial to change the metering mode. This must be set before you start recording video.

20. *Frequency response* – This symbol will appear to let you know whether you have the microphone's frequency response set to Wide or Voice. Wide will capture a much broader range of sound for when you want to record all sounds in a scene. The Voice setting limits the sound recording sensitivity to ranges encompassing human voice frequencies, making it best for recording human speech, such as during a public discourse or lecture. This function is controlled by the *Shooting Menu > Movie settings > Frequency response* setting, or by the Frequency response setting in the *i* Button Menu, as described in the upcoming **Preparing to Make Movies** section.

21. *Microphone sensitivity* – This setting allows you to adjust the current Microphone sensitivity setting. As shown in figure 12.2, #21, there are three symbols associated with this setting. The top symbols of a mic and the letter A means that I have the mic set to Auto. The two side-by-side lines of bars show a live view of the left and right sound channels in action, and the L (left) and R (right) symbols indicate which channel is which. For the side-by-side sound level bars, white means normal sound, yellow means loud sound, and red means too-loud sound that may be distorted. The Mic sensitivity is controlled by *Shooting Menu > Movie settings > Microphone sensitivity*, with the choice of Auto sensitivity, Manual sensitivity (in 20 steps), and Microphone off. You can also adjust this setting before a recording session begins with the Microphone sensitivity setting in the *i* Button Menu, as described in the upcoming **Preparing to Make Movies** section. The D810 does not allow mic sensitivity adjustment during a video recording session.

12

22. ***Headphone volume*** – This setting lets you adjust the volume output by the camera to a set of headphones. You can also adjust this setting before you start shooting a video with the *i* Button Menu, as described in the upcoming **Preparing to Make Movies** section. You can adjust the volume level anywhere between off (level 0) and level 30. You adjust the volume level by holding down the Thumbnail/Playback zoom out button and scrolling left or right with the Multi selector until you have selected Headphone volume. You then scroll up or down with the Multi selector until you have selected a comfortable volume level. You must adjust the volume before starting a movie recording session.

When you press the Movie-record button, the screen removes several of the controls in the overlay along the top, as shown in figure 12.3. You can tell this is a screen from a video being recorded by the REC symbol in the top-left corner, next to the red dot. REC blinks the whole time you are recording.

Why do some of the controls disappear during a video recording? Basically, to clean up the screen a bit so the overlay is less distracting while you are concentrating on your subject. During the video recording, you can still change some of the control functions shown in figure 12.2, with the exception of the following functions (see numbers in previous list):

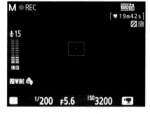

Figure 12.3 – Movie live view screen overlay 1, during a video recording

- Picture Control
- Frame size/frame rate
- Headphone volume
- Metering mode
- Movie destination
- Sound level
- Exposure mode

The MENU button has no effect during a video recording, so you are locked out of even attempting to make any serious camera adjustments that have no button/dial combinations on the camera. However, you can still adjust many of the control functions shown or not shown.

For instance, if you press the AF-mode button while recording a video, the Auto-focus and AF-area mode symbols will reappear, allowing you to turn the rear Main command dial to change the Autofocus mode or the front Sub-command dial to change the AF-area mode. Try it.

Likewise, if you press the WB button during a recording, you can change White balance on the fly. According to which Exposure mode was previous selected (P, S, A, or M), you can adjust the aperture, shutter speed, and ISO sensitivity. Finally, you can always add or subtract Exposure compensation with the +/- Exposure compensation button.

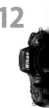

Shooting in Manual (M) mode gives you the greatest control over the camera during a video recording. In Manual, you can adjust the following functions (see previous list again for numbers):

- Autofocus mode
- White balance
- Shutter speed
- Exposure compensation

- AF-area mode
- AF point (focus)
- Aperture
- ISO sensitivity

Manual mode (M) gives you full control of the camera while recording a video. Aperture-priority auto (A) allows you to control the aperture, while the camera controls the rest. Shutter-priority auto (S) and Programmed auto (P) give you much less control and could almost be considered point-and-shoot modes when recording video.

Now, let's consider the other available screen overlays and their purposes. Press the info button when you see screen 1 (figure 12.2 or 12.3) and the camera will switch to screen 2 (figure 12.4).

Movie Live View – Screen 2

Screen 2 in the overlay series is a very bare screen for those times when you want very little distraction while making a still image or recording a video (figure 12.4). You can still see the most important controls at the bottom of the screen (aperture, shutter speed, and ISO sensitivity), but everything else is stripped out of the overlay.

Nikon calls the screen in figure 12.2 the *Information on* screen, while the screen in figure 12.4 is called the *Information off* screen.

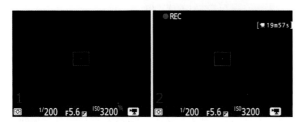

Figure 12.4 – Movie live view screen overlay 2, for still images (1) and video recording (2)

Movie Live View – Screen 3

Most photographers have a tendency to tilt their cameras to the left or right slightly. The *Framing guides* screen is designed to help keep things level in the Viewfinder (figure 12.5). The grid lines are very useful for keeping horizons level and architecture straight.

12

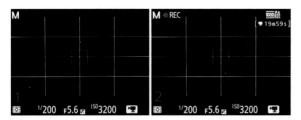

Figure 12.5 – Movie live view screen overlay 3, for still images (1) and video recording (2)

I leave these grid lines turned on in my Viewfinder-based photography all the time and use them in Live view mode when I need to level things in comparison to a feature in my subject, such as the horizon.

Movie Live View – Screen 4

The *Histogram* screen gives you a live histogram to help you judge exposure during video recording (figure 12.6). In Manual (M) mode, you can adjust the aperture, shutter speed, or ISO sensitivity to correct for under- or overexposure. In other Exposure modes, you can use the +/- Exposure compensation button to push the exposure toward the dark or light sides, making the exposure better.

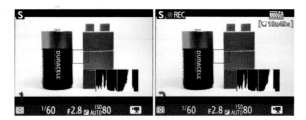

Figure 12.6 – Movie live view screen overlay 4, for still images (1) and video recording (2)

If you are a video perfectionist who wants to control all aspects of the video production, you will certainly enjoy having a live histogram to keep you informed immediately when light levels change in a way that will damage your video's quality. This is a truly professional tool and one all serious videographers should use regularly, especially in Manual (M) mode!

Movie Live View – Screen 5

The *Virtual horizon* screen displays roll and pitch from the camera's built-in tilt sensor (figure 12.7). If the lines are green, it means the camera is level. The tilt sensor senses left and right tilts and forward and backward tilts. When the camera is not level in one direction or the other, the line for that direction turns yellow and signifies the approximate degree of tilt.

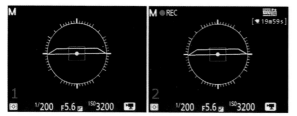

Figure 12.7 – Movie live view screen overlay 5, for still images (1) and video recording (2)

This is very useful when setting up a camera on a tripod to shoot a video. You can start the video with the knowledge that the camera is level both left to right and front to back. While you're shooting a video handheld, this screen may be invaluable to prevent introducing tilt into an otherwise excellent video.

Preparing to Make Movies

(User's Manual – Page 49, 57)
The Movie mode in the D810 is one of the best video recording systems Nikon has put in a DSLR. It has automatic or manual focus, 1080p HD recording, stereo sound, 10, 20, or 29-minute 59-second recording segments according to frame size and rate, a 4 GB movie length maximum, and excellent rolling shutter correction.

Another excellent improvement is the fact that you can control the D810 in a fully manual way while recording video, just as when taking still images. This is an important level of control for serious video mavens. If you want to buy all the cool attachments, like stabilization frames, bigger external video monitors, external streaming video recorders, a headphone set, and an external stereo mic, this camera has the ports and controls to support them.

Let's examine how to prepare for and record videos and then how to display them on various devices. Keep in mind that the D810 offers two levels of video recording; first, to the camera's memory card as a compressed (b-frame H.264/MPEG-4 AVC) QuickTime MOV file; and second, as an uncompressed 4:2:2, clean (overlay-free), broadcast-quality HDMI video stream through the HDMI port to an external recording device.

Basic HD Video Information

Before shooting your first movie, you'll need to configure the camera for your favorite video frame size and rate. We'll look into the actual configuration in a later section. For now, let's briefly discuss some basics.

A video frame is much smaller, in terms of pixels, than a normal still-image frame. Although your D810 can create beautiful 36-megapixel still images, its best HD video image is just above 2 megapixels (2,073,600 pixels).

Whoa! How can 2 megapixels be considered high definition (HD)? Simply because it matches one of the high-definition television (HDTV) broadcast resolutions. In the good old days of standard-definition television (SDTV) that we all grew up watching, there was even less resolution. Would you believe that the old TV you have stored in the garage displays only 345,600 pixels, or 0.3 megapixels?

I've been talking about the number of megapixels, but that's not normally how HD devices are rated. Instead of the number of pixels, most HD information talks about the number of lines of resolution. There are several HD standards for lines of resolution. The most common standards are 720p, 1080i, and 1080p. The p and i after the numbers refer to *progressive* and *interlaced*. We'll talk about what that means in the next section.

The D810's best Movie mode captures video at 1080p, which is a display-quality HDTV standard. At the time of this writing, most over-the-air broadcast-quality HD is 720p, but 1080p is growing in popularity. The 1080p designation simply means that your camera captures and displays HD images with 1,080 lines of vertical resolution. Each of those lines is 1,920 pixels long, which allows the D810 to match the 16:9 aspect ratio expected in HDTV. An older SDTV usually has an aspect ratio of 4:3, which is taller and narrower than the HDTV 16:9 aspect ratio.

Progressive versus Interlaced

What's the difference between progressive and interlaced? Technically speaking, progressive video output displays the video frame starting with the top line and then draws the other lines until the entire frame is shown. The D810 displays 1,080 lines progressively from the top of what the imaging sensor captured to the bottom (lines 1, 2, 3, 4 . . . 1,080).

Interlaced video output displays every even line from top to bottom, then comes back to the top and displays every odd line (lines 2, 4, 6, 8 . . . 1,080, then 1, 3, 5, 7 . . . 1,079).

Progressive output provides a higher-quality image with less flicker and a more cinematic look. I'm sure that's why Nikon chose to make the D810 shoot progressive video. Now, let's set up our cameras and make some movies!

Camera Setup for Making Quick Movies

The D810 is capable of creating movies at any time and with little thought, by simply using the following settings and actions:

- Select Autofocus mode AF-F (Full-time servo AF).
- Set the Exposure mode to Programmed auto (P).

- Flip the Live view selector lever to Movie live view.
- Press the Lv button to enter Live view.
- Press the Movie-record button.

Setting up the camera in this way makes it act like a standard video camera, where you give little consideration to camera settings and simply shoot the video.

However, you have purchased an advanced-level camera, and you may want to do more than just take automatic movies. The D810 can do it either way. Let's discuss how to set up the camera for more professional movie creation. First, we will consider the 10 primary settings found on the *i* Button Menu and then we will consider a few more settings that are critical for proper video capture.

Using the *i* Button Menu in Movie Live View

Pressing the *i* button while in Movie live view mode gives you access to 10 convenient control functions, including:

- Image area
- Frame size/frame rate
- Movie quality
- Microphone sensitivity
- Frequency response
- Wind noise reduction
- Destination
- Monitor brightness
- Highlight display
- Headphone volume

Let's examine each of these settings individually and prepare for recording premium-quality videos. Some of the settings are fully covered in previous chapters of this book, so we won't go into extreme detail about how to select the settings; only the screens are necessary. If you need more detail about a particular setting, refer to the chapter that covers it; for example, *Shooting Menu > Set Picture Control* is covered in the chapter **Shooting Menu**.

These 10 setting are all available in the *i* Button Menu (found by pressing the *i* button while the camera is in Movie live view mode).

Image Area

The camera has four Image area settings available for still images. However, when shooting video the camera limits you to two video areas: FX and DX.

The FX choice takes data from the camera's 7360x4912 sensor pixel array and subsamples a 1920x1080 subset of the FX image data for the video. FX also gives

12

you very shallow depth of field for pulling focus—changing focus to a different subject while recording—a technique that makes HD-SLR video very interesting.

The DX choice uses data from a 4800x3200 pixel rectangle in the center of the D810's sensor, subsampling a 1920x1080 subset of the DX image data for the video. DX also matches the aspect ratio and depth of field found in many other digital video cameras, so many videographers prefer using the DX mode when recording video.

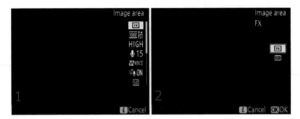

Figure 12.8 – Choosing an Image area

Use these steps to choose a video Image area (FX or DX):

1. Make sure the Live view selector lever is set to Movie live view mode (figure 12.1) and that you have pressed the Lv button to enter Movie live view.
2. Press the *i* button to open the *i* Button Menu. Select Image area from the list (figure 12.8, screen 1). Scroll to the right.
3. Choose FX or DX from the Image area menu (figure 12.8, screen 2).
4. Press the OK button to lock in the setting.

Settings Recommendation: I like to use the FX setting because I enjoy pulling focus, and the shallow depth of field of the FX mode makes that easy. Of course, when I need more depth of field than FX can easily provide, I use the DX mode. You should shoot video in both modes and see which look you prefer.

Frame Size/Frame Rate

There are two *Frame size* settings available in *Shooting Menu > Movie settings > Frame size/frame rate*, and five *frame rate* settings. The frame sizes are both HD standards at 1920×1080 and 1280×720. The frame rates are 60, 50, 30, 25, and 24 fps.

The camera records video using the progressive (p) scanning method (sequential lines) and can output both progressive (p) and interlaced (i) standards through its HDMI port to external devices. Choose your favorite rate and size using the menu screens shown in figure 12.9. For more information on choosing a Frame size/frame rate, see the section **Movie Settings** in the chapter **Shooting Menu**.

Use these steps to choose a video Frame rate and frame size:

1. Make sure the Live view selector lever is set to Movie live view mode (figure 12.1) and that you have pressed the Lv button to enter Movie live view.
2. Press the *i* button to open the *i* Button Menu. Select Frame size/frame rate from the list (figure 12.9, screen 1). Scroll to the right.
3. Choose one of the seven choices from the Image area menu (figure 12.9, screen 2).
4. Press the OK button to lock in the setting.

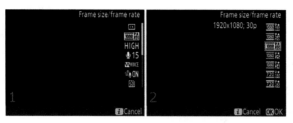

Figure 12.9 – Choosing a Frame size/frame rate

Obviously, you must set the Frame size/frame rate before you actually start recording video. The Frame size/frame rate setting changes how large the resulting movie will be when it's stored on your memory card and computer hard drive. The maximum the camera will allow is 4 GB in any single movie segment. All frame sizes and rates are limited in recording time length to 10 minutes, 20 minutes, or 29 minutes 59 seconds, per the Movie quality bit rate in table 12.2:

Frame Size/ Frame Rate	Bit Rate HIGH Quality	Bit Rate NORM Quality	Maximum Length High Quality/Normal
1920x1080; 60p	42 Mbps	24 Mbps	10 min / 20 min
1920x1080; 50p	42 Mbps	24 Mbps	10 min / 20 min
1920x1080; 30p	24 Mbps	12 Mbps	20 min / 29 min 59 sec
1920x1080; 25p	24 Mbps	12 Mbps	20 min / 29 min 59 sec
1920x1080; 24p	24 Mbps	12 Mbps	20 min / 29 min 59 sec
1280x720; 60p	24 Mbps	12 Mbps	20 min / 29 min 59 sec
1280x720; 50p	24 Mbps	12 Mbps	20 min / 29 min 59 sec

Table 12.2 – Frame size/frame rate, Movie quality bit rates, and Maximum movie length

We will discuss how to choose the bit rate, or Movie quality, in the next subsection, **Movie Quality**. The Movie quality affects how much data is collected by the camera, and directly affects the resulting video's file size along with the maximum length of time you can record in one video clip.

12

Why Different Frame Rates?

The NTSC encoding format, established in the 1940s, originally used two frame rates: 30 and 60 fps. In the 1960s a new German standard was created called PAL, which used 25 and 50 fps. Today, frame rates of 24, 25, 30, 50, and 60 are common in DSLR cameras. These rates can also be expressed as a hertz (Hz) rate on progressive scan monitors. The primary frame rate used in the movie industry is 24p.

A video is many still pictures joined together and moved past your eye at a very fast rate. The human eye maintains an image at about 10 to 16 fps (1/10 to 1/16 second), so frame rates faster than that do not flicker for many people. However, some people's eyes are more sensitive and can see flicker in slower frame rates. I am afraid to say much more about this issue because it can rapidly degrade into an almost religious discussion, with people having very strong opinions about their favorite frame rates.

Let me just say that many people prefer 24 fps because that is normal for cinema movies. This rate is called a cinematic rate. Other people like the faster frame rate of 30 fps due to its lack of flicker. I suggest that you try all the frame rates and see which you like best. You might even want to shoot some video at 60 fps and play it back at 30 fps for cool slow-motion effects.

Video File Format

The file format used by the D810 is the popular Apple QuickTime MOV format. This format is handled by virtually all computer movie players. The video compression used inside the MOV file is H.264/MPEG-4 Advanced Video Coding.

A computer should display any of the Movie quality modes. Using a mini-HDMI (type c) to HDMI standard (type a) cable, you can play full HD videos on an HDTV. An HDMI cable is not included with the camera. They are easily available online and in many electronics stores. We'll talk more about how to display video in a later section, which includes pictures of the cables.

Settings Recommendation: There are three considerations when selecting a Movie quality setting: First, how much storage capacity do you have on your camera's memory cards? Second, what type of display device will you show the movies on? Third, are you a video fanatic?

If you are fanatical about video, you'll shoot only at the fastest rates and highest quality. Others may want to shoot a lot of family videos and hate storing the huge files that result from high frame sizes and rates. In that case, the normal quality setting and lower resolutions may be sufficient.

If you can't stand watching a non-HD video on YouTube, maybe you should stick to maximum quality. If standard YouTube videos are sufficient for your needs, nearly any quality setting from the D810 will look great on your computer.

This is a personal decision, and you'll need to experiment with video modes to find a balance between quality and file size.

Movie Quality

The Movie quality setting has to do with the Maximum bit rate (Mbps) that the camera can flow while making the movie. The higher the bit rate, the higher the quality of the movie. The bit rate can go as low as 12 Mbps in Normal quality mode and as high as 42 Mbps in High quality mode. Here is a table that shows the Mbps flow in High (HIGH) and Normal (NORM) quality modes (table 12.3):

Frame Size/ Frame Rate	Bit Rate HIGH Quality	Bit Rate NORM Quality
1920x1080; 60p	42 Mbps	24 Mbps
1920x1080; 50p	42 Mbps	24 Mbps
1920x1080; 30p	24 Mbps	12 Mbps
1920x1080; 25p	24 Mbps	12 Mbps
1920x1080; 24p	24 Mbps	12 Mbps
1280x720; 60p	24 Mbps	12 Mbps
1280x720; 50p	24 Mbps	12 Mbps

Table 12.3 – Bit rates per Movie quality setting

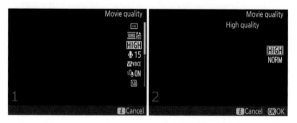

Figure 12.10 – Choosing a Movie quality (bit rate)

Use these steps to choose a Movie quality (bit rate) for your video:

1. Make sure the Live view selector lever is set to Movie live view mode (figure 12.1) and that you have pressed the Lv button to enter Movie live view.
2. Press the *i* button to open the *i* Button Menu. Select Movie quality from the list (figure 12.10, screen 1). Scroll to the right.

12

3. Choose HIGH or NORM from the Movie quality menu (figure 12.10, screen 2).
4. Press the OK button to lock in the setting.

Changing the bit rate is one way to control the amount of data the video contains. The higher the bit rate, the better the movie quality—but the larger the movie file size. You will need to decide which is more important, quality or size.

Note: You can also set the Movie quality by using the *Shooting Menu > Movie settings > Movie quality* menu.

Settings Recommendation: Unless I am just shooting a video for the Internet only (Facebook or YouTube) and of a subject with no commercial value, I shoot with the camera set to Maximum frame rate, frame size, bit rate, and whatever other maximums I can find and max out. If a video has potential to make me some money or is of an interesting subject that others will enjoy watching, I want the best quality I can wring out of those little 2 MP frames. However, that comes with a trade-off of much larger file sizes, so I have committed to buying larger and larger hard drives each year or two. One thing about the D810, it will certainly increase the stock prices of the hard drive manufacturers. The quality from this camera is amazing, and so are the file sizes!

Microphone Sensitivity

The Microphone sensitivity setting is designed to give you the ability to set how sensitive the Microphone is to surrounding sound. This setting affects the Built-in microphone until you plug in an external Microphone in the camera's Microphone jack under the rubber Connector cover (figure 12.11D). Let's look at the best way to set the Microphone level just before recording a video.

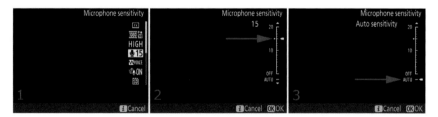

Figure 12.11A – Manually setting the Microphone sensitivity with camera controls

Use these steps to choose a Microphone sensitivity:

1. Make sure the Live view selector lever is set to Movie live view mode (figure 12.1) and that you have pressed the Lv button to enter Movie live view.
2. Press the *i* button to open the *i* Button Menu. Select Microphone sensitivity from the list (figure 12.11A, screen 1). Scroll to the right.

3. Choose from as low as Off to as high as level 20 from the Movie quality slider on the right side of the screen (figure 12.11A, screen 2, red arrow). I have selected Microphone sensitivity level 15.
4. If you would rather have the camera decide which Microphone sensitivity to use, the D810 offers an Auto setting at the bottom of the sensitivity slider (figure 12.11A, screen 3, red arrow).
5. Make a selection and press the OK button to lock in your chosen mic sensitivity level.

The Microphone must be set before you start recording a video, so you may want to test the level to see if the sound gets into the yellow or red zones. Keep the indicator in the mid to upper white zone for normal sound (figure 12.11B, red arrow). As the sound increases, the indicator hits the yellow zone and finally the red zone, where clipping may occur.

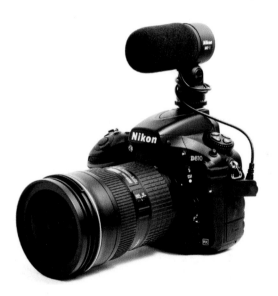

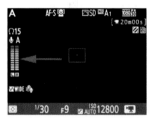

Figure 12.11B – Monitoring the sound level

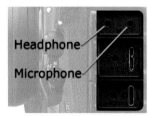

Figure 12.11C – Nikon D810, AF-S Nikkor 24-70mm f/2.8G ED lens, with Nikon ME-1 microphone in Accessory shoe

Figure 12.11D – Headphone and Microphone plugs

The D810 offers the ability to plug in an optional stereo microphone (figure 12.11C). It disables the built-in mono mic and overcomes some of its limitations. There are several microphones available for the D810, including a few that mount onto the camera's Accessory shoe like a flash unit does. I like Nikon's ME-1 microphone, shown in figure 12.11C.

In figure 12.11D you can see where an external Microphone plugs into the camera. The right-hand plug is for a microphone and the left-hand plug is for a headphone.

12

If you decide to simply use the Built-in microphone, just be sure you don't accidentally cover it with your finger while recording a video. The Built-in stereo microphone is a series of three holes, one set on either side of the prism housing on the front of the camera (figure 12.11E, red arrows).

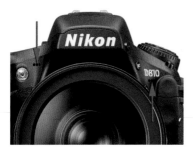

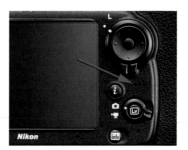

Figure 12.11E – Nikon D810 Built-in stereo microphone (red arrows)

Figure 12.11F – Nikon D810 Speaker

Sound Output from Camera

When you are not using headphones, the video's sound is output through a small speaker on the back of the camera during camera playback. You'll see three small holes between the Live view selector and Multi selector (figure 12.11F). This little speaker can put out an amazing amount of volume.

You can control the volume output of the speaker with the Thumbnail/playback zoom out button (volume down) and Playback zoom in button (volume up). The setting range is 1 through 30, and Off. I find that level 20 is about right to hear well in a normal environment.

You can use headphones to listen to the sound from the video, too. I find that 12 or 13 is plenty loud for my headphones. For more information about using headphones with the D810, see the upcoming subsection titled **Headphone volume**.

Note: You can also set the Microphone sensitivity from the *Shooting Menu > Movie settings > Microphone sensitivity* setting.

Settings Recommendation: First of all, I strongly suggest that you acquire the Nikon ME-1 external microphone. I have really enjoyed using it. It vastly improves the quality of sound flowing into the camera during a video and isolates the camera's clicking and whirring noises more effectively. The ME-1 is relatively inexpensive—well, compared to a lens, anyway.

I leave the sound level set to Auto (A) most of the time. However, if I am in an especially loud environment, I will set the sound manually to about 15. When there are sudden loud sounds in Auto mode, the camera seems to struggle and often clips the sound as it overwhelms the camera's sound circuitry.

I suggest experimenting with this because normally it's not a problem. Where the problem occurs is at something like a ball game. You will be recording the game and someone scores, to the crowd's great yelling and stomping happiness. Auto may not be the best setting under those circumstances. I wish Nikon would just give us control of the sound *during* a video shooting session, not only before!

Frequency Response

Sound is a very important part of video recording. Maybe you want to record a video while visiting a national park and would like to pick up the sound of every bird song, leaf rustle, and gurgling stream. Using the wide frequency option will allow this type of sound recording. On the other hand, using the voice frequency option while recording a video of a wedding ceremony is a good choice because it won't pick up the sounds of a bird singing outside the window and road traffic outside.

With a combination of the Microphone sensitivity and Frequency response functions, you can capture some very high-quality sound. Microphone sensitivity affects how sensitive the microphone is to sound, and Frequency response affects which sound frequencies the mic is most sensitive to. We've already considered Microphone sensitivity, so now let's see how to make the mic sensitive to a wide frequency range (national park) or a human voice frequency range (wedding ceremony).

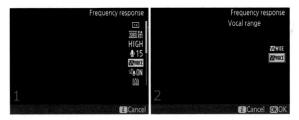

Figure 12.12 – Choosing a Frequency response for the mic

Use these steps to choose a Frequency response range for the microphone in use:

1. Make sure the Live view selector lever is set to Movie live view mode (figure 12.1) and that you have pressed the Lv button to enter Movie live view.
2. Press the *i* button to open the *i* Button Menu. Select Frequency response from the list (figure 12.12, screen 1). Scroll to the right.
3. Choose WIDE (Wide range) or VOICE (Vocal range) from the Frequency response menu (figure 12.12, screen 2).
4. Press the OK button to lock in the setting.

12

Settings Recommendation: If you are recording a human speaker, use VOICE, and for about anything else use WIDE. I leave my camera set to WIDE most of the time because I am a nature photographer and enjoy hearing natural sounds.

Wind Noise Reduction

Have you ever recorded a video on a beautiful, breezy summer afternoon, only to later find that you have recorded that distinctive rumbling sound of wind blowing across a microphone instead of the clear sound you desired?

While that sound may not be completely eliminated without using special microphones designed to deal with it—such as the Nikon ME-1—it can be significantly reduced with the Wind noise reduction function, which removes or cuts low frequency noises like wind rumbles.

Let's see how to enable and disable the Wind noise reduction low-cut filter.

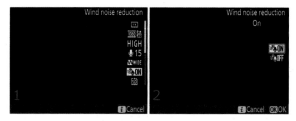

Figure 12.13 – Enabling or disabling Wind noise reduction

Use these steps to enable or disable Wind noise reduction:

1. Make sure the Live view selector lever is set to Movie live view mode (figure 12.1) and that you have pressed the Lv button to enter Movie live view.
2. Press the *i* button to open the *i* Button Menu. Select Wind noise reduction from the list (figure 12.13, screen 1). Scroll to the right.
3. Choose ON or OFF from the Wind noise reduction menu (figure 12.13, screen 2).
4. Press the OK button to lock in the setting.

Settings Recommendation: I use this wind noise filter selectively. Most of the time I am using an external Nikon ME-1 hotshoe microphone, which has a foam screen around the mic to reduce or eliminate any wind noise. I do use Wind noise reduction when I am using the built-in stereo mic to record family events outside.

Destination

The D810 allows you to choose which of your camera's two card slots will receive the video. It also gives you an estimate of available video recording time for each card, based on the current Frame size/frame rate and Movie quality settings.

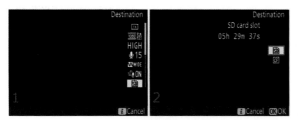

Figure 12.14 – Choosing a Destination for your video (SD or CF)

Use these steps to choose which memory card the camera will use to save your new video:

1. Make sure the Live view selector lever is set to Movie live view mode (figure 12.1) and that you have pressed the Lv button to enter Movie live view.
2. Press the *i* button to open the *i* Button Menu. Select Destination from the list (figure 12.14, screen 1). Scroll to the right.
3. Choose SD or CF from the Destination menu (figure 12.14, screen 2).
4. Press the OK button to lock in the setting.

Settings Recommendation: Deciding which card to use is based on the speed and quality of your current cards. CF cards often have better transfer rates, so you may want to default video output to your CF card. However, SD cards are cheap, plentiful, and fast enough that you may want to have several with you to swap out as you create video.

This boils down to personal preference. All I can advise is to have either big (16 or 32 GB minimum) cards or a bunch of smaller ones because the Nikon D810 can quickly fill up a memory card with its video files.

I generally relegate video to the secondary slot, which is my SD slot. I don't shoot as much video as I do still images, so it's SD for me. Memory cards, especially SD, are getting cheaper every day. With a D810, that's a good thing!

Monitor Brightness

The Monitor brightness function is for your convenience when shooting in very light or dark environments. You can quickly turn the brightness up or down with camera controls. The brightness setting in no way affects the video recording itself. It is just for your Monitor viewing comfort while recording video.

Use these steps to choose a Monitor brightness level for video recording:

1. Make sure the Live view selector lever is set to Movie live view mode (figure 12.1) and that you have pressed the Lv button to enter Movie live view.
2. Press the *i* button to open the *i* Button Menu. Select Monitor brightness from the list (figure 12.15, screen 1). Scroll to the right.

12

3. Use the Multi selector to scroll up or down and set the brightness to a comfortable level (figure 12.15, screen 2). You can scroll up or down over a range of 10 steps (-5 to +5). The yellow indicator at the point of the red arrow in screen 2 is set to 0 (factory default), a medium setting.
4. Press the OK button to lock in the setting.

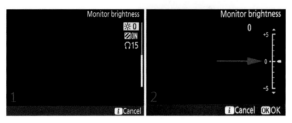

Figure 12.15 – Setting the Monitor brightness to a comfortable level for viewing

Note: You can also adjust the Monitor brightness with *Setup Menu > Monitor brightness*.

Settings Recommendation: I generally leave my camera set to the middle setting (0) unless I am out in bright sunshine, when I may crank it all the way up to the + sign on top of the indicator (maximum). At night, when I am out shooting star trails, I will crank it all the way down to -5, to save my night vision. The 0 setting is about right for normal use.

Highlight Display

The Highlight display or Zebra stripe mode is a welcome addition to the Nikon D810's features. This display allows you to determine when an area of your video has lost all highlight detail (it is blown out to pure white).

In figure 12.16, screen 2, you can see the zebra stripes in the white background of my deliberately overexposed image. See how the small Zebra stripes show exactly the area that has no highlight detail left? If there is any detail left, even a small amount, the zebra stripes will not show in that area, as can be seen by the very faint shadow areas to the left of the subjects and a triangular shaped region on the top right of the frame.

This can be a useful function for shooting video in high-contrast lighting conditions.

Use these steps to enable or disable the Highlight display (zebra stripes) for video recording:

1. Make sure the Live view selector lever is set to Movie live view mode (figure 12.1) and that you have pressed the Lv button to enter Movie live view.
2. Press the *i* button to open the *i* Button Menu. Select Highlight display from the list (figure 12.16, screen 1). Scroll to the right.

3. Select ON or OFF from the list (figure 12.16, screen 2). Screen 1 shows a normal picture that has clear overexposure but no zebra stripes. In screen 2 you can see the same image as in screen 1, except the Highlight display's alternating black-and-white zebra stripes are enabled and show the blown out (pure white) areas with no detail.
4. Press the OK button to lock in the setting.

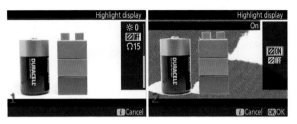

Figure 12.16 – Using the Highlight display (Zebra stripe mode)

Settings Recommendation: I generally leave Highlight display enabled because I want to know when the highlights are blown out in certain areas of my videos. I can then reduce the exposure quietly and save the video from looking bad.

Headphone Volume

The Headphone port under the rubber Connector cover is an excellent addition to the Nikon D810 (figure 12.17B). It allows you to plug in a headphone set to isolate yourself from surrounding sounds and focus on hearing what the camera is actually recording. This is important for those who are concerned about maximum sound quality.

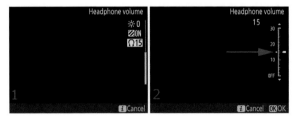

Figure 12.17A – Choosing a Headphone volume output level

Use these steps to select a Headphone volume to use while recording your video:

1. Make sure the Live view selector lever is set to Movie live view mode (figure 12.1) and that you have pressed the Lv button to enter Movie live view.
2. Press the *i* button to open the *i* Button Menu. Select Headphone volume from the list (figure 12.17A, screen 1). Scroll to the right.

3. Choose a level from Off to 30 for the Headphone volume (figure 12.17A, screen 2). Be careful not to have it turned up high when you use the headset or earbuds or you could damage your hearing. The camera is set to level 15 on the volume range in screen 2, which is a medium setting.

4. Press the OK button to lock in the setting.

Settings Recommendation: The headphone you use doesn't have to be an expensive outfit to be effective. I often simply use a set of normal isolation ear buds, like the ones you would plug into your smartphone or iPod. Ear bud headsets can be stored in a small pocket in your camera bag, so they will always be with you. I like the type that have good bass response and can be inserted in your ear, instead of the type that kind of hang off of your ear (like the ones that come with an iPhone).

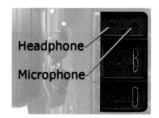

Figure 12.17B – Headphone port under rubber Connector cover

I have found that output level 15 is about right for my ears while recording and for playback. However, I hear less well than I did when I was young due to listening to my Walkman (remember those) at high volume as a kid. Be careful not to go too loud because sudden sound increases might damage your hearing. You may be more comfortable with the volume around 10 or 12.

The really cool thing is how people react when you have a set of ear buds connected to your camera. Invariably someone with a cheap point-and-shoot camera will ask me why, and I tell them, of course, that my camera has a built-in iPod so I can listen to music as I take pictures. They are amazed and don't even realize I am recording video as we talk!

Additional Settings Before Shooting Video

In addition to the 10 controls found in the *i* Button Menu, there are a few more that you should consider before shooting a video:

Picture Control

Using different Picture Controls can give you powerful control over the look of your videos. Since videos are not still-image RAW files that can be adjusted as easily after the fact for color errors, it's a good idea to carefully choose a look based on a Picture Control that you are comfortable with and that matches the current situation.

For instance, let's say you are shooting a video on an overcast, low-contrast day and you want to add some snap to your movie. You can simply preselect the Vivid Picture Control, which will saturate the colors and darken the shadows.

Or you might be shooting on a very high-contrast, sunny day and want to tone down the contrast a bit. Simply preselect the Neutral Picture Control, which will open up the shadows for a lower-contrast look.

If you are an experienced video editor and know how to do color grading, you might consider shooting the video with the Flat Picture Control. This will give you greater dynamic range and lower-saturation colors for better color grading with professional video-editing software.

Just remember, you must select the Picture Control before you start recording the video. Here's how.

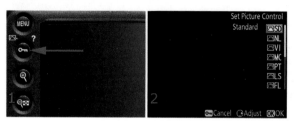

Figure 12.18 – Choosing a Picture Control for best movie look

1. Using figure 12.18 as a guide, while in Movie live view mode, press and release the Protect/Picture Control/Help button (figure 12.18, image 1)
2. Choose a Picture Control with the Multi selector (figure 12.18, screen 2).
3. Press the Multi selector center button or OK button to choose the control.

Fortunately, you can actually see the effect each Picture Control will have on your video. Use the Movie live view screen to select Picture Controls and see how they look by pointing the camera at your subject. When you have found a Picture Control that benefits the subject, use it for the video.

Settings Recommendation: I like to shoot with the Neutral Picture Control for most of my videos that involve people because I like the skin colors better with that control. However, when I am outdoors enjoying the beauty of nature, I will often select the Landscape (LS) Picture Control, or if I am feeling a bit frisky in the autumn colors, I might even use the Vivid (VI) Picture Control. The key is to use the Picture Controls enough to know what you'll get with each one. That way, you are in command of your camera.

Choosing a White Balance

White balance sets the color tint of the video. It is very important to use a White balance that matches the light source where you will be shooting the video. Auto WB works most of the time but can sometimes have problems with mixed lighting.

You should be aware of the White balance and even experiment with it for your videos. Maybe you should switch to Shade White balance when in the shade or

Direct sunlight when in the sunlight. If you pay careful attention to your camera's White balance, your videos will have superior quality.

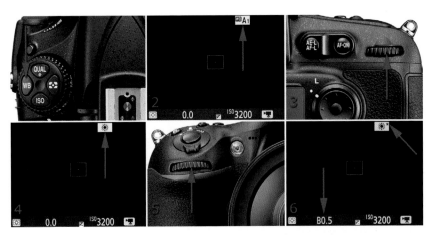

Figure 12.19 – Choosing and fine tuning a White balance

Use the following steps to set the White balance before or during a video recording:

1. Using figure 12.19 as a guide. While in Movie live view mode, press and hold the WB button (figure 12.19, image 1).
2. Notice that the Movie live view screen shows a White balance (WB) setting with a yellow background (figure 12.19, screen 2). Auto1 (A1) is currently selected.
3. Choose a White balance by rotating the rear Main command dial (figure 12.19, image 3).
4. In figure 12.19, screen 4, you will see that the WB value is no longer set to A1. Instead, the Direct sunlight symbol is selected.
5. You can fine tune the WB value by rotating the front Sub-command dial (figure 12.19, image 5).
6. Fine tuning allows you to add amber (warm) or blue (cool) fine tuning to the standard for that WB setting. You can fine tune the colors in a range of from 0.5 to 6.0 steps of amber (A) or blue (B). Notice in figure 12.19, screen 6, that B0.5 is selected (left red arrow), which means ½ step of blue is added to the normal Direct sunlight value, cooling it down a little. Also, notice that an asterisk has appeared after the WB symbol (right red arrow). This shows that you have fine-tuned the WB value. The asterisk will stay until you reset the WB value back to 0.0 (where B0.5 is currently set). Figure 12.19, screen 2, shows the fine tuning value still set to 0.0.
7. Release the WB button to select the White balance.

Watch carefully as you select the different White balance settings. You will see the color tint of the current White balance on your camera's Monitor. You can change

12

the White balance during the actual video recording, as well as fine tune the color tint. This shows how serious it is to use a correct White balance. Fortunately, the Nikon D810 makes it easy.

Note: You can also use the *Shooting Menu > White balance* setting to manage the WB value for your movie. Refer to the section on the White balance setting for more information.

Settings Recommendation: I often use Auto WB (A1) unless I am in tricky lighting situations, such as inside under fluorescent lighting with some outside lighting coming in the windows. In situations like that, I try to match the camera to the most prevalent light source.

The camera does well outside in natural light, although I have at times seen a little blueness in the shade. If the look seems a little blue in shade, I might use Shade WB. The critical thing is whether the color tint in the video you are seeing on the Monitor looks like the scene you see with your own eyes. If not, try to make the camera match what you see.

Selecting an Autofocus Mode

The Autofocus modes available in Movie live view are AF-S and AF-F. AF-S is single-point AF and you control it. AF-F is camera-controlled Autofocus. There are no other Autofocus modes available for Movie live view. You can move the focus square to any point on the Monitor to focus on the best area of your subject in either Autofocus mode. If you are using AF-S, you can focus with either the Shutter-release button or the AF-ON button. You can even change Autofocus modes while recording a video. Here's how to select the AF mode with external camera controls.

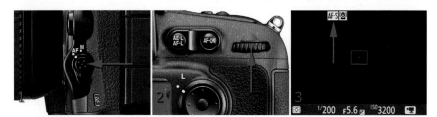

Figure 12.20 – Choosing an Autofocus mode

Use the following steps to set an Autofocus mode before or during a video recording:

1. While in Movie live view mode, press and hold the AF-mode button (figure 12.20, image 1).

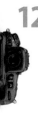

12

2. Choose an Autofocus mode by rotating the rear Main command dial (figure 12.20, image 2).

3. In figure 12.20, screen 3, you will see that the AF-S mode is selected. As you rotate the rear Main command dial this value will change between AF-S and AF-F.

4. Release the AF-mode button to select the White balance.

Settings Recommendation: Many people use Full-time-servo AF (AF-F mode) for fun video shooting. However, for commercial purposes, AF-F mode is lacking. It struggles to remain in focus in low light, and even in the best light it tends to rack in and out on a frequent basis, which is very distracting to viewers. That's why many serious videographers use manual focus lenses, so they can control the focus with great smoothness—after much practice, of course.

I like videoing with my manual and autofocus prime lenses, such as my AI Nikkor 35 mm f/2 or AF-S Nikkor 50 mm f/1.4G in MF mode. I'm sure you already have, or will soon have, several favorite lenses that work well for video. Just be sure to try them in Manual mode for best focus results.

Choosing an AF-Area Mode

The AF-area mode lets you choose *where* the camera will autofocus on your subject (see the chapter **Autofocus, AF-Area, and Release Modes**). The setting modifies the basic way autofocus decides what part of the subject is important. Let's examine each screen and AF-point style and then see how to select one of the four AF-area modes.

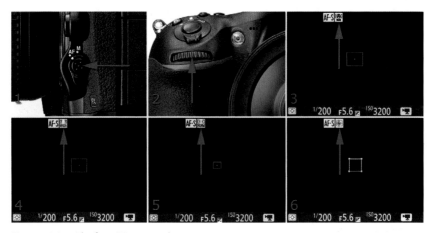

Figure 12.21 – The four AF-area modes

Use the following steps to set an AF-area mode before or during a video recording:

1. While in Movie live view mode, press and hold the AF-mode button (figure 12.21, image 1).
2. Choose an AF-area mode by rotating the front Sub-command dial (figure 12.21, image 2).
3. In figure 12.19, screens 3 to 6, you will see the four AF-area modes. Use the upcoming list to choose the best mode for your video making.
4. Release the AF-mode button to select the AF-area mode.

The following list explains the four available AF-area modes (figure 12.21):

- **Face-priority AF** (figure 12.21, image 3) – The camera has the ability to track focus on the faces of several people at the same time. It is quite fun to watch as the little green and yellow AF point squares find faces and stay with them as they move. Nikon claims it can detect up to 35 faces at the same time.
- **Wide-area AF** (figure 12.21, image 4) – For the landscape shooters among us who like to use Live view mode or shoot movies of beautiful scenic areas, this is the mode to use. The camera will display a big red (out of focus) or green (in focus) AF point square on the Monitor. You can move this big AF point square around until it rests exactly where you want the best focus to be. The camera will sense a wide area and determine the best focus, with priority on the area under the green square.
- **Normal-area AF** (figure 12.21, image 5) – This is a mode primarily for shooters who need to get very accurate focus on a small area of the frame. This is a great mode to use with a macro lens because it gives you a much smaller AF point square that you can move around the frame.
- **Subject-tracking AF** (figure 12.21, image 6) – In this mode you have to autofocus first with the Shutter-release button or AF-ON button (AF-F mode does this automatically). Then you start subject tracking by pressing the Multi selector center button once. To stop subject tracking, press it again.

Settings Recommendation: Why not leave the AF-area mode set to Face-priority AF if you photograph people a lot? If you are using Movie live view for macro shooting, Normal-area AF gives you the smallest, most accurate area mode for detailed, up-close focusing. Landscape shooters should use Wide-area AF, and wildlife or sports shooters should use Subject-tracking AF.

There is more detail available on this subject in the chapter titled **Autofocus, AF-Area, and Release Modes** in the subsection **AF-Area Mode**.

Selecting an Exposure Mode

The Exposure, or Shooting, modes—Programmed auto (P), Shutter-priority auto (S), Aperture-priority auto (A), and Manual (M)—give you various levels of control over the D810. It is best to use Manual (M) mode when possible if you want complete control over the camera. Every other mode has limitations.

12

When you control the aperture in M or A mode, you can also control depth of field for cinematic blurred backgrounds in videos containing people and deep focus in landscapes. When you adjust the shutter speed during the video (in M mode only) you can capture a beautiful blur effect for a waterfall (slow shutter speed) and quickly switch to a fast shutter speed to get that deer leaping over a fence. With ISO sensitivity control (in M mode only) you can select the best ISO for the current video and vary it only when needed.

Or, you can relinquish part or all of the control to the camera. The Nikon D810 lets you decide. The following list provides information about using the aperture, shutter speed, and ISO sensitivity settings during a movie. Unlike previous Nikons, the D810 gives you full control of the camera in Manual mode only, including all three corners of the exposure triangle: aperture, shutter speed, and ISO sensitivity.

- **Aperture** – When using Aperture-priority mode (A) or Manual mode (M), you have complete control over the aperture of the mounted lens. You can change the aperture anytime you want while shooting the movie when in those two modes, allowing you to change depth of field throughout the video. You simply turn the front Sub-command dial anytime you need to change the aperture. Be careful, though, because the camera makes an audible noise that can be picked up by the internal stereo microphone for each aperture change when using the Sub-command dial. Fortunately, you can use the Power aperture setting provided in Custom settings g1 and g2 while recording a video. It is very quiet! See the sections **Custom Setting g1 – Assign Fn Button** and **Custom Setting g2 – Assign Preview Button** in the chapter **Custom Setting Menu** for more information on using the Power aperture setting.
- **Shutter speed** – Manual mode (M) is the only mode where you have complete control of the shutter speed during the video recording session. This allows you to control the level of motion blur by simply rotating the rear Main command dial, thereby changing the shutter speed to any value between 1/30 and 1/8000 second. You cannot reduce the shutter speed to below 1/30 second when in Movie live view mode. Shutter-priority mode (S) does *not* allow you to change the shutter speed when in Movie live view mode.
- **ISO sensitivity** – You have full control over the ISO sensitivity of the camera only when using Manual mode (M). You control the ISO sensitivity by holding in the ISO button on top of the camera while rotating the rear Main command dial. Use this in conjunction with the shutter speed or aperture to make adjustments when conditions change. You can adjust ISO sensitivity to anything between ISO 64 and H2.0 (51,200).

Note: It is best to shoot in Manual (M) mode for full camera control, or Aperture-priority auto (A) mode to control the aperture while the camera automatically adjusts the rest of the exposure controls.

When using Shutter-priority mode (S) or Programmed auto (P) mode, the camera acts like a consumer video camera and leaves you little control over any of the exposure controls, with the exception of using the +/- Exposure compensation button to add or subtract exposure.

Also, remember that the D810 allows you to use Auto ISO control (mode M) in Manual (M) mode, in which the camera adjusts the ISO sensitivity to maintain a correct exposure. You can select Auto ISO control (mode M) in the *Shooting Menu > Movie settings > Movie ISO sensitivity settings* function.

Let's examine how to select an Exposure mode.

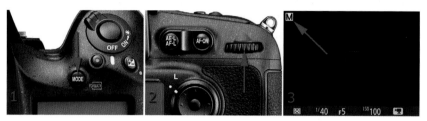

Figure 12.22 – Selecting an Exposure mode (P, S, A, or M)

Here are the steps to select an Exposure mode:

1. While in Movie live view, press and hold in the MODE button (figure 12.22, image 1).
2. Rotate the rear Main command dial (figure 12.22, image 2) to the left or right to select one of the four Exposure modes: P, S, A, or M. As you rotate the rear Main command dial, each of the four modes will appear in the position indicated by the red arrow in screen 3. In screen 3, Manual (M) mode is selected.
3. Release the MODE button to set the Exposure mode.

Note: If you use semi-automated Exposure modes (P, S, and A), the camera will change the ISO sensitivity to maintain a good exposure. The Nikon D810 uses the ISO sensitivity as a failsafe to make sure the video is usable. It will raise the ISO up to noisy levels pretty quickly when light starts falling, so be aware of that and use artificial light (e.g., LED) to prevent having noisy videos.

If you are shooting in Manual mode and change the aperture or shutter speed quickly, the camera cannot adjust the ISO to compensate, *unless you have enabled Auto ISO control (mode M),* so your video will get dark or overbright until you change the ISO or opposite control to match the new settings. Video is a little harder to shoot in Manual compared to still images because it is live and everything you do to affect exposure is immediately apparent to all viewers. Practice, practice, practice!

Settings Recommendation: The Nikon D810 is a truly professional video camera. It can do things that even expensive pro video cameras cannot do because the

12

large sensor makes such shallow depth of field and the lens selection is so great. However, that puts a burden on you when you use the camera manually. You now have the control you need for expert usage, so go practice and make the camera's controls second nature so that you can react well to changes.

I recommend shooting most videos in Aperture-priority auto (A) mode until you are fully comfortable with operating the camera manually and understand what will happen. As a videographer, you now have complete control to make masterpiece video or really bad video. Get some books on the subject and learn your new skills well. We are no longer just still photographers!

A couple of books I highly recommend are *How to Shoot Videos That Don't Suck: Advice to Make Any Amateur Look Like a Pro* by Steve Stockman (Workman Publishing Company, 2011) and *Mastering HD Video with Your DSLR* by Helmut Kraus and Uwe Steinmueller (Rocky Nook, 2010). These books set me on the path to much better videos by not only discussing the formats and cameras involved but also offering great advice on video technique.

Recording a Video with Your D810

(User's Manual – Page 52)

Now let's look at the process of recording a video to the camera's memory card. There are several easy steps, as shown in the upcoming description. This is assuming you've gone through the configuration process discussed in the first part of this chapter that readies your camera to record video in the modes you prefer to use. Let's record a video!

Here are the steps to start recording a movie:

1. Flip the Live view selector on the back of the camera to the bottom position to enable Movie live view (figure 12.23, image 1).
2. Press the Live view button to enter Movie live view (figure 12.23, image 2).
3. Press the Movie-record button to start recording (figure 12.23, image 3).
4. The video will now start recording with the REC icon blinking in the upper-left corner, the time-left counter counting down in the upper-right corner, the Microphone sensitivity indicator moving as the camera records sound, and your new video recording being written to the camera's selected memory card (figure 12.23, image 4).
5. To end the movie recording, simply press the Movie-record button once again.

Amazingly, that's all there is to it. You have a powerful, professional video camera built into your still camera. It is available with the flip of a switch and the press of a button.

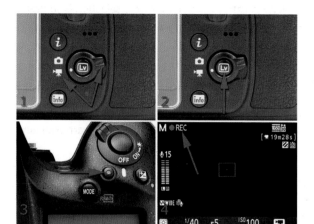

Figure 12.23 – Recording a video

Settings Recommendation: In most cases, unless you really want to try to control the camera manually, just shoot your video in a semi-automated mode and enjoy what you have captured. The camera will make a good exposure in almost all circumstances. When you are ready to move into high-end video production, the Nikon D810 is ready to help you move up.

Recording Video from the HDMI Port

(User's Manual – Page 270-271)

The Nikon D810 has a unique ability in the 35 mm camera genre: streaming uncompressed, broadcast-quality video out of its HDMI port to an external recording device. Doing so is a fairly complex process, requiring knowledge of wrappers, containers, formats, and interfacing with expensive recording equipment. The process of creating commercial video is beyond the scope of this book.

For those of you who are interested in learning about the much more complex process of streaming uncompressed HDMI video, I have prepared a document that should get you started. It is called **Streaming Uncompressed HDMI Video from Your Nikon D810** and is available at the following websites:

http://www.nikonians.org/NikonD810
http://rockynook.com/NikonD810

Please download this document and consider it. I give you the basics on working with the HDMI port along with format information to make your learning process

12

easier. I also list several websites and forums where you can gain very deep knowledge on using your D810 for high-end video creation.

Displaying Movies

(User's Manual – Page 65)
Now the fun begins! You have created a video on one of your memory cards.
What next? You can always simply transfer the video to your computer with Nikon
View NX 2's Transfer button and view it there or upload it to Facebook or YouTube
directly, both of which know how to convert the QuickTime MOV file to display on
their respective sites.

Let's also discuss how to enjoy one of your movies directly from the camera,
either on the camera's LCD Monitor or on an HDTV.

Displaying a Movie on the Camera LCD Monitor

Viewing a movie on the D810 Monitor is simplicity itself, just like video capture. Videos are stored on the camera's memory card just like still pictures. All you have to
do is select the video you want and press the Multi selector center button to play it.

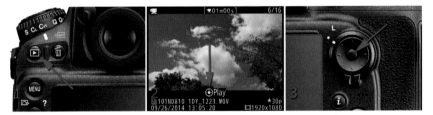

Figure 12.24 – Playing a movie on the Monitor

Use the following steps to play a movie on the Monitor:

1. Press the Playback button to display images on the Monitor (figure 12.24, image
   1, red arrow).
2. Locate the video you want to play by scrolling through your images and videos
   with the Multi selector. When the video appears on the camera Monitor, you'll
   be able to identify it by three signs: a small movie camera icon in the top-left
   corner, a minutes and seconds (total time) counter at the top center of the
   screen, and the word Play at the bottom of the screen. The image you see is the
   first frame of the video (figure 12.24, screen 2).
3. Press the Multi selector center button to start playing the video (figure 12.24,
   image 3).

Settings Recommendation: The Monitor on the D810 is big enough for several people to enjoy one of your videos. Don't be afraid to show off a bit because your camera creates excellent high-resolution videos. Set it up on the kitchen table, put a jar next to it for tips, and start a video. You'll find viewers!

Displaying a Movie on an HDTV

To display a video from your camera on an HDTV, you'll need an HDMI cable with a mini-HDMI (type C) end to insert into your D810; the other end will have to match your HDTV's HDMI port, which is usually HDMI standard (type A). We'll talk more about the cable specs in a moment, but first let's discuss your camera's HDMI output frequencies.

Before you attempt to connect your Nikon D810 to your HDTV, be sure that you've correctly configured your HDMI output to match what your HDTV needs or you won't get a picture. Use the *Setup Menu > HDMI* setting to select a specific Output resolution, or just select Auto so the camera and HDTV can figure it out for you. Here is a list of formats supported by your camera for video playback:

- Auto – Allows the camera to select the most appropriate format for displaying on the currently connected device
- 1080p – 1920×1080 progressive format
- 1080i – 1920×1080 interlaced format
- 720p – 1280×720 progressive format
- 576p – 720×576 progressive format
- 480p – 640×480 progressive format

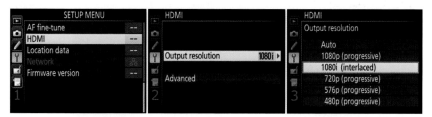

Figure 12.25 – Selecting an HDMI Output resolution

Here are the steps to select an Output resolution:

1. Select HDMI from the Setup Menu and scroll to the right (figure 12.25, image 1).
2. Choose Output resolution from the menu and scroll to the right (figure 12.25, image 2).
3. Select one of the five output resolutions (figure 12.25, image 3). I suggest using Auto initially because it works well in most cases.
4. Press the OK button to lock in your selection.

12

Settings Recommendation: If you have any difficulty getting your camera to interface with your HDTV, please refer to the section **HDMI** in the chapter titled **Setup Menu**. In my experience with the camera, most of the time it just works when you plug it into the HDTV and video flows immediately. However, sometimes there are some configuration issues that involve using the Advanced setting on the HDMI menu. I won't go back over those here because most of the time the camera interfaces well, and you can always refer back to the chapter on the Setup Menu if you have any problems.

One thing I will recommend is to make sure you have the correct HDMI port selected if your HDTV has more than one HDMI port. Often there is a control on the HDTV's remote that lets you select a particular HDMI port. Until that port is active, you will see nothing from the camera.

If the video appears too big to fit on the HDTV screen, you can reduce the size of the D810's video output by five percent with *Setup Menu > HDMI > Advanced > Output display size*. If the colors appear washed out in your video, you may have to try a different Output range (Full or Limited) with *Setup Menu > HDMI > Advanced >Output range*. Finally, if you don't want the camera to display its control overlays on the screen, just the pure video, you can turn off the overlays for the HDTV display with *Setup Menu > HDMI > Advanced >Live view on-screen display* (set to Off).

Now your camera is ready to output video on a compatible HDTV. Figure 12.26 shows what compatible HDMI cable ends look like. Unfortunately, you'll have to purchase an HDMI cable because you don't receive one with your D810. You'll need to use a mini-HDMI (type C) to HDMI standard (type A) cable. And, of course, you'll need to plug your HDMI cable into the correct port on the D810.

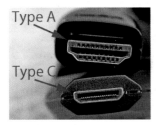

Figure 12.26 – HDMI connectors, types A and C

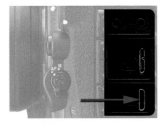

Figure 12.27 – HDMI connector, type C (mini-HDMI)

In figure 12.27, you can see the port you'll need to use with your mini-HDMI (type C) connector. Before it is plugged in, here are the steps to display a video on your HDTV:

1. Turn your camera off. Why take a chance on blowing up your camera from a static spark?

2. Open the rubber flap on the left side of your D810 and insert the mini-HDMI (type C) cable end into the HDMI port (figure 12.27, red arrow).
3. Insert the HDMI standard (type A) cable into one of your HDTV's HDMI ports. (Both video and sound are carried on this one cable.)
4. Your HDTV may have multiple HDMI ports, and you may have other devices connected, like a cable box or satellite receiver. When you plug the D810's HDMI cable into your HDTV, be sure to select that HDMI input port on your HDTV or you won't see the D810's video output. You may have to select the input from your HDTV remote or use another method. If in doubt, check your HDTV manual. (If your HDTV only has one HDMI port, please ignore this step.)
5. Turn on the camera and press the Playback button; then locate the video you want to show off.
6. Press the OK button to play the video on your HDTV.

The Nikon D810 can display movies on both progressive and interlaced devices.

Settings Recommendation: Unless you are heavily into HDMI and understand the various formats, I would just leave the camera set to Auto. That allows the D810 to determine the proper format as soon as it's plugged into the display device and the HDMI input port is selected—if the HDTV has multiple ports.

Author's Conclusions

The video capability in the Nikon D810 is simply amazing. You will create some of the best videos of your life with this camera. When you are out shooting still images, why not grab some video, too? Years from now, actually hearing and seeing friends and family who are no longer with us will mean a lot.

Pictures are important, but so is video. Your camera does both, and either is available at a moment's notice. Carry your camera with you and record your life. Hard drives are cheap compared to the memories you will lose if you don't record them. Make good backups and give away family videos to your family. Share the good qualities of your powerful camera with others, and the goodwill will come back to you later.

Now, let's look into our last chapter in the book, **Speedlight Flash**. Pop up the built-in Speedlight on your D810, or plug in your favorite external Nikon Speedlight, and let's see how best to use a flash directly and to control banks of Speedlights with Nikon's Creative Lighting System (CLS).

Speedlight Flash

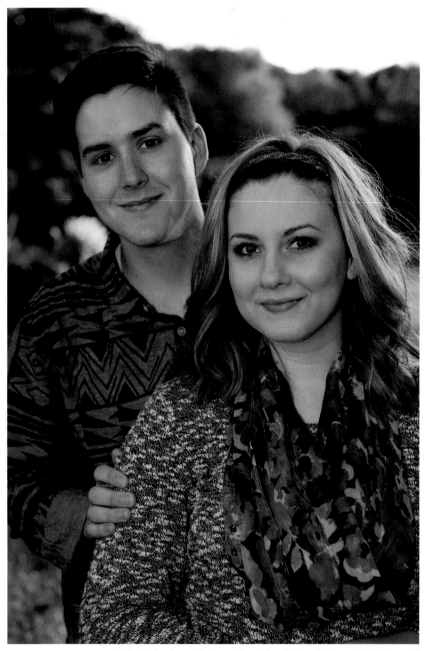

Ode to Youth and Autumn Sunshine © Darrell Young (*DigitalDarrell*))

Light is the photographer's friend! Controlling light is the primary thing that separates excellent from not-so-excellent photographers. On beautiful, balmy summer evenings, the light wraps around the land and gives us that so-called golden hour that we crave. However, some days are rainy, and some are dark and gloomy.

As photographers, we want to take pictures. We don't want to stop just because the sun won't cooperate. We need light that we can take with us, and we want it to be available quickly. We need a Speedlight!

Fortunately, your D810 has a built-in Speedlight (figure 13.1). The little pop-up **13** unit that's built in to your camera is a Nikon Speedlight flash. Speedlight is Nikon's name for its flash units, large and small.

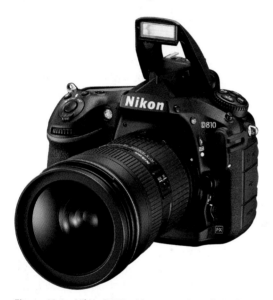

Figure 13.1 – Nikon D810 with pop-up Speedlight flash open

You have several choices, from the tiny pop-up Speedlight flash on your camera to the flagship Nikon SB-910 Speedlight flash. You can even create a wireless flash array using your camera, a commander unit, and several Speedlight flash units. This type of setup is called the Nikon Creative Lighting System (CLS). We'll look at CLS later in the chapter. First, let's examine some general flash information and explore how the D810 uses flash. How can you determine which flash will work best for your style of shooting? Will the pop-up flash be enough with its limitations in range, or do you need more power to reach out and light up more distant subjects? How is the power output of a flash unit rated?

This chapter contains information that will help you make a good choice in flash units. First, we'll look at how to rate the power output of a flash by examining the guide number.

What Is a Guide Number?

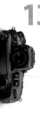

13

The guide number (GN) for a flash unit measures how well it can light a subject at a specific ISO sensitivity and with a precise angle of view (wide angle versus tele- photo). To put it simply, a higher guide number means the flash is more powerful, all other things being equal.

Be careful when you are deciding on an external flash unit, whether it is a Nikon Speedlight or an aftermarket unit. Simply comparing the GN is not enough. You must understand the settings on which the GN is based. Many flash units have zoom capability and can light up subjects farther away when they are zoomed out. However, imagine buying a flash unit from a manufacturer who publishes the GN based on a longer zoom position, and then comparing it to a different flash unit based on a shorter nonzoom position. The GN rating on the flash that is zoomed out would seem to be higher than the same unit not zoomed out. Unless you are comparing flash unit GNs with exactly the same settings, it is truly like comparing apples to oranges. For instance, to get an exact comparison of GNs, you would have to know the following:

- Distance from flash head to the subject
- Aperture in use on your camera
- ISO sensitivity of your camera's image sensor
- Angle-of-view setting on the flash zoom head
- Actual angle of view your lens provides (must match flash head)
- Temperature of ambient air

In reality, the camera has little to do with figuring the GN other than providing an f-stop number and ISO sensitivity. So how can you decide what GN is best without whipping out a scientific calculator? Just look at the flash unit specifications to see what the GN is based on. Here are the most important figures:

- Flash zoom angle-of-view setting (e.g., 24 mm or 75 mm)
- ISO sensitivity

If you see a flash unit advertised as GN 98, realize that this is not enough informa- tion to make a decision. In this instance, 98 is the GN. It represents the number of feet from the flash head to the subject (98 feet). In countries that use the metric system, the equivalent GN is 30, which is the number of meters from the flash head to the subject. That number by itself is simply incomplete. Don't buy a flash unit based solely on a GN like 98 or 100 or 111.

Let's think about this for a second. Let's say I'm a manufacturer who is desperate to sell you a flash unit. I might stretch things a little bit. I might say my Super-Duper flash unit has a GN of 98 (feet) or 30 (meters) and hope you won't ask about the settings I used to arrive at that number. Here is a comparison of two flash units with a so-called comparable guide number:

Super-Duper flash unit GN information:

- GN 98 (30)
- 80 mm zoom-head setting
- ISO 200 sensitivity

Nikon SB-400 flash unit GN information (real values):

- GN 98 (30)
- 35 mm zoom-head setting
- ISO 100 sensitivity

Both of the flash units have the same GN, so which one is really more powerful? The Nikon SB-400 will literally blow away the Super-Duper unit. Yet the Super-Duper manufacturer lists the same GN! The Super-Duper unit must have its zoom head set to 80 mm, a much narrower beam, and have twice the camera ISO sensitivity to equal the Nikon SB-400 unit. Mr. Super-Duper is hoping you won't check the fine print at the bottom of the specifications so you'll think his much less powerful unit equals the Nikon SB-400. Surprisingly, there are flash unit manufacturers who do exactly this.

What can you learn from this example? The GN itself is not enough to make a decision on which flash unit to use. You must know what the GN is based on in order to make an informed decision. Take your time when buying a flash unit. You're safe in sticking with Nikon Speedlights, because the ratings are well known and they're designed to support all the features of your D810.

There are also excellent aftermarket flash units available from manufacturers like Vivitar, Sigma, Sunpak, Metz, Braun/Leitz, and others. Examine the underlying settings and not just the GN. What the GN is based on is as important as the actual number.

For comparison purposes, the GN of the D810's pop-up Speedlight is 39 (feet) or 12 (meters) at ISO 100. Nikon's flagship Speedlight, the SB-910, is 111.5 (feet) or 34 (meters) at ISO 100. Obviously, the larger external flash unit has a lot more power and can light up subjects that are farther away.

Now, let's examine the various flash modes found in the Nikon D810. Since I have no way of knowing which flash unit you'll be using, I'll write from the perspective of the built-in flash. Almost everything mentioned next applies to the built-in flash and most Accessory shoe–mounted Nikon-brand Speedlight units, plus many Nikon-specific aftermarket flash units.

Note: The built-in flash unit provides coverage for the angle of view of a 24 mm lens in FX mode and a 16 mm lens in DX mode.

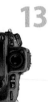

13

> ### Technical GN Information
>
> The GN is based on a specific formula: GN = distance × f-stop. It is based on the inverse-square law, which states that doubling the GN requires four times more flash power. So, a flash with a GN of 100 is four times more powerful than a flash with a GN of 50. The guide number represents an exposure constant for a flash unit. For example, a GN of 80 feet at ISO 100 means that a subject 20 feet away can be completely illuminated with an aperture of f/4 (80 = 20 × 4) using a sensitivity of ISO 100. For the same guide number and an aperture of f/8, the light source should be 10 feet from the subject (80 = 10 × 8). Fortunately, your camera and flash combination is capable of figuring the correct values for you when you use TTL mode.

Flash Modes

(User's Manual – Page 191)

The built-in pop-up flash has two types of flash metering:

- **i-TTL balanced fill flash** – The flash fires in two stages. Nikon calls stage 1 *monitor preflash*. The built-in flash emits a series of almost invisible flashes before the main flash burst fires (stage 2). The preflashes allow the 1,005-pixel RGB flash sensor to examine all areas of the frame for reflectivity. The camera uses the Matrix meter and distance information from a D or G lens to calculate a flash output that is balanced between the main subject and the ambient lighting. You must use Matrix or Center-weighted metering to use this mode.
- **Standard i-TTL** – When the Spot meter is used, the camera automatically switches to standard i-TTL. This mode ignores the background and concentrates on whatever the camera's selected AF point is focused on. For the most accurate flash output for a specific subject, just set your camera to use its Spot meter, and the flash will meter for the subject only.

In addition to the types of flash metering, the camera has several Flash modes that affect how it controls light. We'll consider each of them shortly, but first let's talk about how the shutter blades work when the flash fires. This is basic information that will help you understand the Flash modes. To fully know what's happening when the flash fires, you must understand a little bit about the shutter curtains in your camera.

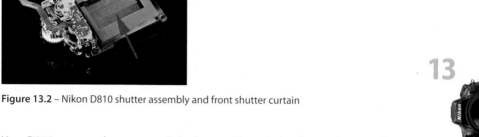

Figure 13.2 – Nikon D810 shutter assembly and front shutter curtain

Your D810 exposes the sensor to light for specific periods of time. This is controlled by the camera's shutter speed. The actual exposure is handled by two moving objects called curtains. The D810 has two shutter curtains. You can see the front curtain in figure 13.2 (red arrow). It's composed of several narrow blades and is in the closed position.

How do the curtains work? One curtain gets out of the way of the sensor to start the exposure, and the other curtain replaces it to stop the exposure. The first one is called the front curtain, and the second one is called the rear curtain. In this context, front and rear are not important as indicators of position but as indicators of which moves first and which moves second. The flash must fire when the first, or front, curtain is fully open and before the second, or rear, curtain starts closing. The time between the front curtain opening and the rear curtain closing is the actual shutter speed.

The whole sensor must be uncovered when the flash fires in normal Flash modes (non–Auto FP). If the shutter speed is too fast, the rear curtain will closely follow the front curtain and partially block the sensor when the flash fires. That's why the shutter speed is normally limited to a maximum of 1/250s on the D810 when a flash is used. With faster shutter speeds, the sensor is always partially covered by one of the shutter curtains. If the flash fires while one of the curtains covers part of the sensor, then that part of the sensor will not get a proper exposure from the flash and there will be an underexposed black band in your image.

The whole point of the Flash modes is to determine at what point during shutter curtain movement the flash fires and whether it's the main source of light or whether some ambient light is mixed in. Keep this information in mind as we discuss the Flash modes.

Be sure to read the upcoming sidebar called **Auto FP High-Speed Sync** because Auto FP affects the maximum shutter sync speed, allowing you to take it higher than 1/250s. Also, see the section **Custom Setting e1 – Flash Sync Speed** in the chapter titled **Custom Setting Menu**, where this mode is discussed in great detail.

13

Auto FP High-Speed Sync

The D810 has an additional mode that lets it exceed the normal flash sync speed of 1/250s. It is called Auto FP high-speed sync mode. Remember how normally both the front and rear shutter curtains must be out of the way before the flash fires? Auto FP high-speed sync mode lets you use shutter speeds all the way up to 1/8000s. At these speeds, the rear shutter curtain follows the front shutter curtain so closely that only a traveling narrow horizontal slit exposes the sensor at any given time.

When you select a sync speed faster than the normal 1/250s, the camera fires the flash in thousands of short pulses instead of one big flash. The pulses fire as the narrow shutter curtain slit moves across the face of the sensor. The faster the shutter speed, the less power the flash can manage. You must be able to depend on ambient light in addition to flash when using Auto FP high-speed sync mode, especially at higher shutter speeds. However, this lets you use your fast lenses (e.g., f/1.4, f/2.8) wide open while in direct sunlight, due to the very fast shutter speed.

You can expose properly with a very shallow depth of field due to a large aperture, even though the light is very bright. We covered this mode in detail in the chapter titled **Custom Setting Menu**, under the heading **Custom Setting e1 – Flash Sync Speed**.

To set your camera to Auto FP high-speed sync mode, choose *Custom Setting Menu > e Bracketing/flash > Flash sync speed*. Select 1/320 s (Auto FP) or 1/250 s (auto FP) from the menu. Afterward, use Shutter-priority auto (S) mode or Manual (M) and adjust your camera's shutter speed to any speed between 30 seconds and 1/8000 second. An external Speedlight will fire its pulses to match the shutter blade slit traveling across the imaging sensor. The maximum shutter speed the built-in flash will allow is the Auto FP mode you've selected (250 or 320). You must use an external Speedlight flash unit (such as the SB-910 or SB-700) to use Auto high-speed sync mode.

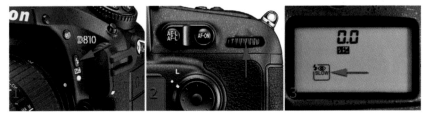

Figure 13.3 – Selecting a Flash mode

Here are the steps to select one of the Flash modes:

1. Hold down the Flash mode button on the front of your camera, just below the D810 logo (figure 13.3, image 1).
2. Turn the Main command dial while watching the various modes change on the Control panel (figure 13.3, image 2 and screen 3).
3. Release the Flash mode button to lock in the Flash mode.

The five basic Flash modes and how they work are described next. The camera will often combine these Flash modes as you use different shooting modes on the Mode dial.

Front-Curtain Sync

In *Front-curtain sync* mode, the camera tries its best to balance the light if you're using a lens that has a CPU in it (figure 13.4). Older non-CPU lenses cause the camera to ignore the ambient light completely and use only the flash to expose the subject. A CPU lens, like an AF-S Nikkor G or D lens, can balance ambient light and light from the flash equally and makes the lighting look very natural. If you use this correctly outdoors, it will be hard to tell that you were using flash,

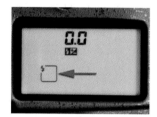

Figure 13.4 – Front-curtain sync

except for the catch light in your subject's eyes and the lack of damaging shadows. The flash simply fills in some extra light without overpowering the ambient light. In a situation where there is very little ambient light, the camera will use only the flash to get a correct exposure. It balances with ambient light only if there is enough.

There is a side effect to using this mode with slow shutter speeds. Front-curtain sync causes the flash to fire as soon as the front shutter curtain is out of the way before the rear shutter curtain starts closing. If there is some ambient light, the shutter speed is long (like 1/2 second), and the subject is moving, you'll see a well-exposed subject with a blurry trail in front of it. The flash correctly exposes the subject as soon as the front curtain gets out of the way, but the ambient light continues exposing the subject before the rear curtain closes. Since the subject is moving, you may see a ghostlike blur before or in front of the well-exposed moving subject in the picture. This can be seen at shutter speeds as fast as 1/60s if the ambient light is strong enough and the subject is moving.

13

Red-Eye Reduction

Red-eye reduction is not really a flash mode, per se (figure 13.5). It simply means that the AF-assist illuminator on the front of the camera shines brightly in the face of your subject for one second before Front-curtain sync flash fires. The intention is that the bright AF-assist illuminator will cause your subject's pupils to close somewhat and reduce the red-eye effect. Otherwise it performs the same as Front-curtain sync.

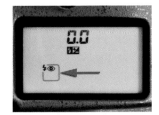

Figure 13.5 – Red-eye reduction

Red-Eye Reduction with Slow Sync

Red-eye reduction with slow sync combines two modes, Red-eye reduction and Slow sync, so that you can take portraits at night while still recording some of the surroundings (figure 13.6). Slow sync flash allows the camera to leave its shutter open for a normal non-flash exposure time in low ambient light, thereby exposing the surroundings well, and just before the flash fires to light the subject, the AF-assist illuminator shines in your subject's face for one second to reduce pupil size.

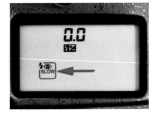

Figure 13.6 – Red-eye reduction with slow sync

When you are shooting with a slow shutter speed in a dark environment, you should have your camera on a tripod to prevent blurry pictures. You should also ask your subject to stand perfectly still, or there is a chance of subject ghosting.

Slow Sync

Slow sync mode lets the camera use ambient light to make a good exposure and then fires the flash to add some extra light, rounding out the shadows or better exposing a foreground subject (figure 13.7). Use this mode in people shots outdoors or where you want ambient light to provide the primary exposure and the flash to add a sparkle to your subjects' eyes and remove dark shadows from their faces.

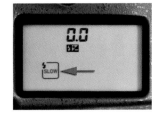

Figure 13.7 – Slow sync

This is closely related to Fill flash, except the ambient light is more important than the light from the flash. Be careful when using this mode indoors because it will expose for ambient light and only assist with some flash light. You can get some terrible ghosting and blurred handheld shots when using Slow sync indoors. Ambient light rules in this mode!

Rear-Curtain Sync

Rear-curtain sync (figure 13.8) is the opposite of Front-curtain sync. The flash waits to fire until just before the rear curtain starts to close. The entire shutter speed time is just ending when the flash fires. This causes a ghosting effect for moving subjects in higher ambient light with slow shutter speeds.

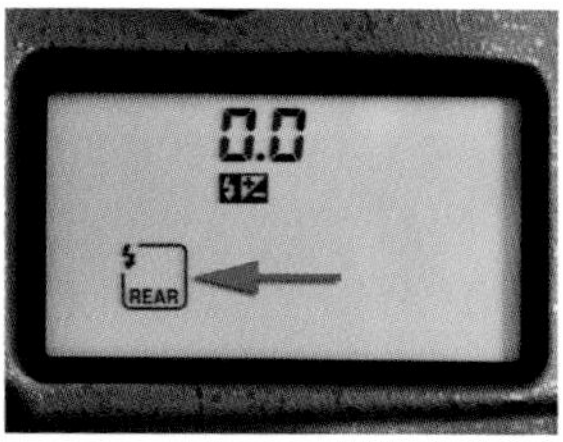

Figure 13.8 – Rear-curtain sync

When you press the Shutter-release button, the front curtain opens, ambient light starts hitting the sensor, and the sensor starts recording the subject. Just as the shutter's rear curtain is about to close, the flash fires, exposing the subject at its current position. The subject was fully exposed by the flash at the end of the shutter speed time, so the ambient light had time to register the subject before the flash fired. If the subject is moving, this can produce a blurred ghost behind or after the well-exposed subject.

Settings Recommendation: I use Front-curtain sync (Fill flash) for normal, everyday flash. It balances ambient light with flash light. I'll often switch to Spot metering mode when using Fill flash for extremely accurate exposures of a particular subject.

External Speedlight flash units offer modes like TTL BL, TTL BL FP, TTL FP, or just TTL. TTL stands for "through the lens" and represents an i-TTL mode (intelligent though the lens). BL stands for balanced. FP stands for Auto FP high-speed sync mode. Refer to the user's manual for your flash unit for exact details on how to switch between modes on the flash unit.

When I'm shooting outside (only) and want a great exposure of my subject's surroundings, along with the subject, I often use Slow sync mode. The only caveat is that you must be aware that slow shutter speeds will cause ghosting and blurring as the light falls.

I don't use the Red-eye reduction modes often because they seem to confuse people. They think the initial shine of the AF-assist illuminator is the flash firing and then look away just as the main flash fires. If you are going to use Red-eye reduction modes, you might want to tell your subject to wait for the main flash.

Rear-curtain sync creates a cool effect if you want to show a ghosted image stretching out behind your subject when you use slow shutter speeds. Rear-curtain sync is sometimes used by sports shooters in situations where there may be some blurring from fast movement in low light. It is much more acceptable to have a ghosted blur after the subject since it implies motion. Front-curtain sync makes the blur show up in front of the subject, which looks just plain weird.

I suggest experimenting with all of these modes. You'll want to use each of them at various times.

Flash Compensation

No metering system works well in all conditions. When you are having some mild subject overexposures due to shooting against a dark background, you may want to dial in -0.3 EV or more *Flash compensation*. The D810 makes adding or subtracting flash exposure very simple.

13

You can add up to one full stop of overexposure to your subject (1.0 EV) and up to three stops (3.0 EV) underexposure.

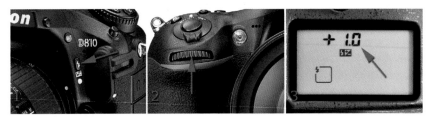

Figure 13.9 – Dialing in Flash compensation

Following are the steps to dial in Flash compensation with the Flash mode/compensation button and other camera controls (figure 13.9):

1. Press and hold down the Flash mode/compensation button (figure 13.9, image 1).
2. Turn the front Sub-command dial while examining the Control panel for changes in the flash compensation (figure 13.9, image 2 and screen 3). In figure 13.9, screen 3, I have + 1.0 EV compensation dialed in.
3. Release the Flash mode/compensation button and take your pictures. Be sure to set Flash compensation back to zero (0.0) when you are finished shooting.

Settings Recommendation: Any camera will tend to shoot a bit hot (overly bright) when photographing a light subject against a dark background. In that case you might want to dial in -0.3 or -0.7 EV compensation, especially when shooting up close. It can be hard to expose for a bride's white dress in a dark area, such as the romantic dance with the new husband. You will often have to use Flash compensation that varies with each shot. Learn to use this feature well, and your event images will be better for it.

Shooting flash with the subject over 10 feet away is not as critical for compensation with an external Speedlight. Most of my difficulties arise when up close. Your camera may respond differently, so experiment before shooting a wedding or event. Also, use the Highlight-weighted metering mode for excellent results.

Now let's look into the Nikon CLS, which allows your camera to control multiple flash units in a wireless array.

Nikon Creative Lighting System (CLS)

(User's Manual – Page 428)

CLS is an advanced wireless lighting technology that allows you to use your imagination in designing creative lighting arrangements. No wires are used because the CLS-compatible remote flash units are controlled by a commander device, or what Nikon refers to as a master flash unit. You can use the Commander mode built into the D810; an Accessory shoe–mounted commander, such as the SB-910, SB-900, SB-800, SB-700, and SB-500 Speedlights; or the SU-800 Wireless Speedlight Commander unit. The SB-600 has only a remote mode, so it cannot be used as a commander unit.

We'll consider only the camera's built-in Commander mode in this chapter. I suggest buying a copy of *The Nikon Creative Lighting System, 2nd Edition*, by Mike Hagen (Rocky Nook and Nikonians Press, 2012). It goes into excellent detail on how to use CLS with multiple groups of external Nikon Speedlight flash units. I have read Hagan's book cover to cover and really enjoyed learning all about CLS. If you want to successfully control complex arrangements of Nikon Speedlights easily, you need this book. It's worth the price merely for the knowledge you gain on configuring your complex flash unit(s).

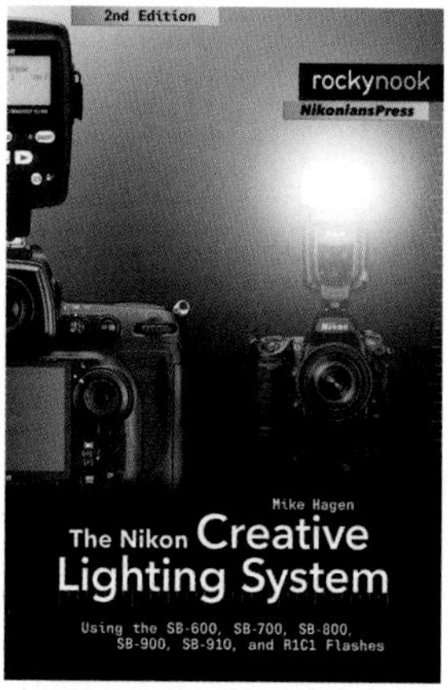

Using CLS, you can easily experiment with setups and flash output. You can obtain a visual preview of how things will look by pressing the Depth-of-field preview button, which will fire the pulsed modeling capability within Nikon Speedlights.

Figure 13.10 – *The Nikon Creative Lighting System, 2nd Edition*, by Mike Hagen, Rocky Nook and Nikonians Press

There is no need to calculate complex lighting ratios when you can control your flash banks right from the camera and see the results immediately. CLS simplifies the use of multiple flash-unit setups for portraiture, interiors, nature, or any situation in which several Speedlights need to work in unison.

You can simply position the flash units where you'd like them to be and let CLS automatically calculate the correct exposure, or you can change the lighting ratios directly from the *Custom Setting Menu > e3 Flash cntrl for built-in flash > Commander mode* menu of your D810.

Nikon's CLS is world class in power and not too difficult to use. The Nikon D810 contains everything you need to control a simple or complex CLS setup. Let's learn how to use it!

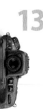

How Does the D810 Fit into the CLS Scheme?

In Commander mode, the camera functions as a controller for multiple Nikon Speedlight flash units. Although the professional-level Nikon D4S/D4/D3/D3S/D3X requires the separate purchase of an Accessory shoe–mounted commander device, the D810 body has full Nikon CLS technology built right in.

You can use normal i-TTL flash technology with the camera's built-in flash, or use Commander mode and the built-in flash to control up to two groups of an unlimited number of external Nikon Speedlight flash units. Nikon currently makes the powerful SB-910 flash unit, along with its slightly less powerful SB-700 or SB-500 brothers, and other smaller Speedlight units such as the SB-300 and SB-R200. You can also still acquire older flash units such as the SB-900, SB-800, and SB-600. The small SB-400 is not CLS compatible, while the SB-R200 is designed especially for CLS.

Many people who use the D810 have an external flash unit or two—usually the SB-910, SB-900, SB-800, SB-700, SB-600, or SB-500. The SB-R200 flash is designed to be used on various brackets available from Nikon and will work in conjunction with the bigger Speedlight flash units. The Nikon D810 is happy to let you arrange professional lighting setups using these relatively inexpensive and very portable Speedlights.

The cool thing about the D810 is that it can serve as a CLS flash commander device or use Nikon's other CLS flash commander devices at will. You have great control with this fine camera!

What Is Commander Mode and How Does It Work?

Commander mode is controlled through a menu on your D810. If you examine the Commander mode screen shown in figure 13.11, you'll note that you have controls for the built-in flash and two groups (A and B), or banks, of external flash units. You'll also see that you can set Exposure compensation for either of these groups (Comp.). If the main flash is too bright, you can either move it farther away or dial its power down by setting Exposure compensation (Comp.) to underexpose a little. You can set Comp. in 1/3-stop increments, so you have very fine control of each group's flash output. You can experiment until you get the image just the way you want it. Sure, you can do things the old way and use a flash meter, or get your calculator and figure out complex fill ratios. Or you can simply use CLS to vary your settings visually until the image is just right (figure 13.12).

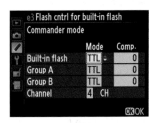

Figure 13.11 – Commander mode

Isn't it more fun to simply enter some initial settings into your Commander mode screen and then take a test shot? If it doesn't look right, change the settings and do it again. Within two or three tries you'll probably get it right, and you will have learned something about the performance of your CLS. In a short time, you'll have a feel for how to set the camera and flash units and will use your flash/camera combo with authority.

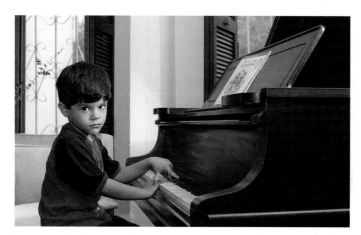

Figure 13.12 – J. Ramón Palacios (JRP) used a Commander device and two SB-800 Speedlights to take this CLS photo

Note: If you leave *Custom Setting Menu > e Bracketing/flash > e4 Modeling flash* set to On, you can test fire the built-in modeling light of your single Speedlight—or all Speedlights in Groups A and B—by pressing and holding the camera's Depth-of-field preview button.

Using Commander Mode

Let's start by putting your camera into Commander mode. We'll do that by changing *Custom Setting Menu > e Bracketing/flash > e3 Flash cntrl for built-in flash* to Commander mode (CMD). Look at figure 13.13 for the steps to set this option.

Since this section is about controlling multiple flash units, we'll have to change the settings in Commander mode, using the screen shown in figure 13.13, screen 4. We'll examine each of the settings available in Commander mode.

First, we'll consider TTL. It's the easiest to use because it allows you to set Exposure compensation for the built-in flash as well as each of your flash groups. Second, we'll briefly look at AA mode, which is an old-fashioned mode not often used by new photographers. Third, we'll look at M mode, because that gives you fine control of your flash from full power (1/1) to 1/128 power. Finally, we'll consider the – – (double-dash) mode, which prevents the camera's built-in flash from firing the main flash output but does not stop the necessary monitor preflashes or the firing of the external flash units. Double-dash mode turns off the main flash bursts for a group of Speedlights when it is selected; however, it does not turn off the monitor preflashes.

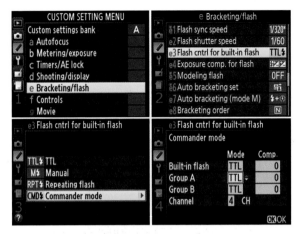

Figure 13.13 – Setting the camera to Commander mode

When your camera is controlling external Speedlights using its built-in Commander mode, you must raise the built-in flash on your D810. The camera communicates with the external flash units during the monitor preflash cycle.

Always position the small round sensor windows on the external Speedlights where they will pick up the monitor preflashes from the built-in flash. Take particular care when you are not using a tripod.

Commander Mode Settings

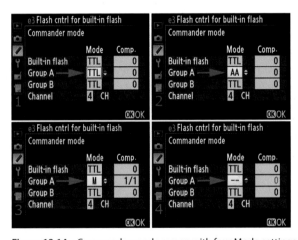

Figure 13.14 – Commander mode screen with four Mode settings

Basically, the Mode fields on the Commander mode screen will display the selections in the following list. Use the Multi selector to change the values, as shown in figure 13.14. Here are the four Commander mode settings:

- TTL, or i-TTL mode
- AA, or Auto Aperture mode
- M, or Manual mode
- – –, or double-dash mode (What else would one call it?)

13

You'll find each mode in the Mode box shown in yellow in figure 13.14. Use the Multi selector to scroll up or down and select a mode. AA mode is not available for the Built-in flash, so you will see AA only in the Mode boxes following Groups A and B. Now, let's examine each mode in more detail:

- **TTL mode** – The TTL setting allows you to use the full power of i-TTL technology. By leaving Mode set to TTL (as shown in figure 13.14, screen 1) for the Built-in flash, Group A, and Group B, you derive maximum flexibility and accuracy from all your flash units. In this mode, the Comp. setting will display exposure values from -3.0 EV to +3.0 EV, a full six-stop range of exposure compensation for each group of Speedlights. You can set the Comp. in 1/3 EV steps for very fine control.
- **AA mode** – The AA mode is an older non-i-TTL technology included for people who are accustomed to using it. It is not available for the built-in Speedlight on the D810 or for the SB-600. You can safely ignore the AA mode unless you want to experiment with it. It may not provide as accurate a flash exposure as TTL mode because it is not based on the amazing i-TTL technology. Otherwise, it works pretty much the same as TTL mode.
- **M mode** – This allows you to set different levels of flash output in 1/3 EV steps for the Built-in flash or the Speedlights in Group A or B. The settings you can put in the Comp. field are between 1/1 (full) and 1/128. The intermediate 1/3-stop settings are presented as decimals within the fractions. For example, 1/1.3 and 1/1.7 are 1/3 and 2/3 stops below 1/1 (full). Many people are used to working with flash units this way, so it seems more familiar to them. CLS is willing to oblige people who have experience with working manually.
- **- - mode (double-dash mode)** – The built-in Speedlight will not fire the main flash burst in this mode. It will fire the monitor preflashes because it uses them to determine exposure and communicate with the external flash groups. Be sure you always raise the camera's built-in flash in any of the Commander modes; otherwise, the external flash groups will not receive a signal and won't fire their flashes. When you set Mode for Group A or B to double-dash (– –) mode, that entire group of flashes will not fire any flash output. You can use this mode to temporarily turn off one of the flash groups for testing purposes.

13

> ## What Are Monitor Preflashes?
>
> When you press the Shutter-release button with the pop-up flash open, the cam-era's built-in Speedlight fires several brief preflashes and then fires the main flash burst. These preflashes fire whenever your camera is set to TTL mode, even if your D810 is controlling multiple flash units through CLS. The camera can determine a very accurate exposure by lighting your subject with a preflash, adjusting the exposure, and then firing the main flash burst.

Since the preflashes of the built-in flash always fire, be careful that they do not influ-ence the lighting of your image. Use a smaller aperture, or move the camera farther away from your subject if the preflashes add unwanted light.

Setting the Channel (CH) for Communication

Look at figure 13.15, the camera's Commander mode screen, and you'll notice that just below Group B there is a Channel (CH) selection (red arrow). The number 1 that is selected in the yel-low box is the communication channel my D810 will use to talk to the external flash groups (the factory default is 1).

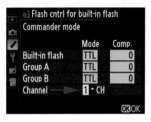

Figure 13.15 – Commander mode channel selection

There are four channels available (1 through 4), just in case you happen to be working in the vicinity of another Nikon photographer who is also using Commander mode. By using separate channels, you won't interfere with each other.

Note: It is important to realize that all external flashes in all groups must be on the same channel. This involves setting up your individual flash units to respond on a particular channel. They might be in separate groups, but they must be on the same channel. Each external Speedlight flash will have its own method for select-ing a group and channel.

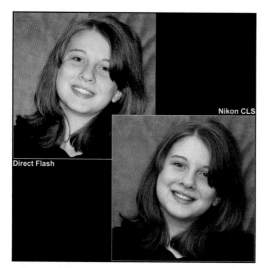

13

Figure 13.16 – Nikon CLS compared to direct flash

Author's Conclusions

The Nikon D810 gives you control over the world-class Nikon Creative Lighting System. It is the envy of many other camera brand manufacturers and users.

I recommend that you buy a copy of Mike Hagen's book *The Nikon Creative Lighting System, 2nd Edition*, as an excellent way to increase your knowledge of the Nikon CLS. It goes into great detail on using Nikon cameras to control several of the major Nikon flash units. *Mastering the Nikon D810* covers CLS only in relation to the Nikon D810 camera body. With these two books and some practice, you can become a Nikon CLS expert!

I also suggest that you find a good book on lighting techniques and study it well. You'll have to learn how to control shadows and reflections, plus you'll have to understand lighting ratios so you can recognize a good image when you see one.

Buy a couple of light stands and some cheap white flash umbrellas and set up some portrait sessions of your family, or even some product shots. With the Nikon D810 and just one extra Speedlight, you can create some very impressive images with much less work than ever before.

The really nice thing is that the Nikon CLS—executed by your camera's Commander mode and external Speedlight flashes—will allow you to shoot without worrying so much about detailed exposure issues. Instead, you can concentrate on creating a great-looking image.

Afterword

Check the book's downloadable resources section from time to time because I intend to keep on adding material to supplement *Mastering the Nikon D810*. The downloadable resources are found at these two web addresses:

13

http://www.nikonians.org/NikonD810
http://rockynook.com/NikonD810

Stay in touch with me by using the following points of contact:

- Website: **http://www.pictureandpen.com**
- Facebook: **https://www.facebook.com/groups/MasterYourNikon/**

Thank You!

I'd like to express my personal appreciation to you for buying this book and for sticking with me all the way to the end of it. I sincerely hope that it has been useful to you and that you'll recommend my books to your Nikon-using friends.

Keep on capturing time . . .

Credits for Chapter Opening Images

Chapter 1 – Jackie Donaldson (*bhpr*), *Elmer the Skinny Juvenile Blue Grosbeak*
Nikon D810, AF-S Nikkor 500mm f/4 (non-VR) with a 1.4 TC, 1/4000 sec at f/7.1, ISO 1600
I took this cute picture the first week I shot with the D810, while at Bombay Hook National Wildlife Refuge in Smyrna, Delaware, which is a favorite spot of mine. Blue Grosbeaks can be pretty skittish, but this juvenile was kind of brave and let me shoot him for a minute or so. Maybe he was just a ham.

Chapter 2 – Richard Higgins (*HigginsR1*), *Gulf Fritillary Butterflies on a Burnt Log*
Nikon D810, AF-S VR Micro-Nikkor 105mm f/2.8G IF-ED lens, 1/6 sec at f/32, ISO 800
Life returns after a forest fire. I was able to catch these two Gulf Fritillary butterflies resting on a burnt log in this devastated area. I was shooting in Manual (M) mode using Mirror-up (MUP) and Electronic front-curtain shutter set to enabled, with a mechanical release and tripod.

Chapter 3 – Jim Austin (*Jimages*), *Spinnaker Sail Multi-Exposure Resembles a Flying Tern*
Nikon D810, AF-S Nikkor 28mm f/1.8G, 1/200 sec at f/7.1, ISO 32
I live aboard a catamaran. After raising the spinnaker, we headed downwind. Sailing out Five Fathom Creek toward Bulls Bay north of Charleston, South Carolina, I took advantage of the in-camera multiple exposure feature and made a handheld, four-shot, multiple exposure of the backlit sail. Nikon D810 set to Multiple Exposure = On (series), Number = 4, Auto Gain = On.

Chapter 4 – Matti Remonen (*MRe*), *Sailboats by Suomenlinna*
Nikon D810, AF-S Nikkor 85 f/1.8G at 85mm, 1/400 sec at f6.3, ISO 64, handheld
This image was taken from a cliff at Suomenlinna in the early afternoon. I had just one day left of my summer holiday and decided to spend it playing tourist in my hometown of Helsinki. I took a ferry from the mainland to UNESCO World Heritage site Suomenlinna—old fortress island—and immediately I was welcomed by the sight of sailboats at sea. Afterward, I was quite amazed that the D810 was able to capture the whole dynamic range of dark cliffs and almost direct sunlight.

Chapter 5 – Greg Jones (*gregor1*), *Hail! The Balloons*
Nikon D810, AF Nikkor 70-200mm f/2.8 VR lens at 70mm, 1/100 sec at f/5, ISO 64
This late afternoon image was one of hundreds I shot at the 2014 New Jersey Festival of Ballooning. At least 100 balloons flew over in the three-day affair. I selected this particular shot because of the yin-yang, S-curve negative space. It's just bold and crisp, and no other camera besides the D810 would have achieved this clarity.

Chapter 6 – Jonathon Bloom (*jbloom*), *Running Back Carries the Football through the Line*
Nikon D810, AF-S Nikkor 400mm f/2.8D IF-ED lens, 1/320 sec at f/4, ISO 1600
For this image of Glastonbury, Connecticut, junior running back Donevin O'Reilly, the Nikon SB-800 Speedlight (in TTL mode) was mounted approximately two feet above the lens and connected to the camera via an SC-28 cable, to provide the main illumination. I had Auto ISO enabled, with a maximum ISO of 1600, to extend the reach of the flash. The field was dark enough that ISO 1600 did not produce enough ambient exposure to cause significant ghosting.

Chapter 7 – Jackie Donaldson (*bhpr*), *El Galeón Andalucía at Baltimore Port*
Nikon D810, AF-S Nikkor 24-120mm f/1.4G ED at 24mm, 1/6 sec at f/4.5, ISO 1600
I was seeking a place to shoot the fireworks during the Star Spangled weekend in the Baltimore Inner Harbor. The ship, El Galeón Andalucía, was really cool looking and the lighting against the evening sky was perfect. I had no tripod and had owned the D810 for only a couple of weeks, but I felt I would get a great shot with it. I used VR to steady my handheld shot at ISO 1600 and captured this image. It is one of my favorites!

Chapter 8 – Michael Kawerninski (*qanik*), *Grizzly Takes a Salmon at Fish Creek in Alaska*
Nikon D810, AF-S Nikkor 500mm f/4 VRIII lens at 24mm, 1/2500 sec at f/4, ISO 1000
I enjoy shooting outdoors, especially wildlife, but for me photography is an objective manifestation of my love of nature. It is the act of picture-taking rather than the finished result that affects me most. The day I took this picture there was good morning light instead of rain, for a change. I used Aperture priority rather than my usual Manual mode, specifically sacrificing depth of field to gain shutter speed, hoping to catch the water from all the splashing of the grizzly and the dripping fish.

Chapter 9 – Larry Loar (*folkloar*), *Giant Fresnel Lens in Pensacola Lighthouse*
Nikon D810, AF-S Nikkor 14-24mm f/2.8 G ED lens at 14mm, 1/50 sec at f/16, ISO 64
I had the rare opportunity to photograph the Pensacola Lighthouse from the top lantern room while on vacation in Pensacola, Florida. Knowing this was a once-in-a-lifetime opportunity, I was looking for an interesting angle. I had to be extremely careful because of the age and fragility of the Fresnel lens. The challenging part was that the lens is constantly moving, with a 20-second gap between each section, so my timing had to be just right.

Chapter 10 – Brian Tilley (*briantilley*), *Hawker Dragonfly in Flight*
Nikon D810, Tamron SP 150-600mm f/5-6.3 Di VC lens at 600mm, 1/800 sec at f/8, ISO 1400
I took this image at Stover Country Park, near my home in Devon, England. In August, dragonflies are quite active around the margins of the lake and I spent

some time stalking them. As anyone who has tried it knows, catching a dragonfly in-flight is a pretty tough task, and really tests the autofocus abilities of the camera and lens. I was very pleased with how the D810 handled things.

Chapter 11 – James T. Keenan (*Lomcevak*), *Heermann's Gull at Tamarack*
Nikon D810, Nikkor 400mm f/2.8 VR lens, 1/4000 sec at f/4, ISO 200, DX mode
This image was captured at the Tamarack State Beach in Carlsbad, California, during a morning shoot of the local high school's Surf Physical Education class. Between waves, this little guy made himself available for a few shots. I shoot the D810 with the MB-D12/EN-EL18a grip and battery at 7fps in DX mode, which doesn't give up too much to the D3S and D300S, while having a deeper buffer than the D300S for those extended sequences. Wide angles and sweeping vistas produce stunning resolution and 16 MB files in DX mode.

Chapter 12 – David Jolley (*DAJolley*), *Autumn Splendor on Dunlop Creek*
Nikon D810, AF-S Nikkor 24-70mm f/2.8G ED lens at 24mm, 1/15s at f/11, ISO 64
This beautiful scene was captured along Dunlop Creek in the New River Gorge National River area of West Virginia. I had a trip planned to this area later in October but got a tip that color was peaking early, so I left the next day on a four-hour drive to see what kind of fall color I could find. A narrow road follows Dunlop Creek for several miles to the abandoned coal-mining town of Thurmond. There are many waterfalls along Dunlop Creek and it makes a wonderful drive any time of year.

Chapter 13 – Darrell Young (*DigitalDarrell*), *Ode to Youth and Autumn Sunshine*
Nikon D810, AF-S Nikkor 24-70mm f/2.8G ED lens at 70mm, 1/60 sec at f/5, ISO 64
I took this shot during a baby bump photo shoot at UT Gardens in Knoxville, Tennessee. This is the sister of the pregnant woman and she was using a Nikon D750 to shoot alongside me. At the end of the shoot, the sun was setting and the evening golden-hour light allowed me to take some excellent portraits. The Nikon D810 and AF-S Nikkor 24-70mm f/2.8 lens are an amazing combo!

Rear Cover – Don Ridgway (*dridgway*), *Aspens in Full Color at Maroon Bells*
Nikon D810, AF-S Nikkor 14-24mm f/2.8G ED lens at 24mm, 1/100 sec at f/16, ISO 200
This was my first outing with my new Nikon D810 and I was very fortunate to be at Maroon Lake in Aspen, Colorado, just when the aspens were in full color. Using the D810 is like shooting with a medium format camera because there is such incredible detail in every image. The camera also has very wide dynamic range.

Index

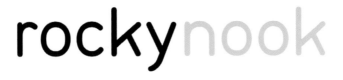
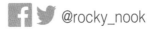